Also by William Greider

*The Education of David Stockman
and Other Americans*

SECRETS OF THE TEMPLE

How the Federal Reserve Runs the Country

WILLIAM GREIDER

A TOUCHSTONE BOOK
Published by Simon & Schuster
New York London Toronto Sydney Tokyo Singapore

Touchstone

Rockefeller Center
1230 Avenue of the Americas
New York, New York 10020

Designed by Helen Granger/Levavi & Levavi
Manufactured in the United States of America

7   9   10   8
17   19   20   18   Pbk.

Library of Congress Cataloging in Publication Data
Greider, William.
Secrets of the temple: How the Federal Reserve runs the country/William
Greider.—1st Touchstone ed.
p.   cm.—(A Touchstone book)
Bibliography: p.
Includes index.
1. Board of Governors of the Federal Reserve System (U.S.) 2. Federal
Reserve banks. 3. Monetary policy—United States—History—20th
century. 4. Banks and banking—United States—History—20th
century. 5. Finance—United States—History—20th century. I. Title.
[HG2563.G72   1989]
332.1'1'0973—dc19   88-26696
                                                  CIP
ISBN 0-671-47989-X
0-671-67556-7 pbk.

Portions of this book appeared originally in *The New Yorker*.

FOR LINDA FURRY GREIDER,
whose intellect and social sensibilities
have informed this book

CONTENTS

—PART ONE—

SECRETS OF THE TEMPLE

1

THE CHOICE OF WALL STREET

In the American system, citizens were taught that the transfer of political power accompanied elections, formal events when citizens made orderly choices about who shall govern. Very few Americans, therefore, understood that the transfer of power might also occur, more subtly, without elections. Even the President did not seem to grasp this possibility, until too late. He would remain in office, surrounded still by the aura of presidential authority, but he was no longer fully in control of his government.

The American system depended upon deeper transactions than elections. It provided another mechanism of government, beyond the reach of the popular vote, one that managed the continuing conflicts of democratic capitalism, the natural tension between those two words, "democracy" and "capitalism." It was part of the national government, yet deliberately set outside the electoral process, insulated from the control of mere politicians. Indeed, it had the power to resist the random passions of popular will and even to discipline the society at large. This other structure of American governance coexisted with the elected one, shared power with Congress and the President, and collaborated with them. In some circumstances, it opposed them and thwarted them.

Citizens were taught that its activities were mechanical and nonpolitical, unaffected by the self-interested pressures of competing economic groups, and its pervasive influence over American life was largely ignored by the continuing political debate. Its decisions and internal disputes and the large consequences that flowed from them remained remote and indistinct, submerged beneath the visible politics of the nation. The details of its actions were presumed to be too esoteric for ordinary citizens to understand.

The Federal Reserve System was the crucial anomaly at the very core of representative democracy, an uncomfortable contradiction with the civic mythology of self-government. Yet the American system accepted the inconsistency. The community of elected politicians acquiesced to its power. The private economy responded to its direction. Private capital depended on it for protection. The governors of the Federal Reserve decided the largest questions of the political economy, including who shall prosper and who shall fail, yet their role remained opaque and mysterious. The Federal Reserve was shielded from scrutiny partly by its own official secrecy, but also by the curious ignorance of the American public.

It was in midsummer of 1979 when this competing reality of the American system confronted the President of the United States and discreetly compelled him to yield. Jimmy Carter, in the third year of his Presidency, was engulfed by popular discontent and declining authority. The public that first embraced the simple virtues Carter expressed in his gentle Georgia accent—earnest striving and honest, open government—was by then overwhelmingly disenchanted with his management. Despite its accomplishments, the Carter Presidency had come to stand for confusion and inconsistency. His stature was diminished by a series of ill events, from failed legislation to revolution in Iran. A Gallup poll asked Democrats whom they would prefer as their party's nominee in 1980 and they chose Senator Edward M. Kennedy of Massachusetts over the incumbent President, 66 to 30 percent.

In early July, Jimmy Carter set out to restore his popular support. The political crisis had been developing for many months but was now dramatized by the President's own behavior. He scheduled an address to the nation on energy problems, then abruptly canceled it and, somewhat mysteriously, withdrew from the daily business of the White House. He and his closest advisers gathered in private at Camp David, the presidential retreat in the Maryland mountains. For ten days, the President remained there in isolation, conducting earnest seminars on what had gone wrong with the Carter Presidency and, indeed, what had gone wrong with America itself.

A stream of influential visitors was summoned to the President's lodge to offer advice. They were diverse opinion leaders from politics, education, religion and other realms, and their talk skipped across the landscape of American life. In his methodical manner, Carter filled a notebook with their comments. Each day, the press speculated extravagantly on what the President intended to do.

On Saturday, July 14, the isolation ended and Jimmy Carter returned to the White House. The next evening, more than two-thirds of the national audience gathered before their television sets to hear his report. After two and a half years, Carter's unusual mannerisms were familiar to the public, the rising and falling cadences that sounded like a Protestant preacher, the cheerful smile that sometimes oddly punctuated stern passages. This speech was different, more somber in tone, more desperate in content.

The President began with a startling ritual of confession—revealing excerpts of the private criticism he had collected at the Camp David meetings. "Mr. President," a southern governor had told him, "you are not leading this nation—you are just managing the government." Others' comments were equally critical. "You don't see the people enough anymore." "Don't talk to us about politics or the mechanics of government, but about an understanding of our common good." "Some of your Cabinet members don't seem loyal. There is not enough discipline among your disciples." "Mr. President, we are in trouble. Talk to us about blood and sweat and tears."

A religious leader had told him: "No material shortage can touch the important things like God's love for us or our love for one another." Carter said he especially liked the comment from a black woman who was mayor of a small town in Mississippi: "The big shots are not the only ones who are important. Remember, you can't sell anything on Wall Street unless someone digs it up somewhere else first." The President was candid about his own shortcomings as a political leader: "I have worked hard to put my campaign promises into law—and I have to admit, with just mixed success."

The present crisis, however, was not really a matter of legislation, Carter declared. America faced a crisis of the soul, a testing of its moral and spiritual values. "The threat is nearly invisible in ordinary ways," the President warned. "It is a crisis of confidence. It is a crisis that strikes at the very heart and soul and spirit of our national will. We can see this crisis in the growing doubt about the meaning of our own lives and in the loss of a unity of purpose for our Nation."

Spiritual distress was an abstraction, but the source of America's political discontent was actually quite tangible. It was the lines at gas stations that made people angry and gasoline at $1.25 a gallon. It was the constantly rising prices on supermarket shelves, prices that seemed to change every week and always higher. In the spring of 1979, after the revolutionary upheaval in Iran had interrupted its oil production, the cartel of oil-producing nations, OPEC, had seized the opportunity of temporary shortages to raise world petroleum prices again. OPEC, which had roughly quadrupled oil prices during its embargo of 1973–1974, more than redoubled them through 1978 and 1979. This second "oil shock," as economists called it, automatically fed price increases into nearly every product, every marketplace where Americans bought and sold.

The latest oil-price shock, moreover, occurred at an especially bad time, when the inflation rate in the United States was already abnormally high. In the first three months of 1979, the government's index of consumer prices, covering everything from food to housing, had risen at an annual rate of nearly 11 percent. In a year's time, a dollar would buy only 89 cents' worth of goods. A $6,000 car would soon cost $660 more. And every wage earner would need a pay raise of more than 10 percent simply to stay even with prices. Through the second quarter of 1979, April to June, as the OPEC price increases took hold, the inflation rate had worsened, reaching 14 percent. By early summer, motorists in some regions were once again waiting in line at gas stations and Jimmy Carter's political popularity had reached a dangerously low point. In July, according to public-opinion polls, barely a fourth of the voters approved of his performance as President.

Carter and his advisers hoped that the dramatic speech, followed by swift and decisive actions, would turn things around. His message was daring. In similar circumstances, a different political leader might have blamed the economic distress on others—on an easily recognized villain like the Arab nations of OPEC or the multinational oil companies—and deflected Americans' resentment toward them. But polarizing politics, the technique of "us against them," was not Carter's style. Instead, he asked the people to blame themselves, just as he had done. The speech did outline an ambitious six-part energy program, designed to overcome the nation's dependency on imported oil. But the central message, the one most citizens would remember, was a critique of their own materialism:

> In a nation that was proud of hard work, strong families, close-knit communities and our faith in God, too many of us now tend to worship self-indulgence and consumption. Human identity is no longer defined by what one does, but by what one owns. But we have discovered that owning things and consuming things does not satisfy our longing for meaning. We have learned that piling up material goods cannot fill the emptiness of lives which have no confidence or purpose.

The President called the country to sacrifice and spiritual renewal. He asked his audience for cooperative self-denial, to forgo the excesses of material pleasures in the national interest. Carter's speech did not even mention the Federal Reserve and its management of money, the government's handle on interest rates and credit expansion by which Washington ultimately influenced both prices and the pace of private economic activity. His stern message sounded especially strange coming from a Democratic President, leading the political party whose majority position was founded on the promise of prosperity for all. The news media quickly labeled it derisively the "malaise speech," a term that Carter himself never used.

But Carter's somber sermon was at first warmly received by the public and, in terms of popular reaction, was one of the most successful speeches of his Presidency. Contemporary Americans were devoted to the pursuit of their own affluence, but they still hearkened to spiritual themes. From the earliest days of the Republic, Americans had always been stirred by the jeremiads of puritan preachers warning of moral decay and calling them back to the old values. In this instance, the public quickly endorsed Jimmy Carter's diagnosis.

New public-opinion polls, taken right after his speech, reported that more than three-fourths of the voters agreed with the President's warnings of spiritual crisis. Carter's own popularity improved dramatically. One survey found that public approval for his Presidency increased overnight by 10 percent, an astonishing shift considering that it was generated by a single speech. At least 40 percent of the vast television audience said that Carter's address gave them greater confidence in his leadership.

This was a promising start, though White House advisers understood that more needed to be done. A Democratic political consultant in Washington remarked optimistically that the President's dramatic appeal to conscience "takes him from three touchdowns behind to one touchdown behind."[1]

A jewelry manufacturer in Cedarhurst, New York, understood something about the American public that did not fit the President's message. Eugene Sussman had observed a new pattern of behavior among consumers which made it most unlikely that ordinary citizens however much they agreed with the President's sentiments would actually act upon them. Sussman kept raising the prices on his luxury jewelry to keep up with the rising costs of gold and diamonds as well as wages. Each time he raised prices, he worried that he would kill his sales. Each time, his sales increased. The higher he set prices on the pins and rings and brooches, the more people bought.

I'm talking about average working girls [Sussman said with wonder]. I see them on the street, wearing my jewelry. They're making $250 or $300 a week and they're spending it on jewelry. They have to have it. It's like food.

I'm paying 120 percent more for my diamonds than I did last year, my labor is up 35 to 40 percent. My product gets marked up again and again. Rings that sold for $170 four years ago are $350, maybe $400. I can sell all I can make.

The "working girls" who bought Sussman's fancy jewelry were on to something new in American life, the awareness that in this era of constant inflation it made sense to buy now and pay later—to buy before prices went up again, even to borrow now and repay the debts in depreciated dollars. Most Americans could not pause for long to contemplate the President's warning about the emptiness of materialism. They were too busy buying things, buying them sooner rather than later.

In the Los Angeles suburb of Sun Valley, a union machinist named Roland Murphy and his wife borrowed $10,000 to redo their kitchen. They were still paying for the Dodge Aspen they bought the year before. When the price of hay got too high, the Murphys sold their horse. In Chicago, an English teacher named Derotha Rogers and her husband, Bev, a pipe fitter, bought a $19,000 Cadillac even though he was temporarily out of a job. Across town, Stephen C. Mitchell, an engineering executive, and his wife postponed remodeling their town house because of inflation, but they bought a $2,000 oil painting and were paying the gallery in installments. In Houston, a young computer analyst named Jack West and his wife, Roseann, used credit cards to take their daughter on a $1,500 vacation at Disneyland.

Mrs. West explained: "For our parents, everything went to the kids and nothing for themselves. But I think those of us who have grown up since World War II just don't want to live like that. We want to enjoy some of it too." Roland Murphy explained how easy it was for him to buy things on his $25,000-a-year income: "I have more credit than money. I could buy far more things than I could ever pay for. When I think about what Sears says I could buy on credit, it's frightening. We could cart away $7,000 of their stuff."

American consumers, having lived with constant inflation for more than a decade, had absorbed a new common wisdom, now shared by the rich and poor and middle class alike. Steadily rising prices were considered a permanent fixture of American life, a factor to be calculated in every transaction. For years, a succession of political leaders in Washington had promised to do something about inflation, and the public became quite cynical about those promises. Each government campaign against inflation had eventually failed and, each time, prices had resumed their steady escalation. Each time, the inflation rate ultimately reached an even higher peak.

By the late 1970s, most citizens had drawn their own practical lessons from the experience. It not only made sense to buy now rather than later; it also made sense to borrow money in order to buy things now. Even with higher interest rates, a loan made today to purchase an automobile or a television set or a house would be paid back tomorrow in inflated dollars that were worth less. So long as wages continued to spiral upward in tandem with prices, one stayed ahead by borrowing. If inflation persisted, as everyone assumed, debtors would be rewarded and savers would be penalized. Jay Schmiedeskamp, research director of the Gallup Economic Service, saw the new behavior reflected in surveys of consumer attitudes. "The brake is off," he said. "Inflation doesn't slow people down the way it always has. That's a rather historic change. There used to be a brake—inflation came along and people stopped buying. That isn't happening now."

The prudential wisdom inherited from the past—a grandfather's old-fashioned warning to save for the future and avoid debt—was turned upside down. Smart young consumers now did the opposite. The overall effect was neither irrational nor antisocial. What grandfather did not understand was that borrowing and buying drove the American economy.

While inflation unsettled economic assumptions in the marketplace, it was also destabilizing in the political arena. As consumers, people were compelled to focus more immediately on short-term decisions, rather than to plan for the distant future. Despite the spreading abundance generated during Carter's term, the rising prices produced anxieties for nearly everyone. Daily chores as routine as grocery shopping induced a sense of running on a treadmill that was moving faster and faster.

As voters, people expressed the same insecurities. Their daily lives might be prosperous, but they found themselves uncertain about the future, more skeptical of distant political promises. While Americans continued their borrowing and buying, they also assumed that the good times must soon end. A Gallup survey found that 62 percent of the public expected a recession sometime in 1979—all the more reason to buy now while prosperity continued. The political effect of inflation, like the economic effect, was to drive citizens toward a foreshortened time horizon in their thinking. A President who urged the nation to sacrifice for long-range goals was addressing an audience pushed in the opposite direction—concentrating on today because it was unable to rely on tomorrow.[2]

. . .

On Monday, amid the popular response to Carter's speech, the financial markets in New York expressed their own reaction to his message. It was negative. The interest rate on short-term borrowing among banks rose abruptly from 10.25 percent to 10.75 percent—50 basis points, in market talk, a very sharp swing for a single day. The rate subsided only after the Federal Reserve took action to supply more money to the banking system. The interest on three-month Treasury bills, the government's own short-term borrowing, also went up sharply. Such small fractional changes in the price of credit might appear insignificant to outsiders, but not to investors. A tenth of 1 percent in market rates would become the multiplier for tens of billions of dollars of other transactions.

The reaction of Wall Street was a troubling political signal—an expressed nervousness about the future and skepticism about Carter's ability to regain control over inflation. The daily fluctuations of Wall Street were often read as implicit political messages, the numbers characterized as curbstone comments on the affairs of government. The day after Carter's speech, market specialists reported that the sudden increase in interest rates expressed "investor uncertainty over President Carter's energy proposals."

Assigning political interpretations to the results of financial markets was, of course, highly subjective. No one could claim to know exactly what combination of economic factors and political anxieties caused lenders and borrowers to bid up interest rates on a given day. Any market participant was free to assert his own analysis of what it meant, and these experts frequently disagreed among themselves. Still, over time, the collective opinions from Wall Street had real meaning to the government in Washington and could not easily be ignored. Pessimistic expectations in financial markets, both at home and abroad, might become self-fulfilling. Political reactions from Wall Street, whether they were right or wrong, could eventually influence the real economy, everything from the price of home mortgages to the pace of industrial expansion, in short, the economic well-being that every President seeks to achieve.

The markets, it was said, wanted reassurance from the President, a promise that he would act decisively to curb the inflationary pressures. For two weeks before Carter's speech, the financial numbers had sounded almost panicky, like nervous warnings to the White House. The American dollar, bought and sold daily in huge volumes on the currency exchanges, had been sliding in value, almost every day. This meant that the currency traders—banks, multinational corporations, wealthy investors, perhaps even other governments—expected the U.S. dollar to continue to lose its value in the coming weeks and months, and they, therefore, found it safer to hold their wealth in other currencies, Deutsche marks, yen, francs and pounds. Roughly translated, the dollar's steady decline amounted to an inflation forecast—a prediction that, unless Carter acted swiftly and convincingly, U.S. price increases would grow even worse. After the "malaise speech," the dollar promptly fell further.

On Tuesday, Jimmy Carter took action to demonstrate his resolve —he asked for resignations from his entire Cabinet and White House staff. Each top-level appointee would be reviewed, and the President would decide "expeditiously" which ones to keep and which ones to dismiss. It was meant to signal a new beginning for the Carter Presidency, a dramatic shake-up that would show he was in charge.

The financial markets drew the opposite conclusion. They were rattled further, both at home and abroad. On Wednesday, the dollar declined again and the price of gold reached a historic record in European markets—moving above $300 an ounce. By comparison, a decade earlier, the official value of gold in American currency, then guaranteed by the United States government, had been $35 an ounce. Its dramatic increase in value was another surrogate measure of U.S. inflation. Gold was an ancient form of wealth, associated with the fabled kings of antiquity, and very few modern Americans ever thought of owning it, aside from jewelry. But the precious metal was bought and sold daily in global commodity markets, in part to serve wealthy investors who saw gold as another safe haven against U.S. inflation. Paper dollars might keep losing their value, but gold was forever. As more and more investors opted for the security of gold, the increased number of buyers naturally drove up the price, thus confirming the expectation that gold would become more valuable as the value of the dollar steadily declined.

Stuart Eizenstat, director of the White House Domestic Policy Staff and an intimate adviser on Carter's economic policies, thought the markets completely misunderstood the President's reorganization. "When the President asked for the resignations of his Cabinet unexpectedly, the financial markets became very jittery," Eizenstat said. "Interest rates were already high and the markets did not really know what was going on. They were thinking of the European model where governments fall."

Nevertheless, the White House was worried by the Wall Street reaction. The Secretary of the Treasury, who is usually a reassuring figure for financial markets, acknowledged that the "climate of uncertainty" in the government was contributing to the dollar's decline. W. Michael Blumenthal was regarded by Wall Street as one of its stronger advocates in the Carter Cabinet, but Blumenthal was himself unsure whether he would continue in office.

On Thursday, President Carter announced wholesale changes in his

Cabinet. Blumenthal would be replaced, along with Attorney General Griffin Bell and the Secretary of Health, Education and Welfare, Joseph Califano. The next day, Energy Secretary James Schlesinger and Transportation Secretary Brock Adams were also dismissed. Each change was inspired by particular reasons, some of which were largely personal. Taken together, they provoked a storm of complaints from Congress. Democratic leaders and committee chairmen rushed to defend the Cabinet officers who had been fired and to express new doubts about Carter's direction. The swiftness of the startling shake-up convinced many political commentators in the press that the President had only aggravated his problems.[3]

But neither the critics nor the White House staff itself focused on the most significant change—the one that concerned Wall Street. It was the resignation of the chairman of the Federal Reserve Board. G. William Miller had served only seventeen months as chairman, since being appointed by President Carter early in 1978 to succeed Arthur Burns. Now, the White House announced, Miller would leave the Federal Reserve and replace Blumenthal as Secretary of the Treasury. But who would run the Fed? The White House did not have an answer.

Miller had been a corporate manager, not a banker or economist, before he became Fed chairman, and his stewardship at the central bank was widely criticized among Wall Street professionals. He was a former chief executive officer of Textron Inc., a mildly conservative Democrat who supported Jimmy Carter for President in 1976, and was warmly regarded by the President and his economic advisers. They thought of him as a "team player," a Fed chairman who cooperated closely with the President's economic goals, though the Federal Reserve was formally independent of the executive branch, not required by law to take orders from the Oval Office. Wall Street analysts complained that Miller was much too cooperative, too timid about raising interest rates high enough to suppress inflation.

Miller's loyalty was one reason why the White House selected him to replace Blumenthal, who was distrusted by the White House inner circle. But the choice of Miller for Treasury Secretary was more happenstance than deliberate, undertaken without much thought about its implications. Eizenstat explained the accidental sequence:

The President "accepts" the resignation of Blumenthal. Blumenthal is known as a voice against inflation and this adds to the confusion. So we were without a Treasury Secretary. So the President makes calls. Reg Jones of General Electric, Irv Shapiro of Du Pont, David Rockefeller of Chase Manhattan—all are asked and turn it down.

This becomes a grave situation. The idea surfaces—I'm not sure where —that Bill Miller take the job. Bill takes it. That then creates a hole at the Fed. And that makes the financial markets even more nervous.

The daily financial numbers got worse. The President had started the week with a fresh glow of public approval and an intention to demonstrate renewed strength as the nation's leader. By Friday, he had created an entirely new problem for himself—finding a new chairman for the Federal Reserve, one who would calm the financial markets.

An obscure banker from Florida, Frederick H. Schultz, meanwhile found himself caught in the middle of the great confusion. On Wednesday, July 18, after a nasty fight, the Senate had finally confirmed Schultz's nomination as vice chairman of the Federal Reserve Board, one of the seven governors who regulate the nation's money. The next day, with William Miller resigning, Schultz was theoretically left in charge—a newcomer unknown to financial markets. This added an alarming new dimension to their nervousness.

Fred Schultz was an investment banker from Jacksonville, Florida, a tall man with a rumpled face and a southerner's amiable directness. He sounded less like a banker than an energetic entrepreneur. In fact, Schultz was one of those driven types who was born to wealth, then went out to make another fortune on his own. As a venture capitalist, he had picked several winners, among them Florida Wire & Cable, initially capitalized at $250,000, later sold for a little over $20 million. As a banker, he had run the investment management subsidiary of Barnett Banks, the largest chain in Florida.

When the President nominated him to be the Fed's vice chairman, the White House staff had told Schultz he was the wealthiest man Jimmy Carter had appointed to federal office. To avoid any conflict of interest, Schultz would have to sell his bank stocks, government bonds and other financial assets whose value might be directly affected by Federal Reserve decisions; the rest of his holdings would be placed in a blind trust. Despite his experience, some critics in Congress had thought he was too parochial for the job.

What bothered them was not Schultz's personal wealth or even that he was a banker, but that he was also a politician. He had served eight years in the Florida legislature, the last two as Speaker of the House, and run unsuccessfully for U.S. senator. Afterward, he was Florida chairman of the Democratic Party and in 1976 had helped raise money for Jimmy Carter's presidential campaign. Since the Federal Reserve's control of money was supposed to be above politics, protected from narrow partisan interests, Schultz's appointment aroused suspicions. On the surface, it looked as though Carter might be naming an old crony from southern politics to be second-in-command at the Fed —just as the President would be heading into the 1980 re-election campaign.

"Some people went around saying, 'This guy is a political hack,' " Schultz acknowledged good-naturedly. He made no apologies for his political experience; he thought it would be an asset for the Fed.

Despite his background in Florida banking, Schultz was not well known in Wall Street. Nervous rumors spread through the financial districts of New York and London that Schultz would now be elevated to Federal Reserve chairman. To some in Wall Street, the Cabinet shuffle in Washington began to look like a clever plot intended to give President Carter political control over the independent central bank so it would pump up the economy for the campaign year.

Frederick Schultz assured the financial press that these rumors were untrue. "It was like asking a new swimmer to serve as lifeguard on his first day at the pool," Schultz said. "When the financial markets opened in Europe on Monday, the dollar dropped like a stone."

The President could not allow this to continue. "Things were beginning to get a little dicey," Schultz said. "They needed to find someone to settle things down. I don't think the White House had the vaguest idea of how bad things were going to get."

By the weekend, the White House was hearing from a wide array of political counselors and friendly business executives, all of whom amplified on the daily messages from the financial markets. The President would be gravely damaged if he did not quickly appoint a new chairman for the Fed, a chairman whom Wall Street trusted.

"It became obvious," Eizenstat said, "that we had to quell the nervousness of the markets."

Political tension existed inevitably between Wall Street and Washington. They were separate capitals, in a sense, representing two different sources of power in the American society. One spoke for capital, the accumulated financial wealth generated by private enterprise. The other spoke for popular democracy, the collective desires of the voting population, rich and poor, owners and workers. The two constituencies were overlapping, of course, and in harmony on many issues. But the two centers of power were often in conflict on the most fundamental questions, particularly in the one area where they both exercised authority, the management of the American economy. A strong President might choose to ignore Wall Street's demands and pursue his own agenda and perhaps prevail. A weakened President did not dare.

"Washington doesn't understand interest rates and Wall Street doesn't understand Washington," Eizenstat observed. "That two-hundred-mile gap is like a giant chasm. They travel in different circles. They just don't speak the same language."

Over the weekend, Carter's White House staff switched its attention from angry politicians in Washington and addressed the complaints from the capital of finance.

On Broad Street, as it curled through the heart of Wall Street, the corporate banners of great banks flew from the façades of elegant old buildings, like the flags of ancient guildhalls in London. The financial district at the foot of Manhattan was one of the oldest urban settlements in America, alive with commerce many decades before there was a government in Washington, and it still felt like an old city of Europe, with narrow, irregular streets and the random congestion of its buildings. The history was still visible. Federal Hall, the Greek Revival temple at the intersection of Nassau and Wall Streets, was built on the site of New York's colonial city hall. George Washington, who took his oath of office here in 1789, stood on the steps, a bronze statue beckoning to tourists. One block west, framed by the tall buildings, the Gothic spires of Trinity Church and its colonial graveyard evoked the shadows of history. But Wall Street also expressed the power and ambition of the contemporary American experience. Office towers of shimmering glass loomed over the old landmarks like intimidating mirrors, physical assertions of modernism's ambition. The old and the new, clustered so close together, created a sense of action. The excitement of eclectic architecture was amplified by the swirl of clerks and brokers always in the crowded streets. No one could visit Wall Street without sensing its importance.

The people who worked there, typically, held a low opinion of Washington. The political capital in Washington, they thought, was egotistical and self-indulgent, detached from reality. People who lived with the markets every day thought of themselves as quite the opposite.

"Washington has political power combined with the insider illusion of being in control," David Jones, an economist with the bond brokerage of Aubrey G. Lanston & Company, complained. "In Wall Street, no matter how big you are, the markets are humbling. If you bet wrong in the markets, you get your ass handed to you. No matter who you are. And that's true every day of the week. In Washington, they think they probably have some control over the outcome."

Unlike any other institution of government, the Federal Reserve was uniquely positioned between these two worlds, and the Fed was obliged to listen to both power centers—the demands of private capital from Wall Street, the democratic ambitions expressed in Washington. Every important decision by the Fed altered the rewards in both domains, the returns of capital and the broad vitality of the American economy, upon which political fortunes depended. The capital of finance understood this relationship much better than did the capital of government, and since many in Washington did not truly grasp Wall Street's function in the American system, they could not understand the Federal Reserve's either. Among bankers and brokers, however, the Fed was regarded as another of life's large uncertainties, a force in the marketplace capable of embarrassing even the largest players.

The humility of Wall Street traders was well concealed. To outsiders, they often sounded arrogant, cavalier about their awesome responsibilities. When financial markets gyrated, perversely changing directions without any obvious logic, the traders often made brash jokes among themselves. They talked in a brisk, loose shorthand of insider jargon and flip clichés. Bond prices did not rise or fall, they "plunged" or "soared." The stock market did not suffer a sharp decline, it "fell out of bed." In a season of losses, a financial institution or a corporation or an investor was said to be "under water." The traders' hyperbole was reflected by the financial press, which transformed the dull numbers from markets, daily changes in price and profit, into animated prose that mimicked the sports pages. Market analysts often spoke the same way, in hyperactive metaphors that sounded lighthearted and knowing. An economist at Crain & Company: "The market is becoming so bearish it can't see straight." A research director for Dreyfus Corporation: "This market is being lashed by flickers of fear."[4]

Wall Street's glibness was a mask. It concealed the daily insecurity that David Jones termed "humbling." The competition that traders described so vividly was not so much among rival firms and financial experts as against the market itself. The most prestigious and powerful banks and brokerages were gamblers, making judgments about the direction markets would take and betting huge stakes on their forecasts. Each and every day, given the nature of markets, some of them would be wrong. Still, they were well compensated for their anxiety.

When outsiders saw the imposing buildings or heard the famous names of finance, they most likely imagined the legendary "Wall Street" of American political history, the "Wall Street" of arrogant financiers who amassed tainted fortunes through ruthless manipulation of the productive economy. By the late twentieth century, the legend of the robber barons had lost most of its force, but politicians still occasionally invoked "Wall Street" as the symbol of irresponsible greed. The American mass culture—movies, popular music, television—continued to resonate with the folk prejudice against bankers, a distrust of financial power as old as the nation. The Populist resentments were echoes from America's agrarian past, particularly the nineteenth century when most citizens were self-reliant farmers and their sense of freestanding individualism struggled, unsuccessfully, to resist the encroaching complexities of corporate capitalism.

In the enduring folk wisdom, for instance, the entrepreneur who invented a new product was more virtuous than a banker; so were the workers and managers hired for his factory. They manufactured real goods that people could buy and use. But what did a banker make— other than pieces of paper and occasional misery? The resentment of finance was still satisfying to many Americans, but of course utterly irrelevant to the daily reality of the American system. In modern capitalism, finance and production were inseparable. Business could not function without credit and neither could consumers. Except perhaps on the smallest scale—a craftsman alone in his shop—economic enterprise did not occur without bankers and borrowing.

The legendary "Wall Street" survived in one respect: New York City was still the center of financial power in America. Despite the rise of new banking centers in other regions, New York remained dominant, rivaled only by California. A crude map of the nation's financial concentration could be drawn from the locations of the largest commercial banks, the core institutions of the financial system. Across the fifty states, there were more than fourteen thousand banks, but most of them were very small enterprises. Only one hundred and fifty or so banks held deposits of more than $1 billion. In 1979, only sixteen banks held deposits totaling $10 billion or more. Together, these sixteen mega-banks accounted for nearly one-fourth of all the bank deposits in the nation.

The geography of financial power looked like this: eight of the sixteen largest banks were in New York. Five were in California. Two were in Chicago, one in Pittsburgh. A less arbitrary map might also include Boston, whose First National Bank (better known as the Bank of Boston) had $8.7 billion in deposits, and Texas, which had four banks with deposits between $4 and $6 billion. In 1979, the nation's largest bank was the Bank of America in San Francisco ($86 billion in deposits), but New York had much more aggregate girth than California, led by Citibank ($70.5 billion), Chase Manhattan ($49 billion), Manufacturers Hanover Trust ($38 billion) and Morgan Guaranty ($30 billion).[5]

Wall Street's banks were surrounded, moreover, by hundreds of brokerages and investment-banking houses that traded stocks and bonds for clients, and, more importantly, raised large blocks of new capital for corporations and governments. A handful of these firms were large enough to be regarded as peers, if not quite equals, of the largest New York banks. Merrill Lynch, leader of the all-service brokers that tended large national client lists, managed $70 billion in money-market accounts for more than one million customers. Even the largest brokerages, however, depended on the commercial banks as a source of credit, for loans to finance their own investment packaging in stocks and bonds and other ventures.

The aristocrats of finance, more prestigious and powerful than their dollar volume indicated, were the major investment-banking houses— led by Salomon Brothers, Morgan Stanley, Merrill Lynch Capital Markets, First Boston, and Goldman, Sachs. Some decorated their office suites to express the confidence of wealth—darkened paneling and fine old antiques, precious artwork and silver tea services for visiting clients. This is where the nation's most important corporations, along with state and local governments, came in search of capital for their largest projects.

Capital formation—the flow of accumulated savings into the creation of new productive facilities—was arguably Wall Street's most important function. Capital formation fundamentally determined the distant future, the pace of expansion that created more products, new jobs and expanding incomes. From their lists of wealthy clients, both individuals and institutions, the investment bankers raised the billions lent for sewers or highways or hospitals, to pay for a new factory or the retooling of an old production line. Many ventures were so large that even the most important banking houses were compelled to collaborate with their competitors, pooling the capital each raised and sharing the risks and profits. In 1979, not an especially good year for capital markets, Salomon Brothers would raise $17 billion for corporations through the sale of bonds and notes and another $1 billion in new stock issues, plus $17 billion in tax-exempt bonds for state and local governments across the nation. Like commercial banking, investment banking was highly concentrated. In 1979, the top five brokers managed 65 percent of the capital market, bonds and new stock issues for corporations. The top ten firms managed 87 percent.[6]

Finance was international, however, and all the largest banks and brokerages operated as multinational financiers. Like oil and wheat, wealth was fungible. It could flow across national boundaries without losing its value, seeking opportunities wherever it found the highest return at the least risk. While the major U.S. banks and brokerages dominated American finance, they were also players on a global stage where they did not seem so imposing. Of the twenty largest banks in the world, only three were American. Germany had six in 1979, Japan had five, France had four and Great Britain had two. The 16th largest bank on the American map, Mellon Bank of Pittsburgh, was 114th in the global geography, hardly in a position to bully its international competitors.[7]

Banking power was less concentrated in the United States partly because America's pluralist tradition and federal law prohibited Citibank or Chase or the others from operating nationwide as the major foreign banks could. Collectively, however, U.S. finance was more powerful than other nations'. Nearly a fifth of the world's five hundred largest banks were American, and they were led and dominated by a mere handful of institutions—the nine largest known as the money-center banks, global institutions that operated worldwide and connected American finance to all the pools of international capital.[8]

Considering its influence on the lives of all Americans, the universe of Wall Street professionals was extraordinarily small. When Dow Jones, publisher of *The Wall Street Journal*, commissioned a census of "finance professionals" in the United States—people who managed finance for corporations and individuals, stockbrokers, securities analysts, bond underwriters, company treasurers, free-lance money managers and the rest—it counted only 405,830 people. This select group was growing rapidly, however, 25 percent larger in just five years. Not all of them worked in lower Manhattan, of course, but, practically speaking, they were all members of the same community, connected by telephone and Telex to the same markets and sharing in the same daily transactions. As the newspaper's survey discreetly noted, 93 percent of them were readers of *The Wall Street Journal*.[9]

All of them, regardless of their positions, devoured information every day—any hard facts or clues that might put them ahead of others in the daily gambles on market directions. But, unlike normal gamblers, most losers in Wall Street did not actually lose their stakes. Most losses were actually only missed opportunities—the failure to maximize the return on someone's invested wealth or to minimize someone else's cost of borrowing. The essence was getting in or out of the market ahead of others, whether it was stocks or bonds or short-term credit. If a firm consistently made the wrong moves, it would lose clients or cost a market trader his job, but there was always an opportunity to catch up. Wall Street was a continuous contest of adjustment and recovery in which players corrected their errors and looked ahead to identify the next trend before others saw it.

Notwithstanding the mistakes and anxieties suffered by the traders, financial markets were described at a distance by academic economists as models of efficiency and rationality. Wall Street was portrayed by them as a living laboratory for the efficient allocation of resources, governed by what they called the "price-auction theory," better known colloquially as the "law of supply and demand." If the proverbial farmers produced 100 bushels of wheat but the bakers needed 150 bushels for their bread, then demand exceeded supply and the farmers were obviously in a position to charge more for their scarce commodity. The bakers would bid up the price among themselves, willing to pay more per bushel rather than be left out. If the farmers produced more grain than the bakers really needed, then supply exceeded demand and the leverage was reversed. The farmers would be compelled to lower the price in order to sell all the grain. At some point, when prices fell sufficiently and the last bushel had been sold, the market would be in equilibrium—every seller had found a buyer and vice versa—"cleared," as economists would say.

The same principle applied to all of the different auctions held daily in the financial markets, only the commodity was wealth itself. In essence, people and institutions who enjoyed a surplus of wealth were willing to let others use it for a while—for a price and usually for a fixed period of time, perhaps for a few days or as long as twenty-five or thirty years. The traders' bidding searched for that same point of equilibrium between supply and demand, the "clearing price" at which the last lender and the last borrower came together on the final transaction. Every market participant would be acting on imperfect knowledge, sometimes erroneous information, and some would always guess wrong. They would borrow just before interest rates fell—a transaction that would have been cheaper if they had only waited. Or they would sell stocks today unaware that market forces would be driving the price upward tomorrow. The economic theory held, nonetheless, that the collective outcome was rational, the most efficient distillation of competing opinions. Traders did not disagree with that orderly description of their work, but some of them resented the bloodless tone. It left out the harrowing days when no one seemed to understand why the markets were plunging or soaring, when psychological impulses or intangible political fears overpowered the simple arithmetic of supply and demand and drove the bidding in perverse directions.[10]

The market participants, the lenders and borrowers who were the buyers and sellers of financial instruments, operated in three great arenas of finance—the stock market, the bond market and the so-called money market. The stock market, strictly speaking, did not involve credit because a stockholder was purchasing a fractional share of ownership in the corporation. But, typically, investors scanned all three markets, compared the potential returns in each and moved their money from one to another as the opportunities guided them. In theory, the stock market lived by the prospect for rising corporate profits, and its natural optimism was depressed whenever downturns in the business cycle wiped out the predictions of company sales and earnings.

The bond market, by comparison, was dour and conservative, yearning for long-term stability, above all, and was often frightened by go-go news that excited the stock market. The bond market dealt in long-term corporate and government debt issues, bonds and notes, ranging from two years to thirty years. This was the place where people were asked to lend their money to the distant future and, therefore, the arena that worried most about the threat of future inflation. A cautious investor who bought blue-chip corporate bonds in 1965, for instance, would have been promised a steady, safe return, an annual interest payment of perhaps 4 or 5 percent on his money. By 1979, the promise was grotesquely undermined by inflation—his wealth was losing value from inflation much faster than it was generating income. The disappointed investor might sell his bonds and invest somewhere else, but he would have to sell at a depressed price.

The money market, in a sense, was the near end of the credit horizon—the short-term borrowing that could be an overnight loan or for a few weeks or months, usually no longer than one year. The money market, unlike stocks and bonds, existed nowhere and everywhere. The trading was done mostly by telephone and Telex and involved a bewildering variety of lending instruments, from verbal swaps of excess reserves among banks to commercial paper issued by corporations to the $100,000 certificates of deposit by which banks raised funds to lend out again. Money-market rates reacted most sensitively to small changes in supply and demand and became the safe haven from inflation, the place to hide when long-term investments seemed too risky. The money market was mainly an arena for large institutional players, banks, brokers, corporations and governments, but it was democratized somewhat in the 1970s by the invention of money-market mutual funds. An individual could put a few thousand dollars in Merrill Lynch's money-market fund and enjoy a return close to the market rates. Merrill Lynch would aggregate thousands of such small deposits and use them to invest in commercial paper, bank CDs and other short-term instruments that were too large for most individuals to afford.

Citizens with only a casual interest in finance perhaps assumed that the stock market was the most important enterprise of Wall Street because it always received the most attention in the news media. Every evening on the network TV news, the Dow Jones average of key industrial stocks was flashed on screen, with up or down arrows, as

the visible barometer of financial news. In fact, the stock market was
dwarfed by the credit markets. The year-end market value of all corporate equities in 1979 was about $1.2 trillion—compared to $4.2 trillion in the credit markets. Most of that vast sum was dedicated to
long-term debt, from mortgages to corporate bonds, but even the
short-term lending in the money market was about equal in volume to
value of corporate stocks.[11]

Every financial institution was, in essence, an intermediary—the
middleman between lenders and borrowers. From the largest commercial banks and bond brokerages on Wall Street to the smallest credit
union or neighborhood savings and loan association, the essential
function was to collect money from people who had accumulated a
surplus, the creditors, and deliver it to debtors, the people who
needed to use it. While banks and brokerages also invested their own
assets for profitable return, the core of their business was managing
the flow of wealth between others, arranging the terms and collecting
a percentage for themselves, either a fixed commission or the interest-
rate spread, the difference between what they paid to borrow the
funds and what they charged to lend them out again.

The essence of finance was, therefore, an exchange across time—
transactions between the past and the future. Old money, the surplus
accumulated from past endeavors, was made available to new ventures, with the promise of future rewards for both. Wall Street, for all
its bewildering complexities, was as simple as that—the meeting place
where past and future agreed on terms and the money changed hands.
The daily auctions of finance determined not simply who would profit
and who would get the money for new enterprise, but whether capitalism itself advanced toward a prosperous future or stagnated and regressed.

Across the three great financial markets, money flowed continuously, in and out of different channels, back and forth from one instrument to another, from lenders to debtors and back again. Sears,
Roebuck paid for its huge retail inventory by short-term borrowing,
issuing commercial paper that it paid off as the inventory was sold. A
savings and loan in California resold the housing mortgages it had
issued to home buyers in order to raise funds for new lending. A small
bank in Arkansas, in effect, borrowed money from its local depositors
and lent some to local consumers and businesses. The surplus it lent
to larger banks in other cities where credit demand was greater and
the larger banks found borrowers for the money. The college housing
authority in New York issued revenue bonds to build new dormitories
and, while it waited to pay the construction company, invested the
money temporarily in short-term commercial paper. A major corpora-

tion like General Electric borrowed billions long term in the bond market for a major plant expansion while simultaneously investing its short-term surplus cash in bank CDs or commercial paper in the money market. The process was repeated in seemingly endless variety and multiplied by millions of transactions.

In this intricate tangle of credit relationships, one customer stood ahead of all the others. The largest borrower in the markets of Wall Street was the government in Washington, which managed a debt of nearly $1 trillion, raised by government securities, from ninety-day Treasury bills to two-year notes to long-term bonds that would mature in 2009. In one dimension, Treasuries were the safest investment available. After all, if someday the U.S. government failed to pay its obligations, then the country would no doubt be in riotous anarchy anyway and no private property would be safe. In another dimension, however, government securities confronted investors with the same risk as other long-term issues—the risk of the dollar losing its value. The price of U.S. bonds, new and old, was, therefore, highly sensitive to the prospects of future inflation.

All in all, the financial system resembled the dynamics of a pump house, not an accountant's static balance sheet, and functioned according to physical laws that a hydraulic engineer might understand. It was like a fantastically complicated labyrinth of pipes and storage tanks and boilers, with pressure valves and plumbing and auxiliary pumps, all elaborately interconnected. Inside this system flowed the financial wealth of the nation, back and forth through many channels and tanks, always seeking higher return and less risk, searching out investments that best promised both. To grasp the larger action of finance, one had to visualize its physics. Indeed, that is how financial analysts themselves spoke of it, using hydraulic metaphors to describe its conditions—the "liquidity" of banks, the "flow of funds" analysis, "circulation" and "float" and "velocity," the surge and ebb of "market pressures."

The Federal Reserve Board stood alongside the system like a governor, like a supervising engineer who had the power to alter the flows inside the plumbing. Its decisions could slacken the pressures of the fluids or intensify them; its policies could stimulate the flow of lending or choke it off or nudge it toward different channels. The Fed accomplished this, primarily, by injecting more fluid into the system or withdrawing it—that is, by creating or destroying money. The ability to create money was the power of sovereigns, almost magical in its simplicity. Central banks inherited the power from kings and, before them, the temple priests of ancient civilizations, leaders endowed by God with the authority to consecrate, en fiat, the currency their societies would accept and use. In the technocratic present, the process of money creation remained a powerful mystery to most citizens.

The Federal Reserve System operated like the modern equivalent of the king's keep—a separate storehouse alongside the private economy and independent of its forces. But the Fed could influence the financial flows inside the plumbing through two tiny valves—mere pinpricks in size compared to all the wealth in circulation. One valve was the Discount window at each of the twelve Federal Reserve Banks, where commercial banks routinely borrowed hundreds of millions, even billions, every day to make up for temporary shortages in their required reserves. The other, more important valve was the Open Market Desk at the New York Federal Reserve Bank in the middle of Wall Street, where the Fed bought and sold government securities in the open market, in daily transactions usually running from $500 million up to several billion. In both cases, the Fed created money with a key stroke of the computer terminal (computer accounting having replaced "the stroke of the pen"). When the Federal Reserve bought Treasury bonds from a dealer or lent through the Discount window to a bank, the central bank simply credited the amount to the bank account of the dealer who sold the bonds or to the bank receiving the loan. In either case, it did not matter which bank or which dealer got the new money. Once it was created, it increased the overall money supply and was free to float from one account to another through the entire banking system. In reverse, when the Fed's Open Market Desk sold bonds or a commercial bank repaid its Discount loan, money was extinguished by the Fed. By a simple entry in the ledger, the money was automatically withdrawn from circulation in the private economy.[12]

As any hydraulic engineer could explain, the impact from the Federal Reserve's actions—injecting or withdrawing money—depended entirely on what was already going on inside the plumbing. When the gauges on a boiler show that pressure is dangerously high, then the slightest hydraulic change can send a strong pulse throughout the system, a displacement that spreads like the ripples on a pond. The financial system was similar. If, for instance, the market demand for credit already exceeded supply and interest rates were rising, then a substantial withdrawal by the Fed would send rates soaring. On the other hand, if credit pressures were slack and interest rates were already falling, the same action might hardly be noticed.

Day by day, the Federal Reserve exerted a powerful influence over Wall Street, but it was not all-powerful. It influenced everything, but it did not control everything. It could set the dials and turn valves, but it could not repeal the fundamentals of economics anymore than an engineer could suspend the laws of physics. Sometimes, despite the

Fed, markets pursued their own direction, driven by contrary perceptions or real economic forces that overpowered the desires of the Federal Reserve Board. Sometimes, trying to change the flow, the Fed turned the wrong valve and produced unintended results. Sometimes, it turned the valve and nothing seemed to happen.

In Wall Street, therefore, everyone watched the Fed. Every bank and brokerage of any size had full-time economists—"Fed watchers" like David Jones—who did nothing else. The scores of Fed watchers analyzed the weekly banking numbers, the credit trends and the general economic news and tried to predict Fed decisions ahead of the crowd. They made daily forecasts of the sales and purchases they expected the Open Market Desk to make, but, more importantly, they attempted to foresee the major "turns" in Fed policy—easing the money supply and credit conditions or tightening. A significant change in direction would send large ripples across the three great financial markets, through the banking system and, ultimately, to the real economy of producers and consumers.

The Fed was most intimate with the commercial banking system, particularly the six thousand banks that were member banks of the Federal Reserve System and entitled to approach the Discount window for loans. Fed regulators examined some banks directly and the Fed was responsible for the overall soundness of the banking system. All fourteen thousand banks reacted to Fed shifts in money supply, however, because that altered their own interest rates and the pace of their lending. Most especially, the Fed concentrated on the fifty or so core banks that held one-third of all the nation's bank deposits, including especially the money-center banks.

Of the three great financial arenas, the money market reacted first to Fed moves. Short-term credit rates rose or fell, almost instantly, in reactions to even small changes in the money supply, and the Fed's strongest, most direct control was over this market. In the stock market, a Fed "turn" could launch a major rally or squelch it, but transient gyrations in the stock market did not much worry the Fed.

The financial market that the Federal Reserve cared about most, respected and even identified with, was the bond market—the place where institutions and wealthy individuals made long-term investments and their commitments were most sensitive to the distant future. If the Federal Reserve failed to maintain stable money values, then the bondholders suffered most dramatically. Like the bond market, the Federal Reserve yearned for order and stability, a reliable future. Consequently, it was the bond market that judged Federal Reserve policy most severely and reacted harshly to errors or transgressions.[13]

In midsummer 1979, the bond market was widely described as

"moribund." As inflation escalated, bond prices declined. Long-term interest rates were rising, but even with the higher return, investors were reluctant to buy. Given the uncertainty, the short-term credit market was the safe place to put one's money. Like citizens at large, the largest investors of Wall Street were concentrating on immediate prospects, unable to count upon the future.

On Sunday afternoon, July 22, Richard Moe, the chief of staff for Vice President Walter Mondale, was at work in the White House, making dozens of telephone calls all over the country. A week had elapsed since President Carter's speech to the nation and Moe was assigned to deal with the President's new problem—checking out potential candidates for chairman of the Federal Reserve Board. The list started with eight or nine names but was quickly winnowed to a few. In Moe's search, one name came up again and again—Paul Volcker.

It was a very intense and compressed process, very rushed [Moe said]. The big factor was: we've got to reassure the markets. That's all we heard. Coming in the wake of the Camp David meetings and the Cabinet changes, people were very nervous about the direction we were going. I wouldn't call it panic but there was clearly a level of concern. We've got a problem on our hands and we have to do it right.

Volcker's résumé was impressive, especially compared with that of William Miller, the man who was leaving the Fed chairmanship to become Treasury Secretary. Unlike Miller, Volcker was an economist who had devoted his entire career to money issues, from banking to the complexities of international finance. For the last four years, Volcker had served as president of the New York Federal Reserve Bank, the most important of the twelve district banks in the System because it served Wall Street. Its president was naturally intimate with the largest financial institutions and international finance, including the central banks of other nations. Before that, Volcker had served as Treasury Under Secretary for Monetary Affairs in the Nixon Administration, the executive-branch official who works most closely with the Fed. He held deputy posts at Treasury under Kennedy and Johnson. He served two tours in private banking at Chase Manhattan. He had even started his career at the Fed, "crunching numbers" as a young research economist at the New York Fed and later trading with dealers on the Open Market Desk. The résumé looked as if Paul Volcker had been training for this job for almost thirty years.

Moe telephoned forty to fifty people and asked for their confidential assessments of the leading candidates. His survey covered business executives and lawyers who were close to the Carter White House, academic economists, a labor leader, other officials in the Administration. Their comments were summarized in a briefing book he was to deliver to the President that Sunday evening. Most reactions to Volcker's name were enthusiastic, but some were quite critical.

A prominent Democratic lawyer: "Excellent. One of my top choices." A liberal economist: "Well respected and has all the experience, but he is rigidly conservative." An Administration official: "No. Arbitrary and arrogant at the New York Fed." The CEO of a major corporation: "Very high on him. Could straighten out the dollar. Has the confidence of the Europeans." The president of a major New York bank: "Good. Number one for professional competence, enormously respected." Another liberal economist: "Very right-wing . . . not a team player."

As Moe summarized his reporting in the memorandum for the President, it was clear that Volcker would give the White House what it desperately wanted—quick reassurances for Wall Street. On the other hand, Moe was bothered by the thread of adverse comments that ran through the conversations: "rigidly conservative . . . very right-wing . . . arbitrary and arrogant . . . not a team player."

As Moe said:

The only real negative that showed up on Volcker was the question of whether he was going to be a team player like Bill Miller. Nobody ever questioned his intellectual credentials and people knew that he was a very conservative fellow, but that never dissuaded the President on appointments anyway. The only question was whether he could work with the White House the way Bill Miller had. Miller was very close to the White House on monetary policy. That's the way any White House wants it.

The Federal Reserve was legally independent of the White House, but it was not cloistered from political persuasion. A Fed chairman consulted and collaborated with a President's own economic advisers. A cooperative Fed chairman pulled in the same direction.

"What people said about Volcker set off alarm bells," Moe said. "He's a very strong-willed, strong-minded person who may or may not be prepared to coordinate policy with you."

Moe decided to share his doubts with the President and suggest that Carter choose one of the other candidates.[14]

When the Dreyfus Fund's proud lion stalked across the TV screen and Merrill Lynch paraded its optimistic bulls, when the actor John Houseman lectured home viewers on the virtues of Smith Barney and everyone stopped to listen to E. F. Hutton, the video images all had the same objective—finding the Americans who possessed a surplus of wealth.

Television fostered a democratic illusion, since virtually every citizen, every household in the land had free access to its commercial messages and absorbed the slogans and visual clichés into daily conversation. Because television was a mass medium, it encouraged the impression that the advertisers were talking to everyone. In fact, of course, Wall Street's TV advertising was aimed at a highly selective audience—the minority of citizens who had serious accumulations of excess money, people who could afford to own stocks and bonds and other financial assets.

Like the television commercials, the financial industry encouraged the impression that investing was a common practice among American households. The New York Stock Exchange boasted of thirty million shareholders nationwide and the growing number of women shareholders. Other commentators described the financial markets as models of democracy in which investors cast their votes each day on the issues of economic progress. In Wall Street, however, democracy operated on the principle of one dollar, one vote, and voting power was highly concentrated among the few.

The advertisers of banks and brokerages targeted their messages at this smaller group, both through the images they conveyed and the type of programs they sponsored. Paine Webber, for instance, bought commercial time on the news and sports shows that attracted audiences with the best upscale demographics—upper income and well educated and male. In sports, that meant golf, tennis and the college football games that attracted more affluent audiences. John Lampe, Paine Webber's advertising director, said:

> We want a relatively small segment of the public. . . . If we had unlimited money, sure, it would be nice to advertise on the Super Bowl. We'd get a larger audience but we'd also get much more waste. We're looking for balance—we would prefer the U.S. Tennis Open or a high-quality golf tournament. It's not *all* sports we want. I can't imagine us ever advertising on a bowling tournament, not that I have anything against bowling or the people who watch it.

Bowlers did not buy stocks and bonds, but tennis buffs did. Paine Webber would create a TV commercial tailored to their ultimate fantasy. A nervous young investor is playing a tennis match with the champion Jimmy Connors. Each time Connors hits a fierce passing shot, a financial consultant from Paine Webber steps in with an auxiliary racket and deftly returns it. As Connors graciously concedes defeat, typical investor exclaims: "Thanks, Paine Webber."

Sears, Roebuck, a newcomer to finance, dissented from the narrower targeting strategies of its more experienced competitors. By combining real estate, insurance and credit at one counter, Sears hoped to develop popular financial centers in its three thousand retail outlets, stores that depended more on bowlers than on tennis players. "Everyone else is going toward rich people by featuring elegant actors, pools and yachts," complained Bob Simon of Foote, Cone & Belding, the advertising agency that designed the Sears campaign. "What they present is not real to 99 percent of the country. It's all coy and cute." Sears, he added quickly, was not against rich people.[15]

A more precise picture of Wall Street's core customers was drawn by *The Wall Street Journal*'s marketing survey of "active investors," defined as those people who generated more than $1,000 a year in commissions for their brokers. Active investors, on the whole, were middle-aged men—57 percent were over fifty, presumably white men. The survey did not ask about race, but one could infer that people of color were not statistically significant in the sample. Only 13 percent of the active investors were women.

The core investors' average income was $84,000 a year, placing them securely in the top 1 percent of household incomes in America. They owned, on the average, portfolios of stocks, bonds and other financial assets valued at $331,000. Five percent of them held assets of more than $1 million. These investments produced, on average, annual returns of about 10 percent. The money they earned from their financial wealth contributed about 40 percent of their total incomes; the rest came from wages.

A similar snapshot of wealthy investors was reflected in the demographics of *The Wall Street Journal* itself. Its own daily readership was a reasonable surrogate for all the people who cared most about news of the financial markets. Of the *Journal*'s two million subscribers, 87 percent owned securities, the average aggregate value of which was $371,900. The readers' average net worth, when tangible assets such as real estate, art, antiques and commodity holdings were added, was $600,000 (the median net worth of *Journal* readers was much lower, $271,000). Ninety-two percent of them had attended college and 44 percent postgraduate schools. Their median age was forty-seven years. Only 11 percent of the *Journal*'s subscribers were women.[16]

The question of who owned financial wealth—or who did not—was the buried fault line of American politics. The wealth holders whose money circulated through Wall Street markets were an untypical minority of Americans, with distinctly different economic interests than the majority. The distribution of wealth was the subtext beneath nearly every important economic question that faced the government, yet it was seldom discussed in politics. Political leaders, instead, treated wealth like a taboo subject, cloaked in euphemisms, as if the hard facts of who owned capital might excite class jealousies they could not satisfy or raise questions about the system for which they had no answers.

Nevertheless, the concentration of wealth was the fulcrum on which the most basic political questions pivoted, a dividing line deeper than region or religion, race or sex. In the nature of things, government might choose to enhance the economic prospects for the many or to safeguard the accumulated wealth held by the few, but frequently the two purposes were in irreconcilable conflict. The continuing political struggle across this line, though unseen and rarely mentioned, was the central narrative of American political history, especially in the politics of money.

The Federal Reserve served as mediating agent for this enduring conflict. On occasion, it assumed the power of independent arbiter, deciding on its own whom the government would favor, enforcing its decisions through its control of money and interest rates. This crucial political role was the essential reason why the Federal Reserve was insulated from public view and popular elections—to protect it from the will of the majority.

Most American families did not own stocks or bonds or even money-market accounts. A majority of the people were borrowers, not lenders. Their net financial wealth was zero or negative. American capitalism was powerfully creative in the twentieth century, generating new jobs and products, expanding wage incomes, distributing prosperity widely in the society. But the system had one major redundancy: it did not distribute the ownership of financial wealth very broadly.

American families, on average, had $24,100 in financial assets, according to a survey of consumer finances conducted by the Federal Reserve Board. But this was an instance where the average of all Americans was grossly misleading, distorted by the concentrated wealth in the upper half. The median was only $2,300, which meant that precisely half of American families owned financial assets, including checking deposits, savings accounts or any others, that totaled less than $2,300. More than a fourth of all families had less than $1,000 and another 12 percent had none.

In fact, those figures overstated the financial status of ordinary Americans because most all of these families were also debtors. They held cash in a checking account or a modest savings deposit, but their outstanding loans were larger than these small accumulations. A second study by the Federal Reserve Board looked at all the financial assets held by individuals (excluding what was held by institutions) and calculated the net financial worth of American families—their assets minus their debts. It reported the lopsided distribution in straightforward terms:

> . . . 54 percent of the total net financial assets were held by the 2 percent of families with the greatest amount of such assets and 86 percent by the top 10 percent; 55 percent of the families in the sample had zero or negative net worth.
>
> Viewed from another perspective, these data imply that fewer than 10 percent of families provided more than 85 percent of the net lending by consumers, and more than half of all families were net borrowers.

In other words, the few lent to the many. The ladder of wealth looked like this: at the top were the 10 percent of American families that owned 86 percent of the net financial worth. Next came the 35 percent of families that shared among them the remaining 14 percent of financial assets. Below them were the majority, the 55 percent of American families that, on balance, had accumulated nothing.

The 10 percent and, to a lesser degree, the larger group below them were, of course, the main customers for Wall Street investments. Their net financial worth amounted to about $1.6 trillion.

Families in the top 2 percent owned 30 percent of all liquid assets, everything from checking and savings accounts to money-market funds and bank CDs. They also owned 50 percent of the corporate stocks held by individuals, 39 percent of corporate and government bonds, 71 percent of tax-exempt municipals and 20 percent of all the real estate.

The top 10 percent owned 51 percent of short-term financial paper, 72 percent of corporate stocks, 70 percent of bonds, 86 percent of tax-exempt municipals and 50 percent of all the real property.[17]

Individual investors were only half of the marketplace, however, and not the largest half. Alongside them stood the institutional investors—corporations, banks, insurance companies, pension funds, foundations and university endowments—which owned or managed huge accumulations of wealth on their own. American households directly owned about $3 trillion in financial wealth, stocks, bonds, savings accounts and other financial instruments, But the institutions controlled about $5 trillion in financial paper (most of that wealth ultimately belonged to other parties, stockholders, pension-fund beneficiaries, depositors or insurance-policy holders). The largest pool of assets, by far, was held in the commercial banks ($1.3 trillion), followed by savings and loan associations ($580 billion), life-insurance companies ($420 billion) and retirement funds ($410 billion). By comparison, tax-exempt foundations and universities had assets of $50 billion.[18]

Individuals, of course, indirectly owned most of the wealth stored in the large institutions, since individuals directly owned 73 percent of corporate stocks, including ownership of bank holding companies, insurance companies and other financial institutions. Pensions and life insurance were indirect forms of personal savings too, distributed much more equitably among American families than stocks and bonds were.

All investors, large and small, personal and institutional, were united by one fear: the specter of inflation. Millionaires and elderly widows, giant insurance companies and young couples accumulating a modest nest egg—all faced the same anxiety in the late 1970s. There was really no safe place in the financial markets, no avenue of investment that guaranteed to protect their assets against inflation. Many moved their money around restlessly, and some smart traders and investors found profits by being more clever than the rest. But, on average, inflation was eroding their wealth, depreciating the billions of dollars these citizens and institutions had accumulated.

The Dow Jones average of thirty industrial stocks, for instance, was trading around 900 in mid-1979, no higher than the level it had reached ten years earlier. But $900 was worth a lot less now. An investor who bought a portfolio based on the Dow Jones average in 1969 and held on to it for ten years would have lost about half of the value of his money.[19]

Stock prices were stagnant, in part, because corporate balance sheets were undermined by inflation too. The glossy annual reports showed ever-rising profits in current dollars, but this was mostly illusion, concealing the damage to companies' real assets. When a manufacturer's machinery and factory buildings grew old and wore out, these would have to be replaced at current prices. Thanks to inflation, the replacement cost of productive equipment was much greater than the depreciation that companies deducted each year on their existing plants and machines. When corporations confronted this squeeze, many simply deferred the moment of truth. Replacing the old with the new became a costly decision.

By 1979, investors in the bond market were demanding an "inflation premium" in interest rates, a cushion of several percentage points to hedge against depreciating dollars, but even that protection was inadequate. The curve of rising inflation rates suggested uncertainty for long-term lending that was beyond forecasting. If the inflation index hit 5 percent in 1970 and reached double digits ten years later, where would it stop? At 15 or 20 percent someday? No one could say with any confidence what the value of the dollar would be in ten or twenty years.

Investors, therefore, tilted toward short-term commitments of their money, where interest rates responded more sensitively to changes in inflation and where they could retrieve their assets quickly, if necessary. Even the money market was treacherous, however. Sophisticated investors considered, in addition to the nominal interest rate offered by an investment, the so-called real interest rate—interest minus current inflation. If the posted interest rate was 8 percent and the inflation rate was 10 percent, then they were losing money (without even calculating the additional loss from income taxes). In other times, investors would have been satisfied with a real return of only 1 percent or even less on short-term paper, but in the late 1970s the real interest rate on short-term lending was often much lower. The real rate on three-month T-bills, a standard barometer of short-term credit, had been intermittently negative for three years. That is, the interest investors collected from the government was less than what they lost to inflation. At least twice in the 1970s, the real interest rates had dropped as low as −4 percent.

To the owners of wealth, this exchange looked like a form of fraud. If one believed, as most of them did, that the government in Washington was responsible for causing inflation, then the government was stealthily robbing them of their savings. The only remedy to their distress was political pressure to change the government's economic policies and restore the stability of money.

The grievances of investors, however, collided with an opposing reality of inflation, a paradox of winners and losers. While the few suffered loss, the many enjoyed real gains. Rising prices aggravated everyone, but inflation actually improved the financial status of large classes of ordinary Americans, probably the majority of them. Inflation particularly benefited the broad middle class of families that owned their own homes, that depended on wages for their income, not on interest and dividends from financial assets. This consequence was familiar to many economists, but not to most ordinary citizens, including many of those whose personal balance sheets were enhanced by inflation.[20]

Joseph J. Minarik, an economist at the Brookings Institution who made a broad study of how inflation in the late 1970s affected the incomes, wealth and tax burdens of four broad groups of citizens, concluded:

. . . the average middle-income homeowner is the big winner in inflation. His labor income keeps up with prices, his home appreciates in real terms, and his home mortgage payment does not increase at all. The Federal income tax becomes somewhat more onerous, but this effect is far outweighed by the benefits of homeownership. The average middle-income home renter does not fare as well, but overall he nearly keeps up with inflation.

By contrast, Minarik found that upper-income households, then defined as those above $37,500 in income, approximately the top 10 percent on the income ladder, were "left substantially worse off." Their salaries kept pace with inflation too, but their assets were eroded. "The wealthy have no safe and profitable store of value in times of inflation," he explained.

A similar study by economist Edward N. Wolff of New York University measured the effects on wealth caused by the first lag of the modern inflationary spiral, starting in 1969 and ending with the recession of 1974. During that period, Wolff reported: "Inflation acted like a progressive tax, leading to greater equality in the distribution of wealth."

Minarik found that inflation's impact on two other groups—the poor and the elderly—was more ambiguous but also more benign than popular political opinion assumed. Generally, it was believed that these two groups suffered most severely from inflation because they lived on fixed incomes. Minarik found this was not true. With a lag, government benefit programs for low-income families, those under $9,000, generally increased in time to keep up with prices. Many poor people were sheltered from rising costs in two sectors where prices were soaring—health and housing—because of Medicaid and public housing. "Over a short period, low-income households are indeed the most adversely affected when prices increase, simply because they have the least maneuvering room in their budgets," Minarik wrote. "But over longer periods their incomes tend to catch up with prices." The poor were still poor, of course, but inflation did not make them worse off compared to others.

The elderly were partially protected too. Social Security benefits were indexed to the inflation rate, automatically increasing the monthly checks periodically to catch up with prices. Among the elderly, Minarik found, the ones hurt most "are those who rely most heavily on private pensions or their own savings. The notion of the Social Security recipient as the chief loser in inflation is largely incorrect. . . ."

The central explanation for this reversal of fortunes—the many gaining at the expense of the few—was homeownership. Most American families, two-thirds of them, owned only one real asset of any significance, the home in which they lived. During inflation, it was the best investment available. It did not, of course, pay annual interest or dividends like bonds and stocks, but in the 1970s, housing was better than either. The value of homes, on average, increased with inflation and, in most places, appreciated faster than the general price level. Meanwhile, the family borrowed heavily through a long-term mortgage in order to own the home—and for debtors, inflation was a winning transaction. The real burden of its debt was depreciating while the family's wage income was rising. For instance, a middle-income family that purchased a $35,000 house in 1969 would be making monthly payments of $400 or so. A decade later, the house might be worth as much as $90,000 and the family's wages might have doubled. But the monthly mortgage payment was still $400. The mortgage payment, typically the family's largest monthly bill, was not inflating at all—it was actually shrinking as a share of the family's income, leaving more money for other desires.

Broad ownership of family homes was one of the federal government's fundamental social policies and one of its most effective programs. The tax deductions allowed for mortgage interest and property taxes, combined credit subsidies invented in the New Deal, stimulated millions of transactions in which families purchased homes they otherwise could not have afforded. Since the Great Depression of the 1930s, homeownership had steadily expanded from 44 percent to 66 percent of all families.

The government subsidy for housing, in fact, was the only significant program that enabled ordinary families to contract large debts and accumulate real assets. It worked. When equity in homes was added to the family balance sheet, alongside financial assets, the median family's net worth was $24,500—$22,000 of it in the family home. People could not, of course, spend that wealth, but they might borrow against it or save it for old age or pass it on to their children. Debt, in other words, could work to broaden the distribution of wealth. In times of high inflation, it worked even better.

"Households with confidence that their real incomes will rise have used the same technique of borrowing to accelerate their consumption of other goods," Minarik observed. "Such households understand that their debt will depreciate as the price level rises and their fixed repayment schedule will become less onerous as inflation drives up their nominal income." This was the same phenomenon observed by Eugene Sussman, the New York jewelry manufacturer. Ordinary people were borrowing and buying despite inflation, indeed, because of it. Middle-income families increased their real assets while the better-off families lost value in their financial assets. The overall effect was a mild but steady leveling process—pushing wealth to the middle and the bottom.[21]

The wealth redistributed by inflation flowed in many directions, but one of the main channels was across the generations—from the old to the young. Shrinking the real burden of debt assisted young families most directly since, starting out with little or no savings, younger people naturally relied most heavily on borrowing to make the basic purchases of family life—cars, homes, appliances. Their gain was older Americans' loss, at least those older Americans who had accumulated savings and lent their money to others.

This benefit for youth was clear enough in economic terms, but in politics, it was obscured by the general anxiety. Many young people felt like losers too, even though they clearly benefited from the inflationary conditions. Younger voters felt especially threatened by rising prices because they were afraid they would be priced out of the good life—the ability to own their own home and car. The actual effect was the opposite. Despite the rising price of houses, homeownership expanded robustly and without interruption during the 1970s as it became easier for young families to assume debt. Inflation tilted nearly every bargain in favor of the future and nearly always penalized the past.

A social philosopher, searching for a progressive theory of justice, might contemplate the underlying consequences of inflation and conclude that this system was a promising model for social equity. Inflation, after all, discreetly redistributed wealth from creditors to debtors, from those who had an excess to those who had none. It took the most from those who had the largest accumulations of wealth but without subjecting them to real suffering. They were not impoverished, after all, merely made less wealthy. Liberal economists like Minarik, furthermore, warned that the orthodox remedy for inflation —a severe economic contraction that increased unemployment— would be a harmful exchange for the many. For the poor in particular, he noted, a recession "amputates the hand to relieve the hangnail."

Political questions were not resolved abstractly by philosophers or economists. In the real world of politics, the tangible aggravations from inflation seemed to be universal, provoking complaints from every quarter, every class. Despite the averages, millions of workers did not enjoy wage increases that kept up with prices, and, as Minarik conceded, even citizens who benefited most handsomely from inflation did not seem to appreciate the fact. Rising incomes pushed average working families into higher brackets of the federal income tax. While Minarik found that the appreciating value of their homes more than offset the higher taxes, they still resented the increases. Rapidly rising prices and debt allowed millions of middle-class families to acquire more real goods, but runaway inflation also frightened them. Politicians, in any case, did not often hear from voters who were celebrating inflation's egalitarian effects.

Perhaps most importantly, the investors were in revolt. The owners of capital could hardly be expected to passively accept the steady loss of their returns. They would resist by refusing to commit their wealth to long-term ventures, the process of capital formation that was fundamental to future economic prosperity. They would move their money out of financial investments and seek safe havens in real assets —gold, real estate, antiques, art—anything tangible that might inflate in price faster than the dollar lost its value. Finally, though they were a minority of voters, investors naturally had political influence far greater than their numbers. The government, they demanded emphatically, must do something to stop inflation.

On Monday morning, when Richard Moe went into the Oval Office, it was clear that President Carter had already digested the contents of Moe's briefing book on possible choices for Federal Reserve chairman. The news from financial markets continued to be alarming. Gold was heading toward $307 an ounce. The dollar continued to fall. In the last month and a half, the U.S. currency had lost 10 percent of its value against the British pound. An anonymous Administration official told *The New York Times:* "The markets are scared to death. Their fear is that President Carter may now sacrifice economic prudence for political expediency."[22]

The press speculation on whom Carter would select for Fed chairman focused on four names: Paul Volcker, president of the New York Fed; A. W. "Tom" Clausen, president of the Bank of America; David Rockefeller, CEO of Chase Manhattan; and Bruce MacLaury, president of the Brookings Institution and former president of the Minneapolis Federal Reserve Bank.

I was informed that the decision was moving clearly toward Volcker [Moe said]. I had enough doubt in my own mind about this one question about him that I decided to go in and see the President. I thought he should consider Tom Clausen of the Bank of America, talk to him personally and see if he was available. If he thought Clausen was as good or better than Volcker, he ought to talk with him. The President was very attentive to that.

The one question about Volcker was whether he would be sufficiently cooperative, a "team player," as Fed chairman. Carter listened to Moe's argument and telephoned Clausen in San Francisco. Was he interested in becoming chairman of the Federal Reserve? The banker consulted his wife about moving to Washington and came back on the phone to decline. After that conversation, the President's choice seemed inevitable.

The next day, Paul Volcker was summoned to the White House for an interview with the President. Volcker was imposingly tall—six feet seven inches, a full foot taller than Jimmy Carter—though he did not use his great height to intimidate others, as some large men do. His posture was slightly stooped, like the awkward center on a basketball team who is used to being surrounded by people shorter than himself. Bald and rumpled, graying, with lumpy features, Volcker's expression sometimes resembled that of a brooding clown, bemused by the surrounding folly of the world and detached from it.

Volcker did most of the talking. Wall Street gossips reported later that Volcker warned Jimmy Carter that he would be totally independent of the White House, if Carter appointed him. That was not quite accurate. Volcker did deliver a standard speech on the importance of the Federal Reserve System's independence, to which Carter assented. Volcker also elaborated the reasons why the Federal Reserve's money policy should be tightened. The President neither agreed nor disagreed.

The appointment would be announced the next day, subject to Senate confirmation. Paul Adolph Volcker was fifty-one years old, a graduate in economics from Princeton and public administration from Harvard, a familiar figure in Washington policy circles and Wall Street finance but largely unknown to the general public. At that moment, few in the White House appreciated what would become obvious in the next few years, that this was the most important appointment of Jimmy Carter's Presidency.[23]

What the President also did not grasp was that he was inadvertently launching a new era and ceding his own political power. The choice had occurred by accident, driven by political panic and financial distress. In time, it would profoundly alter the landscape of American life, transforming the terms for virtually every transaction in the national economy and the world's, creating a new order. It would also produce ironic fulfillment of Jimmy Carter's sentimental plea for sacrifice and self-denial.

In subsequent months and years, Paul Volcker would effectively seize control of events and force them in a direction of his own choosing. In the course of challenging the inflationary spiral, Volcker and the Federal Reserve would prove to be more powerful, more effective than any element of the elected government in Washington, but the democratic anomaly remained unexamined. Millions of Americans would lose jobs, homes, farms and family savings in the tidal shift that followed. For others, the transformation would create new opportunity and fortune. Virtually every American, indeed the entire world, would share directly in the consequences. Only a few understood what was happening to them or why.

Stuart Eizenstat, the President's domestic policy adviser, explained Jimmy Carter's fateful choice: "Volcker was selected because he was the candidate of Wall Street. This was their price, in effect. What was known about him? That he was able and bright and it was also known that he was conservative. What wasn't known was that he was going to impose some very dramatic changes."

Late in the afternoon, another White House aide, Gerald Rafshoon, got a telephone call about the Fed appointment from Bert Lance, the Georgia banker and political adviser whom Carter had originally appointed as budget director. Lance had been forced to resign early in the Carter term because of scandals surrounding his private banking affairs; it was a grievous loss to the President, who depended on Lance as a personal friend for wise political advice and a banker's insights on economic policy.

Rafshoon knew nothing about the status of the Fed chairmanship, but he took a message from Lance. "I don't know who the President is thinking of for Fed chairman," Lance said, "but I want you to tell him something for me. He should not appoint Paul Volcker. If he appoints Volcker, he will be mortgaging his re-election to the Federal Reserve."

Rafshoon dutifully went in to see the President and repeated Lance's warning. If Volcker was named, Lance predicted, it would mean both higher interest rates and higher unemployment and the outcome of the 1980 election would be "mortgaged" to the Federal Reserve. The President smiled and thanked him.[24]

A few minutes later, Rafshoon stopped by the office of press secretary Jody Powell and casually asked what was going on. Nothing much, Powell replied, except the press release he was preparing on the appointment of Paul Volcker as Federal Reserve chairman.

The next day, the financial markets applauded. The Dow Jones stock average rose 10 points. The bond market rallied. After months of decline, the dollar abruptly improved on international markets. The price of gold fell $2.50 an ounce. The markets were reassured. It was a political event that Wall Street understood better than Washington.[25]

2

IN THE
TEMPLE

When the Federal Reserve System's new building on Constitution Avenue was completed in 1937, the clean, classical exterior of white marble looked much like the neighboring federal buildings going up in the New Deal era. The design conveyed "dignity and permanence," as the architects intended, without the decorative tricks or monumental scale that made older government buildings in Washington seem pretentious or forbidding. An American eagle in white marble, perched over huge bronze doors, looked out at the green spaces of Washington's Mall, just east of the Lincoln Memorial. The doorway led to a lobby displaying portraits of Woodrow Wilson, the Fed's founding President, and Senator Carter Glass of Virginia, who shepherded the Federal Reserve Act through Congress in 1913. The lobby's ceiling was decorated with a plaster relief of Greek coins surrounding the goddess Cybele, symbol of abundance and stability. The entrance was imposing but impractical. Except for rare ceremonial occasions, the bronze doors remained closed. Everyone, from clerks to governors, entered the Fed through the back door on the C Street side of the building.[1]

When the building was still new, Representative Wright Patman of Texas, last of the genuine Populists to serve in Congress, offered a mischievous suggestion. Patman was a brilliant eccentric, self-taught and stubbornly independent in his views, and he devoted nearly fifty years in Congress to methodically assaulting the Federal Reserve System and its privileged powers. This building, Patman observed at a

House hearing in 1939, did not actually belong to the federal government. It belonged to the twelve Reserve Banks of the Federal Reserve System—and the twelve Reserve Banks were owned and controlled by private commercial banks, which held stock in the Reserve Banks as a condition of membership in the System. Therefore, the congressman reasoned, the Fed's headquarters was not tax-exempt like other public buildings. It should be subject to local property taxes, like any other private enterprise.

Inspired by Patman's remarks, the District of Columbia tax collector sent a bill for property taxes to the Federal Reserve's Board of Governors. The Fed refused to pay. The board's lawyers patiently tried to explain the complicated institution created by Woodrow Wilson's legislative compromise, an institution that, they insisted, was a part of the government. The lawyers cited the original legislative history of 1913 and an Attorney General's opinion issued the following year and subsequent federal court decisions, all of which confirmed this. The Federal Reserve was an "independent department" of government.

The D.C. tax collector was not convinced. After all, the Board of Governors had purchased the land from the federal government in 1935 for $750,000 and the Treasury Department had signed over the deed, relinquishing "all the right title and interest of the United States of America." If the Fed was part of government, why would the federal government sell real estate to itself? In December 1941, four days before Pearl Harbor, the District of Columbia government published a notice of delinquent taxes and scheduled a public auction. It would sell the Federal Reserve's marble temple to the highest bidder.

The auction was postponed several times and never occurred, but it took three years of legal wrangling before the Board of Governors could convince the local government that the Federal Reserve System, despite its peculiar structure, was indeed part of the federal government. In the end, each of the twelve Reserve Banks was compelled to execute a quitclaim deed, attesting that they did not own the building on Constitution Avenue, that the U.S. government owned it.[2]

Nevertheless, the Federal Reserve System enjoyed the ambiguity over its status and exploited it. Philip E. Coldwell, who served nearly thirty years in the System, as president of the Dallas Reserve Bank and on the Board of Governors, observed: "To some extent, the Federal Reserve considers itself government. Other times, when it serves, it considers itself not government."

Wright Patman never relented. Twenty-five years later, on the floor of the House of Representatives, he declared: "A slight acquaintance with American constitutional theory and practice demonstrates that, constitutionally, the Federal Reserve is a pretty queer duck." He was correct in that. The Federal Reserve System was an odd arrangement, a unique marriage of public supervision and private interests, deliberately set apart from the elected government, though still part of it. The Fed enjoyed privileges extended to no other agency in Washington —it raised its own revenue, drafted its own operating budget and submitted neither to Congress for approval. At the top were the seven governors of the Federal Reserve Board, appointed by the President to fourteen-year terms and confirmed by the Senate. But the seven governors shared power with the presidents of the twelve Reserve Banks, each serving the private banks in its region, from Boston to Atlanta, Dallas to San Francisco. The Reserve Bank presidents were not appointed in Washington, but were elected by each district's board of directors. Six of the nine directors in each case were, in turn, elected themselves by the commercial banks, the "member banks" of the Federal Reserve System. When the Fed decided the core questions of regulating money supply, its debate and votes were conducted in a hybrid committee that combined the two levels, known as the Federal Open Market Committee. In FOMC decisions, the governors had seven votes and Reserve Bank presidents had five votes, rotated annually among the districts. Only the president of the New York Fed, more important than all the others, did not have to share; he voted at all meetings. Thus, critics complained, the nation's money regulation was decided in part by representatives of private interests—the banks.[3]

To further complicate and darken the picture, the commercial banks held stock shares in each of the twelve Federal Reserve Banks, which misled many into assuming that the Federal Reserve System was "privately owned." In fact, the stock shares were a vestigial feature of System membership that confused and excited Populist critics, but had virtually no practical meaning. The Federal Reserve System was government, including the twelve Federal Reserve Banks, not a private entity. Commercial bankers did enjoy preferred access and influence at the Fed, but the internal power relationship gave the Board of Governors, appointed by Washington, more authority than the presidents of the twelve Federal Reserve Banks. When a regional board of directors selected its new president, the chairman at the Fed's home office could veto the choice.

The American arrangement was quite different from those of the central banks in most other industrial nations, where the appendage of regional reserve banks did not exist. The crucial difference, however, was that other central banks, even the prototypical Bank of England, were democratized in a way the Fed was not. They all operated on the same basic principles of finance, but other central bankers took their orders directly from elected politicians. When the Bank of England wished to raise interest rates, it could not move without approval from the Prime Minister's Cabinet. The same subservient relationship applied in Japan, France and Italy. The one exception was the Bundesbank in West Germany, whose political independence resembled the Federal Reserve's and for good reason. In the reconstruction following World War II, Germany's new central bank was patterned on the American model.

Patman's crusade failed. In a lifetime of tenacious lobbying for reform, the Texas congressman could never persuade a majority in Congress to change the Fed in any way. Year after year, as chairman of the House Banking Committee, Patman held meticulous hearings and introduced reform legislation to make the Fed more democratic and less subject to the influence of major banks. Shorten the terms of the governors so a single President would have more appointments and, thus, more influence. Remove the Reserve Bank presidents from the Federal Open Market Committee so that only public officials who were nominated by the Chief Executive and confirmed by Congress would decide monetary policy for the nation. Force the Fed to open its books for independent audits by Congress. Subject the Fed's operating budgets to regular congressional scrutiny in the appropriations process, like any other federal agency. Above all, eliminate the privileged status of the private bankers. "A bunch of money hucksters," Patman called them. The Fed, he said, constituted "a dictatorship on money matters by a bankers' club." None of his legislation was enacted.

Long after Patman died in the mid-1970s, others continued to raise his complaints. The same reform bills were introduced year after year in Congress, with both liberal and conservative sponsors. All failed to pass, with the single exception of the congressional audit of Fed books, authorized in 1978. Nearly every year, some group somewhere in America filed new lawsuits against the Fed, attacking its secrecy or challenging its legality. None of these lawsuits succeeded.

Neither the hot Populist rhetoric nor careful scholarly critiques made any difference. For all its peculiar features, the Federal Reserve System was remarkably stable among America's political institutions. Over seventy years, its basic design probably changed less than any other important operating arm of the federal government, from the Pentagon to the Postal Service. Most major federal agencies and departments have undergone repeated reorganizations and restructuring, but the Federal Reserve System was "reformed" only once— during the 1930s when control over its decision making was centralized in the Board of Governors in Washington, just as other New Deal reforms consolidated power in the national capital. Regardless of its peculiarities, the Fed's enduring stability as a political institution was evidence that it somehow "worked"—that is, the Federal Reserve seemed to provide what the American system wanted. Otherwise, surely, it would have been changed.

Yet the suspicion and mystery endured too. From the beginning, the Federal Reserve was implicated in nativist conspiracy theories. Homespun tracts and polemical books described it as the secret nexus for sinister forces in the world. The Fed was agent for the "Powers," usually identified as the "International Bankers" and sometimes the "Illuminati" or the "Zionist Conspiracy," echoing the febrile anti-Semitism associated with money since medieval Christianity. The Fed, it was said, was the operating center for a mysterious network of unseen but awesomely powerful people who were manipulating the society for their own purposes—world dominion. In the 1970s, as inflation accelerated, the dark theories about the Fed thrived anew, disseminated in scores of homemade newsletters and privately published books. When Paul Volcker was confirmed by the Senate Banking Committee in August 1979, a citizens' group from Virginia had testified against him, noting his connections with the "top secret" Bilderberg Conference, David Rockefeller's Chase Manhattan Bank, the Council on Foreign Relations and the Trilateral Commission—all of them staples in the popular theories of "one world" conspiracy.[4]

The conspiracy theories were inconsequential in political terms, but in cultural terms, most relevant. The theories contained a revealing message—an expression of spiritual anxiety. Like all conspiracy theories, the ones aimed at the Fed were confused attempts to confront larger mysteries of life, to explain the awesome powers that were shielded from the scrutiny of ordinary mortals yet seemed to govern their lives, like the temple incantations of ancient priests who interpreted divine messages and decreed the course of social destiny. In a twisted sense, belief in a grand conspiracy was an act of religious deference, an acknowledgment by people that someone or something held distant and unexplainable power over them. The believers collected scattered facts and stitched them together to construct a cosmology that explained good and evil, and, like most cosmologies, this one seemed logical to believers and utterly bizarre to everyone else. Somewhere, in a hidden place, there were mortal men who conspired to rule over all—to usurp powers that belonged only to God.

The supposed sacrilege of men who created money was a constant theme in the most virulent tracts attacking the Fed. One of them, *The Federal Reserve Hoax*, written in the early 1960s by Wickliffe B. Vennard, Sr., explained, for instance, a dizzying series of historical connections between money and democracy and Christian faith, the death of Christ, the assassination of Lincoln, and the Federal Open Market Committee:

When our Lord and Master defied them by upsetting the tables and casting the money changers from His temple with a whip, He knew full well that within a week He would be nailed to a cross on Calvary. . . . Abraham Lincoln, whose rash defiance [of bankers] cost him his life, saved this country billions in interest, because the money was not issued against debt as is that issued by the Federal Reserve System. . . . Since the Babylonian Captivity, there has existed a determined behind-the-scenes, under-the-table, atheistic, satanic, anti-Christian force—worshippers of Mammon—whose underlying purpose is World Control through the Control of Money. . . . This book is aimed at the Sanhedrin of today—the 12 men who control this country from behind the scenes.[5]

To modern minds, it seemed bizarre to think of the Federal Reserve as a religious institution. Yet the conspiracy theorists, in their own demented way, were on to something real and significant. Economics was the essence of scientific rationalism; the Fed's analytical techniques were the opposite of metaphysical speculation. But the Federal Reserve did also function in the realm of religion. Its mysterious powers of money creation, inherited from priestly forebears, shielded a complex bundle of social and psychological meanings. With its own form of secret incantation, the Federal Reserve presided over awesome social ritual, transactions so powerful and frightening they seemed to lie beyond common understanding.

Feverish polemics that portrayed the Fed as the "Sanhedrin of today" were ludicrous in their particulars, but they were based on an ancient cultural reality about money that was still valid in the age of enlightenment and computers. Above all, money was a function of faith. It required an implicit and universal social consent that was indeed mysterious. To create money and use it, each one must believe and everyone must believe. Only then did worthless pieces of paper take on value. When a society lost faith in money, it was implicitly losing faith in itself. In the advanced economies of Western capitalist nations, this fundamental social bond had been managed for several centuries by ordinary mortals, working in institutions devoid of religious trappings (though religion still exercised direct influence over money in some less advanced cultures). The money process, nonetheless, still required a deep, unacknowledged act of faith, so mysterious that it could easily be confused with divine powers.

"It is a truism that public confidence is important to banks," an
editorial in *The Wall Street Journal* observed. "That's why early He-
brews did their banking in temples and the later Americans and Europeans built banks that looked like temples."[6] Officials of the Federal
Reserve were themselves the ultimate rationalists—economists who
analyzed numbers, constructed scientific theories to explain economic
behavior and tested the theories against reality—yet they too unconsciously invoked the sacred aura of their institution. Federal Reserve
governors spoke enthusiastically about "the mystique of central banking," without being able to explain it very succinctly. A former officer
of the Federal Reserve Board, describing the confidential fraternity
that economists entered into when they joined the Fed staff, called it
"taking the veil," the expression that describes nuns entering a con-
vent. A chairman of the House Banking Committee sometimes referred derisively to the Fed's senior economists as "the monks."[7]

Richard Syron, a vice president of the Boston Fed who served for a
time as special assistant to Volcker, suggested that the institutional
temperament and structure of the Federal Reserve System most resembled the Catholic Church, in which he had been raised.

> The System is just like the Church. That's probably why I feel so com-
> fortable with it. It's got a pope, the chairman; and a college of cardinals,
> the governors and bank presidents; and a curia, the senior staff. The
> equivalent of the laity is the commercial banks. If you're a naughty parish-
> ioner in the Catholic Church, you come to confession. In this system, if
> you're naughty, you come to the Discount window for a loan. We even
> have different orders of religious thought like Jesuits and Franciscans and
> Dominicans only we call them pragmatists and monetarists and neo-
> Keynesians.

The institution's official secrecy naturally enhanced the mystique.
The Federal Open Market Committee met to deliberate on the money
supply eight to ten times a year, but its decisions were made in secrecy. Only six or eight weeks later, after the FOMC had held its next
meeting, would the Fed release a brief report on what the previous
meeting had decided. Internal reports and memos, the economic analysis that supported the decisions, were kept confidential for five years.
A full transcript of the committee deliberations was never available,
because it was no longer kept. The FOMC used to make a transcript
of its deliberations available to the public after the five-year waiting
period, but even that historical record was discontinued in the mid-
1970s. When Congress was enacting the Freedom of Information Act,
Federal Reserve Chairman Arthur Burns decided to abolish the full

transcript, lest litigation force it into public view prematurely and embarrass Fed officials. No other agency of government, not even the Central Intelligence Agency, enjoyed such privacy.

The Fed would explain itself, but only up to a point and long after the fact. Ostensibly, this was meant to avoid market manipulations and "insider trading" on the Fed's own decisions, but it also provided political cover. The secrecy spawned an infantile anger among the Fed's critics, even from some distinguished scholars whose commentaries on Fed performance frequently seemed harsh and petulant. Not knowing was a form of impotence, and the critics' anger often sounded like the frustrated tantrums of a small child who has been excluded from the family secrets. What is going on behind the closed door? Father does not answer. It must be something important. Mother will not tell. The secret behind the bronze doors was not, of course, sex, but nearly as mysterious.

The anti-Fed polemics liked to quote Henry Ford, Sr., on the mysteries of money and the Federal Reserve: "It is well enough that the people of the nation do not understand our banking and monetary system for, if they did, I believe there would be a revolution before tomorrow morning." [8]

The American public, not unlike its political leaders, depended on familiar clichés for its limited understanding of money. The Federal Reserve controls the money supply. The Fed sets interest rates. When the government spends too much money, the Fed turns on the printing press and then we have inflation. All these crude generalities were either mistaken or too simplistic to describe the reality, and unless one was willing to move beyond them, it was impossible to understand the awesome powers of the Federal Reserve or its frailties.

The public's confusion over money and its ignorance of money politics were heightened by the scientific pretensions of economics. Average citizens simply could not understand the language, and most economists made no effort to translate for them. The dominant mode of modern economic analysis mimicked the methods of Newtonian physics by presuming that economic behavior followed its own self-contained logic, rules and patterns as capable of replication as the natural laws that physicists discovered in the physical world. Most economists, regardless of their particular ideological biases, dwelt rigidly within that narrow definition of their discipline. They cloaked their observations in dense, neutral-sounding terminology that was opaque to nonscientists. The neutral language masked the political content of economics and the social rituals of capitalism—as if all economic players were simple molecules destined to behave according to the same natural order, regardless of their political values or wealth. All economic decisions were made not to reward one group or to punish another but simply to advance the universal objective of "sound economics." John Kenneth Galbraith, an economist with a more supple understanding of human society, drolly observed: "What is called sound economics is very often what mirrors the needs of the respectably affluent." [9]

Economics also tried to ignore the psychological impulses that lay beneath all human behavior. Individually or in large groups, people did sometimes defy the tangible dictates of supply and demand. They behaved in ways that seemed perverse to economics, driven by their own beliefs or emotions, nonquantifiable fears or hopes that existed only in their heads, not in economic data from the marketplace. Every fishmonger in Washington, D.C., for instance, understood the psychology of bluefish. If the price of bluefish was up at $2.20 per pound, the Chesapeake Bay fishermen would likely bring in larger catches. That naturally drove down the price, and as it fell, customers bought more and more bluefish. Then a strange thing happened: when the price fell below $1 a pound, people stopped buying bluefish, even though it was plentiful. Bluefish had become a "cheap" fish, unfit for their dinner table. When the price went up, they started buying again. In larger and much more complicated ways, financial markets were also driven by the nonquantifiable beliefs and emotions.

The ultimate test of soundness for any science was the ability of its rules and theories to predict outcomes, and by that standard, economics was a crude and underdeveloped discipline. When its models failed, as they often did, economists grudgingly acknowledged that political impulses or human psychology had somehow disrupted the equations. These events were usually dismissed as "random shocks" —war or political intervention or social upheavals—that need not be explained since they were nonrecurring aberrations. War and politics were not abnormal events in human society, only in economics. The reigning scientific perspective of economists, in addition to being severely limited in scope, was also outdated intellectually. Economics mimicked physics, but twentieth-century physicists had moved beyond the clockwork laws of Newton to the relativity of Einstein, a vastly richer and more supple conception of reality. Economists seemed unable to follow.

The public confusion about money began at the most elementary level—with the word itself. When academic economists or monetary experts at the Federal Reserve talked about money, they meant something specific and different from what most Americans understood. Money simply meant wealth in the loose colloquial that most people used. "My money is in stocks and bonds." "His money is in real estate."

To economists, money was only what could be used immediately to buy things—that is, the cash in one's pocket, coins and bills, or the demand deposit in a checking account at the bank. When economists talked about the "money supply," or the principal monetary aggregate known as M-1, they meant only the money that could be spent right away—the gross sum of all the currency and demand deposits held by every consumer and business in the country. In August 1979, the spending money called M-1 totaled only $362 billion for the entire U.S. economy. That hardly seemed adequate to sustain a Gross National Product of $2.4 trillion, the annual total of goods and services produced in America. The modest supply of money was adequate, however, because, in the course of a year, this money would turn over many times, as people exchanged it. A factory worker cashes his paycheck and buys groceries. The supermarket pays the wholesaler for produce and the wholesaler buys a new car. The auto dealer pays his employees. The same $362 billion would slosh in and out of many pockets, many bank accounts, turning over more than six times during the year.

Most of the spending money known as M-1 existed as checking-account deposits, about three-fourths of it, and the rest as currency. The proportions did not matter, since the two were interchangeable. If the public for some reason wanted to hold more of its money in hard cash, the Bureau of Engraving printed more bills and the Federal Reserve distributed the currency through the banking system, but the printing itself did not create new money—since the cash was simply substituted for the existing deposits in checking accounts.

If the same factory worker put part of his wages in a savings account at his bank or the neighborhood savings and loan, he would still regard his money as money, but monetary economists would treat it differently. Unlike bank checking accounts, a savings account paid him interest on his money. But it was no longer so easy for him to spend it immediately. He would most likely have to withdraw funds from his savings account, deposit the money in his checking account at the bank, then write a check at the store. Thus, the money moved more slowly into economic transactions—less liquid in the hydraulics of the economy. Economists, therefore, counted it in a second category, a broader monetary aggregate known as M-2. M-2 included all of the small savings accounts and time deposits at banks, credit unions or S & L's plus whatever people had invested in money-market mutual funds. With M-1 added in, M-2 totaled about $1.5 trillion.

Following the same distinctions, M-3 was a still larger category of money—larger and less liquid than the other two. It added such large-denomination financial instruments as $100,000 certificates of deposit that only corporations, financial institutions or wealthy investors could afford to hold, usually for a specified time period like three months or six months. They could withdraw their money eventually, but it was not readily available for spending. The broader M-3 aggregate—which included M-1 and M-2—totaled about $1.7 trillion. (A final measure of money, known as L, for total liquidity, attempted to count all the financial assets that could be sold and converted into spending money —Treasury bills, commercial paper, U.S. savings bonds and a few others—though perhaps at a penalty if market prices were down. L totaled a little more than $2.1 trillion.[10]

The three main blends of money described, in a sense, the fluid that the Federal Reserve attempted to regulate inside the tanks and plumbing of the financial system. Each blend of money had a different viscosity, like three different grades of oil. The spending money called M-1 was light and freely flowing. M-2 and M-3 were more dense and flowed more slowly, like heavier oils that settled to the bottom of a tank. Any businessman or family could shift its money from one blend to another, simply by moving it from one kind of liquid asset to another, and this interaction between the three monetary aggregates was under way constantly in millions of financial transactions. These shifts did not alter the overall size of the money supply, but they were an important element in the money dynamics that the Federal Reserve monitored, a source of continuing uncertainty and occasional error.

America's money, however, did not stop at the national borders. "Our money is the world's money," as Paul Volcker has said. The dollar was the dominant currency of world trade so its value affected global transactions far beyond U.S. commerce. If Saudi Arabia sold oil to Latin America, the transaction was in dollars; if the dollar was declining in international exchange, the Arabs lost real income. "Fundamentally, what disturbs Peoria disturbs Zurich," Volcker argued. In addition, the U.S. financial system also functioned in a "51st state," as one analyst called it—the Eurodollar market. A huge pool of expatriate dollars, at first built up over the postwar decades by the trading and investment of U.S. multinational corporations, existed offshore for lending and borrowing. U.S. banks alone had assets of more than $400 billion in overseas offices—essentially unregulated. Technically, it was not part of the domestic money supply, but every day the major banks, corporations and investors shifted back and forth between the two, seeking the highest rate of return or the cheapest loan. The dollar in Peoria, therefore, reacted eventually to the dollar in Zurich and vice versa.[11]

The economists' definition of "moneyness" was not the heart of public confusion, however. The fundamental source of mystery—the process that so defied common intuition that it did not seem quite believable—was the creation of money. For centuries, as the outlines of modern banking developed, prudent men had condemned its money-creating powers as dangerous and immoral, destined to collapse someday and bring society down with it. The anti-Fed polemics railed at the Board of Governors and the secret proceedings of the FOMC, but what really disturbed the authors was the way in which money was created. For ordinary citizens, who had never before contemplated the matter, the experience could be slightly dizzying. It did sound like magic.

New money was created not only by the Federal Reserve but also by private commercial banks. They did it by new lending, by expanding the outstanding loans on their books. Routinely, a bank borrowed money from one group, the depositors, and lent it to someone else, the borrowers, a straightforward function as intermediary. But, if that was all that occurred, then credit would be frozen in size, unable to expand with new economic growth. On the margins, therefore, bankers expanded their lending on their own and the overall pool of credit grew —and the bank credit turned into money.

A bank officer authorizes a $100,000 loan to a small-business man —a judgment that the businessman's future earnings will be sufficient to repay the loan, that his enterprise would create real value in the future, which would justify the risk and the creation of the additional money. Ordinarily the banker would not hand over $100,000 in dollar bills. He would simply write a check or, more likely, enter a credit in the businessman's bank account for $100,000. Either way, money has been created by the simple entry in a ledger. Implausible as that might seem, it was a reality that everyone would accept, even if they were unaware of its audacity. The businessman would go out and spend the money, writing checks on his new account, and everyone would honor their value. The creation of new money, thus, was really based on bank-created debt. This concept is what baffled and outraged so many critics of the money system. Money ought to be "real," they insisted. It should be based on something tangible from the past, accumulated wealth like gold, not on a banker's hunch about the future.

How could such a system possibly work? Why didn't it collapse and produce social disaster? The short, simple explanation was: trust. People trusted the banks (and, by extension, the Federal Reserve). They believed, perhaps not even knowing the actual mechanics, that bankers would use this magic prudently. Banks would make sound loans that would be repaid, and they would always keep enough money on hand so that any individual depositor could always withdraw his when he needed it.

If enough loans went bad and enough people became distrustful, they all went to the bank at once to withdraw their money and discovered that actually the bank didn't have enough. A "run on the bank" usually ended in failure and padlocked doors, but the legendary bank panics of history were largely unknown to modern Americans; nothing like that had happened in America in nearly fifty years.

This was the original purpose for which the Federal Reserve was created in 1913—to protect the banking system from periodic liquidity crises, temporary shortages of money that led to failure. Through the Discount window, the Fed provided short-term loans to banks that were temporarily strained, helping them through the tight spots. With one spectacular exception, the Crash of 1929 and the banking panic that closed nearly half of the banks in America, the Fed's protection was extraordinarily successful.

Banks, large and small, were the most secure business enterprises in America, sheltered by the government from failure like no other sector of the economy. Year after year, no more than a handful of the nation's fourteen thousand banks failed, usually six or eight a year and sometimes none. In 1979, ten banks would be forced to close, all of them quite small and marginal. This compared to 1,165 mining and manufacturing companies that failed, 908 wholesale goods suppliers, 3,183 retail stores, 1,378 construction companies. Banking was safe and profitable, nearly fail-proof.[12]

Bankers, however, could be dangerous. They were human, after all. Left to their own impulses, they might be tempted to expand their loans and create new money infinitely—collecting more and more interest income, the main source of bank profits, until eventually the system collapsed of its own greed. They were restrained from doing this by the Federal Reserve.

The ultimate purpose of the central bank was to control the society's overall expansion of debt—to decide, in effect, what level of hopes and promises the future could reasonably fulfill. If new credit expanded recklessly, beyond the realistic capacity of the economy to expand its output, then the future would deliver failure and disorder. If the new lending was restrained too severely, then feasible ventures would languish and the future could not realize its actual potential. The Federal Reserve's estimates of the future were calculated by scientific reasoning, of course, but the function closely resembled the prophetic role of the ancient temple priests who were given divine license to look into the future and foretell whether lean or abundant years lay ahead. The Federal Reserve governors also made prophecy, but they had the ability to make their own predictions come true.

The Fed's leverage for controlling the banks' expansion of credit was a mechanism inherited from centuries of banking history, the requirement that each bank hold a portion of its total deposits in reserve, a guarantee that it would always have sufficient funds for normal banking business. The reserves must be deposited at one of the twelve Federal Reserve Banks or held as cash in the bank's vault. Reserves were like earnest money against the possibility of bad surprises, a rash of failed loans or a rush of withdrawals by depositors. The Fed's reserve requirements varied according to the size of the banks and the types of accounts, but the basic requirement set for member banks in 1979 was 16.25 percent. For every $600 a bank held in checking accounts, it must park approximately $100 at the local branch of the Fed —idle money, collecting no interest. Thus, the total reserves held in the Reserve Banks was about $41 billion, backing about $258 billion in demand deposits. When all the currency held by the public was added, the total came to about $362 billion. That was the nation's basic money supply, the monetary aggregate called M-1.

To expand the money supply or contract it, the Federal Reserve created more reserves for the banking system or withdrew reserves— using its two small valves, the Discount lending directly to banks or the open-market purchase and sale of U.S. government securities. When the Fed bought Treasury bills or bonds, it simply credited the newly created money to the reserve account of whichever financial institution sold it the securities. It didn't much matter which bank was the seller, because once the money was in the banking system, it was free to flow to wherever it was needed. If the Fed bought from a brokerage firm instead of a bank, it had the same effect. The Fed credited the reserve account of the broker's bank which in turn credited the broker's individual account.

Either way, the Fed's action increased the total reserves of the banking system—and thus allowed the total money supply to grow too. The Fed injections, whether they came through the Discount window at the Reserve Banks or the Open Market Desk at the New York Federal Reserve Bank, were called "high-powered money" because of this unique property: whatever new money the Federal Reserve added would be multiplied many times through the money-creation powers of the commercial banks.

The act of multiplication seemed dizzying too. If the Fed injected $1 billion in new reserve deposits, the banking system could immediately commit $840 million of it to new loans, setting aside 16 percent to satisfy the reserve requirement. The $840 million in new loans would instantly create $840 million in new deposits. It didn't matter which banks got the deposit accounts; the new deposits would immediately be the basis for new lending. The banks would set aside 16 percent of the $840 million and lend out another $706 million. Those loans would immediately become new deposits again and permit still more new lending, another $593 million, and so on in diminishing sums. This multiplying process in which new credit became new money continued until the banks exhausted the additional lending capacity created for them by the new reserves added by the Fed. The original $1 billion injected by the Federal Reserve became more than $5 billion in new deposits—deposits that were now counted in the nation's money supply, the M-1 aggregate.

Every resourceful banker, every well-managed bank, naturally worked to take maximum advantage of these powers—since more loans meant more interest earnings for the bank—and so the natural state of the banking system was to be "booked up," its reserves fully committed to the last possible dollar. In slack times, if a bank could not find enough borrowers to soak up its credit capacity, then it would buy government bonds that paid interest—using the same money-creating process. The bank simply wrote a check or created a deposit for whoever sold it the securities.

When a bank's portfolio exceeded its reserves, perhaps because its lending policy was too aggressive, it had two choices. It had to get in balance by the close of the Fed's weekly reporting period. It could call in some loans and extinguish the deposits, but that was awkward. More typically, it would simply borrow the reserves temporarily, per-haps overnight or for two or three days, either from other banks that had a surplus in their reserve accounts or, if necessary, from the Federal Reserve itself. The bank-to-bank borrowing of reserve funds, known as the Federal Funds market, sometimes exceeded $125 billion a day, traded in the money market by telephone and Telex.

The price of this overnight borrowing was the interest rate known as the Federal Funds rate—the rate that reacted most sensitively and immediately to the slightest changes in supply and demand. If many banks were short on reserves, they would have to bid up the Fed Funds rate to get them; when credit was slack and the money supply exceeded the banking system's demand for funds, the Fed Funds rate fell. It was the leading indicator of where interest rates were headed, generally.

In terms of control, the Federal Reserve manipulated the Federal Funds rate more surely than anything else in the financial system; the Fed's own daily actions would move the rate up or down quite pre-cisely and almost instantly, as reserves were added or withdrawn from the banking system. The Fed Funds rate also served as a daily barom-eter for other short-term rates, from three-month Treasury bills to commercial paper issued by corporations. It was watched closely by everyone, by the Fed itself to judge credit conditions in the banking system, and by the Fed watchers of Wall Street to figure out whether the Federal Reserve was easing or tightening or holding steady.

The Federal Funds rate provided the most precise model of how the Federal Reserve manipulated interest rates—the price of borrowed money. Its influence was imperfect but powerful. The basic premise was the rule of supply and demand, but the dynamics were more complex than that. If the Fed restricted the inflowing supply of new reserves below the banking system's demand for them, naturally the price went up. The Federal Funds rate rose as banks bid among themselves for the scarce supply of excess funds. That part was straightforward. But the Federal Reserve's control also directly influenced the demand side of the equation. When it forced this interest rate to rise, that discouraged borrowers from taking on new loans and compelled banks, in turn, to slow down the expansion of their loan portfolios. Demand subsided and came back in balance with supply. Reality, of course, did not operate as neatly as the model, since many other independent forces also simultaneously influenced the demand for new credit and the supply.

Given the fluid nature of finance, manipulations of the Fed Funds rate would swiftly ripple across the entire spectrum of short-term lending, with similar feedback effects on supply and demand. With rare exceptions, the hydraulics of the money market faithfully responded to the engineer's direction. When the Fed raised or lowered the Fed Funds rate, bank CDs, commercial paper, T-bills and the others followed.

Long-term interest rates were powerfully influenced by the Fed too, but with less predictable results. The bond market had a mind of its own, and bond investors made their own forecasts of the future, particularly of future inflation. Notwithstanding the immediate conditions of supply and demand, they might decide to bid long-term rates in a contrary direction—if they concluded that the Fed's management of money or other economic factors would alter the dollar's value many years hence. The Fed had the power to pull short-term interest rates up or down, but it had to coax and persuade the long-term investors.

The ideological implications of the money system had to be understood on two different planes. The idea of money created through new debt offended many conservatives because, in essence, it was a forward-looking process, a social commitment to the future. Bankers were not ordinarily thought of as a progressive element in American politics, yet banking itself functioned on the premise of progress, on a working belief that reliable gambles could be made on the future. On this faith rested the process of economic growth, the financing of new ideas and ventures, of change and innovation. The folk wisdom feared debt, yet future prosperity depended on it.

The folk fears were correct in only one sense: if a society contracted too many claims against the future, if it amassed debts that the future economic effort could not possibly pay off, sooner or later it would pay the consequences. Borrowers would fail to meet their obligations; lenders would lose their gamble. Bankers, as a consequence, dwelt between two conflicting commandments: one was to be generous with the future, to take risks and make the loans that businesses needed to expand and consumers needed to buy; the other commandment was to be always prudent in the risk taking. The Federal Reserve was the governor for both.

Yet as a political arrangement, the American money system was profoundly conservative. Control was concentrated in a relatively few hands—the banking system and the Federal Reserve—and was shielded from any interference by other interests. The national government, the democratic equivalent of a sovereign, possessed the unique power to create credit and money, yet it delegated the power to others, a select group of private corporations that were licensed as commercial banks, without any specifications as to how the banks should allocate the credit. Who would qualify for loans and who would be denied? Which projects in the future were worthy gambles and which were speculative or redundant? The choices made by bankers had profound political consequences: which economic sectors would flourish, which cities and neighborhoods and regions of the country would thrive, and which ones would struggle or even perish. The Federal Reserve remained silent on those questions, adhering to a laissez-faire ideology. Those priorities, it maintained, were better settled in the free-market auctions.

The basic mechanics of money regulation, the way in which the Federal Reserve restrained or encouraged the expansion of credit, in turn, regulated the entire American economy. Credit expansion was not the only factor that determined whether production and consumption would expand or shrink, whether new factories would be built or consumers would buy more cars and houses, but expanding credit was the necessary precondition. Neither production nor consumption could grow if credit was not growing too. Too little new credit would starve commerce. Too much new money would eventually produce another ailment called inflation.

In simple mechanical terms, the Fed's money regulation of the economy resembled a series of interlocking gear wheels. The first gear, turning slowly but powerfully, represented bank reserves, totally controlled by the Federal Reserve. The reserves, in turn, drove the faster gear wheel, bank lending. And the pace of bank lending powerfully influenced a huge and vastly more complicated gearbox, the entire economy of real work and enterprise—the borrowing and buying, producing and consuming that were central to every citizen's well-being.

The metaphor of interlocking gears described the basic relationship —reserves to bank lending to real economic activity. But it failed to convey the full flavor of this system, the complexities and ambiguities that existed daily at each stage of the process. At times, the money system resembled not smooth-running gears but large and wobbly flywheels connected only by loose belts—drive belts that were elastic, stretching or contracting on their own or sometimes slipping impotently. At times, the different flywheels seemed to be pulling in opposite directions. At times, even the monetary experts inside the Federal Reserve had difficulty figuring out which wheel was driving the system and which ones were being driven.

Inside the Federal Reserve System, the appointment of Paul Volcker was widely regarded as the restoration. After a long period of diversion and instability, the Fed would be returned to its true values, the style of management and authority that was the pride of the institution. Even career staff members who were not personal admirers felt a sense of relief that Volcker was taking charge.

In its institutional memory, the Fed celebrated only two chairmen from its past, two men who had made a great impact on how the Federal Reserve worked and who embodied its spirit. One was Marriner Eccles, the Republican banker from Utah who became one of the creative minds in Franklin Roosevelt's inner circle. Eccles wrote the New Deal legislation that reformed the Federal Reserve System and he served as chairman for nearly fourteen years. On the seventieth anniversary of the Federal Reserve Act, in 1983, the building on Constitution Avenue was renamed in his honor. The Fed's second office building, across C Street, built in 1974, was already named for the other esteemed chairman, William McChesney Martin, who served from Harry Truman to Richard Nixon. Martin provided the Fed's favorite operating cliché—"leaning against the wind"—which meant that proper money policy should adroitly counter the directions of the business cycles. The Fed would tighten when economic expansion threatened to reach inflationary stages; it would ease when the economy was in contraction. "The Federal Reserve's job," he once joked, "is to take away the punch bowl just when the party gets going." The process was considerably more complicated than the cliché, but Martin personified the Fed mystique of intuitive decision making—looking at all factors in the economy and deciding, season to season, which ones were most important. This discretionary style, whether valid or not, made it nearly impossible for outside critics to know exactly how the Federal Reserve determined its money policy.

For ten years, however, the Federal Reserve had been run by two men who, for different reasons, were considered alien to its traditions. William Miller was regarded as too complacent about inflation and too responsive to the Carter White House. He was a business executive who did not seem to understand the subtleties of Federal Reserve power. Arthur Burns, a conservative economist who served as Fed chairman during the Nixon and Ford years, was remembered in almost the opposite terms, a domineering egotist who bullied and manipulated fellow governors and staff economists, who was not above deliberately mismatching the monetary numbers in order to win votes inside the Federal Open Market Committee.

As a former corporate CEO, Miller was impatient with the unwritten protocol of the Board of Governors and the Federal Open Market Committee, the "collegial atmosphere" in which every opinion was to be respected. Miller was used to running things. Weary of lengthy speeches from the others, he brought an egg timer to the meetings and tried, unsuccessfully, to limit their orations to three minutes. At his first board meeting, the new chairman placed a small sign on the oval table in the boardroom: "Thank You for Not Smoking." The others were not amused. They looked at the sign—and lit up. "Miller was a CEO and he expected people to follow his orders," Governor Philip Coldwell said. "The sign stayed. And we smoked."

On a more substantive level, Miller was considered too sanguine about the outlook for inflation. He also did not seem to understand the special aura of authority that came with his position. Early in his tenure, when the board was considering an increase in the Discount rate, Miller voted against it and lost, 4 to 3. Colleagues gently suggested he reconsider his vote, but Miller persisted. The news shook the financial markets the next day—a sign of weakness in the new chairman. The Federal Reserve chairman always voted with the majority, even if he had to change his own views to do so.

Arthur Burns, a Columbia University professor who was economic adviser to President Eisenhower in the 1950s and was appointed chairman by President Nixon in late 1969, was distrusted, even despised, on a deeper level. In public, Burns gave curmudgeonly sermons against inflation and enjoyed celebrity in Washington as the stern professor, the "Number One inflation fighter." In the privacy of the Fed, many high-level officials considered him an arrogant fraud. Years afterward, professionals who served under him still spoke bitterly about his brutal treatment of them.

The Burns era, furthermore, produced the most damaging accusation of political collusion in the Federal Reserve's history—the economic pump priming that helped Richard Nixon win a landslide re-election victory in 1972. The President's federal budget was highly stimulative, and despite objections from senior governors, the Fed contributed its part to the campaign boom—rapid money growth that reached 11 percent three months before the election. An easy-money policy through the campaign season insured a robust economy and Nixon's triumph. The following year, the nation paid for the excesses —runaway inflation that reached a new peak, then money-tightening by the Fed and a long, painful recession. Even some Federal Reserve governors who argued against Burns at the time excused his 1972 performance as "honest mistakes," not political manipulation. But Washington politicians, particularly the Democrats, were quite cynical about the Fed's denials. They saw a conservative Federal Reserve chairman pumping up the economy in order to re-elect his old friend, the Republican President who had appointed him. The memory of 1972 lingered over the institution like an embarrassing odor.

In Wall Street circles, G. William Miller was blamed for the surging inflation of 1978 and 1979, but Fed insiders understood that Miller had inherited errors made earlier by Burns—excessive money growth in late 1976 and 1977. One Fed official who worked closely with Burns attributed the mistakes to Burns's deep desire to win appointment to another term as chairman from the new Democratic Administration elected in 1976. Money growth accelerated in the months right after Jimmy Carter's election—and Burns began a private campaign to ingratiate himself with the Carter White House. His campaign for reappointment ultimately failed, but monetary economists attributed the subsequent surge of inflation to Burns's overly generous money policy in the opening months of the Carter Administration.

When Volcker was appointed, many older staff members believed that he would revive the Fed's good name and restore the traditions inherited from Eccles and Martin. The tradition called for a dominant leader who, while respecting the internal sensibilities, would produce prudent control of money growth—without yielding to the complaints and pressures from politicians in the White House or Congress.[13]

The chairmanship, in addition to technical expertise, required an adroit political operator, someone who could coexist peacefully with the other power centers of government and thus preserve the Federal Reserve's most cherished legacy—its own independence.

Like most bureaucracies, the Federal Reserve regarded its own survival as a preeminent political goal, not solely as a matter of self-interest, but because its officials sincerely believed (not unlike other bureaucrats in other agencies) that their functions were vital to the nation's well-being. Fed officials were constantly, sometimes obsessively, sensitive to the fact that, in theory, Congress and the President could at any time abolish their privileged sanctuary. If the Fed went too far, if the elected politicians were sufficiently angered, they could simply rewrite the laws and make the Federal Reserve directly subservient to Congress or the executive branch. A wise chairman would know how far was too far.

Volcker was brilliantly prepared, both as technical expert and as political operator. His training was so extensive that he resembled a senior civil servant from the British system, a career man who stays in government while the elected officials come and go, who accumulates great influence because he knows every issue more thoroughly than the politicians whom he advises. That was quite rare in American government where high-level appointees were usually drawn from private careers, lawyers or business executives or scholars who made their reputations outside Washington.

Volcker was a public servant who had served the government in both capitals, Washington and Wall Street. He was a policy maker under four Republican and Democratic Presidents and had spent years on Capitol Hill fencing with congressional committees and lobbying for votes. He was in Treasury when John F. Kennedy proposed the stimulative tax cuts of the early 1960s and when Lyndon Johnson launched the U.S. war in Indochina. Under Nixon, he worked closely with Treasury Secretary John Connally, an urbane Texas politician who frequently complained about Volcker's dowdy appearance (Connally once threatened to fire him if Volcker did not get a haircut and buy a new suit).

Together, Connally and Volcker engineered the most fundamental change in the world's monetary system since World War II—the dismantling of the Bretton Woods agreement that had made the U.S. dollar the stable bench mark for all currencies. The changes that began in 1971 meant the final abandonment of gold as a U.S. guarantee behind its money and the introduction of floating exchange rates among the world's major currencies. Some critics still condemned Volcker bitterly for his role in those reforms, but he himself had originally argued for preserving the system of fixed exchange rates. In the course of those controversies, Volcker traveled the globe, confronting and bargaining with finance ministers and central bankers of every industrial nation. In the policy battles of Washington, his opponents included the Federal Reserve Board chairman, Arthur Burns. Volcker and Connally won.

And there was this wonderful irony about the man: Volcker was not interested in money, at least not in acquiring it for himself. One of the minor absurdities of the Federal Reserve System was that Federal Reserve Bank presidents, whose salaries were set by their boards of directors, not by Congress, were paid much more generously than the governors and the chairman. Thus, when Volcker left the New York Fed to return to Washington as chairman, he had to accept a salary cut of 50 percent—from $116,000 to just under $60,000. He lived comfortably but without the ostentatious consumption that Washington elites often favored. While his family stayed in New York, the chairman commuted on weekends and lived alone in Washington in a small apartment not far from the Fed building. Volcker made a small personal fetish of smoking cheap cigars and seeking out inexpensive Chinese restaurants. If someone took him to dinner at one of Washington's glossier places, he would grumble about the prices on the menu.

Not even his harshest critics questioned his personal integrity. With his résumé and brilliance, Volcker could easily have tripled or quadrupled his income any time he chose to go to work at a Wall Street brokerage or bank. He sounded a trifle old-fashioned, lamenting the fact that so few young people wanted to make the same choice of public service that he had. "The best of our young gravitate toward Wall Street, instead of Washington, our statehouses or our courthouses," he complained to an audience at Harvard. "Or, perhaps more accurately, a great many of them do end up in Washington—to run a lobby or represent a client." [14]

"Everyone laughed because Paul always had shiny suits, but he had to watch his money," Vice Chairman Frederick Schultz said. "His wife had a little accounting business, but he had to watch their spending. He really doesn't care about the things that money buys, a big house in the country, a fancy car. He just doesn't care."

Back in Teaneck, New Jersey, where he grew up, Volcker was known as "Little Buddy." His high-school yearbook noted that he "has an incredible knowledge of politics" and predicted that someday he might rise as high as town manager of Teaneck. Volcker's father was city manager of the Teaneck municipal government for twenty years —an important clue to how Volcker saw himself.

"I never heard him talk about his father in this way," a senior official at the New York Federal Reserve Bank said, "but I suspect he was heavily influenced by watching his father's work. A city manager is supposed to see things in a dispassionate way, to look down the road and propose long-term solutions and continually battle with those who are only pushing their own short-term self-interests."

The Federal Reserve was supposed to do the same thing. The city-manager form of government was a "good government" reform invented in the same historical period that created the Federal Reserve System, the Progressive era of Woodrow Wilson, and both shared the same premise—a technocratic vision of government that was suspicious of politics. City managers would "depoliticize" municipal government by promoting sound managerial solutions—building the new highway where it ought to go, not where some corrupt alderman wanted to build it. The Federal Reserve embraced precisely the same managerial spirit—a sense that government must be removed from politics in order to produce good policy. The Progressive reformers themselves were middle-class managers and civic leaders who distrusted the raw forces of democracy, the popular distempers and appetites. Their reforms were intended, fundamentally, to protect government from the people.

A professional city manager still had to deal in politics, however, pacifying and persuading the mayor and the city council, just as the Federal Reserve constantly must soothe and cajole Congress and the White House. This necessarily required artful manipulation and produced an uneven relationship that was often marked by disdain, even contempt. The technocrat who understands the facts must coax the ignorant politician into doing the "right thing."

In his personal manner, Volcker reflected some of the same perspective and prejudices. He could be charming and droll, joking at a cocktail party about the dour reputation of central bankers: "We have a haunting fear that someone, someplace may be happy." Or, confronting a contentious senator in a committee hearing, he could be brutally opaque. Often, he would lead a hostile questioner deeper and deeper into the esoterica of monetary policy until the embarrassed senator was lost in confusion.

"Volcker has a pretty low opinion of the intelligence of mankind on the whole, both practical and theoretical intelligence," a former close associate said. "Whether he thinks nonbankers are more intelligent than bankers, I don't know, but he certainly has a low opinion of bankers."

If the authors of anti-Fed polemics looked more closely at the personal backgrounds of Federal Reserve governors, they would not find much to corroborate their theories of global conspiracy. They might conclude, instead, that the "Powers" were located not in the eastern Establishment banks of Wall Street but somewhere in the Middle West. The National Association of Home Builders, in fact, undertook such an investigation when its members were particularly outraged about high interest rates. The study was abandoned because the only pattern of connections it found led to small towns and state universities in Indiana, Ohio and Illinois.

Governor Philip Coldwell grew up in Urbana, Illinois, where his father was secretary of the YMCA. J. Charles Partee was from Defiance, Ohio. His father was a mailman. Nancy Teeters, the first woman to serve on the board, was from Marion, Indiana, the daughter of a salesman for a paper-box company. Emmett J. Rice, the second black man to be appointed governor, was raised in Washington, D.C., the son of a Methodist minister. Paul Volcker was also from modest origins, not poor but certainly not born to privilege.

Fred Schultz, the new vice chairman, was an exception, a wealthy banker. So was Henry C. Wallich, at sixty-five the scholarly elder of the board. Wallich was born in Germany in a family with a long history in banking, but emigrated as a young man to seek a different career in America. He was an academic economist at Yale before his appointment in 1974 and better known than his colleagues because he used to write a regular column for *Newsweek*.

A sociologist, examining the backgrounds of governors past and present, as well as senior staff economists, would find this pattern: despite occasional exceptions, most of the people who ran the Federal Reserve were drawn from the broad American middle class, even the lower middle class, without the help of social status or influential connections.

The Federal Reserve governors, it seemed, were splendid proof of an American meritocracy—a culture that rewarded bright and ambitious people regardless of their origins, that allowed them to rise to positions of exceptional authority in the society, without the need for family connections. Many governors thought of their own success as a series of happy accidents.

"I was a music student, a pretty good trumpet player, played in dance bands and so on, but you couldn't make a living at it," said Governor Partee, who was known to colleagues as Chuck. He studied music for a year at Indiana University, then transferred to the business school. He dropped out of graduate school to become a junior economist at the Chicago Federal Reserve Bank, worked six years for the Northern Trust Company, then joined the Federal Reserve Board's research staff in Washington as chief of the capital markets section. In 1969, he became research director and seven years later Gerald Ford appointed him governor. Partee wore tweed jackets and snappy bow ties. With his scruffy little moustache, he looked like a slightly eccentric English professor. His speech was accented with blunt little exclamations—"huh" and "ah," like a lecturer underscoring his point. "The only trouble with this job," he said, "is that it doesn't pay much money."

Philip Coldwell, tall and acerbic, with a creased face that seemed avuncular, was a "System man" for thirty years. He graduated from the University of Illinois in chemical engineering, then switched to economics in graduate school at Wisconsin. As a staff adviser and president at the Dallas Fed, then as governor, Coldwell had attended the closed meetings of the Federal Open Market Committee since 1953, the insider with the longest tenure.

As the biographies suggested, one of the best ways to reach the Board of Governors was to work for the System itself. Most appointees were not career employees like Partee and Coldwell, but nearly all of them had had some prior experience at the Fed or one of the Reserve Banks. Even Nancy Teeters, known as the board's most stalwart liberal and the most consistent critic of the conservatives around her, began her career as a junior economist at the Fed.

Like the governors, the Federal Reserve bureaucracy was cloistered from the normal tempests of politics. The board employed about sixteen hundred people in Washington (plus another twenty-three thousand at the twelve Reserve Banks), but most of them worked at prosaic tasks—collecting and sorting numbers or the "factory" chores at the regional banks, the check traffic, currency management and other services provided to commercial banks. The Fed's elaborate systems for shipping canceled checks back to their bank of origin and balancing accounts daily among banks were essential to commerce, but no more mysterious than what the U.S. Postal Service did for mail.

Still, Fed bureaucrats had a special élan. They were set apart from the regular civil service and even underwent their own elaborate security rules before they could handle the banking numbers. Fortunes could be made if traders knew the money statistics a few days ahead of the market, and despite the temptations, the System had never suffered a major scandal. In the international division, economists were cleared to read CIA and State Department cables too.

The prestige belonged to the economists—about two hundred research economists in Washington and another two hundred and fifty at the Reserve Banks, the largest assemblage in the world. To bright young graduate students looking for jobs, the Federal Reserve seemed as prestigious as a major university, only the Fed's scholars did not have to teach. Most of them were men—white men—and if they did not rise on the Fed's management ladder, they could always turn to much more lucrative careers as Fed watchers or market analysts.[15] "People develop expertise in very narrow areas," a former staff economist explained. "Some may cover the Federal Funds market and they know everything there is to know about Federal Funds or commercial paper. After two or three years, they go on to banking or business with that expertise."

The Fed's "revolving door" with Wall Street created an unofficial fraternity of industry insiders, men who spoke the same language and traded gossip, not unlike the military officers who left the Pentagon to work for defense contractors. Indeed, the professional esprit at the Fed resembled the professional officers' corps of the armed forces. "You almost don't have to give orders," one former economist said, "because the troops already know what the orders will be."

The real power at the Fed was closely held, however. Despite the Fed's vast bureaucracy, only a handful of employees below the Board of Governors—no more than fifty people on the central staff—had access to and actual influence on the most sensitive question, the making of monetary policy. When G. William Miller was Fed chairman, the staff director, Stephen H. Axilrod, became an extraordinarily powerful bureaucrat because he understood the technical issues, and Miller, who did not, followed his advice. When Paul Volcker became chairman, that ended abruptly.

The Federal Reserve Act commanded that a President, when selecting governors, "shall have due regard to a fair representation of the financial, agricultural, industrial and commercial interests and geographical divisions of the country." But there were now no farmers, manufacturers, small-business men or labor leaders on the board. With only scattered exceptions, the Fed governors were drawn from two disciplines—financial economics and banking. In the case of the Federal Reserve Board, the American meritocracy allowed capable people to rise to the top, but it also screened them carefully. There were no radical thinkers or original theorists among them. No one with unorthodox opinions would be chosen.

The institution encouraged its own consensus and conformity. Individual governors were dependent on the senior staff for technical data and professional advice. Inevitably, this tended to narrow the range of opinions on any given issue, and it took a strong-willed governor to stand alone and repeatedly argue for a competing analysis.

Nancy Teeters was one. She was chief staff economist of the House Budget Committee when she was appointed in 1978 and was considered a most unusual choice. Jimmy Carter, anxious to advance women and minorities, insisted on finding a woman for the board (the first black governor, Andrew Brimmer, had been appointed by Lyndon Johnson). Teeters was well known and respected as a liberal economist, a disciple of John Maynard Keynes and the Keynesian principles that had guided the Democratic Party's economic policy since FDR. Yet even Nancy Teeters felt membership in a special club.

At a dinner party in 1978 [she recalled], Arthur Burns was talking to me, asking me questions and it sounded like a job interview. I said, "Arthur, you don't want someone like me on the Board of Governors with my liberal background." Arthur said, "Don't worry, Nancy. Within six months, you will think just like a central banker."

Arthur was right. I think I'm very much a central banker now. You're in a position where your views on money, credit and banking are not really a reflection of your political party or your positions on economic issues. It's not really a political job. I understand the whole milieu of what we are doing, the continuous decisions, the mystique of central banking.

3

A PACT
WITH THE
DEVIL

The new chairman of the Federal Reserve Board sounded a lot like the old chairman and like the chairman before him. An immutable feature of the American political dialogue was that the Federal Reserve chairman always delivered the strongest, most eloquent sermons against the dangers of inflation. After Paul Volcker took the oath of office on August 6, 1979, he continued the tradition.

To be sure [Volcker told the House Budget Committee], the impact of inflation is uneven. Those on fixed incomes suffer, while some people who are well positioned—either by clever design or by good luck—do manage to increase their wealth. Even for the fortunate, however, such a result is at best precarious, frequently built on heavy indebtedness or highly speculative investments. . . .

It is not entirely a coincidence that we can observe in these recent inflationary years a declining tendency in the profitability of investment . . . one estimate indicates that the annual after-tax return on corporate net worth, measured, as it should reasonably be, against the replacement cost of inventories and fixed assets, has averaged 3.8 percent during the 1970s, a period characterized by rapid inflation, as compared to 6.6 percent in the 1960s. . . .

In other areas, inflationary expectations are reflected in a diversion of energies into essentially speculative activities—ranging from the "froth" of investing in art objects to the considered purchase, at the expense of heavy indebtedness, of larger or second homes as an inflation hedge.

The public, if it was listening, was not persuaded. People kept borrowing and buying. The inflation rate was hovering around 14 percent. Consumer debt, the loans to buy cars and houses and other items, was growing faster than consumer incomes, approaching a historic peak. The prospect of continuing inflation seemed more reliable than any political promises to stop it.

Volcker appreciated the public skepticism. "We've lost that euphoria that we had fifteen years ago, that we knew all the answers to managing the economy," he conceded. As he made the rounds of public speeches and testimony before congressional committees, he defined the problem in two parts: first, the tangible effects of inflationary pressures on the economy and, second, the psychological momentum of "inflationary expectations." As long as people believed that rising prices were inevitable, then they would be. Labor unions would demand escalator contracts that protected their members' real wages from erosion. Retailers would try to anticipate next month's rising costs by raising this month's prices. Producers would postpone new capital investment. Creditors would demand higher interest rates. In the long run, Volcker's central challenge was to convince everyone they were wrong.

"For its part," Volcker assured audiences, "the Federal Reserve intends to continue its efforts to restrain the growth of money and credit, a growth that in recent months has been excessive in terms of our own 1979 objectives."[1] The Federal Open Market Committee set annual target ranges for the rate of money growth it expected to allow. For M-1, the basic aggregate of spending money, the Fed wanted growth of only 1.5 to 4.5 percent in 1979. But, for the last three months, money had been growing at an annual rate of more than 10 percent—nearly three times higher than the upper limit the Fed had set for M-1 growth.

Bland as Volcker's remarks might have sounded to outsiders, for financial markets his words translated into a clear signal: he intended to tighten down, holding back the infusion of new reserves until—gradually—the rate of money growth subsided and came back within the target range. This meant raising interest rates—perhaps a lot.

The question was how far Volcker was willing to push up rates. At the second board meeting where he presided as chairman, on August 16, the seven governors unanimously accepted a historic milestone, which in other circumstances might have jarred the markets. They raised the Discount rate from 10 to 10.5 percent—the highest level in the sixty-five-year history of the Federal Reserve System. The Discount rate applied to the hundreds of millions in daily loans that the twelve Federal Reserve Banks routinely made to commercial banks that were temporarily short of reserves. The Discount rate was the floor price of short-term credit. When the governors raised it, that meant other short-term interest rates would be going up too.

The financial markets were barely stirred by the action because they were expecting much more from the new chairman. The governors themselves were divided, however, on how tough the Fed should get. At two successive board meetings in early September, Volcker proposed additional increases in the Discount rate, but had to back off because it became clear he might not have a majority behind him.

Most economists, including the Fed's, were forecasting a recession, but then economists had been expecting one for many months and they had been wrong. Despite the aggravations of inflation, President Carter had presided over one of the longest and most expansive periods of economic growth in postwar history, four years of recovery starting in 1976. In confidential forecasts for the governors, the Federal Reserve senior staff predicted a deteriorating economy in the third quarter, then a recession by the Christmas holidays of 1979. The contraction of economic activity might last as long as nine months, the Fed staff thought.[2]

If correct, the forecast was a terrible political portent for the President—a shrinking economy leading right up to the 1980 election. Of all the many factors that influenced election returns, the most powerful was the ebb and flow of the national economy. A growing economy that increased real personal income and reduced unemployment rewarded the incumbent party and President; a declining economy threatened them with punishment from voters, regardless of other accomplishments or personal popularity.

As with other political issues, timing was everything. Naturally, no President would wish for recession. But, if recession was inevitable, the President might be better off if it occurred sooner rather than later —so the economy would be growing again in time for the campaign season, and the ill effects of the unemployment would be forgotten by voters. Earlier in 1979, at least one adviser, Treasury Under Secretary Anthony M. Solomon, had urged President Carter "to take a recession" now and get it over. Otherwise, Solomon warned, the President would be confronted with both rapid inflation and rising unemployment in the midst of his re-election campaign. Jimmy Carter, ever the optimist, ignored the advice.

By late summer, the President's options looked much worse. Lyle E. Gramley, a member of the President's Council of Economic Advisers and former research director at the Federal Reserve Board, described the bind confronting White House policy makers: "We face a cruel dilemma. If policy actions are taken to offset slow growth and a rising unemployment rate, we will lose some of the gains we expect on inflation. If we tighten budgetary policy to dampen inflation further, we will lower growth and raise unemployment."[3]

The same trade-off that faced the President's budget policy confronted the Federal Reserve and its monetary policy. If the Fed tightened credit in order to brake the inflationary spiral, would it also tip the economy into recession? If the Fed failed to tighten, inflation would likely grow worse.

In public, Paul Volcker did not sound as gloomy as did the predictions from the Fed staff. Economic adjustments, Volcker suggested, "need not by themselves set in motion a deep or prolonged contraction in activity . . . some of the economic and financial dislocations and imbalances that usually have presaged severe cyclical declines have been avoided . . . [the position] that the economy should grow moderately in 1980 still seems reasonable."

In private, Volcker was less sanguine. He was beginning to consider policy options that would provide a sharp brake, not a gradual deceleration, and he shared his thoughts with a very small circle of insiders. Like a cautious politician preparing for a major campaign, Volcker was testing the political climate inside his own institution. If he was going to lead, the chairman first had to be sure that others would follow.

Both the Board of Governors and the federal open market committee were divided and drifting. Miller's weak leadership had produced months of contention and some confusion. Volcker was familiar with the arguments because, as president of the New York Reserve Bank, he had been a regular voting member of the FOMC for the past four years and participated in them. "This is a brand-new chairman," Coldwell said of him. "Sure, Paul had been in the System a long time . . . but he was still a new chairman. Others who had been supporting Miller hadn't been weaned away from that position."

Back in the spring, when the inflation rate was taking off, Volcker himself had challenged Miller's stewardship. Normally, the New York president worked closely with the chairman and tried to support him on policy issues, but at FOMC meetings in March and April Volcker had joined Wallich and Coldwell in formal dissents. The three most senior and respected members were voting against the chairman, pushing him toward a tougher money policy. "That created quite a stir," Coldwell said. "The three of us had never ganged up on the chairman before, and I think we bent things a little bit. Others became a little disenchanted with the chairman. It became a very fragmented board."

At a distance, the arguments seemed to be over quite small differences, even petty distinctions. The FOMC members often split over whether the Federal Funds rate, the key barometer for credit conditions, should be raised a quarter of 1 percent or not. Chairman Miller supported periodic increases, but they were always quite modest. Miller and his supporters feared that more dramatic action on interest rates would depress sectors like housing and autos, which depended heavily on lending for their sales, and that would lead to a general recession.

"They were arguing that the Federal Reserve would be in the position of killing off the whole recovery," Coldwell said with impatience. "We were only talking about a quarter percent increase—and within the year we would be talking about 2 or 3 percent."

The internal conflicts crystallized for Volcker on September 18, confronting him with a delicate dilemma. The twelve Reserve Bank presidents came to town for the regular meeting of the Federal Open Market Committee and joined the seven governors at the huge mahogany table in the boardroom. By meeting time, they had all digested the voluminous staff reports on the economy, including the most important one, the so-called "blue book," which described the policy choices. Through the morning, each governor or president would have a turn to speak, though only five of the bank presidents would have a vote. Usually before a lunch break, the chairman offered a proposition and the twelve members of the FOMC announced their votes.

The "blue book" prepared by the senior staff for the September 18 session described the market effects of what the FOMC had authorized six weeks before, in early August: "In response to the System's tightening actions, short-term interest rates have generally advanced about three quarters to 1.5 percentage points . . . and long-term bond yields have moved up 25 to 45 basis points. The relative sharp response of market interest rates appeared to reflect anticipation of further tightening by the System in the face of continued rapid inflation and monetary growth." For the last three months, the basic money aggregate, M-1, had grown at an annual rate of 10.6 percent, far above what the Fed itself had set as its goal for the year. Only further tightening would bring down the money-supply growth to within the target range. The financial markets, therefore, expected more of the same—higher interest rates to dampen credit expansion.[4]

The question was: how much higher? The senior staff did not make recommendations, but it offered the details of plausible alternatives—one for easing, one for standing pat and one for tightening. None of these policy alternatives suggested anything more than small changes in the Fed's posture. According to the minutes, no FOMC member was in favor of easing credit, not when inflation was close to 14 percent and the money supply was far above the target.

But some members argued for no change at all. Interest rates had risen substantially in recent months and sooner or later that ought to have an impact on credit expansion and the economy. The cautious members thought the Federal Open Market Committee "should avoid policy actions that might intensify the developing weakness in the economic activity."

But the majority opted for "slight additional firming," as the FOMC minutes put it. That meant Alternative C from the "blue book," which called for raising the Federal Funds rate only .5 percent, from 11.5 to 12 percent, with leeway to go as high as 12.5 percent. That was supposed to slow down the money growth in the coming weeks, but only gradually.

To get a majority, Volcker had to soften even that small step. The final proposal, adopted as an operating directive for the Open Market Desk in New York, authorized the traders there to shoot for a Federal Funds rate of only 11.75—an increase of only one-quarter of a percent. Given the roaring pressures of inflation, this was hardly more than a nudge.

The vote was 8 to 4, because several committee members thought the policy was too soft. Three entered dissents—Governors Wallich and Coldwell and John Balles, president of the San Francisco Reserve Bank—on the grounds that the Fed should tighten more aggressively. The Federal Funds rate should be pushed up to 12 percent, they argued, or the money supply would continue to expand excessively. One other governor, Emmett J. Rice, dissented in the other direction —insisting that further tightening, even one-quarter of a percent, might be too much for the economy.

After the FOMC finished its business, the seven governors reconvened in a meeting of the Board of Governors to consider the prerogative it did not share with the Reserve Bank presidents—the power to set the Discount rate, the rate the Fed charged for its short-term liquidity loans to banks. Proposals for increases or decreases were forwarded as recommendations from the boards of directors of the Reserve Banks, but the question was decided only by the seven governors in Washington.

The Board of Governors was split too, 4 to 3. They voted for the increase—only this time the dissenters were pulling in the other direction. Governors Teeters, Partee and Rice argued together for no change at all. "More time was needed," they asserted, "to assess current uncertainties in the economic outlook and the impact of increasing restraint . . . over the course of recent months."[5]

For the new chairman, the situation resembled a squeeze play—dissenters pulling in opposite directions. One faction insisted the Fed must get tougher with the economy and the other feared that the Fed might already be too tough.

Vice Chairman Schultz said:

You have to recognize that Nancy Teeters was the most liberal member of the board, a dyed-in-the-wool Keynesian. She had less concern about inflation than any of the others. She continued to believe that a gradualist approach would work. She thought we ought to wait and see after the FOMC action. Chuck [Partee] was kind of on the fence. The inflationary thing was bothering him a great deal, but he wanted to go slowly. Emmett [Rice] came around a little bit later.

Board members used the labels sparingly, but "liberal" and "conservative" implied distinct philosophical differences about the purposes of monetary policy. A liberal like Teeters would focus on the trade-off between inflation and unemployment, between the benefit that higher interest rates might produce in moderating prices and the damage they would do to the real economy, destroying jobs and businesses. Most of the senior economists in the Federal Reserve had been schooled in the same tradition—a sense that they must balance their choices and weigh the costs. Inflation must be resisted, but easier money policy also produced social benefits—full employment, rising incomes, fewer Americans who could not find work.

"I am one of those who came out of graduate school convinced that a little inflation was a good thing," Governor Partee reflected. "Inflation lubricated the economy and it was better to have low unemployment. People's incomes would adjust."

A conservative like Henry Wallich would argue that there really wasn't any choice. "I regard inflation as a form of fraud," Wallich said, much worse than an ordinary swindle because it was the government itself defrauding citizens—wiping out the value of their assets by debasing the nation's money. From Wallich's perspective, the Federal Reserve had only one choice—to do its best to stabilize the value of money.

These underlying tensions collided in the arguments of September 18, as they often did in the Federal Reserve's deliberations. The Fed was divided between "hawks" and "doves," code words that entered the language during the war in Vietnam to define the political debate over continuing the war. "Phil Coldwell and Henry Wallich were the hawks and I was getting there pretty fast," Fred Schultz said. "Paul was for the Discount increase but the strong arguments were from me, Coldwell and Wallich."

The cautious, gradual incrementalism of the September decisions was exactly what conservative critics had complained about for years. Politicians might pressure the Fed to proceed slowly, but some academic economists, market analysts and bankers argued that the Fed's action was always too little and too late. The Federal Funds rate and the Discount rate would be raised, but never sharply enough to make much difference—"always behind the curve," critics complained. The Fed, they argued, was too worried about keeping interest rates stable, for fear of upsetting the money markets. It should forget about interest rates and, instead, focus directly on the one lever through which it could really control the money supply—the creation of bank reserves.

Federal Reserve officials read the newspapers. They followed quite closely the daily chatter from the financial markets, as reported in the "Credit Markets" column of *The Wall Street Journal* and elsewhere in the financial press. They also read the scholarly critiques published in economic journals, but they listened most diligently to the market talk.

Paul Volcker was not especially upset by the closeness of the 4–3 vote on the Discount increase—but the financial markets were. The reactions from Wall Street the next day interpreted it as a defeat for him. Short-term interest rates fell sharply as investors concluded that the Fed under Volcker would be less aggressive than they had expected, that the dissenters would keep him from any future increases.

The 4–3 split, *The Wall Street Journal* reported, "indicates that Mr. Volcker's drive for a restrictive monetary policy may encounter increasing opposition." Wall Street analysts made a practice of reading the dissenting votes at the Fed like a leading indicator: if the governors became evenly divided on their direction, that meant they would not go any further.[6]

Moreover, if Wall Street was skeptical about the new chairman's ability to halt inflation, so was the rest of America.

Jack Brod, owner of Empire Diamond and Gold, a precious-metals exchange on the sixty-sixth floor of the Empire State Building in Manhattan, had to hire a security guard to handle the crowds. He roped off part of the hallway to make the lines more orderly. Brod could still not keep up.

"I'd get here in the morning and there would be people waiting outside the office in the lobby," he said. "They took blankets and they slept outside until we opened the door. They brought food and ate their breakfast."

The people brought old jewelry and silverware, candelabra, platters, rings, anything that contained gold or silver. A dentist brought a pile of gold inlays and silver fillings he had removed from teeth over five years, a $3,000 sale. Others showed up with fine heirlooms that had been in their families for generations.

"We were getting calls from all over the world, people wanting to sell silver bars," Brod said. "I could have bought a hundred thousand ounces of silver in a day if I wanted, but I didn't want to get stuck with it. The refiners got several months behind. We had to send it to Switzerland where they would process it faster."[7]

The frenzy at Empire Diamond and Gold was repeated in jewelry stores, pawnshops and other exchanges across the country—ignited by the price of gold and silver. Silver had sold for $6 an ounce in January. By August, it rose to $10 and hit $17 in September—nearly tripled in value in nine months. Gold, which sold for $300 in July, was now at $450 and still climbing. In the months ahead, silver prices would triple again, surpassing $50 an ounce, and the price of gold would peak at $875.

Wallace Silversmiths, Inc., which manufactured silverware in Wallingford, Connecticut, would have to lay off more than half of its workers as the price of its basic commodity kept escalating. "We publish a price list to dealers," said Arthur Bowker, vice president of the company, "but we couldn't print the price list fast enough. They had to be printed, then mailed to the main store and they were always out of date."[8]

This was what Paul Volcker called the "froth" of inflationary expectations. In the autumn of 1979, the United States experienced a kind of price frenzy—a flight from its own currency. Americans were in a rush of buying and selling which assumed that dollars would continue to lose more and more of their value. The only safe haven for their wealth—and the opportunity to increase it—lay in tangibles. Buy gold, buy art and antiques, buy real estate. The rush of new buyers drove prices even higher—reinforcing the impression that this was the place to put one's money. The trick was to buy and sell fast while the price was rising and before it collapsed, as bubbles of speculations always did.

In the Middle West, the expectations of continuing inflation led otherwise cautious farmers to make serious long-term investments, to buy expensive new farm machinery or another hundred acres of farmland. When farmers borrowed, they used their land as collateral, and as land prices escalated, their collateral grew, expanding their ability to borrow.

"Lenders would come out to the farm," Jim Clark of Mount Ayr, Iowa, explained, "and they would say, 'That tractor looks a bit aging.'

So a farmer would buy a new one. Why not? Land was going up, machinery was going up." Farm economists from the state universities gave farmers the same advice—increase your holdings, your capital investment, to stay ahead of inflation.

"They were telling us: 'Get that land bought, it won't be as cheap as it is now,' " said Sandy Shields, another resident of Mount Ayr.

"We didn't throw money at anybody," a local banker, Roger Kerndt, president of Hawkeye Bank and Trust, insisted. An economist from Iowa State University, Kerndt said, "was telling people to leverage. Economists were saying you'd better be leveraged 10 to 1. And you could be. People, including bankers, were doing what they thought was the right thing to do. You make your decisions on what you see. There wasn't hardly a soul who didn't think inflation would keep going up."

For farmers, increasing their debt leverage was easy, a simple matter of bookkeeping at the bank, as Kerndt explained. "When that eighty acres went up for sale next to him, of course it looked like a good deal and we went along," the banker said. "Everybody's memory was so short. If a guy's financial statement looked bad and he wanted to buy land, you just add a hundred dollars to the acre on his collateral."[9]

In southern California, the action was in housing. Across the nation, the value of property was increasing monthly at an annual rate of 17 percent, but the truly spectacular boom was in the splendid towns and cities along the Pacific coast south of Los Angeles. The San Diego Board of Realtors had doubled its membership since 1975. In affluent communities like Newport Beach, housing values increased by 100 percent in less than five years.[10]

Herbert Young, president of Gibraltar Financial Corporation, a Los Angeles savings and loan, kept thinking the market would cool off as interest rates on home mortgages continued to rise. In the beginning of 1985, the mortgage rate in California was 9.25 percent. A year later it hit 10.75 percent. By September, it was above 12 percent.

"I would have sworn that the 11.5 would put the nail in the coffin," Young said. "But the buyers out here are voracious." Instead of looking backward, home buyers were looking forward. "People usually look back to six or nine months ago and they see lower rates and they expect those rates to return," Young explained. "But that didn't happen. This time, they were looking ahead and saw higher rates."[11]

People were not simply buying homes to live in or even as long-term investments. They were buying homes in order to sell them again quickly. The Irvine Ranch, a huge housing development in Orange

County, was celebrated for a transaction in which a buyer bought a condominium for $87,050 and resold it two weeks later—before the mortgage closing was completed—for $117,500.[12]

David Parry, an economist studying the real-estate boom in the San Francisco Bay area, overheard a conversation between two buyers in a Contra Costa County subdivision. Between them, they were purchasing six houses on six different streets. The manager of the development conceded that 60 percent of his sales were to people who did not intend to live in the homes.

"You could see the speculation in the advertisements," Parry said. "Homes were advertised for resale that hadn't been built yet. In the ads, they used pictures from the housing brochure."

Like gold and silver, the rush of speculators into housing increased the demand for homes—artificially—and stimulated more construction. "Builders tend to be rather unsophisticated," Parry said. "They build on the me-too syndrome. They see a hundred homes being built on the market and bought. They say, me too, and pretty soon there are a thousand homes. The speculators don't represent real demand, so they exacerbate the oversupply."[13]

In less obvious ways, the same distortions were spreading throughout the U.S. economy. It was not just home builders and silver dealers and farmers who acted on inflationary expectations. The impulses were driving the decisions of major businesses and manufacturers and the lending policies of the largest commercial banks. Even though the economy was growing at a modest rate, total bank lending increased by nearly 22 percent in September—nearly double the already high rate of credit expansion that had occurred in August. Construction loans, home mortgages and farm debt were minor shares. Most of the new borrowing was made up of commercial and industrial loans. In a three-month period, U.S. corporations added $40 billion in additional liabilities to their balance sheets.[14]

It was exhilarating and also a bit frightening. As evidence of the hyperactive economy accumulated, the governors and senior economists of the Federal Reserve Board were having second thoughts about gradualism.

Governor Partee was particularly taken aback. A few days after the Board of Governors had split, 4 to 3, on raising the Discount rate, he went to New York to address a meeting of market analysts. "We had extremely poor credibility," Partee said later. "And I got extremely hostile questions. I was chastised for not voting for the Discount increase. Didn't I realize the metals markets were going wild? Didn't I realize the Mexican peso was now favored over the dollar?"

Partee changed his mind. The hawks were right. Something more had to be done.

Governor Coldwell, among others, was getting unsolicited phone calls from around the country, from fellow bankers who were themselves worried about where things were headed.

"Wild speculation was under way in the financial markets and in banking," Coldwell said. "Some bankers were calling me, saying, 'Look, Phil, this thing is getting out of hand. You've got to do something.' I said, 'I wish you'd talk to some of the other governors.' "

The new vice chairman was alarmed too. "Every day you got this sense that the world was coming apart at the seams," Fred Schultz said. "You saw it in every market. There was a genuine flight from the currency—people investing in tangibles, art, jewelry, stamps, gold. Everything that was tangible was increasing in value. It was just a textbook case."

Only one of the Federal Reserve governors had had personal experience with hyperinflation, when prices double or triple in a single year or even in a single month. Henry Wallich had been a small boy in Germany during the early 1920s when the German currency was rendered worthless by hyperinflation, when prices doubled almost daily and citizens literally had to transport their cash in wheelbarrows. The experience was the political trauma that, coupled with the defeat in World War I, destabilized German society and paved the way for the rise of Nazism and Adolf Hitler. Despite the anxieties of others, Wallich did not himself really believe that America was on the brink of such a disaster. Even if U.S. inflation soared to 20 or 25 percent, that would still not be anything like what Germany had gone through.

"I used to say that I never, never thought this could happen in the United States," Wallich explained puckishly. "But now I only say one 'never.' "

Whatever the numbers showed, it seemed obvious to the Fed that it had to do something more. Governor Coldwell compared the Fed's role in the financial system to a traffic cop at a busy intersection.

"Every once in a while," Coldwell said, "the Fed flicks on the yellow light and people react the way drivers in Washington react to a yellow light—they speed up and get through the intersection. Then the Fed has to flick on the red light, and when it hits red, people come to a screeching stop—after a few of them try to run the light."

The metaphor described the moment. Governors who had been cautious and uncertain a few weeks earlier were now changing their minds. Paul Volcker was talking to them one by one, coaxing them toward a new consensus. It was time, the chairman said, to flick on the red light.

. . .

The bald little professor with the elfin face and the tart tongue seemed a quixotic figure at first, as he trudged cheerfully from one congressional hearing to another with his improbable arguments. No one questioned Milton Friedman's scholarly brilliance, but his ideas seemed hopelessly out-of-date. The press called him an "intellectual radical." Paul Samuelson of MIT, an eminence in the Keynesian orthodoxy that reigned over economics, likened him to "a man with a foil attacking a battleship." [15]

In 1963, the University of Chicago economist had published with coauthor Anna J. Schwartz the magnum opus of his career, *A Monetary History of the United States, 1867–1960*. To professionals, Friedman's work was an awesome piece of scholarship, a dense tome that traced in meticulous detail the entire course of money, banking and U.S. monetary policy from Ulysses S. Grant to John F. Kennedy.[16] To most politicians in Washington, Milton Friedman seemed just a figure with an odd obsession. He kept reappearing in academic and political forums, preaching the same profoundly conservative sermon: the Keynesian orthodoxy that had dominated economics for thirty years was wrong. Not just a little wrong, Friedman insisted, but totally, fundamentally, disastrously wrong.

Many were bemused by his feisty persistence; few took his message seriously at first. Friedman had begun his proselytizing, after all, in the early 1960s, the era of practical triumph for the liberal intellectual inheritors of John Maynard Keynes, the great British economist. The Democratic Administrations of Kennedy and Johnson were aggressively applying the lessons elaborated by Keynes during the Great Depression—that is, manipulating the federal government's own budget in order to stimulate growth in the private economy. Either by cutting taxes or increasing federal spending or doing both, the government could augment the aggregate demand of the private economy, the total spending power of consumers and businesses. In essence, the government put more money in people's pockets—either by taxing them less or giving them cash subsidies or buying more of whatever they had to sell, whether it was labor or paving cement or surplus wheat. The increased aggregate demand induced by Washington would ripple through the private economy and multiply. The newly hired construction worker bought a new car and the auto factory purchased more steel to make cars and the steel mill hired more workers. Rising incomes and profits stimulated buying and selling, production and employment.

Since the government was pumping out more money than it collected in tax revenue, the strategy naturally produced temporary deficits in the federal budget, a source of constant alarm to conservatives. The liberal architects of the "New Economics" argued persuasively— at least persuasively to the political majority—that engineered deficits were therapeutic. The increased economic activity stimulated by federal fiscal policy would more than compensate for the budget shortfall. The increased demand for goods led wealth owners and corporations to invest in new factories, the process of capital formation that was the heart of economic growth. Expanding production meant more jobs and rising personal incomes, broadly distributed in the society. As a consequence, the revenue base of the federal government—all the workers and businesses that pay taxes—would be permanently enlarged.

The New Economics worked. In fact, it produced spectacular returns. The unemployment rate, which was nearly 7 percent when Kennedy took office, began to fall dramatically as the tax-and-spending policies took hold. The American economy entered a long cycle of robust expansion, and unemployment fell below 5 percent, then below 4 percent, where it remained for four years. Eventually, it dropped to only 3.5 percent, the practical equivalent of full employment in America, a job for everyone who wanted to work.

Milton Friedman, meanwhile, worried about inflation. He testified frequently before Congress and patiently instructed important committee chairmen on why they should worry too. At the time, it seemed an odd complaint, even cranky. The Consumer Price Index rose by modest increments each year, but never by as much as 2 percent through 1965. Wealthy bond investors might grumble when the inflation rate hit 1.5 percent, but the rest of the country was more impressed by the general prosperity. Friedman persisted, nevertheless, with his dire predictions.

As a libertarian conservative, Friedman objected fundamentally to nearly any form of government intrusion in the natural functionings of the private marketplace. But he had a more pointed quarrel with the Keynesian perspective that then dominated political thinking. Fiscal policy, the budget choices that Keynesians thought so important, produced only ephemeral results, Friedman insisted. The fundamental source of government influence over the private economy was its control of money—the monetary policy made by the Federal Reserve. The Fed's manipulation of the money supply, Friedman added, was consistently destabilizing and damaging.

To mainstream economists in the sixties, including many who worked at the Federal Reserve, Friedman's essays and lectures at first sounded quaint. His basic ideas were not actually new, as they recognized. Friedman was essentially asking the political community to renounce all that it had learned from Franklin Roosevelt's New Deal. He was audaciously attempting to rehabilitate classical economic doctrines from the nineteenth century, the faith in free markets and an abhorrence of government intrusion. These ideas had themselves been the orthodox wisdom for generations of economists, businessmen and political leaders—until they were brutally discredited by events.

The seminal events that destroyed the old ideology were the Crash of 1929 and the Great Depression that followed. Classical economics taught that free markets would always seek and find a natural equilibrium, a self-correcting capacity that revived production and employment, once prices and wages fell low enough. In the Great Depression, the American economy did not revive. Neither did the rest of the world's. Year after year, as the social misery deepened and massive unemployment stretched on for more than a decade, the popular faith in free markets was shattered. Somewhat haphazardly, the New Deal advanced a new creed: an activist national government must intervene to overcome the shortcomings and weaknesses of private enterprise. This new idea—government's obligation to manage the economy— was legitimized by the national trauma of Depression, embraced both in public opinion and in scholarly theory.

Friedman's old-fashioned preoccupation with the money supply collided with a corollary lesson taught by the Depression years. The new generation of economists, who proudly called themselves Keynesians, concluded from the experience of the thirties that the money supply was not a reliable tool for stimulating growth in the economy. Fiscal policy—taxes and spending—was much more potent and direct. After all, the nation was awash with excess liquidity, an overabundance of savings, during the Depression years. The problem, crudely stated, was not a shortage of money—the problem was that people were afraid to spend it. If consumers would not buy, then capital owners would not invest in new factories or rehire the unemployed. Everyone held back, and the cycle of caution and contraction fed on itself. As the Keynesians' cliché put it, trying to revive the economy by expanding the money supply was like "pushing on a string."

In this contest of ideas, therefore, Friedman's book brilliantly reargued the historical record of the Depression and insisted that the conventional analysis was mistaken. Friedman found that both the original collapse of 1929 and the long contraction of the real economy were probably caused and certainly exacerbated by the Federal Reserve's failure to provide an adequate money supply. In the debates among economists, the Friedman position was summarized with a new cliché: "money matters."

None of this intellectual combat would have counted for much in the lives of ordinary Americans if the good times of the sixties had continued. Milton Friedman might have remained obscure and lonely, an eccentric thinker living in the wrong age. Instead, he won the Nobel Prize for economics in 1976. He became, if not a celebrity, at least widely celebrated as a prophet. Bright young graduate students listened to their Keynesian professors and then to Friedman, and some began calling themselves "monetarists," the label applied to his disciples. Wall Street analysts followed the money numbers more closely, the weekly fluctuations of M-1, and concluded, just as Friedman had said, that M-1 was a more reliable predictor of economic swings than the changing federal budget. Many executives of important banks and corporate economists were converted too, along with reporters and editors in the financial press. Eventually, the converts included important political figures in Washington, even liberal politicians.

Over a decade, starting in the mid-1960s, a remarkable transformation took place in elite opinion—a kind of counterreformation that rose to challenge the hegemony of the Keynesian liberals. More than anyone else, Friedman was its leader. Each generation, it seemed, discovered new truth from its own experience and discarded competing truths from the past. When the tide of events shifted, the collective wisdom shifted with it, sometimes rediscovering what the previous generation had forgotten. Back in the 1930s, with his usual drollery, Keynes had observed that political leaders were, unaware, "the slaves of some defunct economist." Now, the monetarists claimed, Keynes himself was the defunct economist.

The challenge of monetarism, the new respectability of money as a central factor in economic policy, flowed from a single disturbance, a new economic trauma confronting the nation—the rise of price inflation. In 1966, the nation was alarmed when the Consumer Price Index increased more than 3 percent, the steepest inflation in fifteen years. By 1969, the annual rate of price increases was above 6 percent. With a brief recession followed by the wage-and-price controls imposed by Richard Nixon, the inflation rate subsided for a time, but still remained about 3 percent. By 1973, prices were escalating rapidly again and the CPI rose by a new postwar record, 8.8 percent. The following year, 1974, OPEC pushed up oil and the price level rose 12.2 percent.[17]

The presumed remedy was a long and deep recession, an economic contraction induced by tight monetary policy from the Federal Reserve. As recession continued for fifteen months, the unemployment rate rose to a peak of 9.1 percent; the nation's industrial production shrank by nearly 15 percent.[18] Yet, when the economy recovered and resumed its growth, so did inflation. Indeed, the disorders got worse: the rate of inflation rose toward double digits again but the economy never returned to anything resembling full employment. In the Keynesian analysis, these twin aggravations—inflation and high unemployment—were not supposed to occur simultaneously.

What exactly was causing this modern spiral of inflation? Many explanations were proffered, indeed, a bewildering variety of different answers came from the economists. Lyndon Johnson was blamed for overstimulating the economy when it was already at its maximum capacity—adding tens of billions in new spending for the war in Indochina to the federal budget alongside the burgeoning new Great Society spending for education, health and poverty. The Arab sheiks and OPEC were blamed for the oil price shocks of 1973 and later. Workers and labor unions were implicated for demanding wage increases that exceeded the increase in their productivity; corporate managers were accused of giving in too easily to labor's demands and passing on the cost in the price of their products. All of these diffuse factors were relevant to the inflation, yet the very complexity was unsatisfying. Who exactly was to blame? The standard explanations from economists seemed to blame everyone, a bit, and no one singularly.

Milton Friedman offered a much simpler answer to the question: inflation was caused by the Federal Reserve.

His scholarly dictum, often quoted, was actually an accusation: "Inflation is everywhere and anywhere a monetary phenomenon." In translation, that meant: price inflation could not have occurred if the Federal Reserve had not provided excessive amounts of money to the economy. Instead, Friedman said, the Federal Reserve swerved back and forth irresponsibly—supplying too much money and causing inflation, then tightening the money supply abruptly, which choked off the economy and produced recession.

His solution was radical. Congress should strip the Fed of its privileged independence and enact legislative instructions for U.S. monetary policy. The Fed must be compelled to accept a simple rule governing its functions: from week to week, month to month, year to year, without deviation, the money supply should be expanded at a fixed rate, somewhere around 3 percent a year for the basic aggregate, M-1. Thus, money growth would be held to the historic average growth rate for the national economy and would avoid the sharp swings. Private business, financial markets and consumers could then count on a stable future, instead of lurching back and forth from inflation to recession. A monetary rule, Friedman explained, would not eliminate the natural highs and lows of the business cycle, but it would moderate them—and guarantee that government intrusion did not make things worse.

The core of Friedman's doctrine was, in fact, a profoundly conservative statement on human expectations. It reformulated, in the language of economics, the ancient myth of Icarus and Daedalus, in which man tried to escape the bounds of his earthly limitations—flying too close to the sun—and tragedy resulted. Monetarism rested on the same belief, that human society would be better off if it modestly accepted limits for itself. Economic aspirations should not attempt to accomplish more than the historical average of economic growth compiled by the past. There were natural limits to what could be expected from life. If democratic ambitions tried to push the economy beyond those limits, chaos and disorder would follow.

The monetarist prescription, a fixed rule for money, was an alluring solution to the instabilities of inflation, and many rushed to embrace it, but it begged an important question: if Friedman was correct, why didn't the Federal Reserve follow such a rule itself? The Fed portrayed itself as the governing institution most dedicated to the goal of stable prices. If a fixed rate of money growth was the obvious answer, was it plausible that the Federal Reserve would persistently refuse to adopt it?

Friedman had an explanation:

The Federal Reserve System is a political institution, and like every political institution, it is seeking to retain its own power, its own decisions, its own prestige. To what end do politicians want to maintain their positions? To what end does a CEO of a business concern want to run that concern for profit? Because the coin he is interested in is both income and power. In the same way, people who are in the Fed want to maintain their position. Their coin is influence and power.

A strict money rule, if faithfully followed, would make their decisions for them. The Federal Open Market Committee would not have to meet every six or eight weeks in deep secrecy to deliberate on the new economic developments and how it should respond to them.

Let's suppose that over the last thirty years the Federal Reserve System had followed the policies I've been recommending [Friedman mused]. They had produced a steady, stable rate of growth in the quantity of money. I assure you the economy would have been vastly better off. There never would have been a major inflation. There would have been milder business cycles. We would have still had business cycles, but they would have been mild. But all that the Fed would have been doing is making sure that the money supply rose by 3 percent a year.

Is there a chance in the world, under those circumstances, that the chairman of the Federal Reserve would be chosen in a public-opinion poll as the second most important person in the country? The Federal Reserve would be a minor service agency of government. Nobody would know that they had been enormously influential in producing these good results. From a purely political point of view, that would have been a stupid policy for them to follow and that's why they haven't followed it.

In one dimension, Friedman's conservative critique of the Fed resembled the liberal complaints of the Texas Populist congressman Wright Patman. The Federal Reserve, he contended, assiduously served the interests of one important constituency—the commercial banks—and the political power of the banks was used, in turn, to protect the independent status of the Fed. "If I said to you, 'Here I've got a major sector of the economy in which no enterprise ever fails, no one ever goes broke,' you would tell me, 'My God, there must not be any competition there,' " Friedman said. "That's correct. The banking industry has been a highly protected, sheltered industry. That's because the banks have been the constituency of the Federal Reserve."

Only public indignation could alter any of this, Friedman believed. The bureaucratic mentality of the Fed was stubbornly devoted to protecting its own discretionary powers. "They are important people," he said. "It's impossible for them to believe that they are doing harm by being important—and that they would do more good by being clerks."

In the privacy of his office, a Federal Reserve governor spoke with uncharacteristic heat in his voice. "I don't understand why the financial press has such a monetarist bias," the governor said bitterly. "The monetarists are the chiropractors of modern economics."

In public, the Fed's contempt for its monetarist critics was usually concealed by polite technical arguments. In private, most of the senior officials of the Federal Reserve shared the sense of frustration that so many were "taken in" by the Friedman argument. In their view, the monetarists swept away all of the complexities of central banking and blithely pretended they did not matter—questions about the definition of money itself, about seasonal fluctuations in the public's need for money, about the external forces that reverberated through the banking system and the real economy. The Federal Reserve tried to adjust for all these and other influences on the money supply. That was the essence of what the Federal Open Market Committee debated every other month; that was why they thought it was impossible to supply the same amount of reserves each week, each month, without adjusting for change. Human society, in other words, did not proceed by neat historical averages. As Governor Henry Wallich stated:

Milton Friedman implies that there are no fluctuations in the real economy that need affect monetary policy—no investment boom, no housing boom, no oil shocks. We should simply supply a steady growth of money.

The Fed feels it has to smooth out reserves, adjust for seasonal influences. Monetarists say that none of this is necessary. Monetarists say, "The markets will learn to adjust to this—those who were right will prosper, those who were wrong will be punished." I say, "If you accept that, eventually you will have only those left who are wise and prosperous and everyone else will be ruined."

The Fed was enormously vulnerable, however. Fed economists could make technical arguments against the rigidity of Friedman's proposal for a monetary rule. But the reality of the last fifteen years was irrefutable: price inflation had steadily escalated and this could not have happened if the Federal Reserve had not allowed it to happen.

In public, Federal Reserve officials were defensive and evasive. Privately, inside the System, even governors who despised Friedman's caustic attacks had to concede his larger point: in the long run, one way or another, the Fed had at the very least acquiesced to inflation. Either through honest error or by lack of will, the Fed had provided more money than was actually required by the economy.

Lyle E. Gramley, a former research director at the Fed who would be appointed to the Board of Governors by President Carter in the spring of 1980, was one of the most respected senior economists from the System. And Gramley did not deny the Federal Reserve's culpability:

When you look back over the past fifteen years, you find that inflation kept getting worse. It got worse for a whole variety of reasons, but certainly one of them was that the course of monetary policy over this long period had permitted too rapid an increase in money and credit. I don't think that monetary policy was the principal initiating force of inflation. I think it was things like the way we financed the Vietnam War, the oil price shocks in the 1970s, the tremendous increase in government regulations on the environment and the workplace. But, you know, if over twenty years inflation accelerates a lot, you have to say that a good bit of the responsibility has to fall ultimately on the conduct of monetary policy.

The Fed's diligent management of money was complicated by a fundamental political dilemma—the impact of its actions unfolded unevenly in the real economy, which encouraged hesitation and error. As most economists agreed, the first consequence of a substantial increase in the money supply was positive—a surge in economic activity. The negative impact of excessive money growth would not be felt until much later—increased inflation.

The economists disagreed among themselves over how long these two different effects lagged behind the original policy action by the Fed. Some monetarists, for instance, insisted that the relationship was quite predictable: money growth stimulated more output in the real economy within three to six months, but the benefits would be wiped out relatively soon by the subsequent inflation, perhaps nine months or a year later. Others argued that it was not so neat and simple, that the lag time varied from season to season, depending on many other factors besides money. In any case, the mismatch in timing confronted the Fed with a permanent tension in its decision making: it could always produce pleasure in the short run—but at the risk of causing disorder later on.

The temptation was obvious: the Federal Open Market Committee could provide short-term gratification and hope that the negative consequences did not materialize in the long term. As Philip Coldwell observed:

> We're not that tolerant of governors in our society. You build a governor in an automobile to limit the speed and someone's going to find a way to wire around it because he wants to go faster. No President is going to be satisfied with 3 percent growth in the economy, even when you explain to him that over the long term things will be fine for everyone with 3 percent growth. He says: "I'll go for 5 percent growth and let the next guy settle for 3 percent."

The general indictment, supported by many years of evidence, was that the Federal Reserve had yielded too easily and too often to the short-run aspirations. Lyle Gramley believed that this behavior did not stem from political pressures on the Fed from the White House or Congress, but from the common mind-set of the policy makers. "The Federal Reserve shared the beliefs of the economic profession and the aspirations of the public," Gramley said.

The sober reassessment of attitudes inside the System was not at all apparent to outsiders in the autumn of 1979. As a political institution, the Fed felt embattled, surrounded by critics. To them, the Fed seemed obstinate and arrogant, stubbornly refusing to change its methods despite the accumulated evidence of failure. "Monetary control remains a marginal concern basically alien to the Federal Reserve bureaucracy's tradition," the Shadow Open Market Committee declared. The Shadow Committee was a rump forum for monetarist economists from banking and academia who met regularly to issue withering critiques of the Fed's performance.[19]

But the Federal Reserve was under attack from liberals too. In an era of runaway inflation, an outcry from conservatives was natural.

They were the traditional advocates of "hard money," the defenders of capital and the wealthy citizens whose financial assets were being eroded by inflation. Oddly enough, however, many liberal Democrats in Congress found common cause with the conservative doctrine of monetarism. While they never claimed the label, Democrats joined Republicans in pressuring Fed officials to move toward the operating methods advocated by Friedman and his allies—strict and steady control over the basic money aggregate, M-1. A labor-liberal Democrat like Representative Henry Reuss of Wisconsin, who succeeded Wright Patman as chairman of the House Banking Committee, pushed a monetarist approach. Even Patman himself in his last years was drawn to it.

"I was always amazed at the liberal Democrats who fell for the monetarist line," said Daniel Brill, the Fed's retired research director, "because it put them on the wrong side of their own political position."

Despite the contradiction, members of Congress had an appealing motive for embracing the monetarist critique, especially liberal Democrats who had promoted the great expansion of federal budgets. If the Federal Reserve was actually to blame for inflation, then Congress was absolved. If stable prices were simply a question of careful monetary management by the Federal Reserve, that deflected criticism from the free-spending fiscal policies of the executive and legislative branches—the perennial federal deficits of the sixties and seventies and the accumulating national debt. For many in Congress, the comforting notion that they were innocent and someone else was the culprit fed their righteous indignation toward the Fed.

The congressional agitation for monetarism produced an ironic token of how much the mainstream political opinion had shifted. The Full Employment and Balanced Growth Act of 1978, better known as the Humphrey-Hawkins Act, was the last legislative gasp of the Keynesian persuasion, a doomed effort by Senator Hubert Humphrey and other liberal stalwarts to refocus government policy on the suffering of jobless workers. By the time the law was finally enacted, it was an empty symbol; the liberal content had been thoroughly eviscerated.

But the Humphrey-Hawkins Act contained one substantive reform —a monetarist provision ordering the Federal Reserve to make public its annual target ranges for growth in the three monetary aggregates, the three Ms. The Federal Reserve chairman would be required to appear twice a year before House and Senate banking committees to explain these goals and any deviations from the targets. This was intended to give Congress a better handle for oversight, a way to make sure the Fed kept its word on controlling the money supply. Liberal cosponsors ignored the irony, but conservative insiders were amused:

their ascendant doctrine of monetarism was riding to victory on the legislative carcass of the fading orthodoxy of Keynes.[20]

In addition to the Fed's outside critics, the enemy was also within the gates. Over the years, the St. Louis Federal Reserve Bank had made itself into a kind of guerrilla outpost for monetarism within the Federal Reserve System. Its research director, Homer Jones, was a teacher of Friedman's and had recruited a staff of research economists eager to critique the "home office" in Washington and oppose its operating strategy. A succession of presidents at the St. Louis Fed were, likewise, regular nettles inside the Federal Open Market Committee—preaching heretical doctrine directly to the church fathers.

Lawrence K. Roos was a commercial banker who served three terms as the elected county executive in St. Louis before his appointment as president of the St. Louis Fed in 1976. "When I took the job," Roos said, "I didn't know a monetarist from a Keynesian, but I was given basic training quick and felt the monetarist approach made sense to me."

Roos's monetarist speeches became predictable features of the FOMC meetings, eliciting occasional snickers and some irritation from his colleagues. He complained that the Fed refused to set long-term goals and stick to them. He criticized the deliberate obfuscation, the bewildering variety of economic yardsticks that other FOMC members used to justify their decisions. "Even though it's a central bank and central banks love to be secretive and mysterious, I think the Fed should tell the American public where it intends to be in two years, its long-range goals for prices, for output and other things. Instead, you name it and the Fed makes a speech saying that's what it wants too. They really represent a wish list for achieving utopia."

The conflicting philosophies were concretely reflected in competing computer models. Since 1970, the Fed had operated an elaborate econometric model that attempted to forecast the effects of monetary policy and other influences on the American economy. Computer models were essentially a series of mathematical equations linked together in a fashion that allowed them to work through the myriad of variables and report the theoretical consequences. If the money supply increased by 4 percent a month, how would that alter employment, prices, interest rates six months or a year from now? The model worked the numbers through the equations and printed out answers. The Federal Reserve Board's computer model in Washington kept adding sophistication to its analysis, growing eventually to more than 160 equations, including everything from oil prices to housing starts. The monetarists at the St. Louis Fed designed their own model of the economy—it contained only eight equations. Money mattered more than anything else. At each meeting of the Federal Open Market Committee, the central staff would provide forecasts based, in part, on its complicated econometric model. Roos delivered contrary results from the monetarists' computer.

Governor Philip Coldwell, who like Wallich was a "hawk" on tight money but disdainful of monetarism, was less rankled by Roos's dissents than some other governors.

> For some governors [Coldwell said], this was really a fighting matter. Every time a St. Louis man left office, one or two governors would come to me and say, "By God, we're not to let another monetarist in there this time." I'd say, "Well, what's the matter with having one bank out of twelve that is monetarist? Sure, they're obnoxious and they argue a bit too loudly, but that is one view that ought to be represented." St. Louis never created a big problem for me. We could always outvote him.

Over time, this was less and less true. The presidents of other Reserve Banks were drawn toward the monetarist camp too—Robert Black of Richmond, John Balles of San Francisco, Monroe Kimbrel of Atlanta and occasionally others. The other presidents were less doctrinaire, less predictable than Roos, but they too found the Friedman case compelling. If the Federal Reserve did not do anything else, it at least ought to get control over the money aggregates.

"Your little monetarist clique," another FOMC member said of them contemptuously. Nevertheless, they were present and voting and their side was growing stronger. Like it or not, the new Federal Reserve chairman would have to deal with the monetarists.

The thicket of competing theories from economists was most intimidating to outsiders. Otherwise intelligent citizens, who did not have a graduate degree in economics, were bullied into silence. They were compelled to listen passively to the heated arguments among experts, barely able to understand the language of the debate, much less to make a reasoned judgment about which side was right and which was wrong. This barrier of ignorance deformed every political question that required economic expertise, benumbing the normal debate with scientific abstractions.

But many questions of the political economy could be approached in a simpler fashion, an alternative approach that skirted the opaque language of the economists and sought broader answers. The alternative approach was through history: what did the American past reveal about inflation that might help citizens understand their own experience?

On this subject, memory could be misleading. Every generation looked backward with nostalgia, imagining a past when life was simpler and less troubled and, certainly, cheaper. The longing was expressed in the famous quip: "What this country needs is a good five-cent cigar." Modern Americans could remember fondly a time in their own lives when movies cost 50 cents and Hershey bars sold for a dime and a family-sized Chevrolet could be bought for less than $3,000.

The nostalgia for lower prices obscured the actual history of inflation. In the late 1970s, when prices were rising at the fastest pace in twenty years, this was not the worst of times. Inflation in 1979 averaged more than 13 percent, which was alarming, but not so bad as 1947 when the inflation rate was 14.4 percent or 1918 when it was more than 17 percent or 1864 when inflation hit 27 percent.

The American past was not placid and golden. Prices were usually either rising or falling and could have damaging consequences either way. In the entire history of the United States, there were only a few brief eras of what might be called "price stability." Each of those episodes was disastrous for many ordinary citizens—prices and incomes were too low.

If a historian examined the data on prices across the entire sweep of American history, an obvious pattern was visible. What caused inflation? The recurring experience of inflationary spirals strongly suggested that the underlying source of these traumas lay not in economics but in politics—the choices made by government or, more precisely, choices that the government refused to make. This was not a matter of the government deciding in a deliberate fashion to ignite an explosion of price increases, yet the periodic bursts of extreme inflation clearly flowed from the government's decisions.

Through the decades of U.S. history, the price index rose and fell, usually by moderate degree, but there were six distinct episodes when prices escalated abruptly—periods that look like sharp upward spikes on a historical chart of U.S. inflation (see Appendix A, U.S. prices from 1800 to 1986). A historian would ask: what happened in those periods to cause these inflationary spikes?

The first one followed the birth of the Republic, the inflationary frenzy that came after the Revolutionary War. This was before reliable data on prices were collected, but the trauma was still remembered in a colloquial expression—"not worth a Continental." The second spike of inflation occurred in 1813–1814 after the young nation had fought and won another war with the British, the War of 1812. The third and sharpest explosion of inflation came in the 1860's. Lincoln was President and the nation was embroiled in its bloody, costly Civil War.

The next dramatic burst of inflation followed immediately after World War I. A fifth spike occurred at the end of World War II. The final one—the beginning of the contemporary inflation—was associated with the war in Vietnam. In all but the last two instances, each rapid run-up of inflation was followed by long and painful periods of deflation, eras when prices fell drastically. Deflation was unknown to modern Americans, except for those elderly citizens who remembered the economic facts of the Great Depression in the thirties, but falling prices produced a much more severe version of suffering and dislocation, failed banks and businesses, farm foreclosures, widespread unemployment and impoverishment.

These simple facts of history suggested a straightforward answer to the question: virulent inflation resulted when the country went to war. That did not explain, of course, why this was so, and the details were different in each instance. But all the inflationary episodes followed the same pattern of behavior by the government—it mobilized the country and the economy by spending vastly more money than it collected in taxes. In each case, from the Revolution to World War II, from Lincoln to Lyndon Johnson, the national government saw itself confronted with a threat to national survival. In those circumstances, government did what it would not have dared to do in other times—it spent far beyond its means, whatever it thought was needed to win the war, pushing aside the problem of how to pay for the war. It would deal with the economic consequences afterward.

The political choices in wartime were always unattractive. In theory, the government could simply raise taxes high enough to pay for the war, but that would undermine popular support for the struggle. Lincoln, Wilson, Roosevelt and Johnson all raised war taxes, but all of them declined to finance the war primarily from tax revenue. Just as Lyndon Johnson feared that a tax increase would turn the American public against the military conflict in Vietnam, Abraham Lincoln worried that additional taxes would deepen the suffering and sacrifice in the Civil War, further aggravating the opposition. It seemed bizarre to equate Lincoln's struggle to preserve the Union with Lyndon Johnson's doomed venture in Indochina, but the relevant point was that the financial consequences were similar.

For every great crisis of national security, the federal government borrowed the money to pay for the wars. It would accumulate huge wartime deficits in the federal budget and sell Treasury bonds to cover the new debt. In Lincoln's case, the solution was much more direct: the national government simply printed new money, nearly $500 million in a new currency called "greenbacks," and spent it.

The immediate result in every instance was dramatic economic growth and an explosive burst of inflation afterward. It was easy to see the historical connection, but not so easy to explain how the government's fiscal actions were transmitted into prices. Economists argued among themselves on how the linkage worked. Some pointed to the postwar pressures on the real economy. When citizens returned to peaceful pursuits, their pent-up demand for domestic goods exceeded the economy's ability to produce them. The sudden shortages led to higher prices. Others emphasized the role of the money supply—expanded artificially to accommodate the government's wartime spending and to make possible the massive borrowing that financed it. In the postwar environment, the money supply was simply too ample for the economy and the result was inflation. Like many disputes in economics, it was not necessary for noneconomists to choose one explanation over the other. It was entirely plausible that both were true, that the government's fiscal policy and its monetary policy interacted with an overexerted economy to produce the spikes of rapid rising prices.

The modern spiral of inflation was unique in one respect—its unprecedented duration—and, therefore, more puzzling. The contemporary run-up of prices started visibly with the Vietnam War in 1966. Yet, unlike the other episodes, it did not halt after a few years and subside. Inflation continued upward for more than a decade—even in peacetime, even when the economy was slack. The inflationary surge of the 1960s and 1970s was not as steep as others in the past, but it persisted and compounded more dramatically than anything that had happened before in the American past.

The Consumer Price Index was calculated as 100 with 1967 prices. By 1970, the price index was at 116. By 1975, it was 161. Four years later, it was 217. During the Civil War, prices doubled in only a few years, but Lincoln was fighting a war. This time, the price level nearly tripled in less than twenty years. And the nation was at peace.

The historical question had to be turned around: what was different about the modern postwar era that produced this unprecedented trend? The plausible answers were essentially political. As economic historian Walt W. Rostow has explained, the end of colonial domination in the world inevitably gave the newly independent nations, most of them poor and undeveloped, somewhat more leverage over the terms of trade with the industrial nations of the West, including the United States. This meant the poorer nations could demand somewhat higher prices for the raw commodities, from copper to coffee, that they sold to the wealthy nations. The most spectacular case of this new reality of global power was, of course, crude oil. Higher costs for imported raw materials naturally pushed domestic prices upward (though most less-developed countries remained in weak bargaining positions and still complained of exploitation by industrial capitalism).

Another new political condition was the still-fresh memory of the Great Depression. After World War II, neither political party wanted to risk repeating the misery of the 1930s, and that collective fear pushed policy makers in the opposite direction—pursuing economic expansion and accepting the risk of inflation. In fact, a modern triumph of the government's economic management was that after World War II Americans did not have to endure another episode of ruinous deflation, the kind that had always followed previous wars.

There was one other fundamental change: the Cold War with the Soviet Union. After World War II, the U.S. economy never actually returned to a peacetime footing. It demobilized briefly but quickly rearmed for global struggle. For the next three decades, driven by fears of conflict with the Soviets, the United States prepared for war. This was unlike any prior era of peacetime in American history. The armed forces were kept permanently at a strength level consistent with war making, and a burgeoning arsenal of modern weapons was purchased from the defense industrial sector. The government's defense spending for the Cold War absorbed a permanent share of the economy's output, boosting employment and incomes but also competing with other desires.

While the U.S remained mobilized, the country also resumed the full domestic prosperity of a nation at peace—producing and consuming consumer goods in unprecedented volume. The standard of living for typical American families reached a level of comfort and even luxury undreamed of by earlier generations, new homes in the suburbs, dazzling appliances in the kitchen, a new car in the garage or perhaps two cars. For a time, modern Americans had the best of both worlds, the pleasures of peace and the economic energy of war.

Notwithstanding inflation and other aggravations, this period would rightly be celebrated as the American era—an extraordinary time of prosperous progress in both social and economic terms. The economic expansion during the postwar years generated an entirely new standard of abundance and equity in American life. Deprivation was not eliminated entirely but greatly reduced and, in prosperous times, the society felt confident enough to address some of its long-standing injustices, racial discrimination in particular. The ambitious economic goals pursued by the federal government were, of course, fully shared by the nation at large. Great multinational corporations were extending their reach around the globe, symbols of America's new hegemony. The swollen military spending seemed a natural extension of the same impulse. America was the new leader of the world, building the largest arsenal ever imagined, prepositioning American troops in dozens of foreign lands. For many years, it seemed, the United States could indeed afford both war and peace at the same time.

But, in time, the failure to choose between the two caught up with the economy and the government's balance sheet. It was not simply that federal deficits got larger; the question was more complicated than that. For years, after all, despite new deficits, the total national debt was actually shrinking in real terms compared to the size of the nation's economy—a sign of health. Each annual budget added modest new deficits to the total outstanding debt, but the economy was growing much faster than the government's borrowing. In 1945, following the massive deficit spending of World War II, the national debt was 119 percent of the annual Gross National Product. But the burden was shrinking dramatically as the postwar economy expanded robustly. By 1960, the debt was only 58 percent of the GNP. By 1969, it had fallen to 40 percent. In 1974, it was down to 35 percent of the nation's economic output.

Then the historic trend was reversed. In 1975, for the first time since World War II, the national debt did not decline in relation to the economy. The new trend was mild at first, not nearly as dramatic as the debt generated in wartime, but an odd turn of events would aggravate it. A conservative government would assume power in the 1980s, and instead of moderating the fiscal imbalance as conservative governments were expected to do, it accelerated the trend. The government accumulated deficits much larger than before, and the national debt grew much faster than the economy. By 1984, the debt ratio would rise from a low of 35 percent to about 45 percent of the GNP—back above the level achieved in 1969.[21] The government's balance sheet, in other words, began to resemble the financial conditions normally tolerated only during a war.

The political debates did not focus on these numbers, but they returned again and again to the same fundamental question—an argument over national priorities. The basic choice was between war and peace, a question of political values, not economic theory. The Cold War, it was said, threatened American survival and, therefore, the defense spending must take precedence. Or, conversely, it was argued that the Soviet threat was exaggerated, that military spending was excessive and the government's resources should be directed to domestic development. Broad factions formed on both sides of the question and struggled for control. But, in practical terms, a political consensus was fashioned between them, an implicit understanding that endured for more than three decades, through conservative and liberal regimes, under Democrats and Republicans. The government would refuse to choose between war mobilization and peacetime spending. It would do both.

"After years of inflation," Paul Volcker told an audience in the autumn of 1979, "the long run has caught up with us."[22]

The message was clear to every member of the Federal Reserve Board, even to those three reluctant governors who had recently voted against even a modest increase in the Discount rate. In the last half of September, their worries about imminent recession were contradicted by the new data on economic output coming in from the Commerce Department. Despite all the forecasts, the economy wasn't tipping into a contraction; it was accelerating again.

And, despite the Fed's gradual efforts to slow things down with measured increases in interest rates, the banking system was actually accelerating its lending. Bank credit was expanding at an annual rate of more than 20 percent, and, as Fed officials heard from worried bankers, a lot of that new credit was going into speculative ventures —businesses and individuals borrowing in order to buy things on the rising prices, speculative investments from gold and silver to real estate. They were betting that inflation would drive prices much higher. The smart speculator would then sell the commodities or other tangibles, repay the loans and reap a smart, quick profit.

Speculation did not look like a risky bet: the overall inflation rate was near 13 percent and the price of oil was increasing at an alarming rate of more than 6 percent a month—an annual inflation rate of nearly 80 percent. Gold had jumped 28 percent in value in a single month, reaching a new record of $411 an ounce. The price of silver, in the same period, had increased by a staggering 53 percent, up to $16.89 an ounce.

"The specter of 1929 was raised by me and others," Governor Coldwell said. "Look, we're on the verge of going into a hyperinflation in the United States."

While that sounded much too apocalyptic, the frenzy of borrowing and buying did resemble the potential for a classic speculative bubble, one of those fevers that has occurred periodically in economic history. The marketplace loses touch with real value and plunges forward in an orgy of acquisition. Whether it is stocks or bonds, corner lots in big cities or undeveloped swampland in Florida, speculative bubbles all derive from one conviction: the buyers are convinced that in a few days or weeks or months they will become sellers and unload their purchase at a profit. Bubbles always collapsed eventually; the fever broke and prices fell drastically. Then speculators were forced to sell at a loss. They failed and so would banks that lent them money to take their gambles. That is approximately what happened to Wall Street in 1929, when the bubble of financial speculation burst and the stock market collapsed.

It was in this anxious setting that the Federal Reserve chairman began to call on the other governors, one by one, to try out his new idea. Early in his tenure, Volcker had directed the senior staff to begin technical studies on changing the Fed's basic operating method, and after the embarrassment of the board's 4–3 vote on September 18, Volcker pushed the idea more aggressively. Some of his colleagues were taken aback. The new chairman was not just advocating a fundamental change in the way the Federal Open Market Committee regulated the money supply. He was proposing a monetarist solution —the approach advocated by the Fed's angriest critics.

When Volcker dropped by Henry Wallich's office, Wallich told him in his polite but blunt manner that he opposed the chairman's proposition. Wallich's office, down the marble corridor and around the corner from Volcker's, was dark and jumbled compared to the others, cluttered with random stacks of staff papers and books, smelling faintly of old cigar smoke. Wallich read by a low lamp on his desk, constantly fondling a long cigar. He sometimes wore a green eyeshade, the kind that bookkeepers once used, to protect his weak vision. The eldest governor resembled a genially eccentric professor, enjoying the solitude of his lair, a shuttered study lined with books.

The other governors' offices were brighter and less forbidding than Wallich's, but all of them, including Volcker's, seemed more suited to the academic life than to powerful decision makers of government. Each had a wall of bookshelves and a fireplace handsomely faced in black marble, usually with a sofa and chairs grouped around it. Normally, the board chairman did not lobby the other governors in the privacy of their offices; the collegial ethic of the Federal Reserve Board presumed a polite distance among its members, in which each governor was to decide policy questions on his own, free of heavy-handed pressure from others. Volcker's one-on-one visits made his point: the chairman considered this a question of extraordinary importance.

"It's a pact with the devil," Henry Wallich warned Volcker.

Wallich explained his objections. The Federal Open Market Committee ought to tighten money and credit dramatically, Wallich said, but not by adopting a risky new operating system that would create its own disorders. The monetarists had long urged the Fed to abandon its preoccupation with the level of interest rates and, instead, concentrate solely on the money supply itself and the level of reserves the Fed provided for the banking system. Interest rates would then be allowed to rise or fall automatically in reaction. Wallich thought this would lead to extreme swings in interest rates that would destabilize the financial markets and the real economy.

"If you make interest rates automatic," Wallich predicted, "you have no influence over where they are. So long as the economy is strong, you restrain money supply and interest rates go up. But, as soon as the economy weakens, you have to let interest rates go down. We first get very high interest rates, then very low interest rates, then high again. Yes, you control the money supply, but interest rates become very volatile."

"Sometimes," Volcker replied laconically, "you have to deal with the devil."

When Volcker called on Philip Coldwell, the other most stalwart "hawk" on the board, Coldwell was as negative as Wallich. He could hardly believe that the new chairman, who he knew was not a true believer, was seriously advocating a monetarist scheme.

"Paul, I don't understand," Coldwell said. "You want to shift to a monetarist control?" Volcker said that he did. "Well, I don't have any sympathy for that at all," Coldwell said. "It kind of binds our hands. It keeps us from making policy judgments." Volcker insisted he wanted to try it.

The chairman would actually have been content himself not to change anything fundamental, but simply to push forward with the Fed's orthodox approach—tightening credit by pushing interest rates up sharply. But the chairman faced an internal political dilemma: members like Coldwell and Wallich were willing, even eager, to drive up interest rates and halt the inflationary spiral. But others like Partee and Teeters and Rice were much more hesitant to vote directly for such drastic action. Could Volcker assemble a sustainable majority that would vote to raise interest rates two points or much more? And keep them there? Would the FOMC members have the nerve, if it were needed, to push up interest rates by as much as three or four points? Nothing that dramatic had ever been executed by Fed policy makers in the past. The answer seemed obvious.

"We could have just tightened," Volcker acknowledged, "but I probably would have had trouble getting policy as much tighter as it needed to be. I could have lived with a more orthodox tightening, but I saw some value in just changing the parameters of the way we did things."

The monetarist alternative offered a clever solution to Volcker's internal political dilemma: it would serve as a veil that cloaked the tough decisions. If the Federal Open Market Committee declared publicly that it was no longer pegging its policy on interest rates, but on the level of M-1, that would obscure its hand and might deflect the public attacks when interest rates rose sharply. Fed members could explain, disingenuously, that the rising interest rates were attributable to "market pressures." In a narrow sense, that would be correct, but, in a larger sense, an evasion. The "market pressures" that drove up interest rates would derive directly from the Federal Reserve's own actions to tighten the supply of reserves.

As a Reserve Bank president explained:

Everyone could say: "Look, no hands." It was easier to do this with a self-imposed, semiautomatic rule than it would be with periodic decisions by the committee. It wasn't just the perception of outside pressures, but also inside pressures. Internally, nobody really knew how much tightening would be needed to break inflation or how far interest rates would really have to go.

For years, in order to control reserves, the Federal Reserve had dealt with the three Ms obliquely rather than directly. Instead of pegging its policy to the quantity of reserves, it pegged it to the Federal Funds rate, the price that one bank charged when it lent its excess reserves to another bank that was short. In its meetings, the Federal Open Market Committee focused primarily on where to hold this short-term interest rate and then instructed the Open Market Desk in New York to achieve that goal. Each day, as pressures in the money market fluctuated, the Fed managers at the New York desk would buy or sell securities, injecting or withdrawing reserves, in order to keep the Fed Funds rate at the chosen level.

When the Fed Funds rate was raised, it signaled tighter credit availability to all the players and, therefore, was expected to discourage further credit expansion. When banks saw the Fed Funds rate going up, they were supposed to moderate their own lending—or else pay dearly in the money market to raise the required reserves. If the banks did not respond accordingly, the Federal Open Market Committee would move its target for the Fed Funds rate higher and hope that the banking system got the message.

To monetarists, this was backwards. The Fed, they complained, employed a permissive, indirect approach that constantly left it reacting to events after the fact. A simple, straightforward method would be much more effective—directly targeting the quantity of reserves it intended to provide, then sticking to that target.

Milton Friedman, the master teacher, provided a lucid illustration of why the monetarists thought the Fed was wrong:

Suppose I want to control the number of automobiles produced in the United States. There are two ways in which I can do it. I can say, "I'm going to try to figure out at what price people would buy so many automobiles. Then I'm going to peg the price at that level and I'll sell all the automobiles I want. If I find they are buying more than I want, I'll raise the price."

Then there's another way. I can say, "Well, you can't make automobiles without steel. I will limit the total amount of steel that's available to build automobiles and then let the price of autos turn out to be whatever it turns out to be." Those are both ways in which you can ultimately limit the number of automobiles produced.

Exactly the same is true with respect to the quantity of money. One way to limit the quantity of money is to say, "Let me try to figure at what interest rate people want to hold a quantity of money equal to the amount I want to make available." Then I will try to set the interest rate at that level. Or I can say, "The raw material of making loans is reserves—high-powered money. How much high-powered money is required to support the quantity of money I want to see out there?" I will provide that quantity of high-powered money. That's like producing that amount of raw steel.

In principle, if I knew enough, the two approaches would be identical. I'd pick the same answer. But, in practice, I don't know enough. It would be clear to you that it's a lot easier to control the number of automobiles by limiting the amount of steel than it is by trying to guess what the hell the price should be. I think the same thing is true in the money market.

There was one thing wrong with Friedman's metaphor—banks aren't automobile companies, money is not steel. The daily expansion or contraction of money and credit was neither so easily visible and definable as steelmaking and auto selling nor was it so neatly limited in consequence. If the price of autos fluctuated suddenly, that affected auto sales. If the price of bank reserves changed suddenly, that sent tremors through every credit transaction in the economy, from six-month CDs to auto loans to capital investment in new factories. Friedman's system might produce smoother control over bank reserves, but it would also create horrendous zigzags in interest rates, as markets bid the price of money up and down.

The Fed, like all central banks, cared a lot about stability. Traditionally, Fed officials had interpreted their legal mandate to include a responsibility for maintaining "orderly markets." Put another way, they felt obligated to avoid actions that might destabilize the vast and complicated machinery of finance. In practice, when the Fed tightened or eased, it tried to engineer smooth changes in interest rates that would "nudge" the financial markets in the right direction without shocking them into hysterical overreactions. Monetarists claimed this concern reflected the Fed's narrow attachment to one special interest, the money-market traders of Wall Street. The Fed's cautious management of interest rates made life a lot easier for market traders, the monetarists complained, but did not necessarily serve the larger public interest. Nevertheless, the Fed managers traditionally saw the public interest in maintaining stable interest rates and avoiding wild swings that might send wrong messages through the entire economy.

But that was the past. Paul Volcker, though he was schooled as an open-market trader in the Fed bureaucracy and shared its solicitude for "orderly markets," now wanted to accomplish the opposite: Volcker wanted to shock the banks and financial markets, even put a little fear in their hearts. If Wall Street had lost faith in the Fed's will to control inflation, how could he convince them? If money-market traders and cynical speculators were persuaded that the Federal Reserve lacked the resolve to break the inflationary spiral, what message would change their minds? An abrupt change in the operating method, one that would disrupt the financial markets' comfortable assumptions about interest-rate stability, might serve as a therapeutic thunderbolt —an exercise in creative uncertainty.

> This approach had another benefit [Volcker explained]. It injected uncertainty into the system, which, at that point, I thought was desirable. There was a general feeling that the Federal Reserve was going to keep interest rates smooth. The Federal Reserve might raise rates, but the market is not going to be volatile. Banks can continue lending and they would always be able to fund their loans at a rate only slightly higher and the Federal Reserve would not intervene. Now, under this approach, there was uncertainty. Banks had to take the risk that interest rates would go against them.

To sharpen the message, Volcker proposed an auxiliary change designed to chasten the most aggressive banks—an added reserve requirement of 8 percent on the funds that banks borrowed to finance their loan expansion. Traditionally, a typical bank, following the standard rules of prudence, depended on its interest-free deposits as the pool of money for making loans; the bank was the financial intermediary that used the money parked by depositors in order to lend to others who needed it. A bank's expansion of lending was, thus, inhibited by how fast it could attract additional depositors. The old tradition of patience was crumbling.

Over the last two decades, a new go-go spirit had taken hold among American bankers, both in Wall Street and among ambitious regional banks, a driving entrepreneurial zeal for growth. The new spirit was reflected in their architecture. Banks were traditionally designed to look like Greek temples, dour sanctuaries with marble columns, symbols of trust. The new bank buildings of the 1960s and 1970s made a different statement: they were soaring towers of glass and gleaming steel, open and dynamic structures that conveyed a spirit of boldness and optimism. The modern banking buildings reflected the new managerial spirit that had taken hold inside.

American banking had discovered a more aggressive approach to management that evaded the traditional inhibitions of deposit growth, a method for achieving faster growth that appealed especially to the largest and most ambitious banks. Instead of waiting for new deposits, the banks would go ahead and make new loans, then turn around and borrow huge sums themselves, in effect "buying" their deposit base in the money market to finance the expansion of credit. The practice was known as "managed liabilities," since both the regular deposits and the borrowing done by a bank constitute the liabilities on its balance sheet—money it owes to someone else. Conversely, a bank's outstanding loans were its assets—the money it will collect from someone else (exactly the reverse of how families or businessmen would describe their balance sheets). Managed liabilities depended on banks issuing such large financial instruments as certificates of deposit and Eurodollar borrowings of $100,000 and in much greater sums. As long as the banks could count on borrowing new funds at a lower interest rate than they charged for lending them out, the interest-rate spread assured their profits.[23]

Volcker's proposed shift would disrupt the banks' confidence in their interest-rate calculations. What if they made loans at 13 percent and short-term interest rates were suddenly going up sharply? They would lose the spread if they themselves had to borrow at higher rates. The marginal reserve requirement of 8 percent would also make the practice of managed liabilities more expensive for the banks. At all but the smallest banks, the Fed's reserve requirement on the demand deposits in checking accounts was 16.25 percent, but it was much lower or zero on funds raised through large CDs or in the Federal Funds market or the Eurodollar borrowings. Under Volcker's scheme, banks would have to set aside another 8 percent of their borrowed funds as reserves—sterile money held at their local Federal Reserve Bank where it collected no interest. For every $1 million a bank raised in the money market, it would have to set aside $80,000 in an idle account at the Fed. This would not prohibit them from aggressive lending, but bankers, more than other creatures, detested idle money, funds that were not producing interest income. Above all, Volcker hoped the new reserve requirement might scare the more aggressive banks a bit, make them wonder if the Fed was prepared to do even more later.

When Volcker called on other governors, all these elements were made part of his larger argument: if the Federal Reserve took sufficiently dramatic action, that might produce an important psychological victory. If the financial markets were convinced that at last the Fed was prepared to get tough and stay tough on controlling money, the investors who were demanding an "inflation premium" in interest rates to protect themselves against future inflation might change their thinking. Thus, Volcker argued, the drastic action would certainly push up interest rates across the spectrum of lending, both for short-term credit and long-term investments like corporate and government bonds. But, if the markets became more optimistic about the long-range prospects for curbing inflation, then long-term interest rates should drop back down to more normal levels.

"What I hoped," Volcker said, "was that there would be a strong reaction in the markets. Interest rates would go up sharply at first, but that would have a favorable impact on inflationary expectations so that long-term rates would start coming down. The sign of psychological success was whether long-term rates would stabilize and start coming down."

As Volcker made the rounds with his other colleagues, his political dilemma was resolved: the three governors who had been most hesitant about drastic action on interest rates were much more receptive to his proposal. Wallich and Coldwell didn't like it, but Teeters, Rice and Partee were willing to make the shift, well aware that it meant a sharp spike in interest rates—the action they had been reluctant to take directly.

"Under the new system," Nancy Teeters observed, "we could say what we were doing was concentrating on the monetary aggregates. It was perfectly obvious to me that if you set the money growth too low, that would send interest rates up. That was never in doubt. The problem with targeting the Fed Funds rate is that you had to set it. This did let us step back a bit."

Emmett Rice, who had joined the board four months earlier, had questioned interest-rate targeting himself, convinced that it would make more sense to control reserves directly. "I was ready to change it," Rice said. "Most of us were rather pleased that Paul was willing to bite the bullet."

Rice also recognized the political cover that the new operating system offered the governors:

   This meant you were not directly responsible for what happened to
interest rates. This was one of the advantages. If interest rates had to go
to 20 percent—and I have to say that nobody thought they would go that
high—then this would be the procedure doing it. I wouldn't call it a cover,
but I don't think anyone on the committee would have been willing to vote

to push interest rates as high as 20 percent. This was a way to achieve a result, a more effective way to get there.

Chuck Partee, the other reluctant "dove," was attracted to the operating shift by a different argument. Partee was not a monetarist himself, but he thought that the monetarist approach might overcome a flaw in the Fed's institutional reflexes—sticking stubbornly with a strong position too long and causing more damage to the economy than it had intended. Partee had been research director during the long and deep recession of 1974–1975 when the Fed was accused of doing exactly that—holding money and credit tight for so long that it drove the economy into more distress than was necessary, more bankruptcies and more unemployment.

As he said:

It may sound odd, but I would prefer the evenhanded approach of the monetarists. I became very concerned about a mind-set that would lead us right into a recession—get tight and stay tight—and lead us into a recession like the 1930s. I found myself far less hostile to the notion that we might have a fairer approach by targeting the money supply than I was to the idea that we should raise interest rates one time and keep raising them. The problem is, there is also a hesitancy to reduce interest rates once they have been raised. My concern grew out of my reflection on several earlier recessions, particularly 1974–1975. My concern was that we would be slow to respond to weakness and permit a substantial contraction in money and credit to occur. There would be a great chance of that, that we might just get locked into a position of holding tight for a rather extended period.

The automatic quality of the monetarist method promised to avoid that extreme. Presumably, if the economy weakened, the Fed would continue to provide the same supply of reserves, and as the demand fell, the price of money would fall too. Targeting the supply of reserves would, thus, force interest rates higher on an upswing in economic activity, but it would also allow the rates to fall on the downside.

"I considered it a big gamble," Partee added. "You probably would never take such a big gamble under normal circumstances."

Now Volcker had his consensus for change. Wallich and Coldwell, though they didn't like the idea, agreed not to press their objections if this was the only way Volcker could get the others to support a tougher policy. Fred Schultz, the new vice chairman, deferred to Volcker's judgment on the issue, agreeing that something dramatic had to be done. Volcker believed that this was probably the only way to get the tighter money that he and the "hawks" wanted to see.

Wallich did not argue much. "I was not sure people would do it my way," he said. "It was probably wise to use a method that produced a consensus for tightening."

On the last Friday of the month, September 28, the seven governors assembled in the chairman's office, where they would attract less attention than in the boardroom, to thrash out the final details. Only a few of the senior staff members were included. If even a hint leaked out before the chairman was ready to move, it would send wild rumors through the financial markets. The governors all agreed to support the shift to a new operating method, but there were many questions to settle about how it would operate. The chairman was now confident that he could sell the idea to the Federal Open Market Committee when it next met. He had discussed the proposal with several of the twelve Reserve Bank presidents by telephone, but most of them had no idea of what was in the works. Volcker did not worry about getting their support. Given their enthusiasm for monetarism, the Reserve Bank presidents would be delighted to learn that the home office was finally coming around to their way of thinking.

At the White House, the President did not know anything either. Nor did any of Jimmy Carter's advisers on economic policy have any idea that the Federal Reserve was preparing a major departure in monetary policy, intended to deliver a psychological shock to the nation's financial system. As it happened, the President and his staff were busy working up their own anti-inflation initiative. In recent weeks, the White House staff had held uncounted meetings with business executives from major corporations and labor leaders from the AFL-CIO, negotiating a new "accord" on wages and prices that they hoped would moderate the business-labor demands for higher wages, higher prices. White House staffers patiently mediated tendentious discussions over how the voluntary agreement was to be worded, coaxing the labor officials and business leaders to sign. They did not know, of course, that the President's anti-inflation effort would be rendered irrelevant by the new agreement Paul Volcker had just negotiated three blocks away in the privacy of the Federal Reserve building.

Despite its appearance of aloofness, the Federal Reserve kept in close touch with the many political interests that surrounded it. Paul Volcker met regularly with a wide circle of interest groups and their representatives, even some that were hostile to the Fed and opposed to its policies. On a typical day, the chairman might breakfast with a lobbyist from the Independent Bankers Association, then lunch with an economist from the National Home Builders Association. In the evening, he might drop by a congressional reception where he would pick up casual intelligence from the stream of Washington political gossip.

The chairman's personality was not well suited to the style of exaggerated chumminess common to Washington luncheons, but neither was he as austere and remote as his public image. Up close, Volcker seemed friendlier and more casual than the imposingly tall man with the big cigar who appeared periodically on the TV news with ominous pronouncements. He asked many questions and something in his rumpled manner allowed others to feel he was listening earnestly to their answers. This was naturally flattering to those who had his ear; an intimate conversation with Paul Volcker was evidence of one's own importance.

The lawyers, lobbyists and politicians, even some news reporters who encountered him regularly, were likely to sprinkle their conversations with casual references to their recent chat with the Federal Reserve chairman. "As I was telling Paul . . ." Seldom did one hear any of these people say: "As Paul was telling me . . ." Volcker listened a lot, but did not reveal much about his own thoughts.

But one special-interest group, above all others, had preferred access to the Federal Reserve chairman and the other governors—the six thousand commercial banks that were members of the Federal Reserve System. Four times a year, a committee of twelve bankers, elected by the member banks in each Federal Reserve district, met privately with Volcker and other governors to tell them what they thought of Fed policy and how it should be changed. It was a unique arrangement in the federal government—a regulated industry holding confidential meetings with the regulators to complain and criticize and recommend new policies. If this were another area of regulatory government, airline safety or water pollution or industrial health rules, private conversations between the regulators and the regulated business would be suspect and subject to prompt disclosure. At the Fed, the secrecy of the bankers' advice was consecrated in the law.

The Federal Advisory Council had inspired suspicions from the start. It was added to the original Federal Reserve legislation of 1913 as a compromise to assuage the disappointed commercial bankers who thought they alone should have control over the new Federal Reserve System. As a sop, the bankers were given a preferred status as official advisers. Since its meetings were kept secret, the Federal Advisory Council figured prominently in many of the conspiracy theories focused on the Fed. This must be the place, people figured, where the bankers tell the Fed what to do.

Federal Reserve officials shrugged off the accusations with an air of resignation. The meetings with the bankers' council, they said, were useful discussions of banking issues but hardly sinister. After all, Fed officials talked to private bankers all the time and also met with advisory groups of consumers and savings and loan executives.

The official minutes of the Federal Advisory Council revealed a more complicated picture—not sinister perhaps, but not entirely innocent either. The bankers regularly used these private sessions for their own special pleading, repeatedly urging the Fed to be more lenient on them and to adopt more stringent regulations for their competitors.

Among the thousands of small, independent bankers around the nation, many resented the advisory council because it looked to them like a private lobby for the largest banks. In 1979, for instance, the twelve advisory council members included Walter B. Wriston, board chairman of Citibank, second-largest bank in the nation and the most successful example of the new style of aggressive growth management. Wriston was himself an outspoken and bold banker, contemptuous of government interference in banking and also an important convert to monetarism. The twelve council members included eight chief executives from banks that ranked in the largest hundred in the nation, among them Continental Illinois of Chicago, Republic Bank of Dallas, Pittsburgh National Bank and the Girard Bank of Philadelphia. Their perspective on banking issues naturally reflected their size. A reasonably alert banker on the advisory council might infer from the board's questions what the governors were contemplating for the future.

The advisory council's minutes did not corroborate the lurid accusations of conspiracy, but the bankers' reports did offer a rough gauge of how close the Federal Reserve's own perspective on the American economy was to the narrow self-interests of the major commercial banks. In the fall of 1979, the alignment proved to be quite close. When the Federal Advisory Council met on September 7, its members congratulated the governors on their recent increases in short-term interest rates. But the bankers urged them to do more of the same.

"The main concern is whether these rates are high enough to stem the bulge which has occurred in the monetary aggregates," the bankers said. "In recent months, the excessive growth in the money supply suggests that credit creation is rising at a faster pace than desired. . . . In this respect, the need to slow the rapid growth in monetary aggregates should take priority over concerns about further upward moves in domestic interest rates." This was the same policy perspective the governors themselves would agree on later in the month.

The bankers also asked the Federal Reserve to consider changing its operating methods, the same proposal that Volcker was then discussing confidentially with the other governors. The minutes did not reflect who brought up this possibility in the private discussions, but the bankers addressed it in their summary report:

Some members of the council expressed concern over the operational techniques of the Federal Reserve in respect to whether it should focus on interest-rate targets or the monetary aggregates in determining an appropriate policy. This is a difficult question to answer, but it is suggested that a re-examination of operational techniques be made.

This recommendation was striking because it occurred three weeks before the governors would reach their own private agreement on shifting to the monetarist approach—and long before Jimmy Carter was told about the Federal Reserve's intentions.[24]

On Saturday, September 29, the day after the governors resolved their differences over reordering the Fed's regulation of money, the Federal Reserve chairman boarded a plane for Europe, bound for the annual conference of the International Monetary Fund, in Belgrade, Yugoslavia. At first, Volcker had wanted to skip the IMF meeting, because he was so busy with the details of the operating shift and so eager to move quickly to implement it. Other Fed officials persuaded him to go. The IMF conference drew the finance ministers and central bankers of the world, the representatives of 138 nations, rich and poor, and it would look odd if the new chairman of America's central bank did not attend.

The airplane was the Secretary of the Treasury's jet, and the other passengers included Volcker's predecessor as Fed chairman, G. William Miller, who was now at Treasury, and Charles L. Schultze, the liberal economist who was chairman of President Carter's Council of Economic Advisers. Crossing the Atlantic, Volcker took the occasion to inform these officials of the Carter Administration, for the first time, how he intended to change things at the Federal Reserve.

Both of them were immediately hostile to the idea. They agreed that the Federal Reserve must do more to tighten the supply of money and credit, but both argued against the change in operating methods that Volcker was preparing. Miller complained that if the Fed began targeting reserves directly, it would produce more volatility in interest rates, sharp fluctuations in credit costs that would disrupt the economy and might actually exacerbate inflation.

Schultze had more fundamental objections: the new operating system would lock in the Fed, put it on a course from which it could not turn back. And that course would lead, sooner or later, to recession.

No one in the conversation needed to point out that next year was 1980 and Jimmy Carter would be running for re-election.

Volcker listened to the arguments and told them: "I'll think it over." When they returned to Washington, he promised, the Administration would have a full opportunity to react to his plan in more detail before the Fed took action. Volcker believed, however, that changing the operating method was a technical issue of monetary policy, a question that ultimately only the Fed itself could decide.

Under the law, the Federal Reserve chairman had no formal obligation to tell the White House anything or to take its objections into account. As a practical matter of politics, however, Volcker needed to know how the Carter White House might react. If the President was going to attack him when interest rates shot up, joined by a chorus of angry representatives and senators, his initiative might become mired in partisan controversy.

> They're entitled to know what we are doing, if they play the game and don't double-cross you by leaking it [Volcker said]. You've got a direct interest in finding out how they feel. You want to know if there is going to be opposition or not. It might just affect the credibility of the action and the sustainability of the action. You are concerned about the counterforces that might be set in motion that could undermine what you are going to do.

Volcker's informal communication with the Carter Administration illustrated the ambiguous terms that linked the Federal Reserve with the rest of the federal government, the elected President and Congress. The relationship was nowhere expressed in concrete rules and obligations. Instead, its boundaries were vague and subjective, determined by political judgment. In every important instance, the Fed chairman had to evaluate the situation before acting, much the way any elected politician measured his potential opposition before committing himself to a major issue or a new campaign. The Federal Reserve could act independently, but how far should it go? At what point would it provoke such a powerful political reaction that, ultimately, it could be stripped of its cherished independence?

As Volcker explained:

> The Federal Reserve as an institution has to operate within some broad parameters of what people can understand and support. You just can't cut 100 degrees across everything that other people understand. They have to know your purpose and understand if some pain is involved, even if they don't agree in every detail. If you are outside that vague consensus, you're in trouble.

The Carter policy makers were unhappy with his plans, but at least they agreed that something more dramatic had to be done to break the inflationary momentum. En route to Belgrade, the plane stopped first in Hamburg, Germany, where Volcker's sense of urgency received an influential endorsement. The American officials sat through a stern lecture from Helmut Schmidt, chancellor of West Germany, on the need for stronger monetary measures.

When the delegation arrived at the IMF conference, Volcker and the others heard the same message, in the strongest terms, in conversations with the central bankers and finance ministers of Western Europe. The dollar was still sliding in value on international exchange markets and the United States must act forcefully to reverse the decline. Arthur Burns, the former Fed chairman, contributed to the gloomy atmosphere in Belgrade with a lecture entitled "The Anguish of Central Banking." It is illusory, Burns lamented, to expect central banks to extinguish inflation when popular political forces pull the other way.

Volcker left early. He had discussed his plans for a major policy shift in elliptical terms with several of his best friends among the other central bankers, but saw no point in staying longer. On Tuesday, with the conference still under way, Volcker departed for Washington, a development that touched off wild rumors and price gyrations in the financial markets of Europe and the United States.

Among Wall Street insiders, the sequence of events in Belgrade created an enduring myth about Volcker's motivation—that the Fed chairman was so jarred by the complaints of European financiers that he rushed home to do something drastic. That version was mistaken in the particulars—Volcker had decided to act even before attending the IMF conference—but it was not wrong in the larger sense. The American government had been pounded for many months by the leading voices of international finance, both American bankers and European, demanding a halt to the dollar's decline in international exchange. The Federal Reserve responded more sensitively to this constituency than did elected politicians.

The weakening dollar was, in one sense, actually beneficial for the real economy in the United States. It gave American exporters an enormous edge in trading competition with foreign producers, an artificial price advantage in international markets from agriculture to heavy manufacturing. That meant greater U.S. output and more jobs. Foreign governments naturally complained and accused the U.S. of debasing its currency deliberately in order to grab a larger share of global markets.

But the most influential institutions of international finance suffered proportionately—particularly the multinational bankers, both American and foreign, who dealt worldwide in dollar-denominated transactions. The depreciating dollar meant their dollar assets were steadily losing value. The largest U.S. banks, for instance, had lent tens of billions to the developing nations of Latin America, and these loans were all pegged in dollars. When the dollar declined in international exchange, the real value of the international loans automatically declined—reducing the debt burden for foreign borrowers just as domestic inflation eased it for home buyers in the United States. Multinational lenders lost for the same reason creditors at home were losing.

For obvious political purposes, Federal Reserve officials tried to downplay the importance of international finance in forcing their hand. A frontal attack against domestic price inflation might be widely welcomed by the American public, even if it required some pain. But raising interest rates sharply in order to save the assets of the money-center banks and other global financiers did not sound like a popular cause. The two, in any case, were expressions of the same monetary policy. Regardless of its motivation, the Fed could not confront domestic inflation without also affecting the international value of the dollar.

When Treasury Secretary Miller and CEA Chairman Schultze returned to Washington on Thursday, they stepped up their efforts to talk Volcker out of going forward with his scheme. They did not have much time—Volcker was planning a special meeting of the Federal Open Market Committee on Saturday, October 6. Schultze began a series of hurried meetings, trying to persuade Volcker to relent and the White House that it should resist. Schultze took the issue to Stuart Eizenstat, the President's chief adviser for domestic policy, and asked him to help convince the President to intervene.

Over the next two days, in meetings and phone calls, Schultze again urged Volcker to reconsider. Raise interest rates, if you must, he pleaded, but don't change the operating system. "Volcker was going to move very quickly, because if it ever leaked, it would be very bad," Schultze said. "Granting that something had to be done, my objection was that once you do this, you can't back out. Once you tell the world this is the money target and we are going to follow it no matter what happens to interest rates, you have to stick with it and you have no flexibility."

This was more than a technical argument between economists: Schultze foresaw bleak consequences for the election season ahead. "What I could see very clearly, without knowing the exact timing," he said, "was that given the inflationary pressures we were under, if the

Fed adopted a rigid monetary policy and promised its clients to stick to it, very likely we would be driven into a recession and we wouldn't be able to back out of it."

Schultze also recognized the political advantages that attracted the Fed governors to the scheme.

In the mind of the Fed, this whole move was, in the broadest sense, a political move, not an economic move. In theory, the Fed could have kept on raising the bejesus out of the interest rates, but that's what it couldn't do politically. The beautiful thing about this new policy was that as interest rates kept going up, the Fed could say, "Hey, ain't nobody here but us chickens. We're not raising interest rates, we're only targeting the money supply." This way they could raise the rates and nobody could blame them.

The fundamental relationship between the supply of money and the price of money, better known as interest rates, was obvious to economists—if supply shrinks, interest rates go up. It was not so obvious to many noneconomists, including the President of the United States. In fact, Volcker kidded the Administration economists on this point. Charles Schultze recalled: "Paul said to us, 'It was really a meeting with Jimmy Carter that gave me the idea. Carter said to me, "Why can't you control the quantity of credit without raising interest rates?" ' Volcker told us that's what gave him the idea to target money supply instead of interest rates." Volcker's remark was facetious, of course, an inside joke among professionals about a layman's ignorance of the fundamentals.

While Volcker did not yield to Schultze's objections, he was concerned enough about the potential for trouble that he sounded out another Administration official, one who would be more sympathetic to the Fed's situation. Volcker consulted Anthony Solomon, the Treasury Under Secretary for Monetary Affairs, who six months later would assume Volcker's old position, president of the New York Federal Reserve Bank. Solomon had worked closely with Volcker on international economic issues during the 1960s when he was at the State Department and Volcker was at Treasury; they thought alike on these questions. Now Solomon shared the Fed chairman's sense of urgency and wanted to help him avoid a public conflict with the White House. Solomon suggested that Volcker and the Administration officials take their argument directly to the President and let him hear both sides.

When Volcker told Schultze and Miller that he was willing to see the President to explain the Federal Reserve's intentions, they told him not to bother. Instead, the two of them, accompanied by Eizenstat, went to Jimmy Carter themselves—and urged the President to express his personal opposition to the Federal Reserve chairman. "You didn't play fair with Volcker," Solomon complained to them later. "Volcker should have been at that meeting to explain his position."

Jimmy Carter, like all his modern predecessors, did not have a strong grasp of the issues of monetary policy. Nothing in the experience of American political leaders prepared them to deal with the subject; the tradition of Fed independence encouraged the notion that money regulation was something left to the experts, a forbidden area where politicians were not supposed to intrude. Richard Nixon, who was as well trained for the Chief Executive's job as any modern President, told an interviewer years later that one of his greatest regrets was that he never mastered an understanding of what went on at the Federal Reserve.[25] Most of the politicians who served in the White House, as well as in Congress, could make a similar confession. As Tony Solomon observed:

No President really understands these things, but the disturbing thing about Carter was that he tried to use the economic jargon as though he did. He tried to make it seem that he understood the technical arguments when he clearly didn't. A President like Lyndon Johnson never pretended to understand all these things—he was only interested in the bottom line. He would ask: What were the political effects? What would happen to interest rates? What did he have to do in order to deal with it? Carter would enter into technical discussions which he only partially understood.

In the event, Jimmy Carter declined to do anything. Resistance was not possible, Carter told his advisers, given his own weakened political status. The White House had no choice but to acquiesce. The President could not challenge the new economic policy determined independently by the chairman of the Federal Reserve Board. Besides, as Eizenstat said, "The President is basically a very honest guy who believes in the integrity of the political system. He had put that guy in there and, by God, he was going to stand by him."

Schultze's explanation was that

the Fed held all the cards. Unemployment was down and inflation was rising. The general structure of political power was such that all of the business and financial community was solidly behind the Fed. The dollar was shaky. The White House had to be very careful about taking on the Fed. Unless it literally wanted to take on a populist campaign that would drive the dollar down even further, we had to be very careful.

Two months earlier, Carter had chosen Paul Volcker almost by accident. Now the President was implicitly surrendering control to him. The Federal Reserve would steer the national government's economic policy now. Over the coming years, the Fed's true role in the American system would become more and more visible to ordinary citizens, as Volcker asserted its leverage over economic life. He would be personally reviled and praised, recognized in public-opinion polls as the second most powerful person in the land. In hindsight, it would be understood that the autumn of 1979 was a historic juncture in the political course of the nation. What was not understood was that this crucial transaction occurred with an enfeebled President's acquiescence, but not with his approval.

The episode also required deep political judgments by officials of the Federal Reserve. Beyond the tactical arguments, Volcker was implicitly making his own political assessment of the nation: an assumption that the nation was ready for what he intended to do, a sustained assault on inflation, including the economic pain that would come with it. Certainly that is what the bankers and financial markets wanted.

If the general public would support the initiative, perhaps even wanted it to happen, then the potential impact on Jimmy Carter's political future might be irrelevant. In the fall of 1979, Jimmy Carter already looked gravely wounded. His popular standing remained low; his own party was deeply divided about his prospects for a second term. It was plausible to assume that the President's fate had perhaps already been settled by events, by his own errors and weakness and bad luck. In any case, if the Federal Reserve's actions added an election-year recession to the President's troubles, such actions would not necessarily provoke political attacks aimed at the Fed. A recession might simply be one more reason not to re-elect Jimmy Carter.

The boardroom at the top of the marble stairs was a cavernous chamber; subtly bathed in gold. The walls were covered in a pale-gold damask, and a monumental chandelier hung far above the floor on strands of golden chains, decorated with a motif of golden eagles guarding huge gold coins. The seven governors and twelve Reserve Bank presidents, joined by a few staff professionals, sat around the massive table before the fireplace, dwarfed by the awesome proportions of their private place.

"We were summoned to Washington and none of us knew a damned thing," said Larry Roos, president of the St. Louis Fed. "I nearly fell out of my chair when I observed that all of my colleagues, many of whom had been disdainful, were now all supporting a monetarist approach."

The extraordinary Saturday meeting of the Federal Open Market Committee lasted all day, as Volcker and others went over and over the details of the watershed decision. The chairman himself played the reluctant advocate, raising doubts and questions and allowing other members to dispel them. "Paul was masterful," Fred Schultz said. "I knew exactly what he was doing. The others ended up arguing with him, talking him into doing it. By the end of the day, he had them fully committed."

At the White House, Charles Schultze had not quite given up. He phoned Volcker again and made one last plea not to do it. Raise interest rates, if you must, but don't get locked into a rigid system that guarantees recession. The President's adviser, however, did not attempt to bluster. The White House, he confided to Volcker, did not intend to attack the Fed chairman publicly if he proceeded.

The import of their decision was clear to the FOMC members. They were voting, in effect, to put the national economy into a contraction. That was the expected outcome, and Volcker himself confided his own pessimism to colleagues.

"Others would say to me, 'Well, you know this will likely cause a recession,' " Governor Coldwell said. "I told them, 'Yes, I know that. But that's the penalty you have to pay for going out too far on the inflation side.' There wasn't any question that the board knew that recession would follow."

When the press was summoned in late afternoon, that is not what the Federal Reserve told the American public. The announcement was couched in technical language that financial traders might understand, but the words had no meaning for average citizens or even most politicians. There was nothing said about what the Fed intended for the U.S. economy. In fact, when a reporter asked Volcker if the likely result would be slower growth and higher unemployment, Volcker evaded the point and concealed his real expectations.

"Well, you get varying opinions about that," the Federal Reserve chairman replied. "I don't think it will have important effects in that connection. I would be optimistic about the results of these actions. . . . I think the best indications that I have now, in an uncertain world, is that this can be accomplished reasonably smoothly."

4

BEHAVIOR MODIFICATION

Financial markets are like "a collection of overlapping crowds," Albert M. Wojnilower once observed. As chief economist at First Boston, one of the nation's leading investment banks, Wojnilower was one of those rare economists who could see beyond the hard numbers of finance to the human ambiguities that influenced them. Financial traders, he pointed out, gathered literally in "crowds" on the trading-room floors of the stock market and in the commodity exchanges. They milled and gossiped, watched what others watched, calculated where the "crowd" was headed. In credit markets, the "crowds" were assembled electronically—all watching their video screens, reading the same bid/ask quotations, gossiping by telephone.

Traders [wrote Wojnilower] must and do therefore respond literally instantly to all news to which they think other traders might respond. Whether the news is considered economically significant or even true is immaterial. Moreover, it is well known that crowds generate, transmit, and respond to messages (rumors included) very differently from individuals.[1]

When the various "crowds" of Wall Street gathered on Monday morning, October 8, they were jostled by their own ignorance, leaderless and a bit frightened. The Federal Reserve System, including the New York Federal Reserve Bank, was closed for the government holiday, Columbus Day, but the financial markets attempted to digest the meaning of the Federal Reserve Board's dramatic Saturday announcement. Nothing tangible had changed, yet everything was different. The crowds' normal expectations were asunder. The Fed, they knew, had suddenly delivered them into a new world, but none of them pretended to understand it.

The Dow Jones index of industrial stocks, which had momentarily reached the 900 level on Friday, lost nearly 14 points. On Tuesday, the Dow index would fall another 27 points. Bond prices also fell sharply, as much as 2⅜ points on long-term government bonds, the equivalent of $23 per $1,000. Gold prices dropped $17 an ounce, then reversed on Tuesday and rose $49 an ounce in two days. In the money market, the Federal Funds rate, trading around 11.5 percent on Friday, jumped to nearly 14 percent on Monday and other short-term interest rates followed, beginning a zigzag pattern of daily swings unlike anything the traders had ever seen before.

In the next few weeks, the Fed Funds rate, which money traders watched as their key barometer, which the Federal Reserve could control most reliably if it wished, moved like a Yo-Yo—perversely unpredictable. It went as high as 18 percent one day, then back to 14 percent the next, then up again to 16 percent, then plunging briefly as low as 11 percent, then back up again. When the Fed Funds rate jumped above the ceiling that the Federal Open Market Committee had set for it, the committee held a special meeting by telephone conference and agreed to tolerate such divergences temporarily. In the gallows humor of Wall Street, the Federal Reserve's policy shift swiftly became known as Paul Volcker's "Saturday Night Special."[2]

One of America's premier manufacturers, IBM, had the bad fortune to enter the credit markets, seeking new capital, just as the storm broke. The week before, IBM had announced it was floating $1 billion in corporate notes and bonds, the largest debt offering ever made by an American corporation. IBM was a blue-chip company, practically a risk-free investment, and the notes sold briskly at first. By midweek, however, the offering fell apart. Brokers could find no more buyers for the IBM paper, which promised a return of nearly 9.5 percent, because the interest rate on long-term government bonds had already climbed higher, piercing double digits for the first time. Why lend capital to IBM when the U.S. Treasury, the most risk-free debtor of all, was paying an even better return? About half of the IBM issue went unsold, and the syndicate of major brokerages that had underwritten the package had to swallow losses of $45 to $50 million.

The new uncertainty cost many others. One trader at a major investment firm told The Wall Street Journal: "My strategy is to look at the numbers, then run out in the hall so I won't be here to make any mistakes."

. . .

On Tuesday morning, as usual, Peter D. Sternlight walked to work. It took about an hour from his home near Brooklyn's Prospect Park, across the Brooklyn Bridge and through the twisted streets of lower Manhattan to his office at the New York Federal Reserve Bank in the heart of Wall Street. Sternlight was manager of the Open Market Desk, the chief technician of monetary policy. He was a slight man with dark hair and owlish glasses who would be lost in the sidewalk sea of clerks and brokers, though his daily decisions to buy or sell securities made him the most active and important trader on Wall Street, perhaps in the world.

The New York Fed, at Liberty and Nassau, was fondly described in official pamphlets as inspired by the elegant lines of a Florentine palazzo in the age of the Medici, an architectural point that was recognizable only if one looked up at the façade of graceful arches and balustrades on the top floors. At street level, the building looked merely forbidding, even grim. The narrow windows were covered by heavy iron bars, and the gray stones were stained by three generations of New York soot. It looked like a bank in the old-fashioned tradition of austerity, but it could have been mistaken for a prison.

Among other things, the New York Fed was the Fort Knox of international finance. In the basement, five stories below street level and behind a ninety-ton revolving door, the gold vault held about 40 percent of all the gold in the world, thirteen thousand tons valued at $140 billion. Some of it was American-owned, but most of it was owned by the central banks of other nations, carefully stored in separate cages. In international-exchange transactions, the bars of gold were simply moved from one cage to another. Even governments that were quite hostile to the United States found it prudent to keep their gold reserves in America, safeguarded from revolution or other upheavals that might occur at home.

Most of the New York Fed, like the eleven other Reserve Banks, was actually a "factory," as Fed officials themselves referred to it, a processing plant that shipped fresh currency to banks and destroyed the old, a clearinghouse that managed the traffic among banks in canceled checks and kept the accounts that had to balance all the millions of payments flowing back and forth each day. The "factory" functions occupied most of the Fed employees, essential but routine.

On the eighth floor, Peter Sternlight's trading room, staffed with fifteen or so young people, housed the real action—the Open Market Desk. His traders watched video screens and worked telephone consoles connected to the thirty-six dealers who were authorized to trade government securities with the Fed, the major bond brokerages and a dozen of the largest banks. The Fed traders faced eleven large panels hung around three walls which listed every single issue of outstanding U.S. bills, notes and bonds. Thirty years earlier, the trading-room walls held only three panels, a change that nicely conveyed how enormously the government's debt had grown in the intervening decades.

On a typical morning, Sternlight would decide, after consulting with Washington, whether to buy or sell a block of securities or do nothing. The thirty-six private dealers would be asked to make bids, without being told what the action was to be. At about eleven-thirty, the Fed traders would call them back and announce the transaction, who bought or sold how much. In other trading rooms at brokerages and banks all over the city, clerks would cry out the news—"The Fed's in!"—and scores of Fed watchers would immediately set to calculating what the effects would be on the money-market interest rates.

On many days, Sternlight would be adjusting the level of bank reserves for incidental reasons, offsetting random shifts in the money supply for purely technical reasons. A seasonal surge of money, for instance, always accompanied the Christmas holidays, when people drew down their savings accounts to have extra cash, or around April 15, when federal income taxes were paid and refund checks were mailed out. Occasionally, money became too plentiful because of a sudden surge in the "float" between banks. If a bad storm closed airports in the Midwest, daily shipments of canceled checks by the Federal Reserve would be stalled. For a time, until the checks were cleared, banks on both ends would be counting the same money on their books, artificially swelling the total supply of money by billions of dollars.

Sternlight compensated for all these factors and many others, including huge transactions in behalf of foreign governments, which the New York Fed also handled. It took an experienced Fed watcher to judge whether the Fed was "in the market" for technical reasons or for some larger purpose, such as moving the interest rates up or down. Federal Reserve officials believed these "defensive" adjustments were necessary for market stability and for their own control; otherwise, traders would be reacting to random ebbs and surges that had nothing to do with the path of credit expansion.

Critics like Milton Friedman and other monetarists claimed that the New York Fed's constant tinkering was not only unnecessary but amounted to "churning" the public's account, creating heavy transactions as an implicit fringe benefit for the private dealers. In a typical year, Sternlight would execute as much as $700 billion in short-term transactions—yet at year's end the net change in the Fed's holdings might amount to less than $10 billion. Whether the Fed was buying or selling, the thirty-six dealers could count on getting a price marginally better than what was available in the private market. The edge was slight, not greater than 4 or 5 basis points. That would be equivalent to only $80 or $100 on a $1 million transaction in three-month T-bills, hardly a bonanza, but even a slender margin added up when it was multiplied through $700 billion in transactions.[3]

When Peter Sternlight surveyed the market turmoil and rising rates, he first thought he would do a modest repurchase agreement, $1 or $2 billion, to give some reassurance to the frightened traders. Repo's, as they were called, were a standard Fed technique, selling or buying securities with an agreement to reverse the transaction three or four days later—in other words, a temporary withdrawal or injection of reserves that could be erased or continued depending on conditions later. The desk didn't want to put in too much assurance, he figured, because the Fed wanted to show the markets it was serious. After consulting with Stephen Axilrod, the staff director in Washington, he decided to do nothing—let the market find its own way.

In the trading room, William C. Melton, a Fed economist working as one of the open-market traders, heard quick evidence of the money market's confusion. Melton has recalled:

> I got a phone call from a friend at a securities dealer firm who opened the conversation by saying, "Welcome to the free-fall market! There are no bids on the screens!" What he meant was that none of the government securities dealers was sufficiently certain of what was happening to be able to say what a proper interest rate was for a Treasury bill or a government bond and, in those circumstances, they did not want to own any.

That afternoon, Sternlight held a special briefing for the dealers, to explain the new system. The Fed would not be as rigid and mechanical in letting interest rates float freely as its monetarist critics would like, Sternlight explained. It would still assert control over the rates to compensate for short-term variables. The new system, he emphasized, was "still very much experimental." These words did not reassure the anxious traders. Melton heard one of them mutter: "Here's one lab rat who has just dropped a million bucks."[4]

Sternlight, one of those anonymous technocrats who exercised enormous power, experienced a brief moment of celebrity that day. One of the New York television stations interviewed him and he appeared on the evening news with a twenty-second explanation of what was happening in the financial markets. "It has haunted me ever since," he said. "My barber and my postman in Brooklyn saw me on TV and now, every time I see them, they ask me when interest rates are coming down."

The Federal Reserve Board chairman was reassuring a different group that day, the commercial bankers gathered in New Orleans for the annual convention of their major trade group, the American Bankers Association. "Those measures were not designed to make your life as bankers easier," Volcker conceded. But, he promised, money and credit would be kept under firm control as long as the inflationary pressures were building. In the atmosphere of speculation and unsettled markets, Volcker delivered a special admonition for the bankers: "The Board of Governors has particularly stressed its own concern that, in a time of limited resources, banks should take care to avoid financing essentially speculative activity in commodity, gold and foreign-exchange markets."

The banks, he added, were better equipped than federal regulators to decide which loans would be genuinely productive and which would simply finance speculative buying, but the chairman underscored his warning. "This is hardly the time to search out exotic new lending areas or to finance speculative or purely financial activities that have little to do with the performance of the American economy," Volcker said.

Volcker was not dismayed by the volatile indecision of the financial markets. "I think the point may be," he told a TV interviewer, "that we captured their attention and I think that's constructive." The turmoil, he hoped, would eventually produce a new optimism in Wall Street. "A lot of people were skeptical about whether we could deal with inflation," the chairman said. "I hope they're less skeptical now than they were before."[5]

In St. Louis, Larry Roos called a press conference at the St. Louis Fed to celebrate the monetarist victory. "We are elated," Roos said. "The St. Louis view has prevailed." Some of the leading monetarist economists were not so sure. The Federal Reserve had announced strong new policy initiatives in past years that turned out, in practice, to be more of the same. They applauded Volcker's decision but remained skeptical about whether the Fed would truly stick to its money-growth targets. "I didn't send a congratulatory telegram," said Allan Meltzer, a monetarist who was cochairman of the Shadow Open Market Committee. "I'm going to hold my breath and hope they don't mess it up."

The turmoil and losses in financial markets continued. The stock market rose to record volumes of daily trading and, within a month, the Dow Jones index lost 100 points. The bond-market prices swung as much in a single day as they had in a month, and by November, the paper value of corporate and government bonds had fallen by as much as $200 million. The dollar's value increased moderately, and gold, after its initial decline, surged a bit. Short-term interest rates continued to bounce around a lot, but they established a new level much higher than before. Money-market funds, where depositors could earn the rising market rates rather than the fixed-interest rates of savings deposits, began a surge of growth—$14.2 billion in October alone—that would continue for more than a year as more and more citizens discovered them. The prime rate charged by commercial banks for standard business loans rose from 13.5 to 15.5 percent.[6]

Money was tighter. Notwithstanding the markets' confusion and gyrations, the change was clear in the Federal Reserve's monitoring of the monetary aggregates, M-1 and the others. Money growth was slowing down steadily, a welcome change from the runaway expansion that had alarmed the Fed in August and September.

If the money supply was tightening, then credit was tightening too —a shrinking supply of new loans for business and consumers. Inevitably, tighter credit meant that, across America, people who were not financial investors or market traders, who did not read *The Wall Street Journal* or follow the Federal Funds rate, would also be compelled to alter their lives. Millions of citizens would immediately feel the impact in the most intimate terms, including many people who did not know there was a Federal Reserve Board in Washington or understand its purposes.

William Kline, a real-estate agent and home builder in Portsmouth, Virginia, read the newspapers and acted promptly. Kline sold off his last house, laid off two secretaries, dismissed his construction superintendent and shut off the office phone. For twenty years, his small construction company had built about twenty-five homes a year while he sold real estate on the side. Now, Kline decided, he would be only a realtor.

"I read that interest rates were going to be volatile," he said, "and I chose right away to say: no more building. The minute interest rates rise, most people will not buy a home."

As an independent contractor, Kline could be swiftly caught in the middle. When a new house was finished but still unsold, the contractor had to pay regular interest installments on the bank loan that financed the construction—loans that were now costing 16 percent or more. "The big problem is, if you don't sell the house right away, your interest payments are about $100 a week," Kline said. "And that's what we aren't willing to do."

His decision was wise. Other small builders he knew tried to stay active and went broke. "The little guy, who should have been helped by the American enterprise system, got knocked off his feet," Kline complained.

James Woulfe sold Fords and Chrysler-Plymouths at dealerships in Dublin, California, when interest rates took off. He knew he had two big problems: the higher credit costs would drive away customers and would also make it more expensive for him to finance his inventory of automobiles. Woulfe immediately began cutting back on his inventory, ordering fewer of the new models from Detroit than he had intended.

Still, his sales would eventually shrink by 50 percent and he had to dismiss twenty of his sixty employees. His sales tactics shifted from family buyers to business clients who could afford the higher interest rates or even pay cash. "That's what we had to do," Woulfe explained, "just to get our business to 50 percent."

Richard LeCates, president of United Building and Development in Salisbury, Maryland, knew immediately that interest rates would shoot up, but he did not grasp how far. "I'm in the money business," LeCates said. "Any builder who doesn't think he's a banker is wrong." When short-term rates topped 15 percent at the end of October, LeCates thought the worst was over. "I figured we could live with it," he said. "We'd raise prices a little, take a little less profit. I figured wrong."

In the last eighteen years, LeCates's construction company had built and sold thirty-five hundred homes. In the next two years, it would sell only one—a house that remained on the market, unsold, for a year and a half.

In Springfield, Pennsylvania, Marvin Berger laid off half of his twenty-five employees at Rayco Auto Services, an auto-parts store and repair garage. Inflation was eating away at his profits, but he couldn't keep raising prices without driving away customers. Berger described the anxiety felt by thousands of small-business managers: "We open up our stores every morning, turn on our adding machines, unlock our cash drawers, and hope like hell that some invisible hand will bring enough heads through the door so that we, with our products and sales ability, can ring up a sale."

Jimmy Jackson, a home builder in Chesapeake, Virginia, felt the same anxiety. Four of his fellow contractors in the Tidewater area of Virginia were now headed for bankruptcy. "I didn't see the crunch coming," he said. "We had come through a couple of good years. When you have good years, you tend to get more overhead—a receptionist, a vehicle, things you need to expand. You have to do that to expand, but you don't have any control over the economy."

Even with cutbacks, the soaring interest rates threatened his survival. "I was scared I wasn't going to make the payments on things I already had out," Jackson said. "You start a business, work at it, and then something you have no control over comes along and does you in."

In the Middle West, many farmers also did not get the message. Later, many of them would pay dearly for their ignorance. Farmers could hardly be faulted for not instantly grasping the significance of the Federal Reserve's action. Many of the farm economists who advised them did not understand it either.

"I don't think anyone in the agricultural sector was aware of the impact of that move," said Vivan Jennings, associate dean of the Iowa Cooperative Extension Service, which counseled farmers on management decisions. "It was not really something that seemed important at the time. Even our best economists, they were talking about business as usual."

Small-town bankers who served the agricultural sector, likewise, did not perceive any crucial changes in Volcker's October 6 announcement. "When we heard that, we said, 'He can't do that,' " Neal Conover, president of the Citizens Savings Bank of Afton, Iowa, scoffed. "We ought to pay attention to what those people do from now on. We learned our lesson."

Many farmers would learn the hard way, borrowing at the higher interest rates in order to buy land and expand production just as the national economy was being pushed in the opposite direction. "You can't manage your way around this with ultimate effectiveness," Conover conceded. "It's luck. Dumb luck. People decided on October fifth to buy the hundred and fifty acres that opened up next to them. Now, all of a sudden, through bright, sound business judgment, he may be gone."

As interest rates rose in financial markets, two effects rippled through the real economy. First, many potential customers for homes or cars or other goods were discouraged from buying at the higher prices. Second, customers who still wanted to buy despite the higher interest rates found it harder to obtain loans. The tighter credit conditions induced by the Fed compelled the lending institutions, from commercial banks to credit unions, to impose their own versions of rationing—choosing carefully among the many potential borrowers who were competing for the limited supply of loan money, accepting some and turning away others.

Chemical Bank in New York raised its minimum-income requirement for consumer loans from $8,000 to $10,000. The Portland Teachers Credit Union in Portland, Oregon, imposed restrictions on "luxury items"—no more loans for recreational vehicles, mobile homes, furniture, boats, vacations, stock purchases. In Illinois, some savings and loan associations stopped taking applications for new mortgage loans entirely. Others required larger down payments or lowered the maximum loans available.

On Long Island, the Suffolk County Federal Savings & Loan Association decided to lend only to people who already had accounts and to their immediate relatives or to families that were newcomers to Long Island—if they made a savings deposit. Even with those limitations, customers streamed in. "It was quite difficult," said a vice president at Suffolk County Federal. "People heard we were giving loans at all and everyone came knocking on the door."

The smaller credit organizations were forced to shut down their lending because they themselves were losing access to money. As market interest rates escalated, depositors of quite modest means withdrew their savings from their local thrifts or banks or company credit unions and shopped around for some place where the money could earn a higher return. Billions of dollars flowed into the money-market funds operated by the larger brokerages in New York.

The State Employees Credit Union of Virginia lost about $750,000 in withdrawals by its members in a few months. "They don't tell us exactly where they're putting the money," said Dorothy J. Hall, the general manager and treasurer, "but we know many of them are investing it for higher yields elsewhere." In the nation's capital, the Department of Labor Federal Credit Union was in "near panic," according to its manager, Lina Gray. Long lines of Labor Department employees formed up each day to withdraw their savings, but no one made deposits. "It's like having a sickness," Gray said. "It's so awful you can't remember what caused it." Deposits fell from $13 million to $7 million; the credit union stopped making loans for a year.

The nation's savings and loans, which traditionally financed home buying, were in a particularly ominous box. Their portfolios were largely locked into long-term home mortgages—loans they had made at fixed interest rates of perhaps no more than 8 or 9 percent. As inflation and interest rates rose, the S & L's found that their spread disappeared. Meanwhile, federal regulation limited how much interest they could pay on deposits and so S & L's lost depositors too.

The stress would devastate the savings and loan industry, the bedrock lender of America's postwar housing boom. For years to come, a large portion of the forty-five hundred S & L's would remain "under water"—losing money each year as they struggled to stay in business. By 1983, a thousand of them would be gone.

As scarce money became more valuable, it found new homes where it would earn higher returns. Merrill Lynch's Ready Assets Trust,

started in 1975, offered market rates for anyone with $5,000 to buy a
share. The pool of money was then re-lent in the money market to
major borrowers—banks selling CDs, corporations selling commercial
paper, the federal government selling T-bills. As the era of permanent
high interest rates took hold, more and more savers flocked to the
pond. Ready Assets grew in one year from 1.6 million shares to 8.1
million—$8 billion to $40 billion. Other firms rushed to offer their own
money-market funds, and their number would roughly double in the
next three years. In 1979, the money funds held $45 billion. By 1982,
they held $207 billion. The net effect was to shift a huge volume of
credit away from the smaller customers—consumers and small businesses—and toward larger ones who could pay the price.

By mid-November, the cumulative effects of all these shifts in the
nation's lending and borrowing were confirmed in the "red book," the
report on regional economic conditions that the twelve Federal Reserve Banks prepared for the FOMC meeting in Washington. The
tightening was having the expected impact, according to the Reserve
Bank presidents. Their summary report noted:

> Mortgage and automobile lending are generally weak, but business lend-
> ing continues to expand moderately, at least in some regions. . . . Real
> personal consumption expenditures are being depressed by the dearth of
> automobile sales, but continue to show resilience in other sectors.
> . . . Most districts report marked slowing in residential construction and
> in sales of existing houses. . . . Manufacturing activity is particularly
> spotty. The automobile sector is exhibiting pervasive weakness, but there
> exist definite areas of strength. . . .

As the "red book" noted, however, the impact of tighter credit did
not fall evenly on all citizens and enterprises. Some were forced to go
without, while others did not feel any shortage at all.

> Despite the prevailing level of interest rates, more stringent non-price
> lending terms and tighter credit standards, business loan demand contin-
> ues to expand in most areas [the presidents observed]. Funds apparently
> remain available to businesses who are taking advantage of that availabil-
> ity. . . . Mortgage lending, on the other hand, seems to be severely and
> broadly depressed. . . . Some districts report non-price rationing of funds,
> while others find some lenders have withdrawn completely from mortgage
> lending activity.

None of these developments would have surprised any of the Federal Reserve governors. This was, after all, how they expected monetary policy to exert its will over the real economy.[7]

. . .

If the exercise of power were measured in terms of how swiftly and intimately it altered the behavior of others, then the Federal Reserve was arguably the most powerful instrument of government, certainly in the realm of economic behavior. Congress could raise taxes or authorize new spending, but that process took many months of legislative debate and its actual effects would usually not be felt by citizens until many months later. The President established the broad directions for tax-and-spending policies and, in extreme circumstances, might activate emergency controls over the economy. Neither Congress nor the White House, however, could affect private lives with the immediacy and universal reach of the Federal Reserve's power, its ability to send instant signals rippling through every family's financial decisions, to change the incentives in virtually every business transaction. The paradox for democracy was obvious: the Washington institution that was most intimately influential in the lives of ordinary citizens was the one they least understood, the one most securely shielded from popular control.

To understand how the Fed's power worked, it was necessary again to step behind the abstractions of economics and describe the money system in more supple language. An economist, asked to explain monetary policy, would describe the mechanics of controlling the money supply, regulating bank reserves and adjusting interest rates, none of which conveyed very much to citizens who did not understand banking or macroeconomics. But an astute psychologist might look at how the monetary system worked and recognize its essential nature. A psychologist would describe what was going on in these terms: the Federal Reserve was operating a vast national program in behavior modification.

The model defined by behavioral psychology had a simple premise: a series of predictable rewards and punishments could be used as incentives to induce a subject to alter its behavior. A laboratory rat that went the wrong way in a maze would receive an electric shock. If the rat discovered the correct path, the route the psychologist wanted it to take, it would be rewarded with a food pellet. In time, the rat learned how to get to the food without getting shocked. The same principle was applied to human behavior. A truant child received promised rewards, candy or extra allowance, if he went to school. Rewards were replaced with penalties when he cut classes. Thus, behavior modification commanded not by rigid edict but by external pressures. A child (or a rat) was free to ignore the signals and continue the miscreant behavior—and pay a price for the wrong choice.

The Federal Reserve's monetary policy was meant to influence the real economy in approximately the same manner—rewarding or pun-

ishing borrowers in order to change their behavior. When the Fed
pushed up interest rates, this was a negative incentive, intended to
dissuade both consumers and businesses from taking on new loans. If
they did not borrow, then they would not buy things. Cumulatively
their decisions not to borrow money and spend it would slow down the
entire economy. The shrinking pool of willing buyers changed the
incentives for producers too, inducing them to cut prices or to manufacture fewer of their products or both. They closed shop and laid off
workers, just as frightened home builders like William Kline did after
October 6. Smaller payrolls meant fewer citizens with money to spend,
and the demand for goods and services contracted further.

As unemployment rose and personal incomes declined, along with
business profits, the impact on inflation would be salutory: producers
could not keep raising prices when their goods were already in excess
supply; workers could not easily demand new wage increases when
factories were closing and the pool of surplus labor was growing.
Everyone's bargaining position was reversed or at least weakened. If
the process continued, feeding on itself as incomes declined, the national economy would soon be in an actual recession. The gross total
of all output would shrink. And the Federal Reserve would eventually
achieve its original objective: the upward pressures on prices would
dissipate, inflation would slow down.

All of this was obvious to economists, who described the process as
"dampening demand" or influencing the economy "through the demand channel." The Federal Reserve found it awkward to speak in
these terms since the Fed's proclaimed function was to control the
economy's supply of money, not to manipulate the economic desires
of all the nation's families and businesses. Many citizens would likely
be confused, perhaps even upset, to learn that the Fed controlled the
money supply essentially by dampening or stimulating the economy's
aggregate demand for goods and services. Controlling the money supply seemed obscure and technical; manipulating prices was central to
everyone's daily life.

Still, the Federal Reserve's official bulletins made no attempt to
conceal the reality. "When the economy begins to expand too rapidly," the Fed's annual report explained, "the associated increase in
the quantity of money demanded for transactions comes into conflict
with the monetary target, and this results in a rise in market rates of
interest; the rise in interest rates, in turn, damps the aggregate demand for goods and services." In translation, the sentence might read:
When all the potential buyers in the economy want more money and
credit than the Fed thinks is healthy, the Fed refuses to supply the
demand and that drives up interest rates. The higher interest rates, in

turn, depress the public's appetite for spending, and the demand for new loans subsides. The growth of money slows down—returning to the moderate level that the Federal Reserve wanted.[8]

That was the operating theory, at least. On its face, the Fed's approach seemed universal and discreet. It did not try to control anyone's private decisions directly, but it could modify the public's economic behavior through interest-rate incentives. As government policy, the approach appeared to be general and disinterested, imposing the same discipline on all economic players equally, favoring none. That was the broad theory, but it didn't work that way in the real world.

The Fed's disciplinary system, in practice, punished the weakest, smallest players first and most severely, while the largest and more powerful enterprises could evade the ill consequences. Many families, businesses and financial institutions were compelled to alter their behavior swiftly—but others were privileged to continue business as usual. The rats in this laboratory maze, to use a tasteless metaphor, were not all equal.

The real cost of higher interest rates fell unevenly on citizens, banks and businesses, depending inversely on their level of incomes and profits. The wealthiest and most successful suffered least; struggling businesses and families of limited income paid the highest price. That was the most elementary point of political inequity, and it stemmed not simply from Federal Reserve policy but from how high interest rates interacted with the U.S. tax code. Every taxpayer, large or small, was entitled to deduct interest payments from his taxable income, but these deductions naturally became more valuable if one was in a higher-income bracket and was taxed at a higher rate. A corporation saved, for instance, 46 percent of its interest costs on its tax bill. A wealthy individual, paying the maximum tax rate, would recover 50 percent of his interest payments in tax savings or as much as 70 percent if all of his income was from stocks and bonds and other investments. This effectively cut the real cost of higher interest rates in half for them—while others paid the full freight. This differential was always present, but it became magnified as interest rates rose.

The trouble is, it's very uneven in its impact on people [Governor Henry Wallich conceded]. Even at these rates, it's very uneven when you think of real interest rates after taxes. If you are in the 50 percent tax bracket, you deduct half of the 13 or 16 percent charged for a loan and that means the real interest rate is still less than the inflation rate. A company that is making no money pays the full 13 percent. A profitable company that must pay taxes pays less. It's the same with people who have no other income or are in a lower tax bracket. People with high incomes are affected much less than others.

A second element of discrimination penalized the same players— smaller businesses and average consumers. The use of higher interest rates to slow the economy naturally worked most swiftly on the sectors most dependent on credit to continue doing business—housing, automobiles and other durable goods like appliances or washing machines that Americans typically bought on credit. Most consumers, in fact, did not bother to calculate the interest-rate effects when they were thinking of buying a home or a car. They simply looked at the monthly payments they would have to make on the new mortgage or auto loan and compared that obligation with their incomes. When the monthly payments went up, some buyers would be priced out of the market. Small businesses like retailers, auto dealers and home builders were squeezed on both ends: their customers had to borrow to buy and they themselves had to borrow to maintain an inventory of appliances, cars, houses.

As Wallich explained:

Housing is very sensitive to high interest rates, because housing is a very postponable expenditure. I may be able to pay 13 percent on a mortgage, but I don't have to buy that house now. The same effect is felt to some extent on automobiles. Those who can postpone do, and those who are financially very strong say, "I'll go ahead and buy anyway."

The effective consequence was a discreet system of rationing— rationing by price. When the Fed tightened, the limited supply of new credit was allocated by market forces not on the basis of who might need it most but according to the financial girth of the prospective borrowers. In combination with the tax code, high interest rates gave the advantage to the largest customers.

The idea that the government rationed any commodity was naturally repugnant to the free-market ethos of American politics. A system that rationed money in a way that favored the largest enterprises and wealthiest individuals would seem to be especially offensive. Except very few understood that this was how monetary policy worked and the government—both elected politicians and the Federal Reserve— had little incentive to make things clearer for people.

The Fed or Congress could, of course, have devised a more straightforward and equitable method for allocating credit in times of scarcity —one that did not depend on pushing the price so high that some people were forced out of the market. Any number of alternatives were feasible—banking regulations that required banks to apportion their new lending more evenly, tax-code changes that removed the advantage for the wealthier, more profitable borrowers. But, in order to adopt such a direct approach, the government would first have to acknowledge that it already practiced an implicit form of rationing. No one wished to admit that the free market was already, in fact, contaminated by government manipulation.

An alternative system—one that allocated credit according to need or other priorities rather than by price—would necessarily have to restrict the flow of credit available to the largest and most influential players in the economy—both financial institutions and corporations—in order to insure that home buyers, small businesses and others got their fair share. This was another good reason why most politicians preferred not to tamper with the status quo. To correct the inequities, they would have to directly attack the prerogatives of the strongest interests.

Aside from the unfairness, the effectiveness of the existing system was also flawed: when the Federal Reserve attempted to restrain, its primary leverage was directed at the wrong end of the spectrum of borrowers—not at those most responsible for generating new credit. The pressure of higher interest rates was felt first and most potently by the weakest buyers and producers, but it was the strongest and largest enterprises that were the primary source of expanding credit. In order to budge them, the Federal Reserve had to keep raising the threshold of pain for others—squeezing the mice harder and harder, in effect, in the hope that eventually the elephants would respond. The strong, meanwhile, and their bankers managed to continue business as usual.

After October 6, the squeeze was on. Credit unions and savings and loan associations were losing deposits and cutting off loan applications. Banks were rationing consumer loans by raising the eligibility requirements. New mortgages were harder to get. But some financial institutions and their best customers—the largest money-center banks and the major multinational corporations—did not feel squeezed.

The Girard Bank of Philadelphia saw the Fed's tightening of money and credit as an opportunity to win customers away from its competitors. "We'll welcome quality business, reasonably priced," said Robert Williams, vice chairman of Girard Company, the bank holding company that operated the nation's seventieth-largest bank. "We're in the business to get market share."

The Bank of America in San Francisco, the nation's largest commercial bank, also did not feel crimped by Paul Volcker's dramatic policy change. Lloyd Sugaski, the bank's executive vice president for loans, sounded positively bullish. "We've been taking on new business —soliciting good, credit-worthy customers—because that's the only way we can grow. I don't see any need to change that."[9]

Their optimism was well founded. The largest banks in America were not compelled to slow down because the Federal Reserve was slowing the growth of money and credit and pushing interest rates to historic levels. On the contrary, it was an opportunity for them to increase market shares. Some loan customers were shut out, particularly consumers and smaller businesses. But the major banks' most important customers, the great corporations that operated worldwide, wanted more credit in this time of scarcity. And they were promised all they wanted.

After October 6, bank lending slowed down sharply at first, as businesses and consumers were taken aback by the higher costs of borrowing. Then, two months later, the credit expansion began accelerating again—almost as though the Fed had done nothing to limit the supply. Three months after the "Saturday Night Special," the commercial banks were expanding their loan portfolios at an annual rate of 14 percent—a robust pace in any season.

The major banks' self-confident management was expressed even more clearly in their willingness to grant new lines of credit to their corporate clients who wanted assurances that, as money was tightening, they would not face scarcity. These formal loan commitments, which banks made for a fee, amounted to an "invisible money supply," according to Albert Wojnilower of First Boston. The credit lines were legally-binding agreements by the banks to provide the promised funds whenever the customer wanted them. The banks were confident that, one way or another, they could find the money to lend, regardless of how high interest rates went. All through 1979, the banks' loan commitments had been expanding at an alarming pace—an annual rate of 20 percent. After the Fed's edict of October 6, the credit guarantees were actually expanded even faster—by 24 percent. In the first three months of 1980, the banks would add to their credit commitments at the extraordinary rate of 41 percent.

"A veritable credit eruption," Wojnilower termed it. "The increase in these loan commitments relieved companies of any serious concern about a scarcity of spendable funds," he explained. "The October 1979 spurt in interest rates and change in the Federal Reserve's mode of operation to reserve targets exerted no perceptible retarding influence."[10]

Federal Reserve officials were distressed by this contradictory development, but not entirely surprised. The same phenomenon had occurred, less dramatically, in previous episodes of monetary tightening over the preceding fifteen years—the limited supply of money and credit flowed to the top, as the larger banks scrambled to protect themselves and their customers from scarcity. This required the banks, first, to ration funds for the less-preferred borrowers, smaller enterprises or riskier ones, a process that bankers described as "improving the quality" of their loan portfolios. Second, the banks had to find more money somewhere. If the Federal Reserve wasn't increasing the overall pool, they would have to get it on their own.

The effect was to compound the inequities of size that were already present because of higher interest rates. The small players suffered first from the "demand side" effects of monetary policy—priced out by higher interest rates. But they also suffered, perhaps as severely, on the "supply side"—the banks' rationing of loans. Consumers and smaller businesses that were willing and able to pay the higher interest rates found they still could not obtain loans.

When Andrew F. Brimmer was a Federal Reserve governor in the 1970s, he was bothered enough to propose an alternative system—reserve requirements on bank loan portfolios that would force banks to allocate new lending more equitably among potential customers. The present system was not only unfair, Brimmer complained, but it also undermined the Fed's own effectiveness.

One of the inescapable facts relating to the lending behavior of commercial banks—particularly the large multinational institutions—is the extent to which they give priority to satisfying their corporate business customers over the credit demands of other sectors of the economy [Brimmer wrote]. Because of this strong network of customers' relationships, the banks—in fact—set priorities that are not necessarily consistent with the overall objectives of public policy.[11]

The other governors dismissed Brimmer's ideas as unworkable. The private banking system, they argued, must be free to set the priorities for new credit, even if the banks were pushing in a direction contrary to the Fed's own objectives.

When money became scarce, resourceful bankers had ways to obtain more of it, despite the rising price, and to amply finance their new loans. Typically, they would sell off government securities to raise funds for lending and raise the market rate offered on their own certificates of deposit—in effect, luring away the deposit money that was fleeing from credit unions and S & L's.

The bankers also borrowed more from the Federal Reserve itself,

simply by phoning the Discount window officer at one of the twelve
Federal Reserve Banks. Discount borrowing soared shortly after the
October 6 announcement to more than $3 billion a day, subsided for
several months and then reached another peak later of $3.5 billion a
day. The Fed's decision to raise the Discount rate to 12 percent hardly
discouraged bankers from "going to the window," as they called it.
When the alternative was borrowing in the money market where short-
term rates were bouncing as high as 18 percent, the Fed's Discount
rate was still a bargain.

In theory and myth, the Federal Reserve's Discount lending was the
power of life or death over private banks. If a bank relied too much on
the Discount privilege, the Fed could simply refuse its request for a
loan—threatening the bank with crisis and possibly insolvency. In
practice, the central bank rarely, if ever, said no at the Discount
window. A bank might be scolded, perhaps subjected to a rigorous
examination or told to "stay away from the window" until its affairs
were in order. But the Federal Reserve would not refuse to make a
Discount loan unless it had concluded that the bank was already
doomed. The Fed's original purpose was to prevent bank failures, not
cause them, a reality that aggressive bankers regularly exploited.

One other source of new money available to the banks was more
important than all the others—the pool of expatriate dollars that the
Federal Reserve did not control, the unregulated funds known as the
Eurodollar market. For the largest multinational banks, which had
ready access through their own foreign branches, Eurodollar borrowing was a fundamental means of evading the Fed's tightening. Chase
Manhattan, Citibank, Morgan Guaranty and the others borrowed "offshore" to finance their own domestic lending, and they also re-lent the
funds to regional banks, which didn't have direct access to the Euromarket themselves.

The Euromarket pool was as large as $800 billion, according to an
estimate by the Morgan bank.[12] The funds were not subject to reserve
requirements imposed by central banks or any other government regulation, and, therefore, the Eurodollar pool was an attractive place for
international banks, both foreign and American, and the global corporations to park their money. The "offshore" label, in fact, was
largely a bookkeeping fiction. Eurodollar transactions were executed
in New York City or Chicago as easily as in London (the fiction was
largely discarded in 1981 when America's multinational banks were
permitted to operate unregulated "international banking facilities" in
the U.S.—a foreign branch, in other words, that was located right at
the home office).

For monetary policy, the crucial point was that the Eurodollar pool provided the largest banks with a safety valve—a place to raise funds when domestic money was growing scarce. Some of the borrowed money that entered the U.S. economy this way would show up as domestic bank deposits and thus be counted in the American money supply, but a lot of it would not, since the loans could be carried on the books of foreign branches of the U.S. banks or the foreign subsidiaries of the American corporations who borrowed the money.

For the commercial banks, the Eurodollar pool was a safety valve. For the Federal Reserve, it was a huge leak in the plumbing. The money flowed into the American financial system when domestic credit was scarce and interest rates were rising or flowed out again when supply was in excess. The Fed did not control it either way. Even the Fed's experts found it impossible to be precise about how large the leakage from offshore was, but Governor Wallich estimated the added amount for 1978 at roughly $50 billion—imported money that, he said, "to all intents and purposes should be viewed as part of the U.S. money supply."

A leakage of $50 billion could effectively add nearly 15 percent to the size of M-1, the basic aggregate of spending money that was used as the principal measure of the U.S. money supply. The Federal Reserve, in comparison, was attempting to hold M-1 to a growth rate of less than 5 percent. The Fed's technicians tried to reckon with the inflow of Eurodollars and compensate for it. "If we ignore it," Wallich said, "the rate of growth of the total dollar supply, combining the U.S. and the Euromarket, would be rising faster than we think."

But, given the system as it existed, the Fed could only go so far in offsetting the money that banks imported from offshore balance sheets. Wallich acknowledged the inhibition:

> The Federal Reserve could, of course, adjust the domestic targets so as to keep the combined amount of domestic and Euromoney on the right track. But as the Eurodollar market grows, the Federal Reserve would have to bear down increasingly hard on the domestic supply of money and credit in order to offset the expansion of Eurodollars. This would work a hardship on our domestic economy and particularly on U.S. borrowers who did not have access to the Euromarket.[13]

When the Federal Reserve Board adopted the special marginal reserve requirement on managed liabilities at its October 6 meeting, it was trying to plug this leakage—raising the cost for bankers who turned to the Eurodollar market for funds, but it did not seem to have much impact.

The new control on managed liabilities had loopholes and the banks soon discovered them. The October 1979 issue of *World Financial Markets,* published by Morgan Guaranty, explained how corporate borrowers could get around the added cost. Multinationals could borrow from foreign banks, which weren't covered by the new reserve requirement, or they could still borrow from American banks, but with different bookkeeping. "Foreign subsidiaries of U.S. companies could approach banks overseas, including the foreign branches of U.S. banks, for credit and then could re-lend the funds to their U.S. parent companies," the Morgan bank explained. "In this way, domestic borrowers could avoid the cost effects of marginal reserve requirements."[14]

Some of America's most important banks were also ignoring another element of the Federal Reserve's October 6 pronouncements—the Fed's admonition to avoid making loans for speculation. In one of its economic roundup stories, *The Wall Street Journal* reported: "Most banks say they are heeding the Fed's request to avoid speculative lending—and doing so with little difficulty."

Edward L. Palmer, chairman of Citibank's executive committee, assured the *Journal:* "The marginal and speculative borrower has gone to Miami to sit in the sun."[15] In subsequent weeks, Citibank would lend a total of $115 million to Texas oilman Nelson Bunker Hunt, his brother Herbert and their commodities firm, while the Hunts were furiously buying up silver as the price skyrocketed. The Hunt brothers' secret goal was to corner the world market in silver and thereby control the price—an effective monopoly that would have driven others to ruin.

U.S. banks and brokerages, despite Volcker's warnings, joined foreign banks in financing one of the most audacious speculative gambles in history. Silver sold for $10.61 an ounce in August, and by late December the price had nearly tripled. In January, it would peak at $52 an ounce. The price was driven up by inflation, but also by the Hunt brothers' global purchases. Eventually, they would acquire more than 129 million ounces of silver. The Hunts, though fabulously wealthy oilmen from Dallas, bought most of their silver hoard with borrowed money.

In addition to Citibank, First National of Chicago lent them $70 million directly and First National of Dallas lent $35 million. Another $450 million was lent by First National of Dallas and twenty-nine other banks to the Hunts' oil company, which, in turn, lent huge sums to the brothers for their silver buying. Major banks were also involved less directly as providers of credit to the brokerage firms that allowed the Hunts to buy vast quantities "on margin." The banks lent to the brokers and the brokers lent to the Hunts. Bache Halsey Stuart, which nearly went bankrupt when the silver bubble eventually burst and the Hunts could not pay their debts, lent a total of $233 million for the brothers' silver buying, backed by bank credit from First National of Chicago, Bankers Trust and Irving Trust, among others. E. F. Hutton put up $104 million. Merrill Lynch lent $492 million.[16]

The Federal Advisory Council had reassured the Fed governors that commercial banks were adhering to the Fed's warning against speculative lending. "Loans to finance essentially speculative activities in commodity, gold and foreign-exchange markets are being avoided," the bankers promised in their November meeting with the Fed, "but it is not clear how important they may have been. Most banks would not have financed such activity directly in any period. . . ."[17] Their reassurances, to put it mildly, were inaccurate.

The Federal Reserve chairman claimed in later testimony that he was unaware that quite the opposite was occurring. Volcker and the other governors had heard rumors and veiled warnings from the bankers about speculative fever and they read newspaper accounts of the Hunts' extraordinary activities, but the chairman did not learn the full scope of the banks' complicity in the speculation until the venture was collapsing in late March of 1980.

Volcker was called out of a Board of Governors' meeting on March 26 by an urgent call. A desperate executive of Bache, one of the nation's leading brokerages, telephoned from New York, pleading for intervention by the Fed. Bache, he told Volcker, was about to be bankrupted by falling silver prices. As the value of their holdings plummeted, the Hunts could not meet the "margin calls," the requirement to put up more cash against their outstanding loans. Bache would be wiped out if something didn't happen, Volcker was informed, and a number of major banks were going to suffer huge losses too.

Afterward, Federal Reserve officials shrugged off the fact that their warnings to the banks had been ignored. "We are under no delusions as to what our persuasion will do against the forces of the market," Governor Wallich explained. "One individual bank may say to us, 'We would like to go along with you and not make these loans, but everyone else in the market is doing it so we don't see why we shouldn't.' " The Federal Reserve, however, easily could have prevented the silver lending and other types of speculative financing by the commercial banks—if it had been willing to impose real controls on the banks' loan portfolios. Instead, the central bank relied on hortatory messages and voluntary compliance. The banks, for their part, went ahead and lent hundreds of millions for the Hunt brothers' silver gamble.

The commercial bankers on the Federal Advisory Council were undoubtedly right about one thing: if the domestic money supply was held tight long enough, keeping interest rates high, sooner or later that would produce the desired results. The entire economy would slide into contraction and everyone's desire for new loans would subside. Then, the competition for money, the uneven contest that pitted the weak against the strong, would abate.

The American economy was like an untamed bull, restlessly charging forward despite the Fed's best efforts to restrain it. By January of 1980, it was clear that things were not slowing down as expected. The recession, predicted and proclaimed for so many months, was not occurring. Instead, the nation's economic activity was surging forward, regaining the momentum that had so alarmed Federal Reserve governors back in the early autumn. It was as though the Fed had swung a heavy club and momentarily stunned the rampaging animal, knocked it to its knees with the sharp spike in interest rates. Then the bull got up, shook off the blow and charged on.

Disconcerting as this was for the Federal Reserve governors, the experience had one reassuring element. It demonstrated, once again, the extraordinary strength and resilience of the American economy, a point that was often lost in the public debates over economic performance. Political leaders and economists and the public, as well, usually focused on the grievances and afflictions. They did not dwell on the underlying energy.

In this season, however, the bull was stampeding like a crazed animal. The inflationary pressures that had driven anxious people to buy things on borrowed money now became maddeningly intense. Thanks to another oil price increase and the higher interest rates that raised mortgage costs, the Consumer Price Index rose in January at a staggering annual rate—16.8 percent. Everything else flowed from that: the dollar weakened further, commodity prices reached historic peaks. Gold, that had sold for $400 an ounce in early fall, more than doubled in a few months, a record price of $875. Silver, meanwhile, quintupled. The bond and stock markets suffered new losses.

What Paul Volcker and the Federal Reserve had wrought was without precedent in modern experience. In a few short months, the Fed had nearly doubled the price of money. Despite the technical complexities, that was the essential meaning of Volcker's operating shift—the dramatic ratchetting upward in interest rates. A few months before, the governors had been arguing over half-percent increases. Now the Fed was pushing the Federal Funds rate from 11 percent toward 20 percent. And other short-term rates followed in step.

Yet the real economy continued expanding despite the declines in the two most interest-sensitive sectors—housing and automobiles. By

January, auto sales had dropped to their lowest level since 1975. New starts of home building had shrunk by nearly 20 percent. Other kinds of consumer spending remained surprisingly strong, even though unemployment was beginning to rise and personal incomes were declining. The explanation was debt: families were going deeper in debt to compensate for shrinking incomes. With inflation at 16 percent, borrowing still looked like a good deal.

The Federal Reserve's new system for controlling the money aggregates had performed exactly as desired at first. The money growth slowed sharply in October and November. Then, in step with bank lending and economic activity, the money supply started expanding more rapidly again in December and January, despite the new operating system and the Fed's intentions. By February, M-1 was growing at a rate of 9 percent, almost as fast as it had back in September.

One point was painfully clear to the Board of Governors: the psychological shock that Volcker thought might reverberate from the October 6 shift had not happened. The chairman had hoped that the dramatic action would alter the financial markets' cynical expectations about future inflation and, therefore, newly confident investors would demand less of an "inflation premium" for long-term credit. "All those happy thoughts," Volcker acknowledged, "did not come to pass."

The Federal Advisory Council delivered the same message at its February meeting. The bankers reported:

The Council commends the Board's continuing efforts to restrain. . . . However, because of the disparity between past Fed announcements and actual results, whether these deviations were intentional or unavoidable, there is some skepticism in the marketplace that the Fed is resolved to adhere to its stated policies over the long term. This doubt is increased by the simultaneous occurrence of a presidential election and a potential recession.

The other message from the marketplace took the form of a question: if the record level of interest rates induced by the Fed was not enough to slow down the economy, then how high would interest rates have to go in order to do the job? The assumptions made on October 6, when none of the governors imagined that rates would have to go above 16 percent, were clearly mistaken. "The economy was much more resistant to higher interest rates than one would have thought," Governor Wallich conceded.

Volcker agreed. "There is certainly reality to the fact that credit has continued to flow during this period," he said. "I think there is also reality to the fact that, horrendous as these interest rates are in respect to our own history, what those people are telling you is that they are willing to borrow at these interest rates because they are so pessimistic about inflation." [18]

Volcker called it "a kind of tail-chasing phenomenon." Housing, for instance, had been hit hardest by the higher rates, yet lenders were still surprised at how many families were willing to take on home mortgages at 13 percent or even higher. "Perhaps it is not so hard to understand," Volcker said, "when you realize that the prices of houses have been going up at 15 percent or more."

These pressures could not last. The economy seemed to be headed for a blowoff—like a steam engine that finally pops the seals on its safety valves. But it wasn't at all clear when or how that would occur. The Federal Open Market Committee expressed its own confusion in its January minutes: "In the judgment of a number of members, a downturn now seemed to be getting under way, but there was also recognition it could be delayed for another quarter or two." The recession, in other words, might already be started or it might start six months from now.

The FOMC members faced another unpleasant decision. Should they resist the new surge of upward pressures? If they did, it would threaten to push interest rates even higher, way beyond what they had envisioned back in October. If they did not resist, then the skeptics would be confirmed in their assumption that inflation would continue unabated.

In early February, the Federal Open Market Committee agreed to further tighten bank reserves moderately, though the majority assumed that the Federal Funds rate, then trading around 13 percent, would remain below the ceiling of 15.5 percent. The committee's two most conservative hawks, Governor Coldwell and Governor Wallich, dissented. It wasn't enough, they argued.

They were right. Two weeks later, the money aggregates were growing much faster and the Fed Funds rate was up to 15 percent. Volcker called a special meeting of the FOMC by telephone, and the twelve committee members agreed to hold tight on bank reserves and raise the ceiling on the Fed Funds rate by one percentage point. It would be allowed to rise as high as 16.5 percent.

That wasn't enough either. On March 6, that new limit was pierced too—the Fed Funds was trading at 17 percent. Volcker called another telephone conference and the FOMC raised the ceiling to 17.5 percent. The next day, he had to do it again. The Federal Funds rate was now up to 18 percent. The Federal Open Market Committee yielded again and raised its ceiling to match the reality. The Fed Funds rate was allowed to remain at 18 percent—50 percent higher than where it had started in early October when the Fed embarked on its campaign to halt inflation.

Yet the commercial banks continued to pump out new loans at an accelerating pace. They found plenty of willing customers even though the banks' loan rates were marching upward in track with the money-market rate controlled by the Fed. The prime rate for short-term interest rose swiftly to 18 percent, then 19 percent and would peak at 20 percent. Nine months earlier, in the summer of 1979, the prime had been below 12 percent. The basic cost of borrowing, the price for money, nearly doubled.

And still the recession did not come. Economists kept predicting it, yet they could not see any clear evidence to confirm it. The Fed's vaunted initiative of October seemed surprisingly impotent and the chatter in financial markets was filled with rumors of impending government controls.

"There was a wave of cumulative pessimism," the chairman of the Federal Reserve acknowledged. "There was a gathering feeling that things were out of control."

The political reaction was strangely muted, despite the severity of what Paul Volcker was engineering. Both in Congress and at the White House, Democratic leaders seemed confused and divided, not certain whether to attack or remain silent. On Friday, October 19, two weeks after the Federal Reserve's dramatic policy changes, the Senate majority leader, Robert C. Byrd of West Virginia, rose to express his concern. The Fed's new initiatives had some positive aspects, the senator acknowledged, but a regime of tight money and soaring interest rates sounded suspiciously like the bankrupt strategy that Republicans had employed against inflation in 1974, leading to a long, severe recession and massive unemployment. Senator Byrd declared:

> Attempting to control inflation or protect the dollar by throwing legions of people out of work and shutting down shifts in our factories and mines is a hopeless policy.
>
> The Congress will be watching closely to ensure that the recession of 1974 and 1975 will not be repeated in 1979 and 1980. We will be watching to see whether the Fed, in casting a net to catch speculative nonproductive investments, is also restricting the flow of credit into vital, productive areas of the economy.
>
> We will watch with concern the impact of this policy on small businesses which depend on credit markets for financing. We will watch its impact on the construction industry which historically is the first sector to feel the shock of tight credit. The Congress will watch the response of bankers and brokers to the Fed's message of restraint.

The senator's speech, in the nature of congressional politics, was like a polite warning shot across the bow. The Democratic leader of the Senate majority was putting Paul Volcker and the Federal Reserve on notice: if the Fed squeezed too hard, it could expect vigorous opposition from the governing party in Congress, which held ultimate legislative authority over the independent central bank.

But, early in the following week, another important senator rose to deliver a strong defense of the Fed and an implicit scolding for the majority leader. William Proxmire of Wisconsin, chairman of the Senate Banking Committee, had endorsed Volcker's initiatives immediately, conceding that the Fed was applying "strong medicine" but praising its courage. "As strong medicine is needed and as no one else is willing or has the fortitude to bell the cat," Proxmire said, "we should support the Federal Reserve when it acts. The Federal Reserve has no other choice."

Senator Proxmire had special influence, not simply because he chaired the committee that exercised oversight on monetary policy, but because he was among the limited number in Congress who understood the subject. Without naming Senator Byrd as the target of his remarks, Proxmire delivered a short lecture on inflation and interest rates. At 15 percent inflation, an investor lending $1 million at 10 percent "loses" $50,000 a year. "You cannot count on the lender being a complete idiot," Proxmire said. Sooner or later, he will stop lending at low interest rates and invest the money himself in commodities or real estate.

> This policy is going to cause pain [Proxmire emphasized]. Anybody who says we can do it without more unemployment or more recession is just deceiving you or is deceiving himself, because there is no way you can do it without more unemployment, without some business failures you would not otherwise have, without serious farm losses. . . .
>
> As I say, this is a bad policy from the standpoint of sacrifice and it hurts many, many Americans, hundreds of thousands, millions of them. But we ought to either come up with an alternative or say that we are not interested, really, sincerely in fighting inflation. . . .

Thus rebuked, Senator Byrd returned to the subject on the Senate floor the next day. His tone was conciliatory and considerably more generous toward the Federal Reserve.

"I believe we need to give the Fed's new approach a chance to work," Senator Byrd agreed. "I see no reason to declare the program a failure when, essentially, its success or failure depends on the prudence with which it is implemented."[19]

Senator Byrd's uncertain foray into the thicket of monetary policy was typical. Some others in Congress expressed misgivings but did not persist, while the most influential liberal voices—Senator Proxmire and Representative Henry Reuss, chairman of House Banking—endorsed the Volcker campaign as "constructive." Many potential critics were intimidated by these endorsements. Like farmers in Iowa or small-business men in Virginia, many members of Congress simply did not understand the technical aspects well enough to comment one way or the other. And many agreed with Proxmire: if Congress was not going to do anything about inflation itself, then it should hold its tongue while the Fed tackled the unpleasant task.

Some politicians, when constrained by such circumstances, were tempted to seize upon issues they did understand and make the most of them. Less than a week after launching its new targeting system, the Federal Reserve reported an abnormal surge of $3.7 billion in the money supply, then with considerable embarrassment retracted the number when it discovered that one major bank, Manufacturers Hanover, had misreported its own balances. The House Banking Committee held a special hearing to investigate what was an irrelevant aberration.

"The nation can't count on the Fed when the Fed can't count," Representative George Hansen of Idaho thundered. "How do you explain to people who have been hurt by interest and discount rates and lack of available money that it was all a mistake? That the economic doctors at the Fed are so careless that they have miscounted the money supply by nearly $4 billion?" Fed Vice Chairman Schultz patiently endured a barrage of angry denunciations while the committee members demonstrated their zeal as watchdogs of the Federal Reserve.[20]

At the White House, the President's public responses to the Federal Reserve's new policy also seemed confused or evasive. At a press conference, Jimmy Carter offered a vague endorsement but attempted to direct press attention to his own anti-inflation effort, the new "national accord" on wages and prices. His attempt failed; the accord disappeared and was soon forgotten. Carter's political future was immediately threatened by Senator Edward M. Kennedy of Massachusetts, leader of the liberal wing of the Democratic Party, who was about to announce that he would challenge the incumbent President for the Democratic nomination in 1980. Kennedy's central complaint was against Carter's fiscal policy, his refusal to increase spending for the domestic social programs that liberals championed. But a new Gallup poll reported an especially ironic finding: the public, by a 2-to-

1 margin, thought Kennedy would be more effective than Carter at reducing inflation.

In San Diego, addressing the convention of the construction trade unions, Carter tried to distance himself from the Fed. "I reject the advice of those who think the only way to cure inflation is to throw millions of people out of work," the President declared. "This has been done in the past by Administrations before mine, but I guarantee you that I will not fight inflation with your jobs."

Later, when a television interviewer in New Jersey asked him if the Fed had gone too far with higher interest rates, the President replied: "As you well know, I don't have control over the Fed, none at all. It's carefully isolated from any influence by the President or the Congress. This has been done for many generations and I think it's a wise thing to do."[21]

Inside the White House, the gloom was almost palpable. On October 31, the President presided over a senior staff meeting including his economic advisers and Vice President Walter F. Mondale. The economists sketched out their expectations and they were all grim.

Lyle Gramley of the Council of Economic Advisers thought there would be a mild recession in 1980 with unemployment rising close to 8 percent, though he added that some private forecasters expected worse. Charles Schultze, CEA chairman, was more pessimistic. Schultze told the President that unemployment would reach 8 to 8.5 percent, that the Consumer Price Index would hit a new peak of 17 to 19 percent in January or February, accompanied by even higher interest rates and recession.

The President was upset. Weren't there any options, he asked, that might keep the economy from drifting into these consequences? Not in the short run, Schultze said, not by conventional means.

Vice President Mondale spoke up. He was alarmed by these grim forecasts. If nothing was done, he said, the economic suffering would drive the Carter Administration from office next year.

The President agreed. The White House economists, he said, had described a scenario for a change of Administrations in 1980. There must be alternatives, some positive steps that at least would allow him to offer hope to the public.

The economists held back. There were no easy solutions, one of them said. Jimmy Carter pressed them for ideas. All the options haven't been explored, the President insisted. Give us a program. Even if it won't work, at least we can offer hope.

Schultze and other economists listed some unconventional alternatives—the imposition of controls on wages and prices or on the expansion of credit, new tax laws to push business and labor toward greater restraint, a new gasoline tax or decontrol of oil prices to discourage energy consumption.

The President ordered his staff to draw up a program, one that might include several of the alternatives that had been discussed, a tighter federal budget to demonstrate fiscal restraint, a gasoline tax and, finally, some kind of program for government controls over the economy's inflationary pressures.

The grim forecasts offered at the October 31 meeting would prove to be quite accurate. But, for some months, nothing much happened to the President's demand for a new plan of action. Four days afterward, a different sort of crisis distracted the White House. On November 4, a mob of Iranian students seized the American embassy in Tehran and took more than sixty Americans hostage there, the beginning of a drama that would preoccupy Jimmy Carter and his senior staff throughout their final year in the White House.

The political future of Jimmy Carter was also in the thoughts of the Federal Advisory Council. When the twelve bankers met again at the Fed on November 1, they were unanimously supportive of the October 6 tightening. But the bankers pointedly warned the Federal Reserve governors they must resist any election-year political pressures to ease off.

There is wide concern about the Fed's resolve in adhering to this policy in the face of an election year and the increasing likelihood of a recession [the bankers advised]. If strong words and actions are not followed by results, then holders of dollar-denominated financial assets in the U.S. and abroad will conclude that the recent changes are no more significant than the statements and policy changes of prior years which did not reduce inflation. When rhetoric sufficed several years ago, tangible proof is now required of the Fed's intentions.

Otherwise, the bankers' council thought the Fed was on track. Consumer optimism had "cooled" in the last month, the council reported. The outlook for housing was "dismal." Mortgage lending had been tightened and business loans were being monitored and priced more carefully. All in all, the bankers concluded: "The recent changes in the administration of monetary policy are viewed by the Council as both significant and beneficial." [22]

5

THE LIBERAL
APOLOGY

When G. William Miller became chairman in 1978, he decided to break the deadlock on a long-festering problem that confronted the Federal Reserve System. Its membership was shrinking. Each year, a few dozen or more commercial banks would decide that the benefits of Fed membership were outweighed by the cost and they would withdraw. The total had fallen from six thousand to about fifty-six hundred and everyone understood why. The Fed paid no interest on the reserve balances that commercial banks were required to maintain at the twelve Federal Reserve Banks. If bankers withdrew and placed themselves under state banking regulation, the required reserve levels would be lower and, more important, the money would be kept at a correspondent bank, where it could be invested in income-producing securities.

The Fed's refusal to pay interest on reserves "constitutes a discriminatory tax," the Federal Advisory Council complained, expressing a grievance long felt by the member banks. The "tax" on Fed banks was actually only lost opportunity—the interest income they did not earn on the idle reserve funds—but the burden of this "opportunity cost" naturally increased during the 1970s as inflation pushed up interest rates. The bankers' distress increased proportionately.

Since Congress had failed to deal with the issue, Chairman Miller decided to take unilateral action. He informed the chairmen of the House and Senate banking committees that the Federal Reserve would henceforth begin paying interest to its member banks on their reserve balances. The response from Capitol Hill was swift and strong. Representative Reuss called the Fed's congressional liaison with a message for the chairman: if Miller dared to do this, Reuss would introduce a resolution to impeach him.

The bankers' complaints about the "hidden tax" imposed on them by Federal Reserve membership left out several offsetting benefits they enjoyed. Thanks to Fed membership, these commercial banks enjoyed a safety net not available to any other business sector—the emergency borrowing available through the Fed's Discount window. If they got into a corner, a temporary liquidity shortage or more serious problems, relief was only a phone call away. That protection from failure, though impossible to quantify, was worth quite a lot. The member banks also received free services from the Fed in their use of the check-clearing and payments system. And, from the congressional point of view, it took real chutzpa for banks to complain about "taxes" since they paid so little compared to other business sectors. In 1980, the effective federal income-tax rate on financial institutions was only 5.8 percent, compared with 34.1 percent for retailing, 24.5 percent for electronics and appliance manufacturing, 16.4 percent for aerospace, 10.9 percent for utilities. The only business sectors with lower effective tax rates than banks were two that were in serious trouble, airlines and wood products.

Nevertheless, Miller won his point. Since 1913, membership had been voluntary, and now commercial banks were leaving the Fed at an accelerating rate. As interest rates rose, many more banks threatened to follow. If this continued, the Fed argued, its control over the money supply would be weakened. Miller acceded to the congressional objections and agreed not to pay interest on reserves, but Reuss and Proxmire, the two banking chairmen, committed themselves to finding a legislative solution.

The ultimate result was the Monetary Control Act of 1980, enacted just as the Fed was driving interest rates to historic peaks. The legislation required all depository institutions, member banks and nonmember banks alike, savings and loan associations, even credit unions, to maintain reserves with the Fed. The imposition of universal reserve requirements was presented to Congress as an arcane question of monetary management, the sort of issue few members of Congress cared much about or understood. In reality, the Fed membership issue was a political question, only marginally relevant to economics. Passage of the Monetary Control Act had very little to do with how effectively the Federal Reserve could control the supply of money. Its purpose was to protect the Federal Reserve's political base.

The central bank, supposedly above politics, maneuvered as adroitly as any private interest group to secure this prize—a historic consolidation of its institutional power. It mobilized the lobbying support of its own infrastructure, the influential network of bankers and businessmen associated with the twelve Federal Reserve Banks. It reluctantly endorsed lucrative concessions to its own favored constituency, the largest money-center banks. It deftly pressured other financial interests to fall in line and accept the terms. As a government agency manipulating Congress, the Federal Reserve was as formidable as the Pentagon.

Still, it was extraordinary that the Fed could realize this long-sought goal at the very time it was imposing such drastic conditions on the private economy. Its legislative victory was possible because the Federal Reserve's agenda was riding piggyback on a much larger cause whose time had finally arrived—the deregulation of finance. In companion legislation, Congress repealed virtually all of the remaining government limits on interest rates, political regulation of lending that had existed since the New Deal. The price of money was free at last—free to seek whatever level the marketplace dictated.

The prime rate was already above 15 percent in the opening weeks of 1980 when the deregulation legislation reached final passage. The Democratic-controlled Congress went ahead, nevertheless, and voted overwhelmingly for the package, which, in other times, they would have denounced as Republican and retrograde. The social implications were obvious: borrowers, businesses and consumers would pay higher interest rates and creditors would enjoy higher returns on their wealth.

Banks would henceforth be permitted to pay interest on checking deposits—with the so-called NOW accounts—in order to lure deposit money back from the money-market funds. The Fed's Regulation Q, which for several decades had imposed arbitrary limits on how much interest banks and savings and loans could pay on savings deposits, was to be phased out. The S & L's, given an interest-rate edge over commercial banks in order to encourage mortgage lending and broader homeownership, were stripped of their advantage—forced to compete on "a level playing field," as the bankers liked to put it. State usury laws—which prohibited interest rates from rising above acceptable levels—were unilaterally suspended by act of Congress.

If the timing seemed odd, the politics was obvious to even the densest member of Congress. Financial deregulation had been gestating for more than a decade and passage was now assured by the convergence of powerful interests. Inflation had sufficiently damaged the holders of financial wealth, including "small savers" of modest means, that even liberal Democrats felt compelled to offer them relief. Commercial banks, led by the largest institutions, argued for the principle of free-market competition. Those who would be hurt—labor, small businesses, many S & L's and smaller banks—protested feebly, but their voices were lost in the rush to consensus.[1]

And the Federal Reserve joined in the lobbying with its own political objective—achieving the universal reach over banks that it had been denied since 1913. Volcker and other Fed officials actually had fundamental doubts about the wisdom of financial deregulation, knowing that the elimination of Washington's interest-rate ceilings would probably weaken the Fed's own control over the expansion of credit. In the heat of the legislative struggle, Volcker and others at the Fed kept these worries to themselves. For them, financial deregulation offered a rare opening and they seized it.

Paul Volcker, like his predecessors, Miller and Arthur Burns, took up the cause of universal reserve requirements and repeatedly warned Congress that shrinking membership was atrophying the Fed's "fulcrum for the conduct of monetary policy"—the base of bank reserves that it manipulated to control the money supply. "As attrition causes the total amount of reserves held at Federal Reserve Banks to decline," Volcker warned, "the 'multiplier' relationship between reserves and money increases tends to become less stable. Consequently, fluctuations in the amount of reserves supplied—and these fluctuations inevitably have a range of uncertainty—can cause magnified and unintended changes in the money supply."

By early 1980, Volcker portrayed the danger as imminent. In recent months, he testified in February, 69 banks with $7 billion in deposits had left the System. Another 320 banks were "considered certain or probable to withdraw," he said, and 350 more were "actively considering withdrawal." If all of those did indeed leave the Fed, the deposits covered by the Federal Reserve's management would decline from 70 percent of the entire banking system to 64 percent. Eventually, the Fed claimed, its membership coverage would fall as low as 57 percent of U.S. deposits. Congress must act.[2]

It sounded ominous to those who did not understand the complex hydraulics of the money supply. But to monetary economists, Volcker's claims were arguable at best and, to many of them, quite spurious. Logically, they pointed out, it did not matter whether the Fed's "fulcrum" covered 70 percent of the banking system or 50 percent or even much less. Since the Fed was the only source that could originate money creation, its actions to inject or withdraw reserves would be transmitted automatically through every channel of the banking system, affecting credit conditions and interest rates for everyone, regardless of where banks kept their reserves.

Everyone agreed, in any case, that the largest money-center banks would never give up their Fed membership, and they were the core of the banking system. The fifty or so largest banks held half of all U.S. deposits and were intimately linked to all others as their correspondent banks, the place where non-Fed banks held their reserves, where smaller banks parked their surplus funds or turned for help. The money-center banks needed the Fed membership both for the Fed's payments system and because they, most of all, depended on the Fed's Discount lending to manage their own liquidity. As long as these core banks were under the Fed's supervision, it would have a reliable handle on the entire banking system.

Governor Henry Wallich, the most scholarly monetary theorist on the Board of Governors, was among the many economists who thought the Fed membership issue was a nonexistent problem, at least as a threat to monetary control.

"I've always thought this was a red herring," Wallich confessed. "Ultimately, I think we can run the economy without any reserve requirements. Some other central banks do it. When I was a director of a bank in New Haven [while teaching at Yale], I said to the managers: 'Look, it's profitable for us to get out of the Federal Reserve System.' And they later did that."

Even with the October 1979 shift in operating methods, Wallich argued, the Fed could still exercise adequate control over reserves with a much smaller number of member banks. During the congressional debate, Wallich did not broadcast his views. Instead, he deferred to the political position staked out by the Federal Reserve and its chairman. "It's easier for me to say this as a theorist," he explained, "than it is for Paul Volcker, who has to go before the congressional committees and talk to the banks and bear the brunt of the complaining."

A senior executive of the New York Federal Reserve Bank shared Wallich's skepticism about the threat of shrinking membership, as did many others within the System. "It was an article of faith in the System that it did matter," the New York official said, "but a lot of people think it doesn't. I've never been convinced it does myself. Logically, we could operate just as effectively if only a small number of banks had accounts with us or maybe even if only brokers had accounts with us."

The commercial banks, however, were also the core of the Federal Reserve's political base, the clientele whom it served and who, in turn, defended the Fed's independence. As more banks, large and small, resigned from the System, the System lost the supporters who helped to protect it from political attack. "There wasn't any question," the New York Fed official allowed, "that the membership provided us with a constituency we could ill afford to lose."

"It would destroy the Fed's political base," explained Kenneth A. Guenther, who was the Federal Reserve Board's congressional liaison throughout the episode. Guenther compared the Fed's political constituency of large and small banks to a naval deployment—"four hundred of the largest battleships surrounded by thousands of little PT boats." The battleships were the essential element for monetary control, but the PT boats provided crucial protection. They were the smaller banks, scattered across the nation in small towns and cities where the bankers were typically much closer to hometown political leaders, including the local congressman, than a mega-banker like Citibank's Walter Wriston or Chase Manhattan's David Rockefeller would be.

Without the picket ships to protect them, the Fed and the money-center banks would be more vulnerable to political whim and the residual popular hostility directed at concentrated power (the political profile of banking resembled the oil industry: thousands of independent producers surrounded the major oil companies and were often more influential, whereas the "majors" like Exxon or Mobil were convenient symbols of corporate power and greed that political critics invoked when attacking the industry). "If you have four hundred of the largest battleships surrounded by thousands of PT boats," Guenther observed, "then someone is really risking political trouble to tamper with them."

The Federal Reserve's self-interest in maintaining this broad base of support was obvious. But, in more subtle terms, liberal Democrats also saw an interest in preserving it. One of the damning complaints against the Federal Reserve, from the beginning, in 1913, was that it became the captive of the largest banks in Wall Street and the other financial centers. The Fed was too subservient to their demands, critics said, and too indifferent to the concerns of smaller institutions or competing interests in the American economy. Yet the Fed's institutional bias toward bigness would likely become stronger if its constituency was narrowed to only the biggest and most important banks. Democratic cosponsors, in particular, were worried by this prospect.

"I don't think anybody in the Federal Reserve System felt you needed more than the four hundred largest banks to operate," Guenther said, "but the Democrats were totally opposed to that. It would make the Federal Reserve the creature of the four hundred largest banks and destroy its democratic base."[3]

To settle on the final terms for mandatory reserves, the sponsors engaged, over many months, in a three-sided dance of persuasion and bargaining—the Fed, the various banking interests and the congressional leaders, all negotiating with one another. To pass its legislation, the Fed had to assemble an enthusiastic coalition of bankers, and that required first Miller and then Volcker to offer some enticements to the various interests. As it happened, the final terms would resemble the outline first suggested by the Federal Advisory Council in the spring of 1979, though the banker-advisers did not get everything they wanted. When the legislation was finally enacted, the Federal Advisory Council was still complaining that it should have been more generous to the Fed's member banks and more punitive for their rivals.

The most important enticement offered to the Fed's member banks was a substantial reduction in their reserves. The Federal Reserve agreed that if it won universal coverage for all banks, then the existing level of reserve requirements could be lowered for everyone. In the end, after much bargaining, the reserves that banks had to hold on demand deposits, the checking accounts that were the core of their funds, were reduced from 16.25 to 12 percent. The Fed's reserve holdings actually shrank from $27 to $16 billion. In other words, the Fed member banks would enjoy a huge dividend in freed-up funds on which they could now earn interest income—while their competitors, the nonmember banks, would be subjected, for the first time, to the "tax" implicit in Fed reserves. (Bankers on the Federal Advisory Council argued for an even greater bonus—a reserve level of only 8 percent.)

The reserves reduction, if nothing was done to offset it, would mean a substantial loss in revenue for the U.S. Treasury. This could be most embarrassing at a time when Volcker and the financial markets were urging Congress to reduce federal deficits to curb inflation. The Federal Reserve's operating budget was entirely independent of congressional control, but each year the Fed paid a large dividend to the Treasury ($9.3 billion in 1979), which was its surplus income after operating costs. The Federal Reserve's income came mainly from the interest on its holdings, including the reserve balances posted by banks, which were invested in U.S. government notes and bonds. The Fed held a little less than 15 percent of all the outstanding debt paper issued by the federal government. Thus, if its pool of bank reserves was reduced, the Federal Reserve's annual income would be smaller and it would have less money to rebate to the Treasury.

Actually, the Fed's annual dividend to the Treasury seemed like money on a merry-go-round. Every year, like any private investor, the Fed collected interest payments from the Treasury on the U.S. securities it owned. Then at year's end the Fed gave most of the money back to the Treasury. This was more than mere bookkeeping. In effect, as any commercial banker might bitterly point out, American taxpayers were saving money by using the bankers' funds.

The solution for the potential revenue loss was to require the Federal Reserve to start charging banks for its services—the daily check-clearing and allied processes. These banking services cost an estimated $400 million a year, and if the Fed priced them at the full cost, that would restore most of the loss. The final trade-off ended up costing the Treasury about $200 million, rising to nearly $600 million a year by 1985 when the new reserve rules would be fully phased in. The larger money-center banks, though they would pay more for Fed services, welcomed the change. Many of them were launching their own service systems for banks in competition with the Fed, and this would make it easier for them to lure away customers.

At the core of the private bargaining, the Federal Reserve acquiesced to a deal with a delegation from the major New York banks. If the Fed would drop entirely its reserve requirement on time and savings deposits, the bankers proposed to Congressman Reuss, they would use their influence to win a legislative endorsement from the American Bankers Association. The concession on reserve requirements would mean a vast return for these bankers; their balance sheets depended heavily on large-denomination CDs. Reuss accepted and the Fed reluctantly went along—and the money-center bankers delivered on their end of the bargain. The ABA endorsed the legislation, despite many protests from regional banks and state-level affiliates.

"We had to placate the small banks and the regional banks and the money-center banks—all of them," Reuss explained. The Federal Reserve, he added, was simultaneously trying to protect its own interests while also looking out for the banks. "Axilrod [the Fed staff director] would throw new formulas into the hopper," Reuss said. "Volcker, under Axilrod's guidance, was always trying to get something more for the banks."[4]

In congressional combat, the Federal Reserve had what amounted to a secret weapon, an unseen political resource that it mobilized for every crucial roll call—the officers and directors of the twelve Federal Reserve Banks plus the board members for twenty-five branch offices in smaller cities. The central bank, as even Volcker acknowledged when pressed, could function perfectly well without any of these subsidiaries. But, in political terms, they provided a network of influentials strategically scattered across America—available for discreet lobbying in behalf of the Fed.

Coast to coast, the Fed directors included an extraordinary cross section of important people: a sprinkling of academics and at least one labor leader, but mostly corporate executives and bankers. High-powered names in the Fed family included Filene's and Connecticut General Life Insurance in the Boston district, Union Carbide, Allied

Chemical and Union Pacific in New York, Westinghouse in Cleveland, Middle South Utilities in Atlanta, Boeing and Kaiser Aluminum in San Francisco, to mention a few. The Fed's home office in Washington went through elaborate charades to convince the regional directors that their economic advice was vital to the System's monetary decisions. In fact, it was not. What was important was their willingness to support the Fed in politics.

"The banks don't need boards of directors, but this is another way to get the movers and shakers on your side," Daniel Brill, the Fed's former research director, explained. "The chairman will put a lot of personal care into keeping them happy."[5]

When each chamber of Congress prepared to vote on the deregulation legislation, the Fed enlisted members from its grassroots network. Pivotal senators or House members were targeted for personal phone calls and letters from the appropriate community leaders back home. Votes were secured and even switched in a most discreet manner. "It was quite effective," Ken Guenther said. "We got the key players, whether directors or bankers, to move on the situation. They gave us contacts with the key congressional players at the moment of truth."

Congress went along with the Fed's proposal, though many legislators probably did not grasp the true meaning of what they were enacting. In the midst of tight money and record-high interest rates, Congress effectively granted a huge windfall to the fifty-six hundred commercial banks that were members of the Federal Reserve System —especially the largest ones. This point was never mentioned in the congressional debates, but following the bankers' own logic, the Monetary Control Act of 1980 represented a major tax cut for the banks, totaling many billions of dollars. When the new rules were fully phased in, the member banks would be freed of nearly $14.5 billion in reserve requirements—money they could now lend out or invest at market rates. How much was this worth to them? A conservative estimate, assuming the banks earned a return of 10 percent on these funds, suggested that the member banks would enjoy more than $5 billion in added income over the next five years, thanks to this arcane change at the Federal Reserve.[6]

With all the other disorders in the economy, the raging inflation and the banks' prime rate at 20 percent, members of Congress might have found it awkward to vote for the Federal Reserve's measure if it had been advertised as a $5 billion tax cut for banks. The members of the two banking committees were intimately familiar with the implications, however. As the legislative negotiations proceeded, the Fed provided committee members with a running series of computer printouts, listing how much their hometown banks would gain or lose in the bargain.

The biggest winners were the largest banks. The fifty largest banks put up roughly half of the bank reserves, and they would get at least half of the $5 billion. The largest two hundred banks would get nearly three-fourths. The rest, $1.5 billion or so, would be divided among the remaining Fed members, more than five thousand banks.

"It was definitely a big-bank victory," Guenther said, "that was foisted on the middle-level banks and the nonmember banks, who paid the freight." The Federal Reserve advanced their big banks' cause while it also served its own.

A banker and a congressman, typically, felt a natural affinity. Both were civic leaders in their community, and in different ways, both influenced the larger destiny beyond their own affairs. The banker knew the true condition of local commerce on a deep level. The congressman, naturally, consulted him. Despite occasional bombast between them, they needed each other's favor. The relationship was so elementary and natural that it was seldom mentioned.

Governor Nancy Teeters, coming from a liberal Democratic tradition, was surprised to discover this closeness when she served Congress as chief economist for the House Budget Committee. "On the Hill," she recalled, "I was always amazed at the level of support for the Federal Reserve. It was partly because the way we operate is so arcane they don't understand it, but also because the members of Congress are so close to the bankers. They see the bankers when they go back to their districts and they listen to them."

This mutuality—members of the governing elite relying on one another—was reinforced by more tangible forms of symbiosis. Commercial banks and other financial institutions, ranging from the savings and loan industry to major Wall Street brokerages, contributed generously to congressional campaigns, a major source of financing for the politicians. For the 1980 elections, incumbent senators and representatives would receive $2,664,000 in donations from the financial sector. The largest share of that money, nearly $590,000, was given to the members of the House and Senate banking committees, the people who drafted banking legislation.

In addition, many members of Congress were themselves involved in finance. More than one-fourth of the Congress owned a direct stake in financial enterprises. In 1980, 129 House members and 38 senators reported that they earned part of their income from stock shares in commercial banks, S & L's and other financial institutions. As a private interest of congressmen and senators, ownership of financial institutions far exceeded their holdings in manufacturing, law firms, or oil and gas. Even some elected representatives were engaged in finance beyond the passive ownership of bank stocks. Forty House members and four senators were active as directors, officers or partners of commercial banks, S & L's and investment companies.[7]

Finance was, therefore, in the front rank of political influence. As a general rule, if all the various interests in the financial sector reached agreement on banking legislation, then Congress would dutifully pass it. The long stalemate on deregulation essentially resulted from the intramural rivalry among the different financial institutions themselves, each holding out for competitive advantage. Once the contending interests in finance reached a fragile consensus on the terms, the legislation was passed.

Interest rates were decontrolled and commercial banks were free to compete more aggressively for deposits. Small-town bankers resented giving up the "free money" of interest-free checking deposits, but larger banks insisted on it to preserve their competitive position. For years, bankers had portrayed themselves as embattled—surrounded by unregulated competitors like the money-market funds that siphoned off their loan customers and depositors. Their anxieties were no doubt sincere but, as Federal Reserve officers sometimes gently pointed out, not entirely consistent with the facts. Commercial banks were not losing market shares but actually gaining moderately (though perhaps not as fast as entrepreneurial bankers wished). The banks' share of total credit-market debt claims was 30.6 percent in 1979, higher than in 1959, when it was 27.3 percent. Bank profits were down somewhat in the late 1970s but still looked quite strong compared to the long-run performance. The average return on equity was 11.5 percent in 1979, not an especially good year, compared to only 8.3 percent twenty years before. If bankers felt squeezed, they seemed to be coping admirably with their stress.

Most of the four thousand savings and loans were not coping as well. For many years, the S & L's had used their own political clout to hold off deregulation, but inflation and rising interest rates had so weakened their balance sheets that they could no longer resist the bankers' lobbying. "They're going to go out of business anyway if they can't adapt," Senator Proxmire, the banking chairman, said.[8] The thrifts were compelled to give up the interest-rate differential imposed by law that had made their savings accounts more attractive than the banks'. In exchange, they were given limited solace—the right to expand their lending into business ventures that were more profitable (and also more risky) than home mortgages. Most thrifts did not like it, but they did not have much choice. "They were reduced to a state of sullen neutrality," Kenneth McLean, staff director of the Senate Banking Committee, explained.[9]

Traditionally savings and loans had been given a protected status and an implicit subsidy so they would provide adequate financing for homeownership—at affordable rates. Now, in effect, they were told to become more like their old rivals, the commercial banks, and to compete with them head to head. "It's a matter of survival of the fittest," Representative Reuss, the House Banking chairman, proclaimed.[10] More than a thousand S & L's would lose the struggle to survive—closed or merged within the next few years. Instead of improving their balance sheets, another thousand would sink further "under water."

As these weaker lending institutions failed, the larger banking organizations would acquire the remains—a steady consolidation of financial power that enabled Citibank, Chemical, Chase Manhattan and others to build the beginning structures of nationwide banks, preparing for the day when Congress finally would make them legal. During the debates, A. W. Clausen, president of the Bank of America, largest in the nation, complained that America's financial industry was still "dominated by mom-and-pop stores." For better or worse, financial deregulation would hasten their demise.

"Freeing the thrift and mortgage markets from government subsidy and guarantee," Albert Wojnilower observed, "is like freeing family pets by abandoning them in the jungle."[11]

The Democratic majority, given its heritage, might still have resisted deregulation, despite the consensus among financial interests. Organized labor was opposed, as it had always been; so were the home builders and other interest groups allied with the housing industry. But the political resistance was worn down and finally overwhelmed by inflation.

"If you save money, you lose," Senator Proxmire observed caustically in the debate. "It is ridiculous for the savings rate to be a maximum of 5¼ percent at a bank for a small saver or 5½ percent at a savings and loan, when the inflation rate, as we all know, is about 13 percent." The Senate committee report also used strong language: ". . . Regulation Q now sanctions blatant discrimination against the small saver to justify its continued existence. It is grossly unfair. . . . Small savers should not be forced by a system of government rate controls to subsidize borrowers."[12]

Defending the "small saver" sounded like helping the very people the Democratic Party had always spoken for. This was not quite the case, as Senator Robert Morgan of North Carolina and the handful of other dissenters pointed out. "The majority of consumers, with or without savings, particularly families of low income, including one-half of the elderly families, would probably suffer a net economic loss," Morgan predicted.[13]

The "small savers" whom Democrats wished to help were actually a limited group, mostly above the median income. First of all, 37 percent of American families had no savings account at all. Another 29 percent had savings balances below $2,000. If these families received another 1 to 3 percent interest on their accounts, that would return at most only $60 a year in additional income. Meanwhile, as borrowers, they would of course pay higher interest rates. As consumers, they would also pay higher prices since business was a major beneficiary of the hidden subsidy of interest-rate controls. When businesses had to pay more for credit, the costs would be passed on to their customers.

During the debate, the elderly were frequently invoked as the victims of the government controls—widows and retired couples who depended on their savings and were embittered by inflation. The elderly had worked a lifetime to acumlulate their nest eggs and now they were being cheated out of a fair return.[14] The Gray Panthers, among other groups, endorsed the legislation. Citibank put up posters in its lobbies blaming Washington for the bank's inability to pay higher interest.

Yet the elderly were also divided by their financial status into winners and losers. Half of the elderly households, sixty-five years old or older, had no savings account at all. Another 11 percent had less than $2,000 and would gain very little. Only 29 percent of the elderly had more than $5,000 in savings and stood to receive a significant increase in their incomes from deregulation. The group of older citizens who would benefit, in other words, was much smaller than the old folks who would not.

Like other forms of deregulation that eliminated hidden subsidies and assigned the true costs directly to customers, financial deregulation inevitably benefited the largest customers most and penalized smaller customers proportionately. Half of the families in America, for instance, had checking balances of $500 or less—too small to qualify for the interest payments from NOW accounts.[15] But these families would begin paying more for their banking services. To make up the cost of paying interest on NOW accounts, banks introduced a bewildering variety of service fees on regular checking accounts. The consequences were not different from cost efficiencies large users gained from the deregulation of airlines or telephones. The little guys, once protected by government regulation, were free to pay more.

In a larger sense, however, financial deregulation was a contest between the generations, a choice between the old and the young, the claims of the past and the ambitions of the future. Though few focused on it, the issue pitted young people who were just starting out in life against their parents' generation, older families that were already established, that already owned their own home and perhaps by middle age were accumulating financial savings. The old would lend their money to the young at higher prices than ever before. Young families forming in the 1980s, setting out to buy a car or their first home, would confront credit terms and interest rates that would have terrified their parents, double-digit mortgages and floating rates that left them vulnerable to default.

Homeownership, the central component of what was described as the "American dream," the main objective of the political controls imposed on finance, would gradually shrink among the population, most dramatically among younger families. By embracing financial deregulation, the Democratic majority was implicitly voting to protect the established interests of older Americans and to reduce life possibilities for the young.

Liberalism, it seemed, was turned upside down. Every important aspect of the 1980 legislation—repealing usury laws, authorizing interest on checking accounts, abolishing rate ceilings—involved the same exchange. The Democratic Party was abandoning the egalitarian agenda that it had embraced for nearly fifty years. The benefits would flow upward on the economic ladder and the costs would flow downward. The past was defended at the expense of the future. This transformation, overwhelmingly endorsed by Democrats after ten years of legislative struggle, could hardly be dismissed as the transient choices of a few party leaders or even explained by the political pressures from the financial industry. Something deeper was at work.

The party of liberalism, one could say, was apologizing for inflation. The Democrats were offering redress to those who had been hurt most, the owners of financial wealth, large or small, whose assets were eroded by nearly fifteen years of price inflation. For years, the party of Roosevelt and Keynes had ducked the question or deflected blame, but as inflation worsened, the disorder was associated indelibly with the expansionary economic strategies of the Democratic Party. The political message implicit in financial deregulation was addressed to those who felt most injured by inflation, the people of relative means who had not been part of the Democratic Party's traditional constituency. We know you have been hurt, the message said, but we will make it up to you. We will set aside our old agenda and help to restore some of your losses.

Senator Proxmire, who came closest to explicitly stating the new perspective, said:

There is nobody in public office today who does not recognize that the number-one problem of this country is inflation. The way to meet inflation is to encourage people to save money, to give them a reward. Let us use these interest rates. Nobody likes high interest rates, but if you have them, let us make sure that people get a reward for saving their money, so they do the anti-inflation job they are supposed to do.

The Senate committee report, likewise, expressed the changed thinking among Democrats: ". . . saving has become an unrewarding economic experience. Inflation eats away at savings and erodes savings as a store of economic value. Unfairly low returns on savings discourage savings and encourage current consumption. This is the wrong economic policy at a time when inflation is our No. 1 economic problem."

In gross terms, the legislation would reward not simply the fabled "small saver" mentioned so often in debate but all creditors—including the wealthiest 10 percent of American families that owned 86 percent of the net financial wealth. Deregulation would help the elderly widow who relied on her small savings account, but it would also improve the interest income for everyone else who owned financial assets. This consequence was discussed only obliquely in debate, and, no doubt, many who voted for financial deregulation did not understand they were effectively raising interest rates for all wealth holders, regardless of where they kept their money.

The explanation was fundamental to the nature of financial markets, where all opportunities for investment compete with one another. Abolishing the regulatory ceilings on savings and checking accounts was like raising the base rate for money—other, unregulated interest rates must rise too in order to maintain their competitive edge. Increasing the bottom-tier savings return would ripple upward through other financial instruments, much the way raising the minimum wage will push up wages for other workers who are already paid much more than the minimum. If unskilled workers get more, then skilled workers can demand more too. While economists would find it impossible to determine the precise impact on interest rates (it might be anywhere from 1 to 3 percent), the effects of deregulation would be evident. Interest rates across the spectrum of lending and investment would remain historically higher in the years ahead, regardless of the level of inflation.

"Just as the price of gasoline is forced up when the crude-oil price increases materially . . . so the deregulation of deposit and loan interest-rate ceilings has unleashed much higher levels of interest rates than prevailed under controls," Albert Wojnilower explained.[16] As a practical matter, the higher interest rates functioned as a system of income redistribution—in reverse. Instead of distributing income downward, as Democrats traditionally tried to do, interest moved incomes in the other direction, from borrowers to lenders, from the bottom to the top.

The distribution, roughly speaking, would flow to the 45 percent of American families that owned all of the net financial worth held by individuals. The money would be paid by the 55 percent of American families whose net financial worth was zero or negative and by businesses, large and small. On its face, that seemed like an implausible choice for politicians to make, charging the majority to reward the minority, but in electoral terms it made more sense. The American electorate was becoming more and more skewed in favor of the upper-income voters, as Thomas B. Edsall explained in his book *The New Politics of Inequality*. As voting participation declined over the last twenty years, it fell most drastically among the alienated citizens with lower incomes. The atrophied electorate that the Democrats faced in 1980 was top-heavy with upper-income, better-educated voters who could articulate their demands and expect a response. Families that earned less than $15,000, for instance, made up 40 percent of the population, but only 33 percent of the active voters. Conversely, families over $25,000 were 29 percent of the population, but they exercised 35 percent of the voting strength. This distortion in the electorate, as it grew stronger through the 1970s, pushed the Democratic Party toward where the votes were—and Democrats listened more earnestly to the grievances of upscale citizens.

The banking legislation of 1980 was not the Democratic Party's first gesture of apology to these voters. A deep transformation in political values did not begin in one season or with a single issue. The complaints from inflation had been building up for a decade. Fitfully, with rancor and reluctance, Democrats had made a series of limited retreats from their old values, legislative concessions implicitly intended to restore the value of capital lost through inflation. In 1978, Congress cut in half the federal income tax on capital gains, aiding the stockholders whose investments stagnated during the 1970s. The same year, the budget growth for domestic social programs that aided the poor and dependent was halted. Over two decades, the Democratic-controlled Congress had reduced corporations' share of the federal tax burden from 26 to 12 percent and shifted the burden to individual taxpayers largely through regressive Social Security taxes.[17]

One way or the other, all these measures reversed the flow of the liberal tradition. Each attempted to give some relief to those on the upper half of the economic ladder. These were not sufficient to satisfy their grievances against inflation. The political struggle would continue. The contest arose on many fronts, from income taxes to monetary policy, addressed to the same fundamental goal, the restoration of capital.

The financial deregulation legislation proved to be an appropriate prelude to the 1980s. The politics of deregulation accurately forecast the political preferences that would prevail in the new decade, which interests would be served and which would be pushed aside. The free-market terms established by the measure cleared the way for finance; unregulated interest rates allowed an era of unprecedented prosperity to unfold for the owners of financial wealth. Other sectors, the ones most dependent on borrowed money, housing, agriculture, industrial production and labor, consumers, would absorb the consequences. What the Democrats had begun reluctantly, a new Republican Administration would continue with relish.

For some years, American society had been engaged in an era of moral liberation, a period when long-standing religious commandments and inherited social taboos fell before the new popular desires. Protestant disapproval of gambling was displaced by multimillion-dollar public lotteries, sponsored by state and local governments. The Catholic sin of abortion was legalized. Pornography, once forbidden and furtive, became freely available. Homosexuality and even prostitution were reconsidered in a more tolerant light. Moral inhibitions that had held authority for centuries were abandoned. Old notions of sinfulness were redefined as largely private matters, no longer subject to public regulation.

In this climate of moral change, American finance was also liberated to do what had once been forbidden. The sin of usury was legalized, by act of Congress. Religious injunctions against usury were as old as the Book of Genesis and given specific definition in American law: lending at interest rates above certain limits was ruinous to the hapless borrower and therefore prohibited. When it enacted financial deregulation, Congress declared that, given the circumstances of double-digit inflation, the usury laws must be set aside. The interest-rate ceilings imposed by state governments on home mortgages were abolished by federal legislation, and the limits on business and agricultural lending were suspended for three years. Many state legislatures, responding to the same pressures, repealed their own usury limits on consumer loans.

Unlike the eclipse of other moral taboos, usury provoked no great controversy when it was decriminalized. The new leniency toward private sexual behavior inspired storms of popular reaction and political movements, but usury provoked little or no reaction. Lending money at ruinous interest rates would now be regarded, like sex, as a "victimless crime," a private act between consenting adults.

The suspension of the usury laws, though less important than the other provisions, accurately reflected the moral logic that propelled the deregulation package. A deep transformation was under way in the political values shared by American elites, both Democratic and Republican, and it cut across many areas beyond finance. The values inherited from the New Deal—the idea that government would serve as regulator and protector in the raw struggles among private economic interests—were in eclipse. The commitments of liberalism— providing shelter for weaker combatants in the marketplace in order to insure certain social goals—were being displaced. An older faith was reviving and regaining its original hegemony, the belief that social justice was best served by an unfettered free market.

The biblical meaning of usury defined the obligations of those who had accumulated wealth toward others who had none and were in need. It imposed limits on the power that the wealthy could exercise, through lending, over the poor. By 1980, the moral argument was reversed. Creditors were now portrayed in political debate as the victims, the virtuous citizens who were exploited by the political interference. Borrowers were described as morally suspect—people who did not themselves save, whose "speculative" spending was "subsidized" by the virtuous savers. The original social contract implied by the concept of usury—the obligations of wealth toward the needs of others —was inverted. The congressional debate described a new political obligation: the savers must be set free, free to seek the highest rate of return on their money.

Congress, of course, did not debate the moral meaning of usury, but was reacting to the practical consequences of usury laws. As inflation pushed market interest rates higher, the usury ceilings effectively shut down lending in state after state. No one would lend at the old levels, and local commerce was starved for credit. Citizens still believed in the concept, however. In Arkansas, voters twice refused to repeal the usury limit of 10 percent in the state constitution, despite the fact that home mortgages and auto loans were no longer available in the state. Their resistance ultimately was futile. No single state could opt out of the national financial system without paying the unbearable price of economic stagnation.

The moral concept of usury was always in fundamental conflict with the dynamics of capitalism. Usury implied social obligation; capitalism depended on individual gain. When they collided in Western history, the capitalist imperative prevailed. Until the late Middle Ages, the Catholic Church still taught that lending at interest—any interest rate whatever—was a sin against God, "ignominious," as the Second Lateran Council of 1139 described it. Usurers, though they might be wealthy merchants and prominent in Church affairs, were excommunicated and refused burial in Christian ground, condemned with robbers, prostitutes and heretics. Their eternal damnation was described in the most grisly terms: toads and other demons gathered on the usurer's corpse, plucking silver from his purse and driving the coins into the heart and mouth of the cadaver. The moral offense was profit without work. The usurer sold time, which belonged only to God.

Christian theology eventually yielded to the new reality. By the thirteenth century, the primitive networks of capitalism—specialized production that yielded surplus goods for trade—were flourishing across Europe. To function, even in its simplest forms, capitalism required the linkage across time that credit provided—lending today for transactions that would be completed in the future. The merchant princes who led the great transformation were cast as sinners, and yet their enterprise was demonstrably generating new levels of abundance, multiplying income and wealth beyond the ancient, precarious struggle for subsistence. A theological innovation opened the way for absolution of their sins—the elaboration of purgatory. After death, the souls of condemned usurers might yet be resurrected for eternity through the intervention of prayer and other considerations. Many primitive capitalists plunged forward into sinfulness, counting on purgatory for their eventual salvation. "The birth of purgatory," the French historian Jacques Le Goff wrote, "is also the dawn of banking." [18]

By the sixteenth century, the practice of usury was quite common despite the Church's lingering disapproval. Emmanuel Le Roy Ladurie, another French historian, described the account books of an enterprising farmer-usurer in southern France around 1540:

> A typical capitalist at the stage of "primitive accumulation," Masenx reinvested his profits and made money on everything he turned his hand to. In the first place, he made loans of grain or money at short term and high interest for a month or for a week at a time, and he also practiced the cruelest form of usury, "from day to day at his pleasure." He lent his *bordiers* (who did not even have sowing seed) the money to marry off a daughter or a sister, and he also furnished, on credit, the silver, the old wine, and the leg of mutton for the wedding feast. He lent money on land, and in time the fields of his debt-ridden clients would help round out Masenx's own properties. [19]

Moral contempt for bankers and their power over others would endure across the centuries and into the present time, but the process of capital accumulation established its own justification. The morality was exalted in the Protestant ethic of John Calvin; the mechanics were elaborated by the classical economists who accompanied the rise of industrial capitalism. Bankers were assured that by doing what had once been forbidden they were actually doing good for all.

The payment of interest was the core of the capitalist dynamic—it mobilized idle wealth for productive enterprises. Interest lured savings into new risks, new ventures that would multiply the economic rewards. Investment was the opposite of hoarding, the miser counting gold in his storehouse and oblivious to the needs of others. Investment promised a return to the wealth holder, but it also created new work for others and more goods for general consumption. If successful, the new venture would produce its own surplus of wealth, which, in turn, was fed back into the process of growth and accumulation. Even allowing for failures and the natural depreciation of things wearing out, this recycling process multiplied wealth, compounding the original value. Interest-paying investment linked the past to the future and bankers were the intermediaries.

Eventually, the concept of usury was refined to a more practical standard: a political prohibition against ruinous interest rates. Capital deserved a just return, but it was not free to collect a toll that would guarantee failure for the borrowers. Above a certain level, interest actually depressed the capitalist process and produced stagnation and further concentration of wealth as debtors failed and forfeited their property to the usurious lender.

John Maynard Keynes himself wrestled with the moral contradictions. Keynes deplored high interest rates and the inequitable distribution of wealth and incomes, but he nevertheless celebrated the creative possibilities of capital multiplication. "The power of compound interest over two hundred years," Keynes wrote, "is such as to stagger the imagination." In 1930, at the depths of global depression, Keynes wrote a prophetic essay entitled "Economic Possibilities for Our Grandchildren," which predicted a golden future for mankind, thanks to the labor-saving inventions of science and the driving force of compound interest. Amid the gathering despair, Keynes was able to see that the capitalist economies were on the brink of vast breakthroughs in agriculture and other technologies—advances that would dramatically multiply the productive potential.

"All this means in the long run that mankind is solving its economic problem," Keynes wrote then. "I would predict that the standard of life in progressive countries one hundred years hence will be between four and eight times as high as it is today." Ultimately, mankind would be freed of the morbid love of money to confront the deeper questions of human existence—"how to live wisely and agreeably and well."

The wealth holders would eventually lose their power over others,

Keynes predicted in the conclusion of his most famous work, *The General Theory of Employment, Interest and Money*. Economies operating efficiently at full employment would, in time, produce such an abundant supply of capital that the price for it would fall to very low levels—that is, very low interest rates. This surplus, Keynes believed,

> would mean the euthanasia of the *rentier* and, consequently, the euthanasia of the cumulative oppressive power of the capitalist to exploit the scarcity-value of capital. Interest today rewards no genuine sacrifice, any more than does the rent of land. The owner of capital can obtain interest because capital is scarce. But whilst there may be intrinsic reasons for the scarcity of land, there are no intrinsic reasons for the scarcity of capital. . . . I see, therefore, the *rentier* aspect of capitalism as a transition which will disappear when it has done its work.

In the meantime, he cautioned, human society must be patient with the moral flaws of capitalism. Until the abundance of capital was secured, practical necessity required one to tolerate the inequities of wealth and the exploitation of usurers. "For at least another hundred years we must pretend to ourselves and to everyone that fair is foul and foul is fair; for foul is useful and fair is not," Keynes explained. "Avarice and usury and precaution must be our gods for a little longer still. For only they can lead us out of the tunnel of economic necessity into daylight."[20]

Fifty years later, the Keynesian vision was not fulfilled, of course. The *rentier* was alive and well, and his demands, as expressed in interest rates, were many times greater than prices that had disturbed Keynes in his day. Yet Keynes was not entirely wrong either. Despite wars and other calamities, the capitalist dynamic had achieved many of the wealth-producing breakthroughs he had envisioned and others he did not foresee. The general "standard of life" was improved dramatically, at least in the industrial world, though the benefits were still distributed quite unevenly. The disparities of wealth and income —and the attendant "gods" of avarice and usury—were now most dramatic on the global scale, among nations rich and poor.

An alternative vision of interest and capital existed in the developing world, springing from the same religious principles. While Americans accepted high interest rates as necessary to commerce, and their elected representatives set aside the legal prohibitions against usury, people in the Islamic world still believed usury was sinful—in the original sense of the word. The Koran, like the Bible, taught that lending at interest was immoral and for the same reasons. In the Moslem nations of the Middle East, however, the original moral meaning of usury survived as an important article of faith, at least among the fundamentalists. Interest income from loans was forbidden. The Islamic societies, notwithstanding the great wealth produced by oil and the accompanying modernization, have never passed through the stages of capitalist development that changed the thinking of Western Christianity. The banking system that existed in the Middle East was largely superimposed by European colonialism, but its values were never accepted by the Moslem faithful.

Starting in the early 1970s, Middle East economists and political leaders began to devise an Islamic alternative to Western banking—a banking system that would serve as intermediary between depositors and borrowers and would raise capital for new ventures, but would not pay or charge interest. Instead, the investor would share equitably in the risk of the enterprise, profiting or losing as a partner with the entrepreneur. Thus, the relationship between creditor and debtor was more equal, more like a limited partnership in Western commerce. The investor is promised a fixed percentage of future profits, but he is not guaranteed that he will receive income or even the full return of his original principal.

A decade later, some thirty Islamic financial institutions were in operation in Egypt, Sudan and the oil-rich Persian Gulf states. Religious advisers were consulted by the bankers designing new financial instruments to make sure the credit transactions did not somehow conceal the forbidden *ribā,* the payment of interest. The total assets of the Islamic banks were relatively small, depending on deposits from the general public, not the estimated surplus of $100 billion from oil income, but the idea was popular.

A study by the Western industrial nations' Organization for Economic Cooperation and Development explained:

> Islamic concepts are different from capitalism by their opposition to excessive accumulation of wealth and, in contradiction to socialism, by their protection of the rights to property, including ownership of the means of production. . . . A true Islamic society must not be an arena where opposing interests clash, but rather a place where harmonious relations can be achieved through a sense of shared responsibilities. The individual's rights must be equitably balanced against those of society at large.

As in Christendom, of course, the rich did not always live by the articles of their faith. Moreover, the Arab investors were guided in financial affairs by the same moral distinction that once governed Christians and Jews. *Ribā* was forbidden among members of the tribe, but it was perfectly acceptable to collect interest from foreigners.

Thus, for instance, pious citizens of Saudi Arabia would see no hypocrisy in the fact that more than $50 billion of their nation's oil revenues was invested at one time in U.S. government securities, collecting interest from the borrower, the American taxpayer, while simultaneously the Saudi princes promoted the concept of interest-free Islamic banking at home.[21]

Meanwhile, Americans generally did not doubt the superiority of their own system or question its justice. After all, the arguments for repealing the legal limits on interest were based on equity too. After Congress set aside the state usury laws, investors would at last be free to recover a fair return on their wealth. In the United States, the concept of usury seemed an anachronism.

When usury became legal, of course some lenders would demand more than a fair return. In Washington, D.C., Pearl S. Merriwether was desperate for a loan. Disabled and out of work at sixty-two, she was unable to pay her gas and telephone bills and so she turned to First American Mortgage Company. First American provided her a one-year $25,000 mortgage with an effective interest rate of 142 percent. This was now legal. First American reported that over a two-year period it lent more than $2 million at interest rates ranging from 100 to 150 percent.

As state legislatures followed Congress by repealing usury limits on consumer loans, other desperate or ill-informed borrowers would pay more too. In Flagstaff, Arizona, a Navajo family named Keams borrowed $700 from Ideasource Inc. at 127 percent interest. In Richmond, Virginia, an elderly couple, Charles and Gertrude Taylor, borrowing $5,325, was charged 39 points, or $2,100, in order to make the transaction. In South Carolina, car dealers charged up to 150 percent interest. Some of these victims, either gullible or desperate, lost their homes to the lenders—much the way French peasants lost their small plots of land to the avaricious *rentier* in the sixteenth century.[22]

These abuses and many others were lamented, but hardly to be avoided in a free marketplace. Like the other changes in public morality, legal liberation from the sin of usury meant, inevitably, that some lenders would try it.

When the financial legislation was finally enacted, the Federal Reserve had won an important victory for itself. Yet, on a deeper level, the Fed also had lost. For more than fifteen years, the Federal Reserve had staged an awkward stalling action against financial deregulation —a position that put it athwart the ambitions of its own primary constituency, the commercial banks. The 1980 legislation meant its rearguard struggle was lost. The Federal Reserve chairman, whatever he might say in public, knew the legislation would greatly complicate the most important function of the central bank—controlling the expansion of credit.

"Under interest-rate decontrol," a former Fed official explained, "any idiot can buy money, as long as he's willing to pay the price. So you have to push interest rates up very high across the board in order to slow down the economy. So the Fed's control becomes blunter, more difficult."

For a generation, the various ceilings that the government had imposed on interest rates had acted like stop valves in the plumbing of finance. When market forces (or the Fed) pushed interest rates up to the legal limits, the system would shut down. It was not that borrowers such as home buyers or contractors were necessarily unwilling to pay higher interest rates—the shutdown came from investors, who refused to provide the money when they knew their returns were artificially depressed by the government ceilings. An investor who held funds in a regulated account at a savings and loan, drawing 5 percent or so, would withdraw his money and move it to another storage place, one that was unregulated and promised a much higher return.

The results could be dramatic. When the Federal Reserve tightened the money supply and pushed up interest rates, thousands and thousands withdrew their funds and the stop valves closed. Money rushed out of financial intermediaries like savings and loan associations, at which point S & L's were unable to make new mortgage loans. When mortgage lending stopped, the housing industry shut down. The declining sales and employment in housing would spread to other sectors, and the Federal Reserve would get the results it wanted—a subsidence of economic activity that moderated price inflation.

These episodes were known as "credit crunches," and a series of them occurred periodically in the late 1960s and early 1970s (known as "disintermediation" to economists, because the process of financial intermediation, the flow of money from investor through lending institution to borrower, was interrupted). The effects could be brutally swift and particularly harsh for the housing industry. Each time a credit crunch developed, the Federal Reserve was denounced by home builders, S & L managers and others for inducing it. The Fed was "choking" their access to credit, they complained, and essentially they were right.

But the credit crunch had two virtues, from the Federal Reserve's point of view. First, it worked (sometimes more severely than the Fed had intended). Second, it worked at relatively low levels of interest rates. If the Fed pushed rates up a notch or two, the flows of lending into certain sectors would begin to stop. Now that the last of the Reg Q interest-rate controls were removed, the supply of funds would continue uninterrupted, but at what price? How high would the Fed have to push interest rates in order to get the desired response from the economy?

"Before, we zapped the housing industry," the former Fed official said. "Now we have to zap the whole economy. That makes Volcker's life a lot more difficult."

The standard economic models presumed that consumers, businesses and bankers would all react predictably to the negative incentives of higher interest rates. Dense mathematical formulas were devoted to describing how x interest-rate increases would produce x restraint among borrowers and buyers—the behavior-modification model of monetary policy. The trouble was, people did not modify their behavior according to the model.

Encouraged by expectations of inflation or driven by their own reckless optimism, borrowers were shattering the old assumptions about how much they would pay for money. People kept borrowing even despite the record rates—most dramatically in the early months of 1980 when the prime rate rose toward 20 percent and credit continued to expand explosively. Higher rates had bite, but not nearly as strong as the economists would have predicted. Household consumers were the most cautious, according to Albert Wojnilower's analysis of the trend. Families were the first to pull back from borrowing at higher rates because they were risking their own well-being. Business executives, a naturally optimistic group, were less prudent than households. Financial managers, in Wojnilower's judgment, were the most incautious of all—willing to continue lending at prices that some borrowers could not possibly pay. If enough borrowers eventually defaulted, then the generous bankers were in trouble too.

Wojnilower described the threat to monetary control:

. . . no amount of deregulation and innovation can enable a financial system to escape the bear hug of a determinedly anti-inflationary monetary policy. But, if key participants in the economy believe that as a result of their ingenuity they as individuals can escape, they make it much harder for a restrictive monetary policy to succeed. They become willing to take greater risks and to bid up interest rates even higher in an effort to outlast each other and the competition. Every rise in interest rates makes it more politically difficult for the government to press home its restrictive policy. And the greater exposure taken by the private sector, the more the Fed's hand may be stayed for fear of touching off an uncontrollable wave of bankruptcies.

The Federal Reserve could not simply let the foolhardy take their lumps, since it was also responsible for "the safety and soundness" of the financial system. If financial institutions, particularly banks, were undermined by their own carefree lending, the Fed would have to pick up the pieces. As lender of last resort, it was supposed to rescue the drowning swimmers, as Wojnilower put it. "Deregulation," he warned, "is like removing the ropes and depth markers and buoys and putting all the responsibility for safety on the lifeguard. It is a game of chicken with the financial survival of our economy." [23]

In less colorful terms, many of the senior Federal Reserve officials shared some of Wojnilower's concern, including Paul Volcker. Their apprehension was never forcefully stated in public. Financial deregulation, after all, was an issue akin to motherhood in the financial community and all Fed officials blessed the general objective. Occasionally, however, Volcker would hint at his misgivings.

"We have devoted a lot of effort, rightly or wrongly, over the past fifteen years . . . to freeing up the markets from the kind of restraint we once had," Volcker told the House Banking Committee. ". . . We are more reliant, in a sense, on interest rates as that cost factor exerting restraint. We don't have the available constraint that we once had and most people count that as a blessing." Did Volcker regard it as a blessing? "Oh, by and large," he answered. "I think that we needed some freeing up here. I get restive about it now and then because it comes out partially in interest rates higher than they otherwise would be." [24]

Over the years, the deregulation question had put Volcker and his predecessors in an awkward position politically. A forthright defense of the regulatory stop valves would have been most difficult, considering that they were under attack from all sides—the disappointed borrowers, the investors and the financial intermediaries that lost their deposits. Instead, the Fed stalled. It endorsed the idea of deregulation, but urged caution in actually doing it. It held the line on the various Reg Q ceilings as long as possible, then one by one discarded them when the pressures for change became too great.

If the Fed was in the back pocket of the major banks, then why did it resist them on financial deregulation? In many ways, the Federal Reserve did resemble the political scientist's definition of a "captive" regulatory agency—one that was beholden to the industry it regulated, anxious to serve its needs first. Yet here was an issue of great importance to the Fed's core constituency of major banks—financial deregulation—and the central bank pulled the other way, at least as long as it dared.

The explanation was that financial deregulation directly threatened the Federal Reserve's own power. It undermined the central bank's ability to deliver on its most basic obligation—to control the overall expansion of credit. The Fed's deepest institutional purpose was to serve as the economy's governor, the wise regulator who kept things from getting out of control. Yet Volcker and other Fed officials doubted that the banking system would do this for itself. The marketplace, they feared, would not moderate the pace of new lending simply by raising the price.

Without supply controls, price was the Fed's only lever. But if borrowers were willing to pay the going rates, however punishing, what was to stop private debt from expanding indefinitely—beyond control of the Fed, perhaps far beyond any reasonable expectation that the new loans could be paid back? Deregulation gave more freedom to the decisions in the private marketplace, but the Federal Reserve was still responsible for maintaining order. If private debt burdens became swollen and widespread failures resulted, the excesses would be attributed to the reckless lenders and borrowers who had made the unsustainable commitments. But the Federal Reserve itself would also be accused of dereliction of duty.

6

THE ROLLER COASTER

The Federal Reserve chairman often seemed deliberately evasive in his answers, which frustrated and angered many members of Congress. Representative Frank Annunzio, a Democrat from Chicago, once offered a sarcastic compliment. "You would make a very excellent prisoner of war," Annunzio told Volcker, "because you wouldn't tell the enemy a thing."[1]

On one question, Paul Volcker was forthright and clear—he did not think credit controls were the answer. Given the inflation-driven explosion of lending and record rates in early 1980, controls would be "beside the point" and "counterproductive," as well as an administrative nightmare. Besides, he pointed out, consumer credit was already declining and mortgage lending already restrictive. What would be the point of imposing new controls on those sectors?

Still, the Fed chairman kept hearing the same question in the early weeks of 1980. The Consumer Price Index was at nearly 17 percent and the prime lending rate was 16 percent and still rising. With its new operating system, the Federal Reserve had been tightening the money supply for four months, but with no obvious effect on the giddy expansion of borrowing in the economy. The Fed's warnings to the banks had not inhibited the rampaging speculation in silver and gold and other commodities. There was a gathering feeling, as Volcker himself said, that things were out of control. The question was put to him by anxious congressmen and even by some leading financiers of Wall Street: why doesn't the government invoke its emergency powers and impose controls to brake the expansion of credit?

"The problems are absolutely horrendous," Volcker explained to the House Banking Committee on February 19,". . . and I would suggest to you that, after all is said and done, controls don't really deal with the basic causes of inflation."

Three weeks later, on March 14, the Federal Reserve Board announced a program of emergency credit controls—supply limitations that covered not only commercial banks but also the unregulated money-market mutual funds and all retail companies that issued credit cards, from Sears, Roebuck to Mobil and Exxon. The banks, whose lending had expanded by more than 17 percent in February, would be limited to 9 percent growth in new credit. Banks would be further inhibited by other provisions that effectively raised the cost of the money they themselves borrowed to fund new loans. All this was accompanied by broad guidelines to banks and other lenders on how they should allocate their loans—another admonition to avoid the froth of corporate take-overs and commodities speculation while providing credit for small businesses, farmers, homeowners and others.

Volcker's earlier hostility to credit controls was doubtless sincere—he did dislike the idea—but the Federal Reserve chairman was not at liberty to reveal the unusual dialogue then under way between himself and the White House. The President wanted to impose controls. He kept pressing Volcker to agree. After weeks of private negotiations with the President and his advisers, the Federal Reserve chairman did not say no.

The idea of controls had first been raised in the President's councils four months earlier, right after the Fed's dramatic policy initiative, when Jimmy Carter heard the gloomy predictions from his economic advisers. By February, their forecasts had come true, and, belatedly, Carter tried to regain the initiative for himself. Volcker, though independent of the President's control, was invited to participate.

In addition to the frightening inflation rate, Jimmy Carter was now threatened by additional skepticism about his economic policies. When the President sent Congress his new budget for the 1981 fiscal year, he promised it would produce a deficit of only $13 billion. The claim was derided, both in Washington and Wall Street, because the Administration simultaneously revised upward its estimate of the deficit for the current fiscal year, 1980—upward to almost $60 billion. Skeptics could not believe Carter's new budget was genuinely austere (though, relatively speaking, it was). For the bond market, this fueled fears of even worse inflation and, as investors fled, bond prices collapsed.

Some of Carter's advisers believed that direct controls might help the Administration thread its way to safer ground for the election season—pushing down the high interest rates and cooling off the economy without forcing it into recession. Charles Schultze, chairman of the Council of Economic Advisers, was not so optimistic. "Given everything that had happened, the oil shocks and so on, the only question, both politically and in economic terms, was how do we limit the damage," Schultze said. "How do we minimize the damage of what's inevitably going to be bad, either through inflation or recession."

As Volcker talked with the White House, a trade-off emerged that embraced their different objectives. The President would draft a new budget, trimming another $13 billion from federal spending. And, at the President's request, the Federal Reserve would impose an assortment of controls on lending. In the course of working out the details, Volcker was used as a kind of emblem of the President's sincerity. The White House advisers included him in meeting after meeting with Cabinet officers, congressional leaders and others, discussing intimate details of which federal programs should be reduced. These were political questions that did not belong to the Federal Reserve chairman, but Volcker's presence at the table was meant to impress the other participants.

As Charles Schultze said:

It's absolutely implicit and not spoken, but it is unusual for the Fed chairman to be involved in these meetings with the President. You can't play that kind of game and then go out and blast the results. Second, there was never a deal explicitly, but Volcker understood that just as Carter was doing things unpleasant for himself, cutting up his own budget, which would alienate the liberal constituencies, so he too, Volcker, would have to do some things he wasn't quite anxious to do.

Volcker was ambivalent. He thought controls on credit cards and retail credit seemed particularly pointless since consumer borrowing was already subsiding. The President insisted that the controls cover credit cards, Volcker was told, because that was something average citizens could understand. It was intended as a unifying political message, not an economic strategy. On the other hand, Volcker figured the controls could be drafted in a way that minimized ill effects and gave him a new opportunity to stiffen the terms for the banks. "I wasn't entirely allergic to some sort of way of telling the banks to slow down their lending, some sort of moral suasion," Volcker said.

Back at the Federal Reserve Board, Volcker's agreement with the President encountered considerable opposition. With the exception of the vice chairman, Fred Schultz, the other governors were unenthusiastic and three were strongly opposed.

Governor Philip Coldwell was opposed, but he was retiring and would not be around to vote against the proposal. Governor Charles Partee was also opposed, though Partee felt mildly embarrassed because, back in 1969 when he was the Fed's research director, he had helped draft the ambiguous Credit Control Act, which empowered the Chief Executive to ask the Fed to impose controls but did not say that the Fed had to obey him.

Henry Wallich politely declined to go along. "There are always good reasons to do a bad thing, something that is convenient and expeditious and avoids the pain," Wallich said. "In the long run, we can adhere to principle, but in the short run it is difficult and so we push the principle off further into the future and choose the less painful course."

When the governors discussed the question, Volcker conceded that, legally, they could refuse Carter's request. But, the chairman asked, do you really want to go against the President?

Wallich was the only one who did. "It's not an easy thing to vote against a President's wishes," Wallich said. "But what are we appointed for? Why are we given these long terms in office? Presumably, it is so that not only the present but the past and the future have some weight in our decisions. In the end, it may be helpful to remind the President that it's not only his present concerns that matter." Wallich voted no.

The Fed's acquiescence on this issue helped define the actual limits of its institutional independence. While in theory the Federal Reserve could ignore a President's wishes, in fact it was reluctant to do so, at least when the conflict was so visible and well defined. Volcker might easily ignore the private kibitzing from the White House on the direction of monetary policy and he regularly did. It was much harder to say no to the President in public.

"You never want a confrontation where a President says, 'Do this' and we say, 'We won't,' " Partee explained. "Good God, that's in extremis."

Once Volcker had the board's consent, he and Fed technicians began drafting the specifics of the controls—designing them to be as loose and innocuous as possible. The restrictions on consumer borrowing and credit cards, for instance, exempted practically every purchase of substance that a family might make—automobiles, furniture and appliances, home-improvement loans and mortgages. The Fed's broad guidelines on credit allocation by banks were merely voluntary. The new reserve burdens on banks and retailers might provide modest restraint but only a marginal impact. The idea, as one draftsman said, was "to throw a little sand in the system," but not to stop it.

When the President and the Federal Reserve chairman announced their initiatives, most of the Fed's officials were confident they had succeeded. They joked among themselves about the many loopholes written into the controls. They were confident that lenders and borrowers would find them. A senior staff economist offered to bet Vice Chairman Schultz that the controls would have virtually no effect. "What we intended was a pretty cosmetic program," Partee said, "and nowhere was it to be more cosmetic than in the area of consumer credit."

On March 14, with the dramatic flourish available to the Presidency, Jimmy Carter announced to the nation that urgent measures were being invoked. "The actions I've outlined involve costs," the President said. "They involve pain. But the cost of acting is far less than the cost of not acting. The temporary pain of inconvenience is far less, for all of us together, than the still worse, permanent pain of constantly rising inflation."[2]

The next day, Volcker held a briefing at the Fed, outlining the complicated limits that would be imposed on lending. Treasury Secretary Miller, CEA Chairman Schultze and other Administration officials held a televised panel discussion to emphasize the seriousness of the new measures. The TV evening news repeated the announcements portentously and displayed credit cards on the television screen—VISA, MasterCard, American Express and others—to dramatize the President's plea: stop borrowing.

For once, Americans got the message. Within days, consumer spending slowed drastically and so did the borrowing by businesses. The White House mailroom was inundated by cut-up credit cards sent by hundreds of citizens to demonstrate their support for the campaign. The President had hoped to capture the average citizen's attention, and he succeeded far too well. If borrowing was suddenly unpatriotic, then so was buying.

The economy collapsed. The recession, long predicted by forecasters, finally began in earnest. But it was not the gradual contraction that many had expected. The loss of economic activity was swift and alarmingly steep. Within three months, the Gross National Product would shrink by 10 percent—the sharpest recession in thirty-five years. For a time, it looked like a free-fall descent.

The Federal Reserve was as surprised as anyone else. The sudden collapse disrupted all its assumptions and launched the Fed's policy makers on a harrowing trip. Through the year, as they struggled to catch up with events, their regulation of the money supply and the economy began to resemble a ride on a roller coaster.

· · ·

Fred Weimer saw Jimmy Carter's message ripple through thousands of Sears stores across the country and concluded it was psychological. Weimer was assistant general credit manager for Sears, one of the nation's largest dispensers of retail credit, and he was amazed by how swiftly Americans reacted to the President's plea.

"The thrust of Carter's message was that it was kind of unpatriotic to use credit cards," Weimer said, "and people responded. We thought it was overkill. The figures already showed the economy turning. We didn't know how bad the controls would be for our sales, although we knew they would be bad."

The Sears network of stores had recorded sales on credit in February that were up 18 percent over the previous year. In March, the credit sales were down 1 percent—and down 8 percent in April and down 11 percent in May. The new reserve requirement that the Fed imposed on retailers offering consumer credit became instantly irrelevant for Sears. Sears did not have to worry about the lid placed on growth—for the next six months its credit sales were shrinking. "Our total company sales were very bad," Weimer said. "You don't make up those credit sales in cash."

For J. C. Penney, the President's announcement was "an absolute nightmare," according to Duncan Muir, manager of public relations. Penney's at first attempted to get in step with the government's credit-tightening campaign by requiring a minimum payment of $200 for long-term loans on large purchases. In the garbled press coverage, it was said that Penney's was allowing customers to use credit cards only if they made purchases of $200 or more.

"I was on the phone for days," Muir said. "Irate customers called. Newspapers called. There was a sharp fallout in sales. We gradually got it straightened out, but it took several months for things to settle down."

Penney's customers not only stopped "charging." Many of them also cut up their charge cards and mailed them into Penney stores. Other regular customers rushed in to pay off their old charge-account balances.

VISA shrank too. The national credit-card company had been expanding robustly, adding more than seven million cardholders in 1979. In a few months, it lost more than 500,000 of them. During subsequent months, VISA's cash advances fell by more than $600 million, nearly 10 percent of its volumes. Credit-card buying declined generally as banks that issued credit cards stopped soliciting new customers. Dozens of retail companies and banks raised the terms for their customers —higher minimum payments, interest rates and other charges. Many of these added costs for borrowers would remain in place permanently, a continuing dividend collected long after the Fed's controls were removed.[3]

Nothing quite like this had ever occurred before. In February, American consumers had $310 billion outstanding in installment loans, a pool of revolving debt that was growing by more than $2 billion a month. In the four months following the Fed's controls, consumers would not only stop taking on new loans, they would also pay off more than $7.4 billion in outstanding loans. The pool was draining.

At the Fed, the harried governors were dealing with thousands of complaints and questions from bankers and retailers and, at the same time, trying to figure out exactly what they had done. The specific controls were demonstrably weak, yet their impact was overwhelming. "We really didn't think we had hit the mule with a two-by-four," Fred Schultz said. "We thought we were using a light switch. The idea was not to make the economy go into the tank—it was supposed to allow the economy to grow but without the credit excesses. Instead, the consumer got it into his head that the government was telling him not to use credit. The darned economy just fell off the cliff."

As the governors heard the dramatic stories from retailers about plummeting credit sales, many of them also concluded that the source of the sudden collapse was psychological—driven by a powerful medium that was beyond the control of central bankers, television.[4]

Federal Reserve officials, in any case, dismissed the episode as a fluke—a bizarre conjunction between the popular influence of television and the obscure regulatory powers of the central bank. They did not pause to consider whether the experience ought to have taught them something about how to influence the nation's economic behavior. Afterward, many technical studies were conducted by the Fed on the financial complications created by the 1980 recession, but it made no attempt to understand the public psychology of the event.

Yet two back-to-back events posed an illuminating contrast in how the Federal Reserve communicated its objectives to the American public. On October 6, when Volcker launched his major offensive, the announcement had been couched in the obscure language of finance. Not surprisingly, very few citizens who were not financiers understood what he meant. Not grasping the significance, the general public and even sophisticated corporate executives did not change their outlook or behavior. In March, when credit controls were announced, the language was blunt and melodramatic and the message itself became the medium for dramatic results (more dramatic than anyone intended). The Federal Reserve's new credit controls were purposely weak, even meaningless compared to the fundamental policy shift it had undertaken on October 6. But this time the government spoke clearly and ordinary citizens responded. The Federal Reserve, in other words, paid a price for the cloak of mystery it maintained around its policies. The Fed, it seemed, might have more influence on how private citizens reacted to its economic policies if it spoke to people in words they could understand.

Jimmy Carter earned an unpleasant distinction. "For the first time in history," as Henry Reuss complained, "a Democratic President put the economy in recession." And in an election year, barely eight months before the voters would decide whether Carter deserved a second term.

In the classic manner of business cycles, the downturn fed on itself. When the demand for goods falls off, the producers find their backlog of unsold products growing and so they cut back on production. The laid-off workers lose income and the lost income further reduces the demand for goods and leads to still more unemployment. The only difference this time was the speed of the contraction. In the second quarter of 1980, the Gross National Product shrank by $39 billion dollars in real terms, adjusted for inflation. For the past four years, real GNP had grown $60 to $70 billion a year. Industrial production decreased by more than 8 percent. Unemployment rose from 6.3 percent in March to 7.8 percent by July, an additional 1.6 million people who were out of work. Real disposable income per capita—the best measure of what average citizens are earning after inflation and taxes —grew weakly in 1979, but by the spring of 1980, it was shrinking. Real per capita income fell from $4,503 to $4,435 in the 1980 recession —wiping out the gains of the previous year. In a nation where everyone came to expect steady progress in his or her economic status, the average worker was, in effect, pushed back to 1978.

Jimmy Carter, naturally, suffered most in public esteem. The President was winning his struggle against Senator Edward M. Kennedy for the Democratic nomination, but as the recession took hold, he began losing primaries in large industrial states, the heart of electoral power for the Democratic Party. Carter's second effort to produce an austere budget that would reassure financial markets about inflation was turned into another argument against him—more evidence of his inconstancy as a leader. When Federal Reserve officials moved quickly to start rescinding the main elements of the credit-control program, Carter's White House advisers did not object.

The Fed, in less obvious ways, was also under attack. The thousands of small independent home builders across the country held Volcker and the governors personally responsible for wrecking them with high interest rates. Starts of new housing construction averaged

1.7 million units for 1979, well below the industry's potential, but 1980 was much worse. In May, housing starts fell to an annual rate of 940,000. From December to April, the monthly bankruptcies of businesses rose from 2,394 to 3,756 and many of the failed firms were home builders.

Hundreds of the contractors staged an informal protest—they put postage stamps on blocks of two-by-fours and bricks and mailed them to the officers of the Federal Reserve. The lumber and bricks were supposed to remind the Fed of all the new homes that would not be built because of its monetary policy.[5] Like other public officials, the Federal Reserve governors were accustomed to nasty mail, but now the letters became more numerous and abusive, including threats of personal harm aimed at the chairman.

A television interviewer, Jim Lehrer, put the question bluntly to Volcker: "Are you willing to accept parenthood for this recession?"

"No, I'll claim no paternity," the chairman replied. "I don't even like the question being asked that way. You know, if it has a father, any single father, and it never does, I suspect inflation and the distortions that arise from inflation are the father."[6]

Still, that begged the question: what made the bubble finally burst? Was it the Federal Reserve's October tightening, gradually forcing a recession with the record-high interest rates and scarce credit? Or was it the economic trauma created by the credit-controls program? Perhaps it was both.

"You could argue, of course, that the credit controls weren't needed at all," said Henry Wallich, who had opposed them. "The economy was already slowing down. Just give it time. Why should we do this overkill?"

That argument looked more persuasive in hindsight than it did at the moment the controls were introduced. Subsequent accounting by the National Bureau of Economic Research, which tracked business cycles precisely, concluded that the economy's growth actually peaked in January and economic activity began to subside gradually two months before the credit controls were announced. Thus, the sudden shock effect of the credit controls most likely converted a gradual contraction into a sharp and deep decline.

The residual political memory was quite different, however. The Fed's credit controls, it was widely assumed, were an unworkable disaster and Jimmy Carter was to blame. The reality was that, if anything, the credit controls had worked too well.

While the economy was rapidly deteriorating, Paul Volcker faced an ancillary crisis—the collapse of the silver bubble. Speculators led by the Hunt brothers of Texas had driven the price to a peak above $52 an ounce in January. When the bubble burst and prices started subsiding rapidly, the speculators were in trouble and so were the banks and brokerages that had financed their silver buying. As the value of silver declined, the lenders had to demand more cash or collateral from the Hunts to support the loans. If silver fell far enough, not even the billionaire family from Dallas could come up with the ante in time. In the extreme, the loans would be defaulted and the lenders would be left holding a lot of silver that wasn't worth much in a collapsing market.

The moment of crisis came on March 27, remembered in commodity markets as "silver Thursday." A top executive of Bache Halsey, second-largest brokerage in the nation, had phoned Volcker the day before and warned that if the price collapsed further, Bache would not survive. It had lent more than $200 million to the Hunts, and the value of the silver collateral it was holding was shrinking everyday. On silver Thursday, silver fell in value by one-third—from $15.80 to $10.80 an ounce. Volcker and other federal bank regulators began a series of hurried catch-up meetings to determine the extent of the Hunts' borrowing and how seriously the financial system was threatened. Some of the regulators feared they might be on the brink of a historic panic, not unlike the crash of stock-market speculation that launched the Great Depression in 1929.

The initial rumors and misinformation made the banks' exposure sound even larger than it was, but it was still substantial. All told, twelve U.S. banks, the American branches of four foreign banks and five brokerage houses had provided the Hunts' silver-buying venture with more than $800 million in loans—equivalent to almost 10 percent of all the bank lending in the country during the previous two months.

The Federal Reserve's admonitions against speculative lending had been ignored, nor had it used its regulatory powers to actually stop the silver lending. But Volcker did not dwell on that point now. The new question was whether a further slide in silver prices would bring down any major banks. First National of Chicago, ninth-largest in the country, was most vulnerable, having lent the Hunts a total of $175 million either directly or indirectly. If silver prices fell to as low as $7 an ounce, the value of the collateral held by the banks would be worth less than the loans they had made.

On Friday, the silver markets paused in the descent and the price stabilized long enough to allow Bache and some others to sell off silver collateral without absorbing fatal losses. Then a new crisis developed: to augment their price speculation, the Hunts had bought futures contracts for silver totaling 19 million ounces from Engelhard, the giant international minerals firm. Futures were normally used as a hedge against sudden price changes, an agreement to pay a certain price six or nine months later when the commodities were delivered. But futures could also be a high-risk gamble—betting that the price would be higher in the future. The Hunts lost their bet. Delivery was due on Monday, March 31, and Engelhard was demanding cash for its silver—$665 million.

If the Hunts defaulted on Monday, the price of silver would fall drastically again and the entire accumulation of speculative bank loans would doubtless crash with it. While $800 million was a lot of money, the dozen major banks and the foreign ones were large enough to survive a loss of that magnitude. What the regulators most feared was the aftershock—the possibility that such a spectacular one-day debacle would set off a general panic among investors, pulling their huge deposits out of the exposed banks like First Chicago and threatening their liquidity.

In that event, the Federal Reserve had the power, of course, to bail out the threatened bank or banks with unlimited advances from the Discount window—in effect, replacing the lost deposits with government loans until confidence in the banks was restored. That remedy would have been politically awkward, given what was happening to the rest of the American economy. And the Federal Reserve chairman did not wish to find out what would happen if he stood aside and let the banks take their losses.

Instead, Volcker gave his blessing to another solution. That weekend, quite by coincidence, the Association of Reserve City Bankers was gathering in Boca Raton, Florida, bringing together the leaders of all the vulnerable banks and others who might help out. Volcker attended too. On Sunday evening, the bankers held an all-night bargaining session with the Hunts and Engelhard representatives. The negotiations led ultimately to the terms for a private bailout—a new loan of $1.1 billion from thirteen banks which would extinguish the Hunts' old debts, give them the means to settle with Engelhard and stretch out their obligations over ten years.

Paul Volcker was down the hall in another hotel room and the bankers kept him informed hour by hour of their progress. In the end, with certain provisos, he blessed the transaction—a crucial assurance for the banks. If Volcker had not consented, the major banks would have found it difficult to participate, perhaps impossible. After all, the Fed had just imposed new credit controls on the nation and the new loan package for the Hunts directly violated at least the spirit of that program, in effect, rolling over loans that were made purely for speculation. Technically, the Fed did not bail out the Hunt brothers and the banks. No government money was at stake. But, practically speaking, Volcker saved them by granting a huge exception to the rules he had just imposed on the American economy.[7]

Although Governor Henry Wallich was not happy with Volcker's handling of the situation, he did not challenge the chairman's decisions as the crisis manager. "Suppose a large firm had gone bust," Wallich said. "It wouldn't have been the end of the world. It would have been a great tragedy, but it would have been a disaster on a smaller scale. The argument against doing anything was: let the bankers and the brokers take their lumps."

Philip Coldwell, who had just retired from the board, resented the bailout. "I was very unhappy with the chairman that he let Bunker Hunt off the hook," Coldwell said. "Hunt clearly was trying to corner silver, and I thought he should pay the price. In my very simplistic way of looking at it, I didn't see anything wrong with the banks' paying the price too."

As details of the silver bailout became public, Volcker was grilled again and again at hostile congressional inquiries, led most effectively by Representative Benjamin Rosenthal, chairman of a subcommittee on government operations. Why had the Fed been so blind to what was going on? And why had it rushed to the rescue? Volcker provided explanations and endured many harangues, but the congressional anger produced a misleading public impression. The critics were tenacious and sincere, but Volcker well understood that these attacks were less meaningful than the heavy press coverage made them seem. Senators and representatives with much more influence privately supported him. Indeed, the congressional delegations from Texas and Illinois had pleaded with Volcker to save their troubled banks. Volcker was not defying Congress, as it appeared, but cooperating with the private wishes of its leading members.[8]

This illusion was often the case in the relationship between Congress and the Federal Reserve: the public heard the angry critics and perhaps assumed that the Federal Reserve was seriously threatened. The Fed willingly took the heat, confident in the knowledge that private, unspoken support from Congress would ultimately protect it. Well-publicized congressional attacks on the Federal Reserve often had the quality of a charade.

In the silver crisis, Volcker made a distinction common to central bankers but offensive to many outside the financial world. His perspective expressed the Federal Reserve's central purpose: rescuing a major financial institution was in the public interest, but government bailouts for other kinds of private enterprises were wrong. A major banking failure could set off a wave of larger and unpredictable consequences, other bank failures and perhaps a genuine panic that would destabilize the financial system. But the bankruptcy of a major manufacturer or retailer was a limited event, a natural consequence of free-market forces. People would lose money, workers would be out of jobs, but the system would adjust dynamically and create new enterprises, new jobs. If government came to the rescue of every failing business, where would it end?[9]

Given his financier's perspectives, Volcker would see no contradiction in the fact that he promoted a rescue for the major banks that had ignored his directive (and, ultimately, for their customers, the Hunt brothers) while he simultaneously opposed a government bailout for the Chrysler Corporation. The central bank followed a selective definition of free enterprise: economic stability required that banks and other large financial firms must be saved from their own folly. But when other kinds of businesses failed, that was considered a normal, healthy feature of free-enterprise capitalism.

The Federal Reserve, in fact, had the power to lend directly to nonbanking corporations that were in trouble, but it had always refused to do so. Though it was not widely known, the Fed had already turned down Chrysler before the auto company went to Congress for help. Since 1935, the law had given the Federal Reserve extraordinary authority to make special loans to any individual or institution, public or private, in distress. The law required only "unusual and exigent circumstances." Except for a few instances during the Depression, the Fed always said no to such financially desperate parties, rejecting pleas from Midwestern grain farmers, Lockheed Corporation and the City of New York, among others. As lender of last resort, the Fed would stretch quite far to avert failure in financial markets, but it couldn't do the same for anyone in the productive economy.

Simultaneously, the Federal Reserve was acquiescing to risky behavior in another sector of bank lending—one many times larger and more threatening than the speculative loans in silver. Over a period of years, the leading U.S. banks had been committing tens of billions in new loans to the less-developed nations of the world, particularly Latin America. The biggest names in American banking were becoming overexposed. Yet the Federal Reserve did not compel these banks to pull back or even to moderate their loan commitments. From time to time, the Fed did issue mild warnings, usually in private. Most bankers brushed them aside.

At one private session with executives of money-center banks, Paul Volcker expressed his own worries about the expanding foreign loans and urged the bankers to show more caution. "Walt Wriston was first to react," Vice Chairman Schultz recalled. "In essence, Wriston said: 'Mr. Chairman, I disagree with you. These international loans are the best loans I've got. I've had few defaults on them and my profit margin is very good.' Paul said: 'That's true for the past. I'm worried about the future.' "

Central bankers did worry a lot. But the Federal Reserve did very little else, in an effective and timely fashion, to force the banks to behave more prudently. The bankers' optimism and the Fed's lenient attitude were, little by little, setting the stage for world financial crisis.

In April, as commercial banks made their weekly reports to the Federal Reserve, the governors watched the incoming numbers with some amazement. For months, they had struggled with mixed success to slow down the runaway growth of the money supply. Now money was disappearing.

Week by week, as each commercial bank reported its currency and demand deposits, Fed economists calculated the total for the entire system. That figure was the basic measure of the American money supply—the aggregate known as M-1. Instead of growing, M-1 was abruptly getting smaller.

Money was vanishing—and at a very rapid rate. In mid-March, there was $393 billion in M-1. By the last week of May, there was only $376 billion. This did not require any shredding of $100 bills or melting down of coins; most of the money supply, after all, did not exist as cash in people's pockets. Most of the nation's money existed merely as numbers in the account books at banks—the total balances of checking accounts. In a practical sense, more than $17 billion of America's money ceased to exist.

The Federal Reserve had not intended anything like this. Back in February, the twelve voting members of the Federal Open Market Committee had been distressed that, after some months of moderate growth, the money supply was again expanding at the alarming rate of nearly 13 percent. They agreed they must impose more restraint—by providing less generous quantities of reserves to the banking system —and the FOMC set a growth target of 4 to 6.5 percent for M-1. Instead, M-1 was flat in March—no growth at all. By April, as the Federal Reserve watched helplessly, the money supply was shrinking at an annualized rate of 17 percent.[10]

The tumultuous turn of events created a policy crisis for the central bank that would haunt the governors for many years. It also put the American economy through a harrowing series of ups and downs. How much should the FOMC increase the supply of reserves to compensate for the abrupt decline in money? If it did not do enough, it was possible to imagine the real economy contracting further and further in a dangerous spiral. If the Fed overdid it, the banking system could suddenly be awash with more money than the economy needed. The oversupply would drive down interest rates rapidly and perhaps restimulate the economy—like a jump start for a stalled car. All these questions would be argued among the governors and Reserve Bank presidents. Volcker's new monetarist system for control, adopted six months earlier, encountered its first severe test.

But what made the money disappear? Despite popular clichés, the money supply, in fact, was "controlled" by many forces, simultaneously. And no single agent controlled it absolutely, including the Federal Reserve. To appreciate this essential point, one could visualize the money supply as the water in a reservoir, the metaphor suggested by John Maynard Keynes in *A Treatise on Money*. The central bank's function, Keynes explained, was to maintain the supply in the reservoir "at any required level by pouring enough water into it." Yet, as anyone could grasp, there were obviously other factors that could change the level of the reservoir "besides how much water is poured in—for example, the natural rainfall, evaporation, leakage and the habits of the users of the system." [11]

The Federal Reserve, in the same sense, was constantly adjusting the flow through its own valves—pumping or draining— in order to offset the competing influences that were also raising or lowering the water level. This was the daily essence of Fed operations—trying to keep the reservoir as close as possible to the level that the Federal Open Market Committee had decided was desirable for the economy. It was an imperfect science, surrounded by random complications, and constantly correcting itself for past mistakes or new fluctuations. In this contest, a "miss" of a billion dollars or so was close enough to be celebrated as a bull's-eye.

The money that ceased to exist was, in fact, destroyed by everyone —humble consumers, small businesses, banks and major corporations, the vast variety of economic players, millions of them. People paid off their debts—that was one fundamental cause. When the recession began in earnest, compounded by the public's shock reaction to credit controls, millions of consumers not only stopped their new borrowing, but they also rushed to pay off old bank loans or charge accounts. This process extinguished money because it reversed the magical way in which bank lending created money in the first place. When a customer paid off his bank loan, the bank erased the numbers on both sides of its ledger—the loan disappeared and so did the demand deposit from which the customer had drawn the money.

In normal circumstances, of course, millions of borrowers paid off old loans every week, theoretically destroying money, but the banking system was also constantly replacing them with new loan customers —and new money. When the real economy was expanding, both consumers and producers needed additional credit as well as additional money for the expanded universe of transactions. Credit and the money supply grew steadily together. From week to week, the money totals ebbed and flowed in unremarkable degrees. One week, the Fed might report that the money supply declined by $1.5 billion. The following week, M-1 might grow by $2.7 billion. But these fluctuations averaged out over time and normally in a steady, upward direction.

In April, the normal relationship between credit and money was dramatically disrupted. Millions of citizens and businesses paid off their old debts, but the banks could not find enough new borrowers to replace them. With the economy sliding swiftly into recession, neither consumers nor commercial enterprises needed additional loans, at least not enough to make up for the ones being retired. Each week, then, the banking system erased billions of dollars in credit from its "assets"—and also erased the same amounts from its "liabilities," the demand deposits. The banking system's "liabilities," when added to outstanding currency, make up the basic component of the money supply known as M-1. So it was shrinking too.

"The money supply," as Fred Schultz put it, "dropped like a stone."

Private citizens and private businesses were shrinking M-1 in another way as well—simply by moving their money. If a small business, for instance, decided to reduce the daily cash it held in an interest-free checking account and move the funds to a time or savings account that paid interest, the shift would subtract from M-1 and add to one of the broader monetary aggregates, M-2, which included these less-liquid accounts. This did not "destroy" money in the fundamental sense, but it did shrink the M-1 pool, the money available for immediate spending and the Federal Reserve's principal measure of the money supply. If money was fleeing from M-1, that created a serious quandary for the Fed policy makers, who were trying to keep the money supply on a steady path. The assumed relationship between M-1 and economic activity was rendered temporarily inoperative.

In April, over the span of a few weeks, millions of bank customers apparently made the same decision—to get out of money and park their financial assets somewhere else. The driving force was the extraordinary peak in short-term interest rates—making it much more costly for someone to let his money sit idle in an interest-free checking account. The Federal Funds rate, for instance, exceeded 19 percent.

The three-month T-bill, another good measure of short-term returns, peaked above 15 percent. Millions of people moved their checking deposits to where they could capitalize on the opportunity.

Monetary economists disagreed among themselves about which of these two causes—the rapid retirement of debt or the massive shift out of checking accounts—was primarily responsible for the collapse of M-1. Like many arguments in economics, it was not a question that noneconomists needed to resolve in an either-or fashion. Either way, the money collapse was an instance where private economic behavior really was adapting to incentives created by the Federal Reserve, but the behavior modification was not working at all as the Fed policy makers had intended. Instead, it created a new question for them: if M-1 was abnormally low, how could they confidently know what the right level would be?

In Keynes's reservoir, the waters were always roiled and choppy, giving off confusing signals. Sometimes, the water level heaved and tossed so violently that not even the reservoir keepers were sure what was happening.

In theory, the Fed policy makers knew exactly what to do. The answers were provided by the new monetarist operating system the Federal Open Market Committee had adopted on October 6   providing "automatic stabilization" for the money supply by tracking the money aggregates instead of interest rates. If M-1 growth exceeded the target range they had set for it, that meant they must tighten up on the reserves the Fed supplied to the banking system and bring M-1 back down. If the money supply was below its target range, then the Federal Open Market Committee would pump up bank reserves and stimulate money growth. In theory, the approach was continuously self-correcting.

In practice, Volcker and the Federal Open Market Committee were about to commit a grave error—one that would undermine all they were trying to accomplish on price inflation and also destabilize the American economy. When they gathered for their regular meeting on April 22, the operating system called for a swift reversal of the hydraulics—start pumping in more reserves until the shrinking money aggregates revived and stabilized. The worriers on the FOMC were not convinced it would work so smoothly.

Their concern boiled down to this: how far, how fast should they let interest rates fall? The Federal Funds rate had already dropped a full percentage point in the previous two weeks, though it was still very high by normal standards, about 18 percent. If the Fed followed its automatic operating system too rigidly, it might drive rates down too swiftly—and send the wrong message to everyone, both financial markets and the real economy.

Several committee members expressed their fears in the FOMC minutes: " . . . if a large decline in interest rates were to occur over the next few weeks, it was likely to be perceived by some market participants . . . as an easing of monetary policy and could have very undesirable repercussions on inflationary psychology and on the dollar in foreign-exchange markets."

In other words, if the Fed let interest rates fall too precipitously, the skeptics of Wall Street might well conclude the central bank was throwing in the towel in its avowed struggle against inflation—and, instead, trying to rescue the economy from recession during the presidential election season. The chairman, supported by a comfortable majority, wanted to take that chance. If the Fed was too stringent, it faced an opposite risk—making the sharp contraction even worse than it appeared.

Among those arguing against Volcker's position was a new member of the Federal Open Market Committee and one who on most issues would be the chairman's natural ally and collaborator. He was Anthony Solomon, the newly installed president of the New York Federal Reserve Bank. Having lately left a sub-Cabinet post in the Carter Administration, a self-made millionaire of liberal disposition, Solomon might have been expected to take the side for easing credit rapidly. The gathering recession, after all, directly threatened his President's re-election. Solomon, instead, had been shaken by his experience in the Carter government. He felt strongly that only the Federal Reserve could restore order and stability to the economy.

"I've changed over the years," Solomon said. "I have the same liberal social values I grew up with, but I realized over the years that some of my bleeding-heart, knee-jerk policies in the economic area were shortsighted and not good for the country. I realized that we need a sense of discipline."

Tony Solomon's background was different from the others. The son of Lithuanian Jewish immigrants, he grew up in Arlington, New Jersey, where his father for a time was a successful real-estate developer. "He went broke in the Depression," Solomon remembered. "He and my mother worked ten years to pay off all their debts on mortgages. In those days, a developer signed personally for them. He lost all his properties, then eventually wound up with some small business ventures, two restaurants and a cocktail lounge."

His humble origins were striking because anyone who met Solomon might easily have assumed he was the product of a privileged background. He was more urbane in manner than the financial economists or bankers he worked with and more catholic in his intellectual interests. His delicate goatee, going gray, and the melancholy in his eyes made him appear contemplative, like a bookish scholar who had wandered into the high-powered world of finance. Solomon and his wife collected rare art from around the world, and he was himself a serious sculptor. As a bright young student on scholarship, Solomon studied economics at the University of Chicago and Harvard, then, after the war, started a business in dehydrated foods in Mexico. Ten years later, making lots of money but bored, Solomon sold the enterprise to General Foods and began an in-and-out career in government, serving Democratic Administrations in important posts in the State Department and Treasury.

"The change in me came during the Carter Administration," Solomon said, "as I saw the incredible amateurism of a liberally inclined economic policy and the wishful thinking that inflation wouldn't keep going up, the silliness of stimulating the economy when unemployment was already falling, the refusal to tighten monetary policy when inflation was the danger. There was an enormous amount of amateurish, wishful thinking on the liberal side."

Solomon and Volcker were like-minded and had worked closely on various issues for years, but at his very first meeting the New York Fed president disagreed with the Federal Reserve chairman's analysis.

I was dismayed by the potential volatility [Solomon said]. Because we were too tied to M-1, we had to increase reserves rapidly. I thought it was ridiculous to follow the aggregates that slavishly—to let the Federal Funds rate fall drastically was absurd. However, Volcker's position was in the majority. He is always able to command a majority. He has to compromise sometimes, but he basically prevails. Volcker admitted that there was a risk. Nobody can be 100 percent sure. If it were black and white, our job would be easy. He recognized the danger, but he still felt the balance of considerations meant easing.

An aide at the New York Fed said Solomon kept pressing Volcker for more flexibility on the operating system and thought he had convinced him, but when they got into the meetings, Volcker was reluctant to abandon the new rules. "Volcker was the one who was going to have to do the explaining when we were attacked for abandoning our policy," the aide said.

Two arguments compelled the majority toward Volcker's position. First, if the Fed did not conscientiously follow the signals of its own new operating method, that would swiftly become apparent to the discerning Fed watchers on Wall Street. The word would soon go forth that, once again, the Federal Reserve had backed away from its promises. The financial markets had experienced ten years of rising disappointment with the Fed's inconstancy; another sudden lurch in policy would further undermine the central bank's damaged credibility.

The second argument was the recession and its unknown dimensions. For at least three quarters, the Federal Reserve Board's economics staff had been forecasting a moderate contraction and it hadn't occurred. Now that recession was finally here, it didn't look mild at all. Sales and production were falling off so sharply that the staff economists adjusted their outlook. The recession, they now thought, would be larger and longer than anticipated.

"A continued shortfall in monetary growth and persistence of relatively high interest rates could exacerbate recessionary forces in the economy," the committee majority warned in the FOMC minutes. It was one thing for the Federal Reserve to do its duty in an election season and encourage the economy to contract. It would be quite another thing to make the recession worse than it had to be.

"That was a big factor in the decision," Solomon said. "Obviously any Administration in an election year is worried about recession, but I wasn't aware of any communications from the White House."

When the debate ended and the roll was called, the only dissenting vote was cast by Henry Wallich. The Federal Open Market Committee agreed to a policy directive that would allow aggressive injections of new reserves and declining interest rates. For months, the FOMC had set a very loose range for the Federal Funds rate—allowing it to fluctuate by as much as seven percentage points—but the wide range did not matter because the rate was always bumping against the upper limit. Now the committee adjusted the range downward slightly but kept it loose. Depending on market conditions, the Fed Funds rate would be allowed to swing up or down between 13 and 19 percent.

Wallich feared that the rate might plummet from the top of the range to the bottom rather swiftly, pulling other short-term interest rates down with it and restimulating the economy before the inflationary influences were extinguished. "I favored considerably less decline in interest rates," he explained. "I wanted to follow the operating method more rigorously on the upside than on the downside. I saw no virtue in driving interest rates into the ground and then have a resurgence later that would force us to tighten again."

As the most ardent hawk, Wallich was used to making contrary arguments and used to losing. Other committee members regarded him fondly, but also with faint derision. "Henry" was the old-fashioned gentleman among them, unfailingly polite and principled, but also stuck like a broken record—predictably repeating himself regardless of circumstances. Throughout 1980, Henry Wallich would cast dissenting votes nine times—almost every time the Federal Open Market Committee held a meeting. He always voted for tighter money.

It's not a pleasant thing to have to keep dissenting [he said in a sorrowful tone]. It makes one quite useless to dissent so often. Your effect on the others is obviously not through your vote itself, because you lost. Your effect may be because of what you said at the meeting, by persuading others to come along and form a new majority. One dissents less often than you think you should. After all, you're a member of a group and you want to get along with the other members. To be a constant dissenter is a fruitless thing.

Two weeks later, on May 6, Paul Volcker hurriedly convened the voting members of the Federal Open Market Committee for a special meeting by telephone conference call. The money collapse was now in full progress, and the Fed's Open Market Desk in New York was furiously trying to brake it—pumping in more bank reserves by buying government securities and creating new money to offset what was disappearing. With shrinking demand and expanding supply, interest rates "fell like a stone too," as Volcker said. The Federal Funds rate dropped by more than five percentage points in a two-week span, from around 18 percent to below 13 percent. On the morning of May 6, the Fed Funds rate was trading below the bottom limit that the Federal Open Market Committee had just set for it on April 22. The Fed was in danger of losing control.

The Open Market Desk in New York needed new instructions from the FOMC. Peter Sternlight said his desk operators could follow the reserve strategy dictated by the declining money supply and keep injecting more reserves, or they could follow the target range set for the Federal Funds rate, tightening up the supply of bank reserves enough to get the rate back up to 13 percent. They could not do both. The new operating system—following the ups and downs of M-1—was in head-on collision with the Federal Reserve's old disposition to manage the level of interest rates.

Under the circumstances, the chairman proposed that they follow the signals from the monetary aggregate and let interest rates fall further. This would require a telephone vote from the ten FOMC members who were on the line, authorizing a lower range for the Federal Funds rate. The Open Market Desk would be instructed to let the interest rate fall as low as 10.5 percent.

Volcker prevailed, but he encountered more resistance on this vote,

7 to 3. Wallich dissented again, arguing that the Federal Funds rate should be kept at 13 percent and allowed to go down no further. Tony Solomon and Roger Guffey, president of the Kansas City Federal Reserve Bank, were willing to allow some decline, but not as drastic as Volcker proposed.

"Everyone else wanted to ease," Solomon said. "The bank presidents formed a little monetarist clique and they believed in following the monetarist aggregates. Then there are people like Teeters and Partee who were not monetarists but were worried about the recession. They wanted stimulus for the economy."

The rate of inflation was subsiding but still in double digits. If interest rates fell too far, below 10 percent, there was the danger of re-creating the condition of negative real interest rates that had existed in 1979—investors losing more value due to inflation than they gained from interest. Negative interest rates created a potent incentive for people to start borrowing heavily again. Going into debt would once again become a cheap hedge against inflation.

None of the policy makers could be certain how fast the public might react, but Volcker and the majority believed the response to lower rates would lag many months behind the decline. If, however, the public reacted quickly, the Fed could moderate any upsurge in borrowing by tightening again. Tony Solomon was not so sanguine:

My concern was that we didn't know the lags and, therefore, we faced the danger of a real roller coaster. You go too high with interest rates and suddenly it's moving the other way and you are going down. Then it switches on you again and it's suddenly going back up. I kept pushing for decreasing the automaticity of the aggregate targeting. No theory is going to help you decide how much is too much. On the downside, you are pushing into negative interest rates. On the upside, it was hard to judge what was too much.

In Henry Wallich's thinking, the dizzying volatility was the "pact with the devil" he had warned against—the very consequences he predicted when Paul Volcker first proposed the monetarist system the previous autumn. In theoretical terms, Wallich felt vindicated. The policy dilemma was an inevitable outcome of trying to target the fluctuations of reserves precisely while ignoring the impact on interest rates. In his judgment, this was a fundamental flaw in monetarism that its many advocates ignored or denied. As he explained:

There are only two things we can peg, interest rates or reserves. I've always believed that whichever of the two things you don't peg will move around rather drastically. If you peg reserves, interest rates will move more drastically. If you peg interest rates, then the money supply will move more. I never believed what the monetarists believe—that if you stabilize the money supply, you stabilize interest rates. If you stabilize one, you will probably destabilize the other. The supply can be held stable, but the demand always varies—so interest rates are very volatile.[12]

Anyone who has ever flown a kite on a windy day might grasp imaginatively the relationship of supply and demand and price that Wallich was describing. In a high wind, the kite will bounce around the sky erratically as long as the string is held taut. Yet if one lets out lots of slack on the string, the kite will stabilize and remain stationary even though the winds continue. Something similar was happening with the money supply and interest rates. If the Fed tried to hold the string taut on its money supply, interest rates gyrated like a kite— blown back and forth by the varying winds of demand. It is a simple law of algebra: if an equation has three variables and you hold one of them constant, the other two will fluctuate in direct response to each other.

Monetarists would probably reject the kite metaphor. The variability of demand, they would say, is the same old excuse the Fed has always trotted out when it lost control. Besides, the monetarist critics complained, the Federal Reserve had still not succeeded in its stated objective—producing a stable, steady growth rate for the money supply. M-1 was bouncing around like a kite too.

With concurrence from the White House, the Fed began in mid-May to dismantle, one by one, the credit-control rules it had imposed only two months before. By July, the last of the provisions would be lifted, but, meanwhile, the "free fall" in economic activity, money supply and interest rates continued and without any clear evidence that the Fed's countermeasures were having much impact.

The Fed kept pumping furiously. During April, the Open Market Desk at the New York Fed had added reserves at an annual rate of 14 percent. In May, still waiting anxiously for some response from the economy, the Federal Reserve pumped in reserves at a truly stunning pace—an annualized increase of 48 percent in what was called non-borrowed reserves. The May open-market operations added an extraordinary $5.4 billion to the government securities held in the Fed's portfolio. One Reserve Bank president complained:

Volcker panicked. He was completely wrong. He was easing too far too fast. When it got down to negative interest rates, I said that's too goddamned far. The inflation rate was about 10 percent and the Federal Funds rate fell to 8 percent. He was panicked by the swings in the economy, the sudden collapse touched off by credit controls. It was the stupidest thing to do, but we did it.

By the May 20 meeting, Volcker agreed he must compromise a bit on the automatic prescriptions of his monetarist system. But now he drew dissent from the other side—two FOMC members who complained that by restraining the decline in interest rates even modestly, the committee was not faithfully following the operating system it had adopted. The dissenters made an odd couple, because they were coming from opposite ends of the ideological spectrum represented on the Federal Open Market Committee. Governor Chuck Partee was an old Keynesian liberal worried about the rising unemployment of the recession. Larry Roos, president of the St. Louis Fed, was the monetarist stalwart who always defended the pure monetarist approach against the pragmatic compromises. Both of them argued that the Federal Funds rate should be allowed to fall as far as the market forces dictated.

I've always been most concerned that we should avoid making the Big Mistake [Partee said]. There is always going to be a lot of fussing around the edges about what the right policy should be, and that will affect the economy—maybe. But when you make the Big Mistake, then the books are written about what the Federal Reserve did to the economy. The big mistakes usually occur when you hold to a policy too long—you tighten and stay tight in order to fight inflation and you are reluctant to let interest rates come down until inflation has gone away. What most bothers me is that we may have a bias on the high side.

So Partee argued that if the Fed was going to follow the money aggregates to tighten credit and raise interest rates, then it should stick to the same rule when interest rates were falling, even if that meant rates that were temporarily negative.

"What Partee was saying spoke very directly to Volcker's concern about what this might do to the Fed's credibility," a committee aide said. "Partee argued that it was too easy to say, 'Okay, we tried it, now let's go back to the old system—judgment calls.'"

Larry Roos, who had been so pleased when Volcker's monetarist system was adopted in October, was now increasingly skeptical about the sincerity of his colleagues on the FOMC. "I believe there should be a consistent path of money growth," he said. "When money was growing too quickly, I dissented. When it was growing too slowly, I dissented for consistency's sake."

Roos was so consistent, in fact, that other committee members found his repetitious monetarist speeches faintly amusing. A senior staff official said:

Roos's approach was to regard the October 1979 technique as the victory of the monetarists. He would say: "Now we have finally seen the light and it's my role to point out to you that what you're dong here today is a violation of that policy. You can't do that. You told people you were going to follow the money supply and I'm here to make sure you do it."

After a while, others snickered.

What a game little guy Roos is [the senior staff official said]. Volcker was always polite with him, but the others were hooting at him. He would go in there, every meeting, with the monetarist line prepared for him by Anatole Balbach [research director at the St. Louis Fed], and he would put his head down and recite it. It got to the point later where the committee members would literally laugh at him. Never Volcker, but the others laughed in his face. Larry would smile and plow on.

Several of the other Reserve Bank presidents shared Roos's monetarist perspective, but they were less aggressive in pushing it. Roos attributed this to the lopsided power relationship between the Board of Governors and the twelve Reserve Banks. The chairman and governors in Washington had final approval over the individual operating budgets of the Reserve Banks. They also could veto salary increases that the local directors proposed for their officers, including the presidents. As any bureaucrat or congressman would understand, the control of any institution's pay scale and its budget is powerful leverage.

"These are very real influences on how vociferous a Reserve Bank president is going to be about dissenting," Roos said. "It's subtle, but it's real. If one is a young, career-oriented president who's got a family to feed, he tends to be more moderate in his opposition to the governors than an older person like myself who's more independent."

The roller coaster was still in descent. By the first week of June, the Federal Funds rate had again fallen below the Discount rate and hit 8.5 percent—the bottom of the Fed's prescribed target range for it. For one trading day, it dipped as low as 7.5 percent and, for a time, the Federal Reserve lost control—the short-term interest rate that monetary policy regulates most securely was floating on its own. Discount borrowing by the banks fell to a very low level, and the money market was for a time rudderless in determining the rate for Fed Fund borrowing. Wallich explained: "When the Federal Funds rate fell below the Discount rate, there is no clear definition of where the Federal Funds rate should be because it's no longer supported by the Discount rate. On a given day, it could fall to zero. So if you don't lower the Discount rate, you get quite an unstable situation."

In larger terms, the financial markets had never witnessed anything so stark and sudden, so dizzying. In early April, the Federal Funds rate hit a peak close to 20 percent. Ten weeks later, it had fallen to 8.5 percent. Commercial paper, certificates of deposit, three-month Treasury bills—all of the many instruments of short-term borrowing followed the same steep plunge, falling by as much or more in two months' time.

The Federal Reserve, when it seized the initiative in the fall of 1979, had forced up the price of money by nearly 100 percent in order to combat inflation. Now the Fed was allowing the price of money to fall, even more rapidly, back to the original level.

Many things caused the run-up and the descent—the explosive pressures of inflation, the shock effects of credit controls, the abrupt uncertainties of recession. They were also caused, inevitably, by the policy decisions of the Federal Reserve. Paul Volcker would confide to colleagues much later that he considered the dramatic easing of interest rates executed in the spring of 1980 as perhaps his largest mistake as Federal Reserve chairman.

But none of these arguments or errors at the Federal Reserve were known to the general public. It was a presidential election year and the press was busy reporting the campaign rhetoric of Jimmy Carter and his opponents, including their economic policies. Political reporters fully accepted the notion that the central bank was nonpolitical and, therefore, its actions were not relevant to elections. The Fed's great mistake would soon become obvious, however, to those who followed the Fed closely. They could see something was wrong. The roller coaster was about to bottom out and to come lurching back up again.

By midsummer of 1980, the majority of the Federal Open Market Committee was confused. The great national economy was abruptly reviving, despite their forecasts and expectations. Instead of a normal contraction that lasted two or three quarters, as predicted, this one looked as if it was already over. Governor Nancy Teeters described the quandary: "I think I was really misled. I thought we really had broken the back of inflation. For a few months, it looked like the beginning of a classic recession. Durable goods had fallen off, so had housing. I was wrong. It turned out to be sharp but very short. Two months later, I had to change my mind."

So did the others. By July, consumers were buying again and business activity was stirring with new life. Personal-consumption spending, which had fallen by $24 billion in real terms during the second quarter, was suddenly expanding again. Business investments in new plants and machinery were still depressed, but no longer declining sharply. Housing starts, after falling for five straight months, abruptly increased by 30 percent in June—a leading indicator for the rest of the economy.[13]

By early August, it was clear that the 1980 recession had ended. On the charts that record U.S. economic history, the contraction of 1980 looked bizarre—a sharp V on the trend line of economic growth. One quarter, the Gross National Product was contracting by nearly 10 percent; the next quarter it was alive again, expanding by 2.4 percent. This is not what the Federal Reserve had in mind in its fight against inflation. Monthly price increases were not as alarming as the peak earlier in the year, but they continued in double digits. After slowing briefly, the Consumer Price Index returned to an annual inflation rate close to 11 percent. Clearly, the war had not been won.

"By taking controls off and lowering rates," John Paulus, a former Fed economist who was now at Morgan Stanley, explained, "the Fed aborted the recession and got none of the benefits. You could say they were playing politics, but at the same time you would have to say that in a few months they ended up increasing interest rates again."[14]

The Fed, however, was making progress on one of its goals: the dollar's long descent in value in international currency markets was halted. By midsummer, the price of the dollar stabilized against an index of foreign currencies and began slowly to rise, for the first time in many years. It was an important turning point, almost ignored at the time, for both the U.S. economy and the world's. The terms of dollar-traded transactions began to shift gradually. The value of the hundreds of billions held internationally in dollar-denominated financial assets began to appreciate. The trend, once started, would continue with gathering force for the next five years—profoundly altering the patterns of world trade and wealth in the 1980s.

Stabilizing the dollar on world markets was the beginning of success for the Fed, even though domestic inflation continued strong. In part, the dollar's turnaround probably reflected the growing conviction of international money traders that Volcker and the Fed meant what they said. But there was a more fundamental reason—the dollar's new strength reflected the pull of Volcker's high interest rates.

Despite all the complicated factors affecting currency trading, the international investors were driven most powerfully by a simple single question: where could their wealth find the highest return? When the

Fed pushed U.S. interest rates far above the competing rates in other countries, wealth naturally began flowing toward dollar-denominated financial instruments. As more investors traded yen or pounds in order to get into dollar-denominated investments, the increased demand for dollars naturally stiffened the price. As long as the Fed maintained a wide differential—U.S. interest rates well above the foreign rates—the dollar would continue to grow stronger and stronger.

In the meantime, however, the Federal Reserve had undone itself at home. Its error would perhaps not sound like error to most citizens: the Fed had inadvertently restarted the American economy.

Its strategy in the spring had allowed interest rates—in the language of the money market—to fall in a matter of weeks by 1,000 basis points. For the real economy of consumers and producers, this decline amounted to a gigantic price cut. Imagine, for instance, that government policy somehow induced General Motors to reduce the price of its automobiles by 50 percent. A great many citizens would decide it was time to buy a Buick. Less neatly but more broadly, the sharp drop in interest rates worked the same way. When the price of borrowed money was cut in half, the result was a powerfully stimulative impact on aggregate demand. It was time again to borrow money and spend it.

Bank lending began expanding rapidly again and so did the money supply. M-1, which had been flat in May, grew by 11 percent in June. The next month, the money supply was expanding still faster, by more than 13 percent. In August, money growth exploded—the M-1 aggregate increased at a rate of 22.8 percent. The turnaround was extraordinary: just two months before, M-1 growth had been running below the FOMC's objective. Now money was growing nearly four times faster than the Fed's own target for 1980. The Federal Reserve had lost control.

If the governors in Washington set the wrong strategy, the banking system could swiftly magnify the error. The actual mechanics of money involved a subtlety that was rarely, if ever, mentioned in the textbooks but that greatly complicated the daily reality of the Federal Reserve's money management. The textbooks described money creation as beginning with the Fed—it supplied more reserves and the banks made more loans and the loans became new deposits and, thus, a larger money supply. In the real world, the order was usually reversed: the banks made the new loans, then the Fed provided the new reserves to support them.

The typical sequence went like this: commercial banks initiated the process by making new loans, then scrambled around to find the added reserves required to support their expanded portfolios. The banks could borrow the needed reserve funds in the money market, or if excess reserves were scarce, the banks would be compelled to turn to the Discount window at the Fed and get the funds there.

Day by day, the Federal Reserve would always accommodate whatever was needed. The Fed might frown at and scold individual banks that came to the Discount window too frequently, but the Fed could not very well refuse the banking system's need for new reserves. If the Fed refused on any given day to supply the reserves the banking system needed, then the scramble for scarce reserves would become desperate and inevitably some banks would come up short—that is, perhaps fail. That is precisely what the Federal Reserve was created to prevent—the short-term liquidity crises that wiped out otherwise solvent banks. Back in 1913, the Fed's architects called it "elastic currency"—a money supply that could grow or shrink flexibly in accordance with the fluctuating credit demands of the nation.

So, day by day, the Fed would accommodate the loan commitments the banks had already made. In that sense, the Fed was always responding to events that had already occurred—bank loans that had already been made, demand deposits already created—and it had no practical choice except to ratify those existing realities by supplying whatever reserves the banking system needed. Its daily posture was reactive (a condition compounded by its own rule allowing banks to report their reserve and deposit totals with a lag of two weeks).

Yet the Fed was not impotent. Its control over money depended on choosing which method it would use to accommodate what the banking system needed in new reserves. It could pump in more reserves through the Open Market Desk—or it could refuse to accommodate the banks that way and, in effect, force them to come to the Discount window and ask for a short-term advance. The Fed would always lend them whatever they needed; not to do so would force a liquidity crisis. But this was a privilege banks could not overuse without inviting a regulatory investigation. In the meantime, the competition for scarce reserves would have bid up the Federal Funds rate—and influenced the entire spectrum of other short-term interest rates.

In crude terms, the Fed said to the banks: Okay, you can have the reserves you need today, but it's going to cost you more than you expected. And tomorrow it might cost you even more. Today you borrowed at the Discount window, but, as you know, you can't be coming back to the Discount window day after day without inviting nasty regulatory scrutiny of what's wrong at your bank. So you had better adjust your own portfolio accordingly—or pay the price.

If the Fed kept doing this over a period of days or weeks, sooner or later the banks ought to get the message. The Federal Reserve's leverage, thus, depended on coordinating its two money valves—the open-market operations and the Discount window—using them like a carrot and stick to prod or entice the banks. When the Fed tightened money, Discount borrowing soared and the squeeze was on. The process did not work instantly (nor as neatly as this description implies), but over time the Fed usually got its way.

For old hands on the Open Market Desk, this was the essence of central banking—the daily trader's game the Fed played with the banking system and the interrelated money markets. The contest was both tangible and psychological. By adjusting its daily open-market strategy, adding or withholding reserves, the Fed nudged the banks and money markets. It bluffed them and on occasion deliberately frightened them. Eventually, if the strategy set in Washington was correct, the banks and the money traders moved in the desired direction. This time, the strategy was plainly wrong.

"The money supply began bouncing back," Paul Volcker said, "which we didn't mind for a month or two because it was just offsetting the decline. What we did not judge, we nor anybody else, was that economic decline itself was going to be so short-lived." Volcker was expecting the surge of money growth to moderate, but it didn't. The economy itself was expanding much faster than he had anticipated. The Fed had told financial markets to watch the money-supply numbers as an indicator of its policy—now the money supply told Wall Street that the Fed was easing up.

"If it hadn't been the focus of so much attention," Volcker told financial writer Andrew Tobias, "I don't think it would have made much difference, but everyone had come to look at the money-supply figures as the symbol of policy. And we were in the midst of an election campaign, so everybody could attribute political interpretations to everything that happened. That didn't help any." [15]

Governor Partee, who in his off-hours liked to sail on Chesapeake Bay, described the Fed's error in nautical terms: "In sailing, when you turn the rudder, the boat doesn't do anything for a while. So you say to yourself, 'My God, I didn't do enough.' So you turn some more. Pretty soon, you see the boat responding and you say, 'My God, I've overturned. The boat is going way beyond where I wanted to be.' "

The Fed had oversteered in the spring and that produced an unintended feedback: lower interest rates stimulated the real economy and the real economy drove the money supply. This was roughly the reverse of how the monetarist doctrine envisioned the cause-and-effect relationship, but it was the way in which most Federal Reserve governors understood the matter. The experience of 1980 only seemed to confirm how the Federal Reserve had always looked at things: interest-rate movements were the best criterion for judging the impact of monetary policy, not changes in the money-supply numbers.

Henry Wallich later summarized the evidence:

At each turn, movements in interest rates were followed, with a lag of three to four months, by a movement of the economy in the opposite direction. The rise in interest rates during the first quarter was followed by the sharp decline in the economy during the second quarter. The decline in interest rates during the second quarter was followed by an upturn in the economy in the third. To make the case that the money supply, rather than the interest rates, moves the economy, one would have to assert that the money supply affected the economy with a zero lag.

None of these facts was entirely obvious in June, when Governor Lyle Gramley attended his first FOMC meeting. Gramley was replacing Philip Coldwell, and since he had served on Jimmy Carter's Council of Economic Advisers, many in Wall Street dismissed him as another fainthearted liberal. Gramley was, without apology, Keynesian in his perspective as an economist, but, somewhat like Tony Solomon, he had been chastened by experience. The decade of inflation was widely blamed on a failure of will at the Federal Reserve, and Gramley was, above all, a "System man." Except for his stint at the White House, he had served in the Fed since 1955. He did not wish to see it repeat the mistakes of the 1970s. In the next few years, Lyle Gramley would join Wallich as a persistent and influential hawk, the voice of experience arguing for a hard line.

"One of the first things I did when I came in as a board member," Gramley said, "was to argue: We've got to stop trying to pump more money into the system. Putting more money into the system is going to be counterproductive." The majority was not yet persuaded.

Like many of his colleagues, Gramley was from the small-town Middle West. He grew up in Aurora, Illinois, the son of a self-taught electrician, and he originally planned to become an electronics engineer. An inspiring teacher at Aurora College excited his interest in economics and he went on to earn graduate degrees at Indiana University. His first job as a research economist was at the Kansas City Federal Reserve Bank and he joined the Washington research staff in 1964. Twelve years later, he succeeded Chuck Partee as director of research and statistics when Partee became a governor. A slender man with dark brows and a solemn expression, Gramley's manner was formal but cordial. Like some others on the board, his personal tastes had evolved a long way from his lower-middle-class origins. Gramley lived in the town-and-country suburb of Potomac, Maryland, and favored horses and fox hunting. A silver statuette of rider, horse and hounds graced his office mantel.

Gramley had never been in favor of the new operating system, though he appreciated the reasons why the other governors had embraced it. The problems he foresaw were much like those in Wallich's analysis—targeting closely on the money supply would produce large swings in interest rates, and the interest-rate changes, both on the upside and the downside, would produce unintended shifts in the real economy, which would then feed back into the public's demand for money. The Fed could get caught in a circular game—reacting to money-supply changes that had been caused by its own policy. "Chasing your own tail," Gramley called it.

At the mid-August meeting of the Federal Open Market Committee, the majority was still not convinced that this is what the Federal Reserve had been doing. Gramley made his case, but he did not dissent. "I work internally," he explained. "It is not that I would never dissent. I would, if I thought the policy were way off track. But what I try to do is to help shape policy in the course of the meeting, in the discussions, in ways that help it to go in the direction I think is appropriate. The point is, I would not dissent lightly."

By September, the mistake was clear to everyone: the new money numbers showed the money supply had expanded in August by nearly 23 percent and the economy was picking up steam much faster than the Fed analysts had expected. Instead of being at the lower end of the growth range, M-1 shot up toward the upper end of its target and was about to exceed it.

As the numbers became public, the Fed's usual conservative critics became even more agitated. The Shadow Open Market Committee, which from the start had doubted the sincerity of the Federal Reserve's commitment to monetarist doctrine, now had hard evidence to support its skepticism. The Fed, Professor Karl Brunner complained, "has condemned us to hear the litany of excuses obfuscating the failure of policy making. It also condemned us to watch a series of false or broken promises. Something is fundamentally wrong with the Fed's policy making, requiring at this stage some radical action." [16]

The twelve commercial bankers who served on the Federal Advisory Council were only slightly more polite. The bankers complained:

Fed operations to date have generated both greater volatility in interest rates and in money growth. . . . The result of the variability in money growth is a substantial whipsawing of interest rates and also a growing instability in financial markets. High volatility breeds uncertainty, reduces the credibility of Fed policy and raises inflationary expectations.

The bankers were clearly convinced that the monetarist critique was correct, for they urged the FOMC to abandon its focus on the level of interest rates altogether and let the market determine how high or low interest rates would go. This was one instance where the Fed policy makers were not going to follow the bankers' advice. Many of the most respected governors were convinced that ignoring interest rates was exactly what got them into trouble in the first place. Yet the bankers' opinions could not be dismissed, because they were an authentic expression of sentiment in the financial markets.

The FOMC members felt awkward when they looked back at what the new operating system had wrought. In the spring, the money supply declined in one month by more than 17 percent. By late summer, it had increased in one month by a record 22.8 percent. Henry Wallich, while he was too polite to claim vindication, observed the chagrin among his colleagues.

Tony Solomon was not so restrained. "It was embarrassing," Solomon said. "The majority had miscalculated. Someone in my position, who had warned that this might happen, we were saying in a polite way: 'I told you so.' "

Fred Schultz, the vice chairman, acknowledged the mistake. "When the money supply jumped like it did, we maybe didn't move quickly enough. But we really thought it was an aberration."

Instead, it was now clear to the committee members that they faced an unpleasant choice. If they were to correct for their past errors, the Federal Reserve would once again have to tighten down on reserves and raise interest rates sharply—right in the middle of the presidential election.

In season and out, the members of the Federal Open Market Committee did not talk politics at the boardroom table, at least not when they were convened in formal session. A governor or a Reserve Bank president might make an oblique quip about how the politicians in the White House would react to the committee's decisions or members would mull over the political implications in private conversations. But frank talk about elections was frowned upon severely. It was not done.

As a group, the governors had become extremely sensitive to the long-standing accusations that they manipulated the money supply in election years in order to insure a growing economy and help the incumbent party win re-election. Political scientists and economists had analyzed the patterns of money growth over three decades and found a striking consistency: with one or two important exceptions, the money supply always grew faster in presidential election years. When voters "feel good" about their own rising incomes and economic prospects, they are less inclined to throw the rascals out.[17]

Federal Reserve officials testily denied the accusations, year after year, and could point to the particular economic conditions of each election season to explain why their decisions were based on objective analysis, not politics. "There is a very high degree of self-conscious rectitude in the Federal Reserve," a senior official at the New York Fed explained. Monetary policies during presidential election years was a tender subject for officials at the Federal Reserve.

"Our attitude toward the election," said Vice Chairman Schultz, "is that we'd like to dig a foxhole and crawl in until it's over."

This disposition undoubtedly inhibited the policy makers from executing sharp, stringent policy moves in the middle of a campaign if such decisions could be postponed. The majority on the FOMC, for instance, might have been more open to the arguments for tightening sooner in the summer of 1980 if it had not been the season for presidential politics. Some governors, if pressed, would concede that during a campaign they would rather be easing than tightening if conditions permitted them to do so. Most of all, they wished for a smooth policy line that would avoid aggravating either political party.

The bumpy ride of 1980 was the opposite. In fact, the events of the election year simply did not support the theory that the Federal Reserve always tries to help the incumbent party. Some critics, especially Republican campaign advisers, concluded that the summer explosion of the money supply was the Fed's desperate effort to save Jimmy Carter. Democrats knew better.

If the Fed was trying to re-elect Carter, it went about it in a very strange way. Volcker's major policy shift in the autumn of 1979— undertaken despite the objections from the Carter White House— assumed the inevitable result would be an election-year recession, hardly designed to help the incumbent. And the inference that the Federal Reserve was trying to bail out the Democrats by pumping up money in the summer of 1980 assumed that the Fed was in control of events—that it somehow wanted M-1 to grow by nearly 23 percent in August. In reality, the Fed was as dismayed as its critics.

The close evidence, if anything, supported the opposite case—that the Federal Reserve was indifferent to Jimmy Carter's fate and quite willing to let monetary policy contribute to his defeat. That was not to say that the Federal Reserve wished to see Carter lose, only that it did not mind damaging his chances. For many months, the governors had been warned repeatedly by their own primary constituency, the commercial bankers who advised them, that they must not let "political pressures" divert them from a tough money policy. In the fall of 1980, the Fed placed its own prerogatives ahead of the President's.

One former Fed economist, more cynical than most other alumni, said:

The Federal Reserve has its antennae up all the time, testing the highest winds. They saw the winds shifting to the private capitalistic philosophy of monetarism and so they shifted their operating techniques in that direction. What they did was chameleonlike—shifting away from Keynesian liberal philosophy and adopting the conservative monetarist philosophy. They were perfectly positioned for the Reagan election. In fact, they probably concluded from soundings back in the fall of 1979 that the country was headed toward a conservative victory and the country would be ready to accept a tight-money policy from the Fed.

The political implications came to a head in September when the Federal Open Market Committee could no longer defer a choice, regardless of the approaching election. If the committee did nothing, the money supply would continue to grow explosively, not as bad as the 22.8 percent growth in August but still far above reasonable levels. When the FOMC met on September 16, the committee members were in general agreement that they must reduce the money expansion substantially—pushing interest rates up again. Four dissenters, led by Wallich, wanted the Fed to be even tougher.

Committee members made a few weak jokes about the likely reaction from the Carter White House. "Bill Miller's not going to like this," one FOMC member remarked. Miller, the former Fed chairman, was not popular with his former colleagues, and they knew the Treasury Secretary would be upset by their action—along with the rest of the Carter Administration.

"The memory of '72 still rankled enough," said a senior Reserve Bank officer, "that there was determination to make sure that this did not become the case in 1980. There was a lot of talk among the staff about how holding fast in the face of Carter's displeasure would turn the Democrats against us and confirm the old mythology that the central bank, down deep, prefers Republican Presidents." Ironically, the official added, most of the central staff in Washington were Democrats, though this was not true of the senior economists at the twelve Reserve Banks.

The FOMC's decision meant interest rates would be climbing again sharply—in the midst of a close and turbulent campaign. In the week of the FOMC meeting, the Federal Funds rate averaged 10.6 percent. Two weeks later, it was up to 12.4 percent. By the end of October, it was 13.1 percent. By election day, it was 14 percent. Other lending rates followed the same curve. The price of money was going up rapidly again.

As any experienced politician understood, rising interest rates constituted "feel bad" politics. One did not have to grasp the intricacies of monetary policy, the variable lags and all that, in order to know what the impact would be on voters. Bert Lance, the Georgia banker who had been one of Jimmy Carter's most astute advisers, explained the political implications of money for the President early in his term.

"I always told the President," Lance said, "that what you need to be concerned about is the rate of inflation and the direction of interest rates. If they are both going in the wrong direction in 1980, you're not going to be re-elected. Carter understood that, but he never got control of the machinery." [18]

One year before, too late to make any difference, Lance had warned the White House: if Paul Volcker was appointed chairman, the President's re-election would be mortgaged to the Federal Reserve. Now, as interest rates started rising, it looked as though the Fed was calling in the mortgage. The President had both numbers going in the wrong direction, and, at that point, the election looked as if it would be quite close. A Gallup poll reported that Carter, after trailing Ronald Reagan for many months, was closing the gap, pulling even.

The decisions of the Federal Open Market Committee were kept secret for at least a month afterward, and while anyone could observe the rising interest rates, how could the White House attack a secret decision not yet made public? Treasury Secretary Miller had taken an oblique swipe, complaining that the Fed was "not communicating" sufficiently with the Administration.

On September 25, the Fed was compelled to go public. The Board of Governors unanimously approved a one-point increase in the Discount rate, from 10 to 11 percent. Since changes in the Discount rate were announced immediately, the decision served as clear confirmation that the Federal Reserve was driving up interest rates. Fred Schultz discussed the politics with Volcker. "He was worried about the Fed having such a high profile in an election campaign, about being in the eye of the storm," the vice chairman said. "We all were. We just came to the conclusion that we had no choice. The timing was awful."

The next day, Schultz got a call from one of the political operatives at the White House. "What the hell are you doing to us?" he asked. Schultz tried to explain: "The money supply has exploded. Inflation is running away. We don't think we have a choice." The White House adviser sullenly accepted the answer.

A week later, while campaigning at a backyard "town meeting" in Landover, Pennsylvania, the President attacked the Federal Reserve for its "ill-advised" decision to raise interest rates. The broadside was slightly out of character for Carter, who had made a point during his Presidency of not trying to pressure the Fed with public criticism or even allowing his economic advisers to do so.

The Fed is independent of the President [Carter explained to the gathering in Landover]. It's just like the judicial system. I don't have influence on it, but that doesn't mean I have to sit mute. My own judgment is that the strictly monetary approach to the Fed's decision on the Discount rate and other banking policies is ill-advised. I think the Federal Reserve Bank Board ought to look at other factors and balance them along with the supply of money.

The President's attack was an extemporaneous outburst, an expression of tension and frustration, not deliberate strategy. "I don't know what will happen with the new interest-rate increases," he lamented. "My hope is that they will turn downward soon and help me politically and obviously help our nation economically."

Criticizing the Federal Reserve became a repeated theme for Carter in the final weeks of the campaign. Both the Fed and the commercial banks were pushing interest rates too high, Carter complained, "more than economic circumstances warrant." The prime rate, back up to 14 percent by early October, was criticized by Charles Schultze as "unjustified." Treasury Secretary Miller added his own complaints. Volcker tried to soften the controversy by conceding that the banks had perhaps raised the prime too swiftly. "The prime rate is sometimes a little more jumpy on the upside than it is on the downside," the chairman said.

The governors did not like becoming a campaign issue, but they were not exactly quaking either. "I said to myself, 'Well, they've got to say something,' " Henry Wallich mused. "I don't want to seem disrespectful of the federal government but—sticks and stones will break my bones, but words will never hurt me."

In the closing weeks of the campaign, Ronald Reagan skillfully turned the money issue against the President—blaming him both for controlling the Fed and for scapegoating it. "The Carter-dominated Federal Reserve Board has now become Jimmy Carter's whipping boy for at least trying . . . to remedy the damage to the economy caused by the highest budget deficit in the history of the country," Reagan declared.

When Reagan and Carter met in their only debate on October 28, the Republican candidate assailed Carter for economic policies that produced both double-digit inflation and rising unemployment. Carter, he said, has blamed the people for inflation, OPEC, he's blamed the Federal Reserve System, he has blamed the lack of productivity of the American people, he has then accused the people of living too well and that we must share in scarcity, we must sacrifice and get used to doing with less. We don't have inflation because the people are living too well. We have inflation because the government is living too well.[19]

At that moment, a Gallup poll reported, the President was slightly ahead, 45 to 42 percent. In the last week, public opinion broke dramatically for Reagan. He was elected in a landslide, 51 to 41 percent, that swept a Republican majority into the Senate for the first time in twenty-eight years and ushered in a new era of conservative reform.

The incumbent President was, of course, defeated by many things —the hostages held in Iran, inflation and rising unemployment, and his own personal style. The final run-up of interest rates executed by the Federal Reserve was like the last wound. Some of the President's advisers thought it had hurt him a lot. "If Carter could have gotten a down-tick in interest rates," Bert Lance insisted, "he maybe wouldn't have won, but it would have been a very tight election."

After the election, the Federal Reserve continued what it had started, without the anxiety of political attacks. The Carter Administration was a lame duck and the Reagan campaign managers were busy preparing their own transition to power. In this interlude, the Fed engineered another record run-up of interest rates, more dramatic than the last one.

The Board of Governors raised the Discount rate again on November 14 and once more on December 4. It was back up to 13 percent, the same level as in May. At each monthly meeting in the fall, the Federal Open Market Committee agreed to tighten the reserve supply further, pushing interest rates upward toward a new peak. By Christmas week, the prime rate for bank loans would set a new record—21.5 percent.

At year's end, the extraordinary ride on the roller coaster was visible to anyone savvy enough to understand the Fed's money numbers. Money-supply growth rose and fell like a Yo-Yo in 1980: up 13 percent in February, down 17 percent in April, up nearly 23 percent in August, down 10 percent in December (see Appendix B for the monthly record of money, interest rates and the economy).

One year after Paul Volcker had launched his monetarist experiment, the bold initiative seemed a shambles, disparaged by all sides. "I'd give the Fed a 'zero' in both effort and performance," Robert H. Parks, a professor at Pace University's Graduate School of Business, told The Wall Street Journal. "It has been a disaster," said David M. Jones, the Fed watcher at Aubrey G. Lanston & Company.[20]

The same zigzag pattern was visible in interest rates. The prime rate was 20 percent in early April, down to 11 percent on July 25, up to 21.5 percent on December 19. The Federal Funds rate, which the Fed controlled most reliably, began the year at a weekly average of 14 percent, rose to 19.4 percent in April, fell to below 9 percent in mid-July, then peaked again in December at 19.8 percent.

Volcker's first year as chairman ended in embarrassment. He and other governors offered Congress complicated explanations for what had happened, citing all the extraneous factors. They denied that they had lost control. Nevertheless, among themselves, they did not obfuscate. They knew that their management of money in 1980 had accomplished little, except perhaps to deepen skepticism about the Federal Reserve.

Lyle Gramley went out to address business groups in the autumn, trying to convince them. He emphasized the Fed's long-term commitment to hold down money growth until inflation was finally under control. As the Fed stuck to its intentions, he warned, tighter money would necessarily limit the economic growth they might expect from the new recovery. His audiences did not believe him.

I would say, "Now you better believe that the Federal Reserve is serious about this" [Gramley related]. Then the question-and-answer period would come and, after an appropriate lull, I would say, "I'd be very interested to hear from you—what are the inflationary expectations that underlie your business plans?" The common answer from the businessmen would be, "Well, 10 percent, 12 percent inflation, something like that." I would say, "You people are wrong. I want you to know that. You are wrong. You are misunderstanding what the Federal Reserve is telling you and you ought to know that."

I got nowhere. For years, the public had heard these ringing speeches from the Federal Reserve about fighting inflation. The Federal Reserve was always fighting inflation and nothing ever happened. They just didn't believe the words and I can understand their skepticism.

The record created by Volcker's new monetarist operating system was hardly persuasive. Inflation had moderated somewhat but was still above 10 percent. The Fed's decision to let interest rates fluctuate more widely had turned into gyrations that no one at the central bank had foreseen—swings up and down by as much as ten percentage points. Beyond the financial markets, the Federal Reserve's impact on the real economy was equally bizarre—an abrupt up and down of recession and recovery.

Anthony Solomon summarized the year: "If you think of monetary policy in the broad sense, including credit controls, the mini-recession and mini-recovery which followed were both abnormal and they were both caused by monetary policy."

To Henry Wallich, the results were unavoidable, given the system they had adopted—and intolerable. "I thought I understood the nature of the monetarist prescription," Wallich said. "By holding steady to the money supply, you get extreme swings of interest rates, followed by extreme swings of the money supply. The economy is kicked back and forth from floor to ceiling by a stable money supply. This is how this method would stabilize the economy—by kicking it through the ceiling and the floor."

"A false start," Paul Volcker himself conceded privately. The most he would claim in public was that 1980 had been a "holding action" for the Fed. "At very considerable cost, at very considerable turbulence, we more or less held inflation at bay," the chairman said, "prevented it from getting worse."[21]

Should the Fed continue with the money-target system it adopted in October 1979 or abandon it and return to the flexibility of its traditional methods? More and more FOMC members would eventually become disenchanted and yet the Fed stuck with the monetarist system.

"Notwithstanding the trauma of that year," Solomon said, "we did not basically shake the monetarist view, the so-called pragmatic monetarist view that Volcker adopted, to keep the monetary aggregates as targets. There was still a feeling in the markets, notwithstanding the roller coaster of 1980, that if we stick to this monetary-targeting policy, it probably would work and there really was no alternative."

If Wall Street believed, then the Fed must keep the faith. Volcker felt and others agreed that, like it or not, the Federal Reserve's own credibility was now dependent on maintaining the commitment it had made in October 1979 to follow the Ms. Informally, however, a new consensus was developing: the Fed would continue to follow the monetarist prescription, but it would compromise, month to month, making its own flexible judgments. The system would become less automatic. The Fed would adhere to it less rigidly.

"We've seen what the method did," Wallich said. "Some of us concluded we should moderate that. If interest rates went down again, we would not let them go down as far. Clearly, one had to moderate the implications of the system."

The "trauma" of 1980, as Solomon called it, had a profound influence on the subsequent behavior of the Federal Reserve—an embarrassing episode that spooked the governors for years to come. At pivotal junctures in the future, whenever the money signals became confusing and the forecasts unclear, the policy makers would remind themselves of the fiasco of 1980. The memory was invoked repeatedly as their cautionary tale: if the Federal Reserve relaxed too soon, it might be hit with another boomerang and lose everything it had gained. Far better, the policy makers agreed, to hold tight too long.

The new consensus forming in late fall meant that the Federal Reserve must begin again what it had first set out to do in October 1979 —letting interest rates go high enough to retard the economy and break the inflationary pressures. Only this time, the policy makers agreed, they would not let things get away from them. Even more stringency would be required. They would not ease prematurely, no matter what the money aggregates signaled. In reality, the young recovery that had begun in July was already being challenged—and imperiled—by monetary policy.

As interest rates headed upward again, there was one persistent dissenter. On November 18, at the first meeting after the election, Nancy Teeters warned that the higher interest rates the FOMC was authorizing would "risk a major contraction in economic activity with a substantial rise in unemployment." She dissented again and again —five times in all—as the FOMC pushed the Federal Funds rate to 19.8 percent.

"I was very disappointed that we hadn't cracked inflation yet, but I still didn't think we had to go to 20 percent interest rates," Teeters said. "It would have taken longer, we would have stretched it out, but these interest rates were threatening a very serious recession."

Her views were very much out of step with the majority, as she well knew. She cast the dissenting votes anyway. Teeters believed that a gradual approach would take longer but still be effective—and fewer people would be hurt. To others on the committee, her qualms about unemployment and business failures sounded like the old liberal Keynesian mind-set they had discarded.

"Once a consensus is formed, there is a very strong temptation to fall into line," Teeters said. "Nobody pressured me, but I wanted to be on record. I thought rates had gone too high. I wanted to be able to say I voted against it. In retrospect, I don't think I was wrong."

—PART TWO—

THE
MONEY
QUESTION

7

THE
GOD ALMIGHTY
DOLLAR

In the atrium of the Federal Reserve building, where sunlight glistens on cool marble, the artwork on display was both playful and profane. The Federal Reserve regularly circulated exhibits of fine art in its entrance halls, a grace note that enhanced the aura of patrician confidence and relieved the tedium of dry statistics. This exhibit, however, mocked and satirized. The series of collages by a New York artist, Barton Lidice Benes, seemed unexceptional until the viewer grasped the joke. Benes had chosen an odd medium. His art was made of shredded money.

Security Blanket was a visual pun, a seven-foot blanket woven from thin slices of paper that used to be Federal Reserve Notes. *Balls* was a meatball press, wrapped in currency, that turned out funny little balls of ground money. Laundered money disintegrated as it was scrubbed against a washboard. Money became things—a statue of Cupid, a fetish doll, a bust of King Midas—and money disappeared into rich patterns of color. In *Entomology* and *Snacks*, Benes turned the miser's nightmare into a busy scene—dollar bills devoured by rodents, worms and insects, each leaving distinctive piles of detritus. A spider magically consumed a dollar bill and spun it into a fragile web.

"People are so serious about money," Benes explained. "I guess I'm poking fun at that a little." The Federal Reserve cooperated in the send-up by providing the artist with a generous bundle of useless paper, about $6 million in shredded money, some of the old currency that Federal Reserve Banks routinely destroy when it is worn out. Benes was also granted legal dispensation for his art since it is a misdemeanor for anyone to deface American money.

> I'm really not trying to make any messages about money [the artist said coyly]. All the critics look into it and come up with all kinds of things— like money is the root of all evil, money slips through your fingers. Some of that may be true. Money certainly slips through my fingers, I can't get enough of it. But I'm not making any political statements. Money is just a medium. It's just like paint to me. It's fun. I want to have a good time with it.[1]

Despite disclaimers, the artist was reaching for a cosmic joke. Playing with money, treating it "just like paint" in the very corridors of the money temple, was a subversive act. By reducing money to its graphic content, possessing only the tangible qualities of color, shape and texture, Benes was exposing the power of the money illusion. Money has no meaning beyond its concrete existence; it is merely another object with certain physical properties.

The human mind insists otherwise. The mind confers real value and elaborate power on these mere scraps of paper. It infuses money with potent psychological meanings, a surrogate for mortal anxieties and yearnings that lie deep and unexpressed in everyone. The psyche insists that money has meaning. And so does the society. By stripping money down to its natural properties, Bene invites the viewer to escape, for a moment at least, the bondage of his own mind.

The Federal Reserve, quite literally, protected money's illusions. The complex bundle of psychological meanings, the social consent, the fantastic implications attached to money—all were sustained by concealment, an austere distance from popular examination. The Fed provided that, with its secrecy and obscure language, with its tradition of mystery and unknowable processes. Ignorance was comforting, perhaps even necessary for belief, and the Federal Reserve's mystique allowed people not to look directly upon these questions. Beyond politics and economics, the Federal Reserve's odd social powers were also derived from the collective irrationality surrounding money. The Fed's full stature as a governing institution could not be grasped without first glimpsing the hidden content of money itself.

The money illusion is ancient and universal, present in every transaction and absolutely necessary to every exchange. Money is worthless unless everyone believes in it. A buyer could not possibly offer a piece of paper in exchange for real goods—food or clothing or tools— if the seller did not also think the paper was really worth something.

This shared illusion was as old as stone coins and wampum, a power universally conferred by every society in history on any object that was ever regarded as money—seashells, dogs' teeth, tobacco, whiskey, cattle, the shiny minerals called silver and gold, even paper, even numbers in an account book.

Contemporary citizens had difficulty acknowledging that they shared this linkage with the primitive past. Money was now embedded in elaborate technology, electronic accounting and payment systems that operated with dazzling speed and complexity. Today's money seemed real, not at all like those quaint and amusing tokens used by ancient tribes. A dollar bill was rational; seashells were blind faith.

Modern money, of course, required the same leap of faith, the same social consent that primitive societies gave to their money. Modern money, in fact, was even more distant from concrete reality. Over the centuries, the evolution of money was a long and halting progression in which human societies hesitantly transferred their money faith from one object to another, at each step moving farther away from real value and closer to pure abstraction. The cattle used as currency by some African tribes were, after all, valuable in themselves. If the money illusion collapsed for some reason, the coins were still cattle. The seashells that became precious currency among aboriginal tribes in North America and other continents were desirable things. Tobacco, which was used as currency in some pre-Revolutionary colonies like Virginia and the Carolinas, was a valuable commodity in its own right. Even gold and silver were not entirely useless. They could be fashioned by an artist into beautiful objects.

In that sense, modern money was utterly worthless (and, therefore, more efficient as money because its value did not get confused with the value of real things). The money illusion was now refined to a new level of abstract faith, visible only if one consciously paused to consider how the money process had evolved. At each stage of history one could see money retreating from concrete reality.

Paper money, it is said, originated with the goldsmiths of Europe who held the private gold hoards deposited by wealthy citizens for safekeeping. The goldsmith issued a receipt for the gold deposit, and over time, it became clear that the receipt itself could be used in commerce since whoever owned that piece of paper could go to the goldsmith and claim the gold. Modern banking originated in the goldsmiths' discovery that they could safely write more receipts and lend them to people, exceeding the total gold that was on hand, so long as they always kept a responsible minimum in reserve to honor withdrawals. This was the origin of fractional-reserve banking and the bank lending that created money. This private money system endured for centuries and was inherited by the American Republic: privately owned banks created money by issuing paper bank notes, paper backed by a promise that at any time it could be redeemed in gold.

In nineteenth-century America, the money in use consisted mainly of these privately issued bank notes, backed by gold or silver guarantees. The money's value was really dependent, therefore, on the soundness and probity of each bank that issued notes. Banking scandals were recurrent, particularly on the frontier, where ambitious bankers, eager to make loans for new enterprises, sometimes printed paper money that had no gold behind it. Governments imposed regulations to keep banks honest, but the bankers still were free to create their own varieties of money. When banks failed, their money failed with them.

The money illusion was transferred to a new object with the rise of demand deposits, better known as checking accounts. Instead of currency, the paper money created by banks, people hesitantly came to accept that money also existed simply as an account in the bank's ledger, redeemable by personal drafts or checks. In the United States, the transition was inadvertently stimulated by government regulation. The National Bank Act, enacted during the Civil War, placed a heavy tax on new bank notes issued by state banks, and in order to avoid the tax, banks encouraged customers to use demand deposits—writing personal checks instead of drawing out their money in cash. It took generations for the public to overcome its natural distrust of checks, but by 1900 most people were persuaded. Personal checks, written by the buyers themselves, were accepted as just as valuable as dollar bills. Currency remained in use, but demand deposits were by now the bulk of the money supply. The nationalization of currency issuance, completed with the creation of the Federal Reserve in 1913, simply continued this arrangement. A new dimension of trust had added to the illusion.

Finally, the last prop for the money illusion was kicked away in this century: the gold standard was abandoned. Demand deposits had been backed by the same promise that applied to currency—any private citizen could, in theory, go to the bank and redeem his money in a quantity of gold. That promise was extinguished by government edict, starting with the warring nations of Europe during World War I, joined belatedly by the United States in 1933. Without the gold guarantee, money was only money—"legal tender for all debts, public and private," as it says on every Federal Reserve Note. A citizen can still go to the bank and redeem it, but his money will be redeemed only in new, identical Federal Reserve Notes.[2]

In the long sweep of human history, the abandonment of gold was a fairly recent event, cheered by most mainstream economists as a progressive development but still deeply traumatic to many ordinary citizens. Without gold, what is money really worth? The question still troubles a fervent minority sometimes called "goldbugs," people who yearn for a return of the old guarantee—"a dollar as good as gold" instead of the government-issued currency they speak of contemptuously as "fiat money." John Maynard Keynes, on the contrary, described the transition from gold as a historic liberation for the world's economies—an enlightened step beyond the fetishistic values attached to shiny minerals. "Commodity money" was replaced by "representative money."[3]

Keynes agreed with the goldbugs on one point: without the gold standard, money must be managed. Its true value would ultimately be determined by governments, by the judgments of fallible human beings or, more specifically, by the monetary policies of central banks like the Federal Reserve. Many citizens find this itself deeply disturbing. They long for some system that would take money regulation out of human hands and return it to some fixed set of values that is impersonal—the "invisible hand" of market forces or perhaps a higher authority. In the meantime, every American coin, every bill offers them the reassuring motto: "In God We Trust."

The money illusion endures for most citizens, however, because they never pause to examine it. Money becomes transparent only when it is followed through its chain of trusting users. An employee works faithfully through the week without recompense, confident that on Friday he will be given a piece of paper by his employer. The paper is given to his bank and the bank authorizes the worker to write new paper of his own at the supermarket. The supermarket gives him food in exchange and takes his paper to its own bank. The chain of exchanges goes on and on, agreed values moving through pieces of paper.

Next the paper itself disappears. Money becomes truly invisible. Americans are now in the midst of this great transition—transferring their money faith again, this time to objects that are even more intangible. Commerce relies increasingly now on transactions in which the social trust is conferred upon plastic cards. The plastic is not itself money, only a coded key that gives access to money. As computer technology advances and money terminals are placed in every outlet of commerce, the plastic cards will displace both checks and currency as the medium of exchange. The pieces of paper will all but disappear, no longer needed to represent real value.

Invisible money requires a deep faith (especially faith in the machines called computers), because no one can really see its physical presence. Even now, a citizen may purchase goods or send money around the world, for that matter, simply by talking over the telephone and reciting certain numerals from his plastic card—like a secret code that opens the cash drawer at the bank. Only there isn't any cash drawer—only more numbers. When money is no longer represented even by paper, it becomes a pure abstraction, numbers filed somewhere in the memory of a distant computer. In the computer, it cannot be seen by anyone, neither its owner nor the bank clerk who does the accounting. At this point, money has been reduced to nothing more tangible than electronic impulses, recorded on tape, which can be read or altered or activated only by other electronic impulses. A playful artist like Benes who wishes to mock the human illusions of money may discover someday that he has no medium in which to work.

As Benes well understood, however, money is larger than the range of the human eye, more resonant than mere numbers. In human thought and experience, money embodies associative powers that, taken together, resemble religious feeling. Those unseen powers are the real core of the money illusion and Benes offered his own irreverent commentary on them.

The historic connection between money and religion was established in one culture after another: the temple was the first mint, where coins were sanctified by priest-kings and therefore accepted as trustworthy by members of the tribe. *Moneta,* the Latin root for "money," was an epithet applied to the goddess Juno, in whose temple the first Roman coins were made. The state and the deity were synonymous and their powers intertwined. Greeks, Babylonians, Egyptians—virtually every early society conferred sacred qualities on its currency. Centuries later, without benefit of clergy, gold and silver maintained their own religious connotations. The association originated in a mystical correlation with Sun and Moon, supposedly confirmed by the mysteriously stable ratio in their values—1:13.5 gold to silver—which astrologers decided was a precise replica of the heavenly cycles. The religious quality of gold and silver endured long after the astrology disappeared and modern banking began issuing paper. The precious metals were, after all, created by God, not man.

Sophisticated modernity naturally resists the notion that money still retains religious content. On rare occasions, however, the connection is still expressed in the most explicit terms. A conservative Republican congressman from southern California, Bill Dannemeyer, wrote a newsletter to his constituents in which he explained how the U.S. government had offended God when it abandoned the gold standard.

It is not an accident [he wrote] that the American experiment with a paper dollar standard, a variable standard, has been going on at the same time that our culture has been questioning whether American civilization is based on the Judeo-Christian ethic or Secular Humanism. The former involves formal rules from God through the vehicle of the Bible. The latter involves variable rules adopted by man and adjusted as deemed appropriate.

In most circles, the congressman's suggestion—that the gold standard was somehow derived from God's law—would be dismissed as reactionary fantasy. In an enlightened age of high technology, it was unfashionably primitive to believe such things. Archaic civilizations may have been governed by mystical money, but surely not the rational minds of modern times. Money was only money, a medium of commerce, a store of wealth, a unit of measure, nothing more.

When Sigmund Freud was first attempting to chart the geography of the human psyche, he kept encountering an outrageous association —money and excrement. Gold stinks. Miserliness is "dirty." Feces are the infant's coin. "It is quite crazy," Freud wrote to a colleague in 1897, "but completely analogous to the process by which words assume a transferred meaning as soon as new concepts appear requiring definition."

Freud's pioneering research relied principally on two sources of evidence: the dreams and recollections revealed by his early patients in psychoanalysis and the folklore of the ages, the inherited myths and fables, from Oedipus to medieval sorcery, that expressed ancient truths about human experience. These sources, he believed, spoke from the same wellspring, the human unconscious, and they confirmed one another's revelations.

"I read one day," Freud reported, "that the gold which the devil gave his victims regularly turned into excrement." The next day, Freud said, one of his patients innocently recalled an odd memory of his childhood nurse who suffered from "money deliria." Her money, the patient said suddenly, was always excrement. Freud noted other associations. The fabled alchemist who would create gold from dross was called *Dukatenscheisser*, literally "one who excretes ducats." In early Babylon, gold was "the excrement of Hell."[4]

Money and the power of the devil was a recurring connection in human experience. In the Middle Ages, Catholic theologians had denounced usurers as the devil's agents. In the late twentieth century, a sociologist named Michael T. Taussig discovered that rural peasants in Colombia, as they were drawn into the commodity-exchange economy of modern capitalism, would devise their own devil legends to explain the dreadful power money and commerce now held over their lives.[5] Freud would doubtless have regarded the Colombian peasants as confirmation of his original insights (so too would Karl Marx, who decried the human alienation of capitalist money cultures). Freud's basic task was to decode these symbolic connections. "Have you ever seen a foreign newspaper after it has passed the censorship at the Russian frontier?" the doctor asked. "Words, sentences and whole paragraphs are blacked out, with the result that the remainder is unintelligible. A 'Russian censorship' occurs in the psychoses, and results in the apparently meaningless deliria."

The blocked-out messages, Freud concluded, emanated from infantile experience—ideas, emotions, responses learned in the earliest months of human existence and, thus, universally shared by all throughout history's stages. The infant's elemental reactions to life do not disappear as he matures, but are deflected to other purposes, repeated in other circumstances and expressed unconsciously, cloaked by the irrational associations. Thus, for example, Freud traced the money-excrement connection to one of the baby's earliest obligations in life—the act of defecation and the need to control it. It is, after all, one of the first expressions of self.

Freud could only speculate on exactly why the human mind transferred its response to feces to the object called money.

It is possible [he wrote] that the contrast between the most precious substance known to man and the most worthless, which he rejects as "something thrown out," has contributed to this identification of gold with feces. . . . The original erotic interest in defecation is, as we know, destined to be extinguished in later years; it is in these years that the interest in money is making its appearance as something new which was unknown in childhood. This makes it easier for the earlier impulse, which is in the process of relinquishing its aim, to be carried over to the new one.

The public was at first scandalized by Freud's remarkable assertions, but eventually accepting. Freudian overlays became so familiar they passed into the conventional wisdom about human behavior, exaggerated by popular usage into their own stereotypes. The modern version of a miser would be explained as an "anal personality," obsessed with accumulating money but afraid to spend it. In the vernacular, he is a "tight ass." The opposite type was the reckless spendthrift, consuming things obsessively likle a baby sucking lustily at his mother's breast, spending money as though he couldn't wait to get rid of the filthy stuff.

In the Freudian context, the Federal Reserve seems strangely appropriate to its task. The Fed's own style and temperament would obviously be described as "anal." But, more importantly, the central bank's unrelenting rectitude and rationality provide a social mask—a way to translate all of the infantile money impulses into acceptable, serious terms. No one would ever think of babies, excrement and the august central bank as extensions of the same human experience. In a sense, the Federal Reserve made money a suitable object for adults to handle.

As Freud explored further, he realized that the human expectations attached to money were far more complicated than his original definitions—money had multiple meanings. It had to do with life and death, love and power, acts of creation and destruction.

To visualize the Freudian subtext more imaginatively, one could ponder the psychological content in the myth of King Midas. Midas yearned for the golden touch and his desire became a curse. Every living thing he touched turned into gold, glistening but dead, even the food he ate, even his loving daughter. Midas reached enviously for the powers of the gods—the power to create—and it turned into a deadly gift. Money is an exquisite contradiction, uniting desire and dread.

"If one is not aware of these profound connections," Freud concluded, "it is impossible to find one's way about in the fantasies of human beings, in their associations, influenced as they are by the unconscious, and in their symptomatic language." To illustrate the complexity, Freud strung together five simple words, each pregnant with psychological meaning, all depending upon the same symbols: "Feces—money—gift—baby—penis." [6]

Money resonated in the unconscious with all those thoughts and more. The deep connections helped to explain why the money illusion endured over the millennia of history, despite its changing forms or the representative money introduced by modern rationalism. The illusion was freighted with a complex of contradictory ideas, each attached to the most elementary fears and aspirations in human life. As a unified whole, money resembled a man-made answer to divine questions.

When Americans spoke of someone who "worships the Almighty dollar," the intent was disapproval. A wholesome human being did not make money his god. Indeed, that was the point of making lots of money and becoming rich—it enabled one to escape the tyranny. Popular how-to manuals on Wall Street investing promised the readers the steps to "financial independence." Wealthy people, it was thought, can forget money, put it out of their minds and get on with real life. In practical experience, it did not seem to work out that way. Money expresses so many satisfying elements of human existence that even people who have accumulated massive surpluses, more money than they could possibly ever spend, were preoccupied with obtaining still more. If money was not God, it appeared to be the next best thing.

In reality, money in its psychological form, as the absolute means and thus as the unifying point of innumerable sequences of purposes, possesses a significant relationship to the notion of God . . . [Georg Simmel wrote]. The essence of God is that all diversities and contradictions in the world achieve a unity in him, that he is—according to a beautiful formulation of Nicolas de Cusa—the *coincidentia oppositorum*. Out of this idea, that in him all estrangements and all irreconcilables of existence find their unity and equalization, there arise the peace, the security, the all-embracing wealth of feeling that reverberate with the notion of God that we hold.

Money, like religion, unified life's contradictions—the petty and the exalted, the confusing multiplicity of things and the elemental, immutable truths, the limits and the potential described by life and death. Simmel was a German sociologist whose epic work *The Philosophy of Money* was published in the same era when Sigmund Freud was exploring the meaning of money from a different perspective. Simmel anticipated Freud when he observed that only psychology could really get at the true relationship between money and religion since psychology "has the privilege of being unable to commit blasphemy." Money, Simmel concluded, imitates life itself.

There is no more striking symbol of the completely dynamic character of the world than that of money [he wrote]. The meaning of money lies in the fact that it will be given away. When money stands still, it is no longer money according to specific value and significance. . . . Money is nothing but the vehicle for a movement in which everything else that is not in motion is completely extinguished . . . it lives in continuous self-alienation from any given point and thus forms the counterpart and direct negation of all being in itself.

Money's continuous action—"the wild scramble for money, the impulsiveness that money . . . spreads over the economy and indeed over life in general"—would seem to be in conflict with the sacred content, but, as Simmel noted, money's constant motion actually enhances the "religious mood." He explained:

Not only is the whole excitement and tension in the struggle for money the pre-condition for the blissful peace after the conquest, but that calmness of the soul that religion provides, that feeling of standing at the focal point of existence, attains its highest value for the consciousness only at the price of having searched and struggled for God.

Yet, while money seems connected with everything, it is also secretive—a way in which the individual can delineate his private self, separate from the mass, separate even from his close neighbors. With the dawn of money economies, Simmel wrote, "an otherwise unattainable secrecy" became possible to human beings, relying on the qualities of money itself—

> its compressibility, which permits one to make someone rich by slipping a check into his hand without anybody's noticing it; its abstractness and qualitylessness, through which transactions, acquisitions and changes in ownership can be rendered hidden and unrecognizable . . . and, finally, its effect-at-a-distance, which allows its investment in very remote and ever-changing values, and thus its complete withdrawal from the eyes of the immediate environment.[7]

Money confers social and political power, naturally. Those who have more of it than others use their wealth to dominate or control other human beings who have little or none. But money also gives power to a secret self, enabling it to pursue its own self-gratification in a singular fashion. Money's most obvious expressive power is the ability to acquire things that satisfy the imagination—consuming goods that are utterly unrelated to necessity or even usefulness. The things, instead, fulfill elaborate fantasies of selfhood, a visible statement of who-I-am, like the primitive tribesmen who used feathers and facial paints to explain their status and inner character.

In 1899, the American economist Thorstein Veblen described the practice with contemptuous clarity in *The Theory of the Leisure Class* and gave it a name, "conspicuous consumption." Money provided the manly prowess of the gambler, the social distinctions of owning certain dogs and horses, the pious self-congratulations of expensive funerals, the idle wealth of a walking stick, the exquisite subjugation of a woman's corset. Things expressed self and differentiated the self from those who did not have these things.[8]

"Reputable wastefulness and futility," Veblen called it, a predatory form of barbarism. He assumed mankind would shed these primitive fetishes when it evolved eventually to genuine civilization. But, even as Veblen wrote, the age of modern advertising was dawning—refining and amplifying the ability to attach inner fantasies to the things people buy with money. If Veblen were alive in the late twentieth century, he would doubtless shudder at the spectacle of superfluous consumption

—urban dwellers who drive around city streets in pickup trucks pretending to be cowboys, automobiles advertised as sleek and ferocious wild animals, talking toilet bowls in televison commercials that promise social respectability to insecure housewives.

Money buys dreams, even ludicrous ones. In that sense, as Freud suggested, it becomes like food—nourishing the self by gobbling up new things, feeding the fantasies. The prophet Isaiah asked his people: "Wherefore do you spend money for that which is not bread?" Veblen raised the same question.

Yet money also speaks to the self even when it is not spent, and perhaps more powerfully. People find that what is more enjoyable than spending their money is not spending it and savoring its possibilities (not unlike the power felt by Freud's reluctant infant on the chamber pot). Money contains the "notion of possiblity," Simmel wrote.

> Money, like power, is a mere potentiality [he explained], which stores up a merely subjectively anticipatable future in the form of an objectively existing present. . . . If one asserts that one "can" do something, then this means not only the mental anticipation of a future event, but an already existing state of energy, physical and psychic coordinations. . . . Whoever "can" play the piano, even if he does not do so, is different from someone who is unable to do so, not only in a future moment, but even at the present moment.

Money, therefore, contains a continuous illusion of immortal power —the psychic vehicle for defeating time itself by controlling the future. It is only an illusion; no mortal ever conquers time. Even the wealthiest must die eventually, and as American folk wisdom reminds them, "You can't take it with you." Nevertheless, people will try. They devote elaborate attention to what their money will be doing after they are gone—who will get it, what things it will buy, how its power can be preserved. The more money one has, the more serious this question becomes.

"It is really nothing but capability, in the sense of chances for the future, which gives significance to what we presently own," Simmel explained, "but it is real capability in the sense of absolute certainty about the realization of such a future."[9] The certainty of money's future is well understood by striving human beings as they make out their wills. The terms of inheritance allowed one to manipulate the future beyond death, rewarding or punishing the survivors with the leftover wealth. No one can be absolutely certain of living beyond the grave, but they know their money will.

Money and religious faith are intertwined in the most basic human aspiration—to conquer time, to escape the mortal bonds. Religions require rituals of redemption and renewal; money is an important artifact in the process—the gift to the gods to expunge past sins.

In primitive cultures, closely attuned to the cycles of the seasons, ritual gifts were offered at regular annual intervals, the winter solstice, the harvest or the birth of spring, as a form of redemption. The tribe was reconciled with its gods, old debts were extinguished and the cycle began anew, free of guilt. The modern vestige for Christians is the Christmas season, in which everyone redeems himself by buying presents. Jews fast on Yom Kippur and are supposed to avoid worldly goods, but it is also the season when synagogues hold their fund-raising drives. Money is the gift that cleanses.

Norman O. Brown explored the debt-guilt content of money and its other psychological aspects in a challenging essay entitled "Filthy Lucre," published in his book *Life Against Death*, a radical critique of the money complex that synthesized ancient wisdom of the Greeks and the Bible with the modern insights of Marx and Freud, Veblen and Simmel. "Whatever the ultimate explanation of guilt may be," Brown said, "we put forward the hypothesis that the whole money complex is rooted in the psychology of guilt."

Even at its simplest level, money is used like a debt instrument, an obligation exchanged for real value. The action of commerce involves passing around pieces of debt paper, taking them from others and passing them on to someone else. In mass, the money economy represents a dense interweave of obligations that must be filled. Individual guilt may be eased by giving some of it away.

"How then does reciprocal giving help to get rid of the burden of guilt?" Brown asked. "Of course, it does not get rid of guilt, as the whole history of archaic and modern man shows. But it does represent man's first attempt at a solution. Guilt is mitigated by being shared; man entered social organization in order to share guilt."

The rise of capitalism offered if not an escape from mortal guilt at least a powerfully comforting salve. Capital accumulation directly challenged the church's conception of the human condition, which is why the medieval monastics opposed it so vigorously. The old limits on human existence were overrun by new possibilities, not just in the tangible terms of higher living standards, but also in deeper psychic terms. Capitalism redefined the idea of time through the miracle of compound interest—money multiplying itself over time. The system seemed secular and rational, but it also contained the seeds of a new faith. "It is really a demonolatry," Brown complained. "We no longer give the surplus to God; the process of producing an ever-expanding surplus is in itself now God."

Under capitalism, money takes on a new illusion: money itself becomes a living thing. People are attracted to the process of capital formation and economic growth because they can now imagine that their money is alive. It is growing. It is reproducing itself. It lives from the past to the future in defiance of time. It has broken the ancient bounds, the sacred admonitions about man's fate.

Money can become a surrogate life for its owner—treated as a living thing, as some people do. If cared for and encouraged, disciplined and protected, money can become a second self, but one that will not die. Some people are so smitten by the illusion of living money that they look after their accumulated capital with as much solicitude as they devote to their children.

Brown described money's new magic:

. . . things become alive and do what the man would like to do. Things become the god (the father of himself) that he would like to be: *money breeds*. The institution of interest presupposes not only cumulative time but also the displacement of the parental complex from the totemic group to the totemic possession, money. Thus money in the civilized economy comes to have a psychic value it never had in the archaic economy.

Thus, on a psychic plane, the Wall Street investor accomplishes what the alchemist could not—creating gold from dross, real wealth from mere paper, a living organism from raw numbers. Yet it is only an illusion, still. Money is not alive and it does not grant immortality. The myth of Midas endures in the modern money economy in a somewhat different form: the act of fulfilling a need provokes other needs, expanding desires instead of extinguishing them. The "game" of Wall Street—making money grow—has no satisfying conclusion because there is no obvious point at which opportunities are exhausted. Instead, it may only enlarge the hunger. Like the golden touch of Midas, the money illusion drives the investor to worry restlessly about missed opportunities and to renew his anxieties about the future. He will touch one more thing, acquire one more portion of wealth, only to discover that once it is in his grasp, the new money is also dead.

The circle of contradictions, thus, returns to where Freud began— the baby's illusions about excrement. Norman Brown described the linkage:

Money is inorganic dead matter which has been made alive by inheriting the magic power which infantile narcissism attributes to the excremental product. Freud pointed out that it was an integral part of the anal symbolic complex to equate the feces with the penis. The infantile fantasy of becoming father of oneself first moves out to make magic use of objects instead of its own body when it gets attached to that object which both is and is not part of its own body, the feces. Money inherits the infantile magic of excrement and then is able to breed and have children: interest is an excrement.

Interest as excrement—it is difficult to imagine a thought that could be any more offensive to citizens of capitalist societies (or to the temple managers of the Federal Reserve). Interest on wealth was the core of the modern economic process. Brown's assertion, however, was merely a sophisticated restatement, in Freudian terms, of the ancient admonitions, from the Babylonians to Saint Francis to Marx. The devil was present when a dead substance was invested with the illusion of life, when filthy lucre kept humankind distant from its own humanity.

Despite his grim analysis of human illusions, Brown also entertained a millennial vision: human society might someday move beyond the fantasies attached to money. That would require nothing less than a new religious perspective—a reordering of human consciousness in which the fear of death was displaced, and along with it, human guilt, and the predatory money impulses that accompany them. The model for Brown's optimism was the psychoanalytic process invented by Sigmund Freud in which the patient overcomes his repressed fear and guilt by confronting them. If an individual could disarm the power of infantile fears by facing their irrationality, then, Brown believed, mankind in general could do the same.

"If we can imagine an unrepressed man—a man strong enough to live and therefore strong enough to die, and therefore what no man has ever been, an individual—such a man, having overcome guilt and anxiety, could have no money complex," Brown concluded grandly.[10]

A truly radical proposition. The world is not yet "civilized." Genuine humanity lies somewhere out there in an indistinct future—when people will be able to move beyond money. Brown's vision connects obliquely with Veblen's. It coincides more directly with the optimistic prophecy of John Maynard Keynes. In "Economic Possibilities for Our Grandchildren," Keynes first described his hundred-year prediction of unimagined wealth, multiplied through the compounding of capital someday eliminating human want. Then, Keynes warned, human nature would confront a much more profound challenge:

When the accumulation of wealth is no longer of high social importance, there will be great changes in the code of morals. We shall be able to rid ourselves of many of the pseudo-moral principles which have hag-ridden us for two hundred years, by which we have exalted some of the most distasteful of human qualities into the position of the highest virtues. We shall be able to afford to dare to assess the money-motive at its true value. The love of money as a possession—as distinguished from the love of money as a means to the enjoyments and realities of life—will be recognized for what it is, a somewhat disgusting morbidity, one of those semi-criminal, semi-pathological propensities which one hands over with a shudder to the specialists in mental disease.

This was a threatening prospect, Keynes acknowledged. "For the first time since his creation," Keynes wrote, "man will be faced with his real, his permanent problem—how to use his freedom from pressing economic cares, how to occupy his leisure, which science and compound interest will have won for him, to live wisely and agreeably and well." [11]

Obviously, this hopeful vision was not about to be fulfilled in the present millennium. Human societies would live for some while longer with money and its complex illusions. Mysterious institutions would continue as the cloak needed to shield money's mystery—protecting human secrets that everyone shared and yet did not wish to know.

The Federal Reserve was not a sacred temple. The seven governors were not high priests performing mystical rites. Yet the Fed inherited all the resonant feelings that surrounded money, the religious mood and the full freight of irrational meanings. The Federal Reserve's decision making was the essence of secular rationalism, devoted to scientific theory. Yet it was still the modern equivalent of mysterious sanctification, for its officers performed the ancient priestly function: the creation of money. The central bank, notwithstanding its claims to rational method, enfolded itself in the same protective trappings that adorned the temple—secrecy, mystique, an awesome authority that was neither visible nor legible to mere mortals. Like the temple, the Fed did not answer to the people, it spoke for them. Its decrees were cast in a mysterious language people could not understand, but its voice, they knew, was powerful and important.

It is impossible to understand the Federal Reserve's peculiarity as a political institution without this mythic function. The religious quality of money was a crucial element in the cultural expectations that surrounded the Fed. It helped to explain the Federal Reserve's odd placement in the governing constellation of representative democracy —exempted from popular control when American civics boasted that the people were sovereign. While reformers insisted that democratic accountability be imposed on far less important matters of government, all efforts to democratize the central bank consistently failed. The idea was simply frightening.

The anomaly of the Federal Reserve was tolerated by the ignorant American populace, but at some irrational level it was probably also wished for. Reformers perennially complained that the Fed deliberately obstructed democratic inquiry with its evasions and elaborate rules of secrecy, but it was probably likewise true that many citizens preferred it that way.

Some Americans, an agitated minority, regarded the Fed itself as blasphemous—mortals who had usurped the powers of God. The goldbugs, who wished to restore the guarantee of precious minerals behind paper money, really wanted to remove the money illusion from the influence of man-made decisions. The rigid monetarists, who campaigned for a fixed, immutable rule that would govern money growth, wished to accomplish the same thing, only in a rationalistic fashion. Either way, by gold or by a monetarist rule, money would become eternal again—protected from human manipulations. The majority had no opinion on these alternatives, and, indeed, no real understanding of how its money was managed by the Federal Reserve. The majority assumed what it had been taught—that money regulation was an arcane technical matter, an obscure managerial function of government without much importance to the great issues of democratic discourse. The confusing economic language employed by the Fed made it easier for citizens to block out the money question—to accept in stead the powerful mystery.

This was odd but nonetheless true: in a great democracy, where political power depended upon information and every interest clamored for it, the American culture had repressed the knowledge of money. There is no other way to describe the mass ignorance or explain it except as a collective blocking out. Like the censored Russian newspapers mentioned by Freud, the meaning of money remained blacked out, unexamined in a nation that congratulated itself on free political debate. Every important cultural institution cooperated in the self-censorship: the mass media and the educational system, the turbulent community of elected politicians and, of course, the officers of the Federal Reserve itself. By their treatment of money management, all of them implied it was not a subject for general debate. The Federal Reserve was regarded as beyond the understanding of ordinary citizens; money was reserved for the fraternity of experts.

The general ignorance created its own political imbalance, enhancing the influence of the small minority who did understand the subject and cared most intensely. The community of investors—the 400,000 financial professionals of Wall Street and the wealth holders they represented—debated the money issue every day of the week. They conducted a running critique of the money managers at the Fed, and the

Federal Reserve listened closely to their commentaries. The debate itself was not exactly secret, but only the most attentive citizens would know that it was going on, much less understand its relevance to their lives.

To demystify the Federal Reserve, one first had to understand that money did not require religious faith or buried fantasies or impenetrable technicalities. Money was, above all, a political question—a matter of deliberate choices made by the state. Money was like all political questions decided by fallible human beings, subject to the usual variables of political action—understanding and intent, influence and error. Money was an everyday argument among competing interests, in which some would benefit and some would lose, depending on the outcome. Money was a social plan that rewarded or punished, stimulated or restrained. Money might encourage democratic aspirations or thwart them.

Strangely enough, there was a time when millions of ordinary Americans understood this, even humble citizens with little or no education. When the money question was alive in American politics, before its meaning was repressed, before there was a temple called the Federal Reserve, people knew that money was politics and that democracy depended on it.

8

DEMOCRATIC MONEY

The founding assumptions of the Federal Reserve System were first championed by a most unlikely group of Americans—not orthodox economists at prestigious universities, not important bankers on Wall Street and not the elected leaders of Republican and Democratic politics. The modern way of thinking about money and credit was first articulated by plain country people—hard-worn men and women, drearily poor and ill-educated, with barefoot children and bleak futures. Respectable opinion dismissed them as backward and dangerous—"hayseeds" spouting outrageous ideas. Yet, in adversity, these unsophisticated citizens discovered great talents within themselves and, together, they created an original political agenda for the nation. The wrenching irony of American history was that, while many of the Populist ideas eventually triumphed, the people themselves were utterly defeated.

The movement began in Lampasas County, Texas, when a group of desperate farmers gathered in 1877 to form the Knights of Reliance, organized to "more speedily educate ourselves" against impending ruin—the day "when all the balance of labor's products become concentrated into the hands of a few, there to constitute a power that would enslave posterity." The organization, soon renamed the Farmers Alliance, foundered at first, but the idea of cooperative action spread. Within a few years, 120 alliances were meeting across Texas, listening to their "traveling lecturers" explain the economic realities and describe remedies. By 1887, the Texas protest had been carried north to the Dakotas and east to the Carolinas; allied groups sprang up across the cotton belt of the South and the grain states of the Middle West.

By 1890, it was an energetic and angry national movement—electing its own congressmen and governors and meeting in grand conventions to formulate far-reaching demands. The Populist agenda became a source book for political reforms spanning the next fifty years: a progressive income tax; federal regulation of railroads, communications and other corporations; legal rights for labor unions; government price-stabilization and credit programs for farmers. Their core issue, however, the ruinous yoke that united failing farmers in political revolt, was money.

Populism's brief and spontaneous drama was probably as close as the United States has ever come, before or since, to something resembling genuine democracy. It was a coarse and creative politics, in which ordinary citizens chose their own rowdy leaders, oblivious to the bounds set by respectable thinking, unintimidated by the established hierarchy of powerful interests and institutions. Historian Lawrence Goodwyn captured Populism's essence and its substantive ambitions in his authoritative account, *Democratic Promise: The Populist Moment in America*. The agrarian revolt began modestly, Goodwyn explained, with

meetings where the whole family came, where the twilight suppers were, in the early days, laid out for ten or twenty members of the suballiance, or for hundreds at a county Alliance meeting, but which soon grew into vast spectacles; long trains of wagons, emblazoned with suballiance banners, stretching literally for miles, trekking to enormous encampments where five, ten and twenty thousand men and women listened intently to the plans of their Alliance and talked among themselves about those plans. At those encampments speakers, with growing confidence, pioneered a new political language to describe the "money trust," the gold standard and the private national banking system that underlay all of their troubles in the lien system.

How is a democratic culture created? Apparently in such prosaic, powerful ways. When a farm family's wagon crested a hill en route to a Fourth of July "Alliance Day" encampment and the occupants looked back to see thousands of other families trailed out behind them in wagon trains, the thought that "the Alliance is the people and the people are together" took on transforming possibilities.

The struggling farmers were brought together, more concretely, by the price of corn and wheat and cotton—falling prices, year after year, that ruined the most diligent among them. Wheat sold for $2.06 a bushel in 1866 and ten years later for only a dollar. By the 1880s, wheat was down to 80 cents a bushel. By the 1890s, wheat was getting only 60 cents and farmers in the Dakotas were selling theirs as low as 35 cents a bushel. The price of corn, which was 66 cents a bushel in 1866, was less than 30 cents three decades later and Kansas corn sold as low as 10 cents a bushel. Cotton prices followed a similar declining slope. The falling prices were accompanied inevitably by usurious interest rates. Both flowed from the same condition—a scarcity of money.

Price levels for basic commodities fell steadily for more than thirty years—the era known as the Great Deflation. Millions of humble farm families were forced into deeper poverty. Many were compelled to surrender what they thought was their American birthright—ownership of their own modest plot of land, a tangible asset that meant self-sufficiency and freedom to the hardworking yeomanry. Every growing season, as prices fell, their land and labor became worth less. To begin again at the next planting, they must borrow more at punishing rates to buy seed and supplies, but by harvesttime, prices had fallen further and they were unable to pay off their obligations. To continue farming, they must borrow still more. Eventually, when the debt became overwhelming, they would forfeit the land to their creditors, just as the *rentier* accumulated larger and larger holdings when the French peasantry failed. The process—liquidation and consolidation—was as old as capitalism.

As a social arbiter, the great price deflation of the late nineteenth century worked the opposite of the inflationary era experienced by Americans in the 1960s and 1970s. Inflation damaged well-fixed families by eroding the value of their accumulated financial assets, but inflation also spread wealth widely—enabling the broad middle class to enjoy a higher standard of living and to acquire greater net worth, largely through borrowing and repaying their debts in depreciated dollars. Deflation reversed the process: anyone who owned financial assets automatically enjoyed greater wealth as prices fell. Their dollar assets could purchase more in real goods; the value of their accumulated capital was steadily increased. Citizens with little or no savings, debtors who depended solely on their own productive labor for their livelihoods, saw their incomes shrink—and the real burden of their debts grow larger. American folklore described the consequences with blunt fatalism: "The rich got richer and the poor got poorer."

In every era of history, regardless of the changing political language, the money question was, inescapably, the bedrock of political choice. The debate over "hard money" and "easy money," falling prices or rising prices, inflation versus deflation, was really an argument about

which economic class must suffer, creditors or debtors, and which one
would benefit, those who derived their incomes primarily from their
accumulated financial wealth or those who still earned their livings by
"the sweat of their brow." American politics, not surprisingly,
yearned for a golden mean between the two—an elusive state of neutrality called "price stability," in which prices neither rose nor fell and
neither economic class gained at the expense of the other. The ideal
of stable money was held aloft by every generation of political leaders,
regardless of their party or ideological persuasion. Yet neutral money
was rarely realized in fact.

The plain people who carried the banners of the Farmers Alliance
in the 1880s understood these implications in considerable detail.
Modern Americans, educated in the conceit of ever-upward progress
and familiar with complex technologies that were unimagined a
hundred years ago, assumed that in every way they were more sophisticated than their forebears living in a simpler past. The politics of
money was an ironic and important exception. Citizens of the nineteenth century were routinely familiar with the political implications
of monetary policy and debated the question fiercely among themselves. Unencumbered by the veil of modern economics, ordinary people formed their own opinions on complicated aspects of money and
credit, subjects that in the twentieth century became reserved for
experts only. In this one dimension, at least, modern Americans were
more ignorant than their ancestors.

At scores of prairie encampments, the Alliance lecturers explained
to earnest audiences the source of their ruination: it was the gold
standard and the private banking system that enforced its rigid terms.
The money problem really started with the Civil War. Abraham Lincoln, like other presidents and kings before him, was compelled to set
aside the orthodox rules of "sound money" in order to win the war and
preserve the Union. To ensure ample credit, Congress suspended the
gold guarantee required for bank notes. To finance the Grand Army of
the Republic, Lincoln borrowed the then-astounding sum of $2.6 bil-
lion. Even more daring, the President issued nearly $500 million in
paper money that was not backed by gold—the "greenbacks"—currency that was not backed by anything but the government's word
(thus, fiat money is money created simply by government decree). All
together, these actions constituted a gross expansion of the money
supply, and the predictable result was roaring inflation. From 1861 to
1864, prices rose by 74 percent, the steepest inflationary spike since
the Revolution. The period was a flush time for farmers (farmers of
the victorious North, that is) and highly stimulative for manufacturing
too. Great new industrial centers arose rapidly, financed with cheap
money and nourished on the demands of war.

After Appomattox, accounts were settled and farmers slowly began to grasp that the financial balance had been set permanently against them. Farmers of the Middle West voted Republican, but the newly dominant political party listened to the financiers of the East, who demanded a swift return to "sound money." Lincoln's "greenbacks" were gradually retired from circulation, without anything to replace them. The gold standard was reimposed on all currency. Worse, the restoration of gold pegged money's value at its old prewar level of parity—an ounce of gold would once again be worth $20. That meant not just an end to inflation, but that prices must inevitably decline to their old prewar level too. The money supply was, in effect, being shrunk back to its original size—"hardened" dollars that would buy more for those who owned them.

This took some years to accomplish, but it did happen: by 1884, the national price level had declined to exactly where it had been in 1860. Then it fell further. As producers often do, the farmers tried to compensate for the falling prices by growing more wheat and corn and cotton—which only compounded their problems. The new mechanization of agriculture made it possible to produce greater yields, but the excess supply of commodities depressed crop prices still further, even below the prewar level, and the small farmers became even more vulnerable to the demands of creditors. One of the fondest speculations of the Populist rebels was that if Lincoln had lived he would not have let this happen to them.[1]

Whatever its virtues, the gold standard did not guarantee stable prices. Price stability under the gold standard, contrary to what its advocates have perennially claimed, was actually a rare and temporary condition that usually lasted no more than a couple of years. The historical record clearly demonstrated this, yet modern politicians and economists who espoused the gold standard as the only cure for inflation persisted in distorting the actual experience of the past. Typically, they alluded to the nineteenth century as a halcyon time of orderly growth and stable prices, when money's value was anchored by gold. The twentieth century, in contrast, was described as permanently biased toward inflation, fed by the paper money created *en fiat* by the Federal Reserve, unrestrained by the gold standard's guarantee of real value. To illustrate, gold advocates liked to point out that the price level in the United States in 1800 was almost precisely the same more than a century later—when the gold standard was permanently abandoned. This left out what happened to prices in between. The observation was narrowly correct, but fatuous—equivalent to suggesting that an airplane mainly flew on the ground, since, after all, it began and ended its flight at ground level.

Prices, in fact, both rose and fell drastically throughout the nine-teenth century—despite the gold standard and sometimes because of it. Wars interrupted gold's discipline or eras of expansionary credit produced bursts of inflation, in spite of gold.[2] The gold standard's effect was to eventually drive prices back down again, producing eras of disaster and disorder, not political peace (see Appendix A for a graphic illustration of U.S. price history). Indeed, the longest recorded stretch of genuine stability in the U.S. price average was actually one of the nation's most fractious periods—the years from 1885 to 1893 when America's farmers were driven to their desperate political rebel-lion and the fledgling labor movement was struggling combatively to protect workers' wages. The index of prices remained flat for nine years, but farmers' prices were falling while prices for other produc-tive sectors of the economy were rising—a turbulent condition that looked like economic stability only if viewed as a statistical abstraction (and only in distant hindsight).[3]

America's experience with unstable money was typical, not an aber-ration of history. Cycles of price inflation and deflation were recurring rhythms in the world's commerce long before there was a United States of America. They appeared in capitalist economies regardless of whether the currency was gold or silver or copper or a combination of those metals. Inflation occurred regularly both when governments managed the money and also when money was totally controlled by private market forces, with central banks and without them. The mas-ter historian Fernand Braudel, in his epic chronicle of the rise of capitalism, described the enduring competition between gold and sil-ver money and the epochs of unstable prices that swept across conti-nents and centuries:

Their production was irregular and never very flexible, so that depend-ing on circumstances, one of the two metals would be relatively more plentiful than the other; then, with varying degrees of slowness, the situ-ation would reverse, and so on. This resulted in upsets and disasters on the exchanges, and led above all to those slow but powerful fluctuations which were a feature of the monetary *ancien régime*. . . .

Ancient theoreticians would have liked a fixed relationship giving gold twelve times the value of silver for equal weights. This was certainly not the general rule from the fifteenth to the eighteenth century. The ratio at that time varied frequently around and beyond this so-called "natural" relationship. In the long term, the scales sometimes tipped towards one metal, sometimes towards the other. . . . The value of silver increased from the thirteenth to the sixteenth century, until roughly 1550. At the risk of straining the meaning of the word, we might say this was an age of gold inflation, which lasted for several centuries.

Braudel's sweeping and meticulous survey of premodern capitalism demonstrated, in fact, that none of the twentieth century's problems with money was particularly novel. For at least six centuries, the emerging capitalist system of Europe struggled with the same issues associated with an unstable money supply—repeated devaluations of currency, foreign-exchange imbalances between merchant cities and nations, economic depressions induced by a scarcity of money and economic booms stimulated by "easy money." In the sixteenth century, France experienced a century-long price inflation of more than 600 percent (roughly equivalent to U.S. price inflation over the last forty years). The city of Naples had a money stock of 700,000 ducats in 1570, which grew to 18 million ducats by 1751, a huge reserve of excess money, four times greater than what commerce required. When it could not be spent, the surplus money was made into usable objects—silver watches, snuffboxes, cane handles, forks and spoons, cups and plates.

In that context, one of the greatest inflationary acts ever undertaken by a sovereign government was the discovery of the Americas—the money supply of Europe was grossly multiplied by the import of precious metals plundered from the Incan mines. A long inflation resulted. In 1500, Braudel estimated, Europe had twenty thousand tons of silver. By 1650, another sixteen thousand tons had been added to the money supply. The gold inflation that had prevailed for three centuries was displaced by silver inflation as the value of silver currency was cheapened. The era produced the paradoxical maxim known as Gresham's law (named for Queen Elizabeth I's counselor): "Bad money drives out good." In other words, buyers will always prefer to use a watered-down currency to purchase real goods rather than a more precious one, for obvious reasons. It's cheaper. Gresham's law became less relevant once the competition between silver and gold disappeared and governments moved to fiat money, but it still expressed the eternal uncertainty over money's correct value.[4]

In fact, the long and turbulent history of inflation and deflation cycles suggested a heretical proposition: capitalism could not long abide stable prices. Otherwise, the centuries of experiment and innovation would surely have devised a monetary system that could provide stability. Perhaps, instead, the process of capital accumulation actually produced periodic cycles of changing money values—inflationary "easy money" to stimulate economic growth and spread wealth, followed by its depressant opposite, "hard money," which slowed down growth and reconsolidated the ownership of the newly created wealth. Certainly, that described the changing tides under which capitalism had flourished, from its most primitive stages to the present abundance.

If this proposition was correct, then the conventional opinion of both politics and economics was astride a deep paradox of capitalism: price stability was everyone's supposed goal and yet the economic system could not live with it. All economic participants, from consumers to capitalists, from merchants to manufacturers, sincerely wished for stable money, but any government or money system that successfully made stable money a permanent fact would eventually be confronted with political upheaval. No matter how prices were measured, there simply was no golden mean for money where every economic player would be treated with perfect equality. Money that was fixed in perpetual equilibrium, the ideal espoused by Western capitalism for centuries, would in fact be the formula for permanent stagnation and destruction. No government that depended on democratic elections for its authority could impose such conditions on its citizens and long endure.

The political obstacles that confronted the Populists were staggering. Charles W. Macune, one of the movement's most inventive intellectuals, recognized that political realities were fully against their reform agenda. "The people we seek to relieve from the oppression of unjust conditions," Macune observed, "are the largest and most conservative class of citizens in this country." In addition to their natural conservatism, the yeoman farmers were also divided by the inherited bitterness of region and party and the still-fresh memories of Civil War. Southern whites, many of whom had fought in the failed rebellion, were raised as Democrats, the "party of the fathers." The grain farmers of the Middle West were Yankee veterans who rallied to Republican orations invoking the "bloody shirt" and Lincoln's noble crusade to save the Union. To unite these two hostile groups in collective action—and also to include the newly freed blacks who were landless tenant farmers across the South—seemed an impossible aspiration. It was a measure of the general desperation that the Farmers Alliance even tried.

Across the cotton states, small farmers existed in a state of virtual peonage, their everyday lives held in bondage by the crop-lien system, an American version of the medieval usurer. In every hamlet, the "furnishing merchant" provided farm families with staples and supplies and took a lien on the farmer's cotton crop as security. If a farmer bought something for cash, he paid one price, but if he purchased on credit, he would pay 25 to 50 percent more. At the end of the season, when his crops were sold and his account settled, the "furnishing man" would add another 33 percent or so for interest. The real interest rate, thus, approached or exceeded 100 percent. There was nowhere else to turn; other merchants or banks would not extend credit to someone who was already indebted. With falling cotton prices, it was impossible for farmers to "pay out," and so the merchants took notes against the farmers' land. As the debts mounted and forfeiture was inescapable, tens of thousands of farmers—eventually millions of people—"descended into the world of landless tenantry," as Lawrence Goodwyn wrote. They became hired hands, sharecropping on the farms they had once owned, or displaced immigrants who streamed to the cities. This wholesale liquidation was entwined in the South's bitter memory of Reconstruction, the legacy that led Populist legislators, once they had gained power in places like Arkansas, to write stringent prohibitions of usury into their state laws and constitutions.

Usurious lending also afflicted farmers in the Middle West, though less dramatically, as they struggled to stay ahead of falling prices. The age of mechanization was opening and farmers were advised that the only way to maintain their income levels was to increase their efficiency—to produce greater yields from the same land and labor. The new machines they purchased on credit typically carried annual interest rates of 18 to 36 percent—chattel mortgages they would have to pay off in steadily appreciating dollars. When the farmers went to ship their grain, the railroads squeezed them further with arbitrary freight rates. "The farmer in the West," Goodwyn wrote, "felt there was something wrong with a system that made him pay a bushel of corn in freight costs for every bushel he shipped."

But the credit problem was larger than the personal anxieties of farmers sinking deeper into debt. The tight-money conditions imposed by restoration of the gold standard guaranteed permanently high interest rates, and the higher profits naturally flowed to the lenders, the banking system and the owners of wealth. But the money-and-credit system also creaked with rigidity and periodically broke down. When the demand for borrowing surged, typically in step with agricultural seasons, the money supply could not quickly or easily expand to provide additional credit, given the rules of the gold standard. Money creation was based on the quantity of gold in reserve, and, thus, more money could not be produced by the banking system until it acquired more gold reserves, usually by borrowing them from Europe. It took fifteen days for a shipment of gold to cross the Atlantic. In the meantime, the banking system was on its own.

The result, again and again when credit became scarce, was a rolling wave of illiquidity that rippled through the financial system, starving commerce for short-term credit and ruining hundreds of banks.

The squeeze typically started in the South and West—farmers bringing crops to market, merchants and traders needing short-term loans to finance the swollen transactions of local trade. When rural banks exhausted their resources, they turned to larger city banks for temporary loans. When the larger banks ran out of reserve funds, they turned to the money centers of the United States, the oldest and largest banks of New York or Chicago or St. Louis, which were great storehouses for America's accumulated fortunes.

Thus, as country bankers and their farm customers bitterly understood, life-or-death decisions over the economic health of Kansas or Texas or Mississippi resided ultimately in the distant offices of Wall Street, controlled by the dominant financiers like J. P. Morgan. When financial panic threatened, the money-center banks could usually provide sufficient temporary loans to allow the provincial banks to get through. Then as now, the banking system was interconnected by this fluid relationship among individual banks, which, in effect, transferred surplus funds to the institutions that needed them or laid off burgeoning loan commitments on the other banks that could absorb them.

Before 1913, however, there was no central bank to help banks through short-term liquidity squeezes. The only "lender of last resort" available to bail out the banking system was Wall Street—the despised "money trust" of Populist oratory. The house of Morgan would typically organize a syndicate of major lenders who came to the rescue with a package of loans to other banks (and who, not incidentally, charged very profitable rates for their risk). If the money-center bankers decided for their own reasons that they were unable to fill all the nation's demands for liquidity, then somewhere at the other end of the line banks failed and local commerce froze. This experience produced regional resentments and the abiding prejudice against Wall Street that still echoes in politics. Southern or western senators, including conservative Republicans, were likely to be much more suspicious of the financial system's control and more impatient with high interest rates than colleagues who grew up closer to the money-center banks.

Between price deflation and the inflexible money system, the national economy was regularly destabilized—contractions that added unemployment in mines and manufacturing to the woes of the farmers. The severe depression from 1873 to 1879 was the longest in U.S. history. Another contraction occurred in 1882 and lasted more than three years. A full-scale bank panic in the spring of 1893 led to two back-to-back recessions that lasted until 1897. The proximate cause of the panic of '93, according to Milton Friedman and Anna Schwartz, was depositors' fear about bank solvency, but the "deeper cause," they added, "was doubtless the preceding price deflation. Loans that would have been good and banks that would have been solvent if prices had been stable or rising became bad loans and insolvent banks under the pressure of price deflation."[5]

Ruin for some was prosperity for others. Friedman and Schwartz calculated that the national economy's output of goods actually increased fairly steadily throughout the three decades of deflation, despite the deep recessions, despite falling prices. The major source of growth was manufacturing, which was displacing agriculture as the country's premier economic activity. The census of 1890 was the first in which the value of manufactured goods exceeded that of farm products.

The Populists first proposed a solution to the money question in August 1886 at Cleburne, Texas, where the Farmers Alliance met in state convention. The "Cleburne Demands" borrowed heavily from the Greenback Party, which in the previous decade had fought the gold standard and defended Lincoln's fiat currency. The Texas farmers endorsed what for them was a radical departure—federal regulation of the banking system and a national currency that was not restrained by gold. But, unlike the liberal reformers who succeeded them in the twentieth century, the Populists were suspicious of centralized power in any form. They may have despised Wall Street bankers, but they distrusted Washington politicians almost as fervently. The North Carolina leader L. L. Polk once declared: "Congress could give us a bill in forty-eight hours that would relieve us, but Wall Street says nay. . . . I believe that both parties are afraid of Wall Street. They are not afraid of the people." Nevertheless, it seemed to the Populists that the federal government was the only center of power that could remedy the money problem.

The new "greenbacks" that the Populists proposed would provide the nation with a flexible money supply, one that could expand or shrink by government management to meet the real credit needs of the marketplace. The Populists' aim was frankly inflationist—getting prices to increase so they could earn livable incomes from their produce. To achieve that, the money supply must be greatly expanded, both through more silver and gold coinage and the new paper money they proposed. Treasury would issue government dollar bills as legal tender to replace the private bank notes in circulation. Congress would regulate money growth. In a subsequent refinement, the Alliance platform defined the "greenbacks" in the same words that would later appear on every Federal Reserve Note: ". . . legal tender for all debts, public and private."

Orthodox economists, bankers and politicians scoffed. Under the

Populist scheme, what was to keep the government from printing money ad infinitum? Growth of the money supply, the rural leaders explained, would be geared to the reality of the growing economy—"per capita circulation that shall increase as the population and business interests of the country expand." The money supply would be democratically controlled by elected representatives, not by an oligarchy of financiers and not by the mystical values attached to precious metals. At the time, it sounded like a dangerous invitation to anarchy. Three decades later, the Populist proposition was, in rough outline, the same economic principle that the Federal Reserve adopted.

By then, the agrarian reformers were defeated, their popular movement crushed. Their political energy was first co-opted by the Democrats and then vanquished by the Republicans. The central bank that Congress eventually created in 1913 was not at all what the Populists had in mind.

Something in the American character resented the idea of a central bank. It seemed undemocratic, and for nearly a century, the young Republic existed without one. When an embryonic version, the Bank of the United States, began operations in 1817, it was denounced as "the Monster" and was dismantled seventeen years later. Andrew Jackson built the Democratic Party around the question of whether a central bank was compatible with American ideals. Popular will—"the real people," as Jackson called them—agreed with him. A central bank meant "control would be exercised by a few over the political conduct of the many by first acquiring that control over the labor and earnings of the great body of people." In 1832, President Jackson vetoed legislation to keep the Bank of the United States alive. The following year the Treasury withdrew its funds from the Bank and deposited the money in a number of selected state banks, and the nation returned to "free banking" and unfettered economic development.

In the textbook summaries that schoolchildren must read, Jackson's Bank War sounded like a cranky oddment of history, one of those dead controversies from the past for which students are required to memorize the dates, but not to understand. It was, in fact, a seminal conflict in American politics—one of those basic arguments of purpose that did not go away with time, but merely evolved in form and language. Properly understood, the Bank issue raised by Jacksonian Democrats really involved the same questions that political parties always engage whenever they decide economic policy for the nation: How fast can the American economy grow? What is the full potential for an expanding prosperity that will spread its benefits widely? What

are the risks? The subject has now been given an austere title—
macroeconomics—and the presumption of bloodless objectivity. But,
in every era, the dispute is also governed by visceral feeling—a debate
between caution and optimism, between wary moderation and boundless faith.

Optimism won in Jackson's time, as it usually did in American
politics. Aside from the heroic stature of its leader, "Jacksonian Democracy" was a powerful set of ideals, all derived from essential elements of the American spirit—the ambitious striving of individual
enterprise, the celebration of productive labor over finance, an enduring suspicion of centralized power and, above all, the yearning for a
new kind of society in which every citizen would be his own master,
beholden to no other. Jackson's economic program spoke for all those
ideals. The "Monster Bank" was an authentic symbol for the economic forces that threatened them.

In economic terms, the agenda was internally inconsistent. The
Jacksonians described themselves as conscientious hard-money men
who supported the rigid discipline of the gold standard, yet they opposed the newly powerful national Bank because it restrained the
expansion of credit and, thus, thwarted robust economic expansion.
Formal thinkers were always offended when a political leader embraced competing ideas that did not logically go together, but contradiction did not necessarily weaken his popular standing. A political
agenda might actually be strengthened by rhetorical inconsistencies
—the appealing promise that it could accomplish all things at once,
by reconciling opposites, by refusing to choose between conflicting
desires. Andrew Jackson could be for sound money and, at the same
time, be against the autocratic bankers who wanted to hold back
American prosperity by restraining money and credit. The "real people" wanted both. The same political values (and the same contradictions) resonated in the economic debates of the late twentieth century.

The Bank of the United States was chartered by Congress amid the
inflationary surge caused by the War of 1812; its purpose was to restore stability to the nation's money and credit and also to restore the
bondholders who had lent their private wealth to the government to
finance the war. This was America's second experiment in central
banking. The first Bank of the United States had been launched by
Alexander Hamilton after the Revolution, then allowed to expire in
1811. The second BUS was housed in a Greek temple in Philadelphia
and was directed for a number of years by Nicholas Biddle, a brillant
financier from a famously wealthy family. As a matter of institutional
history, the central bank was descended from kings, the inheritor of
the monarch's authority, and the proximate model was the Bank of

England, chartered in 1694. In the United States, however, the people themselves were supposed to be the sovereign.

In a very short time, the second Bank accumulated enormous financial power. It held the federal government's deposits interest free and was also the largest store of private wealth. It became the dominant player in foreign exchange and the domestic money market—the place where other banks turned for reserves and where commercial ventures applied for capital. Thus, in a rough fashion, the Bank performed the same functions that would be assumed by the major financial houses of Wall Street in the Populist era and also the role of the Federal Reserve in the twentieth century—the "lender of last resort" that could save a foundering bank or doom it. Like the Fed, Biddle's Bank also attempted to regulate the economy, restraining credit when it appeared that speculative lending was becoming dangerously excessive or stimulating activity with easier terms if a recession was threatening. The tools were more primitive, knowledge of the economy less sophisticated, but Biddle would be celebrated by later generations of economic historians for his advanced grasp of business and finance.

In his own time, however, Biddle was the reincarnation of autocratic control—the few ruling over the many—precisely what sincere republicans sought to escape in America. Jackson defined his constituency of "real people" as planters, farmers, mechanics, laborers, the individual producers whose restless energies and common sense formed "the bone and sinew of the country." These were the raw and unsophisticated yeomanry who trampled the White House parlors on Jackson's Inaugural Day; he was the first President elected without the genteel credentials of Virginia or Boston. Their values were freedom, equality and the individual pursuit of happiness—unconstrained by a meddling government or anyone else.

Jackson's constituency was alive to opportunity—opening the frontier territory to agriculture and mining, developing roads and canals and railroads that would link up markets, constructing new towns and cities. Yet they also felt threatened. Their aspirations, their economic independence, seemed endangered by an encroaching web of concentrated power—the influence of wealth represented by the Bank of the United States combined with the then-innovative format for organizing economic power, the corporation. The two seemed to conspire against individual enterprise, manipulating economic outcomes with their mysterious paper transactions and using the federal government to enhance their own fortunes.

The key to preserving republican independence was credit. If the control of credit (and money creation) was concentrated in the hands of a few, then all the variety of individual enterprise would be held in thrall by them. On the western frontier, ambitious entrepreneurs and willing bankers were eager to gamble on new projects for development, but they had to turn to the East for financing. Back east, the established wealth holders and their bankers were always more skeptical, having been burned many times by grandiose schemes that failed or by provincial state banks that made loans and issued currency without the required gold reserves to back them up. The banking system, as Galbraith observed, had elastic standards in those times, reflecting the geographic conflict. South and westward, more distant from the eastern Establishment, state banks were less fastidious in their lending practices, more eager to believe in the potential of new ventures. The money-center banks, defenders of the already established wealth, naturally insisted on order. Provincial bank failures were commonplace, confirming the conservative caution of the East. But the looser credit standards on the frontier made possible the great leaps of development—entrepreneurial dreams that came true and bankers who were rewarded handsomely for blind faith. If caution always prevailed, the future might be more orderly and stable, but also stunted, robbed of its full potential.

This difference in perspective formed one of the permanent tensions of American political life—the caution of the money-center interests versus the uninhibited ambition of provincial developers. In modern politics, the regional conflicts became muted as the financial system developed its national scope, but the tension was still present beneath the surface, in a Texas oil boomer's resentment of big-city bankers, in the Middle West's paranoia about eastern dominance, in the small-town banker's complaints about Fed favoritism toward the largest banks. In the twentieth century, the political conflict took a new form in the arguments over federal credit programs. Who should control access to credit? Who should determine the level of risk taking and the potential of the future? When blocs of citizens or economic interests were turned down by the private financial system or found its terms too stingy, they turned to government as an alternative source of credit—for farm purchases, small-business ventures, home mortgages, business export financing, college tuitions and a long list of other investments. In every instance, the underlying political rationale for government credit subsidies was that the private lending system was wrong. If bankers would not or could not underwrite new ventures that the nation needed, then the government would intervene and dilute their control.

In the Jacksonian era, Biddle's Bank was the practical arbiter of these questions of credit. The Bank of the United States's natural posture was in close harmony with the money-center banks, not unlike the Federal Reserve's a century later and for the same reasons. The Bank shared the same cautious perspective of the largest commercial banks and the same fears that runaway lending and expansion by reckless state banks would eventually lead to calamity, inflation or collapse that could undermine the value of accumulated wealth. In an ultimate sense, the Bank could guide, if not determine, the course of development—which new projects would go forward, which states and localities would be held back, how fast the young nation would be allowed to develop its raw resources.

The popular resentments, in other words, were not the misinformed fears of a backward citizenry. Opposition to the Bank reflected real economic complaints, real questions about the practical dimensions of who held power in a democracy. Historian Marvin Meyers provided an illuminating examination of the struggle in his essay *The Jacksonian Persuasion:* ". . . when one speaks of the Bank as a symbol of corporate power, monopoly privilege, complex credit economy, and so on . . . the symbolic relationship is more nearly that of the powerful king to his state than that of the flag to the sentiment of loyality." The Bank was the symbol, but it was also the reality. As President Jackson said, it was founded on "a distrust of the popular will as a safe regulator of political power."

Andrew Jackson became an icon for modern liberalism in the Democratic Party because he spoke for the same people—farmers and workers, the industrious middle class—and he challenged concentrated power in the same institutions, banks and corporations. Yet, as his words suggested, the values of Jacksonian Democracy also infused the thinking of many conservatives in the modern Republican Party. They shared his contempt for centralized government, his commitment to the individualism and the free striving of entrepreneurs, his desire to conserve cherished old values that were threatened by a changing society. Election after election, the contest for votes between the major political parties, between liberal and conservative alternatives, was a continuing redefinition of who exactly was to be addressed as the "real people" at the center of American politics and which of those fundamental values were presently important to them.

When Jackson's "real people" triumphed in 1832 and Biddle's Bank of the United States was stripped of its powers, the results were so dynamic that both sides could claim their arguments were confirmed by events. Without the Bank's overarching control of money and credit, a vast boom developed—followed by a surge of inflation and eventually economic contraction. In that sense, the fears of the eastern bankers were dramatically fulfilled. European wealth was lent to develop America and America defaulted massively, many times. Bray

Hammond, the Federal Reserve's own historian, disparaged the results—a promising monetary system was destroyed, state banks were freed from federal control, rampant speculation was encouraged. The consequence, Hammond lamented, was a "reckless, booming anarchy."

But the Jacksonians were right about America: the country could develop much faster than the cautious bankers of the East had imagined. And it did. A wild economic boom developed, fed by a dizzyingly generous creation of money and credit (created by the banks "more or less out of nothing," as one economic historian complained). Without Biddle's Bank to inhibit them, frontier dreamers and land speculators plunged forward hopefully with new schemes, some sound and some outlandish.

The decade of the 1830s, even with its excesses, became a time of extraordinary development—gambles that mostly paid off and permanently advanced the economic structure of the nation. More than three thousand miles of canals were built between 1816 and 1840— about two-thirds during the thirties. The decade produced roughly the same mileage in new railroads. The transportation systems linked markets and, thus, allowed the division of labor to progress to a higher plane, the specialization of production that was the keystone of an efficient capitalist economy. The developing economic markets fueled a spectacular urban boom as towns and cities grew twice as fast as the overall population. In a single decade, the North Central states doubled in population. In 1830, Chicago was a mere dream of land speculators; thirty years later, it was a bustling reality.

"Reckless, booming anarchy," in short, produced fundamental progress. It was not a stable system, racked as it was with bank failures and collapsed business ventures, outrageous speculation and defaulted loans. Yet it was also energetic and inventive, creating permanent economic growth that endured after the froth had blown away. While some economic historians labored the moot question of how the young economy might have fared if Biddle's Bank had continued as its financial steward, Marvin Meyers thought the balance between excess and progress clearly favored the Jacksonians and their reckless optimism.

"Those who gambled on the future rise of the public lands in the West," Meyers explained, "were madmen only in the short-run business sense—only in thinking that future prospects could be realized all at once by means of an infinitely expansible credit system—and not in their basic sense of direction." The whirlwind creation of credit, wasteful as it was, had the effect of transferring purchasing power from the passive elements in the economy to the activists. "After all

the casualties are mourned, the bankrupt enterprises and the bankrupt states, one still sees reason in the improvement madness of the
1830s, and results of unlimited importance," Meyers concluded.[6]

The phrase that Fed historian Bray Hammond employed pejora-
tively—"reckless, booming anarchy"—in fact rang a joyous chord in
the American character. It sounded hopeful, creative, free. The
"reckless, booming" mentality tempted fate, the risk of inflationary
excess and collapse, but it also defied fate, by insisting that positive
thinkers could shape their own destinies. It was very American—self-
confident and forward-looking and, on occasion, cocky. This attitude
included an assumption about credit that was closely linked to the
idea of equality. Some citizens were wealthy and some were not, but
the adventurous with acquisitive ambitions should not be held back
by those who already had theirs. If credit was the tool for realizing
America's possibilities, then it should be put in the hands of the bold
ones who would use it. Americans wanted order and stability; they
also wanted endless opportunity and growth.

Economic convictions, though cloaked in theory and data, were
nonetheless rooted in one's personal disposition toward the future. It
was these emotions—hope and doubt, ambition and caution—that
formed the psychological subtext for every great political debate. Both
Republican and Democratic parties contested over the same sentiments, in modern times, changing their economic perspectives as circumstances changed, sometimes even trading identities as one
political party became the optimist and the other became the doubter.

For the Jacksonians, the final paradox was this: their political victory led ultimately to defeat for their nostalgic vision of America. The
virtuous yeoman Republic that they sought to preserve was, in fact,
obliterated by the future they made possible. The impersonal corporations that Jackson despised proved to be the most effective vehicle
for organizing the far-flung activities of the emerging national markets.
Quite naturally, the national financial system grew with them, developing its own parallel networks to finance the new order. The new
roads and canals, the railroads and booming cities, provided the physical infrastructure that was the necessary prerequisite for the rise of
corporate capitalism.

"Reckless, booming anarchy" had inadvertently created a new
world, and it was this changed economic reality that threatened the
next generation of "real people." Fifty years after Jackson, the Populist farmers on the plains and prairies found themselves encircled by
its awesome complexity. Reluctantly, the conservative farmers agreed
that they must turn for relief to the one remaining source of alternative
power, the federal government.

• • •

The "Populist moment," as Goodwyn called it, was brief. The movement spread furiously for a few years and then, like a prairie fire, burned itself out. Unable to sell its unconventional ideas to either Republicans or Democrats, the Farmers Alliance created the People's Party and ran its own candidate for President in 1892. The ticket drew more than one million votes, about one of every twelve, and won electoral votes from six states, but that was a long way from attaining real power.

Political realities pushed the agrarian reformers toward fusion with sympathetic Democrats, but the issue on which they united was not the Populists' imaginative scheme for a new national currency system, but a simple inflationist proposition—free silver. If the government minted new silver coins in abundance, that would expand the money supply and dilute the deflationary power of gold, raise prices and bring relief to the farmers. In 1896, William Jennings Bryan of Nebraska became the presidential nominee of the Democratic Party and also the insurgent People's Party. Co-opted by the Democrats and the silver issue, the movement's original agenda was already effectively defeated. When Bryan lost to McKinley in the election of 1896, Populism was finished as a serious threat to the established order.

The indelible memory of the Populist era, the one taught in schoolbooks, was of silver, Bryan and his famous "cross of gold" speech. But, as Goodwyn explained in *The Populist Moment*, these images grossly distorted the real experience and concealed the substantive core of Populist thinking. Bryan was a late convert who made himself leader of an army that was already marching; his "free silver" platform was shallow, even reactionary, compared with the far more radical plan that Populist thinkers had devised.

In 1889, they had proposed a new monetary system for the nation that would create money "in the name of the whole people," that would ensure ample credit for productive enterprises and free producers from the control of commercial bankers. Called the "sub-treasury plan," it was calculated to use the pure credit inherent in the sovereign national government to finance directly the productive efforts of the most humble citizens—a democratic money system, in other words, that was much too radical for the American system, then or now.

The Populists' bold concept evolved, a step at a time, from experience and practical frustration. From the beginning, the heart of the Alliance movement was the formation of farmer cooperatives as the way to escape the deflationary squeeze of tight money and the demands of usurious lenders. The cooperatives would buy the farmers' cotton or corn, store it in cooperative warehouses and then resell it at optimum prices, thus protecting individual farmers from the harrowing losses of a glutted marketplace. The cooperatives also served as purchasing and credit collectives, buying supplies at wholesale and selling them to farmers at low interest rates, insulating them from the ruinous interest rates demanded by merchants. Through cooperative action, the angry farmers believed, they would win back their independence.

The largest and most ambitious cooperative was the statewide Texas Exchange and it was also the first to fail. The problem was access to credit—the carry-over financing that the cooperative needed to stretch from planting to harvest, to pay farmers for their cotton before it could be marketed. To raise its own capital, the Texas Exchange sold stock shares to the impoverished farm families at $2 per capita and collected more than $20,000. For collateral, the cooperative made an extraordinary request of its landowning members: they were asked to put up title to their own farms as security so the cooperative could borrow the funds to purchase supplies and extend crop loans to all its members, including the landless sharecroppers. By the spring of 1888, the Texas Exchange had collected more than $200,000 in collateral, the notes pledged on land and livestock by Texas farmers. With that secure base, the exchange managers confidently went ahead and ordered $108,000 in supplies for the growing season.

But the bankers refused to lend. When Charles W. Macune, business manager for the Texas Exchange, tried to borrow the working capital, he was turned down. He went to bankers in Dallas, Houston, Fort Worth, Galveston and New Orleans, but they refused to advance operating credit in exchange for the farmers' notes. The best he could get was a $6,000 loan in Houston for which the lender demanded $20,000 in farm notes as collateral. Macune concluded that "all those who controlled the moneyed institutions of the state either did not choose to do business with us, or they feared the ill will of a certain class of businessmen who considered their interests antagonistic to those of our order."

The Texas Exchange was suddenly in crisis, unable to borrow or to pay for the supplies it had ordered from wholesalers. It survived, but barely, through a dramatic fund-raising campaign across the state in which farmers put up another $80,000 to save their cooperative venture. The following year, frozen out again by the private banking system, the Texas Exchange went under.

Macune, who was trained as both doctor and lawyer, became a self-taught economist, studying the theories of money and credit, searching for a plausible solution. The cooperatives were doomed, he recognized, unless there was a fundamental change in the lending system. Texas Populists had already declared for fundamental money reforms in their Cleburne Demands of 1886: to halt the price deflation, the nation must abandon the gold standard and move to a fiat currency of Treasury notes, a flexible money supply that would respond to seasonal surges in the demand for credit. Those concepts were already too advanced for the elites who dominated banking and politics; now Macune leaped further beyond them into the realm of government-supplied credit.

At the St. Louis Alliance convention in 1889, Macune unveiled his radical plan for money: the U.S. Treasury would establish federal warehouses and grain elevators in every county with significant agricultural production, and these thousands of "sub-treasuries" would serve as the valves for money creation. A farmer would put his corn or cotton in storage at the sub-treasury and then could borrow against his crops at a 1 or 2 percent rate or he could sell the crops at prevailing market prices or borrow on the value of his land. The farmer would be paid in legal tender, the greenback dollars printed by the government as the new national currency, or in negotiable certificates of deposit that could be used in trade. The government, thus, would be creating new money and putting it into circulation via the loans made to farmers—a money supply that would be based on real production, the tangible goods in storage. In theory, when farmers repaid their loans, the currency would be paid back into the Treasury and extinguished, withdrawn from the circulating money supply—much as the Federal Reserve System creates and destroys money through the medium of bank reserves and bank lending.

The difference, however, is crucial: the Populist plan essentially would employ the full faith and credit of the United States government directly to assist the "producing classes" who needed financing for their enterprises. In effect, it would circumvent the bankers and provide credit straight to the users, particularly the small farmers who needed it most, who were most vulnerable to the demands of the private credit system. The government would provide "money at cost," instead of money lent by merchants and bankers at 35 or 50 or 100 percent interest.

The money-creation system that was adopted in 1913, instead, preserved the banking system as the intermediary that controlled the distribution of new money and credit. When the Fed expanded the money supply, commercial bankers decided who would get to use it and also how much it would cost. The Federal Reserve never interfered in those decisions, despite its occasional pleas to the banking system to favor certain kinds of borrowers or to avoid others. In that sense, the Fed shrank from the full implications of its power and, instead, delegated the allocation of new credit to private interests.

The first consequence of the Populist scheme, if it had been adopted, would have been a dismantling of the old order, the hierarchical control implicit in the private credit system and also the regional conflicts between eastern money and provincial development. In terms of the money mechanics, the Populist solution seemed to reverse what the Jacksonians had wanted. The Populists wanted to abandon gold and create a central bank, exactly the opposite of Andrew Jackson's agenda. Yet, despite the policy differences, both movements spoke for the same aspirations, the same classes of Americans. Democracy, they insisted, required a democratic money system —one that dispersed economic power on a broadly democratic plane, that decentralized the control of credit and gave a free run to the natural economic energies that would spread the opportunities and incomes as widely as possible. The "real people" would be enhanced; the power of wealth holders would be diminished.

The second consequence, just as dramatic, would have been the abrupt reversal of falling prices—an explosive surge of inflation that would have restored prosperity for agricultural producers. The purpose of the land loans, in particular, was to expand the money supply to about $50 in circulating currency per capita—roughly the same per capita money supply that existed during the Civil War. Higher prices would have swiftly followed, doubling and tripling, with the same egalitarian consequences that usually accompanied inflation. In each and every instance, inflation was a political phenomenon—a decision to serve the many over the few.

It was the road not taken. *The New York Times*, reflecting conventional wisdom of the era, denounced the Populist plan as "one of the wildest and most fantastic projects ever seriously proposed by sober man." Yet John Maynard Keynes later saluted these self-taught agrarians as "a brave army of heretics," for Keynes recognized that their economic analysis anticipated his own. Many decades later, William P. Yohe, a monetary economist at Duke University, analyzed the subtreasury scheme and concluded that, despite some flaws, it would have worked more or less as intended—forcing up prices, distributing new wealth more broadly and grossly stimulating the national economy.[7]

For some years, Populist congressmen introduced legislative versions of Macune's original concept, but most mainstream politicians and economists dismissed the Populists as irresponsible cranks (one economist who did not was Richard T. Ely, founder of the American Economic Association). Fifty years later, during the Great Depression, the price-stabilization aspects of Macune's sub-treasury plan were incorporated in the New Deal farm programs—government purchasing and storage of crops, accompanied by subsidized credit for farmers. But the concept was stripped of its deeper implications—the reform of money.

The struggling farmers eventually won relief from the devastating deflation, but by a fluke of history. In the late 1890s, prices stopped falling and started rising smartly again, a steady inflation that lasted for twenty years and restored prosperity to the agricultural producers. The cause had nothing to do with politics or government policy. It was caused by a surge in the supply of gold—new gold fields discovered and developed in Alaska, Colorado and South Africa that doubled the world's stock of gold between 1890 and 1914.

The central element of the Populist plan, a democratized monetary system, was much too radical to be seriously pursued by later generations of reformers. At its core, the plan was an audacious redefinition of money—money was a contract with the future, not an obligation to the past. A free society could determine that contract for itself, in a democratic manner, and fulfill its terms, independent of the demands imposed by the old wealth accumulated from past enterprises. In short, the national government could create money and invest it with a social purpose—promoting greater equality—because the government was the ultimate guarantor of the future. The new money created by government, the Populists reasoned, would be free (save for the costs of printing and handling), yet valuable. Where did its value come from? From everyone—from the mutual consent given by all, and so all should share in its power.

Nearly a century later, "populist" distempers would still echo regularly through American politics, but the core ideas were moribund and the Populist label was randomly claimed with dubious legitimacy. In an especially perverse twist, some discontented Americans who called themselves "populist" campaigned earnestly for a return to the gold standard. Most were middle-class businessmen or professionals, doctors and dentists and ranchers, who were deeply alienated from the governing elites of both Wall Street and Washington. In that cultural sense, they were authentically "of the people." But, in economic terms, they were on the other side of the money question—minor members of the creditor class distressed by inflation. The fact that *The Wall Street Journal* championed this "populist" cause ought to have suggested which interests expected to benefit from the restoration of gold. On the whole, they were the same interests that had defeated the original Populists.[8]

To complete the ironic symmetry, one genuine legatee of the Populist thinking was himself a wealthy investment banker. Louis O. Kelso, a San Francisco banker with libertarian values, tirelessly promoted a modern equivalent of the sub-treasury plan that he had devised—a money-and-credit system that would use the central bank to distribute the ownership of new capital democratically and, thus, restore the economic autonomy that so many had lost. If everyone owned capital, each would be more free—less dependent on both concentrated wealth and the liberal welfare state. Kelso's vision resonated with the same principles (and the same distrusts) that had motivated the original Populism, but his mechanics were adapted to the terms of corporate capitalism. Owning stock had replaced owning farmland as the primary source of wealth and independence, but access to credit was still the heart of the matter.

Despite years of derision from conventional economists, Kelso's invention—employee-owned trusts that held stock in corporations (better known as ESOPs)—was gradually spreading in use, especially among thousands of smaller or embattled companies. But few politicians or policy analysts would listen seriously to Kelso's more radical proposition: the Federal Reserve's money-creation powers could be harnessed directly to the need for new capital, channeling low-interest credit to new enterprises, provided that the stock ownership of these companies was distributed broadly among workers and communities, indeed to all citizens. Instead of only buying government securities when it created money, the Fed would also buy the debt paper of employee-owned or community-owned trusts, which financed new capital formation. When the new ventures paid off the debts on their new machines and factories, the loan paper would be retired and ordinary citizens would hold title to the new capital stock. Over a generation or longer, without confiscating or nationalizing anyone's property, the ownership of wealth would become more broadly distributed.

Kelso's plan envisioned essentially the same money process that Macune and the others had espoused a century before: by gaining access to capital credit, people would have access to owning wealth. Kelso would encounter the same hostilities, the same objections. Like the sub-treasury plan, there was no technical reason why Kelso's scheme (or at least a modest version) could not be made to work compatibly with the Fed's other obligation to control the expansion of money and credit. But there were many political reasons. He was offering a new version of the political choice that American politics had always refused to make.[9]

.   .   .

The Populists had an expansive conception of democracy's possibilities that, from the perspective of the late twentieth century, seemed grandly innocent. Certainly, it was too much for their contemporaries. It was radical enough to abandon gold and silver, the ancient guarantees of money's value, and to entrust the management of money to mere mortals. To go the next step and allow democratic aspirations to shape the money process seemed recklessly idealistic. Popular desires, it was said, would inevitably outstrip realistic prospects and debase the currency, and politics would corrupt the decisions. Accumulated capital—and the political power it embodied—would be the permanent hostage of democracy.

In the American system, it was decided, the people could not be trusted with these questions. Some issues, it seemed, were too important to be decided by democratic process. The Populist vision was rejected and history chose a different alternative. When the Federal Reserve was created in 1913, purposely insulated from the hot breath of politics, the new institution effectively defined the permanent limits of American democracy.

9

THE GREAT
COMPROMISE

The house of Morgan towered above the pedestrian ranks of American finance and business like a great baronial castle, dreadful in its feudal power but also admirable in its way.

The "money trust," as *The Wall Street Journal* insisted in a 1912 editorial, was really just another name for J. Pierpont Morgan. Morgan himself was the prototypal financier whose image lived on as the American caricature of the tycoon—an austere patrician, balding, with a gray walrus moustache, wing collar and cravat, a gold watch chain across his vest. As the object of intense public hatred, he was serenely indifferent to the howls of the mob. In his own world, J. P. Morgan was regarded as something of a hero.

The Morgan banks could execute dazzling and ruthless manipulations in the stock market—cornering, crushing, swallowing their corporate prey. At the same time, Morgan was the ultimate guarantor of stability and order in the banking system, the man whom other bankers turned to in distress. With a few confident strokes, it was said, J. P. Morgan could stop bank panics. Some critics were convinced that he also started them.

Morgan was among those masterminds of capital—men like Rockefeller, Harriman, Du Pont and others—who organized the new century. They saw the emerging shape of things and moved boldly to seize control. It was not a pretty struggle, and in their own time, these men were denounced for greed, power lust and a brutal indifference to human suffering. But they invented the structure of industrial produc-

tion that would dominate American commerce in the twentieth century—consolidating whole sectors into mammoth corporate organizations with names like Standard Oil, AT&T, U.S. Steel and General
Motors. In social influence, they were America's closest approxima-
tion of European royalty.

As the banker of bankers, Morgan also assumed a mantle of noblesse oblige. When the banking system was swept with panic and
illiquidity, it was Morgan who organized the loan syndicates among
major banks that came to the rescue. Morgan and his men made the
choices about which banks would be saved and which ones allowed to
fail, a function that won limited gratitude from the survivors (since
they paid dearly for the assistance) and lasting enmity from the
doomed. At his zenith, J. P. Morgan was so powerful that even the
federal government came to him for help and he agreed to save it from
impending financial ruin. Naturally, he was hated. He was also indis-
pensable.

> The condition that has developed in Wall Street in the past fifteen years
> is to a considerable extent a personal one [the *Journal* editorial explained],
> and the authority which centers in the hands of Mr. Morgan, a man
> seventy-five years of age, is by no means something which can be passed
> down to his successors. Such men have no successors; and their work is
> either left undone after they are dead or the world devises other means
> and other works to take its place. There were no successors to Napoleon,
> Bismarck, Cecil Rhodes or E. H. Harriman, and their authority was not
> perpetuated.[1]

The commentary seemed prescient. By the following year, 1913,
J. P. Morgan was dead, and on November 16, 1914, the Federal Reserve opened its doors and effectively replaced him by "other means."
The mantle of Morgan's private authority was inherited by the Fed—
and also his sense of noblesse oblige. Morgan's informal stewardship
was formalized in law and depersonalized as a remote agency of government. While many citizens would continue to rail at the mysterious
powers of the Fed, it was, on the whole, more difficult to blame an
institution than an individual. The public wrath directed at the handful
of bankers associated with the "money trust" was much harder to
sustain once the object of attack was a faceless bureaucracy.

The paternalistic attitude that would permeate the Federal Reserve
as an institution reflected the same sense of exalted public mission
felt by the "Morgan men." Indeed, the two institutions would remain
intimate through future decades, so much so that Morgan Guaranty
became known informally as the "Fed bank."[2] One was private and

the other was public, but they thought alike. Outsiders were rankled by the aristocratic clubbiness. Inside the Fed, it was regarded as a legacy of honor.

The Federal Reserve System would not, of course, continue Morgan's brutal stock-market forays for the control of private corporations or the aggressive profit taking that had caused so much resentment. But the Fed did assume his place as the castle, overseeing the fields of finance. Like Morgan, the Federal Reserve would be the ultimate defender of stability, with the power to protect and also, implicitly, to destroy. And officers of the Federal Reserve would fully understand, as J. P. Morgan had, that they would not be loved for their efforts.

Sometimes in human events, momentous decisions were driven by the wrong question and based on mistaken answers. Was there really a "money trust" that controlled everything? The idea that a Wall Street financial monopoly had gained a stranglehold on the American economy absorbed the nation in 1912, stimulated by two decades of bewildering financial turbulence and brutal corporate consolidations. People wanted explanations. A sensational investigation conducted by a House banking subcommittee early that year seemed to reveal them. Twelve banks in New York, Boston and Chicago, the investigators found, held a total of 746 interlocking directorships in 134 corporations —railroads, insurance, manufacturing, public utilities, trading companies, other banks.

The implications were frightening. The public's alarm provided the necessary political steam that led to reform of the nation's money system, the legislation enacted in 1913 to create the Federal Reserve System. As a matter of cold logic, however, the solution did not answer the popular discontents surrounding the "money trust." Whether by accident or design, the Fed may have actually preserved the financial power of those very bankers who the public thought were at last being brought under control. Great moments in history were often surrounded by a confusion of purposes.

Representative Robert L. Henry of Texas, one of the last genuine Populists to serve in Congress, summarized the evidence from the congressional investigation:

It is sufficient to say that, during the last five years, the financial resources of the country have been concentrated in the city of New York, until they now dominate more than 75 percent of the moneyed interests of America, more than 75 percent of the industrial corporations which are combined in the trusts, and practically all of the great trunk railways running from ocean to ocean; until these great forces are in such combi-

nation and agreement that it is well-nigh impossible for honest competition
to be set up against them.

The popular sense of conspiracy was greatly enhanced when George
McC. Reynolds, president of the Continental Bank of Chicago, the
largest outside New York, testified before the House investigation.
"The money power now lies in the hands of a dozen men, of whom I
plead guilty to being one," Reynolds confessed. But when J. P. Morgan himself was called to testify, he dismissed the talk of a "money
trust" as nonsense. "All the banks in Christendom could not control
money," Morgan insisted. "There could be no 'money trust.' "

Morgan was essentially correct—or at least closer to the reality than
the melodramatic accusations against him. Contrary to what the public and congressional reformers believed, the problem was not that a
few well-placed tycoons were in control of the nation's money system.
The problem was that no one was in control of it. As the leading
bankers of Wall Street appreciated, the United States must now at
last devise what its citizens had so long resisted—a central bank,
invested with the authority of government, to manage money and
credit.

In the decade after 1900, as the Populist revolt faded, bankers
replaced farmers as the leading voices for monetary reform. For the
distressed farmers, the money question had been primarily a complaint about prices. Their central grievance had been alleviated in the
late 1890s when a sudden surge in the world's supply of gold from the
Yukon and South Africa had produced a prosperous era of rising
prices. But the money question always had a parallel component to it
—the issue of instability in the banking system caused by the inflexi-
bility of money and credit. This was the concern that persuaded nervous bankers of the East and industrial Midwest that the system must
be altered. With considerably more political clout at their disposal,
the bankers picked up the cause that western and southern farmers
had futilely championed and refashioned the reform goals to coincide
with their own interests. Not surprisingly, the bankers neglected to
acknowledge any intellectual debt to the agrarian agitators whose wild
proposals they had denounced only a few years earlier.

For two decades, the banking system was shaken by periodic
tremors, the panic in 1893 and again in 1895 and, most severely, the
panic of 1907, which even closed an important bank in New York City.
The troubles usually started with seasonal surges in the demand for
agricultural credit. Across the country, the thousands of nationally
chartered country banks were required to maintain their reserves on

deposit at larger banks in forty-seven "reserve cities," and these reserve banks, in turn, kept their reserves at the largest banks in the
three "central reserve cities" (principally New York but also Chicago
and St. Louis). In theory, the nation's total supply of reserves was
ample enough to support the periodic surges in lending, but in practice, the reserves were spread out widely and in the wrong places—
immobile money that could not be quickly redirected to where it was
needed.

When the autumn demand for loans increased, the country banks
drew down their reserve cash on deposit in the forty-seven reserve
cities, and the reserve banks, in order to restore their own depleted
balances, would have to withdraw funds from the three central reserve
cities. If lending continued to expand in the countryside, the pressure
to supply more reserves intensified in New York—"much like a whip,
where a little force at one end produced a tremendous force at the
other," as historian Roger T. Johnson put it.[3]

New York banks held vast fortunes in their vaults, and up to a point,
Morgan and the others could satisfy the expanding demand, perhaps
raising their rates in order to discourage further lending. When
pressed, they could organize far-flung loan syndicates, mobilizing the
idle reserves on deposit at many scattered banks. If they had enough
time, they could turn to London or Paris and borrow more gold from
Europe, permitting the money supply to expand and re-lending the
new funds to the American banks that were in need.

When all these contingencies failed, a panic began. New York
would begin saying no to the next requests and somewhere in America
banks would begin to fail, unable to meet loan commitments or to
honor their depositors' withdrawals. When the word of a bank failure
spread, depositors everywhere panicked—rushed to their banks and
demanded their money. These "runs" multiplied the crisis many
times, often toppling otherwise solvent institutions that did not have
enough cash on hand to pay out all their checking deposits. As failures
cascaded through the system, closing large and small banks almost
randomly, many innocent people lost their savings and, without credit,
normal commerce was frozen. Deep recessions accompanied the
money crisis, collapsing prices and "smashing" the financial markets.

Given the pivotal role of Wall Street bankers (and the accompanying
spectacle of their stock-market manipulations), it was natural that
people blamed them for these waves of destruction. In a narrow sense,
Wall Street financiers did decide when banks would fail and which
favored banks would be saved. When panic struck, Wall Street financiers did take advantage of the collapsing financial markets to enhance
their own profits and gobble up corporations. The monetary problems

were more systemic, however, than mere greed. Imperious bankers of the East may have been as wicked as the people of Texas or Iowa believed, but they were not what caused the recurring crisis.

Two rigidities interacted to create waves of panic: the immobile reserves, scattered too thinly around the country to be redirected quickly to the banks that needed them, and the inflexible money supply tied to gold, unable to expand fast enough to supply seasonal surges in bank lending. These problems were compounded by the public's lingering distrust of account-book money, existing only as a number in a checking deposit (even though by then Americans held $6 in demand-deposit money for every $1 they held in cash). In troubled times, people wanted to have their money in real dollar bills they could see and touch and put under the mattress until the panic ended. So they rushed to the banks.

In 1894, when Populist orators still were pushing the sub-treasury plan and free silver, the American Bankers Association proposed the first version of what bankers regarded as reform—a new national currency, unconditionally guaranteed by the federal government, distributed by commercial banks. The following year, another devastating panic swept the country. It took fifteen more years of debate and crisis before solutions emerged.

As the Populist unrest approached its crest, nervous investors feared that either hyperinflation or even political revolution would wipe out their assets. In 1895, they began fleeing from the American system, withdrawing their wealth from U.S. financial assets, demanding gold and shifting it to Europe. The federal government's own gold reserve was drained so rapidly that it was threatened with depletion. The desperate Treasury turned to J. P. Morgan. He organized a syndicate of bankers and they bailed out the U.S. government with a loan of 3.5 million ounces of gold.

A dozen years later, the bailout was reversed. Morgan and his allies not only failed to contain the panic of 1907, but they were compelled to seek help from Washington. The bank crisis that unfolded that autumn was different—it struck Wall Street itself. The Knickerbocker Trust Company, third largest in New York City, was forced into sudden bankruptcy and two others were driven to the brink. Morgan organized a money pool of $25 million for emergency loans, then another $10 million the next day. But as he tried to contain the Wall Street crisis, alarm rippled across the country. Provincial banks rushed to draw down their reserves, anticipating that dreadful moment when New York would cut them off. The self-protective hoarding of reserves only added to the pressures. Cumulatively, it was more than Morgan and his men could handle.

The Treasury in Washington did what it could to help (prompted in part by Morgan's personal plea to President Theodore Roosevelt). Treasury responded much the way a central bank would react—by pumping liquidity into the banking system. As the crisis threatened in September, the government shifted millions of dollars in federal funds to deposits at commercial banks around the nation and tried to limit government withdrawals. On October 24, the day after the Knickerbocker failure, Washington rushed $25 million to the major New York banks—technically a deposit but effectively an interest-free emergency loan. The bankers could lend out the new funds to whoever was threatened with insolvency (and also collect interest on the loans). In all, the government provided nearly $38 million for New York alone. In November, by presidential order, the Treasury issued $150 million in low-interest bonds and certificates and permitted the banks to use the government securities as collateral for creating new currency—an expedient device for pumping up the money supply in a hurry. The crisis subsided, but the economic effects were again ruinous.

The 1907 trauma convinced Wall Street. The financial system and even the banks' own security could no longer depend on the good offices of a few titans like Morgan. Money reform became not just an interesting ideal but a practical necessity. From that point on, the major banks and financiers applied their political influence to achieving it. Historian Gabriel Kolko described the watershed:

> The panic of 1907 was an indication of the extent to which the ability to control crises had moved out of the hands of the New York bankers. If it was merely a question of raising $50 million in a healthy European financial market, as in 1895, Morgan would have been able to handle the task. But the American economy, and the scale of its needs, had grown tremendously, and it was as much affected by conditions outside New York as in the city itself. By 1907, Morgan, Stillman (of the Rockefeller bank) and other key leaders of finance were old men, and the strain of the situation was more than they could bear financially or psychologically.[4]

The old order was failing. Villainous Wall Street was actually losing its dominant position over American finance. A Treasury Department study in 1913 quantified the diffusion of financial power that was occurring as industrial capitalism dispersed its enterprises across the nation. Despite the periodic banking disasters, the number of banks in the United States increased two and a half times from 1900 to 1912 (roughly from ten thousand to twenty-five thousand), nearly twice as fast as the population. Most of the growth, naturally, was far distant from New York. During these twelve years, the percentage increase in banking capital and deposits was two to four times greater in the West and the South than it was in the East.[5]

There was a good reason why financial power was becoming less centralized. As Kolko noted, ascendant industrial corporations increasingly decided that they could finance their expansion projects from their own growing profits, instead of borrowing the capital from investment bankers. From 1900 to 1910, he found, 70 percent of the new funds for manufacturing were generated internally, making the corporations more independent of finance capital, not more ensnared, as the banks' critics believed. As new companies prospered without Wall Street, so did the new regional banks that handled their funds. New York's concentrated share of bank deposits was still huge, about half of the nation's total, but it was declining steadily. Wall Street was still "the biggest kid on the block," but less and less able to bully the others.

This trend was a crucial fact of history, a misunderstood reality that completely alters the political meaning of the reform legislation that created the Federal Reserve. At the time, the conventional wisdom in Congress, widely shared and sincerely espoused by Progressive reformers, was that a government institution would finally harness the "money trust," disarm its powers, and establish broad democratic control over money and credit (this version became the historian's standard interpretation). As Kolko's reinterpretation argued and the facts would subsequently demonstrate, the results were nearly the opposite. The money reforms enacted in 1913, in fact, helped to preserve the status quo, to stabilize the old order. Money-center bankers would not only gain dominance over the new central bank, but would also enjoy new insulation against instability and their own decline. Once the Fed was in operation, the steady diffusion of financial power halted. Wall Street maintained its dominant position—and even enhanced it—until the trauma of 1929.

When Woodrow Wilson accepted the Democratic presidential nomination in the summer of 1912, his acceptance speech mildly restated the passionate grievances that western and southern Democrats held against the "money trust." "Vast confederacies" had formed among banks and corporations, Wilson agreed, neither illegal nor conspiratorial, but still disturbing. "A concentration of the control of credit . . . may at any time become infinitely dangerous to free enterprise," he acknowledged.

The new Democratic leader, a historian from Virginia, formerly president of Princeton University, was clearly more conservative on the money question than major elements in his own party. Three times the angry provincial Democrats had given their party's nomination to William Jennings Bryan, the Nebraska Populist, and despite his defeats Bryan was still their putative leader. In contrast, Woodrow Wilson had a few years earlier praised the leadership of J. P. Morgan. Wilson also spoke positively about the rise of vast corporations. "The old time of individual competition is probably gone by," he observed. "It may come back; I don't know; it will not come back within our time, I dare say."

As a candidate, Wilson stiffened his rhetoric to reassure his fellow Democrats and took leadership of a political party that was resurgent after nearly two decades of minority status. In 1910, the Democrats had regained control of the House and, among other things, succeeded in blocking the Republicans' major proposal for banking reform, a measure introduced by the patrician senator from Rhode Island, Nelson Aldrich.

The Aldrich plan, it was said, was hatched at an infamous secret meeting at Jekyll Island, an isolated retreat in Georgia where key leaders of Wall Street finance met clandestinely in 1910 to settle on the terms for reform. The Jekyll Island meeting, which became a staple in the conspiracy theories surrounding the Fed, included Frank A. Vanderlip of National City (now Citibank), Henry P. Davison from the Morgan bank and Paul Warburg of the Kuhn, Loeb investment house.

The conspiracy-minded critics exaggerated the importance of the Jekyll Island meeting, since it was hardly a secret that Wall Street wanted reform. But their suspicions were poetically accurate—the bankers met secretly because they knew that any proposal identified as Wall Street's bill would be doomed in the Democratic House of Representatives. The plan worked out by the group did, in fact, become a prototype for the final legislation: creation of a National Reserve Association with fifteen major regions, controlled by a board of commercial bankers but empowered by the federal government to act like a central bank—creating money and lending reserves to private banks. Aside from details, the same fundamentals were to be incorporated in the new central bank. Idle reserves would be consolidated in strategic locations where they could be deployed swiftly to banks that were temporarily illiquid. An "elastic currency" that could grow or shrink in response to credit demands would let the money supply adjust to the changing needs of commerce. A new national currency (eventually called Federal Reserve Notes) would be automatically interchangeable with demand deposits, extinguishing the lingering popular suspicions of checking. Together, these reforms were designed to eliminate the rigidities that had produced perennial crisis.

Once elected, Woodrow Wilson moderated his rhetoric, and instead of consulting Bryan's agrarian wing, he turned for his ideas on bank reform to those who were already quite close to the bankers' perspective. A historical account published by the Federal Reserve Bank of Boston described the new President's shift with evident approval: "It was probably a combination of political realities and his own lack of knowledge about banking and finance that caused Wilson to reflect many of Bryan's views, but after his election to the Presidency, Wilson relied on others for more expert advice on the currency question."

One of the experts was H. Parker Willis, an economist on the House Banking Committee staff who fifteen years earlier had served on a private commission supported by large banks to promote an early version of monetary reform. The bill drafted by Willis and his boss, Representative Carter Glass of Virginia, differed in detail but not in fundamentals from the Aldrich plan: a privately controlled network of regional reserve banks that would be given government powers.

The President accepted their outline, but insisted on one crucial change—a Federal Reserve Board in Washington, appointed by the President, would be added to control and coordinate among the regions. This was to be the "capstone" that would represent the public interest alongside the bankers. Bankers would run the twelve Reserve Banks, and as consolation for being excluded from the central board, they would send their representatives to the Federal Advisory Council that would meet regularly with the Federal Reserve Board to advise it on money issues.

The Secretary of the Treasury and the Comptroller of the Currency would serve on the seven-member board in Washington, guaranteeing a direct voice for the Chief Executive in the making of monetary policy. With that alteration, Wilson explained, the elected government could control the new system—"so that the banks may be the instruments, not the masters, of business and of individual enterprise and initiative."

It was Wilson's great compromise—creating a hybrid institution that mixed private and public control, an approach without precedent at the time. Louis D. Brandeis, the brilliant lawyer and reformer, advised Wilson that the bankers should be excluded entirely from control of the system. "The conflict between the policies of the Administration and the desires of the financiers and of big business is an irreconcilable one," Brandeis warned. "Concessions to the big-business interests must in the end prove futile."

Wilson's conviction that he had struck the right moderate balance seemed confirmed, however, by the reactions to his legislation. It was attacked by both extremes—the "radicals" from the Populist states and the bankers in Wall Street and elsewhere. The bankers feared a dangerous precedent for government control over the private economy. The remnant Populists complained that Wilson's approach did not give the government enough control. Both critiques proved to be correct.

With a few cosmetic changes, the President persuaded Bryan, whom he had appointed Secretary of State, to endorse the measure as a triumph over the "money trust." But other Populists were not taken in. Representative Joe H. Eagle of Texas accurately perceived the economic benefits for banks—they were "to be guaranteed against loss by the establishment of a paternalistic relationship or private partnership with the government." Congressman Robert Henry of Texas, most perceptive of the Populist legislators, described the political balance in Wilson's legislation as "wholly in the interest of the creditor classes, the banking fraternity, and the commercial world, without proper provision for the debtor classes and those who toil, produce and sustain the country."

The most relentless opposition, however, came from bankers. It was a Democratic bill and most of them were Republicans. *The New York Times* derided Wilson's proposal as the "Oklahoma idea, the Nebraska idea." The New York *Sun*, then the reliable voice of Wall Street sentiment, dismissed the President's cautious compromise as "covered all over with the slime of Bryanism."

As traditional conservatives, many bankers were still not reconciled to the abandonment of laissez-faire economics. If government was given a role in finance, they foresaw (correctly) that a creeping process of government intrusion would be legitimized and eventually other aspects of the private economy would be politicized. Moreover, the basic idea behind establishing numerous regional banks was to avoid centralization and dominance by either Washington or the eastern money centers (an essential assurance to placate smaller provincial banks, which were themselves wary of Wall Street power). Some bankers opposed the idea of any central board at all. Others insisted that if there was to be one, its members must be appointed by them, not by politicians.

Through 1913, as the legislation worked its way toward enactment, banking leaders argued these points, offered alternatives and condemned the Administration's bill in the harshest terms. The bankers failed to defeat Wilson's design, but their opposition left the indelible impression that when the Federal Reserve Act was signed into law two days before Christmas, it was a great victory for Democratic reform over Republican special interests, a triumph for the popular will and defeat for Wall Street.

The reality was more ambiguous, as Gabriel Kolko documented

from the private correspondence and public comments of prominent bankers. While banking organizations were adopting resolutions against the measure, many bankers were also writing their senators urging them to vote for it, rather than allow reform to die. They denounced Wilson's "obnoxious" contributions to the bill, but were "extremely favorable to about 80 percent of it," as one of them put it. When the law was enacted, opponents like Paul Warburg swiftly put aside their complaints and agreed to help run the new system.

"For years bankers have been almost the sole advocates of just this sort of legislation that it is now hoped we will have," Frank Vanderlip of National City told an assembly of New York bankers, "and it is unfair to accuse them of being in opposition to sound legislation."

In fact, they were not opposed to the general scheme, only to certain particulars. The banking interests lost their battle to gain full private control over the new Federal Reserve System, but they won the larger struggle to create a money system that would rely upon the commercial banks as its operating partners.

Ultimately, the question of who really won and who lost in Woodrow Wilson's compromise would be answered most persuasively by the subsequent performance and politics of the new central bank. If the money-center banks were truly defeated in 1913, then why did they become so loyal and supportive toward the institution that Wilson had created? If the Federal Reserve was the public master created to control Wall Street, then why did the Fed turn always for political protection not to labor or farmers or small business but to the largest and most influential bankers?

In partisan terms, the Federal Reserve was derived from mixed parentage—inspired by both Republican and Democratic objectives. This helped to explain why the basic terms worked out in 1913 would endure unaltered for many decades afterward. The original idea had started as a conservative reform, sought by Republican interests, but the final design was modified by a Democratic President and a Democratic Congress, imposing a governmental presence on private finance.

This melding of interests gave the Fed a unique posture in American politics, artfully balanced between the two parties and effectively insulated from both of them. Whenever it was threatened from left or right, the central bank would turn to the opposite side for help in blunting the attack. In the same manner, as Fed lobbyists cheerfully acknowledged, the central bank learned to frustrate the occasional challenges from either Congress or the executive branch by playing one off against the other. When the Fed wanted legislation to expand its powers, it turned to Democrats. When its independence was threatened by liberal reformers, it turned to the conservatives of both parties, the natural majority in Congress, to defend it. Wilson's grand compromise had created a kind of permanent stalemate.

As an instrument of government, however, the Federal Reserve's lineage was clearly an institution of the Democratic Party, not the Republican. That seemed to contradict the political stereotypes surrounding it, since Democratic liberals often attacked the Fed for high interest rates and Republican conservatives usually rallied around when the Fed imposed a hard-money policy. But, historically, Democrats invented and nurtured the Fed. During sixty-seven years, there were only three important occasions when the Federal Reserve was established or altered by Congress—the original act of 1913, the 1935 reforms that centralized policy control in Washington and the 1980 Monetary Control Act that gave the Fed universal control over reserves of private banks. In all three instances, the legislation was proposed and enacted by Democrats.

The Federal Reserve was, more profoundly, an important prototype for the modern liberal state. For the first time, a governing arrangement would explicitly mix public and private interests in a manner that was elaborated many times later in different ways. However inadvertently or reluctantly, the creation of the central bank committed the federal government to a direct role in managing the private economy, and, once involved, it could no longer pretend to be aloof. It was, in fact, the beginning of the end of laissez-faire.

The Fed would pursue large public objectives, but it would also serve private economic interests. It was exactly the mixture of purposes—protecting private profit and the public interest at the same time—that was the hallmark of modern liberal institutions. Later on, it became commonplace in the national government as liberals intervened to protect or stabilize other economic sectors, from agriculture and oil to communications and labor unions. The basic terms of debate from 1913—laissez-faire conservativism versus liberal intervention—would echo again and again through subsequent economic issues, but the political choice had already been made and future debates would nearly always be settled in a similar manner.

The Federal Reserve, tradition decided, was to be "independent" of politics. The word itself appeared nowhere in the Federal Reserve Act, but both parties accepted the self-imposed limitations on their own power. These were the terms of truce under which democratic capitalism would function in the twentieth century, suppressing the class arguments that had dominated politics in previous generations.

As Carter Glass promised in the debate, the Fed was to be an "altruistic institution . . . a distinctly nonpartisan organization whose functions are to be wholly divorced from politics." Federal Reserve Board members were given ten-year terms (later lengthened to fourteen years) to insulate them from crass partisan pressures. The mechanics of how the Fed would coordinate its economic policy with the rest of the government's was left deliberately murky. The management of money was presumed to be a technical matter, best sequestered from politics.

One promise was not kept: Carter Glass assured his congressional colleagues that the Federal Reserve Board would operate under "the X-ray of publicity" so that there "can be nothing sinister about its transactions." Instead, the money question receded from political debate and became submerged in a new managerial complexity. When the Federal Reserve was created, the realm of acceptable political discourse shrank.

The competing political claims surrounding money and credit did not, of course, disappear from real life, but only from visible politics. The contest over money continued among classes and interests, but fewer and fewer people could observe the action or understand how to participate. Over the years, in different circumstances, both Republicans and Democrats would find themselves provoked by the Fed's "altruism" and complain that the Fed was injuring their constituencies. But political leaders were unable or unwilling to intervene. Having surrendered political control of the money question (and responsibility for it), America's two major parties could summon neither the energy nor the political imagination to challenge the quarantine.

Rather late in the congressional debate, Senator Elihu Root, a Republican conservative from New York, had expressed an odd complaint about the new money system that Congress was creating. It was, he reasoned, an invitation to inflation. If the Federal Reserve was to provide banks with new money in exchange for their commercial loan paper, what was going to curb the process from printing too much money? The Discount loans, Root warned, would be made "upon security that is good until the time comes when, through a process of inflation, we reach a situation in which no security is good." The standards for money creation, he feared, would "become modified by the optimism of the hour and grow less and less effective in checking the expansion of business."

Senator Porter J. McCumber, Republican of North Dakota, made the same point more graphically. The new "elastic currency," he predicted, would mean a money supply "which will pull out three feet and will come back only one foot."[6]

Their objections were easily deflected in the congressional debate. The Federal Reserve Banks, the sponsors explained, could moderate money expansion at appropriate times simply by raising the Discount rate. Putting a higher price on money would discourage new borrowing by businesses, and as credit expansion subsided, fewer banks would come to the Discount window with new loan paper to exchange for new money. Besides, the "elastic currency" would be self-liquidating. As businesses paid off their loans, the money went back into the Federal Reserve Banks that had discounted their loan paper and the money was thus extinguished, retired from circulation. The answers satisfied most participants.[7]

Inflation, ironically, was only a peripheral issue during the Federal Reserve debates. Aside from Root and a few other skeptical conservatives, no one foresaw that the issue of stable money would eventually become the pivotal question of Federal Reserve performance, the core test of its monetary policies. Inflation did not seem especially relevant to the reformers of 1913 because they assumed that money's value would continue to be stabilized, just as it had always been, by the gold standard. Their reforms would simply add a new flexibility to the mechanics of money and credit, a self-correcting auxiliary that would eliminate the periodic strains that caused bank panics. The new Federal Reserve Notes would still be as good as gold.

Like most momentous decisions in history, this one was loaded down with unintended consequences. The overwhelming majority in Congress who voted for Wilson's measure did not grasp (any more than the President did) that they were creating a new management system that would replace gold as the regulator of money's value and, therefore, would influence prices generally. Nor did they understand that the Federal Reserve Board would become an important throttle for regulating the tempo of the entire economy, stimulating or depressing production and employment with its money decisions. Most of all, they would have been appalled to learn that the new Federal Reserve Notes they were authorizing would become, in fact, the fiat paper money that had been proposed thirty years earlier by the Populist agitators.

The confusion of purpose stemmed in part from fundamental misunderstandings about how the new system would function, but mainly it resulted from unforeseen events no one could have anticipated. The crucial event was World War I. Even before the Federal Reserve Board could hold its first meeting in August of 1914, the great nations of Europe were at war. One by one, in order to finance their armies, the governments of Europe abandoned the gold guarantees behind their own currencies. While no one recognized it at the time, this was the beginning of the end for the gold standard in domestic economies worldwide. The United States would hang on to gold longer than others, but it too finally suspended the right of gold convertibility in the financial crisis of 1933. Until then, citizens could turn in their Federal Reserve Notes for an appropriate quantity of gold. After 1933, the Fed's paper money would be redeemed only with more paper money.

One of the few who had the foresight to anticipate this outcome was Benjamin Strong, the "Morgan man" who was appointed president of the New York Fed and from that position dominated the affairs of the new central bank for almost two decades. In 1913, Strong wrote to his friend Paul Warburg warning that if Federal Reserve Notes were made an obligation of the U.S. government, they would inevitably constitute "greenbacks," the fiat money that the Populists had sought. "If the United States government embarks once more upon the expedient or experiment of issuing fiat paper, although in this case supported by bank assets and percentage in gold reserve, the day will come when we will deeply regret it. . . ."[8]

Without the gold standard, money was on its own, so to speak. Rather, as Strong had feared, money's value in the long run depended on one essential variable—the money-supply management by the Federal Reserve. This was not what anyone had intended—government-managed price levels—but there was no inclination to go back to the original decision and reargue it. Instead, Congress allowed the Fed to adapt to the changing circumstances and, in effect, to discover step by step how it should manage money. This accidental evolution of the Fed's powers was a crucial element contributing to the institution's privileged political status, exempt from intensive oversight, for it allowed the central bank to expand its de facto authority gradually, without first submitting to the test of congressional approval. In the strictest sense, Congress did not create the Federal Reserve System as it later operated; Congress ratified the reality of Federal Reserve power, a step at a time, after necessity had brought it into existence. The mystical reassurances of gold were gone at last. A new secular temple, run by mortals, was entrusted with the secrets.

The original instructions that Congress gave to the temple were vague (and not much improved over the years). The 1913 act said merely that the Reserve Banks should set Discount loan rates "with a view of accommodating commerce and business." Credit should be provided to member banks with due regard to "the maintenance of sound credit conditions, and the accommodation of commerce, industry and agriculture." In later years, subsequent legislation would add similar words and phrases to the Fed's mandate, but always framed so loosely that the congressional intent could be interpreted to fit almost any policy in any season.

For many years, the Fed's critics would complain, with justification, that Federal Reserve governors hid behind platitudes and refused to state the real economic objectives of their policies in meaningful terms. Certainly, Fed chairmen always resisted the occasional legislative efforts to impose more precise objectives on the central bank's functions. The ambiguity and evasion, however, were not solely an invention of the Fed, but an implicit part of the original political bargain. To state the goals of monetary policy in explicit terms would require Congress to make the stark political choices it did not wish to face. If the objectives of money policy were visible and constant, then the class implications would be more visible too. Most everyone could figure out for themselves which groups were to benefit and which ones would likely be hurt, borrowers or lenders, eager entrepreneurs anxious for expansion or cautious owners of capital worried about stability. Keeping things vague was another way to avoid the central argument of democratic capitalism.

The Federal Reserve was not born in isolation. Its creation was the keystone in a profound alteration that occurred in the American culture of self-government—a new sensibility that devalued the potential of representative democracy and imposed limitations on it. The new perspective held that popular will, so turbulent in nineteenth-century politics, must be restrained in the new age of multiplying complexity and scale. Decisions on great public issues that were once left to politics should be consigned to disinterested experts, bureaucratic technicians who had specialized training. "Good government" must be managed. The managers must occasionally ignore public opinion in order to make correct decisions.

This new conception of American governance was a central principle of the Progressive reformers led by Woodrow Wilson, a movement populated by businessmen and professionals, members of the educated middle class that was emerging. They were managers themselves. They distrusted, even feared, the raw, barefoot politics unleashed by Populist agitators; they regarded public opinion as an unstable force, occasionally destructive. The implications of popular control of government were attacked most bluntly by one of the leading Progressive essayists, Walter Lippmann.

It is not possible [Lippmann wrote in 1922] to assume that a world, carried on by division of labor and distribution of authority, can be governed by universal opinions in the whole population. Unconsciously the theory set up the single reader as theoretically omnicompetent and puts upon the press the burden of accomplishing whatever representative government, industrial organization, and diplomacy have failed to accomplish. Acting upon everybody for thirty minutes in twenty-four hours, the press is asked to create a mystical force called Public Opinion that will take up the slack in public institutions. The press has often mistakenly pretended that it could do just that. It has, at great moral cost to itself, encouraged a democracy, still bound to its original premises. . . .[9]

The masses of ordinary citizens, though theoretically sovereign, were incompetent to govern—randomly willful in their opinions, blind to the complexities of modern life. The affairs of state and society would therefore be conducted by new elites of professionals, managers who could communicate intelligibly among themselves on important questions. In the nineteenth century, these autocratic views would have been swiftly denounced as anti-democratic heresy, but Lippmann's disenchantment with popular opinion was widely shared by the Progressive reformers who dominated the first two decades of the new century. They attacked the corruption of big-city political machines with the city-manager form of government, designed to insulate public policy from the whims and greed of elected representatives. They devised a variety of federal regulatory programs, including the Federal Reserve and civil service reform, with the same purpose. A new ethic was born—faith in the technocratic approach to government—and this creed implicitly embraced what Andrew Jackson had denounced eight decades earlier: "A distrust of the popular will as a safe regulator of political power." As the idea of management by experts flourished in twentieth-century politics, new bureaucracies grew up with it, putting further distance between raw public opinion and the decisions made by government.

The Federal Reserve was an exemplar of the technocratic approach. From the beginning, each Federal Reserve Bank and the board in Washington set out to build its own individual research department, staffed with bright young economists who systematized the gathering of banking and business data and began studying the private economy with the same methodological rigor as the academy. In time, the Fed's assembly of economists would rank in size and prestige and seriousness with the leading research universities, though their work was mainly directed at narrow questions of economic management. The System's many research departments did not, as a rule, hire eccentric thinkers who produced grand new theories of economics that might disrupt conventional thinking.

The government's new emphasis on technical expertise only mimicked the trend that was simultaneously permeating American business. The days of the freewheeling entrepreneur were closing, as Woodrow Wilson had said. A new managerial approach was required to rationalize the vast new corporate enterprises thrown together in the generation of capitalist combat and consolidation. The idea of efficiency became enshrined as the test of performance, expressed most eloquently by the "scientific management" doctrines of Frederick W. Taylor, apostle of the "time study" approach to industrial production. A factory worker's every step was carefully clocked and analyzed; then his work routine was modified to save time and motion and, not incidentally, labor costs. The assembly line merged men with machines in a continuous production process that need not pause for rest or reflection. Efficiency placed a premium on systematic coordination and duplication; it discouraged the "costs" of individual deviations.

The managerial ethic provided the cultural atmosphere that welcomed the new central bank as a legitimate departure from democratic accountability. It helped explain why Progressive reformers were so eager to insulate the Fed from politics. The money issues that were formerly political questions could be better resolved by disinterested technicians dedicated to the objective science of economics. Money was too complicated, too important, to be left to blind opinion.

But why did the general public acquiesce so meekly to managerial culture and the depoliticizing of the money question? After all, it was yielding control over issues that had stirred furious popular passions only a few years before. Jacksonian Democrats had attacked the anti-democratic implications of a central bank and rallied public opinion against the idea. The unwashed Populists had demonstrated that "plain people" did not need a college degree to understand the politics of monetary questions. What changed in the American character that allowed Americans at last to accept what for a century they had resisted?

In the demonological version of Fed history, the ordinary citizens—Jackson's "real people"—were innocent. They were hoodwinked by elite conspirators, betrayed by feckless politicians. They were tricked into accepting an arrangement for money control that, as Henry Ford declared, would cause rioting in the streets if Americans ever understood its true nature. Certainly, there was abundant confusion and ignorance surrounding the Fed; but the notion of an ongoing conspiracy by governing elites, somehow thwarting the public's true desires, does not satisfy the question.

The public acquiescence involved a complicated psychological transaction in the popular mind. The transition was connected emotionally to a deeper wound. Millions of citizens were already accepting a traumatic transformation in their own lives and values, adapting to a new order that would have appalled their ancestors. From 1890 to the 1920s, American life crossed a cultural watershed, one that produced giddy prosperity in everyday lives and also a lingering sense of loss and personal guilt. "The United States," as historian Richard Hofstadter put it, "was born in the country and has moved to the city." [10]

By 1900, only four in ten American workers were still on farms. A few decades earlier, the figure had been eight in ten. The economic dimensions of America's transition from an agricultural society to an industrial society, the rapid and dramatic shift of population from rural to urban, were well understood. The emotional transaction was not. It left a deep cultural imprint of contradictory memory and emotion, still visible in popular values, a painful nostalgia for something that was lost and also a sense of liberation from old burdens.

Everything changed, even the language. In the Populist era, when the grassroots speakers appealed to the "producing classes," they were speaking of farmers and factory workers, individuals who made things with their own hands, the "bone and sinew of the nation" in Andrew Jackson's rhetoric. In twentieth-century usage, "producers" were no longer people; the term now meant those anonymous corporate enterprises that controlled most output, distinguished from their employees, the "workers." In 1900, a rural census taker in Pennsylvania innocently listed all of the farmers in his district as "unemployed," since all of them worked for themselves, not for someone else.

The American sense of loss was expressed most directly—and stubbornly—in the nation's literature. In 1855, when Walt Whitman celebrated the national experience in "Song of Myself," his poetry made music out of the sweaty diversity of American workmen: "Blacksmiths with grimed and hairy chests environ the anvil . . . The carpenter dresses his plank, the tongue of his foreplane whistles its wild ascending lisp . . . The farmer stops by the bars as he walks on a First-day loafe and looks at the oats and rye . . . The machinist rolls up his sleeves, the policeman travels his beat . . ."

Two generations later, the lyrical celebration had been silenced, replaced by a dark and brooding literature of loss and corruption. Poets were no longer able to romanticize the American experience. The heavy novels of Theodore Dreiser, *Sister Currie, An American Tragedy* and others, told, over and over in different story forms, the same moral tragedy: innocent Americans who left their simple country past for the dangerous excitement of the city, where they were ensnared by a brutal new system of economic organization, forced to cooperate with it, robbed of their native virtue.

This literature of alienation has endured throughout the twentieth century, for serious poets and novelists in America have never reconciled themselves to the terms of the modern economic system. They remain hostile to it and pessimistic, mocking the values of corporate bureaucracy, lamenting the soul-deadening materialism. Instead, literature and popular culture continue to celebrate what seems lost— the free-ranging individualism, the honesty and simplicity of rural life, the idyll of self-reliance. A familiar story line, repeated endlessly in novels, films and rock 'n' roll lyrics, depicted the lonely rebel who resists and somehow beats the system—romantic tales that mourned the idea of America's lost Eden.[11]

With loss, however, there was also reward. Millions of American families willingly traded roles in life: they ceased to be the independent yeomanry of American tradition, self-reliant and proud and skillful in the practical arts of self-sufficiency. They became, instead, employees and consumers. They went to work for someone else, usually a corporation, and their labor produced wages—pieces of paper in place of the "real things" of country life. The energies of individual expression, once devoted to daily survival, were diverted instead to consuming—buying things and using them, things made by others in some distant place. Both new roles—consumer and employee—made people more dependent on the abstractions of the money system than they had been as self-sufficient farmers, producing real goods. Money belonged to the city and its complexities. Country people, as they were drawn closer to the ancient mystery, were uncomfortable confronting money. Money was the everyday symbol of what they had given up.

Whatever people lost emotionally in the exchange, the compensating rewards were staggering in material terms. Before 1900, most households in America lacked the simple amenities of indoor plumbing and central heating, not to mention the luxuries of electric lights, telephones or automobiles. The new prosperity made possible by the industrial system would have stunned the Populist farmers of 1885, notwithstanding the continuing conflicts between labor and owners, consumers and producers, borrowers and lenders. The rush to the cities unleashed a virtual frenzy of buying and consuming, notwithstanding the dark portrait sketched by novelists. A proliferation of invention introduced liberating devices that saved time and labor— refrigerators, washing machines, radios, store-bought bread and a new fantasy life offered in the movies. Each was beyond the imagination of the old prairie radicals; all were soon accepted as basic necessities.

The emotional legacy was, thus, contradictory—a combination of pain and gratification, loss and reward. An individualist from the nineteenth century would complain that Americans were seduced by a Faustian bargain. People surrendered control over their own lives, accepted a smaller role for themselves as cogs in the vast and complicated economic machinery, in exchange for mere material goods. From the twentieth century, modern consumers might respond that, yes, but the devil certainly kept his half of the bargain. Ordinary citizens could now fulfill personal fantasies by acquiring things on a scale that in Thorstein Veblen's day was reserved for the "leisure class."

This inherited conflict of cultural emotions seemed quite distant from the technical complexities of monetary policy and the Federal Reserve, but it provided the deepest explanation for why the central bank was permitted to assume its privileged status, outside political scrutiny. The American character, when it moved from country to city, suffered a great wound of the spirit—pain and alienation that were salved with money. People regretted the loss; yet they also welcomed the escape. The new life offered an adolescent release from privation, mingled with the guilt of having surrendered something valuable. These complicated feelings intersected with all the potent psychological illusions surrounding money described by Freud and the others—money's power of dread and potential, guilt and giving, immortality and death, the unity of contradictions. From country to city, citizens gave themselves over to the rhythms governed by this ancient mystery.

The Federal Reserve, as the new regulator of money, served as comforting mediator for the cultural transaction, a miraculous analgesic that relieved people of painful confrontation with their own guilt. The closer they were to money, the less they wished to know about it. The obligation of confronting the operative symbol of their new dependency or even understanding it was taken from their hands and citizens were permitted to repress the guilty knowledge. In time, ordinary citizens would no longer grasp the political meaning of money or even know that it existed. The burden was entrusted to a new technology that was as mystifying as the ancient temples. Like the temple priests, the Fed would satisfy the society's collective sin and error by performing sacred rituals of sacrifice and expiation.

The first recession directly induced by the Federal Reserve began in the spring of 1920, though Fed officials disclaimed any responsiblity for it. A sharp spike of price inflation followed the close of World War I, just as inflation had followed previous wars and for approximately the same reasons. To finance the war, the federal government had borrowed heavily, and the national debt ballooned in a few years from less than $1 billion to $27 billion. By the fall of 1919, prices were rising at the rate of 15 percent a year. Benjamin Strong and his colleagues agreed that they must act to break the inflationary spiral.

Over the next few months, the twelve Federal Reserve Banks raised the Discount rate from 4 to 7 percent, and other market interest rates rose with it. If the Fed's 1920 tightening appeared modest compared with the double-digit interest rates of modern experience, it was not. In a short period of time, the price of money was nearly doubled. Once the Discount rate was raised to a historically unprecedented level, the Reserve Banks kept it there, without relief, for eighteen months.

The result was a swift and dramatic price deflation and economic contraction that lasted for a year and a half, severe enough to earn the label of depression. Commodity prices fell from their early 1920 peak by more than 50 percent over the next two years and farmers were plunged once again into financial crisis. General business activity subsided by nearly a third. Manufacturing volume fell by 42 percent. Unemployment rose fivefold to 11.9 percent—an additional four million people who were out of work. As Jane D'Arista observed in her account of the Fed's performance, "All prices fell except the price of money."

The Fed managers deflected critics with narrowly worded denials. When an angry delegation of Farm Bureau leaders confronted Benjamin Strong, he responded disingenuously: "You inquire as to the man who gave this order for deflation. I know of no order being given." Besides, Strong said, he was out of the country at the time.

Congressional critics, including Progressive Republicans and the out-of-power Democrats, threatened legislation to revoke the Fed's independent charter, but the governors did not yield. Even the new Republican Secretary of the Treasury, Andrew Mellon, who was himself a member of the Federal Reserve Board, pleaded futilely with his colleagues to reduce interest rates, once prices were falling rapidly and the economy was shrinking. The political pressures failed.

Strong, addressing a conference of Reserve Bank officials in the spring of 1921, warned: "What this System requires is protection against misled public opinion, which will be reflected in Congress, in some foolish act by Congress. . . ."

The Fed's objective, as frankly stated in records of its own deliberations, was the restoration of "sound financial conditions," not the restoration of economic growth. Bank failures increased dramatically during the 1920–1921 recession (from 63 in 1919 to 506 in 1921), but, on the whole, a period of stringent credit conditions would be profitable for most banks. The real value of their own financial assets, bonds and outstanding loans, increased proportionately, as prices fell and money "hardened" again.

The Fed policy makers concentrated on eliminating the inflationary fears of financial investors, not on lowering the unemployment rate or restoring farm prices. Indeed, the first objective was necessarily in conflict with the others. From the Fed's perspective, declining prices were the goal, not the problem. High unemployment did not hurt, but helped. A surplus of labor forced wages down generally as more workers competed for fewer jobs; falling wages led to moderating price inflation. Even as late as April 1921, one member of the Federal Reserve Board, Adolph Miller, argued it was still too early to ease credit conditions because, in his judgment, wages were still too high. American industry could not return to a "safe and sound condition," Miller explained, until the contraction produced "what is called the liquidation of labor." The phrase, he conceded, sounded "a little offensive." Strong agreed that labor must yield more before "sound central banking principles" would permit the Fed to relent.

The 1920–1921 depression was prototypal. Its severity was greater than most, but priorities were the same the Federal Reserve pursued in future episodes of contraction. The "dominant guides to policy were financial rather than economic," Lester V. Chandler, Strong's authorized biographer, concluded. "A central banker accepting this set of priorities," Chandler explained, "naturally feared inflation more than deflation and insisted that on some occasions deflation was necessary for the attainment of primary financial objectives."

Though chartered to accommodate "the needs of commerce and industry," the central bank focused its concern on the health of the financial sector over the productive economy. In order to restore one, it was necessary to punish the other.

For those who truly understood monetary policy, a new reality was coming clear: the Federal Reserve System may have been created for the narrow task of providing an "elastic currency," but its actual powers were far greater. The Fed's decisions could turn the broad tides of economic growth and decline for the entire nation. Federal Reserve governors, as a practical matter, were making macroeconomic policy for the federal government before the term was even invented.

Woodrow Wilson's compromise was also swiftly subverted. The Federal Reserve Board did not become the "capstone" Wilson had envisioned, speaking for the public and keeping a leash on the bankers. From the outset, the board's authority was successfully challenged by the presidents of the twelve Federal Reserve Banks, who saw themselves as independent coequals (they were originally called governors themselves). Led by Benjamin Strong at the New York Fed, they united to go their own way. Over fifteen years, whenever the Federal Reserve Board in Washington tried to reassert control, the bankers would accuse it of political meddling.

When the System was first organized into twelve regions and Federal Reserve cities were selected, the choices themselves had not been entirely free of politics. Cincinnati and Pittsburgh were rejected in favor of Cleveland, hometown of Wilson's influential Secretary of War, Newton D. Baker. Baltimore lost to Richmond, capital of Carter Glass's home state. The System map seemed a reasonable delineation of the nation's economic regions with one blatant exception—Missouri. While dozens of other states fought for the honor and lost, Missouri won two Federal Reserve Banks—St. Louis and Kansas City. The Speaker of the House of Representatives, Champ Clark, was from Missouri.

The twelve Reserve Banks formed their alliance against Washington around an issue that, at the time, seemed a peripheral question—the buying and selling of government securities. The original operations of the Federal Reserve did not use the open-market purchases of U.S. securities as the means to create new money or extinguish it. Money was created entirely through the Discount windows at the twelve Reserve Banks. Instead of buying or selling government notes and bonds, the Fed took in "real bills" of trade—the short-term debt notes that banks took when they lent to business and agriculture. When these notes were eventually paid off at the Fed, the money would automatically cease to exist. Creating money for real commercial transactions, it was assumed, would make the money supply self-regulating, growing and contracting always in step with the ebb and flow of private commerce and credit.

When individual Reserve Banks began buying government securities for their separate portfolios, it was not to regulate the money supply but to increase their own earnings. Treasury paper was a safe place to park idle funds and provided a modest return that would help pay for the banks' operations. Most economists, inside and outside the Fed, did not grasp the larger implications—these random transactions were themselves expanding or shrinking the money in circulation. If Atlanta or Philadelphia bought $1 million in bonds, it was pumping high-powered money into the banking system—$1 million that would be multiplied by bank lending. If it sold bonds, the reverse occurred.

The wiser heads, including Benjamin Strong in New York, rather quickly recognized the connection. When Reserve Banks made open-market transactions, interest rates rose or fell, accordingly, in financial markets. On some occasions, there was plain confusion when one Reserve Bank would be buying bonds while another Reserve Bank was selling.

Strong persuaded the other Reserve Bank officials that the twelve Reserve Banks, at the very least, must coordinate their actions, a proposal that became the means for organizing the regional banks as a rival power center, independent of the Federal Reserve Board in Washington. The New York Fed, it was agreed, would handle all sales and purchases for the others, managed in a way that did not disrupt markets. The twelve Reserve Banks formed their own Open Market Investment Committee to decide things. The Federal Reserve Board approved, apparently unaware that it was ceding control of a powerful monetary lever.

For the banking community and for Benjamin Strong, the independent open-market committee provided the arrangement of power they had originally wanted in the new central bank. Before enactment of the Fed legislation, Strong had expressed his preference: "If we ever have a central bank, it must be run from New York by a board of directors on the ground. . . ." Strong, a "Morgan man" and former president of Bankers Trust, had rather deftly circumvented the will of Congress and the intent of Woodrow Wilson.[12]

For years, the System's open-market operations were too small to be significant, and conventional thinking still did not recognize the full implications for the larger economy. The Fed continued to rely on discounting, buying or selling commercial debt paper, raising or lowering the Discount rate to ease or tighten "credit conditions." But these principles of money management contained a fatal and ruinous flaw, one that would eventually become visible to all.

After the recovery in 1921, the decade of the twenties proved to be an era of extraordinary economic growth, despite two more recessions that were much milder than the first. The Fed was implicated in both. One was attributed to the System's excessive tightening of credit in 1923; the other was blamed, less persuasively, on the Fed's failure to ease credit in 1926 when economic activity began to decline.

The 1920s, nonetheless, greatly enhanced the Federal Reserve's stature. Thanks largely to Strong's management, it was an era of relatively stable prices—"the high tide" of the Federal Reserve System, according to Milton Friedman and Anna Schwartz. At the same time, the robust American economy embarked on the "roaring twenties." New technologies increased productivity enormously; the output per hour of labor rose by an astonishing 63 percent during the decade. Mass markets developed for automobiles and timesaving appliances like refrigerators. Sales of radios increased 1400 percent.

The Republican era of good feeling was epitomized by Calvin Coolidge's relaxed sense of the Presidency. "If you see ten troubles coming down the road," Coolidge said, "you can be sure that nine will run into the ditch before they reach you." Treasury Secretary Mellon advanced a more sophisticated rationale for the old Republican doctrine of laissez-faire. Mellon, who dominated economic thinking through three Republican Administrations, argued that the old Populist idea of progressive taxation—higher rates for the wealthy, or "soak the rich," as Republicans called it—was destructive to general prosperity. Instead of using the income tax to compensate for the maldistribution of wealth and income, tax rates on the rich should be reduced drastically in order to stimulate economic growth. The Republicans devised tax credits, refunds and abatements to benefit private corporations, and they enacted four major reductions in income-tax rates, purposely skewed to benefit the upper-income brackets. The Mellon argument —denounced by Democrats as "trickle down" economics—was that everyone would eventually benefit as the wealthy devoted the tax cuts to capital investment and new jobs were created. Mellon fell short of his ultimate goal—complete elimination of progressive tax rates—but his approach seemed for a time to be wondrously effective in stimulating new factories and expanded production.[13]

As the Republican prosperity unfolded, the Federal Reserve shared in the applause. Banking panics seemed to be a thing of the past. Inflation was vanquished. Economic performance was evidently aided by the Fed's stable management. Informed opinion was in agreement: the promises made back in 1913 for the new Federal Reserve System had been more than fulfilled.

In the aura of self-congratulations, the darker portents of the 1920s were largely ignored. Farmers, unlike other sectors, never really recovered from the depression of 1920–1921 and the drastic decline in commodity prices. They remained trapped by deflated prices and glutted markets. In 1920, farm families had received about 15 percent of national income; eight years later, they received only 9 percent.

Labor, less obviously, was also losing ground. As industrial production expanded robustly, workers seemed to be sharing in the new prosperity, but they were also working longer hours for the same wages and borrowing more heavily to keep up. Primitive estimates of unemployment ranged from 5.2 to 13 percent, but the more relevant fact was that the work hours available per person actually fell by 7 percent during the decade. As labor surpluses built up, the struggling labor movement was decimated; unions lost nearly 30 percent of their membership. That and other accumulating evidence suggested deep instabilities in the economy, but most people were persuaded to ignore them. The stock market, after all, was rallying to new heights—a sure signal of more good times ahead.[14]

The Federal Reserve, in this setting, established another precedent for the future—its ability to obfuscate and confuse when under attack. Public discontent was blunted by long and complicated technical answers that diverted attention from the Fed's own role in economic distress. The official answers were usually accurate in the narrow sense, but they grossly dodged the questions. The evasive techniques would become standard procedure in the System.

Following the price collapse of 1920–1921, angry farmers and livestock growers from the upper Midwest addressed a series of hostile questions to the Minneapolis Federal Reserve Bank. The answers were mostly huffy denials.

"The Federal Reserve Banks were responsible for inflation," the farm representatives complained. "Why should they attempt to place the burden of deflation upon the farmer, cattleman and wool grower?" The Minneapolis Fed responded: "Deflation is not chargeable to the Federal Reserve System or to any group or aggregation of banks, bankers or financiers. It is the natural and inevitable national reaction from war conditions."

But, the farmers asked: "Was it not unfair and unjust to the farmers for the Federal Reserve Bank to help big banking interests in their conspiracy to advance interest rates?" The Fed replied: "Neither the Federal Reserve Bank nor the big commercial banks nor any group of banks in this district has the power to make interest rates high or low. Few subjects are more simple, but there are few that are so generally misunderstood." A long and not-so-simple explanation followed on how market forces of supply and demand determined the price of money.

Well, then, the farmers asked: "Is the Federal Reserve Board more responsive to the money power than to the farmer?" The careful answer was meant to reassure: "Congress was largely influenced in the adoption of the Federal Reserve Act in 1913 by a determined purpose to break up the centralization of the financial power in this country in New York. In view of the history of the Federal Reserve Act, it is more than unlikely that the Federal Reserve Board would show special consideration to the so-called money power even though it had the ability to do so."[15]

High interest rates were an act of nature—caused by impersonal market conditions, not by anyone's conscious decision. This became the stock response offered by successive Fed chairmen in subsequent decades, whenever rates went up.

Ben Strong, the dominant central banker in America during the Fed's first formative decades, understood the political advantage in blurring the central bank's influence over prices and the economy. The Fed would always be caught between the conflicting interests of consumers and producers, between finance and farmers, between lenders and borrowers. "There you are," he said, "between the devil and the deep sea."

"It seems to me that if the Federal Reserve System is recognized as a price regulator," Strong explained, "it is going to be somewhat in the position of the poor man who tried to stop a row between an Irishman and his wife. They both turned in and beat him." [16]

Benjamin Strong died in October 1928, and one year later, the Federal Reserve System suffered its historic disgrace. The stock market crashed and the American economy collapsed with it. The "new era" of permanent properity was abruptly demolished, followed by the Great Depression with unemployment at 25 percent and desperate poverty for tens of millions of Americans. Tens of thousands of businesses were bankrupted, and the panic of bank failures also returned —destroying more than forty percent of all American banks. The Federal Reserve was blamed for failure to act on both sides of the Great Crash—first for letting it happen, then for failing to reverse the devastation. The Fed's defenders liked to imagine that had Benjamin Strong lived, maybe the worst of the disaster could have been averted. It sounded like wishful thinking in hindsight.

Certainly, Strong saw the outlines of the gathering crisis before others did. In the summer of 1928, three months before his death, he warned a colleague that banks and investors were caught up in a dangerous frenzy of speculation, borrowing heavily to make speculative stock-market forays, bidding up prices so high that the rosy expectations could not possibly be fulfilled. The nation was giddily enjoying the Republican prosperity. The New York Fed was privately worrying about its collapse.

"The problem now," Strong wrote, "is so to shape our policy as to avoid a calamitous break in the stock market, a panicky feeling about money, a setback to business because of the change in psychology, and at the same time accomplish if possible some of the purposes enumerated above." The Reserve Banks, he said, must dampen credit and restrain the speculative lending, but without setting off that "calamitous break."

This was a tricky business, though Strong thought it could be done. After his death, his successors tried fitfully and failed. They applied "moral suasion," pleading with commercial banks to stop making loans for stock-market speculation. When that failed, they argued among themselves. Without Strong to impose his will, the Reserve Banks and the Federal Reserve Board were stalemated through most of 1929. Belatedly, they voted a modest Discount increase in August, intended to slow down the rapacious bank lending. The speculative bubble continued. Stock-market prices went higher and higher.

On October 24, 1929—Black Thursday—the bubble burst, the "calamitous break" that Strong had feared. Within a matter of days, the Standard and Poor's composite index of stocks fell from 245 to 162, wiping out more than one-third of the stock market's value. Something on the order of $7 billion in bank loans to financial investors was rendered worthless. A "panicky feeling about money," as Strong had called it, swept the nation and the world.

In the tendentious postmortems over what exactly caused the Crash of '29, Strong was himself blamed for the debacle. Adolph Miller of the Federal Reserve Board, among others, charged that Strong had personally engineered the major easing of credit in the summer of 1927—Discount-rate reductions and open-market purchases of $340 million—that pumped excessive liquidity into the banking system and permitted the artificial investment boom to take off. Strong's easy-credit policy in 1927, Miller said later, "was father and mother to the subsequent 1929 collapse."

The 1927 error, if it was an error, was at least motivated by Strong's desire to aid the real economy. When he had leaned on his colleagues at the other Reserve Banks to reduce their Discount rates, he was worried. Employment was slipping, wholesale prices were declining again and business appeared to be sliding back into recession. The easier credit was intended to avert another contraction. But Strong had another more controversial motive—helping out the central banks of Europe. Presiding at the New York Fed, Ben Strong regularly collaborated with the central bankers of England and the Continent, trying to stabilize things so the gold standard could be restored internationally. The great international banking houses, from Morgan to Rothschild, had always worked closely with one another, borrowing and lending capital among themselves to balance out the worldwide demands for credit. From the start, Strong discreetly assumed the same role for himself—personal responsibility for representing America in global financial coordination, in an era when most Americans still thought of their nation as totally independent.

In mid-1927, Montagu Norman of the Bank of England called on

Strong and urged him to ease U.S. credit. Strong promptly agreed to do it. The Fed would provide excess liquidity for the American banking system and that money could flow abroad, through foreign loans, to ease credit in the European financial markets, where tightening conditions threatened to push up interest rates. If rates rose sharply in London and Paris and Vienna, that would depress business and perhaps set off a general contraction. The explanation would certainly have rankled citizens of the United States if they had known it. World War I had left a great tide of isolationism in its wake. The suspicion that the Federal Reserve secretly served the needs of international banking at the expense of domestic interests would become a perennial source of resentment.

As Strong himself argued, however, the U.S. assistance was also self-interested—what damaged European business would in time also damage America's. If Europe's economies contracted, for instance, then Midwestern grain farmers would find no buyers for the surplus crops they exported. Like it or not, the world's industrial economies were already closely interlocked, through both finance and production, long before the Federal Reserve came into existence. The "global economy" celebrated by modern commentators was different only in the degree of complexity, the volume and speed of international transactions. Despite his autocratic manner, Strong was ahead of his time in his internationalism.

Strong's maneuver, in any case, did not work. It backfired. Given the weakened state of the real economy, the flush of excess liquidity he had pumped into the banking system was not needed for transactions in real commerce or production. The surplus of money flowed, instead, into financial markets—artificially inflating financial values and fueling the run-up of stock prices that ended abruptly in the autumn of 1929.

After the crash, the Federal Reserve System did nothing. If Ben Strong had been alive and in charge, perhaps he would have acted to stop the collapse. At least, when he was expressing his fears of a "calamitous break" back in 1928, Strong understood that the Federal Reserve could quickly reverse such a disaster.

I think you realize, as I do [Strong had written to a colleague], that the very existence of the Federal Reserve System is a safeguard against anything like a calamity growing out of money rates. Not only have we the power to deal with such an emergency instantly by flooding the street with money, but I think the country is well aware of this and probably places reliance upon the common sense and power of the System. In former days the psychology was different because the facts of the banking situation were different. Mob panic, and consequently mob disaster, is less likely to arise.

Strong was mistaken about the "mob" and its faith in the Fed. When the market broke, the same psychology that had driven banking panics in 1907 and earlier took hold, swept across America and Europe, and ultimately destroyed 9,800 U.S. commercial banks over the next five years. But Strong was making a more fundamental point: the Federal Reserve had ample power to stop such a crisis almost instantly "by flooding the street with money."

That is what his successors failed to do. At first, they accepted the ruinous deflation as a natural, even desirable outcome. As the contraction deepened, they bickered among themselves about the correct reponse. Finally, rather late in the crisis, they tried briefly to reverse the decline, then abandoned the effort before it had a chance to succeed.

Money disappeared on a massive scale. As billions of dollars of bank debt were liquidated by defaults and bankruptcies in the economy, involving farmers and businesses along with the stock-market speculators, the process naturally extinguished money and the supply of money contracted. From 1929 to early 1933, U.S. money shrank in volume by more than one-third. The Federal Reserve could have intervened to reverse the contraction. It could have reduced interest rates sharply to stimulate renewed borrowing and business activity. More importantly, it could have purchased millions or billions in government securities—pumping new money into the banking system to reverse the price deflation and restart the dead economy. Instead, as President Herbert Hoover lamented, the Fed became a "weak reed for a nation to lean on in time of trouble." [17]

Long afterward, the 1929 debacle left the general impression in political circles that it could never happen again. The Fed would not permit it. If another similar collapse ever occurred, the central bank would simply begin pumping up the money supply, creating new money abundantly until the crisis was reversed. When the Great Crash occurred, it was said, the failure stemmed from the Federal Reserve's ignorance and impotence. Fed officials lacked sufficient knowledge of the economy to understand what was happening. They lacked the proper monetary tools to intervene successfully.

Comforting as the mythology was, it was not quite right. It was not that Federal Reserve governors lacked the tools to reverse the waves of failure after 1929. They could have pumped money into the economy by open-market purchases—"flooding the street," as Strong had said—and that would have restarted the economic engine. But the governors argued among themselves over whether to use these powers to halt the collapse—and they decided against it. The Federal Reserve's failure was a failure of human judgment, not the mechanics of money. Unless one assumed that the Fed had subsequently become all-wise, such decisive errors would always still be possible.

The central bankers of 1929 did not view the economic collapse as an unfolding tragedy, at least in its opening phases. On the contrary, they regarded it as a normal correction to excess. Ten months after the stock-market crash, amidst soaring unemployment, collapsing prices and an ominous new wave of bank failures, George W. Norris of the Philadelphia Fed sounded almost pleased by developments.

The consequences of such an economic debauch are inevitable [Norris told his fellow Reserve Bank officers]. We are now suffering them. Can they be corrected or removed by cheap money? We do not believe that they can. We believe that the correction must come about through reduced production, reduced inventories, the gradual reduction of consumer credit, the liquidation of security loans and the accumulation of savings through the exercise of thrift. These are slow and simple remedies, but just as there is "no royal road to knowledge," we believe that there is no shortcut or panacea for the rectification of existing conditions.

The leading commercial bankers who advised the Fed agreed. The Federal Advisory Council urged the central bank to let nature take its course. "The present situation will be best served if the natural flow of credit is unhampered by open-market operations," the council declared in November 1930.

Andrew Mellon made the same case with chilling clarity. The way out of the Depression, he confided to President Hoover, was more failure and unemployment, more liquidation. "Liquidate labor, liquidate stocks, liquidate the farmers, liquidate real estate," Mellon declared. The Treasury Secretary believed, and many other Fed officials agreed, that panic and recession were good for people. "It will purge the rottenness out of the system," Mellon explained. "People will work harder, live a more moral life. Values will be adjusted and enterprising people will pick up the wreck from less-competent people."

Hoover was not so sure this was the answer, but the President had little influence over the independent leaders of the Federal Reserve System. Herbert Hoover, of course, became the political scapegoat for their failure; his name would be invoked by a generation of Democratic orators as the symbol of Republican indifference to human suffering.

As the Depression deepened, the Federal Reserve persisted in its passivity in part because the Fed's money principles—the "real bills" doctrine—called for passivity. Again and again, in their private minutes and memoranda, the Reserve Bank officials insisted that the Fed's role was merely to provide Discount loans to the commercial banks that asked for them—accommodating the credit needs of the economy. Of course, almost nobody was asking for new loans in 1930 or 1931. The economy was contracting and the banking system did not need expanded credit from the Fed. On the contrary, banks found themselves floating in an excess of reserves—a pool of surplus lending capacity—because they could find no customers who wanted to borrow.

When others urged the Fed to inject more money into the financial system, Norris of the Philadelphia Fed reminded his colleagues of the operating principle thay had formally adopted in 1923 on the System's tenth anniversary: "The Federal Reserve supplies the needed additions to credit in times of business expansion and takes up the slack in times of business recession." That was the whole idea of an "elastic currency"—expanding or shrinking the money supply in response to business demands for credit. Norris complained that even the modest steps the Fed had taken on its own initiative would be regretted. "We have been putting out credit in a period of depression, when it was not wanted and could not be used," he warned, "and will have to withdraw credit when it is wanted and can be used."

Logical as it sounded, the theory was fatally flawed. The "real bills" approach meant the Federal Reserve would always be passively following the direction of the economy and exaggerating its cycles on both the upside and the downside—providing more and more new money to banks during a period of expansion and withdrawing more and more money during an economic recession. Thus, the Fed's behavior deepened the great contraction through its self-imposed stance of impotence. The Discount rate, its principal means of control, was like an empty sail on a becalmed sea.

What was needed, as some Fed officials recognized, was an activist money policy that pulled against the economic tide rather than drifting with it—a countercyclical policy, economists would say, rather than the procyclical policy implicit in the "real bills" doctrine. In short, the Fed must be willing to inflate the currency on its own initiative— "flooding the street with money"—in order to counteract the natural forces of deflation and contraction that were under way. The Federal Reserve System had neither the desire nor the courage to do that.

Federal Reserve officers had another reason not to act—a rather ugly reason considering the human suffering abroad in the land. Reserve Bank presidents held back because they were anxious to protect the earnings of private commercial banks. That sounded callous and narrow-minded, but political scientist Thomas Ferguson and economist Gerald Epstein found confirming evidence in their research of the central bank's archives—blunt private statements by the Reserve Bank presidents that no more additional money should be supplied because it was hurting the important banks in their districts.

For two years, some Fed officials, including the board chairman in Washington, Eugene Meyer, had pleaded with their colleagues to inject massively through open-market purchases. That would pull down interest rates and get prices and wages rising again, restimulating economic activity. In October 1931, the Reserve Banks actually did the reverse—raising the Discount rate by two percentage points in two weeks. Industrial production fell another 26 percent in the next six months. The money base shrank by another $90 million.

Finally, by April of 1932, Meyer and others prevailed, supported by the Morgan bank and important Wall Street financiers. They persuaded the Reserve Banks' open-market committee to pump up the money supply and quickly. The New York Fed began buying Treasuries on an unprecedented scale—$100 million a week for eleven weeks, $1.1 billion in additional reserves. If the campaign had continued, it would have produced a turnaround in the economy.

But, in early summer, the Reserve Banks abruptly abandoned the initiative. The bold experiment was over. When the contraction resumed a few months later, a third wave of bank failures swept the country, more severe than the first two. Another five thousand banks would close.

James McDougal of the Chicago Fed was among the Reserve Bank presidents who objected to the Fed's attempted activism. Major banks in the Chicago district, he complained, were suffering an earnings squeeze because of the Fed's easy money. The expanded money supply drove down interest rates on government securities to a minuscule level, and in these slack times, the banks held large portfolios of government securities as their principal source of income. "We believe that the additional (open-market) purchases made were much too large," McDougal wrote a colleague, "and have resulted in creating abnormally low rates for short-term government securities."

Norris of the Philadelphia Fed agreed: "Further increases in excess reserves would adversely affect bank earnings. . . ." Owen D. Young of the Boston Fed, who had voted against the open-market initiative in the first place, was "apprehensive that a program of this sort would develop the animosity of many bankers." [18] All in all, the episode was perhaps the starkest evidence in support of historian Gabriel Kolko's estimate of the Federal Reserve as a political institution: it was created to serve the most important banks and, in this instance, it did, despite the horrendous losses it was to cause the nation at large.

The Federal Reserve backed off. The infusions of new money were halted. And nature followed its course to a climax of destruction. By early 1933, as Franklin D. Roosevelt awaited his Inaugural, a new wave of collapsing banks was under way, accompanied by still higher unemployment and many more business failures. As Democrats came to power, the national economy was ruined and the American banking system was ruined with it. Also destroyed was the reputation of the Federal Reserve System.

——— 10 ———

LEANING AGAINST THE WIND

On a Monday morning in the late summer of 1931, the lobby of the First National Bank of Ogden, Utah, was jammed with nervous depositors—people waiting in line to withdraw their money before the bank ran out of funds. Another Ogden bank, older and more distinguished, had failed to open that morning. Prudent citizens figured First National would be next, one more victim of the bank panics sweeping the country. "We can't break this run today," Marriner S. Eccles, the forty-year-old president, told his tellers. "The best we can do is slow it down. People are going to come here to close out their savings accounts. You are going to pay them. But you are going to pay them very slowly. It's the only chance we have to deal with the panic."

All day, as people waited nervously to get to the window, the tellers moved, as instructed, with maddening lethargy. They paid out withdrawals in small bills and counted slowly. They looked up the signatures of everyone, even customers they had known for many years. As closing time approached, the bank was still jammed and the tension increased. If the bank closed at the regular hour, scores of disappointed depositors were going to be powerfully angry. If Eccles kept his bank open longer, it might well run out of money.

Just in time, an armored car arrived at the door, delivering fresh cash from the Federal Reserve's branch office in Salt Lake City. "As in the movies when the Union cavalry charges in to save all from the Indians," Eccles wrote. He made a great show of ushering the armed guards to the vault. Then Eccles mounted a counter to address the crowd:

Many of you have been in line for a considerable time. I notice a lot of pushing and shoving and irritation. I just wanted to tell you that instead of closing at the usual hour of three o'clock, we have decided to stay open just as long as there is anyone who desires to withdraw his deposit or make one. Therefore, you people who have just come in can return later this afternoon or evening if you wish. There is no justification for the excitement or the apparent panicky attitude on the part of some depositors. As all of you have seen, we have just had brought up from Salt Lake City a large amount of currency that will take care of all your requirements. There is plenty more where that came from.

"This was true enough," Eccles said to himself. "But I didn't say we could get it." The Federal Reserve did have plenty more cash. But none of it belonged to Eccles and First National of Ogden.

Marriner Eccles's theatrics succeeded. The crowd dispersed. Reassured depositors went home without withdrawing their accounts and his bank survived. The nightmare recurred again and again, however. Like thousands of other American bankers, Eccles spent three years in continuous crisis, staving off the periodic "runs" that followed the Crash of 1929. He was more successful than most. The Eccles family's chain of twenty-eight banks, scattered through towns and cities of the Mountain West, did not suffer a single failure. "To do so," he confessed in his memoirs, "we had to adopt a rough and distasteful credit and collection policy. Living with ourselves was not a pleasant experience under these circumstances."

The trauma profoundly altered Marriner Eccles and his view of the world. "I awoke to find myself at the bottom of a pit without any known means of scaling its sheer sides." He was Mormon and Republican, reared in the conservative economic doctrines taught by his father: thrift and hard work and free enterprise. "A business, like an individual, could remain free," his father preached, "only if it kept out of debt, and the West itself could remain free only if it kept out of debt to the East."

David Eccles, the father, was himself living proof of these principles. As an adolescent in the 1860s, still illiterate, he had emigrated from muddy poverty in Scotland to the raw but promising wilderness of Utah. Twenty years later, by ingenuity and the sweat of his brow, he was a millionaire. The Eccles fortune was a classic American triumph, from the stage of development known as primitive capitalism. He began with timber and a sawmill. Labor and raw resources were his only capital. As he earned profits, he put them aside for future ventures. As the West developed its natural resources and attracted population, David Eccles created new businesses to serve the people—railroads, coal mining, Amalgamated Sugar, Sego Milk, the Utah Construction Company and banks, a chain of them.

The critiques of capitalism and the "money trust" heard in political circles "left my father cold," Marriner Eccles recalled. "He had built his works by himself, owned many of them outright, and ran them all in a direct and personal way. He saw no reason why other men could not . . . re-create themselves in his image, providing, of course, they were left free to use their wits and will without government interference."

Until he was forty years old, Marriner Eccles believed the same. His father, a Mormon polygamist, had two wives and two families with a total of twenty-one children. When his father died suddenly in 1912, Marriner Eccles became steward for his mother's eight other children and manager of their share of the vast estate. He was only twenty-two years old, his formal education limited to high school. He was also as brilliant as his father in business. First Security Corporation, which he founded, became one of the nation's first bank holding companies, operating twenty-eight banks in Utah, Idaho, Wyoming and Oregon. Utah Construction became a prime contractor for a jewel of western development, the great hydroelectric project called Boulder Dam. The Eccles enterprises expanded and prospered with the "roaring twenties."

Then, like the nation itself, Marriner Eccles abruptly found himself in the pit of despair. Through eclectic reading and his own native intellect, Eccles gradually came upon explanations for the puzzling collapse of 1929 and the continuing Depression. Bankers like himself, he decided, only added to the problem by calling in loans and forcing the liquidation of their borrowers. Indeed, every individual enterprise, by doing what seemed sound on an individual basis, simply contributed further to the contraction. He arrived at a radical conclusion: "The only way we could get out of the depression was through government action in placing purchasing power in the hands of people who were in need of it."

Eccles's analysis contradicted all that his father had taught him. The robust economy of the 1920s had vastly expanded America's capacity to supply goods—roads, public utilities, oil, manufacturing and other productive facilities, all had grown enormously. The problem was not supply nor inadequate savings for investment, as David Eccles would have assumed. The problem was the opposite: insufficient consumer demand for the products that America could now make. There was too much money channeled into savings, too little into spending.

As mass production has to be accompanied by mass consumption, mass consumption, in turn, implies a distribution of wealth—not of existing wealth, but of wealth as it is currently produced—to provide men with buying power equal to the amount of goods and services offered by the nation's economic machinery [Eccles concluded]. Instead of achieving that kind of distribution, a giant suction pump had by 1929–30 drawn into a few hands an increasing portion of currently produced wealth. . . . By taking purchasing power out of the hands of mass consumers, the savers denied to themselves the kind of effective demand for their products that would justify reinvestment of their capital accumulations in new plants. In consequence, as in a poker game where the chips are concentrated in fewer and fewer hands, the other fellows could stay in the game only by borrowing. When their credit ran out, the game stopped.

The fundamental weakness of the 1920s prosperity, in other words, was not that Americans were profligate, spending too much and saving too little, but the opposite. "We did not as a nation consume more than we produced—far from it," Eccles declared. "We were excessively thrifty." The maldistribution of incomes guaranteed that millions of potential consumers—workers, farmers, everyone who did not earn enough to join the ranks of accumulating wealth—would eventually exhaust their purchasing power. "While the national income rose to high levels," Eccles explained, "it was so distributed that the incomes of the majority were entirely inadequate and business activity was sustained only by a rapid and unsound increase in the private debt structure, including ever-increasing installment buying of consumption goods." When the consumers' chips were gone, when they could no longer borrow or buy things, the producers would naturally curtail their production of goods too. More factories were closed; more people lost their incomes. The game was over.

The solution became dazzlingly obvious to Marriner Eccles. His father's creed of thrifty individualism, perhaps sound in its own time, was no longer valid for a modern industrial economy. As a millionaire himself, Eccles was certainly not hostile to the private accumulation of wealth, though he did resent the stubborn adherence to the status quo preached by his fellow bankers and businessmen. They insisted depressions were "God-given and not man-made" events and that no one should interfere in the process, least of all government. "It became apparent to me, as a capitalist, that if I lent myself to this sort of action and resisted any change designed to benefit all the people, I could be consumed by the poisons of social lag I had helped to create," he explained.

For Eccles, it did not matter greatly who owned wealth or how much they owned. Money itself was neutral as an economic force—positive if it was put into transactions and investment, harmful if it was hoarded in idle savings. What mattered was that people kept their money moving. Wealthy investors or bankers, following individual reflexes for self-preservation in the contraction, would not put their idle money in motion on their own initiative. Why should they reinvest, reopen factories or lend to new enterprises when unsold products were already stacked up in surplus? Why make more goods to sell when nobody had the money to buy anything? The economic problem, therefore, was how to start money moving again—how to get money from those who had a surplus (but could not possibly spend enough of it) to those who did not have enough (and, out of harsh necessity, would spend money promptly if they got some).

The only mechanism that could accomplish this transfer, Eccles decided, was the federal government. The government could borrow idle capital held by the few and put it in the hands of the many— laborers and contractors, farmers and manufacturers, even the unemployed or the destitute elderly—people who would spend it. The government could do this simply by purchasing more things itself— roads, buildings, whatever—or by sending out benefit checks to eligible recipients—veterans, the unemployed, the elderly. Instead of paying for the goods and services or welfare through taxes, the government would borrow the money (if it raised taxes to pay for the spending, that might dilute the intended economic impact, taking money out of the private economy with one hand and putting it back with the other). Thus, by definition, Marriner Eccles proposed to do deliberately what his father, David Eccles, had always preached against—living on borrowed money, better known to later generations as deficit spending.

A policy of adequate governmental outlays at a time when private enterprise is curtailing its expenditures does not reflect a preference for an unbalanced budget [Eccles explained]. It merely reflects a desire and the need to put idle men, money, and material to work. As they are put to work, and as private enterprise is stimulated to absorb the unemployed, the budget can and should be brought into balance, to offset the danger of a boom on the upswing, just as an unbalanced budget could help counteract a depression on a downswing.[1]

The new economic principles that Marriner Eccles happened upon in his earnest research would be enshrined later as "Keynesian economics," the doctrine that reigned over government management of the economy for nearly fifty years. Eccles articulated these new ideas at least three years before John Maynard Keynes would publish his *General Theory* and, for years afterward, boasted that he had never read anything by Keynes (an exaggeration, perhaps, since Eccles quoted Keynes as authority in at least one of his early speeches).

Eccles, in any case, was an untutored intellectual pioneer. An American banker from Utah, a man who had never studied economics or even attended college, was able to see what the great British economist himself saw, and Eccles had the uncommon courage to articulate this thinking before it became fashionable.

When Marriner Eccles testified before a Senate hearing in early 1933, he found a receptive audience. In addition to the new economic principles, Eccles described a specific agenda for how the federal government could spend more money: unemployment relief, public works, agricultural allotments, farm mortgage refinancing and settlement of foreign war debts. He also proposed reforms for long-term stability: federal insurance for bank deposits, a centralized Federal Reserve System, tax reform to redistribute income, a minimum-wage law, unemployment insurance, old-age pensions, federal regulation of the stock market and other economic sectors. In one sitting, a Mormon Republican banker from Utah had described most all of the reforms that would become known as the New Deal agenda of Franklin Delano Roosevelt.

"We shall either adopt a plan which will meet the problem of unemployment under capitalism," Eccles told the senators, "or a plan will be adopted for us which will operate without capitalism."

The left-wing intellectuals clustered around FDR as advisers instantly recognized that here was a kindred spirit. Despite Eccles's background, they invited him to join the inner circle drawing up legislative plans for the new Roosevelt Administration. Only in America perhaps—and then only in crisis—could such an odd political convergence succeed, a creative coincidence that enabled this unschooled but brilliantly innovative mind to collaborate with liberal reformers and closet socialists on how to save America. One summer, Marriner Eccles was struggling to save his small-town banks from failure. The next summer, he was at the center of American political power, an intimate of the President's and a principal architect of the New Deal's reforms.

"I find some pleasure in noting," Eccles later reflected, "that if I was a traitor to my own class, I earned this distinction long before Franklin Roosevelt was called one."

The name of Marriner S. Eccles would be largely forgotten by later generations of political Washington, where few remembered his extraordinary role in the New Deal. In one corner of the capital, however, Eccles was still regarded with appropriate esteem. The Federal Reserve, on its seventieth anniversary, would rename its marble building on Constitution Avenue in his honor. At the Fed, his name was spoken reverently, as if to invoke a patron saint.

Marriner Eccles, in the course of the Great Depression, became the salvation of the Federal Reserve System, the man who rescued it from disgrace. With FDR's support, and despite bitter opposition from his fellow bankers, Eccles personally designed the legislation that re-formed the Fed itself—stripped the twelve Federal Reserve banks of their autonomous privileges and their veto powers and consolidated control of money policy in the seven-member Board of Governors in Washington. Appointed by Roosevelt in 1934, Eccles served as Fed-eral Reserve chairman for fourteen years, while he also functioned as an important collaborator in White House policy making.

In political circles, Eccles restored the Fed's good name. More im-portant, he substantially altered the central bank's own economic sen-sibilities. In fact, as John Kenneth Galbraith described it, the Federal Reserve under Marriner Eccles became "the center of Keynesian evangelism in Washington."[2]

In the legislative upheaval of 1933, the American Bankers Associa-tion led the fight against one particular proposal. "Unsound, unscien-tific, unjust and dangerous," the bankers warned. The New York Federal Reserve leaders and other Fed officials objected that the mea-sure would intrude on their authority. Even the new Roosevelt Admin-istration, reform-minded as it was, declined to endorse it. Congress went ahead and enacted the law anyway, and the measure proved to be the most important banking reform of the New Deal era—federal insurance of bank deposits.

Whatever the promises and expectations, the Federal Reserve Sys-tem had not brought an end to the danger of bank "runs." Federal deposit insurance did. During the 1920s, bank suspensions had fluc-tuated annually from 366 to 975 (from 1929 to 1933, they ranged from 1,350 to 4,000 a year). In 1933, once the Federal Deposit Insurance Corporation was in place, the phenomenon of panic and collapse vir-tually disappeared from American economic life. By the 1940s and the prosperous decades that followed, the number of annual bank failures usually could be counted on the fingers of two hands and often on only one.

The main reason was public confidence—an unconditional guaran-tee by the national government that, no matter what happened or who was to blame, small depositors would get back their money if their bank was closed. At first, the guarantee covered deposits up to $5,000, a limit raised eventually to $100,000. The banks paid regular premi-ums to support the insurance fund, but ultimately it was a good-faith obligation of the federal government (and the American taxpayers). If bank failures should someday exhaust the FDIC insurance fund, Congress would doubtless appropriate the money to make good its guarantee and pay off depositors. With the FDIC sticker in the bank's window, citizens need not rush to make withdrawals whenever they heard rumors of collapse; the panicky crowds that Eccles had faced no longer appeared. Their money was safe. Despite their original opposition, commercial banks now enjoyed a double layer of government protection—the federal guarantee that reassured customers and the Federal Reserve's Discount lending that relieved temporary crises of liquidity.

Other reforms enacted in 1933 were aimed at the behavior of the bankers themselves and were intended to eliminate the self-destructive impulses that had contributed to the Great Crash and worsened the subsequent contraction. By law, banks were prohibited from paying interest on checking accounts—a control designed to stabilize the banks' balance sheets and avoid the kind of earnings squeeze that had encouraged risky lending and, in bad times, led bankers to accelerate the forced liquidation of their loan customers. Banks would now enjoy "free money" from their checking depositors, which they could lend out, presumably at somewhat lower rates, with less pressure on their earnings. With this implicit subsidy from depositors, banks were expected to be more prudent in lending and also more tolerant when recessions made it harder for borrowers to keep up the payments.

Other measures were designed to insulate banking from the runaway speculation in the stock market, which had finally collapsed in the autumn of 1929. The Federal Reserve was empowered to set collateral rules for credit in the stock market, eliminating the highly leveraged transactions in which speculators could buy as much as $100,000 in stocks with only $10,000 in cash. With the margin requirement set at 50 percent, an investor could borrow no more than half of the purchase price from his broker (who would, in turn, obtain the credit from a commercial bank). By raising the margin rule, though it rarely did so, the Fed could curb the bank lending devoted to financial adventures.

At the same time, the banking industry was effectively split in half —compelled to choose between the short-term lending of commercial banking and the long-term capital raised by investment banks through issues of stocks and bonds. Before 1929, when the major banks typically did both, they were frequently accused of conflict of interest— floating a new issue of corporate stocks or bonds, then hyping the sales by pushing dubious securities off on their own deposit customers and trust accounts. The Glass-Steagall Act of 1933 forced a separation. The house of Morgan, for instance, chose to continue as a commercial bank (known later as Morgan Guaranty), despite its prominence in the capital markets. The same year, three Morgan partners (including J. Pierpont Morgan's grandson) formed a new investment-banking firm called Morgan Stanley, which inherited most of the old Morgan clients, corporations that raised large blocks of capital through stocks or bonds.[3]

In their perennial rhetoric promoting deregulation, the commercial bankers were understandably silent about the government's two most intrusive roles in their marketplace. Commercial banks longed to be "freed," but not from federal deposit insurance or the Federal Reserve's Discount lending. Yet to establish a genuine free market in finance, a "playing field" that was truly level, banks would have to give up both of those protective subsidies. Without those privileges, commercial banking would doubtless be more competititve. There would also be many more failed banks.

When Marriner Eccles laid out his blueprint for reforming the Federal Reserve, FDR bought the whole package and added one condition of his own—Eccles must agree to serve as chairman of the reconstituted central bank. "It is only fair that you should know that formidable opposition has developed. . . ." Roosevelt told him. "However, I don't give a damn. That opposition is coming from the boys whom I am not following." Eccles replied: "Well, Mr. President, if you don't give a damn, I don't see why I should."

Wall Street banking fought him on both fronts—Senate confirmation of his appointment and the legislation reforming the Fed—but Eccles won both struggles. The essence of the 1935 act was to acknowledge the reality that had already emerged haltingly over the previous two decades: the Federal Reserve's money-supply regulation directly and powerfully influenced the course of the entire economy. If that was so, then these decisions could not be left to willful bankers operating twelve scattered Reserve Banks, each trying to defend his own local interests apart from the whole. Control must be centralized in one place—the seat of the national government in Washington, D.C.

The Board of Governors was given bureaucratic authority over the Reserve Banks, the power to oversee their internal affairs and to override or ignore their policy decisions, on everything from plans for new buildings to staff salaries to changes in the Discount rate. Western banks, led by the Bank of America, supported Eccles's reforms because they too resented Wall Street's domination of the Fed. The twelve Reserve Bank presidents, with the practical exception of the New York Fed, became subordinates to the seven political appointees in Washington. The Fed's protocol of elaborate courtesies attempted to obscure this relationship, but everyone at the big conference table understood it.[4]

At the same time, however, the Board of Governors was given further insulation from political control. The Secretary of the Treasury and the Comptroller of the Currency, both representing the elected Chief Executive, were removed as members. This change seemed minor to Eccles since he himself was a close adviser and political ally of the President's, with the practical status of a Cabinet officer. Under Eccles's successors, however, the distance between the Fed and the White House would grow wider. With no Administration representative involved in the making of monetary policy, the lines of political communication became fuzzier and less reliable. Public accountability became murkier too. Practically speaking, a President was held politically responsible for the results of Fed policy, but had no direct hand in shaping it.

The control of monetary policy was formalized in a new creature, the Federal Open Market Committee, in which, despite their reduced status, the Reserve Banks retained some clout. Eccles wanted the Reserve Bank presidents consigned to a lowly advisory capacity, with no voting power, but Congress compromised with the bankers and created the odd hybrid known as the FOMC. With seven of the twelve votes, the governors could dominate the FOMC, but consensus required more than a bare majority. If the governors were divided, the five votes of Reserve Bank presidents could be decisive.

The Reserve Bank presidents, who voted in annual rotation, could still exert some pull on policy—usually in a conservative direction. When political scientist John T. Woolley examined FOMC decisions covering the 1960s and 1970s, he found that 90 percent of the dissents cast by Reserve Bank presidents were in favor of tighter money. The governors, in contrast, cast 60 percent of their dissents to promote an easier policy. Governors were conservative-minded people themselves but, on balance, less conservative than their colleagues from the Reserve Banks.[5]

In purpose and operations, the modern Fed began in 1935. Eccles did not use the economists' term "countercyclical," but that is what he meant—a money policy that stimulated the economy in recession and restrained it when an expansion threatened to become an inflationary bubble. The Fed's duty, he said, is "to assure that adequate support is available whenever needed for the emergency financing involved in a recovery program, and to assure that a recovery does not get out of hand and be followed by a depression." His successor, William McChesney Martin, expressed the idea more succinctly: the

Fed's role was "leaning against the wind," whichever way it was blowing.

Discount lending, as the great contraction had demonstrated, was an impotent tool for this purpose. Indeed, the rise and fall of Discount borrowing followed the trends of economic cycles rather than pulling against them. On both the upside and the downside, the Federal Reserve would henceforth rely principally on open-market operations to regulate the money supply and influence the economy through interest rates. The Discount rate, though still important to the money market and to the Fed technicians who monitored it, would cease to be the main valve by which the Fed added or withdrew liquidity from the banking system. Government debt securities replaced short-term commercial notes as the principal financial paper in Fed transactions. U.S. Treasury notes and bonds became the main assets in the Fed's own portfolio.

This change in the composition of the Fed's portfolio sounded obscure and technical, but it had a profound political resonance. The central bank was shifting its primary focus to Treasury bonds and notes at the very time the federal government would be issuing lots of them—entering a new era of managed deficits that, in time, would swell the national debt and create a vast financial market in government debt securities. The timing of these transitions was a coincidence of history, but the shifts in monetary and fiscal policies interacted with one another, subtly encouraging the expansion of federal debt. The Fed, as lender of last resort, now bought and sold Treasury debt paper and accepted it as collateral against its own Discount window advances to banks. The central bank, thus, had a direct self-interest in maintaining the stability of the government-securities market, for both prices and trading practices. When the government borrowed, the Treasury and the Fed routinely collaborated in the marketing of the new debt issues, anxious to ensure that the pool of private buyers could absorb the new bonds and that prices would not gyrate wildly.

The change in Fed operations inevitably pulled the Federal Reserve closer to the financial world—the bond traders of Wall Street, who would purchase U.S. securities—and allowed the Fed to be more distant from the commercial sectors of the real economy. The Fed's own market interest was now mainly government notes and bonds, not the short-term commercial and agricultural loans that it was originally founded to serve. The political consequences were impossible to measure, but it seemed likely that this shift would influence the Fed's monetary decisions. Central bankers worried about all things, but they would worry first about the temperament of financial investors in the bond market, less about the consequences of Fed decisions for businessmen leading commercial ventures.

In the simplified hindsight of political memory, the Great Depression was summarized as one long decade of uninterrupted bleakness. New Deal reformers perhaps salved the pain with their vast public-works projects and welfare checks, but Washington's deliberate deficit spending failed to produce economic recovery. The general misery was finally relieved only by the vigorous stimulation of World War II. This collective summary was crudely accurate, but the actual thread of events was more complicated and more instructive.

In strict economic terms, the great contraction that began in October 1929 ended in the spring of 1933 and a wobbly recovery began. The nation's economic output slowly expanded over the next four years and prices began rising, but the recovery was too weak to restore the pre-1929 prosperity or even to reduce unemployment substantially. In 1933, 15 million were unemployed; four years later there were still 11 million out of work. The recovery was real, nevertheless, and the stock market, buoyed by reviving profits and prospects, enjoyed one of its greatest "bull markets," doubling stock prices in two years' time.

Then another sharp recession hit in 1937, less traumatic than the Great Crash but still punishing. It was as though the battered nation had struggled to regain its senses, but was then benumbed by a second blow. The causes seemed plain: the federal government, after running unprecedented peacetime deficits for three years, opted for balanced budgets. It cut the federal deficit in half in 1936 and again in half the following year. The Federal Reserve, for its own reasons, was simultaneously raising reserve requirements on banks, soaking up excess reserves and raising interest rates. The combination was devastating —a tightening fiscal policy and a more restrictive monetary policy. Together they wiped out the fragile recovery and put millions more out of work. It was this second recession of 1937 that finally and completely discredited the old orthodoxy of balanced-budget economics. It also confirmed the political hegemony of Keynesian doctrine.

The combat over ideas within the New Deal demonstrated how difficult it is for a conceptual breakthrough in economics to win respectability against the scorn of established wisdom, particularly the ranks of professional economists. Contrary to legend, the New Deal did not rush to embrace the new theory of deficit spending in 1933; it argued over the idea for years, temporized and compromised. One of the leading skeptics was the President himself.

During the 1932 campaign, FDR had promised fiscal prudence: "I regard reduction in federal spending as . . . the most direct and effective contribution that government can make to business. . . ." This was not altogether insincere. Roosevelt left himself a loophole: he would tolerate federal deficits, he declared, only "if starvation and dire need on the part of our citizens make necessary the appropriations . . . which would keep the budget out of balance." That was his justification for the vast public-works projects launched during his first months in office, for the emergency employment programs and other relief measures that created large deficits. The President was still ambivalent about the theory, however, and he salted the government with tenacious advocates from both camps—big spenders versus budget balancers—who tugged back and forth for control of government policy. FDR sometimes sounded loyal to one camp and sometimes to the other. "The contradictions between the afternoon and the evening positions made me wonder whether the New Deal was merely a slogan or if Roosevelt really knew what the New Deal was," Eccles complained.

From his pulpit at the Federal Reserve, Marriner Eccles led the fight for greater federal deficits by the Roosevelt government and was usually frustrated by the compromises that FDR settled on. "It seems certain," Eccles said, "that the President assented to two contradictory policies because he was really uncertain where he wanted to move." To help bolster his side, Eccles recruited as Fed research director a young Harvard economist named Lauchlin Currie, whose thinking also anticipated Keynes. Currie recruited and converted others.

Eccles also helped launch the era of liberal credit, the easier terms for borrowers that became standard for American consumers. As a banker who understood leverage, Eccles argued that the government could have more impact on housing through mortgage guarantees and interest-rate subsidies than through direct spending. The funding for public housing, he said, "was just a drop in the bucket so far as need went." But Washington could stimulate millions of housing starts by leveraging the credit market—knock a percentage point off mortgage interest rates with a direct subsidy and provide government guarantees to induce lenders to make long-term mortgages available, loans running for an unheard-of twenty years. Home mortgages had typically been limited to seven or ten years—which meant prohibitive monthly payments. The New Deal changes in mortgage finance laid the basis for delivering the "American dream" to millions of ordinary families —a home of their own, purchased with long-term mortgages and payments they could afford.

When Keynes published *The General Theory* in 1936, he was not announcing new ideas to the world. He was formulating them in the rigorous scientific terms that other economists could not so easily ignore. "The effect of *The General Theory*," Galbraith explained, "was to legitimize ideas that were in circulation. What had been the aberrations of cranks and crackpots became now respectable scholarly discussion." The pre-Keynes Keynesians included Adolf Hitler. After 1933, Hitler initiated the Third Reich's version of government-induced recovery—borrowing vast sums to build superhighways and armaments. He was so successful that by 1936 the Depression was substantially over for Nazi Germany.

The profession of economists seemed permanently conservative in its mode of thinking—always the last to know when old verities were crumbling and new ones emerging. As a group, they defended the status quo, whatever it was, until real events destroyed it. In the Populist era, most economists had derided the agrarian reformers who described the liabilities of the gold standard. In the 1930s, they dismissed original thinkers like Marriner Eccles. A generation later, having embraced the new Keynesian orthodoxy, mainstream economists would be blindsided again by changing realities.

John Maynard Keynes's many-chambered masterpiece was courageous in that sense, for with densely technical arguments he was systematically refuting what his profession had believed since the days of Adam Smith. Classical economics taught that free markets, constantly self-correcting, would always find a natural equilibrium for wages, production and prices. Unemployment was a temporary dislocation, naturally eliminated as wages fell to match the demand for labor and prices adjusted accordingly. The premise was not exactly wrong, Keynes argued, but equilibrium was the exceptional condition, only rarely realized, rather than the general rule. He described how the mechanics of finance and capital formation, in fact, regularly left industrial economies operating below full employment and well short of their full potential.

In particular, Keynes upended a bedrock principle of classical economics known as Say's law (after J. B. Say, a French disciple of Adam Smith's): supply produced its own demand. The process of economic activity, according to Say's law, began with producers investing and making things, then finding markets for them. In the modern economic system, Keynes explained, it was more the other way around. Manufacturers would not produce if they could not first see a market for their goods. The "demand side"—not the "supply side"—was where the action began.

The ruinous disequilibrium known as the Great Depression, Keynes argued, flowed from an excess of savings that could not find viable investments in production. The morbid capital would not be invested in creating new supply until it was clear that there was sufficient demand—buyers who could purchase things. The solution, therefore, was to manipulate the level of aggregate demand in order to stimulate production, to convince savers that it was profitable again to invest and restore the miraculous process of capital formation and compound interest which multiplied the world's wealth.

Despite his Cambridge education, aristocratic manner and wealth, Keynes was also an outsider in his own way. He was an aesthete who enjoyed describing himself as an "immoralist," a leading member of that sparkling circle of British intellectuals known as the Bloomsbury group that defied Victorian mores in both art and love. Keynes was married but was also homosexual, a fact that automatically put him in defiance of social convention.

Keynes's rebellion against economic orthodoxy, as he explained himself, was not derived from the political discontents of socialism and class conflict. It was based on a psychological insight: capitalism was ripe for unprecedented abundance, universally distributed, if only human society could get beyond the stern dogma of the Protestant ethic, the Calvinist ethos that insisted self-denial and suffering were good and necessary for the human spirit. Save for the future, the Calvinist creed taught, and you will be rewarded in the long run and certainly in heaven. "In the long run," Keynes observed, "we are all dead." Enjoy the here and now, he insisted. Pleasure is good. Suffering is mostly unnecessary.

The Keynesian ethic won the argument. In most modern economies, dependent on mass consumption, pious rhetoric was still devoted to Calvinist themes of thrift and self-sacrifice, but everyday reality followed Keynes to the pleasurable life of easy credit and self-gratification. The conversion was embraced, most dramatically, in the hearts and habits of Americans.

As a political idea, Keynesian doctrine was equally influential. Conservative critics decried it as the advent of socialism, but the core of Keynesian politics was quite different. What Keynes proposed was not class conflict, but reconciliation. His economic prescriptions suggested the terms for peaceful resolution. By intervening judiciously to correct capitalism's flawed mechanism, government would save the marketplace from the political struggles that threatened it, labor versus capital, consumers versus producers, poor versus rich. Keynes's remedy, as Robert Skidelsky explained, "avoided having to choose between capital and labor. Keeping demand buoyant would simultaneously underwrite high profits, full employment and rising wages, thus eliminating or at least easing the conflict over the distribution of wealth."

Crudely stated, his formulation offered something for everyone—a promise bound to appeal to both politicians and voters. Instead of the ancient war of class interests that divided citizens into winners and losers, here was a political approach that suggested everyone could gain. In loftier terms, Keynes (and Eccles and the others) provided the political community with a unifying principle for economic decisions: everyone rides in the same boat. Given the complex relationships of the modern economy, everyone will prosper together or, ultimately, everyone will languish. Capital will not collect its rewards unless labor gets its due. Workers cannot be healthy if producers are sick. Savers cannot reap profit if no one is able to borrow their savings and use them productively.

Enlightened self-interest required cooperation, a negotiated sharing of rewards. The Keynesian perspective became the unstated premise for most bargaining in modern politics. The perennial arguments over taxes and spending were mainly contests over the size of the shares, who got how much and what the likely effect would be on economic growth, but class arguments were considered passé. Fundamental questions about the American system, like those raised by the Populists or labor socialists, receded. Fierce political struggles between labor and management and other competing interests continued, of course, after Keynes, but his ideas were a moderating influence. Like the creation of the Federal Reserve in 1913, the advent of Keynes helped to submerge the class conflicts embedded in American politics.[6]

This generous political spirit—the truce implicit in Keynesian doctrine—closely resembled the practical principles by which Franklin Roosevelt governed. Despite the fractious politics and FDR's derisive attacks on Wall Street's "economic royalists," the true spirit of the New Deal was conciliatory and collaborative. He was remembered as labor's champion, but Roosevelt was also supported by important elements of Wall Street, including leading investment bankers. FDR's many reforms were, in a sense, a series of "new deals" worked out with various sectors of the economy, both the injured and the prosperous. His bargains did not put an end to conflict, but they did lower the intensity.

In addition to the uneven efforts to increase aggregate demand, the New Deal also worked on the other side of the equation—programs to limit supply. Farmers, vulnerable to supply gluts and drastic market fluctuations since the Populist era, were protected against price instability with a subsidy program that, in exchange, imposed limits on how much they produced. Organized labor, vulnerable to competition from the nonunion workers willing to accept lower wages, was given labor-law enforcement for its efforts to restrict the supply of labor available to employers. In exchange, labor surrendered its own freewheeling tactics of disruptions and accepted the orderly regulation of disputes.

The New Deal regulatory schemes developed for various sectors—oil production, trucking, communications, airlines—imposed government supervision over these private industries, but they also stabilized them by controlling supply. Competition was limited by setting prices and restricting access to the markets by new ventures that might undercut the arrangements. Conservative critics called them government cartels, but the arrangements resembled the protection that government already had provided to banking.

Once the 1937 recession hit, the economic argument among the New Dealers was settled. Keynes won. The lesson was that balanced budgets could do real harm to the economy. The only thing wrong with the New Deal's deficits was that they had not been large enough to get the job done.

Marriner Eccles refused to accept any of the blame for the 1937–1938 recession, but economists spanning the conservative-liberal spectrum from Milton Friedman to John Kenneth Galbraith agreed that the Fed itself had inadvertently helped unravel the nation's fragile recovery. In 1936 and early 1937, thinking it would cause no harm, the Federal Reserve doubled the level of reserve requirements for commercial banks—at the same time the executive branch was tightening its fiscal policy. By August 1937, a new contraction was under way.

Until then, the central bank had followed a "passive" monetary policy, allowing plenty of room for economic expansion to take hold. Interest rates were low; excess bank reserves were abundant. Eccles was convinced, like other Keynesian liberals, that monetary policy could not be the main engine driving the recovery. The Fed could make plenty of money available, but the Fed could not compel people to borrow it. The most potent contribution the Fed could make to stimulating aggregate demand was through interest rates—keeping the price of money cheap while fiscal policy did the main work of encouraging business activity. On these assumptions, the Federal Reserve developed the operating approach that prevailed for several decades and would come under attack a generation later from Milton Friedman and the monetarists. The central bank focused its control primarily on interest rates and "credit conditions," instead of money and the money supply.

The irony of Eccles's leadership as Fed chairman was that while he restored the Federal Reserve's stature as a governing institution and was honored ever after by its officers, Eccles himself believed the central bank should play a subordinate role—complementing the fiscal policy set by Congress and the President and aiding the government in its borrowings.

The Fed simply cannot be isolated as the cause of our economic problems [Eccles once explained]. It is not all-powerful. Its overall objective is to maintain an adequate rate of economic growth, low levels of unemployment and reasonable price stability. But its principal job under present conditions is to supplement fiscal policy. The fiscal problem continues to be one of heavy deficit financing, and the Fed, whether it likes it or not, is required to provide adequate reserves to the banking system in order for the government to finance its needs, even when that is inflationary.[7]

Eccles's large mistake was the tightening he began in 1936. The reserve requirement was raised, in a series of increases, from 12.5 percent to 25 percent. Most banks could meet the higher requirement with their excess reserves, but the action also produced a general increase in interest rates in financial markets. When the new recession unfolded, Eccles lost some of his esteem as a member of FDR's inner circle. "A mood of near panic took hold of some highly placed people in the Administration," Eccles said, "and with very few exceptions they cast sour looks in my direction."

The episode seemed to confirm what the Keynesian liberals already believed about monetary policy—the best thing the Fed could do for economic growth was to get out of the way. Money should accommodate the economy and stop interfering with it. In the turmoil of World War II, the Federal Reserve did, in fact, adopt a policy of total passivity.

"The 1937 action was the last error of the Federal Reserve for a long time," Galbraith wrote. "That was because it was its last action of any moment for fifteen years."

When Paul Volcker was an undergraduate at Princeton University in 1949, majoring in economics, he chose to write his senior thesis on the topic "The Problems of Federal Reserve Policy Since World War II." The 256-page essay was a scholarly account of how America's central bank, yielding to the financial imperatives of World War II, had lost its power to control money and prices. Volcker predicted—correctly, as it turned out—that something had to give. Either monetary discipline must be restored or the United States would face continuous inflation.

"Although the inflation problem continually raised its head in a disconcerting manner and demanded attention, the countermeasures taken have not appeared to be a realistic attempt to combat the danger," Volcker wrote. "The policies followed have been largely passive."

If Marriner Eccles had read the young undergraduate's analysis, he would not have disagreed. During the war, as the federal government borrowed hundreds of billions, the Federal Reserve explicitly supported the Treasury debt financing with its monetary policy, pumping more liquidity into the banking system so that private buyers would be able to absorb the new government securities. The Fed followed Treasury's instructions, yielding any pretense to independence. The central bank's money-supply management was "pegged" to one purpose—low interest rates. The interest rate on the longest-term government bonds was held at a steady 2.5 percent throughout the war and short-term rates were correspondingly lower (ninety-day T-bills paid less than .5 percent).

If market pressures threatened to push rates higher, the central bank simply bought more Treasury issues itself, thus adding more money to the financial system and preventing the price of money from rising. In effect, the Fed guaranteed that if there was any Treasury paper that the private market would not buy, then the Fed itself would buy it. In 1933, when FDR took office, the national debt was $22 billion. When Pearl Harbor was attacked in 1941, it was $48 billion. By V-J Day, when the war ended in 1945, the national debt was $280 billion.

Paul Volcker, the economics major, concluded that the Federal Reserve must stop "pegging" interest rates at a fixed level and allow rates to rise to reflect market pressures "in order to have an anti-inflation policy worthy of the name."[8] Inside the government, Marriner Eccles was making the identical argument—and becoming increasingly unpopular for it. "I regret that the Federal Reserve did not take a more independent position despite Treasury resistance," Eccles wrote in his memoirs. "There was no justification for our continued support of the Treasury's wartime cheap-money policy."

During the war itself, Eccles quarreled regularly with Treasury on how to finance the mobilization, but he was compelled to acquiesce. The Federal Reserve had played a similar role in supporting the government's borrowing for World War I. Lincoln had printed "greenbacks" to pay for the Civil War. History and politics argued that a nation at war, threatened with survival, will do whatever it needs to do in order to win and worry later about the financial consequences.

Eccles did not disagree with that general proposition, but he objected in particular to the financing methods. The periodic Victory bond drives staged by Treasury, he said, meant "outrageous profits" for banks and large investors because the arrangement allowed a daisy-chain exploitation of the Fed's money creation. To ensure a successful bond sale and stable interest rates, the Fed expanded bank reserves by buying up outstanding government securities. The commercial banks lent the expanded money supply to private customers who would in turn lend it to the government by buying the new Treasury issues. The customers then sold their new government securities to the commercial banks—and they eventually sold them back to the Fed when the central bank was again required to expand the money supply. In a roundabout way, the government was borrowing its own money—and paying a fixed fee to middlemen for the privilege.

The bankers, of course, were delighted with most aspects of Treasury financing, as were government bond dealers and the brokers [Eccles complained]. The practices followed ensured them a windfall of profits, as they did to countless corporations and insurance companies. A substantial part of the buying did not come from genuine savings; it came from money created by the banking system through the very process of buying the securities held by nonbank investors.

Eccles wanted to prevent the "free riding" by limiting bank participation in the market chain of government securities and by issuing government bonds that could not be resold. He was never able to prevail. Eccles also pushed for a policy that every political leader found difficult to sell in wartime—the additional sacrifice of higher taxes. Federal taxes were raised sharply, but World War II was mainly paid for with loans to the government. From 1940 to 1945, about 60 percent of the federal government's expenditures were financed through borrowing, not revenue.

Marriner Eccles, the original advocate of bold deficit spending, now became the "sound money" scold of the Roosevelt Administration. He continually urged FDR to borrow less and tax more, to finance the war from the swollen savings of consumers rather than the artificial expansion of money. Inflation was largely avoided by the wartime controls on wages and prices. But once controls were lifted, he warned, the grossly expanded money supply would become an "engine of inflation."

The economic consequences of World War II were, nonetheless, extraordinarily bountiful for America. Keynesian liberals looked upon the experience, justifiably, as the finest hour for their doctrine—full confirmation of what was possible with central planning and government manipulation. Every war had produced robust economic growth, but World War II resembled an industrial revolution. In only five years' time, the nation's annual output increased by more than 75 percent. In 1942 alone, the Gross National Product expanded by 16 percent and the next year by 15 percent and another 15 percent the following year (annual growth of 5 percent would be considered exceptional in later decades). The Federal Reserve was totally accommodating throughout. It never let money or interest rates get in the way of economic growth.

The operative principle was Keynesian economics on the grand scale: create new supply by first creating new demand for it. The government borrowed and spent in unprecedented volume, and the government's spending created the market for new products and newly emerging technologies. To meet the necessities of war, the government, in effect, force-fed the rapid development of new productive facilities across many industrial sectors. These would become the basic industries of America's postwar prosperity—electronics, petrochemical synthetics, aircraft frames and engines, shipbuilding, steel and nuclear power, among others. The new industrial base created by World War II was the platform that launched America's global hegemony, the era of multinational corporations based in the U.S. and astride the world economy. This revolution might also be called "supply side" economics, but it was done from the gospel according to Keynes.

For consumers, the war mobilization was a time of sacrifice—automobiles, houses and appliances were simply not produced, meat and sugar and gasoline were rationed, wage levels and prices were administered by Washington bureaucrats. For the 12 million citizens who served in the armed forces, the economic sacrifice was especially severe—lost years of work and wages (not to mention the risk of getting killed or wounded). Overall, however, the self-denial of the war years was laying the groundwork for an abundant future. During the war, per capita income rose more than 40 percent above the 1939 level. With so many millions conscripted for war, unemployment vanished and labor scarcity became the problem. World War II was "an equal opportunity employer"—women and blacks filled prime industrial jobs previously reserved for white males. With limited ways to spend their rising incomes, families saved more of their money (partly by buying war bonds, lending the money to the government). In 1943 and 1944, personal savings reached extraordinary levels—25 percent of incomes. After 1945, this pent-up consumer demand would drive the postwar prosperity, private citizens replacing the government's war as the principal customer for American production. Once again, people could spend their money on the things they had been denied—cars and vacation trips, suburban houses and appliances, a new cornucopia of goods to buy.

World War II was a model of the possible. In theory, if a national consensus of purpose developed, if people would accept temporary limits on their economic choices as well as regulatory controls on wages and prices, the nation could literally rebuild itself, almost overnight. With the right choices, America could practically double the productive capacity of its economy and advance innovation and dramatically multiply new wealth and incomes. These economic choices, however, were really political questions: who would take the sacrifices and who would reap the rewards? Whose consumption would be restrained and whose production would be encouraged? All this consigned extraordinary powers to government, perhaps tolerable only in war. No one, including the most ardent Keynesian planners, has ever figured out how to re-create a comparable combination of creative sacrifices in peacetime or how to sell it to a free society.

As controls were gradually lifted, the predictable postwar price inflation did occur—8.5 percent in 1946, 14.4 percent the next year. Yet, despite the huge swell in government debt, the inflation after World War II was notably less intense than the price spirals that had followed other major wars. A substantial share of the government debt, vast as it was, had been spent on real capital formation—investment in new factories and new technologies that raised the productivity of the nation in real terms. If real production increased more or less in step with the expansion of money, it would not be inflationary. Debt was a gamble on the future, and in this instance, the bet paid off.

The prevailing political consciousness after World War II, in any case, was still preoccupied by the searing memories of the Great Depression—not by the risk of inflation. Many assumed that without war as a stimulus, the suffering of economic contraction would resume. If mistakes were going to be made in economic management, they would be on the upside—keeping the economy going and avoiding a repeat of the 1930s calamity. One economic fundamental was different, however, after World War II. The government did not really demobilize for peace. After a brief interlude, the Cold War began in earnest and defense budgets rose again. A vast arsenal and a standing army of war-fighting capability became a permanent commitment of federal spending—and a permanent contribution to aggregate demand.

The postwar dilemma for the Federal Reserve intensified, however, as the swollen public debt was now joined by rapidly expanding private debt. As consumers, investors, manufacturers and other businesses were gradually freed from the wartime controls on borrowing, their demand for bank credit added pressure on the money supply. If the central bank must continue to acquiesce, providing whatever money was needed to keep interest rates from rising, Fed officials felt impotent to brake inflationary pressures.

"There is no limit to the amount of money that can be created by the banking system," Eccles warned, "but there are limits to our productive facilities and our labor supply, which can be only slowly increased and which at present are being used to near capacity." This was the Marriner Eccles that the Federal Reserve remembered reverently—talking like a worried central banker, not a liberal dreamer.

Yet Treasury wanted to keep interest rates low, both to hold down the cost of government borrowing and to encourage private economic activity. It was, Eccles acknowledged, "a conflict of responsibilities. The Treasury's primary job is to finance the government at the lowest cost at which it can. . . . The Federal Reserve has the job of regulating money and credit in such a manner as to help maintain economic stability."

Something had to give. Eccles and the Federal Reserve Board began halting efforts to declare their independence and break free of their subordinate position. Several times they attempted to let interest rates rise. On each occasion, the Treasury Secretary rebuked them and, as Eccles said, "implied that we were proposing to stage a sit-down strike." Once the hero of liberal reformers for renouncing his conservative Republican roots, Eccles now found himself accused of apostasy: "Insisting on a balanced budget and tighter credit policies, Eccles has forsaken his earlier position in the New Deal years and gone over to the camp of the reactionaries." In 1948, President Harry Truman declined to reappoint him to another term as Fed chairman and named Thomas B. McCabe instead. After fourteen years, Eccles bore his scars proudly—despised by the bankers, no longer trusted by the bankers' enemies.

The Fed's dilemma was still unresolved when Paul Volcker, a future chairman, wrote his senior thesis at Princeton. Volcker proposed a heretical solution. The conflicting responsibilities for government debt financing and the constant tug-of-war between Treasury and the central bank could be resolved by simply extinguishing the Federal Reserve's independence and making it part of the Treasury Department. This would be roughly comparable to other industrial nations like Britain and France where the central banks take their instructions from the elected government. Marriner Eccles would have been horrified by the suggestion. And so would Paul Volcker when he matured as a central banker.

The conclusion seems clear [the young Volcker wrote] that there must be some better method for assigning responsibility for monetary control than at present. Either the monetary authority should be located entirely in the Federal Reserve System or the Treasury and the Reserve System should be combined in one agency. This would seem to be more logical because the fiscal actions of the Treasury are bound to have large monetary implications.

Admittedly, past actions of the Treasury have not always indicated that it could be safely entrusted with discretionary monetary authority; but, since its influence cannot be excluded anyway, the unification would give some promise of eliminating the indecision, conflict and irresponsibility which tends to make any policy result in failure.

Political accountability would thus be located in one place, the executive branch, which was answerable at elections for the economic consequences of its decisions. Fiscal policy, the government's spending and taxes, would necessarily have to mesh with its monetary policy, the regulation of money and credit expansion. If a President used this power to ensure cheap money, he would also have to accept the blame for whatever price inflation resulted. If an overly stringent credit policy caused a recession, the President could not point impotently at the Federal Reserve as his excuse.

The solution proposed in Paul Volcker's undergraduate thesis was not seriously considered when, early in 1951, the conflict reached its crisis point. The Federal Reserve Board announced again, more forcefully than before, that it would no longer hold down interest rates. Harry Truman called the entire Federal Open Market Committee to his office for a chat and, afterward, the White House announced that all was resolved amicably—the Fed would continue to fix interest rates at the same old levels.

But the argument was not resolved. A few weeks later, the Fed again resisted and the President assented to a negotiated settlement between officials of Treasury and the central bank. The results were announced in March 1951 as the Treasury–Federal Reserve Accord. The agreement was a delicate compromise in which Treasury acceded to slightly higher rates and granted minor flexibility to the Fed. Eccles, no longer chairman but still a board member, took part in the bargaining. The principal negotiator from Treasury was Assistant Secretary William McChesney Martin, a former president of the New York Stock Exchange, who would soon be named himself as the new chairman of the Federal Reserve Board. Appointed in 1951, Martin held the chairmanship through five presidential elections.

The initial impact of the Accord was quite small—a slight upward creep in interest rates. Within two years, however, Martin and other Federal Reserve officials claimed for themselves a more sweeping interpretation of the Treasury–Fed agreement—it was, they attested, a declaration of full independence for the central bank. By that point, the liberal Democrats were gone from the White House, defeated by Dwight Eisenhower in 1952. The Democratic policy makers who wanted easy credit and low rates were replaced by conservative Republicans who shared the Fed's anxieties about "sound money" and supported higher interest rates.

Esoteric as it sounded, the Accord became a crucial juncture in the life of the Federal Reserve—and the course of the postwar economy. In practice, the Fed did become independent again. The central bank no longer felt required to hold interest rates down or to follow the executive branch's direction. The independent Federal Reserve would ease or tighten, whenever it thought necessary. The price of money rose steadily in subsequent years, directly influenced by supply-and-demand perceptions in the financial marketplace and by nudges from the Fed. "Our purpose," as William McChesney Martin put it, "is to lean against the winds of deflation or inflation, whichever way they are blowing."

Martin's relentless critic, Representative Wright Patman, described the consequences somewhat differently. "The Federal Reserve," Patman complained, "would spend the next ten years sending interest rates in orbit."[9]

The new Federal Reserve chairman was disarmingly witty, capable of neutralizing political attacks with blunt colloquialisms. The Fed's main role, William McChesney Martin once confessed cheerfully, was "to take away the punch bowl just when the party gets going." His liberal critics howled at the thought. That, they complained, is precisely what William McChesney Martin did during the 1950s—blunting the postwar expansion with high interest rates so that the economy never reached its full potential.

From the other side, conservative critics of the monetarist school complained that the central bank operated with baffling imprecision, leaning this way or that, dampening credit or easing, with no clear definition of what guided its decisions. "There was essentially no discussion of how to determine which way the relevant wind was blowing," Milton Friedman and Anna Schwartz wrote.

Martin's eclectic approach and his self-confident style muffled the blows. He fenced energetically with Wright Patman at congressional hearings and responded amiably, if sometimes opaquely, to scholarly questions. But the Federal Reserve's management never became the decisive political question that critics demanded. Inflation was moderate, the 1950s were bountiful and the general public was not much interested in abstract economic debates. During Martin's tenure, the central bank was able to recede further into its own mystique. The subject was too vague and complicated for most people to understand; money seemed too remote from politics to become a serious source of controversy.

Many years after his retirement, Martin reminisced with good humor about the mysteries of his institution. When he took office as chairman, he told himself: "My gracious, here I am the new chairman of the Fed and I'm doing my best—I'm not the brightest fellow in the world but I'm working hard on this—and I haven't the faintest idea of how you control the money supply. Yet everyone thinks I have it at my fingertips." [10]

Martin's frequent warnings about the dangers of imminent inflation seemed precious in hindsight. The Fed's anxiety, however, repeatedly interrupted the postwar expansion. Three recessions occurred during the prosperous years of the Eisenhower Presidency, and the Fed was directly responsible for at least two of them. In 1953, when the inflation rate was less than 1 percent, the Fed imposed a drastic tightening on money markets; then it reversed itself—too late to avoid a recession in 1954. Four years later, the Fed began leaning the other way, expanding money rapidly to head off a contraction. But it was too late again—a brief and mild recession occurred anyway. Exactly two years later, in April 1960, the economic recovery was halted, one of the shortest on record, and another recession began—six months after the Fed had virtually stopped growth in the money supply.

Whatever else liberal critics might say against Martin's cautious stewardship of money, they could hardly accuse him of trying to help the incumbent Republicans. All three recessions in the 1950s occurred during election years. The higher unemployment helped Democrats take away Republicans' seats in Congress—and eventually the White House. Vice President Richard M. Nixon had urged the Eisenhower Cabinet to push Martin for easier credit during his 1960 campaign for President. After the election, Nixon called on Martin at the Fed and told him precisely whom he blamed for his defeat—the Federal Reserve.

The "New Economics" that triumphed during the Kennedy-Johnson years was a blunt reversal of the political climate surrounding the Fed—an optimistic declaration that the stodgy conservatives of the Eisenhower era had underrated America's potential. During his campaign, John F. Kennedy obliquely criticized the Fed itself, but his winning theme conveyed the essence: a promise "to get the country moving again." The liberal indictment of Federal Reserve policy was spelled out in more detail by Wright Patman, among others: excessively tight money had nearly doubled the interest rates on government bonds over the preceding decade, from 2.3 percent in 1950 to 4 percent in 1960. Yet unemployment had crept steadily higher, approaching 6 percent, and the nation's economy was operating far below its capacity. Inflation, meanwhile, was a bogus fear—prices were rising at the unthreatening rate of only 1.5 percent in 1960.

It has become painfully clear [Patman declared] that the monetary policy carried out by the Fed was not sufficiently expansionist to keep the country moving at a rate justified by the increase in the working force and the industrial capacity. . . . Interest rates have climbed steadily, with slight interruptions, during the entire post-Accord period. The period has been marked, then, by a continual shift of income to the banks, other major financial institutions and individuals with significant interest income. The rest of the country provided this income.

Patman was a distinctive critic because he was one of the very few politicians, even among liberal Democrats, who were willing to attack the money question on old-fashioned terms—the gross redistribution of income that flowed from higher interest rates, shifting wealth from the many to the few. For this, Patman was called the "last Populist," a label that mixed nostalgia with derision. In an era of general abundance, his attacks on bankers and high interest rates were dismissed as cranky demagoguery from the distant past. Interest rates were now regarded as a question to be resolved by scientific management and natural market forces, not by the raw politics that pitted haves against have-nots.

But Patman's complaints also spoke to the broader economic goal articulated by John Kennedy and his Keynesian advisers. "By instituting a high interest policy," Patman explained, "a country chooses to grow more slowly than it otherwise could." The economic policy launched by Kennedy and fully implemented by Lyndon Johnson asked monetary policy to stand aside or at least not to interfere with the increased growth that an activist fiscal policy would make possible.

Patman foresaw inevitable conflict between the two—the government's fiscal policy versus the government's monetary policy. "As things stand now," he warned, "economic policy making is run like a dual-control car driven by two drivers, one of whom insists on his independent right to use his own brakes and accelerator as he and he alone sees fit. It is pure luck if the motor is not constantly stalling. To say the least, that is a most inefficient way to get anywhere." [11]

The New Economics worked. As the Kennedy-Johnson tax cuts and spending increases delivered more aggregate demand to drive the economy, it seemed for a time as though economists really could "fine tune" endless prosperity. For 106 months, from February 1961 to December 1969, the nation enjoyed its longest era of uninterrupted economic expansion. The stock market soared in a long bull market, driven by rising corporate profits, and workers enjoyed steady real growth in personal incomes and declining unemployment. In a generous mood, the national government expanded its commitment to help those who were left out of capitalism's growing bounty—the poor and elderly and racial minorities.

As the nation approached full employment, a discreet combat developed between the White House and the Federal Reserve. Martin and his colleagues worried that when the economy reached its full capacity and could no longer absorb rapid growth, then the natural law of supply and demand would produce inflation, as various markets bid up prices for scarce materials and wages for scarce labor. The Fed tried to restrain without provoking open conflict; the White House leaned on the Fed to be more accommodative. The clash became public briefly in late 1965 when Lyndon Johnson summoned Martin to his ranch for a melodramatic lecture on the danger of raising the Discount rate.

The White House economic advisers devoted considerable energy —and memo writing—to the question of whether the Fed chairman was "on the team." They also selected new governors for the Federal Reserve Board who would be more liberal and perhaps pull Martin in their direction. When Lyndon Johnson was thinking of replacing Martin as Fed chairman in 1967, Gardner Ackley of the CEA sent the President a reassuring memo. Ackley had talked privately to other Fed governors and was assured that "Bill [Martin] was increasingly becoming a follower of the 'New Economics.' . . . Now that the 'New Economics' is firmly in the saddle in both places, Bill can be counted on to cooperate." [12]

Martin and his colleagues did periodically resist the inflationary impulse from the pumped-up federal spending, but not as forcefully as some wanted. Philip Coldwell, then president of the Dallas Fed, said:

The System attempted to fight back, but in those days a dramatic event was when you raised the Discount rate a quarter of one percent. You just didn't attempt a swing in interest rates big enough to contain those pressures. . . .

Johnson set the Fed up for the blame if anything went wrong. That's all right. Every President has to have a scapegoat. His argument was that the economy is very flexible and the Fed shouldn't be stiff-necked. It was perfectly all right for him to triple spending for arms—because he wanted the Fed to monetize the debt. A number of us on the Federal Open Market Committee argued very strongly that we should have greater restraint. But others were saying, "Well, we are in a war and we have to support the war effort," We never did it.

In fact, the New Economics was already unraveling, but not because of William McChesney Martin or the Fed. The hubris that led the United States into the war in Indochina may have also infected some liberal economists. The chairman of the Council of Economic Advisers, Arthur Okun, boasted in 1968: "When recessions were a regular feature of the economic environment, they were often viewed as inevitable. . . . Recessions are now generally considered fundamentally preventable, like airplane crashes and unlike hurricanes." [13]

Yet, by 1968, the confident managers of the economy had already waited too long to take the necessary measures that their own Keynesian doctrine prescribed—raising taxes or reducing spending in order to dampen aggregate demand and avoid an overheated economy.

Paul Volcker was one who recognized the error early. In the autumn of 1965, after he had resigned as Deputy Under Secretary at Treasury and returned to Wall Street banking, Volcker sent an anguished memo to his former boss, Treasury Secretary Henry Fowler. Volcker's message, as he paraphrased it from memory, was: "My God, if taxes aren't increased now, the whole of the New Economics is going to be in disrepute."

Volcker was a "team player," sharing the Administration's goals, but not entirely swept away by its presumptions.

It is almost impossible to reconstruct the mood, but there was a feeling of exuberance in the economics profession [he recalled], because it really thought it had the business of the cycle of boom-and-bust licked. Everyone was caught up in it, though I don't think I shared it entirely. But I was from a different background, more financially oriented, and in the Treasury we were naturally more cautious than the advisers in the White House. [14]

The crucible for Keynesian economics came early in the war, as Volcker's memo suggested, when military costs escalated rapidly alongside the Great Society's new spending commitments for domestic programs. The test was whether the managers of the New Economics, politicians and economists, had the steel to do the hard part—restraining fiscal policy when inflationary pressures became evident in the economy. It was one thing to ask Congress to cut taxes and increase spending, not exactly a sacrificial act for elected politicians. But would they be willing to do the reverse when the economy required it? The answer was, they would not. In American politics, the Keynesian idea seemed to work fine on the upside, but it couldn't work at all on the downside.

The political flaw was fundamental, though at the time it was blamed on the deceit and evasion of Lyndon Johnson. The President first concealed the true costs of the Vietnam War, then stalled when his advisers urged him to raise taxes. When Congress finally enacted a tax surcharge in 1968, it was too little, too late. Arthur Okun, one of the leading Keynesians, described the liberal debacle as the "defeat of the New Economics by the old politics."[15]

The Keynesian failure, however, was larger than one President's foibles or the budget dilemma created by war in Vietnam. A postmortem by John Kenneth Galbraith described in fundamental terms why the political system found itself unable to follow the Keynesian rule. The composition of federal spending had changed drastically since the 1930s, for one thing, and now included a large and permanent base of Cold War military expenditures plus the maturing commitments of New Deal social-welfare programs. Both types of spending, practically speaking, were not subject to discretionary reductions. In an increasingly unpopular war, the famous debate between "guns and butter" was left unresolved: the people got both. Tax revenues, likewise, were not as flexible as the New Deal reformers had supposed. "An increase in taxes at a time when prices are rising appears to all but the most enlightened citizens as a peculiarly gratuitous action," Galbraith observed. "More is being paid for goods; now the government adds insult to injury with higher taxes."

The political reality, confirmed in later years by subsequent episodes of congressional inaction and presidential evasion, was that the New Economics could not keep its promises. "If taxes cannot be increased except under the *force majeure* of war and public expenditures cannot be decreased much for any reason," Galbraith concluded, "it follows that Keynesian policy is unavailable for limiting demand. It can expand purchasing power but it cannot contract it. . . . The goals were there; the instruments for reaching them were becoming distressingly inoperative."

The failure of fiscal policy left it to monetary policy to do the nasty chore. By 1968, price moderation had disappeared; inflation was approaching 5 percent. The "war tax" belatedly enacted by Congress in the election year failed to restrain the overstimulated economy. In early 1968, members of the Federal Open Market Committee fought privately for months over how tough they should be—and the "hard-liners" lost to Martin and the moderates. By 1969, with the Democrats defeated and Richard Nixon in the White House, the inflation rate was above 6 percent.

The Federal Reserve asserted itself again. When the Fed tightened money and credit more vigorously in 1969, monetary control proved to be more effective than the limited fiscal restraint that had been tried (persuading more young economists that Professor Friedman was right and their liberal teachers were wrong—money did matter, power-fully). The confirming evidence was the new recession that began late in 1969, the first contraction in more than eight years.

The 1970 recession was different. Unemployment rose, as expected, but price inflation did not recede proportionately. When the recession ended, both aggravations persisted together—high unemployment and steadily rising prices. Economists called the puzzling combination "stagflation." Politicians argued over which affliction bothered the public more.

The era of confident economic management was over. Richard Nixon, among other misfortunes in his Presidency, had the bad luck to announce his conversion to the Keynesian orthodoxy at the very moment when that doctrine was eclipsed by new realities.

If historians searched for the precise date on which America's sin-gular dominance of the world's economy ended, they might settle on August 15, 1971. On that day, President Nixon abruptly changed the monetary rules under which nations had traded with one another for twenty-five years. From World War II onward, the United States was the wealthiest, most productive and most stable of the competing economies in the world. Its currency, the dollar, was the guarantee for everyone of order and stability in international trade and finance. President Nixon's announcement, without saying so explicitly, meant the dollar was now too weak to lead.

In the United States, the next-day headlines and political reaction focused mainly on Nixon's dramatic domestic measures, the imposi-tion of wage and price controls to brake inflation. But the truly historic content was his decision that the United States would no longer honor the terms of the Bretton Woods agreement, the arrangement that had stabilized the exchange of foreign currencies since 1946 by pegging them to the dollar. Nixon's decision was a momentous change, sowing global controversy and economic dislocation over the next fifteen years.

Paul Volcker, Nixon's Treasury Under Secretary for Monetary Pol-icy and International Affairs, was on a plane to Europe that night, off to reassure foreign central bankers and finance ministers. "We had to have a breathing space," Volcker said, "but I looked hopefully for a reconstruction of the orderly system." He would spend the next two years in globe-trotting negotiations, trying to patch back together the orderly system of international currency exchange, but the efforts failed. Afterward, Volcker saw the breakdown of Bretton Woods in larger terms: it was a failure of American leadership, an unwillingness to confront the nation's economic excesses and to impose self-discipline.

The essence of foreign exchange, when all the daunting complexities were set aside, was an ancient quarrel among trading nations— how to keep everyone honest, how to ensure that a nation's money actually had the value it claimed. A government willing to water its own currency by inflation could gain enormous windfalls at the expense of other nations—both in currency exchange and in trade advantages. A sound coin would be exchanged in trade for a dishonest one. Country-to-country disputes over relative currency values were older than capitalism itself. For centuries, the neutral arbiter had been gold, a precious substance that did not lose intrinsic value and, unlike paper money, could not be manufactured at will.

Every nation understood that international trade needed a system of mutual discipline, for temptation was always present. By manipulating its money values, a government could win large markets overseas for its exporters and thus create satisfaction at home with expanding production and employment. If, for example, France's money was normally valued at five francs to the American dollar, a $4 bushel of wheat from Nebraska sold for 20 francs in Paris. A bottle of perfume worth 100 francs in Lyon sold for $20 in New York. Then, suppose, an inept or capricious or scheming French government watered the value of its own national currency drastically, reducing the actual value of francs by 25 percent. Its francs would be worth less at home as price inflation resulted, but the $4 wheat exported from America would now be effectively priced in France at $5—a boon to the grain farmers of Normandy who had to compete with U.S. agriculture. Likewise, the French perfume could now be exported profitably to the U.S. at a much cheaper price, perhaps as low at $15 a bottle. That would stimulate sales in American stores and take market shares away from competing brands.

In global financial markets, where currency traders were alert to every slight and imagined deviation in money values, the French manipulation would set off protective action, probably long before the effects on trade were so obvious. Investors would rush to get out of any financial asset, bonds or stocks or currency itself, that was denom-

inated in unreliable francs and losing its real value. They would shift
their wealth to assets in other currencies, dollars or yen or Deutsche
marks, whose value was stable or increasing. These shifts of capital
wealth across the international spectrum of currencies often exacerbated the trade imbalance—the increased demand for dollars and
dollar-denominated investments would push up the international price
of dollars and weaken the franc further.

Foreign-exchange arguments flowed constantly through both finance and trade, reflected daily in the changing prices on international
currency markets, where banks, corporations, large investors and
even governments bid on their own estimates of reality. However, the
value of any nation's money in international transactions was not ultimately determined by currency traders in New York or London or
Tokyo. The foreign-exchange value of a currency reflected how that
nation conducted its own domestic economic policy. Was it being
responsible or spending beyond its means? Was it buying and borrowing more than it could really afford, expanding its money supply more
than was justified and inflating the currency? What most Americans
saw as an arcane subject for international economists really originated
in their own behavior at home and in Washington.

The Bretton Woods treaty, devised in 1944 by Keynes and his American counterpart, Harry Dexter White, used the dollar as the disciplinary system to punish dishonest currencies—and the ultimate enforcer
was gold. The value of the franc, the pound, the Deutsche mark, the
lira and other currencies was fixed at agreed-upon ratios to the American dollar. If Britain or France or any other country watered the value
of its currency, it would be forced back into line by the fixed exchange
value with the dollar. In extremis, the wayward nation could be compelled to redeem its francs or pounds in gold, not at the watered-down
value, but at the fixed value against the American dollar. To cushion
the process, the International Monetary Fund was created as a financial pool for short-term loans among nations. Instead of shipping gold,
a nation could draw funds temporarily from the IMF to settle its foreign accounts while its government worked to get its domestic house
in order.

The dollar was the rock of certainty for all nations, just as the British
pound sterling had imposed stability in the nineteenth century when
Britain's economy dominated world trade. And gold kept the dollar
honest. To guarantee the dollar's own constancy, the United States
agreed to pay gold for dollars (at $35 to the ounce) whenever any
foreign government had accumulated a surplus of dollars and wished
to exchange them. Every other currency was anchored to the dollar
and the dollar was anchored to gold.

What Richard Nixon did on August 15 was to "close the gold window." The United States unilaterally declared it would no longer pay out gold for dollars in foreign exchange. The reassuring guarantee was suspended—temporarily, Nixon said at the time, but permanently, as it turned out. For more than a generation, the dollar had imposed discipline on the rest of the world, but now the dollar itself was unreliable. What happens when the rock itself crumbles?

In the short term, Nixon did not have good choices. The United States had been paying out billions in gold for foreign claimants for more than a decade, and the reserves stored at Fort Knox had rapidly depleted. By 1971, foreign financial institutions had amassed dollar claims totaling $36 billion—double the $18 billion in gold reserves the United States still held for international convertibility. If the President let events play out, the guarantor of world monetary order—the American government—would soon find its own storehouse empty. Its guarantee to the world would become meaningless by default.

In broader terms, the crisis reflected the consequences both of American success and of the excesses of its domestic inflation. The United States, undamaged by World War II and much stronger for it, had led the industrial world to spectacular recovery (while it also paid most of the cost of military defense for the non-Communist alliance). Western Europe and Japan were rebuilt. American dollars spread around the globe for foreign aid, corporate investment and trade. Just as the dollar became the dominant currency used in trade by everyone, American interests dominated international commerce. For two decades, the United States supplied generous foreign aid and exported capital for global development, expenditures a wealthy nation could easily afford. Compared with the destructive turmoil that followed World War I, the American hegemony after World War II was brilliantly effective.

By the late 1960s, however, all these factors matured into real problems—just when the New Economics was allowing America's price inflation to take off at home. The industrial allies were no longer weak and malleable, but aggressive competitors for world markets. The buildup of exported dollars—now known as Eurodollars—became a permanent alternative source of finance, interacting with America's domestic money supply and complicating control over it. The annual trade deficits had built up a backlog of real economic claims—claims that could be satisfied ultimately only if Americans sold more abroad and bought less themselves or if they surrendered their store of immutable wealth, the gold at Fort Knox.

For two years, the Nixon Administration struggled to make adjustments that would restore the old order and allow the dollar to resume

its role as the fixed star in the international constellation of currencies.
In December 1971, after intense negotiations with foreign finance ministers and central bankers, Nixon devalued the dollar 7.9 percent (now
an ounce of gold would be worth $38). Other nations agreed grudgingly
to revalue their own currencies at higher levels, thus further reducing
the dollar's. But the imbalances continued and so did the market
pressures of a weakening dollar. Early in 1973, the government devalued the dollar again (now pegged to gold at $42 an ounce, an 11 percent
devaluation).

Finally, by March 1973, exhausted and unable to keep the international bargaining alive, officials conceded that the old order was dead
beyond resurrection. The U.S gold guarantee was permanently abandoned and so were the fixed exchange ratios among the other major
currencies. Henceforth, a dollar would find its own value in the currency markets. So would the franc, the yen, the pound and all others.
Fixed exchange rates were replaced by a system of "floating exchange." A dollar was still a dollar, but its international value would
fluctuate daily, depending on the judgments by millions of economic
players on what a dollar was really worth compared with other kinds
of money.

Paul Volcker was at the table throughout the saga of retreat and
unraveling (and would be stigmatized somewhat unfairly among central bankers for his role in dismantling the certitude of the dollar
backed by gold). Volcker himself, however, was a reluctant advocate
of the new system of floating exchange rates. He proposed alternatives
but could not persuade the political leaders.

I didn't think floating was a good policy, though obviously we did some
contingency planning for it [he said]. I was concerned as an economist
about it because it conveniently removes the need for internal economic
discipline to protect the external value of the currency. But I also thought
of our political situation in the world. You couldn't just walk in and say,
"We have a system that has been operating pretty well for twenty-five
years, but we've decided to change it."

The United States wasn't in extremis, and I believed that floating would
be a tremendous source of political tension. But you have to remember
that a half or even two-thirds of the academic community were in favor
and so were some people on Capitol Hill and in the Administration.

Milton Friedman, among others, was triumphant. Conservative
monetarists saw floating exchange rates as an excellent free-market
solution—let the private markets decide the value of the dollar. Their
judgments, based on hard facts in the marketplace rather than on

political sentiment, would force the government to behave. More importantly, Friedman argued, the Federal Reserve would at last be free to concentrate solely on the one thing it could control—the domestic money supply. Monetarists wanted the central bank to ignore the international complications—all else would fall into place if only the Fed got its domestic money regulation right. In practice, their promise was never fulfilled. Floating exchange rates produced, instead, an era of constantly shifting currency values that meant perpetual instability in the terms of trade among nations.

These subtleties were lost on the President who made the choice. "Poor old Nixon," Volcker said, "was not a deep thinker in these matters. He had no intellectual conviction about floating. His position was, 'You tell me which rules you want to play under, fixed or floating, and I'll play it that way, but you're to make sure the best interests of the United States are taken care of.' "

Indeed, from abroad, the abandonment of the U.S. gold guarantee looked like a blunt political gambit—a way to hang on to American hegemony when the fundamentals were going against the United States. With floating rates, the dollar would continue its decline through the 1970s as U.S. inflation escalated, and this trend was vastly stimulating for American export industries, including agriculture, at the expense of their foreign competitors. Advocates of the floating system would argue that, though it would take several years, the free-market approach would finally force the United States to discipline itself. The process finally began, they would argue, when Paul Volcker took office in 1979 and imposed his tight-money regime.

In the meantime, floating exchange rates permanently destabilized global commerce, creating artificial advantages and real losses almost at random. Currency values were pushed back and forth in unpredictable ways that no business executive could reasonably foresee. Every multinational corporation became, perforce, a gambler in currency markets. The American devaluation, furthermore, altered real returns for everyone else conducting international transactions in dollars.

The immediate consequence was dramatic and frightening. In the fall of 1973, six months after the dollar was permanently "floated," the oil-producing nations of OPEC quadrupled the price of crude oil. Americans blamed the higher gasoline prices on greedy Arab sheiks, but, in truth, they could have justly blamed their own government's monetary policy. The OPEC price escalation was a direct and logical response to Nixon's fateful decision. Oil traded worldwide in dollars, and if the United States was going to permit a free fall in the dollar's value, that meant the oil-producing nations would receive less and less real value for their commodity. The dollar had already lost one-third of its value in only half a dozen years and seemed headed toward even steeper decline. In substantial measure, Saudi Arabia and the other OPEC nations were grabbing back what they had already lost—and tacking extra dollars on the price to protect themselves against future U.S. inflation. *The Wall Street Journal* observed: "OPEC got all the credit for what the U.S. had mainly done to itself." [16]

The abrupt run-up of oil prices fed instant inflation into the price of everything else. Poorer nations that could not pay the bills borrowed heavily—the "recycling" of petrodollars by major banks. Banks collected the deposits of revenue-rich OPEC governments and lent the money to developing nations so they could avoid bankruptcy and keep their economies growing. The global system adjusted to the trauma and carried on, much better than many had expected, but the dynamics were different. A game of money combat had now been established among nations—a contest to protect narrow self-interests in a newly precarious world.

Paul Volcker speculated that it might have turned out differently if there had been sufficient political will in the United States. The old system might have survived if the U.S. had been willing to restrain its own domestic economy—the discipline of higher interest rates and higher unemployment, less spending and slower growth—until the dollar was stabilized. On the other hand, America's ability to dominate the other economies of the world was inevitably waning. Although America was still the wealthiest and most powerful nation, its luxurious margin for error and excess was becoming much smaller.

When Richard Nixon was elected President in 1968, he innocently assumed he could immediately appoint his own chairman for the Federal Reserve Board. William McChesney Martin, who had held the job for nearly twenty years, informed the President-elect that he was mistaken. Martin's term did not expire until early 1970, a year after Nixon's Inaugural, and Martin said he intended to serve out his time. The Fed chairman, in the President's mind, was the man responsible for his first political defeat, in 1960. The President's displeasure deepened in 1969 as the Federal Reserve tightened credit forcefully, despite White House complaints, and the nation entered recession late in the year. On January 31, 1970, Nixon was finally able to put his own man in charge of money and credit and presided proudly as the oath for the new Federal Reserve chairman was administered to his longtime adviser, Arthur F. Burns. Nixon wished Burns success in his new job, then added a touch of deadly-serious humor.

"I respect his independence," the President assured the audience gathered at the White House. "However, I hope that independently he will conclude that my views are the ones that should be followed." The audience applauded vigorously. Nixon smiled and turned to the new Fed chairman. "You see, Dr. Burns, that is a standing vote for lower interest rates and more money."

Burns, as it happened, delivered promptly. Two weeks later, presiding at his first meeting of the Federal Open Market Committee, Burns argued forcefully that the weak economy needed a substantial and overt easing of credit. In the first "go-round" of discussion, when governors and Reserve Bank presidents expressed their preferences informally, the majority favored only a moderate relaxing of credit. On the final vote, after Burns reiterated his strong convictions, the majority voted with him, 8 to 4, and the Fed provided the "lower interest rates and more money" that the President wanted.

Inside the Fed, Arthur Burns would be both admired and despised for his force of character. Unlike Martin, he was blunt and blustery, an autocratic leader who trampled on the traditional "collegial atmosphere" of the Board of Governors. As a Columbia University economist and former Eisenhower adviser, Burns had credentials and intellect that were not questioned, but his bullying manner was. He could be cruel, associates said, humiliating staff economists with nasty remarks on their competence. He was also capable of shamelessly juggling the monetary numbers—deliberately mismatching interest rates with money-growth projections—in order to achieve an FOMC consensus for the policy directive.

"Arthur just hated dissents," Governor Philip Coldwell said. "I guess it wasn't three months after I came on the board, I threw a dissent at him, along with Alfred Hayes, president of the New York bank. For the next five meetings, Al Hayes and I would be brought into Arthur's office beforehand for little prep sessions—a lecture from Arthur on the importance of consensus."

Outside the Fed, Burns won an exalted reputation as the stern enemy of inflation. He delivered many eloquent lectures on the subject, scolding Congress and other audiences for their lack of self-discipline. Among his colleagues at the Fed, however, there was considerable cynicism about the chairman's pious rhetoric. If it was fair to indict the central bank for regularly yielding to inflation over a period of years, for failing to resist the short-term political pressures for economic growth, then Arthur Burns was as guilty as any chairman. When he took office in 1970, inflation was running above 5 percent. Eight years later, when he left, despite a long and severe recession in 1974, the inflation rate was headed toward 9 percent and higher. His stewardship was recorded indelibly in America's prices: the Consumer Price Index was at 116 when Burns took charge of the central bank. When he retired, the price index was at 195 and rising. His reputation as an inflation fighter seemed to inflate right along with the value of money. In retirement, Arthur Burns began lecturing on the "anguish of central banking."

An uglier accusation surrounded his tenure—the conclusion, shared especially among Democratic politicians, that Arthur Burns had deliberately manipulated monetary policy in order to help re-elect his old friend Richard Nixon. Burns and his fellow governors strenuously denied it, including governors who had opposed Burns's policy persuasions at the time. If Burns made mistakes in 1972, and the governors all agreed that he did, the mistakes were based on honest convictions about where the economy was headed, not partisan bias. No one, of course, could definitively settle questions of motivation, but politicians could interpret the evidence for themselves: when Arthur Burns erred, his errors were all tipped in the same direction— providing a prosperous climate for Richard Nixon's re-election campaign.

Nixon's White House staff, which liked to play "hardball" with both its allies and its adversaries, did not trust Burns to deliver on his own, and in the year before the re-election season, they threw several blunt messages at him. Early in 1971, concerned that the new Fed chairman was behaving as independently as the old one, two White House staff members called on Burns separately and told him what the President wanted—money expansion that would allow the economy to reach full employment by 1972. Burns protested that their behavior was improper and he complained to the President. That summer, the White House managers fired another "shot across the Fed Chairman's bow," as one presidential aide put it. A fictitious story was planted in the press that Burns had asked for a $20,000 pay raise at the same time he was urging wage and price controls for the rest of the nation. The story also claimed the President was considering a proposal to double the size of the Federal Reserve Board—a not-very-subtle threat to dilute the chairman's power.[17]

The tactics were crude, but Nixon's broad political strategy for 1972 was brilliantly successful. The President's popular standing and his re-election prospects were being undermined by the new and puzzling performance of the economy—a listless recovery in which both unemployment and inflation lingered on at awkwardly high levels. Nixon's strategy was to pump up the economy for the campaign year with larger federal deficits while keeping a lid on inflation by imposing wage and price controls. In August 1971, the President announced the controls—freezing the rising prices that were so troublesome. Simultaneously, the Nixon Administration embraced a stimulative fiscal policy—increased federal spending that would drive the economy faster. Thus, for the short run at least, voters would enjoy relief from both afflictions—inflation and unemployment—in time for the 1972 elections. To succeed, however, the strategy depended upon a cooperative Federal Reserve.

The Fed must be willing to provide "a rate of monetary expansion sufficient to move the economy up on the desired path," as Nixon explained in his memoirs. "The word went out that 1972, by God, was going to be a very good year," confessed a high official at Treasury, where Paul Volcker was in charge of monetary policy.

The Federal Reserve came through. Money growth, which averaged only 3.2 percent a month in the last quarter of 1971, jumped to a monthly average of 11 percent in the first quarter of the election year. Given the usual time lag of monetary stimulus, generosity in winter meant the economy would respond robustly by the summer and fall. Overall, the Fed permitted money expansion throughout 1972 that was about 25 percent faster than the year before. The Federal Funds rate crept upward slightly, but the Federal Reserve Board did not raise the Discount rate. The Discount rate was lowered to 4.5 percent and held there until after the election, despite repeated pleas for increases. During 1972, the Board of Governors rejected twenty-two recommendations from the various Federal Reserve Banks for an increase in the Discount rate.

Inside the Federal Open Market Committee, Arthur Burns argued repeatedly with his colleagues through the spring and summer about the potential consequences of their policy. A determined minority warned him that a new breakout of inflation was ahead in 1973 if the Federal Reserve did not apply restraint now. The White House, they pointed out, was already hinting that price controls would be lifted early the next year. Once the regulatory lid was taken off prices, an inflationary burst would surely follow—fueled by the generous money policy that preceded it. Their warnings, expressed in minutes of the FOMC meetings through 1972, proved to be an accurate forecast of what did occur after Nixon's electoral victory.

In meeting after meeting, however, Arthur Burns successfully stared them down. At one point, according to the minutes, the chairman answered their anxieties by remarking that "he was not afraid of prosperity." Unemployment was still relatively high, Burns observed, and he did not see an "economic boom" ahead. Each time the argument was joined, a distinguished minority voted against Burns's direction, including a spectrum of governors from the conservative Philip Coldwell to the more liberal Andrew F. Brimmer. Each time, the chairman prevailed. The Fed declined to tighten forcefully.

By August, when the portents of future inflation were even more evident, the dissenters tried again. Andrew Brimmer expressed the worry that some comments made by Burns and others about "constraints on interest rates" might "be interpreted as suggesting political constraints." Brimmer hoped that was not the intended message.

No, Burns assured him, he did not mean to suggest there were any "political constraints" on the Fed's policy. "Nevertheless," the chairman added, "the Federal Reserve System was a part of the government." He meant this: the President's anti-inflation controls did not apply to interest rates (though lenders were urged to follow voluntary guidelines). However, if the Fed pushed up rates, that might provoke an outcry for mandatory controls on credit too. "In the circumstances," Burns warned, "the Federal Reserve should not be eager to raise interest rates." A majority of the Federal Open Market Committee yielded to this logic and its implication of political repercussions. The majority did not wish to tempt collision with Richard Nixon's re-election strategy.[18]

And 1972 was a very good year. Inflation was held in check while unemployment declined steadily. The government accelerated its distribution of benefit checks to families and happy citizens spent the money. Real disposable income per capita, the best statistical indicator of voter satisfaction with the economy, rose by a robust 3.3 percent. America seemed headed in the right direction again. In November, Richard Nixon won re-election in a historic landslide. And, for the next ten years, Federal Reserve governors would labor, with scant success, to convince skeptics that the Fed's policy errors of 1972 were not based on politics.

The American public felt the eventual consequences, even if it was unaware of the causes. For 1973 was a very bad year. As the Nixon Administration phased out its controls, prices renewed their escalation. The embattled dollar weakened further on international-exchange markets and the U.S. government abandoned its two-year struggle to stabilize it. In the fall, the Organization of Petroleum Exporting Countries responded to the devaluation of its dollar income by employing the long-threatened "oil weapon"—a boycott that traumatized Americans with lines at their gas stations and quadrupled oil prices, feeding naturally into higher prices for nearly every other product. The U.S. inflation rate reached 8.8 percent in 1973, more than doubled from the previous year, and would rise above 12 percent. For its part, the Federal Reserve pushed up interest rates—trying to restrain the boom it had helped to stimulate the year before. By November of 1973, confronted by tight money and the "oil shock" from OPEC, the economy sank into contraction.

The nation had not experienced anything like it since the 1930s. Industrial production shrank by nearly 15 percent. Unemployment accumulated each month for nearly a year and a half, reaching a peak of 9.1 percent, nearly 8 million workers without jobs. In all, the economy's output declined in size by nearly 6 percent. As the contraction continued, price inflation eventually began to moderate, yet it hardly went away. As the buildup of idle labor and surplus goods retarded wage and price increases, the inflation fell from above 12 percent to below 5 percent. But that left inflation still well above the inflationary conditions that had prompted Richard Nixon to impose controls in 1971. There seemed to be a new plateau of distress in which neither unemployment nor inflation subsided to "normal."

Arthur Burns and the Federal Reserve got more than their share of the blame. Once the contraction was under way, the central bank allowed it to take its course, hoping that as the recession deepened, it would break the curve of runaway inflation. After nine months or so, the Fed began easing money and credit modestly, but without much effect. The recession finally ended in March 1975 and, even then, the recovery was painfully slow.

Frustrated congressional critics zeroed in on Burns, their anger heightened by the partisan overtones of the 1972 performance. Democrats, for instance, proposed a congressional directive early in 1975, ordering the Fed to provide "substantially higher" money growth. "Congress has received expert evidence," the resolution declared, "that money supply growth of nearly 9 percent per year in mid-1972 and mid-1973 contributed to the present inflation and the barely 2 percent per year in the second half of 1974 as contributing to the recession and increase in unemployment and the decline of gross national product."

Burns objected testily to Senator William Proxmire of Wisconsin, one of the sponsors. "I think it is most unfortunate and, if I may say so, shortsighted and even unfair on your part, Senator, to suggest, as the resolution does, that the Federal Reserve is largely responsible for the ills of this country," Burns said.

"We do not say that," Proxmire replied. "We say 'contributed.' "

"You do not mention anybody else," Burns snapped. "You do not mention what Congress has contributed or what the President has contributed or what business firms have contributed."[19]

Burns, for his part, tightened up on Fed secrecy. He abolished the long-standing practice of keeping verbatim minutes of the Federal Open Market Committee meetings. These minutes were normally kept secret until five years had elapsed—and were unlikely to embarrass anyone so long after the fact. Even so, they were the only record of who said what in the private policy meetings, the central bank's only decent accounting for history of how it had determined policy for money and credit. Arthur Burns discontinued the practice. In the future, the Federal Reserve's secret deliberations would remain secret forever. FOMC minutes were reduced to mere summaries of its meetings.

"The word 'sordid' is probably too strong," a former aide to the chairman reflected, "but what Burns did immediately after Jimmy Carter's election in terms of monetary policy can be documented. There was a rapid shift in monetary policy and it was designed to ingratiate Burns with Carter so he would be reappointed chairman."

The records did indicate that shortly after the election of 1976 the Federal Reserve eased. The Discount rate was cut and money growth accelerated smartly. In fairness to Burns, the same evidence demonstrated that he did not play political games to help re-elect Gerald Ford. The recovery that began in 1975 was frustratingly slow, but as the economy gradually gathered momentum, Ford's prospects steadily improved. He lost narrowly in the end—without the extra monetary stimulus that might have put him over the top.

Burns was a Republican, appointed by a Republican President. According to one Fed associate, he "wanted desperately to be reappointed by a Democrat and go down in history like Bill Martin as a bipartisan chairman." Like Martin, Burns had one more year to serve before the new Democratic President could appoint a chairman to a new four-year term. During that year, Burns discreetly courted key members of the Carter Administration, hoping to win their friendship and approval.

A memorandum from one staff aide advised the Fed chairman in November 1977:

> Carter can be seduced . . . reappointment would make Carter out to be a high-minded statesman, would reassure the national and international financial and business communities, would rally financial markets, etc. . . .
> Carter will have to be reassured that, if you are reappointed, you will not continue to publicly criticize everything that is near and dear to him. . . . Any seduction program would have to reassure the President that you won't criticize him publicly every six months.

The courtship failed. Carter and the liberals in his White House, particularly Vice President Walter Mondale, distrusted Burns on several levels. They were not about to take the risk of letting him control money and interest rates during their term in office. In early 1978,

Carter appointed G. William Miller, chief executive of Textron, as Burns's successor.[20]

The Burns campaign for reappointment had ironic consequences for the Carter Presidency, though Carter himself seemed oblivious to them. The easy-money policy begun by the Fed in late 1976 and extended through 1977 laid the groundwork for the inflationary run-up that would engulf President Carter a year later. The double-digit price inflation that would ultimately help defeat Carter was widely attributed to inept management by G. William Miller. In hindsight, many officials at the Fed privately conceded that Arthur Burns himself deserved a larger share of the blame.

In 1978, as inflation escalated again, Paul Volcker brooded about the future of the American economy. He was now president of the New York Fed. A lecture he delivered at New York University was a gloomy meditation on what lay ahead. The future would not be like the past, he warned. Something was changing in the collective psychology that shaped everyone's economic choices. After a long era of prosperity and confident risk taking, Americans were shaken—by inflation, by the oil-price shock, by the 1970s' long, severe recession. A "long cycle" of caution and uncertainty was unfolding.

The evidence, Volcker explained,

seems to me pretty clear that there is some tendency toward swings in the tempo and mood of business activity over long periods of time—say periods of ten to twenty years. Those swings may be influenced by a variety of more or less objective events, such as changes in population, wars and their aftermath, waves of technological innovation and so on. But those swings also appear to be influenced by less tangible, even psychological, phenomena. . . .

A long period of prosperity breeds confidence and confidence breeds new standards of what is prudent and what is risky. For a while, the process is self-reinforcing, sustaining investment and risk taking. But it may also contain some of the seeds of its own demise: eventually natural limits to some of the trends supporting the advance are reached and the advance cannot be sustained so easily. We find ourselves with more houses and shopping centers and oil tankers and steel capacity than we can readily absorb. Financial positions are extended and the economy has become more vulnerable to adverse and unexpected developments. . . . The mood turns conservative and uncertain. . . .[21]

The Bible spoke of seven good years followed by seven lean years. A controversial Russian economist, Nikolai Kondratieff, had once theorized that capitalism underwent "long waves" of fifty years or so —an extended cycle of innovation and upward thrust, despite the occasional setback of minor recessions, followed by a long era of general collapse and decline. The long cycle of growth, he claimed, would eventually exhaust itself, and then capitalist enterprise required a consolidating period of depression and retrenchment before it could regain vigor and growth. Modern economists, including Volcker, did not embrace the idea of a "Kondratieff cycle," but they did accept what students of business cycles, Arthur Burns among them, had identified as "long swings" of ten to twenty-five years when economic growth and capital formation reached a peak and then retreated to eras of slower expansion.

Volcker, in his careful manner, added a particular insight of his own: if a new "long cycle" was unfolding, its duration would be crucially influenced by what was inside people's minds—the psychology of investors, consumers, businessmen, even government. They could resist the new reality and plunge on confidently with risk taking that would be disappointed. Or they could adjust to the inevitable and accept the more modest prospects that the new reality imposed.

Volcker's rumination was, thus, a profoundly conservative statement. He rejected the euphoric optimism of the New Economics or even the belief that human actors could somehow alter the deeper tides of economic fortune. If people failed to honor natural limits, he warned, they were destined to suffer turmoil and crisis. Volcker was articulating, in a sophisticated manner, the classic perspective of the central banker—order and stability required a moderation of aspirations. The essence of his essay might have been written by Nicholas Biddle in 1830 in rebuttal to Andrew Jackson's attacks on the "Monster Bank" or by Benjamin Strong in the 1920s to silence angry farmers.

"If it is true that the difficulties of the recent past can be traced in part to a kind of overconfidence generated by a long period of prosperity—and that is the burden of my lecture—then it can also be true that a more conservative and cautious approach can help lay the base for renewed and sustained growth of the economy," Volcker said.

The dour admonitions were the philosophical key to Paul Volcker's mind, the framework that would guide his own performance as Federal Reserve chairman. Volcker would position himself in confrontation with this intangible core of mood and feelings. His goal, as he saw it, was to persuade the economic players, including financial markets and political leaders, to change their minds about the future, to rein in their expectations and accept less. The balmy, confident days were over. The new era of caution was for real. The "long cycle" of retreat and disappointment and failure would continue, Paul Volcker figured, until everyone got the message.

——PART THREE——

THE LIQUIDATION

——11——

A CAR
WITH TWO
DRIVERS

On the unseasonably warm morning of January 20, 1981, the broad avenues of Washington were wreathed in Inaugural bunting. The city's marble monuments glistened in the winter light, and galleries of expectant citizens lined the streets, waiting for a glimpse of the new leader. Marching bands, horses, military units paraded by, from the Capitol to the White House, and Washington became randomly alive with spontaneous tableaus—democratic vistas formed by the swirl of patriotic colors and exuberant crowds and imposing edifices of government.

The presidential ceremony was always a ritual of renewal for the nation, refreshing the faith in popular sovereignty, but this year's Inauguration generated a special excitement. That very morning, the American diplomats held hostage in Iran for more than a year were finally freed to come home. The news ended a humiliating ordeal for the nation and added a cleansing spirit to the celebration. Even jaded lobbyists and bureaucrats in Washington, permanent operatives in the permanent government, sensed that this new President would be different. Ronald Reagan, taking his oath of office on the west front of the Capitol, called it a "new beginning."

These United States [the new President declared] are confronted with an economic affliction of great proportions. We suffer from the longest and one of the worst sustained inflations in our national history. . . . It threatens to shatter the lives of millions of our citizens. Idle industries have cast workers into unemployment, human misery and personal indignity. Those who do work are denied a fair return for their labor by a tax system which penalizes successful achievement and keeps us from maintaining full productivity.

The economic disorder that had helped to elect Ronald Reagan reached a new pitch just as he was taking office. Price inflation remained in double digits. Interest rates, driven by inflation and the Federal Reserve's stringent money policy, were again at unprecedented levels. The prime rate for bank loans, after falling so sharply in mid-1980, had climbed back to an even higher peak—above 21 percent. The national economy was recovering from 1980's brief contraction, but uncertainly. Housing and autos were still depressed; the unemployment rate was 7.4 percent.

"In this present crisis," the new President asserted, "government is not the solution to our problem; government is the problem."

This conservative theme had been Ronald Reagan's battle standard for twenty years as he rose in national politics, but it had special force now that he had attained the ultimate office of government. The man beside him on the Inaugural platform, Jimmy Carter, had blamed inflation on the excesses of popular appetites, the citizens themselves. Carter had admonished Americans to temper their own desires for material goods. He had promised government action to halt the inflationary binge. And the government had so far failed.

Now, with Ronald Reagan, the logic of guilt was reversed. The public was absolved and the government itself was blamed. It was Washington, not the people, that had ruined the American economy, Reagan assured his audience. Instead of scolding private citizens, the new President celebrated their enterprise and applauded their ambitions for personal gain. Instead of dour sermons on spiritual malaise, Ronald Reagan offered sunny optimism.

His indictment of the government started with the complaint that burdensome federal taxes on workers and business had stifled their initiative and depressed the engine of capitalism. Furthermore, the government had failed to balance its own accounts, spending more each year than it collected in revenues. "For decades," the new President complained, "we have piled deficit upon deficit, mortgaging our future and our children's future for the temporary convenience of the present. . . . You and I, as individuals, can, by borrowing, live beyond our means, but for only a limited period of time. Why, then, should we think that collectively, as a nation, we're not bound by the same limitation?"

Reagan promised to deliver a new program for economic recovery that would overcome the "negative economic forces" and reverse the damage caused by his predecessors. "It is time," he vowed, "to reawaken this industrial giant, to get government back within its means and to lighten our punitive tax burden."

Four weeks after his Inaugural, the President announced the details of his plan. To increase incentives for wage earners and business enterprises, Reagan asked Congress to approve a three-year reduction in individual income-tax rates, totaling 30 percent. To foster business expansion, he proposed additional tax relief for corporations as well as relief from federal regulations. The formulation known as "supply-side economics" was actually an updated version of the tax philosophy first articulated in the 1920s by Andrew Mellon, Treasury Secretary for Reagan's boyhood hero, Calvin Coolidge. The intent was to scale back the progressive income tax; the assumption was that, once in private hands, the money would flow into capital investments, building up the supply side of the economy—new factories and technologies, a larger base of productive capacity. All together, however, Reagan's tax cuts would reduce the federal government's revenue by a total of $540 billion over five years, raising a specter that would have alarmed the conservative orthodoxy of Andrew Mellon and Calvin Coolidge—huge federal deficits, in peacetime and under a Republican President.

To avoid that outcome, President Reagan promised simultaneously to shrink the federal government and drastically reduce its spending. Initially, his economic recovery plan outlined budget cuts totaling $41 billion, an unprecedented cutback for a single year, with more huge reductions promised in subsequent years. Big government would get smaller; private enterprise, as well as individuals, would keep more of its own money to spend and invest as it wished.

Reagan promised that, given several years of cumulative budget cuts and revived economic prosperity, his blueprint would produce a balanced federal budget by 1984. The claim seemed dubious on its face since, by the President's own accounting, the federal deficits would actually grow substantially larger in the immediate future, if his program was enacted. The Reagan agenda also included a massive increase for defense—hundreds of billions in new spending that would largely offset the savings he envisioned from budget cuts for domestic programs. Meanwhile, his proposed tax reductions would lose, on average, $100 billion a year in government revenue. Taken together, Reagan's proposals appeared to produce the opposite of what he promised—much larger federal deficits. As financial markets had learned painfully over the previous fifteen years, huge federal deficits were usually the predicate for continuing price inflation.

But Ronald Reagan was as dedicated to restoring "sound money" as he was hostile to centralized government. Modern inflation, in fact, was an important particular in his indictment against Washington. Though it was not generally known, Reagan was the first modern President who could fairly be labeled a monetarist. He was a disciple of Milton Friedman's, the monetarist economist whose scathing critique of the Federal Reserve had persuaded so many others. For years, Reagan complained, reckless liberal politicians had pushed the Federal Reserve into pumping up the money supply to provide short-term economic stimulus at the expense of long-term price stability. In order to break the raging price inflation, the President explained, money must be disciplined at its source—the central bank—and Reagan fully endorsed the Federal Reserve's commitment, already under way, to gradually slow down the growth of the money supply. What Paul Volcker had begun in October 1979 Ronald Reagan wanted too—confronting inflation by reducing money growth.

"Now, we fully recognize the independence of the Federal Reserve System," Reagan said, "and will do nothing to interfere with or undermine that independence. We will consult regularly with the Federal Reserve Board on all aspects of our economic program and will vigorously pursue budget policies that'll make their job easier in reducing monetary growth." The outcome, Reagan predicted, would be lower inflation, lower interest rates and restored vigor for financial markets and the productive economy.

The more Ronald Reagan talked about his "economic recovery program," the more confident he sounded. "This plan will get our economy moving again," he declared, "create productivity growth, and thus create the jobs that our people must have."

Two weeks after the plan was announced, Reagan thought he saw his own optimism spreading throughout the land. "There is a kind of glow out there among the people," the President told Walter Cronkite in a television interview, "and a confidence that things are going to be all right, where, a short time ago, polls were revealing that the people didn't think things were going to get better."

The explanation, Reagan thought, was that his economic program gave people a new sense of certainty about the future. "Our program gives a stability down the road ahead," the President explained. "A person can say, 'I know what's going to happen for the next few years. . . . Someone can say, 'I have confidence to do this, because I have been told and I know what's going to happen. . . .' "[1]

The chairman of the Federal Reserve Board did not, of course, deliver an independent State of the Union address of his own, but he did make public speeches, from time to time, and his estimate of the future sounded very different from the new President's. During the fall campaign, when the Fed was pushing up interest rates and Jimmy Carter was attacking it, Volcker had kept a low profile. Starting in November, immediately after Reagan's landslide victory, the Federal Reserve chairman began a series of brooding public lectures, speeches that sounded dark and skeptical compared with the President-elect's engaging optimism. Ronald Reagan spoke confidently of restored vigor and prosperity for the American economy. Paul Volcker talked about pain.

"Let us not be beguiled into thinking there are quick and painless solutions," Volcker told a banquet audience in New York City.

"There is no way we can avoid a clash between monetary restraint . . . and the growth of economic activity," he warned a university gathering in Milwaukee.

"If monetary policy is going to do it alone," Volcker asked gloomily, "how long is it going to take and what are the unnecessary costs going to be in financial market pressure and lost output, in unemployment and deferred growth? I think there is a lot of evidence that it could be considerable. . . ."[2]

Volcker's ominous remarks—veiled warnings he repeated for several months following Ronald Reagan's election—were ignored by the news media, newspapers and television. The Washington press, like the rest of the capital, was caught up in the excitement and euphoria surrounding the new President and his bold plans for conservative reform.

The news media rarely paid much attention to what was said by Federal Reserve governors. The Fed was a central political institution of the American system, capable of altering the lives and fortunes of private citizens more directly and forcefully than most other components of government, yet the press covered it sparingly and deferentially, as though the Fed's decisions were of interest only to economists and Wall Street technicians. Most stories about monetary policy ran on the financial pages and were written in the jargon familiar to financial specialists but impenetrable for average readers. Above all, the press treated the central bank as a benevolent nonpolitical institution, somehow divorced from the normal combat among interest groups in Washington and utterly uninterested in the politics of winners and losers. If one judged the central bank solely on the basis of its uncritical press coverage, the Federal Reserve appeared to be the only agency of government that never made mistakes. Reporters and editors, who considered themselves such skeptical observers of government, submitted unblushingly to self-censorship in this realm.

They too deferred to the cultural taboo that surrounded the creation of money.

The central bank, in most seasons, encouraged the press to keep a respectful distance. In addition to the Fed's secrecy, Volcker and the other governors spoke in the dry and cautious language of economists, technical talk that was not very quotable. Their pronouncements were usually hedged with dangling qualifiers and framed in bland euphemisms that required expert translation to be understood. Volcker, for instance, would never use the word "recession" to describe what he expected for the American economy. Fed governors, instead, spoke of the "pain" and "significant problems" that they foresaw, the "sacrifice" and "substantial adjustments" that would be required—vague code words that did not lend themselves to shocking headlines.[3]

Yet, given his cautious nature, Paul Volcker was being remarkably forthright now. He was describing the "clash" he saw coming, as the Fed pursued its goal of restraining the economy while the new President promised the opposite. Notwithstanding the optimistic forecasts emanating from the Reagan Administration, breaking inflation would not be a painless process. "The likelihood of a squeeze is apparent," Volcker warned.

No one was listening. It was as if Volcker were trying to remind everyone what the Fed was in the process of doing—"leaning hard" on the money supply and on the struggling economy, forcing interest rates to extraordinary levels. If Volcker's intention was to counter the euphoric promises being made for the new Reagan program, to provoke second thoughts about massive tax reductions, he failed. All eyes were on the Chief Executive. The second-most-powerful officer of government, the independent chairman of the Federal Reserve, was ignored.

The basic arithmetic that Volcker spelled out for his audiences described the collision he foresaw—and suggested the likelihood of another recession. The Federal Reserve, by limiting the growth of money, was ultimately determining the size of the nominal Gross National Product for the nation—the sum of all U.S. economic output as measured in dollars. The Fed could control the growth of nominal GNP. What the Fed could not control, at least in the short term, was how much of the nominal GNP would simply reflect price inflation, more dollars paid for the same old goods, and how much of it would represent real growth in the economy's output. Real growth, of course, was what counted—the real value of expanded production after discounting the dollar inflation—the familiar measure reported each quarter in the newspapers.

The distinction between nominal GNP and real GNP was more visible in microcosm: an auto factory that turned out a thousand cars one year and sold them for $5 million might produce the same number of cars the next year but sell them for $6 million. The company's real output increased by zero, contributing nothing to growth in real GNP, but its dollar volume grew by 20 percent, which would be reflected in nominal GNP. By selling its cars at higher prices, the company did not necessarily come out ahead, of course, because its own costs were rising too—the price of labor, the price of raw materials. The same distinction between real value and dollar volume, repeated millions of times throughout all the economic sectors, determined the sums known as real GNP and nominal GNP for the nation.

For the Federal Reserve, the squeeze was obvious: as it applied its restraint on the money supply, the central bank in essence set an upper limit on how much growth would be possible for the nominal GNP. If so, something had to give—either the price inflation or the real output. But which one? Volcker and other governors patiently explained the arithmetic to various audiences: inflation was now running at 10 or 11 percent. A healthy economy would add another 3 to 5 percent on top of that in real growth—requiring a total of 13 to 15 percent in nominal GNP. But the Federal Open Market Committee was setting a much lower goal for 1981—targets that would hold nominal GNP between 9 and 12 percent. The "squeeze" was the gap in those numbers.

"That discrepancy," Volcker said, ". . . is suggestive of the problem." If inflation continued in double digits and the Federal Reserve kept its word on limiting nominal GNP, there was no room left for real growth. In fact, real growth would probably be negative—a fancy way of saying that the economy would actually be shrinking. America would soon be back in recession.

But what if inflation abated instead? Fed officials could not prove this wouldn't happen, but experience taught that it would be the real economy that declined first, not escalating prices. Theoretically, if every economic player, from labor unions demanding higher wages to corporate planners setting prices on products, were to decide abruptly and unanimously that inflation was over, that they no longer needed to seek additional wage and price increases to protect themselves, then inflation could indeed abate suddenly. Inflation would miraculously melt away and the economy could flourish, regardless of the Fed's restraint.

Unfortunately, as Volcker explained, it had never worked that way in the past. Human nature argued against it. Even if people wanted to forgo another round of price or wage increases, they could not easily do so. Prices were embedded in contracts—labor wage contracts, loan

agreements, marketing and investment plans. When a farmer borrowed for the spring planting, he counted on getting a certain price for
his crops in the fall. So did his banker. Labor unions, corporations,
even individual families entered transactions following similar assumptions.

Furthermore, after years of enduring inflation, Americans were
deeply cynical about the government's frequent promises to end it.
"Skeptical Americans," Volcker noted, "are all too likely to claim
Missouri residence: they will want to be shown." If so, skeptical businesses would continue to demand higher prices and employees would
expect higher wages and the dollar chase would continue. If the Fed
held tight, as promised, the economy would have to slow down first.
Price inflation would subside later.

The Federal Reserve chairman was more circumspect in describing
his other anxiety: while the Federal Reserve was confronting inflation
with tight money and high interest rates, the Reagan government was
embarking in the opposite direction. The President's across-the-board
tax reductions would be stimulating the economy, while Volcker was
trying to restrain it. And the prospect of much larger federal deficits
might encourage the expectations of more inflation, just as the Fed
was trying to persuade financial markets of the opposite. To use the
Presidents' metaphor, Ronald Reagan wanted to "reawaken the industrial giant" while Paul Volcker wanted to sedate it.

"Before I join the 'taxpayers' revolt,' in the name of anti-inflationary
policy," the Fed chairman said, "I must emphasize the necessary
corollary. We cannot proceed without concern about the size of the
deficit. Prudent tax reduction, in the end, depends on expenditure
restraint."

Sophisticated listeners appreciated that the Federal Reserve chairman was implicitly arguing against the new President's economic
agenda. If fiscal policy was stimulative, that meant monetary policy
alone would carry the burden of enforcing restraint and must overcom-
pensate to get results. Volcker's dissent sounded like a lament: "I
sincerely question whether monetary policy *by itself* can or should be
asked to carry the entire load."

The potential mismatch of government policies—the President and
Congress determined to accelerate economic growth, while the central
bank simultaneously tried to brake it—could produce its own damage
to the economy, Volcker warned.

I know [he conceded] that, in concept, a case can be made that restraint
on money and credit alone, sustained long enough and strongly enough,
could control inflation and thus lay the ground for renewed growth. But is

that a realistic, tolerable, believable course *if* other instruments of policy and opinion are running counter to our purposes? Will the sustainability of the policy be credible if the costs in growth and employment seem excessive? And the costs fall unfairly on the industries and elements of the population most dependent on credit?

The chairman's troubled questions were the core issues that confronted Ronald Reagan's economic agenda in 1981. The President wanted to encourage economic growth with tax cuts, but the President also wanted the Federal Reserve simultaneously to restrain the economy with tight money and high interest rates. In plain language, did it make sense for the federal government to attempt both things at once? If the President pushed one way, would the Federal Reserve feel compelled to pull even harder in the opposite direction?

The consequences, as Volcker elliptically suggested, would be even higher interest rates, more severe "pain" and "sacrifice" than would otherwise be necessary. The millions of Americans who depend on borrowing would suffer additional distress—consumers, farmers, home builders, auto dealers, businesses of every type—without ever understanding its source. People and institutions that lend money would naturally be the beneficiaries.

The chairman's questions did not excite a great debate. The President and Congress and the Federal Reserve were not obligated to confront the disparity in their economic policies. Given the independent status accorded to the central bank, there was no forum anywhere in the government, no existing mechanism, that compelled the executive branch and the Federal Reserve to sit down and formally reconcile their differences. The Federal Reserve's regulation of the money supply and the President's control over spending and taxation were both powerful levers for manipulating the private economy, yet they could theoretically push in opposite and uncoordinated directions —regardless of the unintended side effects for private citizens.

Volcker's questions, therefore, could be easily evaded by the community of Washington decision makers. And evasion was the essence of what occurred in the fateful political battles of 1981. Congress, responding to the President's confident optimism, declined to choose between the contradictory impulses of stimulus and restraint. It accepted both. The decisions would become a kind of threshold for the decade of the eighties that, once crossed, would create utterly unprecedented conditions for the American economy—a bewildering new order for how rewards and penalties were to be allocated among private citizens.

After the Inauguration, Paul Volcker muted his message. As Ronald

Reagan campaigned brilliantly for his economic program, building toward dramatic victories in Congress, the Fed chairman's public expressions of dissent became even more discreet. He eventually dropped the stark warnings about an impending "clash" and also the broad hints of likely recession. The political momentum in Washington was clearly running in favor of the President. The train was rolling down the tracks and Paul Volcker was not about to stand in its way.

The chairman of the Federal Reserve, powerful as he was, lacked the political standing to challenge a popular new Chief Executive in frontal debate. To do so, Volcker would have had to put his own institution's independence at risk, inviting retaliation from the ascendant Republicans. The Fed chairman already felt politically exposed because of the stringent money policy and high interest rates he was imposing on the American economy. Instead, Volcker's gloomy predictions, his arguments against the Reagan tax cuts, were confined to confidential conversations with senators and congressmen. His timely warnings remained virtually unknown to the general public.[4]

For Bruno Pasquinelli, the political changes in Washington offered no comfort. His construction company in Homewood, Illinois, was already in recession. For twenty-five years, Pasquinelli Construction had built modestly priced homes, under $50,000, as many as six hundred a year. Since 1979, when the Federal Reserve started to escalate the price of money, his net worth had shrunk by 70 percent. "Those interest rates have killed me and my business," he said, "killed the small home buyer.

"I am tremendously frightened," Pasquinelli said. "I don't sleep at night anymore. I owe money. I don't have government guarantees. I don't have a pension fund. I put my pension fund up as a guarantee for notes. I don't have anything. When I come to negotiate with a banker, I don't negotiate. It is a card game, but I don't have any cards."

In Atlanta, Georgia, David Chatham was preparing to lay off one-fifth of the regular employees at his home-building company. In 1979, he had sold seventy-nine new homes. This year, 1981, he would sell only fifty-four and it would take three times longer to find buyers, which meant the builder had to extend his own borrowing. "We came to the conclusion," Chatham said, "that our company has become a nonprofit organization."

William Cahill, a real-estate broker in suburban Chicago, saw his sales dwindle by two-thirds. In 1979, his firm handled 640 homes. Within the next years, it was down to 214 sales. "We are in the worst times we have ever been in," Cahill said. "We have had recessions, slowdowns, other things before, but never as bad as this."

When the housing industry collapsed, so did its suppliers. In Aberdeen, Washington, Lucille Sajec was laid off by the plywood mill where she worked. The mill's crew shrank from 220 workers to 85. "Now all we are doing is stockpiling plywood," she said, "because we can't sell the plywood."

Mrs. Sajec worried about the future. "In this mill," she said, "there is a high rate of divorce. There is people losing their homes. It just has gotten to a point where it is not even funny anymore."

Housing, automobiles and other interest-sensitive sectors—where both the buyer and the seller rely heavily on borrowed money—never really recovered from the roller-coaster recession of the previous year. Early in 1980, the combination of high interest rates and credit controls had forced the economy into a sharp but brief contraction. When the Federal Reserve eased money rapidly in the spring, however, interest rates fell dramatically—from a high near 20 percent to below 9 percent—and the economy turned around abruptly. By fall, however, the Fed was progressively tightening again and driving interest rates to a new peak. The Federal Funds rate rose past 12 percent in October and by January it crested at 20 percent. In the first quarter of 1981, the nation's real GNP was still expanding, in the aggregate, but housing and the auto industry remained depressed.

The practical impact of the Fed's initiative was to jack up the price of homes, nationwide, driving millions of potential buyers out of the housing market. Herman J. Smith, a Fort Worth, Texas, builder who was president of the National Association of Home Builders, calculated the arithmetic for typical home buyers. A $60,000 home, purchased with a mortgage interest rate of 9 percent, would commit the family to a monthly payment of $483. When the mortgage rate went to 15 percent, the monthly payment rose to $758—an effective price increase of nearly 60 percent. At the level of 15 percent mortgages, Smith complained, about 90 percent of American families could no longer afford a $60,000 home. Yet, in the opening months of 1981, mortgage rates rose above 17 percent.

Bruno Pasquinelli, like thousands of other businessmen in distress, appealed to his congressman. "Hell, we are talking about the Fed, Volcker, all these guys," Pasquinelli told members of Congress at a House hearing. "You are the lawmakers. Change the law. What makes the Federal Reserve System sacrosanct? Why is Congress not represented on the Federal Reserve Board? You are the people. I put you there. I vote for you. Why aren't we represented there?"[5]

Every Thursday morning, the Federal Reserve chairman had breakfast with the Secretary of the Treasury and aides. Every Wednesday, officials from Treasury and the White House lunched at the Fed with governors and senior staff members. Every other week, the President's Council of Economic Advisers sponsored a similar luncheon at the White House.

Paul Craig Roberts, Assistant Secretary of the Treasury for Economic Policy in the Administration, said:

> Anybody on the outside with a conspiratorial frame of mind would think we were in there plotting interest rates for the country over lunch. That's bullshit. If you brought up interest rates, the Fed people let you know that you were an impolite boor even to ask. They think that's their job, not yours, and they won't talk about it with you. Why not be a polite guest and talk about pleasant things like baseball or basketball?[6]

William Niskanen, a business economist whom President Reagan appointed to the Council of Economic Advisers, felt the same frustration. "It's very difficult," Niskanen said, "to get the Fed to talk about monetary policy. We talked about wine, which is Henry Wallich's specialty. We talked about baseball, about vacations. They were more than willing to talk about what we were doing—but not about what they were doing."[7]

Frederick Schultz, vice chairman of the Federal Reserve Board, was one of those who steered the conversations away from the substance of Fed policy.

> When the Reagan Administration first came in [Schultz explained], they said we'd like to have better communications with the Fed, a way to talk regularly. But Paul said to me: "You've got to be very careful not to have a situation where they are making overt attempts to influence our policy." They would try to argue with us about monetary policy and I would explain what we were doing—nothing more. I tried to stay away from a situation where they could think they were influencing our policy.

The Federal Reserve, in fact, did not tell the Reagan White House much about what it was doing. Sophisticated outsiders assumed that, despite its official independence, the central bank regularly coordinated with the executive branch in a private manner, seeking informal approval for its decisions. This assumption was particularly important to those political scientists who defended the Fed's odd position in democratic government. Despite appearances, they argued, the Federal Reserve was discreetly responsive to elected government, through unseen channels of private collaboration.

But the unseen consultation did not seem to exist, at least not during the Reagan Administration, despite all the private lunches and breakfasts. The strongest proof of this, ironically, was contained in dozens of confidential memoranda on the Fed written by Reagan's economic advisers. Since these memos were intended solely for the private reading of the President and his staff, there was no reason to omit sensitive information. Yet none of the confidential memos contained even a hint of inside knowledge of the Fed's decisions. The President's policy makers were compelled to discuss the central bank's actions and intentions in the same uncertain tone used by Wall Street's Fed watchers—offering expert hunches, but no sure knowledge of what was happening.

The Reagan Administration and the Federal Reserve were, ostensibly, in agreement on the correct course for money-supply regulation. In their private relations, however, the two centers of governing power were mutually suspicious, even contemptuous of each other. Volcker's wariness was well founded—key positions in this new Administration were filled with some of the Fed's most zealous critics.

Beryl Sprinkel, a Chicago banker and monetarist economist, was appointed to Volcker's old job at Treasury, Under Secretary for Monetary Affairs, the official responsible for liaison with the central bank. For years, Sprinkel had been a leading voice on the Shadow Open Market Committee, the private group of banking and academic economists who regularly assaulted Volcker and his predecessors with such harsh critiques. Jerry Jordan, an economics professor named to the Council of Economic Advisers, was also an alumnus of the monetarists' shadow committee.

The disciples of Milton Friedman, like the master himself, regarded stable money as the core issue of government management, and they were inclined to dismiss competing factors as relatively inconsequential, even deficit spending by the federal government. For a sound economy, what mattered was money, the monetarists insisted, a focus that seemed narrow and obsessive to other economists who did not share the faith. Sprinkel himself once used a metaphor to describe money that evoked the same psychological overtones that Sigmund Freud had identified in dreams and infantile transference—money was food. "Stuffing a kid with too much food doesn't make him grow faster; it makes him sick," Sprinkel explained to a congressional committee. "Similarly, injecting a lot of money into an economy does not make it grow faster; it just makes it sick."[8]

While Beryl Sprinkel endorsed the Fed's commitment to steady reduction in money growth, he doubted the central bank's sincerity. "I've heard those beautiful words before," he said. "Excessive and erratic growth of money has plagued the economy for more than fifteen years." Jerry Jordan of the CEA likewise disparaged the central bank's capabilities. "The Federal Reserve Board's reputation as an effective inflation-fighting institution has been so severely damaged by events of the past decade," Jordan said, "that I doubt that their views on the economy and the appropriate policies for the circumstances carry much weight with the public."

Others in the Reagan White House, who were not monetarists themselves, shared the skepticism. Murray Weidenbaum, the new chairman of the CEA, complained about the Fed's "stop and go" monetary policy. David Stockman, the new budget director, warned in a memorandum to the President that if the Fed accommodated the rising prices in 1981, "the already tattered credibility of the post–October 1979 Volcker monetary policy will be destroyed. . . . The markets have now almost completely lost confidence in Volcker and the new monetary policy."[9]

The Reagan team had ample grounds for skepticism—the roller coaster of 1980. As outsiders, these economists had watched the gyrating money supply and interest rates through 1980 and concluded, variously, that Volcker's management was either politically motivated or incompetent. In 1979, Paul Volcker had promised a monetarist approach, rigorously controlling the money supply to provide modest, stable growth. The money numbers had caromed up and down wildly ever since. Given that shaky performance and the Fed's long-standing hostility to monetarism, the Reagan monetarists doubted the sincerity of Volcker's conversion to their faith.

Not very subtly, in public and private forums, the President's advisers put the Fed on notice: they would be watching closely to make sure that the Federal Reserve kept its word. If the central bank really did slow down the rate of money expansion, the Reagan Administration would lend its full support. But if the money numbers continued their abrupt surges and declines, the executive branch would not hesitate to criticize.

"The Federal Reserve has said consistently over the past ten years that they have a policy of bringing money under control," Sprinkel observed in an internal memorandum for the Cabinet Council on Economic Affairs. "The fact is that they have failed to match action with intent."[10]

At first, Sprinkel proposed a weekly consultation between the Fed chairman and himself, but Volcker refused. "Volcker said he doesn't report to the Under Secretary—he held that job once himself," Paul Craig Roberts related. "So Sprinkel set up the regular Treasury breakfasts including all the heavyweight players from the Administration. It was more difficult for Volcker because he didn't have his senior staff there to change the subject. But Volcker has a way of talking for an hour and not telling you much."

Sprinkel kept delivering the message any way he could, usually by urging his boss, Secretary of the Treasury Donald Regan, to demand better performance from Volcker. In public, the Reagan Administration espoused a gradual approach, steadily reducing money growth year by year. In the Administration's private councils, however, Sprinkel advocated a sterner policy—the faster the Fed tightened, the better.

> The pattern of money growth which is implied by the gradual approach should be considered as a ceiling for the rate of monetary expansion [Sprinkel argued in his April 24 memorandum]. Any under-shooting of this long-term target path, such as in the first quarter of this year, should be accepted. No effort should be made to boost money growth in order to make up for such under-shooting and instead the target for the future rate of monetary expansion should be reduced accordingly.

Quite aside from his political triumph, Ronald Reagan's ascension to the Presidency made possible a historic watershed—the rehabilitation of classical economic doctrines that had been out of fashion for fifty years. Reagan's economic program restored to influence three strands of conservative thinking that were once the conventional wisdom of economics. All three had been discredited by the debacle of 1929 and eclipsed by the Keynesian doctrine that came to power with Roosevelt's New Deal.

Monetarism was one of them, the classical theory of money reasserted and popularized by Milton Friedman. The Depression experience, including the failure of the Federal Reserve, had persuaded the mainstream that control of money was a "weak reed," as Herbert Hoover had put it, for managing the economy. Friedman devoted his career to convincing the nation that this was wrong. Another strand was the "supply side" argument for shrinking the progressive income tax, an approach inherited directly from Andrew Mellon's "trickle down" economics in the 1920s. In order to stimulate savings and investment, just as Mellon had argued, the supply-side tax relief would be provided disproportionately to upper-income families, since, the theory held, the wealthiest citizens would obviously be most able to devote their tax windfall to investment in new production. The third strand was the conservative orthodoxy that the Republican Party had preached stubbornly (and unsuccessfully) ever since the New Deal—deficit spending was ruinous in itself and the federal government must balance its budget.

Ronald Reagan comfortably embraced all three doctrines, and for twenty years his speeches had elaborated all three themes. He attacked the "printing press" money promoted by liberals, the burdens of the progressive income tax and the profligacy of deficit spending.

Like Reagan himself, the three schools of conservative thought were united by their aversion to big government, a generalized commitment to laissez-faire economics and "the magic of the marketplace," as the President called it. They also shared an active contempt for the ideas of John Maynard Keynes and any who espoused them.[11]

Yet the three strands of conservatism contained theoretical conflicts and were potentially incompatible—particularly if all three were vigorously pursued at once. What divided them was the practical reality outlined in Paul Volcker's cautionary speeches—a collision of purposes. How could the supply-side tax cuts pump up economic growth if the monetarists' money policy was simultaneously retarding it? How could the Reagan program lead to a balanced budget if the tax cuts were at the same time increasing the deficits?

Reagan's team of economic advisers was drawn from all three schools of conservative thinking, and despite their unity in public, they argued intensely among themselves over which priorities truly fulfilled the President's mandate. In fact, the monetarists and supply siders did not agree at all on how to control inflation. The disciples of Friedman wanted stable regulation of the money aggregates; the supply-side camp thought the monetarist theory was inoperable (for approximately the same reasons that Fed officials disparaged monetarism). The supply siders argued that the only solution to inflation was a return to the gold standard. Yet Milton Friedman devoted a large portion of his monetary history to explaining why the gold standard was a failure.

The Administration's internal disagreements were papered over in public, but, ironically, they were most visible to Paul Volcker and the other Fed officials. When they met periodically with the Reagan advisers, listening to the luncheon conversation, the Federal Reserve governors quickly grasped that these new policy makers from the White House and Treasury did not agree with one another on economic policy, much less with the Fed.

If you don't think that wasn't a zoo [exclaimed Fred Schultz, the Fed vice chairman]. Beryl was taking the monetarist line. Paul Craig Roberts was the Savonarola of supply-side economics. Larry Kudlow [assistant budget director for economic analysis] had the arrogance of youth. He and Stockman were bright young guys and they thought they were going to solve the problems of the world. Jerry Jordan was another monetarist. Every Administration comes in with a fairly strong ideological position and this one came in with more ideology than most.

The Reagan advisers agreed to resolve these fundamental contradictions by evading them. In constructing the President's economic recovery program, they designed a forecast of how the economy would respond that defied historical experience—and ignored the "clash" of purposes cited by Paul Volcker. But it met everyone's particular objective. "Our original forecast was not an exercise in economic analysis," David Stockman conceded. "It was a statistical argument between the various doctrinal sects. The numbers became the medium by which those contradictory doctrines were harnessed together." [12]

The supply siders, in order to sell Congress on the tax cuts, insisted that the forecast show vigorous real growth. The monetarists demanded a year-by-year deceleration of the money supply. Meanwhile, the forecast must predict that inflation would subside and the federal budget would swing into balance. Both inside the White House and out, the blueprint became known as the "rosy scenario." Those who questioned it, however, were dismissed as retrograde Keynesians who did not understand the new economic principles at work.

"The original forecast," said William Niskanen of the CEA, "had inflation coming down without any real trade-off in growth. In other words, it was costless. I don't know any economist who really believed it."

"The problem was that the process was political," said Paul Craig Roberts, who represented the supply siders in the argument. "We were trying to preserve the tax cuts. Marty Anderson [a White House policy adviser] would pop in and say, 'Remember the President's campaign promise to balance the budget.' Murray Weidenbaum would argue about the core inflation rate. Stockman tried to resolve the argument by adjusting the numbers."

As the congressional debate unfolded in the spring, budget experts around Washington zeroed in on the implausible claims made for the Administration's fiscal policy—balanced budgets, despite massive tax cuts and increased defense spending—but few people recognized that the President's blueprint for monetary policy was illogical on its face. That the economy could enjoy such expansive real growth while the money supply was simultaneously shrinking defied nature: people would have to start spending money faster and faster—circulating the available money supply at a higher and higher velocity. Even the monetarist architects did not defend this. In private, they conceded, the President's monetary numbers made no sense.

The intellectual confusion and evasion within the Reagan Administration became a crucial fact that shaped the politics of the 1980s, for the ultimate effect, ironically, was to enhance the stature of Paul Volcker. In the community of Washington decision makers, ideas did matter and mattered especially if the advocate seemed coherent and self-confident. Volcker could play that role brilliantly. In contrast, it swiftly became clear to congressional insiders that the Reagan White House was in constant turmoil and flux—bickering with itself over its own economic policy. Volcker seemed to know what he was doing while his critics in the White House did not, and political deference naturally gravitated toward the strong-willed leader.

Subtly but surely, this undoubtedly strengthened Volcker's hand throughout the Reagan years, particularly among members of Congress, and made it easier for the Federal Reserve chairman to dominate events. Even liberal Democrats, who might have been expected to challenge the Fed's harsh strategy, were frightened by the chaos in the Reagan Administration and reassured by Volcker's strong hand. Volcker himself may have been affected too. A friend and admirer explained: "Paul is at his best when he has an intelligent opponent who can challenge his thinking. When he doesn't have intelligent opposition, that's when Paul tends to make mistakes."

The only rationale offered by the Reagan team as to how its contradictory policies were supposed to meld successfully was a wishful claim that people would change their economic behavior—once their confidence in government had been restored. This seemed an odd argument for conservatives to make, but it was advanced most enthusiastically in the early months of the Administration, particularly by Treasury Secretary Donald Regan, the former CEO at Merrill Lynch. Usually, the Treasury Secretary was drawn from Wall Street and served as the dour voice of caution in a President's Cabinet. But Regan was from the ranks of Wall Street's ebullient optimists—the stock-market traders—and he was as bullish as the President.

> I believe the President's program will begin to bear fruit even before it is enacted [Regan enthused in late March]. . . . As people see the program unfold, as permanent changes in spending programs and tax rates move through Congress and are enacted into law . . . we expect the public will respond. This will not be some sort of mystical response based on faith and psychology. The expectations we are referring to are the public's logical computation of what they expect to happen in the future.[13]

"The whole thing is premised on faith," as David Stockman explained it. Once financial markets are convinced the Reagan team is serious about its multiple goals—slower money growth, reduced spending, tax cuts and a balanced budget—investors will begin acting on their new expectations. "The inflation premium melts away like the morning mist," Stockman predicted. "It could be cut in half in a very short period of time if the policy is credible. That sets off adjustments and changes in perception that cascade through the economy. You have a bull market in '81, after April, of historic proportions." [14]

The respectable name given to this reasoning was "rational expectations"—borrowed from a conservative economic theory which held that private economic players would always anticipate and adjust their actions to compensate for changes in government policy. Less grandly, it amounted to an existential wish: by changing people's minds, Ronald Reagan would change their behavior.

At the Fed, the premise seemed so specious—utterly unrealistic—that it merely heightened suspicions that the Federal Reserve was being "set up" as the political scapegoat. The President was promising irreconcilable goals for the economy, and when these promises failed to materialize, the Fed would be blamed.

"One may wonder," Henry Wallich dryly observed, "how an increase in this year's deficit, accompanied by a promise to rescue it next year, would affect expectations." [15] If the past was any guide, the financial markets' fears of continuing inflation would be aggravated, not alleviated, by the Reagan program, once the larger deficits became obvious. Instead of accepting lower interest returns, investors would demand even higher rates to protect their wealth against the future.

As an economic document, the Reagan plan seemed incoherent. The budget projections were dubious. The money-supply numbers simply didn't add up. Yet, as a political document, it seemed brilliant. It promised relief from the anxieties of inflation, without the attendant costs of recession and unemployment. It asked Americans to enlist in a great struggle to restore the nation's economic health, but instead of demanding sacrifice and self-denial as Jimmy Carter had, Ronald Reagan demanded only that citizens accept a reduction in their taxes.

For eight weeks, the Federal Reserve had eased off a bit, though it was still extraordinarily stringent. The Federal Funds rate, which the Fed had pushed to a historic peak of 20 percent in January 1981, was allowed to subside notch by notch. By the first week in March, it had fallen below 16 percent. Interest rates for other forms of short-term credit—corporate commercial paper, three-month Treasury bills, bank CDs—all followed the same trend line downward. Money was still very tight, but somewhat less so.

The bond market refused to go along. While the Fed was letting short-term rates subside, the interest rates on long-term investments were heading in the opposite direction—rising, instead of falling. From the second week of January to the end of March, while short rates fell, the average interest rate for corporate bonds rose from 13.65 to 14.25. U.S. Treasury long-term bonds went up 90 basis points in the same period. The upward creep of long-term rates might have seemed modest to outsiders, but it was the contrary direction that was disturbing. The bond market was contradicting the Federal Reserve —and President Reagan.

Usually, Wall Street's financial markets spoke in a babble of contradictory opinions, but this was one of those instances where the message was clear. Investors in the bond market, in a manner of speaking, were casting their ballot—and it was a veto of the euphoric promises being made in Washington. Far from being reassured by the Reagan economic program, they were instead increasingly nervous about the future—demanding higher returns before they would put their money into long-term financial assets. Despite Ronald Reagan's optimism and Donald Regan's predictions, the bond market was betting there would be more inflation ahead, not less.

In case anyone in Washington missed the point, one of Wall Street's leading gurus delivered the warning directly. "Rallies in the bond markets will be just interruptions in a bear market setting," predicted Henry Kaufman, chief economist at Salomon Brothers, the investment-banking firm. Long-term interest rates, he said, would continue to rise—along a "rocket trajectory"—if the President's expansionary tax cuts were enacted, accompanied by massive new spending for defense.

Among irreverent Wall Street traders, particularly from the stock market, Kaufman was known as "Dr. Doom," because the dour economist was always issuing depressing predictions—higher interest rates, higher inflation and bearish financial markets. Most of the time, for the previous decade, his predictions had been right. "One of the problems of achieving credibility," Kaufman warned Washington, "is that you just cannot promise to balance the budget three or four years from now." [16]

Treasury Secretary Donald Regan, an old Wall Street hand himself, scoffed at the bond market's pessimism. "Never look to a bond trader for economic advice," Regan said. [17]

Federal Reserve officials were not so sanguine. Among all the various "crowds" that gathered as Wall Street's financial markets, the bond market was considered the noblest "crowd" of all, sober and judicious compared with other markets. This was the place where judgments were made about the long-term future. Its function, aside from making money for traders and investors, was the core process of capitalism—capital formation, the flow of old wealth into the creation of new productive capacity.

And the Fed listened most attentively to the bondholders' concerns. In daily operations, the Fed executed its policy moves in the money

market, manipulating short-term interest rates by adding or withdrawing reserves from the banking system. But it was the bond market—
whose long-term interest rates the Fed could not directly control—
that mattered most to the success of monetary policy. When bond
traders bid on investments of ten or twenty or even thirty years' duration, whether it was government bonds to cover the federal debt or
corporate bonds to raise capital for new factories, they were implicitly
making a forecast on future inflation. Their inflation forecasts were an
implicit judgment on how well the Federal Reserve was doing its job.

The bond market and the Fed were kindred spirits, both cautious
and conservative, both wanting the same things—stable prices, sound
money, order. Bondholders depended on the Federal Reserve to protect their wealth, because as inflation cheapened the value of the
dollar, it directly eroded the value of their long-term financial assets.
For the last decade, long-term inflation had devastated the market for
corporate bonds.

But the bond market was also a critic, a skeptical audience that
continuously assessed the Fed's performance and regularly scolded
errors or lapses. When governors from the central bank worried aloud
about their "credibility," they meant in particular: did the bond market really believe their promises to control inflation? When bond traders bid up interest rates, it meant that, all things considered, they did
not trust the Federal Reserve to protect the future value of money.
Volcker and the other governors worked continuously to persuade
them and win their good opinion.

Bondholders, in particular, did not necessarily want the same thing
everyone else in the country wanted from the economy, and they often
seemed perversely narrow-minded in their reactions to events. Bonds
rallied on bad news and sulked over good news. If the government
announced a sharp decline in retail sales or manufacturing output, the
price of bonds rose. If Washington reported a quarter of healthy
growth for the Gross National Product, bond prices sagged. Bond
investors were preoccupied with one question about the nation's economic performance—not the actual results in production, income and
jobs, but how everything would affect the future value of their dollars.
An economy expanding robustly heightened their fears. A weak economy assured the bondholders that their money was safe.

The bondholders were one of the oldest, most influential interest
groups in American politics, yet their presence had nearly vanished
from political discourse. Financial wealth, like so many other aspects
of American life, had become bureaucratized over the years; wealth
was now held in large, impersonal institutions that diffused its visibil-
ity. In crude terms, nevertheless, the bondholders had not much

changed since Andrew Jackson's time—they were the wealthiest individuals and financial institutions that owned most of the capital invested in long-term debt paper, including the U.S. government's.

Among individuals, for instance, the top 10 percent of American families owned 72 percent of corporate and federal bonds held by individuals plus 86 percent of state and local bonds. Among institutions, commercial banks owned about 20 percent of the outstanding Treasury debt (roughly the same share held directly by wealthy families) and another 10 percent was owned by insurance companies and other corporations. Private wealth was, of course, redundant—the same people likely to hold the bonds in their personal portfolios also owned, disproportionately, the stock of the corporations and banks that owned bonds. The wealth holders represented the conservative hand of the past, but capitalism had no future without their cooperation. Paul Volcker preferred to call them "the forces for stability." [18]

The bondholders functioned like any other political interest group, even though they were not formally organized as such. They actively sought to influence the government policy that would benefit their interests—in particular, the money regulation by the Federal Reserve. They had many channels of influence, but the bond market was their principal voice—the lever by which they influenced public policy most directly.

What was good for this affluent minority of citizens, of course, might or might not be good for the rest of the country, and, very often, the bondholders sought the opposite of what the majority wanted. In the early spring of 1981, the nation at large would not likely have urged the Federal Reserve to raise the price of money still further, but that is what the anxieties of the bond market demanded. Like all special-interest groups, of course, bondholders saw their own self-interest as synonymous with the national interest.

Officials at the Federal Reserve listened closely. They monitored the daily prices and interest rates from the bond trading, but they also listened to the random chatter of market participants. When "Dr. Doom" said that inflation and interest rates would likely increase, when the market's behavior seemed to agree, the message rippled immediately through the policy discussions at the marble temple on Constitution Avenue.

Indeed, Volcker and his colleagues were frustrated because the bond market seemed hypersensitive to the Fed's slightest move. Since 1979, when Volcker had initiated his monetarist approach, the financial markets tracked even the slightest wiggle in M-1—the basic money aggregate that included checking deposits and currency in circulation. The long-term credit markets reacted anxiously to the new money-supply figures reported by the Fed each week, trying to read long-range portents from every minor fluctuation. Some days, bond prices and rates swung dramatically if M-1 surged or fell modestly but contrary to the Fed watchers' predictions.

As it happened, M-1 started expanding rapidly in early April, after months of below-normal growth. New jitters were expressed daily by traders in the market. If M-1 grew too fast, they reasoned, then the Fed would have to tighten soon and that would send interest rates higher—thus depreciating the value of the bonds already purchased at lower rates. The traders began bidding up rates in anticipation.

"People are very nervous about a money-supply explosion this month," said a senior vice president at Drexel Burnham Lambert. "You're going to have another false explosion in money growth, which will set off inflationary expectations beyond reality," an economic consulting firm warned. The chief economist at Philadelphia's Fidelity Bank complained that the M-1 surge, if left unchecked, would "spew a considerable amount of destabilizing inflation into the economy." A Citibank executive predicted: "I think we will have a blip upward in rates for a while. The Fed may have been surprised at the recent money-supply increases and the continued strength of the economy."

The comments were implicitly a running critique of how the Fed was doing and what adjustments it ought to make in the weeks ahead to satisfy opinion in the bond market. Volcker and other Fed officials constantly pleaded with the market specialists to be more patient—not to jump to extreme conclusions based on one or two weeks' changes in the money supply. But, in a sense, the Fed had created the problem for itself: the central bank had promised Wall Street that its money policy would faithfully adhere to the M-1 trend line and give only secondary attention to everything else. So the markets concentrated on M-1 as the leading signal of the Fed's actions. Whether their interpretations were right or not (and they were frequently wrong) hardly mattered. The bond market reacted nervously to M-1 and the Federal Reserve reacted nervously to the bond market.

For curious outsiders, the most convenient window on this circular chatter was the daily "Credit Markets" column in *The Wall Street Journal*. It tracked the trading in the bond markets and, with scrupulous neutrality, provided a daily sampler of opinions from traders and bank economists. Most of the time, they were predicting short-range changes in prices and interest rates important only to the traders and investors themselves. On most days, the experts were issuing utterly contradictory opinions. But their forecasts always focused on the largest variable in their world—what they thought the Fed was going to do in the coming weeks or months.

Most citizens would find the information useless, if they were able to comprehend it at all. But Fed economists earnestly followed the running commentaries, like performers reading their reviews, and occasionally governors contributed comments of their own. The dialogue held enormous political consequences for the entire country, yet it resembled a closed loop: financial experts in Wall Street communicating with the government's financial experts in Washington in a language that few other citizens could penetrate.

"Just as the financial press watches the Fed, the Fed watches the financial press, much more than people imagine," a Federal Reserve Board research economist explained. "A lot of our analysis of markets actually comes from the press."

While the financial press was highly specialized and inaccessible to most citizens, it represented one of the last surviving forums for public debate on the money question. The dialogue of opinion was quite exclusive, however, restricted to those who shared the same assumptions as the bondholders. Stability and order and "hard money," they agreed, ought always to be the Federal Reserve's first priority—to be served ahead of economic growth or full employment or rising wage income. In that regard, the wealth holders had become disenchanted with their protector. After fifteen years of continuing inflation, the chatter of the bond market was laced with a permanent tone of suspicion and resentment toward the Federal Reserve.

Now the Federal Reserve was attempting to make amends. The country was exhausted by the anxieties of inflation and ready to tolerate drastic action to stop it. The new political climate, enhanced by the election of a conservative Republican, allowed the Fed to do what in other times it might not have dared. It could serve the interests of the bondholders and the much larger group of citizens who held more modest portions of financial wealth but nonetheless felt the same sense of loss, the 45 percent of American families whose savings made them net creditors. The Fed would push the price of money high enough to break inflation and restore a stable dollar—and, perhaps, win eventual applause from the general public too.

At the beginning of April, the Fed discreetly yielded to the judgments from the bond market. Long-term rates were rising, contrary to the direction of the short-term rates influenced by the Federal Reserve. Though the real economy was weakening, the Fed changed directions itself. The Federal Funds rate, instead of declining further, was allowed to inch back upward again. The Fed had been unable to lead the market and so now it would follow the market.

As April unfolded, the bond market experienced a traumatic seizure that resembled an anxiety attack. President Reagan's legislative program began its advance through Congress, gathering enthusiasm and preliminary victories, and long-term investors reacted with a panicky feeling. To compound their fears, the money supply was growing rapidly again. Either the Fed was losing control, as it had in 1980, or the Fed would soon have to tromp down even harder on money growth, driving rates higher. Either way, taken together, events in Washington shook up the bond market. "Prices tumbled," as the financial news put it. Day after day, bond prices fell sharply, and their interest rates climbed correspondingly, even faster than their ascent during previous weeks. The average market rate on high-quality corporate bonds jumped 100 basis points over a month's time, and so did the rates on long-term government bonds.

For many in the bond market, the jitters turned into debacle. Michigan Bell Telephone, with a triple-A credit rating, offered a new bond issue at a record interest rate of 15.9 percent, and yet brokers still had a hard time moving it. Alabama Power offered bonds at 17.5 percent. The U.S. Treasury marketed $4.3 billion in new two-year notes and received only $5 billion in bids, about half the normal response. The State of California failed to get any acceptable bids on a proposed $150 million bond issue.

"Apprehension is the only word you can use to describe this market," a senior economist at San Francisco's Crocker National Bank said. "Nobody wants to buy bonds yet," said a vice president at Pittsburgh's Mellon Bank. "There is a buyers' strike because investors don't like the outlook for inflation."

"There's a lot of blood around, a lot of losses," said a government securities trader on Wall Street. An executive at First Boston added: "There are two emotions that move markets—fear and greed. Well, fear has become the dominant emotion."[19]

Amid the turmoil, Federal Reserve Board members heard directly from one of the most important investors in the bond market—the commercial banks. The asset portfolios of America's banks included more than $115 billion in government bonds, and when bond prices collapsed, bank assets shrank in value accordingly. The bankers' Federal Advisory Council met privately with the Federal Reserve governors on April 30 and scolded the Fed for contributing to the disorders.

"The failure of long-term rates to decline, even when short-term rates were falling, is indicative of deeply entrenched inflationary expectations," the bankers warned. "Apparently, the financial markets remain skeptical that the monetary authorities [the Federal Reserve] can or will maintain a steady but restrained growth of the money supply."

The banker-advisers repeated an admonition they had delivered many times before: "The board must avoid a repetition of 1980 when explosive growth of the money supply occurred . . . To allow such an occurrence again would greatly hinder the badly needed restoration of the financial markets' confidence that a proper monetary policy will be carried out."

A few months previously, the advisory council had speculated on the potential for what Wall Street called a "double-dip recession"—another contraction in 1981 right after the brief one of 1980. At their April meeting, however, the bankers revised their outlook. The economy, they estimated, is "likely to weaken but unlikely to fall into a full-blown recession."

The Fed was under fire on many fronts. Its most important constituency, the commercial bankers, was upset with its performance. The bond market was panicky. On Capitol Hill, Democrats were attacking the Fed for high interest rates while the Republican advocates of supply-side tax reduction blamed the Fed for the roiled financial markets. "One has to question," said Representative Jack Kemp, "whether or not they know what they're doing."[20]

At the White House, privately at least, the President's economic advisers conceded that Wall Street was not buying their "rosy scenario." Treasury Under Secretary Beryl Sprinkel acknowledged, in a briefing for the Cabinet Council on Economic Affairs, that the bond-market disruptions reflected doubts about President Reagan's program. The rising long-term rates, Sprinkel reported, "indicate significant skepticism about the likelihood of the budgetary, tax and monetary policies delivering all that has been promised. In particular, financial markets show a deep concern about the outlook for the budget deficit and the potential effect on monetary policy."

But the deeper problem, Sprinkel contended, was the Federal Reserve's own lack of credibility—"the skepticism about future monetary policy in the face of impending budget deficits." Many years of disappointment had persuaded the financial markets not to count on the central bank to hold the line against an aggressive fiscal policy.[21]

Lawrence A. Kudlow, chief economist for the Office of Management and Budget, offered a similar analysis: "Significant increases in long-term interest rates cast doubt over the credibility of the Administration's program."[22]

But Sprinkel warned the White House policy makers to resist complaints from Congress and stand fast for a rigorous monetary policy. "Critics of the Administration's economic policies have been calling for an easing of monetary policy as the solution to the current situation," Sprinkel said. "Unfortunately, this view has been reinforced by the repeated references by Congress to the evils of high interest rates. This is simply an example of confusing a symptom (high interest rates) with the disease (inflation)."[23]

Sprinkel and the other monetarists believed, in fact, that interest rates were ultimately determined by market forces, not by Federal Reserve manipulation. The focus of monetary policy must be exclusively on M-1 and the money supply, they insisted, and any attempts to bring down rates by injecting more money into the banking system would be quickly canceled out by the financial markets' fears of inflation and upward pressure on market rates.

Economic history suggested, rather forcefully, that monetarists were simply wrong about the Fed and interest rates. After all, for a full decade in the 1940s, the Fed had demonstrated that it could hold interest rates absolutely flat if it wished—both short-term and long-term rates—despite the market pressures created by the huge wartime deficits. The Fed did so by pumping in more money—holding down the price by increasing the supply.

The monetarist logic, nevertheless, allowed the White House to blame the central bank's performance for the bond-market debacle—not the President's own program. By insisting that interest rates did not matter and only money did, Sprinkel and the others narrowly focused their critique on a single factor—the Fed's month-to-month control of M-1.

And when they looked at M-1 in early spring, the evidence seemed most disturbing. For three months, the basic money aggregate had expanded but it was still running well below its target for the year. If anything, money was already too tight in terms of the Fed's own goals. But now, suddenly, M-1 looked as if it were growing explosively again. During April, the primary money aggregate started expanding at an annual rate of 25 percent. White House suspicions seemed confirmed.

Was the Fed deliberately pumping up money again, despite its promises to the White House? Or was the Fed simply losing control, as it had in 1980? Either way, Sprinkel warned, if the surge continued, financial markets would be rattled further and long-term interest rates would be bid still higher. The President's economic promises would be defeated by incompetence at the Federal Reserve.

Inside the White House, the monetarists sounded the alarm. Volcker and the Fed bureaucrats had never really believed in controlling the money aggregates, they complained. The Fed was targeting interest rates again, despite its public denials. At the weekly meetings with Fed officials, Sprinkel and others complained repeatedly about the central bank's inconstancy.

There were strong arguments, strong debates [Fred Schultz said]. Beryl and Jerry [Jordan] would argue that we weren't being tight enough. Kudlow was hammering on us too. I would say, "Look at M-1 growth, it's quite low for the year." They would say, "Yeah, but you're not really staying on those targets. You're deviating." We would say, "No, Beryl, if we stick closer to the targets, we will get more volatility [the lesson that Fed officials had learned from the 1980 roller coaster]." He would say, "You've got to stick precisely to the targets. If you do that, it would make things settle down."

At the White House, the circle of senior presidential advisers picked up Sprinkel's complaints and soon they were buzzing with indignation. Volcker was undermining the President. He mustn't get away with this. Treasury Secretary Regan confided to an aide one day that he and the President had actually discussed "abolishing the Fed." [24]

"We worked ourselves into a frenzy," an important White House official said. "Volcker has to be told. First, we have to let him know he's got to have a working relationship with us. He needs to work in harness with the White House. Second, we don't want any more of his zooming money supply like we had in 1980, that caused the mess we're still in."

The Federal Reserve chairman would be called to account. Only the President himself could make Paul Volcker shape up.

The President sat in one of the big wing chairs in the Oval Office and opposite him, sprawled in the facing chair, was the chairman of the Federal Reserve Board. Lined along the couches were the President's senior advisers: James A. Baker III, the White House chief of staff; Treasury Secretary Donald Regan; CEA chairman Murray Weidenbaum; Edwin Meese; Martin Anderson; and David Stockman, the budget director.

"It was like a meeting with a visiting head of state from a foreign country," Stockman complained. "Brief and formal and there wasn't much real communication."

Paul Volcker was an intimidating figure to these men. The Fed chairman was not ten feet tall (he was only six feet seven), but his reputation and expertise were as imposing as his physical stature. Volcker had more practical experience in governing than any of those who had just taken charge of the executive branch. He had served at Treasury when Lyndon Johnson entered the war in Indochina; he was devising international economic policy when Richard Nixon resigned from the Presidency. Volcker knew the real history of every issue and understood the subtle interplay of politicians and bureaucracies in Washington, the submerged game of power relationships. Furthermore, Paul Volcker's domain—monetary policy—was itself a large mystery to most of the men gathered around the President.

Ronald Reagan, ironically, had a surer grasp of the subject than any of his senior political advisers—ironic because, in most realms of government policy, Reagan was a passive executive, with a weak grasp of details. He often left both the particulars and the strategic choices to his circle of advisers. They worked out a consensus among themselves, then brought the decision to him for ratification. When it came to money, however, Reagan knew what he wanted and expressed it forcefully.

"Most of the major players in the White House—Baker, Meese, Mike Deaver—don't know much about monetary policy," one of their colleagues explained. "The President probably has the most developed understanding of any of them."

David Stockman elaborated the point:

The President has two metaphors he uses when he talks about monetary policy. One is "zooming the money supply," which meant money was too easy. "Pulling the string" meant it was too tight. The President doesn't have a lot of things right in his head. He is kind of selective about what facts he takes in. but one thing he really believes in deeply is anti-inflation. He used the same cliché over and over: "Inflation is like radioactivity. Once it starts, it spreads and grows."

Ronald Reagan was a monetarist himself. That label had never been publicly applied to him in all his years as a candidate (perhaps because most political reporters were oblivious to the distinction), but Reagan's campaign bromides clearly reflected his monetarist perspective. Inflation originated with the "printing press" money at the Federal Reserve, he said, and in order to brake inflation, the government must halt its excessive production of money.

This was one thing that the President knows in detail [Stockman said]. He could take a piece of paper and draw a line tracing the money-supply growth all the way back to the sixties. He had one thing that he knew and he always made the same point about the Federal Reserve. The money supply "zoomed" in every election year—"flooding the economy with money," he said—and then, after the election, the Fed "pulled the string" and the economy went into recession.

Ronald Reagan had been tutored on the subject by Milton Friedman himself. Now that Reagan was President, Friedman continued as an outside economics adviser, one who dropped by the Oval Office regularly to offer his analysis and advice. The President did subscribe to one principle on money that conflicted with the Friedman doctrine. Like the supply siders in Congress, Reagan privately advocated restoration of the gold standard as the ultimate way of guaranteeing stable money. "You can't control inflation as long as you have fiat money," he told his aides. The President's attachment to gold was almost never mentioned in public, however. His political advisers feared that it would sound "kooky" and "old-fashioned" to voters.

The President was fully prepped for the meeting with Volcker, but he delivered to the Federal Reserve chairman the same speech on money that White House aides had heard many times in private. The problem, Reagan told Volcker, was the "zooming" money supply, following by "pulling the string" too tight.

"The President took his finger and drew the chart of the money supply in the air for Volcker," Stockman said. What was needed, the President told the Fed chairman, was not a line that zigzagged up and down, but a smooth, steady line that moved upward at a moderate pace.

Volcker, another Administration official remarked, "would have found the President rather abstract. In terms of dealing with the President, Volcker could get a sense that this guy is just interested in the abstractions and the abstractions are sufficiently trite that he could live with it."

Volcker had already taken the measure of the Reagan advisers in his regular meetings with them. "If the President asked him to listen to his advisers," the official explained, "Volcker could say to himself: 'This Administration does not have a coherent view and, if we want one, I know more than these jokers.' "

The Federal Reserve chairman listened respectfully to the President and responded with his own clichés. He gave a rambling, disjointed discourse on the Federal Reserve's policy goals. He emphasized the uncertainties surrounding M-1 and the other monetary aggregates. He discussed potential operating problems associated with the various technical changes demanded by the monetarists.[25]

"I said to myself, 'The President isn't going to understand this,' and, sure enough, he didn't," Stockman related. "The President went into his own circular arguments about controlling money. Volcker replied, 'Yes, we're controlling the money aggregates, but we think the numbers may be high for other reasons and these other operating procedures are overrated and so on.' "

When Volcker departed, Stockman thought the Oval Office showdown was a great disappointment. "The meeting turned into mush— all mush," he said. Volcker had not given his commitment to cooperate with the White House economic policy. He hadn't even been asked for one.

Some of the other presidential advisers, however, were pleased. The message had been delivered with sufficient force and clarity that Volcker would have to respond. Within a few days, the grapevine of monetarist economists, inside and outside the government, was gossiping about the stern lecture that Ronald Reagan had delivered to Paul Volcker. The President, they were told, demanded that the Fed shape up.

Beryl Sprinkel, for one, expressed a new confidence that the Fed would bring money growth under control. "They can," Sprinkel said. "The question is: will they? I believe they will."

"We have had many frank discussions about the Federal Reserve in the last few months," Sprinkel told a meeting of financial executives in Chicago. "I am now convinced that the Fed will meet its stated objective." [26]

Volcker himself did not remember any stern lectures from the President, then or at any other time. But the chairman certainly got the drift of what the White House wanted. He must have also recognized an implicit political threat for the Federal Reserve.

Stockman, initially disappointed, concluded that the summit meeting with Volcker had some effect, after all. "Volcker is now trying to make peace with the White House," he reported to colleagues. [27]

The President's message, technical details aside, was not that complicated. "Volcker couldn't have come out of that meeting," Stockman said, "thinking anything but that the White House wanted tightening."

In mid-April, before a university audience in Kansas, Paul Volcker was explaining once again what the Federal Reserve was doing. The money-supply growth rates would be steadily reduced, year by year, until inflation was squeezed out of the economy. But the chairman added a reassuring promise: the reduction would be done gradually, he said, "not all at once, but over a period of years."

This was an important point. If money was squeezed abruptly, that might produce a dramatic decline in inflation, but it would also overwhelm the people and enterprises whose prices were bound up in contracts and commitments—wage agreements, bank loans, sales contracts. Gradualism would be slower but less wrenching for innocent economic players who had entered transactions in good faith, assuming that price inflation would continue into the future.

"The purpose," Volcker explained, "is to permit some time for the economy, for personal behavior and for existing contracts to adjust to the prospect of a slower rate of growth of price increase and eventual stability. 'Shock treatment' may be more dramatic—but not necessarily more effective over time."

People would be given time to adjust. Businessmen would see that the steady deceleration of prices was real and revise their expectations for future loans, wages, prices. Once everyone understood the new direction, the inflationary fever would subside. The economy would back off its demands for higher wages, higher prices. "What is essential," Volcker said, "is that there be widespread appreciation of our intentions and our ability and will to carry them out."[28]

Among the Federal Reserve governors, Nancy Teeters was the most persistent advocate of the gradual approach. She did not argue that a recession could be avoided, but she was more sensitive than the others to the particular groups that would suffer most directly from a sterner policy.

> I invoked every argument I could think of [she said]. Small business was suffering because they had to borrow at the prime plus. Housing was dead and autos. The consumer didn't have any strength left at all and unemployment was rising. My intuitive feeling was that the same results would be accomplished with lower rates. It would take a little longer but probably more small businesses would survive.

Teeters's perspective did not prevail. The Federal Reserve chairman did not keep his promise.

Assuming Volcker's assurances were sincere, either he changed his mind abruptly or he erred in his execution of money regulation. For in the coming weeks, for whatever reason, the Fed did the opposite of what the chairman had promised. By May, the economy was slowing down appreciably, weakened by the high interest rates that the Fed had imposed for nearly six months. The Federal Reserve, nevertheless, decided to tighten further. The Fed would push interest rates even higher.

That was what the White House said it wanted. That was also what the bond market wanted, as well as the commercial bankers on the advisory council. Any hesitation among the Fed governors was brushed aside. The technical doubts were resolved in favor of an even sterner policy. Promises of gradualism were permanently discarded.

About the same time, thirty or forty Wall Street financial experts were invited to the Fed for a private two-day seminar on monetary policy. John Paulus, the analyst from Morgan Stanley and a former Fed staff economist, was struck in particular by what Volcker had to say to the group. It was a clear signal of his intentions.

"Volcker told us," Paulus said, "that since the policy mistakes in the past have been made on the side of excessive ease, in the future, if we err, it makes sense to err on the side of restraint."

That was what happened at the next meeting of the Federal Open Market Committee.

America's money always became confused in April. Families were paying their income taxes, many drawing down savings accounts in order to mail a check to Washington. At the same time, the government was sending out tax refunds to millions of other citizens. With all these billions of dollars sloshing back and forth in the mail and between bank accounts, the April statistics on the money supply were notoriously quirky. In any other year, when M-1 surged abruptly in April, the Fed might simply have tolerated it, waiting to see if this was a real trend or merely a statistical aberration of the tax season.

This year, they were not so patient. On May 6, members of the Federal Open Market Committee were consulted in a telephone conference call on how to deal with the M-1 problem. They agreed to let the Federal Funds rate rise above its target range. The expansion of money and credit would be dampened by making money more expensive. In the second week of May, this key interest rate controlled by the central bank jumped more than 260 basis points—above 18 percent.

Notwithstanding the sudden surge of M-1, every other visible signal indicated that money and credit were tightening—not easing. Short-term interest rates were being bid up in the money market. Commercial banks were borrowing more heavily at the Discount window. The rate of inflation, moreover, was already beginning to moderate. In March, inflation fell below double digits and stayed there for the first time in two years. By April, inflation had subsided to 7.2 percent. The Fed, nevertheless, made money tighter still.

When the Federal Open Market Committee gathered for its regular meeting on May 18, the debate was preoccupied with technical confusion over exactly what the money numbers meant. In addition to April's usual uncertainties, the money-supply aggregates were now distorted by the banking innovations authorized in the financial deregulation legislation of 1980. At the beginning of 1981, NOW accounts became available nationwide at commercial banks—checking accounts that paid interest. That altered the economic meaning of M-1.

Billions of dollars flowed into the new NOW accounts, some transferred from the regular demand deposits counted as M-1 and some from savings accounts counted in the less liquid aggregate known as M-2. NOW accounts were included in M-1 because people could write checks on them and spend the money in immediate transactions. Yet, because they paid interest, the NOW accounts also resembled the old-fashioned savings accounts or money-market funds counted as M-2—

invested money that would not flow quickly into the transactions of regular commerce. What did this hybrid brand of M-1 mean for the economy? Did people intend to spend this money promptly or were they just parking idle savings in NOW accounts for the added convenience?

For many months, various Keynesian economists had complained that if the Federal Reserve was going to follow the monetarist approach to regulating money, it had chosen the worst possible time to do so. Financial deregulation permitted all sorts of innovations in banking habits and the money numbers were scrambled by them, not just the meaning of M-1 but the other aggregates too. The Fed would be led into error again and again, the liberal critics warned, as the composition of M-1 and M-2 changed in new and unpredictable ways.

Frank Morris, president of the Boston Federal Reserve Bank, agreed with the critics:

> You could see what was happening to money [Morris said]. People would have a NOW acount and a savings account, both paying practically the same interest rate. But the NOW account is checkable. So you close down the savings account and put the money in NOW. You now have money counted in M-1 that is not really a transaction account. As time goes on, we get more and more of these things. With various innovations, you can write checks on accounts that are counted in all three Ms.

The traditional definitions of money were literally breaking down. The fine distinctions that monetary economists relied upon to decide money-supply questions were being obliterated, in unpredictable ways, as private depositors changed their behavior, reacting to the new banking possibilities authorized in the 1980 legislation. The economic relevance of M-1 was now unknown.

Yet the Federal Reserve had committed itself, starting back in 1979, to faithfully adhere to M-1 as its policy guide. Volcker's conversion to a monetarist operating approach was premised on the confident assertion that a given quantity of M-1 would produce a predictable level of activity in the larger economy. Some Federal Reserve officials doubted this from the start. But now they knew for certain it was not true.

Just as the Keynesians had warned, the Fed was trying to steer the economy by an inherently unstable variable—an economic number that had lost its meaning. Once M-1 was contaminated by the idle savings money alongside active spending money, the basic aggregate looked artificially larger than it really was, in terms of what level of economic activity it would permit. The statistics could be dangerously misleading if the Federal Open Market Committee continued to follow

M-1 obediently. By holding down M-1 growth, the Fed might be squeezing the American economy tighter than even it intended.

The private reaction at the Fed was anguish and a little chagrin. It seemed ludicrous for the central bank to continue following a wayward lodestar, especially since several of the leading governors had never themselves believed that the money aggregates were a reliable guide. Yet to admit the dilemma and abandon Volcker's operating system would be embarrassing too. The FOMC members decided instead to plunge forward, improvising and rationalizing.

In the technocratic tradition, the problem would be resolved by rational calculation. Fed technicians had devised a new money aggregate called "shift-adjusted M-1B" that attempted to compensate for the distortions caused by NOW accounts. Except no one, including the Fed technicians, really knew how much distortion there was. So they made an estimate. The M-1 debate could now continue, using a new label, M-1B, that suggested more scientific certitude than existed. Some senior Fed officials began to worry about where Volcker's commitment to monetarism was leading them.[29]

"A lot of us talked privately about getting ourselves into a monetarist trap," said Peter Fousek, executive vice president at the New York Fed. "We had the whole world looking at the money numbers and taking them too seriously. How are we going to get out of the monetarist box after the country has been sold on the idea that the money numbers are so important? Yet you know they are giving you wrong signals."[30]

At the May meeting of the FOMC, however, Volcker and the two governors most respected for their analytical skills stoutly defended the operating system and offered a different interpretation of what the Ms were signaling. Prior to the April surge, M-1's growth had been running below target for months. But the broader aggregate that included savings accounts, M-2, was running in the middle of its target range. People were also pouring funds into M-2's money-market accounts in order to reap the returns offered by the high interest rates. This included not just savings but money they probably intended to spend. Thus, the governors reasoned, the rapid growth of M-2 was signaling that money was actually too loose. The Fed, they suggested, should temporarily focus on M-2's high growth, instead of M-1, as the correct indicator.

When Lyle Gramley and Henry Wallich both came to the defense of Volcker's monetarist approach, their opinions carried special weight with their colleagues on the FOMC—since neither of them, it was understood, was a true believer. Wallich and Gramley, however, improvised similar interpretations of the Ms that would justify tightening the money supply still further. People, they theorized, were dumping funds into M-2 money-market funds to collect the extraordinary interest returns, but actually these people intended to spend a lot of this money. Therefore, Wallich proposed, the FOMC should arbitrarily assume that a portion of M-2 was really M-1.

"I argued," Gramley said, "that the effective money growth was actually faster than what the numbers on the aggregates showed." Both men, as it turned out, were grossly mistaken.

Their rationales were influenced, however, by another factor unrelated to the mechanics of money—their fear that the Federal Reserve might be embarrassed once again if it did not stand by its promises and try to make Volcker's techniques work. "Had one known we were going into a pretty sluggish period," Wallich conceded afterward, "we might have had a policy that was less tight. But the effectiveness of the new techniques was being called into question and that was very much in our minds. What else could we do?"

Frank Morris, for one, argued the question repeatedly with his colleagues on the Federal Open Market Committee and always lost. "We were following a false god," Morris complained. "The others would say to me, 'Granted, we're having some problems with M-1, but this is only a temporary phenomenon. The dust is going to settle soon and we will return to normal.' I heard this at every FOMC meeting. I think it's a lot of baloney."

Morris had been president of the Boston Fed since 1968, which made him senior among the twelve Reserve Bank presidents. Educated at Michigan by Keynesian economists, he came to Washington to work in the Truman Administration and stayed through John F. Kennedy, with a tour in between doing international economic analysis for the Central Intelligence Agency. Morris was more urbane than most Fed bankers and his sophisticated taste was reflected in the Boston Fed's extraordinary building near the waterfront. The gleaming tower won architectural prizes, but the design seemed audacious for a public building, too smart and handsome for such a staid old institution as the Federal Reserve. For economic advice, Frank Morris stayed in close touch with the liberal Keynesians on the faculties of Harvard and MIT.

Morris's perspective on monetary policy, in fact, was the traditional view at the Fed—before Chairman Volcker had converted everyone to the money aggregates. His colleagues, Morris grumbled, were now enthralled by the same "mystique of money" that had so long obsessed their monetarist critics. It was as if Fed policy makers had been taken in by their own propaganda. Many of them had opted for the monetarist approach mainly because it would give them political cover for imposing high interest rates—the Fed could say it was regulating M-1, not interest rates. Now the Fed seemed hooked on the money numbers too.

Morris couldn't shake the faith, though he insisted that most of his colleagues, including Volcker, knew better. The Fed could not control M-1 fluctuations as monetarists imagined. More to the point, the M-1 fluctuations did not matter to the real economy. Interest rates and credit expansion were what guided things.

I don't think money itself has any causal relationship to nominal GNP [Morris explained]. The dominating causal force is interest rates. If rates go up, you can naturally expect the money supply to go down because economic activity declines and because you've raised the opportunity cost of holding money. Most members of the FOMC, if you faced them with this causal question, would not disagree.

Morris's arguments were never a match for the authority of Paul Volcker, seconded by influential governors like Gramley and Wallich. The Federal Open Market Committee accepted the chairman's interpretation of events and agreed to come down hard on the surge in M-1. Ironically, if the Fed had been basing its policy on interest rates instead of monetary aggregates, there would have been little argument: credit conditions obviously were already abnormally tight and growing tighter, even as they met. The Fed, instead, stuck with the money numbers. The policy makers adopted a directive that ordered a "substantial deceleration" of money growth—strong language compared with the bland phrases usually contained in the FOMC's policy decisions. As Volcker saw it: M-1 was rising again. He decided to step on it.

The results were dramatic: the year-old expansion of the American economy was finally broken. By July, the nation's gross economic output would peak and the country was once again plunged into recession—a second contraction in two years, both induced by the punishing interest rates imposed by the Federal Reserve.

For whatever it was worth, the Fed did get M-1 under control. M-1 —or, rather, shift-adjusted M-1B—not only stopped growing in May, it declined sharply, by $4 billion. The basic money supply shrank in May at an annual rate of 11 percent. It shrank by an additional 2 percent in June. In fact, it would be six months before the Federal Reserve allowed M-1 to grow again. Not until November would the money aggregate return to the same level it had reached in April.

This was equivalent to slamming hard on the brakes—driving up interest rates by choking off supply. Interest rates responded accordingly. The Federal Funds rate climbed above 19 percent and stayed there through most of the summer. The economy was already weakening under the cumulative burden of six months of high interest rates. The additional jolt administered by the Fed in May became the final blow that finished the job.

Within a few weeks after the May meeting, it became obvious that the FOMC's reading of the monetary aggregates had been mistaken. The Fed had misinterpreted its own money signals rather than conceding that they were too confused to be reliable.

"By July," said Governor Charles Partee, "you could see that April had been just a seasonal blip and there was considerable slackening in the aggregates."

"What else could we do?" Henry Wallich lamented. "We could have abandoned the reserve technique. Then we would have avoided the recession. And what rate of inflation would we have wound up with?"

The Federal Open Market Committee was wrong about the economy as well as the money numbers—an error of judgment that led to large and painful consequences for the nation. The dimensions of the mistakes were defined in the Fed's own words, its published reports and minutes. Month after month in the first half of 1981, the FOMC minutes revealed misinterpretations of the diverging monetary aggregates, and also misjudgments of what was happening to the real economy. In its report to Congress at the beginning of the year, the FOMC had agreed to hold M-1 growth to a target range of 3.5 to 6 percent. In the event, the Fed actually held adjusted M-1 to only 2.3 percent growth. After years of overshooting the money targets, this time the Fed erred on the hard side.

Nothing in the Fed's official record would suggest, furthermore, that the Federal Open Market Committee expected that its decision to tighten would tip the economy into recession (see Appendix C for minutes of the May 18, 1981, FOMC meeting). On the contrary, the FOMC reported: "While generally anticipating a substantial slowing of growth from the exceptionally rapid pace now indicated for the first quarter, a number of members expressed the view that expansion in activity over the rest of the year was likely to continue to exceed the rates typically being forecast."

Michael G. Hadjimichalakis, a University of Washington economist who was a visiting scholar at the Federal Reserve Board for two years during this period, published a meticulous analysis of the policy record of FOMC decisions and arrived at harsh conclusions. "The Fed became lost in a maze of unnecessary detail, mostly of its own creation, in order to follow the monetarist prescriptions," he wrote. Hadjimicha-lakis's critique was virtually unknown to political Washington, but his analysis was widely read among the Federal Reserve's staff econo-mists, with a mixture of agreement and rejection and injured pride.

Leading up to the recession, he noted, the FOMC consistently ig-nored the contractionary signals coming from M-1 each month and misconstrued the meaning of M-2 as well. Each month, the policy makers found new reasons for disregarding the deterioration of the real economy and, instead, searched for evidence of expansionary dangers. Hadjimichalakis's scholarly analysis of Fed errors, couched in the neutral prose of economics, added up to a devastating commen-tary:

> We must emphasize that the Fed's intended disinflation is not at issue here. At issue is the extra and *unintended* disinflation that resulted from the Fed's errors. Of course, it is true . . . that the members of the FOMC, following monetarist prescriptions, repeatedly preferred to err on the side of fighting inflation rather than fighting the looming recession. Neverthe-less, the economic depression of 1981–82 was mostly unintentional.

Hadjimichalakis surmised that the Federal Reserve was driven into its fateful mistakes by embarrassment over its own inept performance of 1980—when Volcker attempted to apply monetarist procedures and wound up producing even more erratic swings in money growth and interest rates. "Although the economic consequences of these errors [in 1980] were relatively minor," Hadjimichalakis explained, "the Fed became vulnerable to monetarist criticism and the Fed's reaction to criticism of these errors, the adoption of even stronger monetarist principles, later caused additional and crucial errors. These latter errors were responsible for the economic depression of 1981–82."[31]

For modern Americans, taught to believe in the efficacy of techno-cratic government, this presented a disturbing picture—the failure of powerful experts. The faceless technocrats of the central bank, priestly regulators of money, had committed a series of miscalcula-tions and wrong predictions. Their mistakes were compounded as they kept adjusting their own operating premises, struggling to defend the logical appearance of what they were doing. For the nation, the result would be economic distress on an epic scale—a deep recession, rising unemployment, personal and business failures rippling through the society. Was it all, then, an accident?

The Federal Reserve governors were not as incompetent as their own technical record made them seem. While the critique of the Fed-eral Reserve's decisions was documented in the Fed's own official reports, this evidence did not tell the whole story of the logic driving the Federal Open Market Committee's decisions. There was another dimension to the Fed's policy making, one that was largely unspoken and subjective and never—never—reflected in the FOMC's official minutes. The Federal Reserve was not simply a group of neutral technocrats exercising its best expertise on money and banking. It was also a political institution, a distinct power center within the government, defending its own prerogatives and reacting to the political currents surrounding it.

The other, unspoken dimension was politics. When the political context was considered, the Fed's supposed errors began to make more sense. As economic choices, the monetary decisions made in the spring of 1981 were clearly flawed. The technocrats failed in terms of their own analysis. As bureaucratic politicians, protecting their own institution from political harm and pursuing larger goals, on the other hand, Volcker and his colleagues knew what they were doing.

In political terms, the Fed was on precarious ground, pressured from several angles at once. The White House had staked out its hard-line critique, both in public and in private. The financial markets remained deeply skeptical that the central bank meant to keep its word. Economists generally were warning that the Reagan tax cuts and large deficits would give new momentum to inflationary expectations. Bankers and the bond market agreed. The Fed's own shaky performance in 1980 was very much on everyone's mind. If inflation came roaring back, the Federal Reserve would be blamed, more emphatically than ever before.

The political nervousness at the Fed was reflected in Vice Chairman Frederick Schultz's trip to St. Louis. Larry Roos, president of the St. Louis Fed, the bastion of monetarism inside the System, had been making many speeches, complaining that his colleagues on the FOMC were not being sufficiently faithful to the doctrine and echoing the same criticisms heard from the Reagan White House. Volcker worried that Roos's constant attacks were undermining the Fed's position. Fred Schultz said he would deal with it.

The vice chairman called on the St. Louis Fed's board of directors and, in so many words, asked its members to muzzle their feisty president. "Look, we're in a helluva battle now," Schultz told the Reserve Bank directors, "and we're all in the same boat. We at the board in Washington may not be as monetarist as you would like, but we're all on the same side. We should argue in the board meetings, but close ranks in public."

The St. Louis board prevailed on its president "to be less of a maverick," as Roos himself put it.

When the governors and Reserve Bank presidents convened as the Federal Open Market Committee, they observed "a very high degree of self-conscious rectitude," as one FOMC staff assistant put it. Politics was never discussed in the formal meetings, except in the most oblique manner. It was not done. To bring up outside political pressures at the board table, when the subject was disinterested economic analysis, would be an affront to the independent posture of the institution.

This did not prevent FOMC members from talking politics during the lunch break, however. As the staff assistant said:

After the vote, there's a break with lunch eaten at the board table, and very often that's the only time when the presidents and governors will discuss political contacts. They will have a more explicit discussion of political reactions then, but it's not part of the official meeting. This is part of a deliberate effort to have the meetings appear to be completely free of political discussion. The politics doesn't get articulated until after the meeting, but everyone understands that the politics is involved in the decisions.

During the lunch break at the May meeting, the FOMC members talked at length about the political subtext for their decision—the pressures confronting them, particularly the monetarist attacks from the Reagan Administration. The discussion, according to the FOMC staffer, went like this:

What do these attacks mean for the future? We are going to see more of this, probably. Are we happy enough with the 1979 policy to use it to resist pressure to move in a direction we don't want to move? We don't want to be seen as responding to the Administration, so we must be sure we have a sound, theoretical basis for our policy. In other words, do it for the right reasons, not because they are leaning on us.

All of the outside pressures pushed the Fed in the same direction—toward a tougher policy. The safest ground for the Federal Reserve would be to demonstrate that, whatever else went wrong, the Fed was diligently keeping its word. If doubts persisted about the Fed's commitment and competence, better to err on the hard side. If Reagan's tax cuts threatened to reignite inflationary fever, better to lean against it in advance.

"The White House drumbeat did encourage us to be tighter than we would have been without it," said a senior officer of the Boston Fed who attended FOMC meetings.

"I guess I would be harder on the Fed than that," his colleague, a senior economist, interjected. "If we had wanted to be easier, we could have been easier. This was the time when the economic miracle was going to happen and tight money was supposed to be part of that. It was very hard to argue against it. This was a new Administration having its honeymoon—give them what they want and hope for the best."

Dan Brill, the retired research director and mentor to many of the Fed's senior officers, was critical too. "I accuse the Fed of having a circle-the-wagons mentality," Brill said. "All the Sprinkel crowd did was confirm that mentality. All that happens at the Fed when you get that kind of attack is you circle the wagons tighter."

Even so, the White House pressure might have been resisted if the bond market had been pulling in an opposite direction. In this instance, both institutions wanted the same thing from the central bankers. Political scientists liked to search for evidence of political influence on the Fed, and when they found it, they concluded that, by and large, the Fed did respond to the White House or to Congress. This legitimized the anomalous arrangement, they suggested, since, in a vague and shadowy manner, the central bank did seem responsive to the elected government. But there was a more interesting question about the Fed's independence, a more fundamental test of its political behavior. It was posed in situations where the political community and the financial markets were in conflict, demanding contrary policies. Whom did the Fed listen to then—when it had to choose between Washington and Wall Street?

In the fall of 1979, when this test occurred, the answer had been Wall Street. Jimmy Carter's advisers had urged Paul Volcker not to adopt the rigid monetarist approach, but the Fed chariman had felt secure enough to go ahead with his initiative, despite White House objections, knowing that the financial markets would applaud. The same test would be posed again at crucial moments in the Reagan Presidency, but in the spring-of-1981 instance, the Fed policy makers were protected on both flanks. Their interpretation of the money numbers, however flawed as economic analysis, permitted the Federal Open Market Committee to tighten money again, which was precisely what both the bond market and the White House wanted.

Paul Volcker was often praised for his political courage, but in this instance, it might have taken more courage to resist. In any case, the other FOMC members usually deferred to his political judgments. They had the luxury of arguing technical issues, but he represented the Fed in politics. "The chairman is the daddy," an FOMC staff assistant explained. "He is the one who's got to make the decision and live with it. He is the one who will have to do the explaining when we get attacked. The others on the FOMC have more freedom to be irresponsible . . . but they leave it to the chairman to say, 'That won't wash in the real world.' "

Volcker's sensibilities nearly always shaped the final decision. "Volcker didn't decide to take away the punch bowl just as the party was getting good," one of his aides joked. "He came in and hit it with a hammer."

Earlier in the spring of 1981, the French ambassador called on Anthony Solomon, president of the New York Fed, and asked him what his outlook was for the American economy. The new government of François Mitterrand was taking power in Paris and France's economic policy would necessarily be influenced by what direction the United States, the locomotive of the world's economy, intended to take.

> I told him the U.S. was going into recession [Solomon said]. The French finance minister asked the same question at Treasury and was told that a great boom was ahead in America. I later learned that Mitterrand, at his first Cabinet meeting, announced that his government could pursue an expansionist policy because the U.S. would be booming. He was told that I was predicting a contraction. Mitterrand said, "Let's go ahead and take the expansionist route because the Treasury has given us irrevocable assurances." He was warned that it was a gamble. They went ahead anyway and, of course, they got clobbered.

The awkward little secret of the American system was that modern recessions did not flow ineluctably from mysterious natural forces in the business cycle. Recessions were induced by the federal government. In the seven recessions since World War II, the same transaction had preceded each contraction: the Federal Reserve's decision to force up interest rates to an abnormal level. If it kept them there long enough, the economy would inevitably decline. Given that power equation, it was natural for Tony Solomon to understand what lay ahead for the American economy even if the Secretary of the Treasury did not.

For months, Nancy Teeters had also assumed recession was imminent. So did Governor Charles Partee and Governor Emmett Rice. "Nobody wishes to see hardship," Rice explained. "Nobody likes to see people lose their jobs and GNP stop growing. But, sometimes, given developments, it's inevitable."

The crucial development, of course, was at the Federal Reserve itself. In broad terms, the governors could argue that they had no choice, given their commitment to curb price inflation. In specific terms, however, it was not price inflation that broke the economic expansion and forced a contraction. It was the high interest rates engineered by the Fed.

"You're always going to take a risk of a recession when you're in this process," Volcker acknowledged. "It's always a question of when. If you're never going to take that risk, you're not going to do anything and end up with recession anyway."

This distinction was an important refuge for Fed governors. Yes, they would concede, they put the economy at risk, pushed it toward the cliff. But that's not the same as saying they deliberately provoked recession. To people who experienced the consequences, it would seem a distinction without much difference.

For obvious reasons, the Fed never declared their expectations in advance. Its policy makers might agree informally among themselves that their policy was steering the economy into recession (or they might confide in the French ambassador), but they never informed the public of what was about to happen to it, except for those oblique comments on "necessary pain" and "substantial adjustments" ahead. If Americans clearly understood the connection, the Fed would find it much more difficult to do what it wanted to do. Secrecy and evasion were considered necessary to the task.[32]

Other branches of government also had an interest in obscuring the reality. If people understood the government itself was inducing recession, the President and Congress would also be in an awkward position —dodging angry questions from the public about why they let the Fed do this to it. If Washington was planning a recession, why didn't the government at least say so in clear, straightforward terms so people could protect themselves? The independence of the Federal Reserve was, in fact, a way for elected representatives to evade responsibility for these events. If things got bad enough, politicians would attack the Fed and the Fed would stoically accept its role as public scapegoat. That was part of the arrangement too.

The government's general silence on this question, the absence of fair warning and full debate, preempted all the reasonable questions that might have been asked about whether the Federal Reserve was doing the right thing. The general public undoubtedly agreed that double-digit inflation must be curbed somehow, but if the question was examined fully, it was not at all clear that a deep recession was the best way to deal with this disorder. Certainly, it was not the only way. The 1981 inflation, for instance, was driven by escalating prices in oil and agriculture, both of which might have been contained temporarily by direct controls and other aggressive government policies. Some people would have been hurt but far fewer people.

By evading the question, the political community did not have to examine the alternatives or which interests would be most injured by the Federal Reserve's method. Every solution, of course, had costs, but the political debate was never asked to compare them, was never in a position to choose which solution might do the least damage to the largest number of people or to the economy as a whole. Instead, the Federal Reserve went ahead and applied its own familiar remedy for inflation—inducing a deep recession. Millions of citizens and hundreds of thousands of business enterprises would discover that this particular cure was far worse than the affliction.

While ordinary citizens could not expect a timely warning from any part of the government, they were not entirely defenseless. People could watch interest rates for themselves and make their own curb-stone judgments about what the Federal Reserve really intended for the economy (though without much help from the press—it obscured the reality too). One reasonably simple rule applied: when the Fed pushed short-term rates higher than long-term rates and held them there long enough, recession was sure to follow. If three-month T-bills, for instance, were paying a higher yield than twenty-year bonds, then people should expect the worst. Short-term financial assets logically earn smaller returns than long-term ones, and so it was an unnatural condition when short rates were pushed higher than long rates—an "inverted yield curve" in the market parlance. It did not happen unless the Federal Reserve made it happen.

Like most economic rules, this one had blind spots. It could not, for instance, predict exactly when the recession would begin. Twenty years before, an inversion of short and long rates could produce a contraction after only two or three months. As inflation escalated and people became inured to higher and higher levels of interest, the impact took much longer. In 1981, the Fed held short-term rates well above long-term rates for eight months before the burden finally exhausted the economy. Fed governors could say, quite sincerely, they did not know when the recession would start. But they were being disingenuous if they claimed to be surprised.

"I don't think anyone could think for one minute that you could produce a sharp deceleration of the money supply without causing a recession," Frank Morris of the Boston Fed said. "It can't be done. . . . I don't think anyone in the Federal Reserve was naïve enough to think that."

In early June, the President's senior advisers gathered in chief of staff James Baker's office and listened to the gloomy portents from the economists. Jerry Jordan, the monetarist member of the CEA, and

Larry Kudlow, Stockman's economic analyst at the budget office, joined to deliver their warning: the "rosy scenario" devised back in February for the U.S. economy had failed to materialize. It was time to face facts, before it was too late.

"This forecast is garbage," Kudlow declared. "We're going to take a recession and have huge deficits."

Jordan and Kudlow summarized the situation for a group that included Baker, Edwin Meese, Treasury Secretary Regan and assorted economists. The Federal Reserve, they explained, was vigorously restraining money and growth in nominal GNP, just as the President and his men had asked. But the miracle of "rational expectations," the vast psychological shift of investors and other interests, had simply not occurred, and Volcker's predicted collision was at hand. Inflation was slowly subsiding, yes, but the real economy was sinking faster, headed for recession.

Lower nominal GNP and a shrinking economy naturally meant smaller tax revenues for the federal government. In Kudlow's estimate, the bottom line was: the Reagan program was going to produce not a balanced budget but larger and larger federal deficits—in the range of $100 billion or more in each of the next three years.

Kudlow and Jordan urged the White House to accept reality and acknowledge the effects in its midyear revision of the budget forecast required in July. For Jordan and the monetarists, this downward adjustment in economic prospects would eliminate the embarrassing monetary-policy numbers that didn't add up. For the Office of Management and Budget, such an acknowledgment would begin to reconcile the public to the prospect of much larger deficits than anyone in the Reagan Administration had previously intimated.

"There's no such thing as a painless cure for inflation," Kudlow said. "Jordan and I argued that the costs were coming first and the long-term benefits would come later. It would be better to acknowledge it instead of being embarrassed later."[33]

But Treasury's supply siders argued strenuously against any changes in the Administration's published forecast. "Lowering the growth projections," Paul Craig Roberts wrote, "would widen the deficit at an inopportune time—just at the point of congressional decision on the President's tax bill. Treasury did not think Congress would pass the tax bill if it seemed that the Administration expected the deficit to grow rather than the economy." Roberts even proposed that the Administration *raise* its growth estimates—making the future look even rosier.

An extended, intense argument developed between the two sides: should the President disclose an honest account of what the Administration expected or maintain the public fiction at least until Congress approved the massive tax cuts? It was one of those pivotal moments in political history when the decision would cast its shadow forward over many years to come—much as Lyndon Johnson's deception about the true cost of the Vietnam War in 1966 had distorted the economy for the decade that followed.[34]

If the Reagan White House had chosen to state the true consequences of its tax reductions at that moment, the 1980s might have been utterly different. Congress might well have balked at the tax cuts. Or the President might at least have been compelled to moderate his tax proposal. At the very minimum, federal deficits would not have soared to $200 billion a year, doubling the national debt in five years. The recession still would have occurred, but as Paul Volcker had warned obliquely six months earlier, interest rates might have been considerably lower. Less damage would have been inflicted on debtors generally and on the interest-sensitive sectors of the economy.

Between Baker and Meese, the President's senior policy makers decided not to disclose the new deficit forecast. The "rosy scenario" would be maintained as the official version of what the Reagan program would do for the economy, at least until after the tax bill was enacted. Afterward, they could deal with the problem of what the Reagan program was doing to the federal budget.

Kudlow described the fateful decision: "Baker said to me, 'Kudlow, I believe you're right, but I'm going to have to deal with that later. The President wants a tax cut and I can't publish this forecast now.' I said to him, 'Once the die is cast, you can't turn back.' "

David Stockman also concluded, with hindsight, that this decision was a final turning point that led inexorably to the massive deficits of the 1980s. "Passage of the tax bill was by no means certain at that point," Stockman said, "and the political decision was made to stick with the old forecast even though it was wrong." The Reagan White House's short-term political objective prevailed over the long-term truth, much as had occurred fifteen years earlier in Lyndon Johnson's White House.

The President himself was not consulted. He was not even informed by his own economic advisers that they now realized the Reagan economic recovery program was going to produce disastrous fiscal consequences. This omission partly reflected Reagan's distance from the real strategic decisions of his own government, his indifference to the operational complexities of managing the economy. But it also reflected the jockeying for favor among all the President's men.

Kudlow, for one, thought that somebody should have at least told Ronald Reagan. Let the President make the decision. "All these guys were trying to curry favor with the king," Kudlow explained, "and they said to themselves: 'The king wants to cut taxes, let's figure out how to do that.' None of them wanted to give the king the bad news."

Through the weeks of early summer, the budget estimates turned steadily worse for the White House. As the Reagan program advanced toward congressional approval, the original package of budget cuts proposed in February grew smaller and smaller as Congress moderated and rejected many of the reductions. Meanwhile, the President's proposal for tax cuts got larger and larger. Reagan had asked for $41 billion in spending cuts, but the final package would be roughly half that size. The original tax proposal would have cost $540 billion in lost revenue over five years, but it grew by roughly $200 billion. In the political competition with Democrats, a bidding war over tax breaks developed between the two political parties. The personal-income-tax reduction was scaled back to 25 percent over three years, but both sides offered more and larger tax concessions to business interest groups in order to win votes in the House and Senate. The final tax measure would lose approximately $750 billion. The net effect—greater loss of revenue combined with smaller savings on the spending side of the ledger—meant that even Kudlow's $100 billion deficit estimates would prove much too low.

Paul Volcker was as distressed as anyone else by the unraveling of the Reagan promises. Officially, the Federal Reserve endorsed the Reagan tax program, at least in general terms. Nevertheless, Volcker and his vice chairman, Fred Schultz, began discreetly lobbying senators and representatives, warning them to think twice before they voted for such a massive loss of government revenue.

Representative Henry Reuss, chairman of the House Banking Committee, thought that Volcker should have been much more forthright in his warnings. Public opposition from the Federal Reserve chairman might have changed the political atmosphere, made it easier for members of Congress to resist. "If Volcker had that much independence in his system," Reuss said, "he would have showed it in the summer of 1981. Instead, he supinely went along with the Administration's fiscal policy and he certainly didn't object to the instructions he was given."

In private, at least, Volcker did voice his alarm to the politicians. "As the tax bill became more and more distorted, we got more and more concerned," Schultz said. The vice chairman lobbied House members and Volcker worked the Senate side. They were careful to state that they were not declaring against the Reagan program, but they wished to warn Congress of the likely consequences—higher interest rates.

The message, Schultz said, went like this: "We are in favor of a tax cut, but you must recognize that if you can't accomplish this with much bigger budget cuts than you are contemplating, it's going to put much more pressure on us and that means higher interest rates." The Federal Reserve's own computer model of the economy had run a test and estimated that the likely effect of the Reagan tax cuts would be to raise real interest rates anywhere from 100 to 250 basis points (the estimate proved roughly accurate).

A lot of people had a tendency to disbelieve us and hope for the best, many Republicans in particular [Schultz said]. They told us, "Well, the old approach didn't work. Let's give this a try." Later on, as it got closer to the vote, they said to us, "Well, we can't do anything about it. We want to vote for tax cuts and we can't get the spending cuts up, so we're going ahead with the package as it is." The political pressure was so strong, they were just willing to engage in wishful thinking.

At the White House and Treasury, the Reagan advisers were particularly rankled when they discovered that the Fed chairman was on Capitol Hill, saying ominous things about the President's tax bill. Manuel H. Johnson, a supply-side economist and Treasury deputy (who himself would be appointed to the Federal Reserve Board five years later), complained that Volcker and the Fed were misreading the economic impact of the tax cuts. "The Fed argued [with the White House] all summer long about the tax bill being highly inflationary," Johnson said. "They were going to have to lean against this tax policy all the more. We got quite frustrated with them. 'Look,' we said, 'this is a phased-in fiscal policy. The tax cuts go into effect over three years.' "

Johnson and other supply siders thought the Fed's misjudgment of the tax cuts led directly to an overly zealous money policy—and higher interest rates than were necessary. "I don't think this was a planned recession by any means," Johnson said. "The Fed was probably as surprised as anyone. They sincerely believed that we did have an excessive, inflationary fiscal policy—and they were going to have to resist it."[35]

The supply siders' criticism was supported by the Fed's record of miscalculations and also in the comments from governors who acknowledged they were "leaning harder" against the economy in order to offset the supposed inflationary effects of the tax bill. Of course, the supply siders in the Reagan Administration tended to overlook the fact that it was their own colleagues, the monetarists, and their own President who had leaned on the Fed and demanded a tighter money policy. Still, they had a valid point about the inflationary impact of the tax cuts. Alan Blinder, a Keynesian economist at Princeton University and unsympathetic with the supply siders' economic theory, nevertheless agreed with their complaint.

"The Fed panicked about the supply-side tax cuts," Blinder explained. "The tax cuts weren't really coming in fully until 1983, but the Fed overreacted to them. The tax bill had no effect on the economy immediately, but the Fed was worried about the inflationary effects and it beat them to the punch—they dampened down the economy and caused a recession."[36]

As Schultz and Volcker lobbied Congress, they encountered complaints in the weekly meetings with Reagan economists, who accused them of trying to undermine the President. "I said, no, that's not true in any way," Schultz related. "We're not speaking against the tax cuts. We favor tax cuts for investment. We are arguing for greater budget cuts."

Shortly before the final vote in the House, Schultz had breakfast with the "boll weevils," the thirty or so southern Democrats whom the White House was counting on as the swing votes that would give the Republicans a majority on the tax bill in the Democratic-controlled House. Schultz told them: "You should know, if you vote for this bill, it is going to result in higher interest rates." His warning was not persuasive. "I only changed one vote," Schultz said. "The rest were all committed."

On July 27, the eve of the legislative showdown in the House, Ronald Reagan addressed the nation via television. "For nineteen out of the last twenty years, the federal government has spent more than it took in," the President said. "There will be another large deficit in this present year . . . but with out program in place, it won't be quite as big as it might have been. And starting next year, the deficits will get smaller until in just a few years the budget can be balanced." The President's senior advisers knew this was untrue.

The President was also upbeat about economic developments. "Businessmen and investors are making decisions with regard to industrial development, modernization and expansion—all of this based on anticipation of our program being adopted and put into operation," Reagan reported. White House economists knew that this also was untrue.

The President urged citizens to wire and phone their elected representatives in behalf of the Administration's tax bill, and a vast outpouring of popular support followed in subsequent days. Despite the months of partisan infighting, Congress did not need to be bludgeoned into voting for the across-the-board tax reduction. The House, where Republicans and Democrats fought for control, passed the Administration bill, 238 to 195, but even the rejected Democratic alternative was itself a statement that President Reagan's tax-cutting, antigovernment politics had triumphed. In the Senate, only eleven of the one hundred senators voted no.

The tax measure, aside from the deficits and other economic consequences, represented a profound change in political values. For the first time in many decades, Congress embraced an income-tax measure that was frankly regressive. Andrew Mellon's economic vision was triumphant again. The largest benefits in reduced tax burden would go to the wealthiest taxpayers, and the tax relief became proportionately smaller and smaller for families that were less well off. The poorest families in America, when Social Security taxes and the effects of Reagan budget cuts were considered, actually lost money.

Tax breaks for businesses were so generous that scores of major corporations would enjoy "negative tax rates" on their profits in the years ahead—the federal government literally owed them money. The effective tax rate for financial institutions, for instance, would drop from 5.8 percent in 1980, already one of the lowest rates for American industries, to −3.8 percent in 1982. Famous corporate names like General Electric were effectively relieved of taxation.[37]

As manager for the national economy, the government in the summer of 1981 provided a literal fulfillment of Wright Patman's old metaphor—the car with two drivers at the wheel. One was stepping on the gas and the other was stepping hard on the brakes. And the car, so to speak, was in the ditch.

The 1981 tax legislation proved to be regressive in a more fundamental way, hardly noted at the time. It became the pretext for a vast redistribution of incomes, flowing upward on the income ladder, through another powerful channel—interest rates. The price of money determined how the fruits of capitalist enterprise would be apportioned—the division of shares between creditors and debtors, between investors and entrepreneurs, between the old and the young, between workers and owners, The immediate consequence of the 1981 tax bill, virtually from the moment it was enacted, was higher interest rates. Paul Volcker's warnings proved correct. The division of wealth was tilted toward the top—a larger share would flow to those who already had accumulated wealth. There would be less for everyone else.

In July, the Federal Reserve, anticipating passage of the tax bill, decided not to ease, even though most committee members now understood that the economy was on the brink of recession. Interest rates should have been falling since business activity was slackening. Instead, the Federal Open Market Committee let the Federal Funds rate move a full point higher, adding more tension to the banking system, more pressure on the economy. The prime rate charged by commercial banks responded by rising to 20.5 percent.

The bond market tightened too. Long-term interest rates moved up as much as 200 basis points in two months' time as the tax bill was passed by Congress and signed by the President. Long rates should also have been declining as the economy's demand for investment funds subsided. Instead, investors were demanding extra protection against the future.

But what caused interest rates to go still higher? Both the Federal Reserve and the bond market blamed the surge on the Reagan Administration—the tax cuts and the prospect of huge deficits—and their argument was widely accepted as the standard explanation, regularly invoked in the political debates of subsequent years. As a matter of logic, however, the tax legislation could not itself have been the cause. Larger federal deficits, after all, did not appear instantly in midsummer of 1981 with enactment of the tax bill. The deficits emerged gradually over several years. Thus, there was no supply-and-demand squeeze on credit markets in July 1981 that could have pushed the interest rates upward. On the contrary, the demand for credit was actually slackening as the economy sank into recession.

The direct cause of the higher rates was the bond market and the Federal Reserve, reacting together. Both feared the same thing—the inflationary potential of the deficits—and both moved protectively, ahead of the fact. The Fed moved short-term rates higher, expressing the same anxiety as the bond market.

When a senator asked Volcker about the Fed's role, the chairman was typically opaque. "I certainly do not think in any fundamental sense that our policies are producing high interest rates," he said. "What's producing high interest rates is the situation we face, which is an inherited, deeply imbedded inflation, heavy credit demands, a pattern of high deficits." [38]

This became the standard line of evasion. The Fed itself had not initiated anything. It was merely reacting to conditions as it found them. And one of the principal conditions was the fragile psychology of the bond market—where investors were alarmed by the prospects of future inflation fueled by the Reagan deficits. The only way to assuage these fears ultimately was to eliminate the deficits. In the meantime, the Federal Reserve would demonstrate its own resolve by rigorously controlling money—keeping interest rates high.

And were these fears of inflation justified? The Fed's theoretical arguments were never confirmed by real events. The inflation rate was already moving lower and would continue to decline, notwithstanding larger and larger federal deficits. The Fed and financial markets, meanwhile, took real interest rates the other way. Perhaps someday the investors might be proved right about their fear of future inflation; one could hardly prove they were wrong. In the meantime, they would be well compensated for their anxieties—collecting a larger and larger real return on their capital.

For Wall Street, the reaction to the tax cuts was enormously hypocritical. Aside from sober investment bankers like Henry Kaufman, who had warned against the tax cuts, wealthy investors and major financial institutions were among the most ardent supporters (and beneficiaries) of the supply-side tax reductions. Yet they were the first to react negatively, once the President's legislation had triumphed.

Paul A. Samuelson, an elder eminence among Keynesian economists, observed caustically: "Wall Street, in early 1981, panted for the tax cuts simply for their favorable income effects. . . . Once Wall Street got its heart's desire, it quickly worked out the consequences. . . . So, immediately in mid-1981, Wall Street did what came naturally. It dumped its bonds, bidding up interest rates in the process. . . ."[39]

For the next five years, the anxieties presumed by the financial markets—and by the Federal Reserve—produced an additional toll on American economic life, one that would collect hundreds of billions of dollars in added interest costs. People and enterprises were compelled to pay an "inflation premium" to creditors—even though inflation was falling—in order to borrow their money. Between Congress and the President and the Federal Reserve, the federal government had made possible an income-transfer program of vast dimensions, only it did not appear on the books anywhere as a federal program.

The inexorable shift of wealth shares was reflected most precisely in what happened to the real price of money—the real interest rate, determined when the nominal interest rates were discounted for inflation. If the nominal interest rate was 10 percent and the rate of inflation was 6 percent, then the real price of money would be 4 percent. Years of inflation had benefited the debtor classes and businesses with cheap credit in real terms; now the advantage was shifted sharply to the creditors. When a family bought a home and took on a mortgage, they typically looked at the nominal interest rate. Wise lenders looked, instead, at the real rate of interest.

In normal times, for instance, the rule of thumb among commercial bankers was that the spread between their prime rate for loans and the inflation rate should be 3 to 4 percent. Early in 1980, when the Fed first pushed up interest rates, the bankers' real-interest spread grew above 4 percent. By early 1981, the real interest rate on bank loans climbed above 8 percent. By the sumer of 1981, it was briefly above 9 percent.[40]

The real return on long-term credit was likewise pushed up dramatically. A Federal Reserve staff economist calculated that the real interest rate on twenty-year government bonds averaged only .6 percent when inflation was soaring in 1979—well below the historic norm for a fair return, around 2 percent or less. In the summer of 1981, the real rate on long bonds jumped from 2.9 to 5.1 percent—roughly double the historic return.[41]

The explanation was not complicated. Inflation was abating—while the nominal interest rates were increasing. When a family or small-business man borrowed at 11 or 12 percent in the late 1970s, it sounded expensive but was actually a good deal. The 11 percent money was cheap because inflation was running at 8 or 9 percent or even higher. In the 1980s, the real cost of the same transaction became steadily more and more expensive.

In broad terms, this represented an ever-expanding share for those with money to lend and invest and the transfer of real wealth from anyone who borrowed. One did not have to be rich to benefit. Elderly widows with savings would enjoy the rising real return on their bank CDs too. But millionaires and giant financial institutions would profit most substantially. The financial sector would flourish and the productive economy would pay a heavier price in order to function. Young families, just starting out in life, would confront higher hurdles than anything their parents had faced. By the summer of 1981, the real price of money was higher than it had been in fifty years and it would go still higher.

Whether people profited or lost from these new terms depended, in large measure, on where they stood in the spectrum of economic interests, less on their personal skills or energy. A farmer, after all, could not simply stop being a farmer and decide to be a bond investor. A home builder or an auto worker could hardly quit and go into banking. Many of them would be ruined, and after the fact, their failure would be blamed on their own miscalculations. American finance, meanwhile, would enter its most profitable cycle of the century.

12

THAT OLD-TIME
RELIGION

"The furniture industry is dead," Elizabeth Brock declared. "That means my sawmill is dead." Brock operated a lumber company in north Georgia, International Hardwoods. The gathering recession had reduced her work force by 60 percent. "I have a small pallet plant that we take the low-grade lumber that the furniture factories cannot buy and we make hardwood pallets for the manufacturing and warehousing industries," she explained. "Wooden pallets are a capital investment for most warehousemen. They cannot afford to make any capital investments right now."

Brock described the poignant reality facing her employees and herself:

Yesterday was a cold day in the mountains of north Georgia. I had men standing around a barrel fire begging me to put them to work. I have no work for them. I cannot buy logs to cut lumber because I cannot sell the lumber. My loggers are standing there in their underwear and mackinaws freezing to death saying, "Find us some trees to cut."

I cannot find money to buy logs to set the lumber on my yard. I do not have that kind of money. I cannot borrow it because the money is too expensive. If I could, who is going to loan the woman money to set the lumber on a yard when God knows when she is going to sell it?

Like other small businesses, Brock's company was now threatened with the possibility of failure, at which point its productive assets would typically be sold to a larger corporation. Companies that were strong enough to weather the depressed conditions would be in a position to buy up real estate or machinery from smaller, failed enterprises at bargain prices. Recession encouraged the consolidation of ownership.

In the sawmill business [Brock explained], it is a rough man's world and 40 percent of my friends in the business have sold out to larger companies because they could not hang on any longer. Some of them have just shut their mills down, walked away, laid their people off and said to the bank, "There it is." I hope I do not have to do that, but it is getting scary.

The bigger conglomerates are having a tough time too. They are shutting down some mills. But they can afford to right now, so far. The Georgia-Pacifics, International Paper, Weyerhaeusers are standing like vultures over us little people, waiting until we say we have had enough, swooping in, paying us twenty-five cents on the dollar for machinery that is terribly expensive. Then we are left there with a hard life that we have lived, trying to put these businesses together.[1]

The logic swept across America, like a deep and irresistible wave. The high price of credit, engineered by the government, drove away customers and also raised the cost of doing business. Retailers found themselves burdened with swollen inventories of goods they could not sell. Manufacturers, in turn, received dwindling orders for new production. At a certain point, they closed the shops and mills and mines and sent the workers home. As more and more workers were severed from their jobs and incomes, consumer demand naturally declined further, the backlog of unsold goods grew larger. Soon everything would be in surplus, particularly the workers themselves.

Eventually, the process would produce the intended results. Sooner or later, both labor and business would have to yield, however reluctantly, to the ancient law of the marketplace: when supply exceeds demand, prices fall. More precisely, neither workers nor business managements could continue raising the price of whatever they sold, whether the commodity was labor or oil or automobiles, in the face of burgeoning surpluses. There was nothing subtle or mysterious about this. The process did not depend on intangible psychology or arcane theories of money. If the Federal Reserve succeeded in breaking inflation, it would be accomplished by the brute mechanics of surplus and failure.

General Electric's Appliance Park in Louisville, Kentucky, was considered a good bellwether for the entire economy. In six sprawling factory buildings, the mammoth manufacturing plant supplied the nation with GE washers and dryers, electric ranges, refrigerators, dishwashers and room air conditioners. All of these products were sensitive to the changing moods of the buying public, to housing starts and the formation of new households, and to consumer interest rates. Appliance Park employed fifteen thousand men and women, union machinists, metal fabricators, electricians and other workers who earned premier industrial wages. Some savvy economists made a practice of checking the production schedules for Appliance Park as a way to test their macroeconomic forecasts against everyday reality.

In August 1981, Appliance Park ordered its first layoffs, 850 workers. In November, another 1,150 would be sent home. During 1982, another 3,000 employees would lose their jobs. Through the course of the recession, each of the appliance divisions would be temporarily shut down at least once. All told, five thousand jobs were eliminated, one-third of the work force. Afterward, when Appliance Park eventually returned to its full capacity, none of these people would get their old jobs back. They were displaced by automation and other cost-cutting improvements. For General Electric, the lull of recession was an opportunity to become more efficient and profitable. For five thousand workers, it meant searching for other permanent employment.[2]

The linkage of retrenchment rippled through the economy in diverse and circular ways, as Eldon Kirsch, an official of the United Steelworkers, understood. Kirsch's district represented iron-ore miners on the Mesabi Range of northern Minnesota, where the taconite mines laid off three thousand, but it also included fabricating plants in Duluth and St. Joseph, where employment was reduced to skeletal maintenance crews.

When we talk about jobs, how we are going to get jobs in the taconite industry, the only way to get jobs is to produce taconite [Kirsch said]. To produce taconite, there has to be a need for steel. To have a need for steel, you have to have cars to buy and houses to build. The housing industry is down 40 to 50 percent. The car industry is down 40 to 50 percent. There is no demand for it. The reason there is no demand—put yourself as an employee in a fabricating plant, iron-ore mine, making from $20,000 to $30,000 a year. How could you afford to pay 20 percent interest? I think it was twice that other car companies came out here a while back at 13.8 percent. How can you afford to pay that? Can you afford to pay $800 a month for a car payment or $600 for a car payment?[3]

In a sense, the iron miners lost their jobs because, first, the government raised the price of cars. When working people like themselves could no longer afford to buy cars, the miners were put out of work.

Many of them understood what was happening intuitively, without the need for sophisticated economic analysis. The favorable balance had shifted from production to finance, from labor to capital, and they could see this clearly enough in their own lives.

Robert Williams, a laid-off miner from Nassau, Minnesota, testified:

I am so scared now as far as what is going to happen. If I buy something on loan, how will I pay for it if I don't have a job tomorrow? I am living in constant fear of tomorrow. I am hoarding my money. Say I am lucky and I have $10,000 in a T-bill. Will I buy a new car or secondhand car? If I can get 18 percent interest on a "money market" on my $10,000, that would be an annual raise of $2,400 a year. So I would be a fool to buy a new car. I will put my money in the bank and let it sit. The guy with the money has it made. The little guy will take his knocks from now until who knows when.[4]

Personal fear was a necessary element of the process too. Unemployment was rising. Home building was approaching a fifteen-year low. The more anxious people became about their future incomes, the less likely they were to borrow and buy. Their insecurities would moderate the demands of their union contract negotiators and contribute directly to braking the escalation of wages and prices.

I have been out of work since May [said Arthur Estrella, a fifty-five-year-old steelworker at Washburn Wire in Providence, Rhode Island]. My benefits are very small. I get unemployment right now. I was getting $130, then I got $143. I have a mortgage to pay—$166.42. I have fuel bills now I can't pay. In fact, I had no food last week in the house. I had to pay my mortgage of $166. You can tell me how you can pay it out of $143. That is pretty rough. I have put applications into plants which, after I put them in, they laid off several people. There is no jobs around. The economy is very, very poor.

Arthur Estrella's co-worker at Washburn Wire, James McCafferty, also lost his job after thirty years at the plant, but he counted himself lucky. "I was fortunate," he said. "Through a friend of mine, I was able to get employed as a security guard. But that is about half of what I would normally be making."[5]

Rhode Island, like other states, experienced a rising tide of bankruptcy. In 1979, 226,000 families had filed and in 1980 the number jumped to 360,000. By 1981, personal bankruptcies reached 519,000 in the state. Rhode Island's business bankruptcies increased from 29,500 to 66,000. Bankruptcy was the forced liquidation of credit, a legal declaration that the borrower could no longer sustain his obligations and the creditors would have to settle for less and extinguish the debt.

A bankruptcy lawyer from Tucson, Arizona, Lowell Rothschild, described what he called the "domino effect" of failure:

If you have high interest and people do not buy houses, the builders don't build them. If they don't build them, the subs cannot work on them. If the subs cannot work on them, the carpenters, the masons, the plumbers have no work and they cannot pay their consumer debt. And that is the domino effect. You don't have to be an economist. It is a very simple process. There are no jobs.

In Clarkston, Washington, Durward DeChenne was sixty-five years old and preparing to retire when the high interest rates hit—driving customers away from his marine-equipment store, raising the carrying costs of the boats and snowmobiles on his display floor. "I thought it was a short-term deal, that we might be able to carry it over," DeChenne said. He was paying 24 percent interest on his inventory. His sales fell from $2 million a year to $600,000. DeChenne worked a year without pay, trying to save his business, then he closed the doors.

"We lost half of what we ever had, of everything we made in twenty-one years," he said. "We just had to close it up and take our lumps."

Like many victims, DeChenne did not blame Washington, neither President Reagan nor the Federal Reserve. "The President is on the right track, even though he put me out of work," he said. "He had to put somebody out of work and somebody out of business."[6]

But, in Mount Ayr, Iowa, a salesman named Jim Clark thought the government should have applied the pressure more gradually—or at least told people what was coming. When Clark bought the local Allis-Chalmers dealership in April 1981, he had no way of knowing that it was absolutely the worst moment to realize his dream of owning his own business. The local bank that financed the purchase and the Small Business Administration that guaranteed the loan did not seem to know it either. When the recession finally ended, Jim Clark's store would be padlocked and he would be $225,000 in debt, working as a laborer at F & S Feed Grain.

"The government is at fault," Clark said. "When they decided to stop inflation, it needed to be slowed down. But they should have used the brakes instead of the wall."[7]

Some Americans reacted to their distress with a jaunty good humor. Dan Issa, a city councilman from Central Falls, Rhode Island, was among 150 people who lost their jobs at the Corning Glass plant. Issa joked about a cartoon he had seen in the newspaper. "I may not be an economist," the man said, "but I know when I am broke."

And many ordinary citizens felt frustration and confusion and anger. All of these emotions boiled up in Manny Dembs, a home builder from Detroit, Michigan, when he appeared before the Senate Banking Committee in Washington. Dembs was testifying with a panel of fellow builders, but when his turn came to speak, he was choking with outrage. His rambling outburst was a coarse soliloquy on the impotence of citizens like himself.

Excuse me, but I am angry and I'm hot [Manny Dembs told the senators]. Let me go into something here that bothers the heck out of me—on October the sixth, 1979, two years ago, two years ago, when the policy of the Federal Reserve Board decided to change the rules, instead of going on interest, they went on reserve requirements, et cetera. At that point, they made a decision and for two years we have been up and down, prime up, prime down. When I buy land, I buy a land contract and I can't buy every day changing my mind. . . . I kept reading *The Wall Street Journal* every hour, every second, every minute, to see M-1 and M-2. I didn't know what the hell M-1 and M-2 meant. . . .

I am telling you, it cost me $20,000 in interest on overhead on fifty-two houses, $1 million in thirty years. I am going out of business. Thirty years, with my wife and three kids, and I got to worry about what the Reserve Board is going to do. I want the Reserve Board to retire themselves, the overall Reserve Board. We got the executive, we got the judicial, but we don't have the Federal Reserve Board as a form of government. They're economists, but they're running our country.

We have got to do something to change it. What I would like to ask you, do something to change it. What I want you to do, I think all the Republicans, all the Democrats in Congress, stop playing politics with my life. I say: "Mr. Volcker, you are chairman of the board. Resign, resign! I don't care if you are right or wrong. You are in charge, get out!"

I'm not a politician. I am just a builder, ready on the line, trying to make a buck. I don't know these people, the Milton Friedmans, Beryl Sprinkel, the Volckers. I'm reading about all these people. These people scare me. I am worried about my country. I am worried that I am going to go down the drain. . . .

The bankers, who are these bankers? They're running our country. I don't know why. But it isn't a person. I am Manny Dembs and I compete with Wall Street. I'm not dumb. I'm not powerful enough. I'm a single citizen. I vote and I come to Washington. I talk to you people, I talk to bankers . . . I respect you people in Congress, but what you should do, stand up, all of you. Federal Reserve Board, don't run my country. Don't run me.

Manny Dembs paused, out of breath, exhausted by his anger and in tears. "I could go on and on," he said, "but I want to give somebody else a chance." The senators expressed sympathy and thanked him for his testimony.[8]

One commodity remained in scarce supply—bank credit. While other producers struggled with their unsold surpluses, the purveyors of credit continued to enjoy a sellers' market. Incomes and profits shrank in virtually all other economic sectors, but commercial banks prospered from the general distress. Recession, perverse as it seemed, actually increased the profits of banking.

Like other aspects of the contraction, this phenomenon was almost never discussed by government economists, but it was still visible to ordinary citizens who could figure out the reality for themselves. Martin Bacal, for instance, president of a family business, the Pioneer Paint & Varnish Company in Tucson, Arizona, was taken aback by a newspaper article reporting that the profits of Tucson banks were going up as the recession took hold.

> And they were up very substantially [Bacal said]. Very substantial. I begin to wonder. I talk to my own banker and have been told, "Yes, the bank is doing very well." Yet the rest of us are not. It kind of makes sense. We are paying 20 percent, 24 percent, and can only earn 7 or 8 percent. We cannot be doing very well. But they are. And I have never understood. The Federal Reserve seems to be banker-oriented. And I wonder if ever we are going to see, as long as that board has the autonomy to determine interest rates and in effect economic policy, if we are ever going to see a return to lower rates.[9]

What was true in Tucson was true everywhere in America. Starting in 1979, when the Fed first pushed up interest rates, commercial banking entered its most profitable era since World War II. Banking's net operating income increased 10.3 percent in 1980, despite the brief recession, and grew by another 9 percent in 1981, while the economy as a whole contracted. The basic measure of bank profitability—the return on equity—reached a historic peak, far above banking's best years in the previous three decades. The largest gains in profit were made by the largest banks.

This striking change in the fortunes of bankers was reflected in the Federal Reserve's reporting on bank holding companies. For the previous decade, the banks' return on equity had averaged slightly more than 11 percent. In 1979, it jumped to a new record of 13.9 percent. The profit rate for banks remained nearly that high through the next three years while the economy at large struggled with failure and retrenchment.

Stated another way, bank profits increased by more than 25 percent while the returns on other kinds of enterprise were headed in the opposite direction. Professor Gerald Epstein, an economist at the New School for Social Research, worked out this comparison: the before-tax profits of the corporate sector, excluding finance, declined to an average of 10.7 percent for the recession-plagued years of 1979 to 1982, compared to the long-term average of 15.9 percent profits for the years 1960 to 1978. Commercial banks, during the same four years, increased their average return on equity to 13.2 percent, up from the long-term average of 10.4 percent.[10]

The mechanics of recession virtually guaranteed this outcome, especially for larger banks that depended on the managed-liabilities strategy, borrowing funds in the money market in order to lend them out again to bank customers. On the upside, as interest rates were rising, banks could increase their interest-rate spreads. But the real profits came on the downside—when the economy was declining and interest rates were subsiding. At that point, the banks would still be collecting payments on old loans made when interest rates were at their peak, but they would be raising funds in the money market at the lower interest rates now available as demand slackened. Their incomes remained high while their operating costs declined—a widening spread that translated into greater profits.

Efficient bankers naturally tried to maintain the mismatch as long as they could. Typically, they decreased their loan rates as the economy went into recession—but more slowly than the decline of money-market rates on which banks themselves borrowed. In short, as the recession unfolded and gathered force, banks lent expensive money and funded the loans with cheaper money.

Paul Volcker's initiative against inflation, whatever other long-term benefits it promised for the general economy, was, first of all, good for the banks, the Federal Reserve's primary constituency. This was not peculiar to Volcker's regime—recessions always improved bank earnings, at least for a time. Similar though milder increases in bank profits had accompanied previous contractions when the Fed pushed up interest rates and induced recession. Volcker's offensive against inflation was more aggressive than any in the past, pushing interest rates to historic levels, and so his era produced a profit surge for banking that was more extreme too.

Eventually, if the recession continued long enough and the business failures spread too widely, the banks would also suffer. When their loan customers were forced to the wall and could no longer pay their debts, the bankers would be forced to write off more and more loans at a loss, losses subtracted from the profitable aspects of recession. For a time, however, the recession strengthened banking.

This economic reality—banks profit in recessions—cast a some-what different light on the confidential advice that the Federal Reserve received regularly from the bankers. The twelve commercial bankers of the Federal Advisory Council, who met privately with the Federal Reserve Board four times a year, were not exactly disinterested con-sultants, devoted solely to the goal of "sound economics." When these bankers urged the Fed to tighten its money control, to tolerate high rates and recession, and, above all, to ignore the inevitable "political" complaints from other interests, they were in fact arguing for the policy that would enhance their own profits. For two years, without surcease, the Federal Advisory Council had been imploring, warning, scolding Volcker and his colleagues. The tough monetary policy the bankers had advocated was now in place and, as a businessman might say, it went straight to the banks' bottom line.

As the recession got under way in the third quarter of 1981, the Fed asked its advisory council of bankers to evaluate "the present condi-tion of financial institutions under the stresses they are encountering." In response, the Federal Advisory Council did not mention the "stress" of record-high profits, but the bankers modestly allowed that banks seemed to be holding up all right. "Although earnings are lower than desirable," they reported, "large banks generally have been able to cope with uncomfortably high interest rates."

According to the Fed's own statistics, the larger banks "coped" with high interest rates in 1981 by producing a return on their equity of 13.66 percent—a banner year, despite the stresses and strains, far better than anything the major banks had enjoyed in the 1950s, 1960s or 1970s.

Their customers were not doing so well, the bankers added. Neither were their competitors, the savings and loan industry. The S & L's were saddled with portfolios of long-term home mortgages, issued years before at lower interest rates, and so the interest-rate peak damaged them severely. The thrifts were suffering operating losses of growing proportions, their capital positions were weakening.

As for business, generally, the Federal Advisory Council took note of the developing distress: "Overall, high interest rates have created additional financial strains on bank customers, including a significant increase in bankruptcies. Existing loan portfolios show some quality deterioration and this has persuaded banks to adopt more cautious lending policies."[11]

When Vice President George Bush returned home from an overseas trip in midsummer, 1981, he expressed his puzzlement. In Paris, Bush had met with the French government's senior economic officials and they had complained about "the high U.S. interest-rate policy," Bush told a Cabinet Council meeting at the White House. They had used the phrase, he said, "as if U.S. policy was aimed at trying to raise and keep interest rates high." The socialists in Paris appeared to have a clearer grasp of what was happening to global capitalism than did the conservative Republican.[12]

The mechanics of money pay no respect to national boundaries, and the Federal Reserve's high interest rates were forcing great shifts in commerce and finance upon the entire world. The global economy was sinking into recession too, large nations and small ones alike. When the richest market in the world, the American economy, declined, exporters around the world lost their best customer. Moreover, the central banks of other industrial nations raised their interest rates too, supporting Volcker's initiative against inflation and depressing their own domestic economies. When the locomotive pulled the world's economy forcefully in one direction, the rest of the train followed.

France, with its new socialist government, tried for a time to go the other way. François Mitterrand attempted to stimulate his domestic economy as the U.S. and others were dampening theirs and discovered painfully that it couldn't be done. Capital fled from French enterprises in search of the higher returns available overseas; the French franc was depreciated rapidly. Instead of faster growth and full employment, the Mitterrand government got stagnation and inflation.

The ascendant U.S. dollar was now the symbol of restored American hegemony. Once derided by the Europeans as weak and unreliable, the dollar was becoming harder and harder, as U.S. inflation moderated. The higher interest rates available in the U.S. attracted more and more foreign wealth to dollar-denominated financial assets (including foreign wealth held as overseas capital by America's own multinational corporations). The worldwide demand for dollars was increasing, but the supply of dollars was still held tight by the Fed, so naturally the international price for dollars went up—the foreign-exchange rate at which other currencies were converted into U.S. dollars. An international bank or a corporation or private investor who wished to buy dollar assets would have to pay with more francs or pounds or Deutsche marks.

From July 1980 to September 1981, the dollar appreciated by 36 percent in its international-exchange value with the German mark. It appreciated by 5 percent against the yen, 26 percent against the Swiss franc, 34 percent against the British pound.[13] Now the allied governments were complaining that the dollar was being driven too high on foreign-exchange markets and they urged the United States to moderate its policy.

The hapless bystanders in the process were the less-developed nations of the Third World, whose economies still depended largely on primitive capitalism, selling their raw commodities, from coffee and sugar to copper and rubber, to the industrialized nations. What was to become a severe recession for Americans would be catastrophe for the citizens of these poorer countries in Africa and Latin America and Asia. Their economic output and real incomes fell disastrously, as much as 10 percent in some instances, as their export markets dried up and commodity prices began to fall sharply. These producers were stuck with surplus too.

Falling copper prices helped reduce the cost to American manufacturers and consumers; it meant crippling losses for Chile or Zaire. Unlike the diverse American economy, the underdeveloped nations could not simply shut down the factory and wait for the recession to be over. Mining raw materials and the production of agricultural commodities were, in many cases, the core of their economies and the major employers. Closing the copper mines was an invitation to social rebellion. Instead, they kept mines operating and sold their production at a loss.

Simultaneously, the debt burdens of the less-developed countries—the LDCs in common parlance—expanded dangerously. The worldwide spike in interest rates had raised the cost of the debt, the hundreds of billions in outstanding loans from the banks of Europe and America. Both governments and businesses in the struggling nations were compelled to borrow more and more, simply to keep up the payments on their old loans—at the very time their economies were contracting dramatically.

But the stronger dollar also came home to the United States. It was another channel through which the Fed's monetary policy depressed the American economy. Just as high interest rates drove away the domestic customers for goods and services, the stronger dollar drove away foreign buyers of American products. It made U.S. exports proportionately more expensive for overseas customers, and at the same time, the appreciating dollar made foreign imports cheaper in the American marketplace. The grain from Iowa or Kansas now cost much more in France. The machine tools made in Germany could underprice American competitors from Cincinnati and take away customers in their own domestic market.

By the autumn of 1981, the damage was already considerable and obvious. American farmers saw their grain exports declining—a crucial outlet for the abundant overproduction of U.S. agriculture. U.S. manufacturing, meanwhile, was losing both exports and domestic market shares. Through the 1970s, the constant complaints about the weak dollar had overlooked the fact that the currency imbalance permitted an export boom for America's mercantile interests. Strong trade had meant higher employment and an expanding productive base. The trade-off was inflation. Now, in the interest of halting price inflation, the boom was over.

The Federal Reserve governors were concerned enough to ask the Federal Advisory Council for an assessment of the dollar's impact on trade. At its September meeting, the bankers' council provided a grim summary: an expected decline of 1.3 percent in U.S. exports this year and another $25 billion loss next year.

New England's high-technology merchandise has experienced sluggish export activity [the council reported]. Textile manufacturing representatives report a 35 percent rise in American textile prices, coupled with 5 percent decline in domestic output. A major Midwest chemical and textile manufacturer is struggling with a significant 15 percent falloff in overseas shipments.

The nation's steel industry has been especially hard hit; imports now represent 17.5 percent of the American steel market, resulting in price restraints on domestic products and a depression in the export market. U.S. agricultural exports, both food and fiber, are slowing. The expected value of those exports will be several billion dollars below forecasts made by the U.S. Department of Agriculture just four months ago. These downward adjustments have been linked directly to the stronger international value of the dollar.

But what damaged American production was rewarding for American finance, especially for the major banks active in international markets. The rising dollar meant simply that the value of their overseas dollars was rising too. It also meant that market demand was growing for the commodity that American financial institutions traded —U.S. financial assets. As long as the Fed held interest rates high— higher than competing returns in foreign countries—capital naturally flowed across boundaries, seeking the higher returns available in American financial instruments. And, as the demand for dollars increased, the dollar would naturally get harder and harder in foreign exchange. In other words, the stronger dollar was good for business— if your business was finance.

In political terms, the Reagan Administration had the power to intervene with the Fed, but did not use it. The dollar's international value was one of the few areas of monetary policy where both law and tradition gave the executive branch higher authority than the Federal Reserve. The Treasury Secretary was responsible for U.S. dollar policy, and if he wished, he could advise the Fed to adjust its domestic interest rates accordingly.

Or Treasury could coordinate interventions in foreign-exchange markets—buying or selling dollars by both Treasury and the Fed—to push the price of the dollar up or bring it down. Given the fundamentals, interventions would not likely have changed the basic trend launched by the Fed, but the Reagan Administration didn't believe in them anyway. It was committed to laissez-faire—let the markets decide what the dollar is worth and don't interfere.

With this attitude, the Reagan Administration was, ironically, surrendering its one legitimate avenue for political leverage over the central bank. It was not clear that senior political advisers at the White House, none of whom was especially sophisticated about money politics, understood the implications. The men in charge at the Federal Reserve certainly did. As Anthony Solomon of the New York Fed explained:

If Treasury wants a monetary policy that strengthens the dollar or weakens it, we have to listen to that. But, when you have a Treasury that doesn't care, then it cannot expect to tell us what domestic monetary policy should be. If you have a Treasury that doesn't care about the dollar, you've removed the one legitimate channel of executive-branch influence over the Federal Open Market Committee.

Jude Wanniski was one of those rare characters who hung around the edges of political power and, without portfolio, bombarded the incumbents of government with his complaints and suggestions. In the 1970s, Wanniski's articles in *The Wall Street Journal* and elsewhere had helped to create political acceptability for the idea of supply-side tax cuts. He was a relentless advocate for gold. He was a close adviser to Representative Jack Kemp and other conservative reformers. Now, with Ronald Reagan in power, Wanniski kibitzed his friends in the White House and at Treasury and even dined infrequently with the chairman of the Federal Reserve. No one could say whether Wanniski had any actual influence on government policy, but important people listened to him.

"I've sworn I'd never write to you unless the news was really bad. It's now bad enough," Jude Wanniski wrote to President Reagan in the fall of 1981. He enclosed a magazine article he had written on the economic disorders and urged the President to read it carefully because "it represents the viewpoint of the supply siders outside your Administration, a viewpoint you have not been getting inside. . . .

"We are on the verge of a global depression," Wanniski warned, "but your economic advisers are blinded by the slide in interest rates into predicting prosperity just around the corner."

He explained that the world economy "has been led into recession and the path of a gathering financial storm by obsolete U.S. monetary policy." To avert disaster, the government must abandon the monetarist doctrine of Milton Friedman and swiftly adopt a new gold standard.

The President's reply, a few weeks later, left Wanniski dejected.

DEAR JUDE,
Thanks very much for your letter and for the script of the *Business Week* article. I've read it and assure you it is being distributed "in house."

I know there is great difference on this subject among top economists, even with one of my favorite people Milton F. opposed, but I'm looking hard at it. As you know, I have a task force studying gold, so will refrain from comment until they report in.

Please believe me, there is less disarray among our family here than the press would lead you to believe. I'm totally pledged to our economic program (the tax cuts), and no one is pushing the other way.[14]

Wanniski was crestfallen. Reagan's letter was a polite brush-off. To Wanniski, the meaning was clear: Milton Friedman would remain the regnant intellectual guiding the President's thinking, the monetarist approach at the Fed would continue with White House encouragement and the rigid control of the money supply would play out to inevitable consequences—a long and severe recession.

On October 18, for the first time, the President had personally announced the recession. Unemployment was ratcheting upward each month, above 8 percent and headed for double digits (in the 1980 campaign, Reagan had decried the "Carter depression" when unemployment was at 7.6 percent). Interest rates were subsiding at last and price inflation too, but the economic contraction was the visible event. Responding to reporters' questions on the White House lawn, Reagan said, "I think there's a slight recession and, I hope, a short recession. I think everyone agrees on that."

The President's rhetoric now shifted perceptibly. His predictions of an imminent surge in investment and growth disappeared, replaced by an emphasis on the sins of the past. Jimmy Carter was to blame. Carter had allowed the inflation and, therefore, Carter was responsible for the recession.[15] Instead of robust claims, the President offered anecdotes of heroic sacrifice. A blind veteran of World War II had written in Braille, Reagan said, to volunteer a cut in his disabled veteran's benefits if that would help the country get back on the right track.

We're going through a period of difficult and painful readjustment [the President acknowledged in a television speech to the nation]. I know that we're asking for sacrifices for virtually all of you, but there is no alternative. Some of those who oppose this plan have participated over the years in the extravagance that has brought us inflation, unemployment, high interest rates and an intolerable debt. . . . I believe we've chosen a path that leads to an America at work, to fiscal sanity, to lower taxes and less inflation. . . .[16]

The rhetoric of shared sacrifice and necessary pain, the price that must be paid for previous extravagance, was the moral center of what Ronald Reagan really believed about the gathering recession and the American economy. His optimistic rhetoric notwithstanding, the President could not have been surprised by the spreading economic distress that was closing businesses and putting people out of work. In a deeper sense, this was what he had always expected and, indeed, what he had long recommended. The optimism was genuine enough, but Ronald Reagan also believed in a sterner economic doctrine that politicians referred to as the "old-time religion."

Before he became President, Reagan had articulated this viewpoint regularly in his syndicated radio talks and speeches. The nation, he would warn, faced a big "bellyache" of unemployment and recession as punishment for its inflationary excesses. In 1978, Reagan confided to a newspaper interviewer: "I'm afraid this country is just going to have to suffer two, three years of hard times to pay for the binge we've been on."

As a presidential candidate, Reagan had been persuaded by advisers to drop the line about a national "bellyache." The ominous talk would drive off potential voters; people did not want to elect a President who promised them two or three years of hard times. The "old-time religion" was derided by supply-side apostles like Kemp and Wanniski and economist Arthur Laffer, who complained that adherence to "root-canal economics" had defeated a generation of conservative Republican doomsayers.

The "bellyache" prescription disappeared from Reagan's speeches, but not from his thinking. "Reagan learned from Carter," one aide explained. "You don't get any mileage out of telling people how hard it's going to be." But, in the Oval Office, as the recession gathered force, the President frequently expressed his conviction that the suffering was inevitable and necessary.[17]

The purgatory view of inflation was out of sight, but not out of mind [David Stockman said]. It was never articulated in public, but privately the President was tolerant of the circumstances. It fulfilled the old Ronald Reagan's expectations of what would happen when you shifted from

Keynesian liberalism to a sound policy. The President would say to us: "We've been on a binge for thirty years. This is the price you have to pay."

William Niskanen, a member of Reagan's Council of Economic Advisers, said many others shared the faith: "There was a fairly widespread consensus within the Administration that we had to tolerate a mild recession to get inflation down. We were Calvinists in a way. The feeling was that good things don't all come in a package, that you have to have a little pain."

The metaphors these public men chose to describe their secular ideas—"old-time religion" and "purgatory" and "Calvinist"—revealed the religious content of their economics. Unlike the abstract language of economics, the religious phrases suggested the deeper emotional context of what was happening. Purgatory meant purposeful suffering to achieve redemption.

"Capitalist rationality does not do away with sub- or superrational impulses," Joseph Schumpeter wrote. "It merely makes them get out of hand by removing the restraint of sacred or semisacred tradition." Capitalism also adapted sacred tradition to its own uses, inventing a rationalistic logic that corresponded with the oldest rituals of worship and cloaked the nonrational impulses in scientific garb.

Every important economic theory, one could say, relied upon an unstated subtext drawn from religious convictions. To declare correct principles for the functioning of the economy, one would first have to make certain assumptions about the larger nature of life itself—about God's purpose and humanity's obligations and the moral law that derived from the relationship of deity and mortals. Monetarists, for instance, assumed an immutable natural order, knowable limits that worldly existence imposed on human behavior and predictable penalties for folly and error. The money rule was described as a golden mean: a society that faithfully adhered to it would enjoy the maximum of what was possible in life. If society strayed too far from its path, like Icarus daring to fly too close to the sun, disorder and retribution would result. The advocates of gold relied upon divine authority to enforce this natural order. If humankind pledged obedience to God's indestructible metal, it would be rewarded with an eternal assurance of stability. Both doctrines, gold and monetarism, were expressions of premodernist fundamentalism, simple and certain moral formulas for life, and their certitudes had deep appeal, especially in anxious times.

In this context, Keynes and his followers were the heretics. They were secular humanists who claimed that men and women could responsibly manage human affairs for themselves. They were rationalists who dismissed the "old-time religion" and its false moral commandments. Universal human pleasure, Keynes announced, did not require a requisite measure of Calvinist pain. It required the application of human intelligence.

When Americans judged economic events or political agendas, they worked off the same subtext, the same set of religious assumptions. Like the President himself, citizens were capable of simultaneously embracing conflicting sensibilities, both the old-fashioned Protestant ethic and the humanist faith of abundance. They believed in the here and now—easy credit, full employment and the economic guarantees of the welfare state. But they also still believed, down deep, that sinful excess must be punished, that suffering was necessary for redemption. The recession fulfilled their expectation.

The "old-time religion" was unacceptable as an explicit theme in a political campaign, but it connected with deeply held beliefs—and a large reservoir of collective guilt. The disorders of inflation produced complicated anxieties that included a sense that, as Reagan put it, everyone must pay for the "binge."

These underlying attitudes were suggested, at least obliquely, in the public-opinion polls on inflation. During the 1980 presidential election, when political candidates were accentuating the positive, the public expressed an overwhelming pessimism: the country would have to undergo a recession in order to slow down inflation. By a 2-to-1 majority, people agreed with Ronald Reagan's unexpressed conviction that the nation must endure a "bellyache" in order to cure itself. According to a Harris poll, 55 percent even said they would favor measures to bring on a recession if that would stop inflation.[18]

With a politician's intuition, Ronald Reagan perhaps grasped that his Calvinist dogma was not altogether out of step with what the electorate really believed. A prudent candidate would not speak of these things directly, but people understood the moral commandment better than they acknowledged. In the spring of 1981, public opinion swung to a much more optimistic frame of mind, as the President campaigned for his economic agenda. The majority appeared to believe his promises of economic recovery. By the fall, however, most had returned to their original pessimism. They could see for themselves that the society was beginning to pay for its collective guilt. The suffering was what they had expected all along.

In the political economy, as in the church, ritual atonement required the elements of convincing theater. For the vast audience of faithful, an ancient religious drama was performed by two figures of mythic authority, the President and the Federal Reserve chairman, who presided like priest and prince on a stage of darkness and light. One was shadowy and remote, an ominous figure; the other, bright and cheerful. Paul Volcker was the stern father who admonished and prophesied, uttering mysterious incantations of numbers. Ronald Reagan was the generous king who inspired hope, whose rhetoric evoked streaks of sunshine across the darkened sky. Together, they promised redemption—if only the faithful flock would first accept the penitential sacrifice.

The ritual of atonement could even be satisfying. Most Americans, after all, would not suffer grievously from the economic contraction. They would witness the dislocations and failure around them, but they would not themselves have to endure the worst of it. Millions of wage earners would lose their livelihoods, but the majority would not. Tens of thousands of businesses would be driven to bankruptcy, but most would survive. For most Americans, the recession meant at most a postponement of their economic ambitions, a time to pull back and wait until the "bad times" passed. In exchange, they received an expunging of guilt.

The real burden of cleansing pain was borne disproportionately by a defenseless minority of Americans. The rest accepted this as morally wholesome or else pretended not to know. The political rhetoric of the leaders emphasized shared sacrifice, a period of national penance in which all participated, and this pretense enabled citizens to ignore the true moral content of the exercise. There was something bracing, spiritually invigorating, in the knowledge of "hard times," especially if one averted one's eyes and pretended that all were sharing in the sacrifice together. The social deception required a complicity of ignorance between citizens and their leaders.

The economic liquidation, in fact, resembled the form, though not the content, of a primitive religious practice—the pagan ritual of human sacrifice. Some individuals were chosen to serve as victims for the good of the entire society, sacrificed in order that the tribe would be restored to harmony with its gods. In moral terms, the process was sadistic, an example of what Thorstein Veblen called the enduring barbarism of modern society.

The economic victims were chosen at random, but mostly from among the weaker groups in the society. The methodology employed by the Federal Reserve to induce contraction—rationing credit by raising its price—insured that the strongest individuals and enterprises would be able to evade selection. There was this hierarchy within democracy—a hierarchy of vulnerability.

Many victims, ignorant of society's larger purpose, innocently protested. Such was the power of economic faith that some victims accepted their fate and even endorsed it as necessary. The moral justification was expressed in Schumpeter's ringing phrase, "creative destruction," which suggested that, from time to time, capitalism must burn off its dead and obsolete parts in order to grow freely again. The implication was that only deserving victims would be destroyed, punished for their inefficiency. But this article of faith did not correspond to reality. It would be more precise to say that victims were punished for not being stronger or larger. For the most part, their inefficiency consisted of not having the accumulated financial resources to protect themselves.

The religious subtext of economic recession helped to explain why people put up with it. The public's tolerance for the contraction and loss was conditioned by a deeper sense of religious awe. Moral objections and democratic qualms were stilled or at least moderated by primitive fears. The gods would be angry if the price was not paid. For a time at least, most Americans acquiesced, with pious sympathies, to the necessity that some among them must be punished. The authority to perform the sacrifice, whether people realized it or not, was implicit in the powers they had conferred, by democratic process, on their national government. The secular temple on Constitution Avenue fulfilled its sacred purpose.

Public acceptance of recession declined proportionately, however, as the ritual continued and the suffering spread. The longer it went on, the more distressing it became to people. Atonement was necessary, but perhaps the priests were going too far. The sacrifices began to seem greater than the burden of guilt required. As failure and unemployment spread through the society, it occurred to more and more citizens that they too might be chosen as victims.

The President's senior advisers were confronted by guilt of a more personal nature—their own guilt over the massive federal deficits they had created. By October, when the recession was well recognized, the President's chief of staff, James Baker, and his inner circle of legislative strategists were confronted with the reality of what their congressional victories had accomplished—budget imbalances on an unprecedented scale. In other circumstances, the White House might have turned its attention to the Federal Reserve's monetary policy and pushed for a speedy recovery. But Baker and his colleagues were preoccupied with the mess they had created themselves—a fiscal deficit that would grow to $200 billion a year.

The deficits became so big, so fast, the numbers traumatized the politicians, both in the White House and the Congress [David Stockman said].

It made the politicians in the White House feel so guilty. Baker's attitude was that deficits caused inflation and something had to be done about them first. The 1982 elections—my God, we're going to get wiped out. We have to do something to get the economy off its knees.

The embarrassment became their ruling preoccupation, which effectively muted the political pressures on the Fed. "The White House went into sheer panic over the deficits," a Treasury aide said, "and that panic drove economic policy. The Secretary of Treasury was frustrated about his inability to get anyone at the White House to focus on monetary policy."

Stockman added: "The effect of the triple-digit deficits was that it really forestalled or dulled what might have been the usual attacks on the Fed. There was a sense of guilt among the politicians. Because they were out of line so far on fiscal policy, they couldn't attack the Fed. It really produced a window of maneuverability for the Fed."

A consensus was quickly developing among Republican leaders in Congress and the President's senior advisers (though not including the President himself). One way or another, Congress would have to take back some of the generous tax cuts that it had enacted only a few months earlier. This question—how to reduce the massive deficits—became the absorbing issue for all of Washington.

Frederick Schultz, the Fed vice chairman, was at a Washington banquet when he fell into a dinner-table debate with Walter Wriston, CEO of Citibank. While Schultz and Wriston argued over the projected supply-side deficits, Senator Robert Dole, chairman of the Senate Finance Committee, sat at the same table and mostly listened.

I argued: you had to expect this [Schultz said]. It was clear that this was going to happen. If the Fed sticks to its guns, there was no way for interest rates to go but up. Wriston argued that it didn't have to happen. Walt believed in the supply-side thesis. He said there would be more capital spending and this would bring in more revenue and there was no reason the deficits should affect interest rates.

A few days later, Senator Dole encountered Fred Schultz in an elevator and informed him: "You won the debate. I think we are going to have to do something on the fiscal side."

Paul Volcker made the same plea in public. "We can't shrink from considering new revenue sources," he said. While the deficits temporarily cushioned the effects of the recession, they also heightened the long-term fears of financial markets. Short-term interest rates were declining, Volcker noted, but long-term rates remained "stubbornly high." Credit markets, he said, were worried that once economic expansion started again, the federal government would soak up the available capital for its own borrowing.[19]

In economists' circles, the collision was described respectfully as a "fiscal-monetary mismatch." The government was pulling the economy in opposite directions, stimulating and suppressing simultaneously, and monetary policy had won—overpowering fiscal policy. The predicament, however, actually enhanced the Federal Reserve's power. By enacting huge fiscal deficits, Congress and the President had effectively checkmated themselves. Practically speaking, they were confronted with only one option, the issue they would debate endlessly for the next five years—how to restore some balance to fiscal policy.

Given the box that elected politicians had put themselves in, they were impotent to control things. The Federal Reserve was the only lever of macroeconomic management that remained flexible and, henceforth, it would be the Fed that drove the car, virtually alone. While Congress wrangled over the deficits, the Federal Reserve would decide on its own whether and when the economy would be pushed forward or pulled back.

"You sit there and try to run the entire economy—that's what we're trying to do," Vice Chairman Schultz brooded. "It is wrong for the Federal Reserve to try to run the economy, but that's the position we were put in. It's wrong, but there we are—struggling to be the economic czars for the entire country."

The economic news was not all bad, however. The process of liquidation was beginning to show its effect on prices and the progress was substantial. For most of the previous two years, the monthly Consumer Price Index had hovered close to 10 percent or even higher. In October, it fell abruptly to just below 5 percent, seasonally adjusted. In November, the monthly CPI went back up to 6 percent, but subsided again the following month. The era of double-digit inflation was coming to an end.

No one was more pleased than the President. "Ronald Reagan's selection process is that out of twelve items in the news, he will pick the two that are good," Stockman said. "The inflation numbers were really starting to look good. Everyone in the White House was talking about that and bragging."

As for the recession, Treasury Secretary Donald Regan predicted confidently that it would be over soon. In early November, Regan conceded that "this current quarter may be a real downer," but the contraction would be less severe by the opening months of 1982 and the economy would resume real growth by the spring.[20]

His monetary adviser, Beryl Sprinkel, also took a sanguine view of the contraction. On November 12, Sprinkel reported to the Cabinet Council that everything seemed on course, as though he had been predicting recession from the start:

> Recent developments confirm that the economy is in a recession. This is not surprising or alarming because a slowdown in economic activity is the expected, short-run effect of a deceleration of money growth. . . . The economy is likely to remain weak for several months, but this is not a sign that the program is "failing." On the contrary, a temporary slowdown in economic activity is the predicted, immediate effect of the transition from excessive and inflationary money growth. . . .
>
> It is important that concern about the recession not lead to quick-fix attempts to reverse the economic slowdown, such as a rapid reacceleration of money growth. . . . The restrictive effect on output and employment of the monetary slowdown is temporary and the economy should recover quickly.[21]

In political terms, everything seemed on course too. A recovery by early spring would be perfectly timed for the 1982 congressional elections in the fall.

"It was important to take your licks now," Lawrence Kudlow of OMB explained. "The President wasn't up for re-election for three more years. This was the time to take your pain and get it over with."

The majority leader of the Senate normally operated with a calm, affable demeanor and so his remarks to the strategy conference of Republican congressional leaders sounded especially harsh.

"Volcker's got his foot on our neck," Senator Howard Baker of Tennessee complained. "And we've got to make him take it off."

The other Republican leaders were upset too. Senator Baker assured the group that he intended to deal personally with the chairman of the Federal Reserve. Volcker would be told what Congress wanted, without a lot of obscure discussion about M-1 and all that.

Members of Congress live according to their own electoral calendar. The President's men might be unalarmed by the "temporary slowdown," but some senators and all representatives faced re-election every two years and their patience with economic distress was understandably more limited. If the recession lasted through 1982, with no sign of relief, Republicans would lose congressional seats and possibly the majority control of the Senate that made Howard Baker floor leader.

Most congressional politicians in both parties did not pretend to a sophisticated knowledge of monetary policy, but they understood one big thing—interest rates. The high interest rates were suffocating their constituents, both businesses and consumers. As a practical guide, the legislators usually followed the prime rate charged by banks —and the prime remained desperately high. Until mid-October, banks kept their basic loan rate at 19 percent, even though other short-term rates had fallen substantially. With inflation falling but the prime rate staying high, the real return for bankers naturally increased. The banks, of course, held on to the wider spread and the larger profits as long as they could.

To Baker and other Republicans, this looked like gross ingratitude. They had just enacted generous tax cuts for business and finance; now Wall Street was repaying the favor with punishingly high interest rates and surging bank profits.

"It's time indeed that the financial markets realize that they're playing a dangerous game," Baker complained publicly. He and Representative Robert H. Michel, the House Republican leader, announced, none too subtly, that if interest rates didn't decline soon, Congress might be compelled to enact credit controls.

"The future of our program and our chances of getting control of the House are, right now, tied to interest rates," Representative Guy Vander Jagt, chairman of the Republican Congressional Campaign Committee, conceded. "In sixty to ninety days," Michel insisted, "something's got to give." [22]

The odd spectacle of Republican conservatives threatening Wall Street bankers with the sort of government intervention usually espoused by liberal Democrats was a measure of their alarm. But some Republicans were infected with a dash of the old Populist spleen traditionally associated with the Democratic Party. Republican attitudes toward Wall Street depended primarily on where the Republicans were from—from the Midwest farm states and the developing provinces of the South and West or from the financial citadels in the money-center cities. Howard Baker, for instance, appreciated the South's lingering resentment. His threat to impose government controls on Wall Street may not have been genuine, but his irritation was.

> They are interest-rate junkies [Baker complained]. They all love it, they love the widening spread between interest rates and inflation. I told a bunch of them that if interest rates didn't come down, there was going to be bloody retribution, not from government, but from people. I got a lot of criticism for that. People told me it was market forces and nobody could interfere with that. I said, "Sure, yes, but the market likes high rates. The market's keeping the price artificially high to increase profits."

Senator Paul Laxalt of Nevada was an orthodox conservative in most respects, but he was also a westerner, and on the subject of interest rates, Laxalt sounded like an "easy money" man. As the Republicans' anxieties increased, Senator Laxalt urged his good friend, the President, to sponsor an anti-usury bill—a measure that would impose a new cap on interest rates. Laxalt's proposal was circulated in the White House, but sober conservative economists scotched it.

The two prominent Texans in the White House—Vice President George Bush and Chief of Staff James Baker—were themselves wealthy, urbane men, yet, in private councils, they too sometimes expressed mild echoes of the old regional resentment toward money-center banks, high interest rates and the Federal Reserve. The White House economists' elaborate explanations of monetarist principles did not entirely satisfy them. At one point, the Vice President proposed that the Administration impose an excess-profits tax on banks if the prime rate did not come down. Nothing came of the suggestion.

While the White House policy makers remained relatively passive, Howard Baker followed through on his promise to confront Volcker. He invited the Federal Reserve chairman to his office for a heart-to-heart conversation on interest rates and monetary policy. It was the first of many intense meetings between the two men, and White House officials were told that the Senate majority leader "really put the wood to him," as one of them said.

"It was me lecturing Volcker on how bad things were for us and how he had to get interest rates lower," the senator said. "Volcker never said much at all. I knew the meeting was over when he stood up to leave."

The Republican leader tried to impress upon the Fed chairman that the political situation would deteriorate if the Federal Reserve persisted. Sooner or later, a majority would form, among both Republicans and Democrats, that might enact punitive legislation—stripping the Fed of its independence and relaxing the central bank's tight-money policy by congressional edict.

"I was genuinely frightened that I would lose control over the Senate if we didn't get some movement on interest rates," Baker said. "I fussed at Volcker regularly and warned him, but I never said it publicly. He began to understand that I meant what I said. I was going to beat hell out of him until he changed these policies, but I wasn't his enemy." [23]

The Fed chairman, however, could make his own assessment of the political threat facing the central bank. Congressional temper was rising, as one would expect, but this did not necessarily mean that Congress would actually do anything to the Fed. As Volcker well appreciated, much of the political outcry over interest rates was merely showing the flag to appease angry constituents. A congressman would issue a blistering statement and the hometown press would report his attack on the Fed and the distressed home builders in his district would feel grateful. Nothing of political substance was involved.

The inhibitions against taking direct control over money policy were deep and historic. Congress could set interest rates and money growth if it wished, but then it would also be responsible for interest rates. Instead, the job was delegated to the Federal Reserve. As Nancy Teeters observed: "There is a widespread perception on the Hill that they don't want to do it . . . and most members like it that way."

Volcker also knew, from his own discreet lobbying on Capitol Hill, that many of the key legislative players were on his side. Senators like Jake Garn of Utah, the Republican chairman of the Senate Banking Committee, and the ranking Democrat, Proxmire of Wisconsin, supported what the Fed was doing, and, if it became necessary, they and many others would defend the Fed against legislative assaults. The Fed's chairman personally worked hard at cultivating congressional friends, senators and representatives from the natural majority of moderates and conservatives who were always reluctant to tamper with the long-standing institutional arrangements. Volcker was more impressed by the reservoir of congressional support for the Fed's tough policy than he was by the inevitable critics.

As Senator Baker's frustrations increased, the Federal Reserve chairman was summoned regularly for consultations. The private dialogue continued month after month, without much change in its outline or intensity. So did the majority leader's exasperation.

"One day," Baker said, "when I hadn't gotten so much as a grunt out of him, Volcker stood up to leave—here I was five foot seven and he's six seven—and I told him: 'I've finally figured it out. For a man who is six foot seven, 16 percent interest doesn't seem so high.' "

Like any good central banker, Paul Volcker worried a bit about everything, but one economic factor worried him more than most— wages. The Federal Reserve chairman carried in his pocket a little card on which he kept track of the latest wage settlements by major labor unions. From time to time, he called various people around the country and took soundings on the status of current contract negotiations. What is the UAW asking for? What does organized labor think? Volcker wanted wages to fall, the faster the better. In crude terms, the Fed was determined to break labor.

This preoccupation turned up repeatedly in his public speeches, though never stated so bluntly. He told a National Press Club audience that the "signs of progress on the inflation front" were heartening. But, Volcker added, "I would be less than frank if I failed to point out those signs have not yet been confirmed by clearly visible and significant progress toward wage deceleration."

By the fourth quarter of 1981, the inflation rate had fallen well below double digits, but compensation for employees was still increasing at a rate of more than 10 percent. "The fact is a conflict may be brewing between high nominal wage expectations and economic policies needed to curb inflation," Volcker warned.

When White House officials congratulated themselves on how swiftly inflation was declining, Volcker pulled out his card on union wages and warned them not to be too optimistic. Until labor got the message and surrendered on its wage demands, the underlying rate of inflation would continue to push prices upward—and collide with the stringent reality imposed by the Fed's money policy.

"Volcker wanted to break the back of wage trends just as much as he wanted to break commodity price speculation," David Stockman said. "Kudlow and I were telling him that inflation would come down fast. He said, "Nope, it can't happen. Wages are about two-thirds of GNP, and inflation can't come down faster until labor unit costs come down faster.' "

With his public messages, Volcker was trying to persuade both labor and management that they had to retreat from the wage and price assumptions of the inflationary era. The Fed really was going to stop inflation, he assured them, and workers would no longer need the protection of generous cost-of-living clauses in their contracts.

In fact, Volcker repeatedly held out this promise: " . . . the prospect for sustained economic growth and increases in *real* wages for all Americans will improve as we achieve greater productivity and moderation in the demand for nominal wage increases."[24] Give up your wage demands today in order to guarantee brighter prospects tomorrow.

After a decade of inflation, labor leaders were skeptical, like virtually every other group of economic decision makers. Weak unions had no choice but to yield; but the stronger industrial unions would not graciously grant concessions based on vague promises. If labor and business ignored the warnings, Volcker predicted they would be confronted by a squeeze on corporate profits and, therefore, the loss of jobs. The cost of wages would continue to rise, but in the disinflationary economy, businesses would no longer be able to pass on their rising costs in higher prices. That squeeze would reduce profits, and when profits fell, businesses closed the factories and laid off their workers.

Though Volcker did not say so explicitly, his decisions on monetary policy would necessarily be influenced by this contest of wills with organized labor. For the Federal Open Market Committee, it was not just a question of watching the monetary aggregates or interest rates or even the falling production in the depressed economy. The Fed figured that if it eased credit conditions in response to those indicators, this might be interpreted by labor and business as a sign that the pressure was off.

Inflation would not be securely defeated, Volcker insisted, until all those workers and their unions agreed to accept less. If they were not impressed by words, perhaps the liquidation of several million more jobs would convince them.

At its October 5 meeting, the Federal Open Market Committee chose not to seek faster money growth, even though the recession was now obvious and the basic money supply was still running below its target range. In the past, when recessions took hold, the Fed normally turned its money policy and "leaned against the wind" the other way —injecting more liquidity into the financial system and pulling down interest rates. This time, it held to course.

"The members generally agreed that the evidence currently available did not portend a sharp cumulative contraction in activity in the coming months," the FOMC minutes said, "though a few nevertheless commented on the risks of a more significant decline."

At the November 17 meeting, for the first time, the FOMC agreed to use the word "recession" to describe the economic conditions across the nation (five months after the fact). But, again, the policy makers asserted that the contraction should be neither long nor severe. "It was generally thought . . . that the scheduled reduction in federal income tax, the projected increases in defense spending along with other elements in the federal fiscal outlook, and the decline in interest rates most likely would generate an upturn in economic activity by the middle of 1982," the committee concluded.

In the meantime, the committee members still worried about whether they had convinced the country—organized labor and management, workers and producers—to abandon its long-held inflationary expectations. "Some encouraging signs . . . were noted, but it was also emphasized that such expectations tended to change slowly," the FOMC warned. "They would be sensitive to judgments about federal budgetary developments, to the nature of the newly negotiated collective bargaining agreements and to perceptions of the course of monetary policy."

Once again, the FOMC agreed not to raise its short-term targets for its money-supply management. The committee's directive permitted "somewhat more rapid growth of M-1" but it also advised the operations desk in New York that "moderate shortfalls from the growth path would not be unacceptable." The complicated syntax and delicate shadings boiled down to the same message: Senator Baker and other critics notwithstanding, the Fed was not ready to let go.[25]

At first glance, the new banking regulation issued in December looked as if federal regulators were at last getting tough with those go-go bankers who were obsessed with maximum growth. Henceforth, the Federal Reserve and the Comptroller announced jointly, banks would be required to keep a higher minimum of their own capital on hand—the shareholders' equity, retained profits and loan-loss reserves—as a hedge against reckless expansion. A bank's capital was its own money, the cushion it relied upon when loans went sour and borrowers failed to meet their obligations. Since the mid-1960s, as banks expanded their lending aggressively and inflation depreciated the value of their capital, the ratio of bank capital to outstanding loans had declined steadily, particularly at the largest banks. The major banks were operating, in effect, with a smaller and smaller safety net.

The Fed, in cooperation with the Comptroller, was now establishing a higher standard of minimum prudence. A bank would be required to maintain a minimum ratio between its capital and its assets or total loan activity—5 percent for larger banks and 6 percent for small-town banks. For every $1 million in its portfolio of outstanding loans and bonds, a large bank would have to hold at least $50,000 as its capital base. Thus, if an aggressive management expanded a bank's lending rapidly, it would also have to go out and raise more capital, presumably by selling stock, to maintain the basic guarantee of its soundness.

The Fed's new regulation had one glaring weakness: it exempted the seventeen largest banks in America. These multinational banks were the ones with the weakest capital-to-assets ratios, the megabanks that were most exposed to risk by their own aggressive growth strategies. The list of exempted institutions included all the famous names—Chase Manhattan, Citibank, Manufacturers Hanover, Bank of America, Chemical, Irving Trust, even Morgan Guaranty. They could not meet the new capital standards and so, for the time being, they were given a pass.

The largest single factor responsible for their weakened capital condition was their aggressive lending to the less-developed countries of the world, mainly in Latin America and Asia, the so-called LDCs. For the previous decade, the leading international banks of the U.S. had pushed for a larger and larger share of this global loan market and their capital base had shrunk proportionately. Brazil, Mexico, Argen-

tina, South Korea, the Philippines and Taiwan were the leading borrowers. Collectively, Third World nations had amassed about $400
billion in debts to foreigners, as of 1980, and U.S. banks held about 40
percent of the bank loans.

But the American loans to the developing nations were highly concentrated among a few big banks. More than four-fifths of the lending
was done by only twenty-four banks. Their LDC loans constituted a
full tenth of their overall business—and added up to 180 percent of
their capital base. The nine largest money-center banks were the most
aggressive of all. Their risk exposure in less-developed countries had
mushroomed to 204 percent of their capital by 1980. In other words, if
the Third World nations were to default for some reason, that catastrophe would wipe out—twice over—the capital of the biggest names
in American banking.

Medium-sized regional banks and small banks were, on the average,
already in compliance with the Fed's new capital standard. The major
banks were far short. In 1981, the seventy or so largest banks averaged
a capital-to-assets ratio of only 4.37 percent and, of course, some of
the very largest banking institutions were below that average. In order
to meet the new minimum, they would have had to raise huge blocs of
new capital in a hurry—selling new stock or retaining their profits and
cutting back the quarterly dividends for shareholders. Either way, the
banks' stock prices would be sharply depressed. And the bank executives might be confronted by angry stockholders demanding a change
of management.[26]

The major bank executives did not seem the least embarrassed by
their aggressive position in the less-developed countries. On the
whole, they were proud of it. Walter Wriston, the most forthright
among them, openly boasted that these countries were his best customers. The interest-rate returns were higher and loan losses were
lower than on domestic lending to American enterprises. In public and
in private, Wriston scoffed at critics who perennially warned that
America's largest banks were dangerously overcommitted.

"In my view," Wriston predicted, "this fear that banks have
reached a limit will turn out to be wrong tomorrow, as it always has in
the past." Citibank's vice chairman, G. A. Costanzo, derided the
"doomsday fantasies" of defaulting nations and failing banks. "The
concept of banks, flooded with OPEC deposits, chasing loans of deteriorating quality is an Alice in Wonderland fantasy," he wrote.[27]

The voices of caution included that of Governor Henry Wallich, the
Federal Reserve Board's leading expert on international finance. Wallich had been gently admonishing the major banks in recent months,
without apparent effect. In June 1981, he gave a speech entitled "LDC

Debt—to Worry or Not to Worry," and answered his own question in the affirmative.

> . . . today we are in a transitional phase that in the long run is not sustainable [Wallich warned]. In the short run, it is made to appear sustainable in some degree by inflation, which causes a country to amortize its debts via interest rates. Fundamentally, a good number of countries are borrowing amounts that cannot be continued far into the future without leading to burdens that appear unsustainable from historical experience.[28]

Wallich was discreetly suggesting to the banks that they slow down, but the major bankers were heading in the opposite direction. According to the executives from Citibank, the biggest LDC borrowers—Brazil and Mexico—were the countries with the brightest prospects for the future. Citibank's Costanzo declared: "Mexico, after Brazil the second-largest debtor among the LDCs, is in a particularly favorable position as it enters the 1980s. . . . On the basis of present trends, Mexico's external debt may surpass that of Brazil during this decade, reflecting not an uncontrolled deficit but the recognition of unparalleled investment opportunities."

As a central banker, Wallich felt restrained from challenging these claims more precisely. "You don't ordinarily publicize the fact that a country's credit isn't any good," he said. "It's counterproductive and stupid. So it's not very easy to sound warnings."

Anthony Solomon, president of the New York Fed and an intimate of Wall Street's most important bankers, privately lamented their lack of caution:

> What I don't understand is why the major commercial banks pay so little attention to their own country-risk assessments. My guess is that it isn't the country-risk experts who are too optimistic. It's the top lending officers of the banks, the senior officers themselves. They watch what other banks are doing. They rely too much on imagery, not enough on risk analysis.
>
> The real cause is the enormous need to be competitive—to show as good a profit sheet as your peers, to show steady growth in the size of the bank. That's the only way to get the right price-earnings multiples in the stock market. Second, they are consoled by fashion. If everyone else is lending to sovereign LDCs, they feel a little better even if their own country-risk department is suggesting otherwise.

But Volcker himself said very little in public about the dangers inherent in the LDC lending, though he and his colleagues worried in private. At the November meeting of the Federal Advisory Council, they posed a blunt question to the twelve bankers: "Are our banks getting into trouble?" Recession was profitable for banks, but only up to a point. If the liquidation continued long enough, the failure of their loan customers would be multiplied rapidly, and the mounting loan losses would threaten the banks' own profits and even their solvency.

The bankers on the FAC acknowledged the deteriorating position of their customers, both American businesses and the foreign borrowers. "Credit quality abroad is suffering from the prolonged period of slow economic growth and high interest rates as well as—for some countries—political disturbances and lower export earnings," the bankers reported, but they added confidently: "The council believes there is a low probability of any significant number of sizable banks getting into serious trouble."

As for the question of weakening bank capital, the advisory council again saw no cause for alarm. "While there are exceptions among individual banks," it said, "on balance the council believes that the capital position of the banking system as a whole is adequate."[29]

The bankers were looking backward, with confidence. Ever since the first oil-price shock of 1973, the multinational banks in the U.S. and Europe had heard these warnings of impending disaster in the debtor nations. As the oil-producing nations built up hundreds of billions in surplus wealth, the banks recycled the money to the needy, taking deposits from OPEC countries and lending the money to Third World nations that were oil importers and underdeveloped. Men like Wriston figured the LDCs had weathered the first run-up of oil prices in '73 and there was no reason why they could not adjust to the second oil-price shock of '79.

Optimistic bankers like Walter Wriston also understood something about the global financial recycling that the carping critics rarely mentioned: the actual result was extraordinarily positive for most of the poorer countries—a decade of high growth rates for their economies, rising levels of income for their citizens, greater productive capacity and the emerging presence of middle-class consumers, the hallmark of social stability. In broad terms, this was the essence of how capitalism was supposed to work—accumulated wealth investing in new enterprises in order to create new jobs and income, new wealth.

Some of the money was wasted and some of it was stolen. But, on the whole, the tens of billions in loans to countries in Latin America and Asia purchased real assets for those regions—new roads and factories, new dams and office buildings and electric-generating plants, the basic components of industrial development. The process was not different from America's own development in the nineteenth century—when U.S. enterprise borrowed its capital from abroad. Just like an American family borrowing money to buy a home or a farmer buying more land and equipment, it made sense for Brazil and Mexico and most others to go heavily into debt as long as U.S. inflation persisted. The loans would purchase real growth for their economies and would be paid back with cheapened dollars. As long as the LDCs expanded their exports as fast as their foreign borrowing, their capacity to carry more and more debt was undiminished.

"The real news today," Wriston proclaimed, "is that life is much better for the mass of the world's population than in any other period of history. In some LDCs, the standard of living has doubled in the last ten years—a feat that even the most dedicated optimists could not have predicted and the pessimists have still not recognized."

On some occasions in history, private finance could accomplish things on a scale that elected national governments would not dare attempt directly. The foreign aid appropriated by the industrial nations, particularly the United States, was meager compared to the vast flow of capital directed to the development of poorer nations through the commercial banks. Ultimately, the money came from the same people—citizens who lived in the wealthy industrialized nations of the Northern Hemisphere. Consumers in these wealthy countries, America included, paid OPEC higher prices for oil. OPEC's money piled up in deposits at the banks. And the banks then lent the money to the developing countries of the world.

In bare outline, the global recycling was like a vast program of foreign aid that effectively transferred wealth from rich to poor, without formal political sanction. The industrial governments, including the United States, encouraged financial institutions to carry on the recycling, but kept a discreet distance from the actual decisions. The pace and priorities were controlled by the private bankers. The portable wealth, of course, was owned by the oil-exporting nations, not by Americans, and the international banking system collected its own profitable tolls on the transactions. Still, American and European consumers, unaware of where their money ended up, were underwriting Third World development on a scale they would never have authorized as taxpayers and voters.

"One by one," Wriston proclaimed proudly in 1981, "we are seeing developing countries finally breaking through the vicious circle of poverty. Far from despairing, I have great hopes for the future of the LDCs in the remaining years of this century."

But Wriston's optimism looked backward. Worried experts like Henry Wallich were looking forward, convinced that the future was not going to look like the past. For one thing, the LDC debt had begun to escalate more rapidly in the late 1970s and the quality of the projects it financed became increasingly questionable. Closer to home, some of the largest U.S. banks were now stretching the rules on their country-by-country risk exposure—putting too many eggs in one basket, as bankers would say.

The financial condition of the borrowing countries was, meanwhile, deteriorating. They were compelled to pay the higher real interest rates imposed by the Fed's tight monetary policy, rolling over loans at higher and higher prices, going deeper into debt just to stay even. Yet their economies were no longer expanding robustly as they had in the 1970s, but sinking. Their best market for exports, the United States, was in recession itself.

In a direct sense, the Federal Reserve itself was inducing crisis through its unrelenting campaign against inflation. If inflation really was brought to a halt, as the Fed intended, a financial bind of epic dimensions could unfold. The fundamentals of credit would be reversed for these nations, just as it would for domestic borrowers in the United States. The real value of their debts would appreciate with the U.S. dollar, rather than decline. The LDCs might be stuck with a mountain of debts they could no longer repay, and America's most prestigious banks would be stuck with a mountain of bad loans they could no longer collect.

The Federal Reserve was, in effect, risking global financial disorder, hoping the conflicting forces would work themselves out without a collision. As a staff economist in the Fed's international division explained:

The problems of the Third World debt were crystal clear to the sophisticated people at the Fed. When they disinflated, they knew the disinflation would reduce the imports we were taking in from those countries. At the same time interest rates were going up, LDC exports were falling. They were in a squeeze. The Fed knew this was going to be a dangerous side effect—the Achilles' heel of the whole process.

The dilemma was itself a source of some guilt among the Federal Reserve governors, or at least regret. The bind that now confronted less-developed countries (and ultimately their bankers) could have been avoided if the Federal Reserve had asserted its regulatory authority earlier and more forcefully. The central bank failed to restrain foreign lending by the commercial banks and, instead, allowed them to keep expanding their LDC risks while their bank capital declined. In the late 1970s, an interagency council composed of the Fed and the other regulatory agencies had adopted guidelines for country-by-country risk exposure and issued mild warnings from time to time, but the major banks paid little attention.

"Winking and nodding" at the banks did not really have much effect, as Volcker himself acknowledged. If the Fed wanted the banks to moderate their foreign-loan risks, it might have adopted hard-and-fast rules and enforced them. The new regulation on capital ratios—in addition to exempting the seventeen largest banks that had the largest problems—came much too late in the game to make a difference.

"It's really regrettable," Henry Wallich admitted, "that we didn't put any teeth in the country-exposure regulations. The banks reported to us regularly, but we didn't do anything about it. Examiners raised questions. In some cases, they got a response. Other banks said, 'These stupid examiners—what do they know?' "

The Federal Reserve, for all its legendary power, behaved in this crucial matter much like other regulatory agencies of the federal government. It yielded to the ambitions of the industry it was supposed to regulate, instead of enforcing the larger public interest. Federal Reserve officials might worry that the largest commercial banks, the Fed's primary constituency, were pursuing a dangerous course, but the Fed lacked the will to discipline them.

The explanation offered by some was bureaucratic. "What people don't realize is that bureaucrats live in the same culture as everyone else," an assistant to Volcker said. "Who do bank examiners talk to? They talk to bankers. There was a general lack of skepticism." But the Federal Reserve's failure did not originate with the bank examiners. It started at the top.

Paul Volcker did not hold a high opinion, at least privately, of bankers' capacity for prudent judgment. "Volcker sees bankers as subject to fad and whim, almost incapable of making short-term sacrifices for their own long-term interest," one of the chairman's close associates said. "I suspect he sees that as an aspect of American businessmen generally."

Yet, aside from occasional attempts at private persuasion, Paul Volcker did very little to forestall the developing crisis. He did not sound a general alarm. He did not ask Congress to support the Federal Reserve in a frontal effort to restrain the banks. He did not, until late in the day, impose new rules that would compel the banks to pull back. His predecessor, William McChesney Martin, offered a harsh assessment of Volcker's performance as Federal Reserve chairman: Volcker was "very good" in conducting monetary policy but "a complete flop on bank supervision."[30]

Charles Partee, the Fed governor in charge of the board's subcommittee on bank supervision, conceded:

It's true we didn't force these people to act better. But Bill Martin knows better than anyone else in the world how difficult it is to get the community of big banks to change its behavior. You say to Walter Wriston, "Walt, you've got to get your ship in order." Why, hell, Wriston thinks he's bigger than the government. You don't get him to do anything by persuasion and argument, that's for sure.

When Fed officials did try to warn the banks about their growing exposure on foreign lending, they were brushed aside, Partee said. "You look at the bank's portfolio and try to point out the potential problems," he said. "When this was done in 1980 and 1981, our examination people were told: 'You don't understand the situation. We know better than you.' There was almost no decent response from the banks—until, of course, their loans got into great difficulty."

By itself, this explanation represented a damaging admission. The mystique of the Fed held that commercial bankers trembled at the slightest frown from the central bank and dared not offend it. The reality, at least for the largest and most influential banks, was quite the opposite. The Fed was too weak to make its word stick. The regulators' pleas of impotence contradicted the myth, but they were also an evasion. The Federal Reserve was empowered by Congress to attend to these dangers. When it failed to do so, the excuses did not sound so different from those offered by other regulatory agencies that fell captive to the regulated.

The defensive explanations disclosed a deeper reality about the Federal Reserve, however, that was even more devastating to the mythology. The Federal Reserve's regulation of private banks was conditioned and restrained by politics and political influence. Governor Partee, among others, cited the inhibition of political pressures to explain why the Federal Reserve had not been tougher on the banks.

We're not talking about the little banks; they're pretty well behaved [Partee said]. We're talking about the top fifty banks. They have extraordinary clout in the financial and business and political worlds. They will speak back to you. "You're being unreasonable. You're trying to retard economic development." They'll go around to back doorways and complain to senators that the regulators are being too tough. It's like pulling teeth to go against them.

The chairman himself did not disagree. The Fed, he conceded, was "too passive generally in regulation and supervision of banks, particularly through the seventies." In his own defense, Paul Volcker pleaded the same argument—politics.

Anyone who thinks you can run bank regulation independent from the general political climate doesn't understand [Volcker said]. Suppose the

Federal Reserve would have decided to be tougher in the seventies. There would have been an outcry, from the banks and the congressmen who get their contributions, from everyone who was sold on deregulation. "What the hell are you talking about? We haven't had a banking loss for thirty years. So what the hell are you doing with new regulations?" Congressmen would come at us. "Why do you regulators think you know more than our bank CEOs?"

The Fed would get tougher with the major banks only if Volcker could think the "general political climate" would support him. This is not the disinterested and aloof institution described in most literature on the Federal Reserve. The Fed responded to the political influence of bankers, as the Department of Agriculture responded to agricultural interests, or the Interstate Commerce Commission responded to truckers.

In the meantime, Volcker and the other governors did not see that they had much choice but to go forward with what they had started and hope for the best. If inflation abated and the Fed could restart the economy soon enough, the debt crisis could be averted. If the Fed held tight long enough, some major borrowers would be in deep trouble and so would their bankers.

The leading candidate for failure was a nation of 68 million people —Mexico. By the close of 1981, Volcker and other senior Fed officers recognized the danger signs on Mexico's national balance sheet— declining export income and rising spending and borrowing. "It was as clear as the hand before your face that Mexico was getting into trouble," Volcker said, "but there wasn't much you could do for Mexico."

An exquisite predicament confronted Volcker and the other governors. After all the promises they had made about breaking inflation and all the public skepticism about the Fed's commitment, how could they back away from what they had begun? Yet the largest risk in proceeding against inflation was to the financial system, whose soundness they were supposed to protect. Wisely or foolishly, they decided it was too late to turn back. Their former colleague Philip Coldwell, who had retired from the Board of Governors the year before, described their thinking:

The banks still believed that the world was made of green cheese and that it was going to go on forever. A number of people were raising warning flags, but the Fed was embarked on a major recession to take care of inflation. You were going to kill off inflationary fervor and you had to keep it going. You could play at the fringes with capital ratios and warnings to the banks, but you couldn't reverse the policy.

Throughout 1981, the Federal Reserve clearly overdid it, restraining money growth so tightly that it undershot its own goal for the year. The Federal Open Market Committee had set its target range between 3.5 and 6 percent, but M-1 grew by only 2.3 percent in 1981. If the statistical difference seemed slight, the damaging effects multiplied through the entire economy, depressing it further than the Fed had intended.

While home builders, labor unions, small-business men and others complained, the bankers of the Federal Advisory Council congratulated the governors on their performance. "The council is unanimous in the belief that the current monetary policy is appropriate," the FAC declared at its November meeting. ". . . The conduct of monetary policy during 1981, which has avoided the large variations in growth experienced during 1980, has strengthened the credibility of the Fed in the marketplace."[31]

Yet, a few weeks later, the Fed's credibility was under attack from financial markets and the White House as well. After six months of sluggish growth, M-1 began surging again, abruptly and somewhat mysteriously. The basic measure of the money supply started accelerating in November, then expanded by nearly 13 percent in December and grew even faster—by nearly 20 percent—in the opening weeks of 1982. To monetarists, it looked as though the Fed was losing control again, or else its nerve. Cries of alarm went up in many quarters, from the bond market to the President himself.

At a January 19 press conference, President Reagan was asked about declining capital investment and how that affected his economic program. His answer directed blame to the Federal Reserve's inconstant monetary policy.

"I think there's a little caution at work," Reagan said, "and perhaps part of that is waiting to see what the Federal Reserve is doing, because there's been an upsurge, for example, in the money supply just recently, which sends, I think, the wrong signal to the money markets."[32]

A few days earlier, Representative Jack Kemp had called for Paul Volcker's resignation. If the President was upset with the Fed's performance, did he agree with Congressman Kemp? Reagan sidestepped the question but did not offer an endorsement of the chairman. "I can't respond to that," Reagan said, "because the Federal Reserve System is autonomous . . . They're not serving at anyone's pleasure."

Four months earlier, when the recession was first visible, officials of the Reagan Administration had suggested belatedly that the Fed was too tight. Now, deep into the recession, they complained that the Fed was too loose. "Some have accused us of being unable to make up our minds," Treasury Secretary Regan acknowledged. "Nothing could be further from the truth. We supported the Federal Reserve's targets and consistently urged them to keep money growth even and steady within the target ranges."[33]

It was not a big deal to get the President's statement made [a senior White House official said]. It came up in the weekly economic group. Don Regan would come in and report on monetary policy, influenced by Sprinkel, and give a heavy argument about the Fed's volatility. Stockman was partly a monetarist and partly happy to create economic disaster in order to get fiscal action. Stockman would generally support the notion that we had to worry about the Fed loosening too much. The rest of the players were skeptical of the monetarist wisdom, but not yet confident of an alternative wisdom.

The President's shot at the Fed reflected the monetarists' anxieties about the money numbers. Beryl Sprinkel had first warned in mid-December about the "burst of money growth." "Recent increases in money combined with public speculation about the budget have reinforced fears about the prospects for long-term monetary control," he had advised the White House. Like many other economists, Sprinkel was convinced that economic recovery would begin in the early months of 1982, but only if the Fed remained loyal to the principle of steady and moderate money expansion. By January, the alarm over M-1 had become stronger, and the President's advisers had agreed that, once again, Volcker must be scolded, not only in private but also in public.[34]

"Perhaps the jump in money is only a temporary phenomenon, a result of technical problems . . . ," Lawrence Kudlow had advised the senior White House counselors just prior to the President's press conference, "but there are numerous other signals suggesting a basic change in monetary policy from steady restraint to alarming expansion."

Kudlow saw a second danger lurking in the situation—one that could blight Republican prospects in the '82 congressional elections. If the Fed continued to let money grow too rapidly now, it might be forced into a sharp tightening a few months hence and thus stifle the new economic recovery just as it was beginning.

"As a best guess," Kudlow said, "real growth in the first quarter of 1982 is likely to be flat, but this could represent a turning zone for the economy and lead to much stronger growth in the second quarter. However, a combination of rising interest rates and a belated monetary correction could create a 1982 second half which is more sluggish. The recovery could become a nonevent."[35]

The monetarist critique led the White House to turn the heat on Paul Volcker again. For the Fed chairman, it must have seemed an odd moment in his political relationships. On Capitol Hill, Republican leaders like Howard Baker were imploring him to bring down interest rates. At the White House and Treasury, Republican officials were insisting that he bring down M-1. It was not evident that politicians at either end of Pennsylvania Avenue recognized the contradiction. Volcker could please one group or the other, but there was no way in the physical world that he could please both.

Even if the Federal Reserve chairman chose to ignore the politicians, he still had to deal with the message from financial markets. Over several months, as business activity declined, so had interest rates. The Federal Funds rate, once hovering near 20 percent, was allowed to decline to 12.5 percent by December. When M-1 started accelerating, however, the financial markets began bidding up both short-term and long-term rates.

The Federal Reserve had taught the money-market traders to take M-1 seriously and so they did. When M-1 surged, the markets assumed the Fed would soon have to tighten again and that would raise interest rates, and so they anticipated the tightening by bidding up rates themselves, just for self-protection. Volcker's monetarist operating system had created a strange circle of existential reality surrounding money: if the Fed said M-1 was real, then financial markets thought so too, and the Fed reacted to what the financial markets thought was real, even if the Fed privately thought the markets were mistaken. The money market and the bond market were "calling for" higher interest rates. Yet the real economy was in recession. Did it make sense to tighten money again in the midst of a contraction?

"Increasingly," Volcker said, "the market commentary was that the money supply was too high, inflation was still too high and inflation was going to revive if the money supply didn't come down."

The chairman might be privately disdainful of the "market commentary," but he was not prepared to go against it. M-1 might well be giving off a false signal. Certainly, the sudden surge was not caused by a resurgent economy or by any change of policy at the Federal Reserve, as the White House economists suspected. Fed economists didn't fully understand it themselves, but they recognized that the shifting composition of the monetary aggregates—actually, the changing patterns of where people stored their money—scrambled the traditional meaning of M-1. During 1981, the FOMC had tried to follow the money aggregates as the gauge for its policy and had been seriously misled. That might be happening again. Yet, if the financial markets and the banks believed in M-1, how could the central bank suddenly announce that it had lost faith?

All through January, Fed officials had long conversations among themselves, trying to figure out the puzzling surge in money growth. It might be simply that people were "parking" their savings in interest-bearing NOW accounts, thus swelling M-1 artificially. Or perhaps the fears induced by rising unemployment were making people more cautious and so they kept more idle cash on hand, but did not spend it. Or maybe it was the steady decline in interest rates over the previous four months. As rates fell, the "opportunity cost" of keeping large balances in noninterest-bearing checking accounts was reduced and so businesses and individuals felt less incentive to move the money elsewhere. All these factors could explain why M-1 was growing rapidly in December and January, yet was irrelevant to the real economy.

When the Federal Open Market Committee met on February 1, the puzzlement over money's true meaning was the main grist of the committee's lengthy discussion. The public's demand for money seemed to be increasing, but not the desire to spend it. Indeed, if the public was holding on to its money longer, that meant money velocity, the rate at which it turned over in new transactions, was actually slowing down. If that was the case, it would undermine all the careful calculations about M-1 and its relationship to the economy. The money supply might actually be tight compared to demand, even though it appeared money was easy because M-1 was growing so fast.

"We faced a giant-sized dilemma," Governor Lyle Gramley said. "We had horrendous increases in M-1 growth. We knew that some of this had to be explained by the new types of accounts and the greater response to interest rate changes. But we can't know how much. Meanwhile, we were very concerned that we not accommodate too much money growth because we were anxious not to lose our credibility."

Gramley, considered one of the most astute forecasters on the board, was among those predicting a relatively mild, brief recession. He thought it would be over by the first or second quarter of 1982.

"I agonized over what to do with these goddamned money numbers," Gramley said. "In fact, it was very hard to determine whether we were implementing a very tight monetary policy or a rather accommodative one."

This was the "monetarist box" that some Fed economists had feared. For lots of reasons, the monetary aggregates were suspect. If the Federal Reserve faithfully followed M-1 as the basis for its policy decisions, it could create a large and damaging error for the economy. Yet, if the Fed abandoned M-1 and based its monetary policy on other factors, it would be denounced for apostasy by the Fed watchers of Wall Street and the monetarist critics in the Reagan Administration.

"Volcker understood the shifts in the aggregates," Fred Schultz said. "He understood that, but he had to balance it off against the goal of really changing inflationary expectations. If we moved away from the rather mechanical system we were using, we did so at the risk of some loss of credibility we'd been trying to build up."

The chairman was still haunted by the experience of 1980 when the Fed had lost control of money. "I think Volcker would tell you that one of his biggest mistakes was in the summer of 1980," said John Paulus, the former Fed staff economist at Morgan Stanley. "He gave away all of the benefits of that recession in 1980. In February 1982, they were concerned that somehow they had initiated another explosion of money—and, remember, they had already blown one of these things before. The Fed asked itself: are we going to do it again?"

This time Volcker would respond faster to the surging M-1. "Most of the business forecasts were calling for a recovery soon," Volcker explained. "There was a fairly common feeling that the money supply was very high. It took a big bounce. We were not easing. That would run against the projections. The best thing to do was sit there and sort it out and see if the money supply got down."

Inside the FOMC, Volcker's position was sold as the middle-of-the-road approach—not clamping down as severely as some of the monetarist Reserve Bank presidents wanted to do, but also not easing, as conditions in the real economy seemed to require. The Fed would keep the faith and continue to follow M-1 as its guide, thus reassuring the skeptics in Wall Street.

In practical fact, the Federal Reserve did tighten, however, despite the depressed state of the American economy. "Taking account of the recent surge in growth of M-1," the FOMC directive stated, "the committee seeks no further growth in M-1 for the January-to-March period. . . . Some decline in M-1 would be . . . acceptable in the context of reduced pressure in the money market." In hard, straightforward terms, this was a decision to let interest rates go higher.

For Frank Morris, president of the Boston Fed, it was too much. Morris had been disenchanted with Volcker's monetarist targets for many months and now he saw the operating system forcing the Fed into serious error. Given the voting rotation for Reserve Bank presidents, Morris did not get to vote on the February directive, but he could speak against it. He urged his colleagues to recognize that the M-1 target was misleading them again and they were about to make a most improbable choice—raising interest rates anew when the economy was still declining.

Morris took the unusual step a few weeks later of repeating his arguments in public. "The thing that really made me decide to go public was when the money supply increased and the Federal Reserve pushed short-term interest rates higher, even though there was a recession," Morris said. "I thought that was a mistake. But it was a mistake demanded by the rigid system we had adopted."

In a speech before an economics conference at the Atlanta Fed, Morris described in theory and in fact why the monetary aggregates were no longer reliable and again urged his colleagues to abandon the system. "We are in a Catch-22 situation," he said, "in that the one thing we are well positioned to control through bank reserves, M-1, is no longer a meaningful target for monetary policy."

Morris proposed that the Fed instead base its policy decisions on other indicators—the growth of all liquid assets or total debt in the real economy or even a broad goal for the size of nominal GNP. If the confusing mystique of the Ms was discarded in favor of more familiar economic guideposts, the public (and the politicians) would at least have a better grasp of what the Federal Reserve was actually doing—regulating overall credit and growth for the entire national economy. "One advantage of the nominal GNP as a goal is that it would upgrade the quality of the dialogue on monetary policy," Morris said.[36]

The Boston Fed president did not make much headway with his colleagues, some of whom did not believe it would make the central bank's job any easier if the general public understood monetary policy. Solomon of the New York Fed shared Morris's doubts on the Ms but was not yet prepared to abandon the monetary aggregates. Others were also troubled by the "monetarist box," but they were more worried that the Fed's reputation would suffer with financial investors, traders and bankers if it changed its operating methods.

With Volcker, they voted for a middle course and hoped it would dampen money growth moderately, preserve the Fed's credibility with financial markets and not interfere with the recovery they expected soon for the real economy.

The decision was perhaps the single gravest error that the Fed policy makers committed during the liquidation of 1981–1982. Their misinterpretations of money and policy mistakes back in early 1981 were at least in step with their general intentions. Volcker and the others were willing then to "err on the hard side" and they were not exactly surprised by the recession that followed their decisions. But, this time, the excessive tightening was not intentional. The consequences for the economy were far more damaging than anything they anticipated.

The result of the February directive was not the moderate holding action described by Volcker and other FOMC members. Instead the Federal Reserve allowed the Federal Funds rate and other short-term interest rates to climb as much as 300 basis points over a few weeks, rising from about 12.5 percent to a peak of 15.6 percent. For the struggling economy, it was as though the Fed had waited until the bull was staggering to its feet, then hit the beast with another hard blow and knocked it to its knees.

The extreme nature of what they did was reflected most starkly in what happened to the relative levels of short-term and long-term rates. Previously, when the Federal Reserve had pushed short rates higher than long rates and held them there, that eventually had induced an economic contraction. Then, as the economy declined and the demand for credit subsided, short-term rates fell back to their normal position, below the long-term rates. This time, in the middle of recession, the Fed actually pushed the short-term rates back up again to contractionary levels above long-term rates. Three-month Treasury bill rates, for instance, exceeded the composite rate for the long-term Treasury bonds. It was as if the central bank had decided to start the recession all over again.

Roughly speaking, that was what occurred. The American economy did not turn around in the next few months and begin growing again. It sank lower and lower. The recovery predicted by so many forecasters, including Federal Reserve governors, for the second quarter of 1982 did not appear.

Instead, the recession would continue many months longer than anyone had expected, multiplying the personal losses and business crises as the economy contracted further. Several million additional jobs would be liquidated and tens of thousands more businesses. Perhaps most alarming and embarrassing for the central bankers, the financial system itself would become frayed and shaky as banks and other lending institutions were pushed to the brink by the deepening failure of their customers, the debtors.

No one could say, of course, what might have happened if the Federal Open Market Committee had chosen a different course. The Fed never acknowledges mistakes officially and always finds other economic explanations for what happens when its own forecasts do not come to pass. It is clear in hindsight, however, that Fed policy makers were especially defensive about this decision. Volcker and his former personal assistant, E. Gerald Corrigan, the president of the Minneapolis Fed, both claimed, for instance, that the Fed had not tightened its monetary policy in the February directive, but merely declined to ease.

The record of what happened to money and interest rates, not to mention the real economy, indicated otherwise. The monthly growth of M-1 decelerated abruptly, from above 19 percent in January to less than 1 percent in February. Interest rates responded accordingly by rising. The Fed Funds rate climbed from 12 to above 15 percent. Still another indication of how tightly the Fed was holding down liquidity was the surge in daily borrowing by commercial banks at the Discount window—Discount borrowing rose to $4 billion as the banks scrambled for scarce funds in a very tight money market. None of this would have occurred if Volcker had been pursuing the neutral, steady-as-you-go monetary policy that he claimed.

Others at the Fed were more candid about their fateful error. Lyle Gramley, for one, regretted the February decision. He had been a System man for nearly thirty years, and inside the institution, Gramley was regarded as the intellectual conscience of the Fed, more representative of its permanent values than perhaps even the chairman.

"In retrospect, if I had it to do over again, I would follow a policy of more expansion," Gramley conceded. "I was deeply concerned about what we were doing, but I was also concerned about the tremendous growth in the aggregates. It seemed to me this might be signaling an upturn in the economy."

But shortly it became clear that the FOMC's analysis of the money-supply surge had been mistaken. "We were tighter than we knew we were," Gramley concluded. "In the midst of recession, interest rates started to go up again. That's very unusual."

Why did the economic recovery not unfold as predicted? Gramley's answer suggested that the Fed itself was to blame. "Interest rates were very high," he said. "Pessimism was widespread. The dollar was beginning to affect the economy. We really didn't perceive the impact."

A senior staff economist at one of the Reserve Banks was more explicit: "We would never have had 11 percent unemployment, we would have had less of a crisis in the Third World, and we would not have pushed the economy down so far if there had been less tightening. We made up for our sins in 1977 and 1978 by overdoing it in 1981 and 1982."

Yet the Reagan White House was pleased when it learned of the FOMC's February decision. The senior political advisers were still listening to the monetarist economists, who assured them that this was the right prescription for economic recovery. Since monetarists believed that financial markets set interest rates, not the Fed, they also believed that reducing the bulge in M-1 would reassure the markets and allow interest rates to subside. From their perspective, it looked as though the President's public complaint and the private hectoring of Volcker had produced the desired result—the Fed was shaping up. Economic theory prevailed over political common sense.

On Valentine's Day, the President and the Federal Reserve chairman met again in the Oval Office and, once again, exchanged vows of mutual commitment to controlling money and halting inflation. Volcker mentioned the federal deficits. Reagan expressed his deep convictions about ruinous deficit spending. A few days later, the President volunteered a hearty endorsement of Paul Volcker and the central bank.

> I want to make it clear today that neither this Administration nor the Federal Reserve will allow a return to the fiscal and monetary policies of the past that have created the current conditions [the President told a news conference]. I have met with Chairman Volcker several times during the past year. We met again earlier this week. I have confidence in the announced policies of the Federal Reserve Board. The Administration and the Federal Reserve can help bring inflation and interest rates down faster by working together than by working at cross-purposes.[37]

Treasury Secretary Regan, feeling bullish again, predicted to reporters that the American economy would come "roaring back like a lion" by springtime. Nervous political advisers at the White House hoped he was right.

On Wall Street, the reaction was also good. John Paulus, chief economist at Morgan Stanley and monetary-policy forecaster for the investment-banking house, was pleased by the tightening because he had predicted it. "I was calling for higher interest rates and I was right," Paulus said. "If you make a big call and you're right, it's not going to cost you anything and it might mean a little reward on your bonus."

As for the real economy, Paulus dismissed the argument that it was wrong for the Federal Reserve to add further injury by raising interest rates in the middle of the recession. "It may sound cruel and cavalier," he said, "but I thought that anything they could get out of the recession in terms of wringing out inflation was worth any pain in the short term."[38]

Neither John Paulus, of course, nor his firm nor most of the financial community in Wall Street would themselves experience any of this worthy "pain," either in the short term or the long term.

————13————

SLAUGHTER
OF THE INNOCENTS

The practice of closing factories and consigning workers to involuntary idleness seemed utterly natural to most everyone in the late twentieth century. Individual workers might plead for reprieve or complain bitterly about their fate, but few questioned the larger logic that produced the disruptions. It was the inherent right of private property. The owners of capital and their corporate managers must be free to withdraw their productive facilities from the economy, to close the doors and send the workers home and wait until business conditions improved.

The principles that governed business economics required them to do so. Lawrence Kudlow had explained it to his White House colleagues: "The heart of the business situation is always the outlook for profits. When the combination of rising costs and falling inflation [prices] squeezes profits, then production and employment must be cut back."[1]

In an earlier era, Thorstein Veblen called this practice "the legal right of sabotage." By sabotage, he meant that business managers must be willing, on occasion, to disrupt the free flow of economic activity in order to maintain the maximum net gain for invested capital. The heart of the management problem, Veblen observed, was always supply—the need to limit the output of goods or services so that the supply would not exceed the market's demand and thus drive down prices and profits. When demand from willing buyers declined and surplus inventories piled up, the managers might first cut prices in order to stimulate sales. When that failed, they stopped producing.

"It is not possible, on sound business grounds, to let the industrial forces of the country go to work and produce what, in the physical sense, the country needs," Veblen explained, "because a free run of production would, it is believed, be ruinous for business. . . . "[2]

"Sabotage" was a word Veblen borrowed from the Wobblies, the radical labor movement of his era that rejected economic orthodoxy and was eventually eclipsed by the more conservative unions that formed the AFL-CIO. The conventional trade unions, in fact, embraced the principle of supply limitation themselves; the central aim of their long political struggle was to obtain the same power for workers. Farmers, once the independent yeomanry, recognized that they too must collectively protect themselves from the ruinous swings of supply and demand in the marketplace. When Veblen wrote his last essays in the 1920s, both of these important groups were vulnerable to periodic catastrophe because neither had the ability to control the supply of what they sold—labor and farm commodities.

The reforms enacted in the New Deal era were intended to overcome such weaknesses. The federal farm programs controlled the production of commodities with acreage limits and price guarantees and thus stabilized agricultural markets. With managed harvests, farmers would not be confronted perennially by the gluts of corn or cotton that collapsed their prices (the oil industry won similar protective legislation designed to limit the supply of oil). Labor unions, likewise, were granted limited legal powers to control access to jobs in the factories they organized. If wage conditions required it, unions could withdraw their labor en masse from the economy by calling a strike. Both reforms, Veblen would have noted, were not different in principle from the business manager's willingness to close the factory. Each group was empowered to "sabotage" production in order to protect its own net gain (public opinion, it was true, seemed more inclined to be morally offended by the spectacle of a farmer who plowed under his cotton or striking workers who withheld their labor than by a corporation that closed its factories).

These elementary facts became particularly relevant to the contraction of 1981–1982 because, by the 1980s, the New Deal reforms that protected labor and agriculture had already lost their effectiveness. For several decades after World War II, the supply-control methods had substantially enhanced wage-bargaining power for major unions and successfully propped up farm prices. Over many years, however, both systems were destabilized—and partly by inflation.

The steady escalation of prices gave every farmer an incentive to increase his production despite the acreage limits imposed by the government—to grow more and more wheat or corn or cotton on the same land. The supply limits encouraged the capital-intensive agricultural methods that could raise per acre yields by extraordinary amounts. American farmers, despite government controls, produced staggering abundance and embarrassing surpluses (surpluses that were sold to the government if the global market could not absorb them). In the process, farmers obligated themselves to larger and larger operating debts—the capital borrowed and repaid every year to purchase the large-scale machinery, fertilizers and pesticides required to turn out the high yields. Even a modest-sized farm might be carrying $500,000 or more in revolving bank loans in order to operate on a few hundred acres. Capital-intensive agriculture required huge debts —burdens mitigated by price inflation. When prices fell in 1982, so did the farm values that supported the agricultural debt. Income and collateral shrank and the farm foreclosures began.

Labor unions, meanwhile, had also lost much of their power to control the access to jobs. Corporations, facing their own cost squeeze on profits, had discovered how to escape the wage demands of organized labor. They simply moved the factories away from the unions. Manufacturing jobs were relocated, first, from the industrial North to the underdeveloped South, where willing workers accepted lower wages and the absence of union protection. Next, the jobs were moved overseas to low-wage countries around the world. When factories were closed by the 1981–1982 recession, union power was already ebbing dramatically. Many of the American plants never opened again because managers concluded that now was the time to find cheaper workers elsewhere.

As Veblen explained, the corporate managers were not entirely free to choose. A sensitive CEO, mindful of the human damage caused by unemployment, might postpone a plant closing for a time, but eventually his softheartedness would be punished. Sooner or later, the stockholders—the "absentee owners," as Veblen called them—would see that he was sacrificing the company's net gain (and their dividends) in order to keep his employees at work and they would simply withdraw their capital—by dumping their stocks. As the stock price declined, shareholders would begin clamoring for new management.

The corporate decisions were also intimately supervised and disciplined by the managers of credit, the banks and brokerages that provided capital and operating loans. In many cases, important bankers sat on the boards of directors of major corporations so they could watch their money more closely. If the banks withdrew their approval and would lend no more, the corporation was doomed to fail.

The principles of "sound business" were, thus, maintained and enforced by a hierarchy of disciplinarians, from the humblest stockholder to the ultimate governor on the credit system, the Federal

Reserve. The corporations were necessarily attentive to what lenders and investors demanded in net gain. The banks were the overseers of business prospects and, at the same time, they were guided in their propensity to lend and in the terms they set by the overall expansion of credit, the monetary policy determined by the Fed. The central bank did not examine the balance sheets of individual corporations, but it did closely follow the broad flows of business growth and debt, prices and wages and unemployment. The pinnacle of the system, Veblen said, was "the conservative surveillance of the Federal Reserve."

Angry factory workers who lost their jobs might blame remote executives at the company's "home office." Or they could blame heartless bankers or the greedy "absentee owners." If they were especially sophisticated, they might even blame the governors of the Federal Reserve. In every case, however, their anger would miss the point. The decision makers, at every level, would reply, correctly, that they were merely agents of the larger logic that governed the political economy. Given the premise of maximum net gain, the choices were required of them. To entertain alternatives, one would have to challenge the underlying principles themselves, to question the dependent relationship between work and capital, to reject the natural supremacy of profit over intangible human cares. Neither farmers nor labor unions were disposed to challenge those deeply held beliefs or able to imagine alternatives that were less insensitive to human suffering.

> The net gain in money values [Veblen wrote] is a more convincing reality than productive work or human livelihood. Neither the tenuous things of the human spirit nor the gross material needs of human life can come in contact with this business enterprise in such a way as to deflect its course from the line of least resistance, which is the line of greatest present gain within the law.

As a practical matter, it was too late for concessions. Once launched, the process of economic shrinkage rolled forward on its own momentum and overwhelmed both management and labor. Every month, for nearly two years, the unemployment rate would increase as hundreds of thousands more were turned out of jobs. Eventually, national unemployment would reach a post-Depression record of 10.8 percent.

The A&P food-processing plant in Horseheads, New York, the world's largest, closed its doors and sent home 1,100 workers. GAF Corporation shut down thirteen roofing plants from New Jersey to California and laid off 1,800 employees. In North Carolina, Wrangler stopped making jeans and another 320 were out of jobs. Texaco laid off 304 workers at its refinery in Tulsa. Ford added another 2,250 to the unemployment rolls from its assembly plant in Lorain, Ohio. General Tire another 1,500 in Akron. On and on, the shutdown proceeded.[3]

Individual workers and their union locals protested and tried to make last-minute concessions to keep their jobs. Some small-business owners attempted to keep their shops open as long as they could. But resistance was futile; this was precisely how the process of liquidation was meant to work. Andrew Mellon had explained the cure in his chilling dictum back in 1930: "Liquidate labor, liquidate stocks, liquidate the farmers, liquidate real estate." Thorstein Veblen, Mellon's contemporary, described it in a different way: "the slaughter of the innocents."

At the peak, in December 1982, 12 million people were out of work, only 4.4 million of them drawing unemployment compensation. Another 4 or 5 million unemployed were not counted in the official statistics because they were no longer actively seeking jobs at the local unemployment office. Another group, at least as large, was working only part time because of the contraction. In all, the dislocated totaled as many as 20 million American workers.

In their idleness, they also served. In the Marxist phrase, they constituted the "reserve army of the unemployed," a visible reminder to those who were still working that their jobs and wages were also insecure. The continuing presence of surplus labor was central to the process of disinflation. By first breaking wages, business could reduce its costs and, thus, retain its profit margins without the necessity of raising prices.

"People didn't talk about it," said Anthony Solomon of the New York Fed, "but it was quite clear. You were going to have to have some recessionary adjustment in wages. You won't get price flexibility without adjustments in labor and other costs."

While the liquidation closed large factories and small shops everywhere, the distress was not evenly distributed across the economy. The millions of unemployed were concentrated in the industrial core of America—manufacturing, mining and construction sectors that traditionally had the strongest unions and the highest blue-collar wages. In the automobile industry, unemployment would reach a peak of 23 percent. In steel and other primary metals, 29 percent. In construction, 22 percent. In appliances and other fabricated metal products, 19 percent. In rubber and plastics, 15 percent. In apparel and other textiles, 13 percent.[4]

In Detroit, radio stations played a wry country-music song for their unemployed listeners. An old favorite had celebrated the independent spirit of the blue-collar worker: "Take This Job and Shove It." The new song lamented: "I Wish I Had a Job to Shove."

The liquidation of business enterprises was, likewise, highly selective. About 66,000 firms filed for bankruptcy protection in 1982, the highest level since the great contraction of 1929–1932, and most of these were smaller companies that could not bear up under the strain that both declining sales and higher interest rates put on their cash flow. Dun & Bradstreet reported 24,900 cases of "business failure" in 1982, in which the company ceased operations entirely, its assets were sold off and creditors were forced to write off their loans as a loss.

This was the worst year for "business failures" that D&B had recorded since 1933 and more than three times the failure rate in 1979. The 24,900 failed companies liquidated $15.6 billion in uncollectible debts. The largest numbers of failures were in retailing and construction, but the largest losses in terms of the dollar value of the defaulted credit were in mining and manufacturing.[5]

The burden of economic loss, nevertheless, was borne mainly by workers and their families. The Urban Institute calculated that the national economy lost $570 billion in output from 1981 to 1983 due to the recession and that 59 percent of this lost income was absorbed by labor—workers who lost their jobs or had their wage gains reduced. Declining corporate profits accounted for 25 percent of the loss, and most of the remainder was absorbed by farmers and small-business proprietors. In social terms, nearly three-fourths of the nation's economic loss was suffered by citizens whom most people would describe as "little guys"—industrial workers, individual entrepreneurs, farmers. These were the later day equivalents of Andrew Jackson's "real people." The bone and sinew of the country, he called them.

In the Urban Institute's study, the actual loss per household was estimated to be an average nationwide of $3,309 (or $3,837 if losses from the 1980 recession were included). The national average was misleading, however, because the unemployment was highly concentrated in certain sectors and the overwhelming majority of American families were not affected by it. In crude terms, the average loss for families that were actually dislocated by the recession was at least three or four times greater—at least $10,000 and for many families much more.

"Recessions are not equal opportunity disemployers," the Urban Institute observed. "The odds of being drafted into the fight against inflation increase steadily the lower an individual's earnings and family income [are] to begin with . . . the 1981–82 recession drove 4.3 million more people into poverty . . . Black men suffered the most of all."[6]

The economic consequences were barely noticed by some groups and, in fact, some sectors flourished throughout the recession. Manufacturing was shrinking, but the so-called service sector of the economy actually continued to expand throughout the 1981–1982 recession, adding 1.5 million jobs. In its broadest usage, "services" meant any work or business that did not produce something tangible for sale. So the general term covered everything from neighborhood drugstores to the largest banks and brokerages, from laundries to airlines and insurance companies. Service jobs ranged from the menial to the most specialized, maids and lawyers, short-order cooks and stockbrokers, key-punch operators and molecular biologists. During the recession, one growth area for service jobs involved the spreading use of computers and high-tech careers. Another growth area was finance and banking, riding the resurgence of financial assets.[7]

The 1981–1982 recession dealt out personal rewards and punishments like an inverted pyramid of economic justice: the least suffered most and vice versa. In contrast to previous contractions, real per capita income, after discounting for inflation, actually increased slightly through the course of the contraction, while the overall economy was shrinking. One reason for this anomaly was the continuing growth of the government's income-transfer programs through which Washington distributed billions to Social Security retirees, veterans, welfare families and others (using borrowed money, if necessary). This increase was normal for recessions as more and more citizens lost their incomes and became dependent.

But the central explanation for the rising incomes reflected the fundamental sea change that was under way in the American economy, rearranging basic patterns. The increase in per capita income was attributable not to wages but to interest. Over the three years since the Federal Reserve had launched its anti-inflation initiative in 1979, there had been an explosive surge in the income families derived from interest payments on their financial assets. The contrast in economic fortunes was stark: industrial production shrank from its 1979 peak by nearly 12 percent, while personal income from interest grew by 67 percent. The real economy was languishing and finance was flourishing.

The increase in interest rates after 1979 produced $148 billion in additional income in 1982 for those who owned financial assets. Naturally, the money was distributed in a regressive fashion—disproportionately benefiting upper-income families since they were the ones who owned the most in financial assets. It was not simply financial intermediaries like the commercial banks that profited in recession, but wealth holders generally, most especially the 10 percent of American families that owned 86 percent of the net financial wealth.

The shifting composition of personal incomes produced an odd juncture for the political economy. If one viewed the Federal Reserve's policy of high interest rates as an implicit government program for redistributing incomes, its magnitude by 1982 was approximately as great as all of the government's other income-transfer programs combined, the redistribution of income that was explicit and controversial. The vast flow of money distributed to various beneficiaries through Social Security, veterans' pensions, welfare and the rest came to $374 billion, now about the same as the income distributed to wealth holders through the high interest rates, $366 billion. Interest payments reached a record share of the nation's personal income in 1982, more than 14 percent, almost doubled from ten years before.

The billions in government checks sent to the poor or the elderly or other beneficiaries generated an endless social debate over whether the recipients truly deserved the money. No questions were raised, however, about the windfall in interest income for the well-to-do, though much of this vast redistribution was also attributable to government policy. Interest income was considered the just entitlement of capital, the reward that was due, under any circumstances, to industrious citizens who had managed to store up financial assets.

The wealth holders, whether they were elderly retirees with modest savings or millionaires with vast accumulations, might claim there was a rough sort of justice in their good fortune. For many years, after all, they were the virtuous "savers" who had lost while debtors had profited at their expense. The federal government had effectively "robbed" them by permitting price inflation. The Federal Reserve, inadvertently or otherwise, had reduced the value of their financial assets by permitting the dollar to become cheapened. Now it was their turn to be made whole.

This moral logic demonstrated the triumph of money over life. In the hierarchy of shared cultural values and political goals, the abstraction of money values was given greater rank than tangible needs of flesh and spirit, just as Veblen had said. The dense web of conflicting social interests would, in effect, be reconciled by an exercise in bookkeeping—justice would be redressed by balancing the ledger of money values. One side would lose and the other would gain, but equity would be served by restoring stable money.

This required implicitly a moral choice of abstraction over tangible reality, a preference that was revealed when one compared the nature of the losses suffered by victims on either side of the equation. What exactly did an investor lose from the inflation that eroded his wealth? In some instances, there was real loss. An elderly couple who depended on interest income from savings to maintain their living standard might experience genuine sacrifices because of price inflation.

Since their asset income purchased less in real goods, they had to give up some things.

More typically, however, wealth holders simply realized less growth than they expected from their accumulated wealth. During inflation, the real return on their financial assets was smaller than they anticipated or, for limited periods of time, even negative. This did not change their material circumstances in any way. With few exceptions, they did not lose their livelihoods or their homes or find themselves unable to buy food and clothing for their families. Their loss amounted to this: their financial wealth did not breed still more wealth as fast as it would have if money's value had been stable. Once money was restored to a stable value, they would again enjoy the full prerogative of capital. They would become steadily, reliably wealthier.

On the other side of the balance sheet, the human distress was not an abstraction. The losers from disinflation did include profiteers, speculators who had gambled on inflating prices by buying farmland or antiques or commodity futures, and their loss was strictly financial. For the most part, however, the victims of the liquidation process experienced tangible privation—the loss of family livelihoods, of homes and businesses and farms—that included incalculable damage to what Veblen called "the tenuous things of the human spirit." It was the general willingness to subordinate these human losses, including life itself, to the goal of sound money that demonstrated the society's true values.

Barbaric as it might seem, people did actually lose their lives so that money could be made sound again. The human casualties from a major economic contraction were comparable in number to the mortalities of a colonial war. These deadly effects were documented by Dr. M. Harvey Brenner of Johns Hopkins University, who made a study of the impact on life and health associated with the deep recession of 1974–1975. That recession, Brenner concluded, produced a 2.3 percent increase in the nation's normal mortality rate. It led to a 2.8 percent increase in the cardiovascular death rate, a 1.4 percent increase in deaths from cirrhosis of the liver, a 1 percent increase in the rate of suicides. In addition, he found a 6 percent increase in admissions to state mental hospitals and in total arrests.

In all, Brenner calculated, 45,900 people had died prematurely due to the swollen unemployment of 1974–1975—casualties in a liquidation that was less severe than the one unfolding in 1982.

John Zanetti, a steelworkers' union official at the Pullman Standard plant in Butler, Pennsylvania, counted nine suicides among his fellow workers and he lost count of the divorces. Pullman Standard manufactured railroad freight cars, sixty cars a day, and when it closed on February 4, 1982, 2,700 steelworkers and others were displaced, permanently as it turned out.

> One guy who shot himself lost his job when the plant closed and his wife was a nurse, making about $7 an hour, I guess, and they had bought a new home [Zanetti said]. They were living high on the hog because, together, they were making $17–$18–$19 an hour—about $35,000 a year. But when he lost his job, he couldn't afford the house payments. His wife didn't want to give up the house and they separated. They were living apart when he shot himself.

At the union office, Zanetti took a phone call from an unemployed steelworker who asked if his wife would still receive insurance benefits in the event his death was a suicide. "I talked to him, another union official talked to him," Zanetti said. "We called his brother who went over and talked him out of it. I talked to him, but I'm not a counselor. You can't put yourself in their shoes. I know what it's like, but still."[8]

In Abilene, Texas, Joan Benigno saw the victims downstream—the thousands of unemployed workers and their families who fled to the Southwest in search of work.

> We averaged two or three suicides' calls a day [said Benigno, director of Abilene's mental-health association]. Sometimes, they were in progress when they called. One woman, she was thirty-two and from Pennsylvania, said to me, "I'm sitting here with the phone in one hand and a gun in the other. Give me one reason why I shouldn't kill myself."
>
> About 80 percent of the callers were from Pennsylvania, Michigan, Ohio, Illinois, that region. One guy, he was twenty-one or twenty-two, was out on the Interstate. He threw himself in front of a tractor-trailer. He's never been identified. . . . They become hopeless. They say you have to hit bottom before you come back, but I don't know if these people will ever come back.[9]

Peter Sternlight, operating manager of the Open Market Desk, the man who bought and sold bonds every day for the Federal Reserve System, worried sometimes about what the Fed was doing to the American people. Sternlight lived in Brooklyn, and on weekends, he took long bicycle rides through the borough, including blighted sections like Bedford-Stuyvesant where the poverty was so visible.

> It can bother me [Sternlight acknowledged]. I ride my bike through these neighborhoods on Sundays and I ask myself: "What the hell are we doing to these areas?" Then I think, "Oh, well, they probably wouldn't be

going much better off if we had a much more stimulative monetary policy. They'll probably be better off in the long run if we do something about inflation." But I continue to be bothered.

The vice chairman of the Federal Reserve Board, Frederick Schultz, felt similar anxieties when he visited at home in Jacksonville, Florida. "One of my good friends was an auto dealer who went under," he said. "I'd go home and see him somewhere and he'd say, 'Schultz, for godsakes, come home.' He wanted me to come home so I would stop doing what I was doing in Washington. It was a little painful for both of us and we didn't talk about it."

The Federal Reserve governors all encountered evidence of the intense public distress that was flowing from their policy decisions and they dealt with these pressures in different ways. "I drink more," one governor explained. His half-twisted smile suggested that he was not joking.

Did I get sweaty palms? Did I lie awake at night? [Fred Schultz asked aloud]. The answer is I did both. I was speaking before these groups all the time, home builders and auto dealers and others. It's not so bad when some guy gets up and yells at you, "You SOB, you're killing us." What really got to me was when this fellow stood up and said in a very quiet way, "Governor, I've been an auto dealer for thirty years, worked hard to build up that business. Next week, I am closing my doors." Then he sat down. That really gets to you.

Governor Lyle Gramley, who had been a senior Fed staff official for many years, realized it was different to be a governor, casting a vote. "It was a very sobering experience for me," he said, "to realize that what I do and decide has horrendous effects on the lives of millions of people." Gramley, like others on the Board of Governors, encountered old friends who were outright hostile to him. "But that's part of the game," Gramley said stoically. "More often, it is teasing."

"What you try to do," said E. Gerald Corrigan, president of the Minneapolis Fed, "is satisfy yourself that, difficult as it may be, the alternative would be far worse. Permitting the instabilities to go on would be the worst thing you could do."

That was the common rationale, repeated by Paul Volcker and the others throughout the liquidation. If inflation was finally brought under control, they promised, then everyone would be better off, including those people who were now suffering. The economy, they said, would be able to achieve higher real growth and sustain its expansion longer without inflation. Workers might get smaller nominal pay raises, but without the constantly rising prices, their real wage gains would be larger. Perhaps most important, long-term capital investment would become more rational and reliable. That would enable the nation to improve its basic productivity—more real output per investment of labor and capital. Rising productivity created the surplus wealth and income that could be distributed among all the players. The human suffering, they reasoned, would be morally justified once these positive results came to pass.

"You just have to tell yourself," Volcker said, "that somehow it's in the larger interest of the country—and even of these people—to get this straightened out."

In Kentucky, the home builders' association printed up "wanted" posters with photos of the seven governors—"for premeditated and calculated cold-blooded murder of millions of small businesses." [10] Three national trade associations—realtors, home builders and auto dealers—joined forces in a silent protest, mailing hundreds of keys to the Federal Reserve Board, representing unbuilt houses and unsold cars. Lapel stickers in the shape of a hangman's noose announced: "Hang tall, Paul."

Volcker reluctantly agreed to a permanent bodyguard after a distraught man entered the Fed with a sawed-off shotgun, a revolver and a knife. Guards stopped the man just outside the boardroom where the governors were meeting. His plan was to take the governors hostage and force the news media to focus on what the Federal Reserve was doing to the country. [11]

"The public criticism was really abusive," an associate of Volcker's said. "It was hard on him. There were a number of personal threats, presumably from kooks, but all of it takes its toll."

Whatever their personal anguish, the Federal Reserve governors were also essentially insulated. They did not personally confront the worst of it; the uglier aspects did not intrude on their official deliberations. Policy discussions inside the FOMC, as political scientist John T. Woolley noted, were rigorously focused on "puzzle-solving" questions—the complex technical issues of money hydraulics. "Questions having to do with income distribution, other inequalities, the appropriate direction of future industrial development and so forth are put aside," Woolley observed. [12]

"I don't think we are very much driven by the question of equity, other than in the broad sense," Governor Partee acknowledged. "We would not back off from an interest rate because we thought there were major inequities involved."

Among themselves, the policy makers talked like financial engineers, working out the abstract problems of money demand and velocity and reserve control. The narrow focus allowed them to distance themselves from the messy reality outside the boardroom. It was considered bad taste to dwell on stories of personal tragedy. Anthony Solomon of the New York Fed said matter-of-factly:

> Once in a while you get a rational letter. The guy's in trouble, it evokes sympathies. Sometimes, the letters are stupid or obscene. But we are sheltered. We are meeting mostly with business people, financial people, government officials, foreign leaders and a little bit with labor leaders. It isn't as though we run into a large number of people who lost their jobs or their car dealerships.

Inside the embattled Fed, the deep contraction produced a comradely élan, a spirit of we-are-all-in-this-together. The angry home builders who had deluged the Fed with two-by-fours, symbols of the collapsed housing industry, would have been aghast to learn that many Fed officials kept the blocks of wood prominently displayed on their desks and showed them off to visitors—like souvenirs of battle. Volcker himself displayed with a smile a huge, brightly painted sledgehammer that was sent to him by citizens of Tennessee to "drive down interest rates."

The Federal Reserve was ruled, after all, by the masculine mystique. This was not simply because nearly all of its senior officers were men. The very purpose of the central bank was anchored in a sense of manly duty: the obligation to make hard and unpopular choices, unswayed by the passions of the crowd. One was expected to exercise a cool rationality. To be strong and stoical in the face of public abuse. To avoid the emotionalism that might contaminate judgment or reveal weakness. Paul Volcker, it was said by a close friend, felt the pressures of social distress as strongly as anyone else, but it would be out of character for him to talk about it. "That would seem like he was appealing to your sympathy," the friend explained. "It would look soft."

The governors' self-conscious "toughness" was expressed most bluntly by Henry Wallich, a courtly gentleman who, nonetheless, took considerable pride in his own willingness to make harsh decisions. "Had one known what the cost of disinflation would be," Wallich said, "it would not be an easy decision to make. But obviously it was worth it—temporary pain for lasting benefits. It's a question of whether you have the guts to take the pain."

Both to his colleagues and to the public, Paul Volcker seemed the very embodiment of this masculine strength and courage. He had "guts." As the recession dragged on, deepening its destruction, the

Fed chairman loomed larger and larger in the popular consciousness —an awesome figure, stolid and unbending and mysteriously knowledgeable. He seemed admirably indifferent to the trivial politics surrounding him in Washington, ominously indifferent to the cries of human pain from ordinary citizens. *U.S. News & World Report* moved Volcker from sixth to second place, right behind the President, in its annual survey of influentials, "Who Runs America?"[13] *People* magazine chronicled his celebrity status. Volcker was photographed at home, sprawled in an armchair, doing a crossword puzzle and smoking his long cigar.[14]

Volcker's character—the strong, silent type—became the public symbol for the wrenching discipline being imposed on the American economy. He was physically imposing, a head taller than most everyone else, including the President. He spoke in a brooding Germanic manner that was intimidating by itself. His intellectual self-confidence was daunting and so were his silences.

On television, appearing before hostile congressional committees, the Fed chairman pulled on his cigar and pouted his lips at a skeptical angle, while the angry congressmen accused him of heedlessly wrecking lives and businesses. Wreathed in cigar smoke, Volcker would shake his head wearily and dismiss every accusation as simplistic. The hostile questions were deflected with rambling, evasive answers that conceded nothing and only added to the politicians' frustrations.

"Paul was worried by the fact that so many groups were rising in righteous wrath," Fred Schultz said. "He's not insensitive. But he is a tough guy."

In the public drama, Volcker was like the stern father, administering punishment to errant children. When the children whined or resisted, he would patiently explain that, for reasons they perhaps did not fully comprehend, this would be good for them in the long run. His manner was aloof. His perseverance seemed to tower heroically above weaker souls around him. Twenty years earlier, Congressman Wright Patman had complained that the Federal Reserve's attitude was "Papa knows best." Volcker filled the same role. He was the father imposing discipline on the family.

The image was more than a metaphor. Many monetary economists actually saw the Federal Reserve in those terms, as the parent of us all, the responsible adult who must occasionally punish the children by inflicting pain. Donald J. Mullineaux, a former senior vice president of the Philadelphia Fed, made the point explicit in a scholarly essay on how the Federal Reserve controlled the economy: "Suppose the central bank announces a target of zero inflation to be achieved through strict control of the money supply. If inflation rises to 5 percent (the economy misbehaves), the central bank needs to slow the growth of the money supply (administer a spanking). But a slowdown in money growth is likely to produce a temporary rise in unemployment (pain)." [15]

Volcker's private character was evidently not that different from his public one. His daughter, Janice, once described a similar distance in her father's personal manner at home: "You'll be talking to him, but he'll sit there reading a book. And you know he hears what you're saying, but he's not acknowledging it." As a small boy in kindergarten, Paul did not talk much either, his mother told an interviewer from *Newsweek.* "His father and I got a report from school complaining that he didn't take part in group discussions—and he hasn't taken part in group discussions in the family since," she said, laughing. Volcker's own recollections of childhood centered on discipline. "My story," he told *Newsweek,* "is that [my sisters] were so conscious of not wanting to spoil me that they were too successful in leaning over backward in the other direction."

As an adult, Volcker disciplined himself. "At the Fed," *People* magazine reported, "Volcker has applied the same strictures to the U.S. economy that he applies to his personal life." The popular accounts of the chairman all focused on this aspect of the man—his frugal life-style. In private and in public speeches, Volcker sometimes ruminated on the popular obsession with getting rich, a desire that was especially popular in Wall Street. "What's the subject of life—to get rich?" he once said. "All of those fellows out there getting rich might be dancing around the real subject of life." [16] In his need for order and control over things, Volcker resembled the classic Freudian character type, the anal personality, but there was this essential difference—Volcker had no interest whatever in accumulating "filthy lucre."

It was a tantalizing irony: the monastic central banker, the spartan father, dedicated to restoring sound money, yet oblivious to accumulating wealth and worldly pleasures for himself. The image lent dramatic depth to Volcker's public persona, but the often-expressed solicitude for his personal sacrifices was misplaced. Volcker was richly compensated for his work. At any time, it was true, he could have left his $75,000-a-year government job for a more lucrative career in private finance, earning many times more than his Fed salary. But Volcker was rewarded in a different coin, the one that mattered most to him. Instead of money, he got power. He got to control things. He was the presiding patriarch for the American economy and, by extension, the world's. No million-dollar salary in Wall Street could buy that for him.

And he had "guts." Even those who detested the Federal Reserve chairman, who objected most strenuously to the stringent regimen he was imposing on the nation, were compelled to concede that much. In early 1982, with public anger rising rapidly, Volcker agreed to address the annual convention of the National Association of Home Builders in Las Vegas. The audience was as hostile as any he could confront, but Volcker did not apologize for their agonies or even promise them speedy relief.

We would all like to see recovery begin [Volcker said to the home builders]. But even more crucial than the precise timing of that recovery is that growth be sustainable for years ahead. It is in that context that I am convinced we cannot let up now in our anti-inflation effort. . . . The pain we have suffered would have been for naught—and we would only be putting off until some later time an even more painful day of reckoning.[17]

Like it or not, the home builders gave Volcker's uncompromising message a standing ovation.

Nancy Teeters, almost alone, resisted. Month after month, as the economy spiraled downward, she repeatedly urged her colleagues to back off. The largest corporations were shutting down more and more of their production. As loan failures accumulated, the financial sector itself was threatened with crisis. The Fed's single-mindedness, she warned, was inflicting deep wounds that would not soon be healed.

"I gave the FOMC a lecture," Teeters said. "I told them: 'You are pulling the financial fabric of this country so tight that it's going to rip. You should understand that once you tear a piece of fabric, it's very difficult, almost impossible, to put it back together again.' "

The metaphor, she remarked caustically afterward, was one that only a woman might use. "None of these guys has ever sewn anything in his life," Teeters said.

But the metaphor hinted at much deeper differences—a moral argument over justice itself. Teeters thought the wholesale destruction of innocents was not simply wrong but largely unnecessary and ultimately dangerous for the society. The other governors thought it was required, unpleasant but therapeutic. Though never stated so directly, they were really arguing about the process of liquidation itself. Was it truly in the society's interest—or morally defensible—to inflict such broad damage when there were other, less brutal ways to restore economic stability? What were the unmeasurable costs of severing so many human relationships at random, the intricate, continuous web of social and economic connections that people and institutions depended upon? Once destroyed, the web might be irreparably lost.

In broad terms, this was an ancient argument over how a society arrived at its sense of justice, an argument made freshly relevant by contemporary feminist critics who were challenging the male-dominated institutions in the society. The feminist critique was aimed in part at the masculine moral perspective, a mind-set that seemed narrow and mechanical, driven by abstract formulations that excluded social complexities and was insufficiently attentive to human loss. When Harvard psychologist Carol Gilligan explored these gender-related moral differences in her study, *In a Different Voice*, she used the same metaphor that Nancy Teeters had used before the Federal Open Market Committee. Women, Gilligan wrote, will usually seek to avoid "the fracture of human relationships that must be mended with its own thread."

The question of "social fabric" was, practically speaking, not an admissible argument at the private meetings of the Federal Open Market Committee. It was not the way its members looked at things, and Teeters's repeated warnings were politely dismissed. She continued to object anyway, month after month. If the Federal Reserve did not swiftly ease up, it might lead to a general unraveling of the financial system and a crisis of much larger dimensions. Some of the men began to share her worries, but they declined to vote with her against the chairman.

It was very difficult for me philosophically to run up the unemployment rate [Teeters said]. It was perfectly obvious to me we didn't need to put interest rates up that high. We couldn't do it without a recession, but recession is still a difficult decision to make, no matter how you dress it up. People get unemployed. People get hurt. All sorts of nasty things can happen if it gets out of hand.

As a successful woman in a profession still dominated by men, Teeters was fully aware of the stereotypes that attached to women who attained positions of power. Women might be dismissed as "soft." Men accused them of confusing emotion with facts. Knowing this, she kept raising her voice anyway. Furthermore, Teeters freely acknowledged what many of her male colleagues would never be willing to admit—the deteriorating economy frightened her. "I was scared and so was everybody else," she said. "That's what it came down to."

Inside the temple, Nancy Teeters was always something of an outsider—a liberal Democrat and also a woman, but more than that a governor who persisted in challenging premises that others assumed were beyond argument. "Nancy never really took the veil," said a senior official on the Federal Reserve Board staff. Another FOMC officer described the distance between Teeters and her colleagues: "She never said 'we.' She always addressed the other committee members as 'you.' 'If YOU do this, you're going to have the worst unemployment.' 'If YOU make this decision, it will guarantee a long recession.' She was very consciously the outsider."

Relations were cordial and correct, but others were increasingly annoyed by her persistence. "She was sounding the alarm about unemployment in a way that irritates people," a senior staff officer said. "Of course they were humane and they were concerned about unemployment, but they didn't need anyone lecturing them on that. It was her tone, her mode of argument."

The irony, of course, was that nothing Teeters said inside the boardroom would have rankled the general public or most public officials outside the Fed. Her position could be described in the terms of the feminine moral perspective, but the values themselves were widely shared among men and women, both in and out of public life. Teeters was trying to make the case for considerations that were broader than the Federal Reserve's narrow preoccupation with money's value. She was invoking the claims of what Veblen called "the tenuous things of the human spirit . . . the gross material needs of human life."

Given its own institutional values, it was not surprising that the Federal Reserve turned away from these claims in annoyance, for the Federal Reserve was a masculine institution. When Teeters became the first woman on the Board of Governors, in 1978, she found two women in senior-grade positions at the Fed. When she retired six years later, there would be only thirteen. Still, the central bank's masculinity was tied not so much to personnel but to its deepest assumptions about right and wrong.

The feminine-masculine distinctions described by Gilligan and other feminist scholars provided a key to understanding the Federal Reserve's own mode of thinking. What was true about little boys playing games at school was also roughly true about the grown-up behavior inside the Fed boardroom. Boys were taught to believe in rules, a hard and concise form of justice that could be calculated. Girls were taught to negotiate and compromise, to avoid harsh judgments that might fracture relationships.

Observed on the playground, small boys will quarrel repeatedly over infractions of the rules, arrive at a decision, then continue the game, Gilligan explained. Girls at play argue much less and are more likely to change the rules to make everyone happy—or even abandon the game if the dispute seems to threaten friendships. Boys, Gilligan wrote, become "increasingly fascinated with the legal elaboration of rules and the development of fair procedures for adjudicating conflicts." Girls, on the other hand, "are more tolerant in their attitudes toward rules, more willing to make exceptions and more easily reconciled to innovations."

This difference, one could say, was approximately parallel to what divided Teeters from her colleagues at the Fed. She was willing to abandon the arbitrary money "rules" that the Federal Reserve was following rather than allow even greater destruction to unfold. For her, the losses were weighing far more heavily than the abstract consistency. She was willing to innovate, to change the rules rather than accept continuing social disintegration.

The other governors could not easily entertain such a trade-off. They sought the "right" decision by deliberating over the economic abstractions of the money formulas. In Henry Wallich's phrase, they were supposed to "have the guts to take the pain." Teeters's dissents kept reminding everyone that it was not they who would take the "pain," but defenseless others. Naturally, this rankled.

The origin of gender differences was woven deeply in everyone's childhood experience—boys taught to separate from their mothers in order to attain a mature masculine identity, girls learning from their mothers' model and assuming responsibility for maintaining unbroken personal attachments in the family. As a result, males tend to have difficulty with relationships and females with a sense of self.

The moral implications were sketched more clearly in Gilligan's example of clinical studies that asked grade-school boys and girls to solve hypothetical dilemmas. If an impoverished man stole medicine to heal his sick wife, should he be punished as a thief? The boys would weigh good and evil and arrive at a straightforward verdict by "logical deduction." The girls attempted to devise ameliorative solutions in which all the parties settled the issue by talking it out among themselves and compromising. In a similar vein, Volcker and the majority would not consider themselves "wrong" in any sense so long as they adhered conscientiously to the economic rules of their system. In the real world, as Nancy Teeters kept pointing out, things were getting dangerously frayed, but the others found refuge from her evidence by sticking to their numbers (while they resented her constant appeals to human sympathy).

In the male-dominated orthodoxy, particularly in economics, the feminine was dismissed as an emotional evasion of hard facts. Yet it was the masculine approach itself that was a form of evasion—a way to block out the complex social realities by focusing solely on a system of mathematical abstractions. As Gilligan and others have suggested, the social ideal should be not to embrace one perspective or the other but to reconcile the two, to seek balance in the way people think about such things, but also in the way public institutions define social justice.

"Sensitivity to the needs of others and the assumption of responsibility for taking care lead women to attend to voices other than their own and to include in their judgment other points of view." This supposed weakness was actually their moral strength—a mediating capacity that could reach beyond the hard-edged adjudications of the masculine. The feminine vision blurred the clear, sharp outlines of justice, and that enriched and deepened the idea of what justice required.

Quite apart from Nancy Teeters and her losing arguments inside the Fed, the feminine-masculine differences framed the moral question that could be asked of the entire process of government-managed liquidation. If they thought about it at all, people could sense easily enough that there was something wrong about a system that, in effect, selected certain victims to serve as the scapegoats for everyone else's benefit. The moral problem became even more obvious when the sacrificial victims were largely chosen from among the weak and powerless.

What was missing from the economics of liquidation—and from the general political debate—was the moral test described by the feminine perspective, the obligation to tend the broader human relationships, the honoring of family responsibilities, the idea of a valuable fabric that must be preserved. If those values were to prevail or were even in rough balance with the masculine, the government would not likely engineer the kind of selective destruction that the Federal Reserve was imposing. It might have to be more patient about restoring stable money values, giving people more time to adjust. It might have to take up other methods of restraint—direct or indirect controls on credit and prices, for instance—that did not require abrupt and massive suffering by a hapless minority but instead spread the sacrifice more gradually and more fairly across the entire society. Most citizens probably assumed there were no alternatives to the destruction because the alternatives were almost never discussed in politics and seldom studied by economists. The ritual of liquidation, brutal as it was, conveyed a bracing sense of manly struggle, and many even found it satisfying. The numbers were hard and certain. The counterclaims were perceived as soft and tenuous.[18]

The Bible taught the same moral lesson about the conflict between abstract justice and human life. Confronted with two women who both claimed a baby as their own, King Solomon decreed a just solution—

the baby would be cut in half and each mother would be given her share. The true mother, as Solomon expected, quickly revealed herself by renouncing her claim to the child. She would not subordinate the baby's life to the logic of the law. "The blind willingness to sacrifice people to truth," Gilligan wrote, ". . . has always been the danger of an ethics abstracted from life."

That was the essence of Nancy Teeters' complaint—that the Federal Reserve was sacrificing people to abstract "truth." If her repeated dissents sounded "soft" to some of her colleagues, the old sexual stereotypes were actually reversed in the behavior of the Federal Open Market Committee. Several other governors, after all, shared Teeters' alarm about the deteriorating economy, but none of these men felt sufficiently alarmed—or strong-willed—to vote with her against Paul Volcker. Even the chairman's own personal courage was more ambiguous than it seemed. In public, he looked heroically steadfast. In private, he worried and hesitated, unable to bring himself to abandon his operating system even though he knew it was flawed. Volcker seemed brave enough in his willingness to stare down the public's complaints. He was not so brave about staring down Wall Street.

Standing alone—opposing Paul Volcker—was not the "soft" thing to do. It took "guts" for Nancy Teeters to vote against the chairman and his majority again and again, knowing she would lose. "It's tough, very tough," Teeters said. "That's why a lot of people don't like to do it. Once Paul has a consensus, people are reluctant to vote against him."

Furthermore, the fact that Nancy Teeters was alone, that she continued to lose the arguments, did not mean that she was wrong. The financial fabric was stretched tight, as she said. In time, as she warned, it would begin to tear.[19]

SENATOR KENNEDY: What is your answer to those who say that the Fed is embarked on a scorched-earth policy with regards to the American economy? Millions of young potential home buyers feel the burden. Millions who are out of work feel it. Millions of small-business men and women feel it. Millions of farmers feel it.

MR. VOLCKER: Let me say, first of all—

SENATOR KENNEDY: Is this your policy or is it the Reagan policy?

MR. VOLCKER: I can only speak for our policy authoritatively. Let me say that monetary policy is an important instrument, but it's only one instrument of economic activity.

*** *** ***

SENATOR HAWKINS: Chairman Volcker, if I were President, I'd have you up for a visit every Monday and we'd have fireside chats or maybe some woodside chats. I know you like to be independent, Mr. Volcker, because we've had this conversation before. You reiterated today that you feel strongly that the Fed should be independent of the Congress because monetary policy is complicated. Yet we don't leave war to the generals over at the Pentagon although that's a complicated subject too.

MR. VOLCKER: Congress has the authority over the Federal Reserve. It's a question of the degree to which they're going to exercise it.

*** *** ***

SENATOR RIEGLE: I think the time has come where stubbornness in one quarter ought not to just be matched by equivalent stubbornness in another quarter. . . . I think the Fed has an obligation in its own right to face up to the damage caused by the high-interest-rate policy.

MR. VOLCKER: . . . I do not think the Federal Reserve is being stubborn in this area. I think we have a very difficult problem. I would be delighted to see interest rates decline, obviously, but you attribute—

SENATOR RIEGLE: You do have something to do with that. I mean, in all honesty, it is not as if you are a helpless bystander.

MR. VOLCKER: It is perhaps not quite as simple as you imply, senator.

*** *** ***

REPRESENTATIVE REUSS: The next subject has to do with the predictions that some are making that, in view of the wretched state of our economic and financial arrangements, there could lie ahead real distress for certain large financial institutions—banks and brokerages. Do you see any peril of that ahead?

MR. VOLCKER: Let me answer that question in general terms, Mr. Chairman. You refer to the "wretched" state of the economy and, in an immediate sense, one can recognize that description.

REPRESENTATIVE REUSS: Ten million unemployed is my wretchedness index.

MR. VOLCKER: Exactly. There's a high level of unemployment. But let me emphasize too that I think this could be a promising period.

*** *** ***

MR. VOLCKER: I think these interest rates are extraordinarily high. If, in the area of monetary policy and fiscal policy we do the right things, I don't see any place for those interest rates to go but down.

REPRESENTATIVE BROWN: But when?

REPRESENTATIVE HAMILTON: When?

MR. VOLCKER: I will not attempt to be more precise.

On Capitol Hill, the "Fed bashing" was under way in earnest. Volcker appeared regularly before numerous congressional committees, where more and more members, Republican and Democratic, liberal and conservative, took the opportunity to denounce his imperiousness or plead with him for relief. Snippets of the angry exchanges appeared on the evening news and made for good television: the vigilant congressman confronts the coldhearted banker on behalf of suffering constituents. Volcker ducked and dodged stoically, repeating

the same bromides over and over again. The most sincere and deferential inquiries elicited no more responsiveness than did the dema-
gogic tirades.

Even some conservatives, who generally supported the Fed against
liberal attacks, were concluding that Volcker had gone too far, that he
must be nudged off his rigid policy. "The man has a certain majesty
in his massive bearing," Senator Lloyd Bentsen of Texas explained,
"but I have never wanted majestic decisions to veto common sense."
Bentsen said his arguments were dismissed by Volcker "with cour-
teous disdain."[20]

The congressional outrage was real enough. The elected politicians
were hearing lots of scary talk, not only from constituents but from
respected economists. Edward E. Yardeni of E. F. Hutton predicted a
30 percent chance of a full-blown depression like the 1930s. If things
did not turn around by May, he warned, the odds would go to 50–50.
Liberal economists like Robert Solow of MIT thought the Fed had
worked itself into a corner and would need help getting out. "They are
stuck in the embarrassing position of having their finger in the dike
and believing they are the country's last hope," Solow said.[21]

The elected representatives and senators were ill-equipped to assert
their authority over the Federal Reserve. Only a handful of them were
truly comfortable with the fundamentals of money, not to mention the
complexities, and their ignorance left them especially vulnerable to
Volcker's evasions. Many of his answers were elaborate non sequiturs,
cloaked in a tone of patient explanation. The infuriated members of
Congress sensed they were being spun around, but they were not
knowledgeable enough to penetrate the chairman's cloud of smoke.

It's really a master fencing with amateurs [said a dispirited staff economist from the House Banking Committee]. Each member gets only five
minutes to ask questions and Volcker can filibuster or fill it up with gob-
bledygook. Volcker is interested in deflecting questions. The members are
interested in cute thirty-second exchanges that will get them on the evening news. They want to be cute. He wants to be obtuse. Plus, most of
them don't do their homework. Members have fifteen hundred things on
their minds. Volcker thinks about one thing—monetary policy.

Democratic senators, led by Robert Byrd of West Virginia, the minority floor leader, summoned Volcker to a private meeting on March
18 in an attempt to pressure him more effectively, away from the TV
cameras. They urged Volcker to lower interest rates and he urged
them to lower the deficits and each side wanted the other to go first.
Senator Byrd, according to one participant's notes, asked: If we cut

the deficit, what would you do? That, Volcker replied, would give the Fed some room for shading of judgment. Byrd pressed for a commitment. The Fed chairman would make none.

Volcker gave the senators in private the same argument he had made so often in public: the Federal Reserve was powerless to bring down interest rates by pumping up the money supply. If the Fed increased M-1, the financial markets would react by bidding up interest rates on their own, canceling out the intended results. That's what had occurred in January, he suggested. What Volcker left out of his explanation was the reason why the markets had reacted this way— because the Federal Reserve's monetarist operating system told them to do so.

"Volcker just said, 'Look, I can't affect interest rates,' " one participant related. "The Fed absolved itself of any responsibility for the recession. It was a great smoke screen."

Liberal Democrats felt stymied by Volcker's argument. They could not see through it at first, not until they were coached by several independent authorities, including Edward Yardeni of E. F. Hutton and Lester Thurow of MIT. The economists explained the game of circular reality played between market perceptions and Volcker's M-1. When M-1 rose above its target, financial markets scrambled for funds and bid up interest rates, anticipating that the Fed would react by tightening. The Fed saw market rates rising in response to M-1, and in order to keep its promises to financial markets, the Fed did indeed tighten—thus ratifying their expectations. The logic formed an absurd game of mirrors but one which the Federal Reserve had the power to break—anytime it wished.

The economists assured the senators that if the Fed pumped enough new money into the banking system, then short-term interest rates would fall—no matter what the markets thought or Paul Volcker claimed. Neither investor psychology nor monetarist theory was capable of repealing the law of supply and demand. A market surplus of anything, including money, would drive down the price, including interest rates.

Senator Byrd and other frustrated Democrats decided to do more than implore and bargain. They suggested subsequently to Volcker that if he failed to act they would sponsor legislation ordering the Federal Reserve to ease its policy. Such an explicit command from Congress would effectively override the Fed's historic independence. It was the ultimate threat.

"To whom are you accountable?" Byrd asked at one point.

"Well, the Congress created us and the Congress can uncreate us," Volcker replied.[22]

The Democratic leader set about organizing a legislative assault on the central bank, a measure that would direct the Fed to take the specific policy actions needed to bring down interest rates. To make his threat credible, however, Byrd would first have to convince his own colleagues. At the outset, only about fifteen of the forty-six Democratic senators were prepared to support such a bill.

Seven decades of history told Federal Reserve officials that threatening gestures from Capitol Hill were usually not meaningful. "Congress doesn't want to control the Fed," Dan Brill, the former Fed research director, explained. "Neither Congress nor the President wants to take the rap for high interest rates." [23]

In spring, Congress fired a mild warning shot—a resolution in generalized language commanding the Fed to re-evaluate its use of the monetary targets in light of the congressional intentions to reduce the deficits. It was an innocuous exhortation, easily ignored.

Senator Byrd, however, was gathering more and more Democratic cosponsors for his legislative weapon—and some Republican interest too. Coached by the outside economists, the Democrats drafted a viable reform measure that would give Congress genuine leverage on monetary policy and force the Federal Reserve to back off its hard position. The central bank was directed by the bill to abandon M-1 and monetarism and begin doing what it used to do—to target interest rates. Furthermore, the Fed's money regulation was to be assessed in the terms that really counted—real interest rates, the true cost of credit after inflation was discounted.

If the measure passed, the central bank would be ordered to keep real interest rates within a range reflecting historic levels—easing or tightening accordingly. If real interest rates on bank lending rose above 4 percent, say, the Fed would be compelled to ease and bring them down. If real rates went negative, the Fed would have to tighten and restore a reasonable return for capital. The immediate practical effect would be easy money. The long-term potential was a monetary policy that avoided extremes on both the upside and the downside.

The idea drew some interesting allies from among the Republicans. Representative Jack Kemp, a regular critic of Volcker's stringent policy, indicated that he would introduce a similar measure, cosponsored by other young conservatives in the House. The odd coalition of liberals and conservatives made the threat to the Fed somewhat more plausible. Democratic reformers had never succeeded, in many years of trying, in harnessing the central bank. Perhaps with gold-standard Republicans on board, they might actually get somewhere.

But Volcker worked the Congress assiduously, cultivating friends and allies in the broad center. Neither the Republican chairman of the

Senate Banking Committee, Garn of Utah, nor the ranking Democrat, Proxmire of Wisconsin, had any sympathy for the Fed-stripping legislation. The solid core of moderate-conservative members could be counted on to defend the status quo.

Howard Baker, the Senate Republican leader, continued to meet regularly with Volcker, pounding on his own impatience with the Fed's high interest rates. Baker, nevertheless, assured the Federal Reserve chairman that he would help block any Fed-stripping legislation.

"I told Volcker flat out that I was not going to support that," Baker said. "I thought it was bad legislation and I did not want the Fed to lose its independence. My gamble was that he would accept, at face value, my warnings that he could only go so far before the system broke."

While Democrats tried to whip up enthusiasm for a legislative assault on Volcker, Senator Baker was trying to negotiate with him. How much more would the Congress have to package in spending cuts and tax increases in order to get the Fed to ease off on interest rates? What were his terms for a truce?

"We're doing our damnedest and it's going to take more," Baker told him, "but pretty soon my troops are going to get disillusioned after spilling so much blood and seeing nothing changed on interest rates. You may be right from the theoretical side, but on the political side, you're getting close to the edge. There's not much more pain the system can take."

Neither President Reagan nor Congress was prepared to come anywhere close to what Volcker wanted. They were engaged in three-sided negotiations—House and Senate and White House, Republicans and Democrats—over how much they would do to reduce the deficits. Volcker kibitzed from the sidelines, pushing Senator Baker and the others to do still more.

"Look, you can't do what Congress won't do," Senator Baker told him sharply at one point. The danger, Baker added, was that the Fed's intransigence would lead to a real political crisis. "First," Baker said, "I will have to fight down an effort to limit the Fed's authority. I thought I could win that fight, but I couldn't be sure. Second, the fragile package of spending cuts and tax increases we had put together would come unraveled. No telling what would happen then, but the deficits would probably soar."[24]

Volcker remained unyielding. Congress was hesitantly moving toward an unusual step—enacting a major tax increase in an election year—and dragging the reluctant President along. But Volcker would make no promises about changing his monetary policy. The hope was born among the politicians, nonetheless, that if Congress passed the tax bill, the Fed would respond by bringing down interest rates.

Congress always thinks there's a deal [Volcker said]. There's a strong feeling in Congress that what we do is negotiate with them. We don't. I always try to avoid that pretext. I will be very careful in what I say. "If this happens, then that will help with conditions that may allow an easing of inflationary pressures and lower interest rates." But then Congress says, "Aha, here's a bargain. If we do this, the Fed will lower interest rates." No matter how carefully I say it, Congress always tries to conclude there is a deal.

Senator Baker, much as he wished for it, had no illusions about having won any quid pro quo. "Volcker and I went through rocky times, but I never thought he made a deal with me," Baker said. "I never claimed I had an impact on the Federal Reserve. It would be nice if I did, but I can't claim that."

The trend line that worried the White House, in addition to the declining economy, was Ronald Reagan's declining popularity in the Gallup poll. The President's approval rating was falling steadily, in inverse ratio to the rising unemployment. Nine months earlier, when the recession began, 58 percent of the American public had endorsed his performance. By the spring of 1982, Reagan's support had fallen below 45 percent and continued downward.

The President blamed Jimmy Carter and stuck to his monetarist principles. "The answer to the recession lies in bringing interest rates down," Reagan told a national television audience on April 3. "To do that, a signal must be sent that, while the political process always requires some compromises, government this time intends to stay the course. . . ."

But some of the President's senior political advisers were ready to change course, the sooner, the better. They were increasingly skeptical of the confident predictions from the Administration's monetarist economists. The recovery the economists had promised for spring not only didn't happen, the contraction was clearly getting worse—six months before the congressional elections. James Baker, the chief of staff, expressed his frustration with Paul Volcker by complaining to colleagues: "How can he keep this misery going on so long?"

But it wasn't entirely clear to James Baker and other White House officials what, if anything, they could do to turn things around. They remained preoccupied with the deficit issue, the problem they had created in 1981, and were less intense about the Fed's tight money.

Treasury Deputy Assistant Secretary Manuel Johnson attended one White House meeting and was struck by the lopsided focus. "The meeting was all gloom-and-doom talk about the need to cut the deficits —and no mention of monetary policy," Johnson said. "When I got upset that this was so one-sided, I was told this is the only way we were going to get spending cuts. The whole focus was, we're not ever going to get out of this recession until we reduce the deficits."

Johnson and other supply siders at Treasury were urging the White House to take a forceful public position in favor of an easier monetary policy at the Fed, but they were frustrated. "Every time we tried to formulate a position on monetary policy, the word came back from the White House that monetary policy is too complicated, too technical to explain," Johnson said. "The public doesn't understand this and the financial markets will get all upset if we talk about it."

The White House staff itself was scattered in all directions on the crucial policy question—what to say to Paul Volcker. Some made the same pitch that Volcker heard on Capitol Hill: give us lower interest rates and we will reduce the deficits. The Administration's monetarists, ever suspicious of Fed intentions, continued to scold the central bank and warn against any deviations from the correct path for M-1. Others like budget director David Stockman were privately encouraging Volcker to hang tough. "Stockman was egging Volcker on," one Administration official said. "He was telling him to screw the Administration, really put it to them and force them to deal with the deficits."

Lawrence Kudlow of OMB said:

It was hilarious. All the major players tried to cut their own deals with Volcker. Stockman would have lunch with him. Don Regan would breakfast with him alone. Weidenbaum would meet with him. In that environment, it's almost like Volcker taking an opinion poll of what the Administration wanted. He learned to filter out the noise and figure out what the consensus was. I'm not saying he would go along with it, but he might go halfway if it was reasonable.

The Federal Reserve chairman kept the pressure on the White House, just as he did on Capitol Hill. The Fed could not possibly move, he insisted, until Congress first acted on reducing the fiscal imbalance. Congressional leaders and the White House, with the President's acquiescence, were approaching a consensus on a substantial tax measure that would raise $100 billion in added revenue over five years, enough to keep the future deficits from rising to a range of $250 to $300 billion. But passage of the tax bill was far from certain.

"Volcker was telling everyone, 'If you give us some relief on the deficits, it will take the pressure off,' " Stockman said. " 'Our hands are tied unless you give us some relief on the fiscal side. We've got to have some room to move.' "

Chief of Staff James Baker and Edwin Meese, the two most important political advisers, lost patience with Volcker's line. The White House was putting full muscle into getting a huge tax bill enacted, yet Volcker acted as though he had no obligation to help out.

"Baker and Meese were running around saying, 'We've got to get control of the Fed,' " one Administration official said. "The message they sent to Volcker was: 'We promise to be good boys on the deficits. So won't you please loosen?' The messages weren't that meaningful because he didn't believe us. Volcker would say to us: 'I'll see you at the signing ceremony.' "

Behind its public façade, the Federal Reserve's self-confidence was shaken. The recovery did not materialize in the spring, as Fed economists had predicted. Instead of bottoming out, the economy seemed to be sinking lower and the damage was spreading rapidly.

At the end of March, the Fed's staff economists had again assured the policy makers that a moderate recovery would be under way soon, but a number of members on the Federal Open Market Committee were no longer buying that forecast. They predicted the opposite— "continuing deterioration in both agriculture and nonagricultural industries and regions."

At the White House, Lawrence Kudlow, who had confidently predicted a turnaround by April, was now not so sure.

At the bottom of a recession, interest rates are much too high [Kudlow reported to his White House colleagues]. Only a year or two ago, present interest-rate levels would have been record highs. With interest rates at or near record levels for over three years, business firms have been unable to secure long-term financing at acceptable rates. Consequently, firms have been forced to rely on bank loans and other forms of short-term debt to meet cash flow and working capital needs. The result has been an unprecedented deterioration in corporate balance sheets.[25]

International Harvester, one of the famous old names of American manufacturing, was a spectacular example of the deterioration. Harvester's sales of tractors, combines, trucks and other heavy farm equipment fell by 31 percent during 1982 and it was compelled to cut its work force worldwide by twenty-two thousand employees. Nevertheless, the Chicago-based company was losing money faster and faster—a staggering $822 million that year. It sold off two divisions to raise cash, it borrowed heavily and it pleaded with its bankers.

A smaller corporation would doubtless have gone under at that point, but Harvester was too big to fail. It owed banks and other lenders $2.2 billion. The company's two hundred creditors, including the leading banks of the Midwest, agreed to defer $200 million in interest payments and to keep lending. The bankers took stock in exchange for the debt and hoped that the company would somehow, someday work its way back to profitability. Over the next few years, International Harvester would survive, but barely. A company with ninety-eight thousand employees in 1979 shrank to one with fifteen thousand by 1985. Agriculture did not recover and the market for tractors and combines never did revive. Harvester would finally abandon the business line that Cyrus McCormick had started in the 1830s, the manufacture of farm equipment, and change its name to Navistar International, a maker of trucks.[26]

At the Federal Reserve, the uncertainties were uncomfortably close to home. The assumptions that had led the Federal Open Market Committee to tighten the money supply again in early February were clearly askew. The surge of M-1 growth in December and January did not presage a pickup in economic activity, as some of the governors had theorized. The opposite was now occurring—industrial production was falling steadily toward a new low. The quantity of money the Fed had supplied to the banking system ought to have been ample to permit economic recovery. Clearly, it wasn't. Judging from the extraordinary level of interest rates, the Fed was still holding very tight. What was wrong with money?

"The economy was spiraling downward," Governor Nancy Teeters said, "and the theories were falling apart on us."

The theory that was falling apart was Milton Friedman's—and, by adoption, Paul Volcker's. The new problem with M-1 was more profound than the confusion of money definitions that the policy makers had encountered and tried to compensate for at previous junctures. Money was now slowing down in circulation—losing velocity, in technical terms—as the money supply turned over in different transactions in the private economy at a declining pace. The slowing velocity disrupted all the standard monetary equations. It meant that a given quantity of M-1 could not possibly produce the level of economic activity expected from it. Indeed, it meant that the money supply was effectively much tighter than the Fed had intended.

Money was slowing down mainly because people were scared. They were holding on to it longer than normal. Under siege, millions of players in the private economy, families and businesses, were storing larger balances in their checking accounts, particularly in the interest-bearing NOW accounts, but they weren't spending their money so quickly. Everyone hesitated, and as the New York Fed put it, everyone felt the "strong precautionary demand for liquidity in the highly uncertain economic and financial climate."

When money velocity departed from the normal expectations, then the Fed's basic calculations—the equations by which it determined the pace for the economy—were rendered inoperable. If a dollar turned over six times in the course of the year, it would produce $6 in nominal GNP. But if the same dollar, for unanticipated reasons, turned over only five times, there would be only $5 in resulting economic activity—a gross shortfall when it was multiplied by the entire money supply.

Though unrecognized at first, that was roughly what began happening to the American economy—and to the economic regulators at the Federal Reserve. In the first quarter of 1982, the Fed had supplied about $450 billion in M-1, the money available for immediate transactions. To illustrate, if $450 billion in M-1 was multiplied by a velocity of six, it would yield $2.7 trillion in nominal GNP. If the rate of velocity fell to 5.5, however, the same money supply would lead to economic activity of less than $2.5 trillion—a staggering loss that no one had intended.

M-1 was a reliable measure, in other words, only if velocity followed its predicted trend line. If people abruptly changed their spending and money-handling habits, for whatever reasons, then velocity changed unexpectedly and M-1 became grossly misleading. The government, including the Federal Reserve, could do nothing to control this wild card in the economics of money. People were not, after all, compelled to circulate their money at a prescribed speed.

Velocity was the Achilles' heel in Friedman's theory—the uncontrollable variable that could throw his confident prescriptions about money totally off track. Nor was this insight especially new. For years, the critics of monetarism (including those at the Fed) had pointed out that Friedman was assigning a constancy to money relationships that did not, in fact, exist. The alluring simplicity of Friedman's doctrine —control M-1 and forget about everything else—was also its central fallacy. Except now M-1's reliability was more than a theory for debate among economists. The Federal Reserve was relying on the same fallacy to regulate the entire economy.

The actual divergence of M-1's velocity was not as dramatic as the simplified example, but it was still unprecedented in modern experience. In the first quarter of 1982, M-1 grew in size by 10.6 percent, but M-1's velocity declined by 10.8 percent—effectively canceling the increase in the money supply. Back in January, when the financial markets and the White House and the Federal Reserve itself were alarmed by the surging growth of M-1, the effective growth of money was actually flat.

The monetarists, those who acknowledged this shift at all, claimed it was a temporary aberration. They felt sure that M-1 would soon regain a predictable rate of velocity. But they were wrong again—it was not an aberration at all. Velocity began dropping in the last quarter of 1981 and it would continue to decline for the next year and a half. What was the Fed supposed to do in the meantime? Nothing in Milton Friedman's monetary rule allowed for this policy dilemma. If the Federal Reserve stuck to the Friedman formula—providing steady, moderate growth in M-1 each month while money velocity was dropping sharply—the central bank would actually be driving the real economy into deeper and deeper ruin.

"This left the monetarists out on a limb," Teeters said, "a limb that just got chopped off."

The emerging reality, however, was not instantly obvious to everyone. There was no meter available where monetary economists could monitor the changing speed of money and adjust the supply accordingly. Velocity was what economists called a "derived" statistic— knowable only after the fact, by dividing the money supply into the economic growth that had already occurred. In the interim, there was confusion and debate. Early on, the Fed technicians recognized that velocity was falling and some thought they understood the reasons why, but that did not settle the question of what would happen next.

Frank Morris of Boston reargued his case for abandoning M-1 altogether, his skepticism shared by a growing number of colleagues. Tony Solomon of the New York Fed also urged the Federal Open Market Committee to back away from rigid adherence to the money aggregate. But the Reserve Bank presidents who were monetarists— Roos of St. Louis, Black of Richmond, Karen N. Horn of Cleveland, among others—argued the opposite case yet again. Abandoning M-1 would be interpreted as the equivalent of abandoning the fight against inflation.

Henry Wallich, though he had disdain for the monetarist doctrine, nevertheless joined the monetarists in arguing for a hard line on controlling M-1. Wallich wanted to wrench out inflation at any cost—"to take the pain," as he said—and keeping stringent pressure on money growth would accomplish that result, regardless of the theory. In Wallich's orthodoxy, holding down the economy could never be a mistake so long as some price inflation remained.

Nancy Teeters, a liberal who had never believed in the monetarist claims, tried once again to convince the committee members that they had made themselves prisoners of a false doctrine. One did not have to look at M-1 or money velocity or any other arcane calculations about the money aggregates to see why the Fed was driving the economy downward. The straightforward explanation was fairly simple: the price of credit. "We had gotten rates too high," she argued, "and we held them too high, too long."

Teeters proposed that it was time to declare victory. Price inflation had abated dramatically. The Consumer Price Index had been running below 5 percent for four months in a row and even briefly dipped to zero. Teeters argued that the Federal Reserve could now justifiably let up—before the damage got worse.

Money was still tight—extraordinarily tight, no matter what M-1 signaled. The Federal Funds rate still hovered around 15 percent, which meant that as inflation abated, the real-interest cost to borrowers was steadily increasing—exceeding 6 percent by springtime. The declining velocity of money should have been accompanied by declining loan demand and falling interest rates. Yet, as Lawrence Kudlow's analysis had pointed out, businesses had no choice but to keep borrowing more and more. The deteriorating corporate balance sheets created a record demand for commercial loans, despite the high real-interest rates, despite the recessionary conditions.

The chairman, to his admirers, was cautious and intellectually strong-willed, but to critics he seemed stubborn and arrogant. In any case, Paul Volcker was not yet convinced it was time to ease. At the March 30 meeting of the FOMC, Volcker agreed that M-1 was increasingly quirky and the Fed would have to back off a bit from the usual formulations it had followed since 1979. The Fed would be somewhat more flexible for a time—and hope that the uncertainties were clarified.

Volcker was not willing to concede that his operating method was now inoperable or that his Keynesian critics had been right. The liberal academicians, joined by some Wall Street voices like Henry Kaufman, had warned Volcker that he had chosen the wrong time in history to impose his monetarist principles. Their critique appeared to be confirmed by the present reality. Still, Volcker clung to the importance of M-1, at least in his public rhetoric, as though nothing had changed.

The monetarist approach had been politically valuable to him and he was reluctant to abandon it. As a management tool for deciding monetary policy, the money numbers had led the Federal Reserve into repeated errors and confusion, some with grave consequences for the real economy. But, as a political argument, M-1 worked. In Washington, it gave the Fed chairman cover for the extraordinarily high interest rates he was imposing, a complicating rationale that most congressmen could not effectively challenge. On Wall Street, meanwhile, Volcker's other audience embraced M-1 as the talisman of Federal Reserve sincerity. The monetarist rhetoric thus blunted criticism from one power center while it nurtured favor from the other.

To discard M-1 now, Volcker would have to announce to the financial system, the banks and the bond market and the money-market traders, that the Federal Reserve was once again focusing attention on interest rates. To skeptical investors, that would sound like the "bad old days" of the 1970s when the central bank allowed inflation to get out of hand. Volcker was afraid the markets might react badly. The Fed would lose "credibility."

The Fed was in control, administering a vast national liquidation in order to eliminate price inflation and stabilize money. Like Henry Wallich and the other hard-liners, Paul Volcker figured that the longer the Fed could hold on, keeping the economy down despite the pain and protests, the closer it would get to the cherished goal, the restoration of sound money.[27]

Jesus Silva Herzog, the finance minister of Mexico, developed a strong memory of the lemon meringue pie served at the Federal Reserve Board's private dining room. It was on the menu every Friday when Silva came by the Fed for his private meetings with Paul Volcker. They met regularly through the spring to discuss their mutual problem: Mexico was going broke.

Given the squeeze of recession and high interest rates, Mexico was fast approaching the day when it could not keep up the interest payments on its loans from abroad. Its currency was inflating wildly and unemployment was at 13 percent. The Mexican standard of living was retreating to the level of 1970—wiping out a decade of progress for ordinary citizens. With the peso falling in value daily, wealthier citizens shipped their money out of the country, converting their capital to stable currencies like the dollar and depleting the nation's reserves. Mexico had to borrow more and more in an effort to stay even.

Mexico's crisis was America's. The two nations were economically intertwined by trade and labor supply much more closely than most U.S. citizens appreciated, but the crucial link was finance. If Mexico went under, so might several of the most celebrated names in American banking. Mexico owed $80 billion to foreign creditors, the largest share to the major American banks. In mid-April, Mexico's largest company, Grupo Industrial Alfa, announced it could not meet the scheduled payments on its $2.3 billion in bank loans, and the banks agreed to work out a restructuring plan (Citibank and Continental Illinois each had lent more than $100 million to the company). In all, the nine largest money-center banks' exposure in Mexican loans was equal to 44 percent of their capital. In the regulatory bookkeeping of banking, when loan payments fell far enough behind, the debt had to be written off, subtracting directly from the bank's capital base. Citibank, Bank of America and others would be instantly imperiled.

When he met with Volcker, Silva did not threaten default nor did he need to. Both men understood that, somehow, they must keep things going. For Mexico, a general default would lead to its expulsion from international finance—no more loans from abroad to finance its trade and development. "We asked ourselves the question what happens if we say, 'No dice. We just won't pay'?" Silva told journalist Joseph Kraft. "There were some partisans of that. But it didn't make any sense. We're part of the world. We import 30 percent of our food. We just can't say, 'Go to hell.' "

For Volcker and his country, the stakes were even larger. A Mexican default would invite the collapse of the American banking system, starting at the top. Nervous investors and money managers would rush to pull their large deposits out of any banks with heavy exposure on foreign loans, and the panic would likely spread worldwide—a global "run" on the largest multinational banks. In theory, the Fed and other central banks of the industrial world could come to the rescue with massive loans to the Citibanks that were losing their liquidity—in effect, pumping up the money supply to save the banking system. This was not a theory anyone wished to test.

The Mexican finance minister had brought the same facts to the U.S. Treasury Department, but he did not get much response from Secretary Regan and his colleagues. At the Fed, Silva found kindred spirits. The Federal Reserve was like a State Department for finance, independently capable of arranging huge international credit transactions and prevailing on other central banks to go along. Volcker's career specialty had been on the international side. At the New York Fed, which dealt directly every day with the global banking system, Anthony Solomon had similar expertise and, indeed, had made his fortune twenty-five years earlier running a business in Mexico. Governor Henry Wallich, the former Yale professor, had had Silva as one of his students in international economics. The Fed under Volcker, as Joseph Kraft put it, formed a kind of "Mexican mafia" within the U.S. government.[28]

At first, Volcker urged Silva to take his problems to the International Monetary Fund. The IMF acted like an international bankruptcy judge, supervising the affairs of debtor nations on behalf of the lenders from wealthy industrial nations. The Fund would make major loans to the financially distressed nations, but it also set the terms on which those countries must clean up their balance sheets—forcing the governments to impose conditions of austerity on their own citizens in order to preserve their status as credit-worthy borrowers. An IMF "work out" agreement meant a debtor government must reduce imports and cut back public spending, raise prices and cut wages. For political reasons, the Mexican president, López Portillo, wanted to postpone the bitter medicine.

Mexico was approaching its presidential election on July 4, and the new president, Miguel de la Madrid, would not take office until December. As the candidate of PRI, the political party that had ruled since the Revolution, de la Madrid was certain to win office, but it was still bad politics, even for PRI, to introduce new measures for suffering in the midst of an election campaign.

"It was clear they were on a trajectory—they were going broke— but what could you do about it?" Volcker said. "You just sat there and wondered: when is Mexico going to blow? Is it going to blow before the election or after?"

The two men agreed on a temporary solution—a huge short-term loan from the Federal Reserve that would keep Mexico afloat until after its election. Then the new Mexican president could approach the IMF and the private banks for new loans—and also confront the Mexican citizenry with the new terms for economic austerity that the lenders would require. For starters, Volcker and Silva settled on the figure of $600 million.

"The money was designed to hold them through the summer," Volcker said. "Then they would go to the Fund and work out new programs."

The Federal Reserve, in addition to its other roles, was authorized to play lender of last resort to other nations. On April 30, it lent Mexico the $600 million, the first in a series of short-term multimillion-dollar loans. Technically, the transactions were called currency swaps, but as a practical matter they were like "bridging" loans. The Federal Reserve would deposit $600 million in dollars in Mexico's account at the New York Fed and Mexico would give the Fed an equivalent quantity of pesos at the going exchange rate, promising to redeem them with U.S. dollars when the swap expired.

Since international accounts demanded payment in reliable dollars, not worthless pesos, the deal gave Mexico enough hard cash to keep paying its bills on time and avoid showing an end-of-the-month depletion of reserves on its books. The $600 million was promptly repaid a

day later. On June 30, Mexico would draw another $200 million over-
night from the Fed's credit line and another $700 million at the end of
July.

The currency swaps had another advantage: they could be done
secretly. Volcker discreetly informed both the Administration and the
key congressional chairmen and none objected. But the public reporting of currency swaps was required only every quarter, so the emergency loan from the Fed would not be disclosed for three or four
months (in this instance, the currency swaps that began in April were
not officially reported until October). By that time, Volcker hoped,
Mexico would be arranging more substantial new financing from the
IMF, and the Fed could discontinue its temporary bailouts.

> The risks are pretty obvious [Tony Solomon said]. The first risk is you
> could have an even greater panic if there was a perception that the U.S.
> authorities weren't talking to Mexico and working on an orderly solution.
> You would have a run on the whole financial system. There were a thou-
> sand banks lending to Mexico. It wasn't just the larger ones. You can't
> afford to underestimate how far a panic might go.
> The only other risk is that the Fed wouldn't be repaid. Technically, it's
> a swap but in reality it's a loan. Their obligation is to reverse the swap at
> the end of three months and pay us back in U.S. currency. But, if the
> country goes bankrupt and they don't repay, their pesos are worthless.

The Federal Reserve's discreet supervision of international solvency could be considered its highest function. The twelve Federal
Reserve Banks, through their Discount lending, protected the fourteen thousand domestic banks against sudden liquidity crises that
might lead to failure. On a higher plane, working with the IMF and
other international lending organizations, the Fed played the same role
for selected nations. The foreign assistance was done as discreetly as
possible to avoid setting off a panic, but also to avoid domestic political
controversy. If, for instance, the Fed had decided to lend several
hundred million to rescue International Harvester (which the Fed had
the legal authority to do), there would have been a great debate about
the implications—and thousands of other parties demanding similar
help. Bailing out Mexico, it seemed, was too grave to be controversial.

In a crunch, the potential for a crisis in the international financial
system came first. It would be placed above all other considerations,
including even the Fed's dedication to controlling the domestic money
supply. Volcker's stringent money control had in fact led directly to
the strains developing in international finance, first by inducing the
global recession that made it difficult for debtors to keep up, then by
creating worldwide the same squeeze on liquidity that existed in the
domestic economy.

The world's vast floating pool of international dollars was flowing to America. Eurodollars ignored national boundaries and went to wherever they could find the highest return. Now this was the United States, where a perfectly safe investment like U.S. Treasury bonds provided historically high yields. This lopsided flow tightened the international market for dollars and left foreign borrowers around the world scrambling for scarce funds—and paying premium prices. The liquidity pressures worldwide were similar to the squeeze confronting corporations inside the U.S., struggling to keep their balance sheets upright by borrowing more and more, despite the high cost of credit. Only, instead of private corporations in danger of failure, these were sovereign nations.

Mexico was the first visible crack in the system—visible at least to those in charge. In April, the problem seemed containable. But the Federal Reserve could not afford to let the crack develop into a full-scale breakdown. It would lend the money to Mexico and hope that things could be worked out later.

"There's a small risk that someone will criticize you," Solomon said. "Why should the Fed do this? On the other hand, most reasonable people would see that this was a crisis. It had all the classic conditions of financial crisis."

On May 17, Wall Street was shaken by a second crack, a smaller fissure to be sure, but still unsettling. An obscure bond dealer, Drysdale Government Securities, Inc., went bust, but the failure sent tremors through several of the most prestigious banks, Chase Manhattan and, to a lesser extent, Manufacturers Hanover and United States Trust. Drysdale, with very little of its own money, had been playing a trader's game with government securities, borrowed from Chase and the others, on the staggering volume of $2 billion—using short-term repurchase agreements on Treasuries to speculate on future prices. When it gambled that bond prices would fall and they didn't, Drysdale's position was wiped out. Chase disclaimed any responsibility for the losses other traders were sustaining on the "repo's," and the traders—who thought they were dealing with the Chase bank, not some obscure and high-flying gambler—panicked.

Bond prices fell sharply, and in the confusion, there was spreading fear that other Wall Street firms would be pulled down with Drysdale. Investors dumped bank stocks, particularly Chase Manhattan's, and the Chase stock price fell nearly 10 percent in two days. Firms scrambled to secure their own clear ownership of bonds and their claims against the default.

It was unsettling, to say the least, that such a huge speculative venture could operate so loosely, depending on the tacit blessing of the most reputable bankers. The government-securities market, largest financial market in the world, was unregulated by the federal government, save for the supervision that the Fed applied to the thirty-six major dealers who were authorized to trade with the Fed's Open Market Desk. Billions changed hands every day over the telephone and the actual paper caught up later. As the only responsible agency of government, the Federal Reserve moved swiftly to calm everyone. Since 1970, when the Fed had intervened in the collapse of the Penn Central Railroad, the central bank had assumed, de facto, a much broader responsibility for itself. In addition to protecting the banking system, the Fed would look out for financial markets generally. When panic or crisis occurred, the Fed stepped forward to reassure and stabilize.

"One of the fears in the market," an assistant to Volcker explained, "was, how did you know the guy you were trading with was going to be in business? If this fear spread, you could have a kind of gridlock in the government-securities market—nobody would dare to trade with anybody."

Volcker, first, had a heart-to-heart talk with the executives of Chase Manhattan and they changed their minds. Chase would cover its share of the losses, about $160 million. The New York Fed also let it be known that its Discount officer would look sympathetically on any banks suffering sudden liquidity problems because of the bond-market scare. In addition, the New York Fed lent several billion dollars in bonds from its own portfolio to the dealer firms to insure that the market had plenty of paper to trade and did not freeze up while everyone sorted out who owned what.

Finally, the Open Market Desk in New York bought bonds itself, in order to provide bank reserves "a bit more promptly than usual . . . to forestall undesired financial pressures," its operations officers reported. The surest way to offset panic was to make certain that ample funds were available to borrowers in the money market, so no one would be caught short. That produced a temporary upward blip in the money supply, but it could be corrected by withdrawing reserves later when everyone had regained his calm. The Fed moved deftly on all these fronts and, with its swift action, the Drysdale crisis was quickly contained.[29]

The underlying strains on the financial system, however, continued. The savings and loan industry was in crisis, hoping for emergency legislation that would restore, at least on paper, the appearance of solvency for thousands of S & L's. Commercial banks were feeling the same pressures as loan defaults accumulated.

William M. Isaac, chairman of the Federal Deposit Insurance Corporation, monitored the bank examiners' reports and was worried by the rising number of troubled banks. Isaac advised Paul Volcker: "I'm not sure how long we can keep this up. We are getting awfully close. We're not going to be able to stand this much longer." [30]

On the day after the Drysdale failure, the Federal Open Market Committee convened for its May meeting. The panicky rumors emanating from Wall Street added an aura of crisis and confusion as Fed officials tried to sort out exactly what had happened. The committee members gossiped about Drysdale and what else might fail. Mexico, they knew, was sliding under. They were already under intense pressures and this episode seemed to raise the stakes still higher.

"It was tense," Governor Emmett Rice said. "I was getting worried about the strength of the financial system. A number of us were beginning to worry whether we had not maintained a restrictive policy too long—and whether we shouldn't ease up a lot."

Anthony Solomon of the New York Fed was frustrated by the confusing variable, M-1, on which the FOMC was trying to base its policy, and he was ready to abandon it. "A few of us more pragmatic types were getting irritated with the monetary handcuffs," he said. "It made no sense."

Governor Charles Partee and Frank Morris, the Boston Fed president, and Nancy Teeters were similarly concerned. Morris, though he had no vote, would repeat his argument that the FOMC's system for decision making was no longer viable. Teeters would warn again about the strains on the savings and loan industry and the financial system in general.

The Federal Reserve, however, was caught in a huge vise of conflicting pressures—the opposing demands of the financial community and the political community, pushing the policy makers in opposite directions. In Washington, the most important voices wanted the Fed to relent. But the financial markets of Wall Street insisted that it hold tight. The members of the Federal Open Market Committee, in addition to resolving the technical complexities of money and the economy, would decide, implicitly, which group they would heed, the politicians or the financiers.

At the White House, James Baker had had his fill of the monetarist economists and their endless talk about M-1 volatility and their wrong forecasts of recovery. If Baker listened to them, the White House would be urging the Federal Reserve to tighten the money supply again. Through April, M-1 growth for 1982 was running at nearly 9 percent, far above the FOMC's target range for the year of 2.5 to 5.5 percent. "We believe firmly if monetary growth is brought back down to the upper end of the Fed's target range, interest rates will come down," said Jerry Jordan, a member of the Council of Economic Advisers.[31]

Tightening the money supply again will lower interest rates? Baker didn't buy it. The President's chief political adviser did not claim any special sophistication about monetary policy, but he belatedly grasped that money was too important to leave to the economists. "Jim Baker has a Texas banker's mentality," David Stockman said. "It starts with the proposition that high interest rates are bad, that the Fed is responsible for them and the Fed has the discretion to lower interest rates and get the economy moving again."

Baker decided to do a little "Fed bashing" of his own. The economic damage was still spreading and interest rates were not falling. Corporate profits had fallen by 17 percent in the first quarter, one of the worst on record. The index of industrial production had declined two points since March. Business bankruptcies were at a post-Depression peak, 280 new ones every day, and now engulfed larger corporations, Braniff International, Wickes Companies, AM International, Saxon Industries, and Lionel, the toy-train maker.[32] "How long can they let this misery go on?" Baker kept asking White House associates.

A memorandum from Lawrence Kudlow of OMB confirmed the gloom: "Looking at the empirical data now in hand, claims for a strong second half recovery are without foundation. Indeed, without immediate relief in the financial sector, claims for any recovery during the second half appear shaky." Why? "The bottom line for the economic outlook is quite simple: interest rates are way too high," Kudlow explained.[33]

Baker and his deputy, Richard Darman, became more and more vociferous in their conversations with Volcker and others, urging the Fed to loosen money and get the recovery started. "We had the fall elections obviously in mind," an Administration official said. "There was a fair amount of frustration, a sense that the Fed was overdoing with too much discipline." Baker was not sure whether private admonitions from him or anyone else, even the President, could budge Volcker, but if there was no economic recovery, Republican candidates would pay dearly in the November elections.

While the most senior officials at the White House were turning up the heat on Volcker, the Treasury Secretary let it be known, not entirely by coincidence, that his department was undertaking a major new study on government reform. The subject: the independence of the Federal Reserve. Among the proposals that would be considered were whether the Secretary of the Treasury ought to have a seat on the Board of Governors (the original arrangement in 1913, when the

Fed was created) or whether the central bank should become a sub-agency of Treasury, fully answerable to the President (the idea that Paul Volcker himself had once endorsed in his senior thesis at Princeton).

"Everybody was just frantic," a Treasury Assistant Secretary said. "They saw the '82 elections coming up and they were desperate for a recovery. It was miserable at Treasury; it was frantic. We could see all these House seats going down the drain."

At the May 18 FOMC meeting, Volcker reported on the various political assaults on the Fed's independent status. Congressional leaders were drafting their version and now Treasury was hinting that it might join the struggle with its own proposal for emasculating the Federal Reserve. Perhaps these were empty threats, but loss of its independence was the most threatening question that could confront the institution.

Still, the message the Fed heard from the financial markets of Wall Street was quite the opposite. Do not quit now, the money traders warned, because we are still not convinced. If the Fed eases prematurely, then inflation will come surging back. It has happened before and it can happen again.

The FOMC will not ease its money policy, Lacy H. Hunt, chief economist at Fidelity Bank in Philadelphia, predicted a few days before the May meeting. "When the Federal Reserve made mistakes in the past, it was to ease too quickly."

But H. Erich Heinemann, a monetarist economist at Morgan Stanley, was skeptical that the Fed would keep faith with the financial markets. The M-1 numbers, he noted, were alarmingly above target.

> These developments are disturbing [Heinemann wrote]. They imply that the Federal Reserve System, despite the vigor of its anti-inflationary rhetoric, may be willing to tolerate considerably faster monetary growth. . . . Should this prove to be the case, it would tend to confirm the worst suspicions of market participants. . . . It would tend to confirm the widespread fear among managers of financial asset portfolios. . . .

A few important voices—Henry Kaufman of Salomon Brothers, Edward Yardeni of E. F. Hutton, George McKinney of Irving Trust and others—were urging the Fed to abandon M-1 and ease its money policy. But the weight of opinion in financial markets was overwhelmingly against any relaxation. Indeed, a survey of 138 money managers, conducted by Oppenheimer and Company, warned the Fed: "The main concern expressed by the executives was fear of renewed inflation—not fear that the recession would be too severe." Bankers of the Federal Advisory Council delivered the same message—don't let up.[34]

The Federal Reserve chairman chose to heed the advice of the financial markets and the bankers. It was still too early to ease. Volcker was afraid of how they might react if he did. He invoked the familiar talisman of "credibility."

Nancy Teeters was tired of hearing M-1 employed as an emblem of the Federal Reserve's "credibility." "People talk about the credibility of the Federal Reserve," she said. "I've never quite known what they are talking about. The monetarists did this big drumbeat that the Fed was no longer credible, but if we just controlled the aggregates, the world would be a safe place. One way or the other, what we control is interest rates."[35]

Furthermore, the "inflation fears" of investors seemed increasingly precious. The Consumer Price Index had fallen in April to an inflation rate of only 2.4 percent. Commodity prices, including food and oil, were flat or falling. Labor was in rout, accepting substantial retreats on wage demands in major new contracts for auto workers and teamsters. How much grief did the bankers and bondholders demand before they would be satisfied? The answer was: they demanded more.

For the FOMC members, the question went beyond the technical uncertainties of M-1 growth or even whether inflationary pressures had truly been broken. The issue was also how to preserve the good name of the Federal Reserve. The Fed had erred in 1980, but, more grievously, it had gone astray in the 1970s and allowed inflation to reach double digits. The bondholders, the money managers, the bankers, had still not forgiven them.

"These markets are incredibly quick to revive inflationary expectations—the banks, the traders and speculators," Tony Solomon insisted. "They would be the first to act on any hint. This is a very nervous group of people and you have to handle them very carefully."

The Federal Reserve was still making amends for sins of the past—still apologizing to the bondholders for the central bank's presumed failure to defend their assets in prior seasons. "Once you have a reputation as a bad boy," Solomon lamented with a bitter trace, "you have to spend ten years being a good boy to change their minds."

The Fed would show Wall Street it was still being a "good boy." After all the debate, all the various doubts and uncertainties, the May directive adopted by the Federal Open Market Committee was essentially designed to comfort the anxieties of Wall Street. Despite the confusion of declining money velocity, despite the visible strains and accumulating damage, the chairman proposed that monetary policy be left unchanged for another six weeks, neither easing or tightening.

The real economy would have to wait a while longer for relief, at least until the next meeting of the FOMC in July.

Volcker's position easily prevailed, despite all the doubts expressed around the table. The Reserve Bank presidents, who were monetarists, were naturally satisfied, since they shared the bankers' fixation with M-1. Hard-liners like Wallich were pleased too. Those committee members who had misgivings—Solomon, Partee, Rice and perhaps others—swallowed their doubts and voted with Paul Volcker.

The only dissenting vote was Teeters's.

Mrs. Teeters dissented from this action because she favored specification of somewhat higher rates of monetary growth . . . with the objective of improving liquidity and easing financial pressures [the FOMC minutes said]. In her opinion, the time had come to foster lower and less variable interest rates in order to enable prospects for significant recovery in output and employment.

Nancy Teeters thought that relying on the financial markets for guidance, in those tense circumstances, was a fundamental mistake. "I don't understand why long-term rates didn't come down, but they didn't," she said. "They stayed very high for a very long time. Why? That's where the psychology comes in. The markets were so pessimistic. The markets had been beaten back to the point where they thought we were never going to ease."

Some of her colleagues concluded—after the fact—that Teeters was right: the Fed should have eased in the spring. In any case, the decision was devastating for the economy—leaving a deeper wound that would take years to heal.

"In hindsight," Anthony Solomon conceded, "we probably should have broken away from the monetary aggregates in the spring and used real GNP and inflation as our targets. If the money supply had been weak, then we could have done that and not had any problem with the monetarists. We could have moved to liberalize and bring down interest rates and get the economy revived."

Governor Emmett Rice agreed with Teeters, at least after the vote. The Fed had held tight too long and the financial system was endangered. But he had decided not to vote with her.

"I thought Teeters was right," Rice said, "but I didn't think she was right enough to dissent with her. It wasn't all that clear she was right or that this was the time to dissent. Too much significance would be attributed to it. People were worried about the pressures on the financial system, but we felt we couldn't back away now."

The chairman and most committee members had no regrets. Holding the money supply tight a while longer—painful as it was for the losers in the real economy—would squeeze a bit more out of prices, more out of labor and commodity producers, small businesses and manufacturers. In the majority's view, the longer the Fed held its position and ignored the complaints, the larger the benefits might be in the future—stable prices, a dollar with certain value, an economic recovery that could proceed without price inflation.

Henry Wallich, for one, was proud of the Fed's performance in this tense season. "People stood their ground," Wallich said. "We didn't stampede."

As for the political attacks on the Fed, Volcker and Wallich dismissed them as inconsequential. "People like to believe the Federal Reserve tries to favor one political party over another," Wallich said, "but here we saw Nancy Teeters, a liberal, voting to enhance the political fortunes of Ronald Reagan, and me, a conservative, voting to enhance the other side. I think that confounds the theory of political influence on the Federal Reserve."

The political influence that was at stake did not belong to Republicans or Democrats, but to the Fed itself. In the course of fighting inflation, the Federal Reserve had gained the high ground and was in control of events. Its influence was superior to that of Congress and of the President, and, like any political institution that has seized control, the Federal Reserve and its chairman were not eager to yield.

14

THE TURN

On June 24, the Federal Reserve Bank of Kansas City dispatched four of its bank examiners to Oklahoma City to investigate a troubled institution called the Penn Square Bank. The managers of Penn Square needed a quick $15 to $20 million in emergency Discount lending to maintain the bank's liquidity, but the Fed examiners had to make sure that Penn Square still had sufficient collateral to qualify—bonds or sound loan paper that the Fed could take as security. It was another bank in crisis, but this was why the Federal Reserve existed, its original purpose, to protect the banking system from sudden failures and spreading panic.

For months, regulators from the Comptroller of the Currency's office, the federal agency that supervised nationally chartered banks, had been alarmed by Penn Square's deteriorating condition. More and more of the bank's loan portfolio was deemed worthless and uncollectible, mainly loans for oil and gas development made in the heady boom time when oil prices were still soaring. The good times would last forever, it seemed then. Now oil prices were falling and the collapsing prospects for Penn Square's borrowers were translating into failed loans. As the Comptroller's examiners ordered millions in bad loans written off at a loss, Penn Square's capital evaporated to the point of vanishing. The bank was insolvent and government regulators would have to close it.

When William M. Isaac, chairman of the Federal Deposit Insurance Corporation, was alerted, he was puzzled by the tone of urgency in the

warning from the Comptroller's supervisor of regulation. The FDIC
was the third partner in federal bank regulation—the insurance
agency that would assume control of a failed bank, pay off the depositors insured up to $100,000, or try to arrange for another bank to take
over the collapsed one and reopen it. In most banking crises, the Fed,
the Comptroller's office and the FDIC worked out the terms coopera-
tively among themselves. On its face, Penn Square did not seem like
a major event.

   I kept asking myself, "Why is he over here talking to me about a $500
   million shopping-center bank in Oklahoma City as if it's a big crisis [Isaac
   said]?" Then he told me. This bank involves a lot more because it has sold
   about $2 billion in loan participations to other banks—Continental Illinois,
   Chase Manhattan, Seattle First, Michigan National. His concern was the
   ripple effect on those other banks, if it's not handled right.[1]

Penn Square was notorious in its wishful thinking. Its executives
were the classic freebooters—entrepreneurial bankers who hustled
new loans for oil drillers based on the most generous assumptions
about the prospects for finding oil and gas, about the future price of
oil, about the borrowers' ability to repay. The federal examiners found
a general recklessness and even fraud in the loan portfolio.

But the hustlers from Penn Square could not have done this by
themselves. Their modest-sized bank simply did not have the capacity. A bank's assets, its loans, were supposed to balance with its
liabilities, its deposits. A shopping-center bank with less than $500
million in deposits could not carry $2 billion in loans on its books. So
Penn Square simply sold the loans—"upstream," as bankers say—to
the larger banks that wished to share in the bonanza.[2]

Continental Illinois, largest bank in the Midwest and seventh-
largest in the nation, picked up more than $1 billion of loan participa-
tions with Penn Square. Lesser amounts, but still in the hundreds of
millions, were absorbed by Chase Manhattan and the others. They
gave Penn Square the capacity to lend more and more and take greater
and greater risks.

Continental was already famous itself as a go-go bank, though on a
vastly larger scale than Penn Square. Its management was driven by
a high-growth strategy so successful that Continental's lending activity
had increased by 50 percent in only five years, a $40 billion bank that
had eclipsed its crosstown rival, First Chicago, and become, in the
words of its aggressive chairman, Roger E. Anderson, a "world-class
bank." Anderson was honored by the business magazine, *Dun's Review*, which declared his bank one of the five best-managed corpora-

tions in the country. Continental Illinois, said *The Wall Street Journal*, was "the bank to beat."[3]

Penn Square, in effect, acted as a business scout in the "oil patch" for Continental and the others. When Penn Square booked loans and reached its lending capacity, it simply offered a share of the action to the larger banks, collected the equivalent of a finder's fee, then turned around and went out to find more oil prospectors who needed money. This was very profitable for everyone, while it lasted, and Continental Illinois's stock climbed from $25 to $40 a share in less than two years. The largest and most admired banks in America were, it developed, as inattentive to the question of loan quality—the prudential rules of banking—as the hustlers in cowboy boots from a shopping center in Oklahoma.

To avert an immediate failure, the Federal Reserve agreed to lend $20 million—and more if needed—to keep Penn Square open until some sort of solution could be worked out. But the officials from the three separate federal regulatory agencies were in fundamental disagreement about how to clean up the mess. The Fed wanted to keep Penn Square going, whatever the cost, until a new owner could be found to acquire it. The Comptroller's staff agreed. Isaac of the FDIC wanted to shut it down, pay off the insured deposits up to $100,000 and teach everyone else a lesson. If no acquisition was arranged by the FDIC, anyone who held Penn Square's CDs in denominations above $100,000 would lose—credit unions, other banks, money funds, private investors. But the biggest losers would be those major banks that had shared in the dubious action of Penn Square's loan portfolio.

The threatened bankers swiftly joined the federal regulators in the private arguments over what the government should do.

> Continental came in, Chase came in and the others, all urging us to handle it in certain ways [Isaac said]. We explored with Continental Illinois and others a merger. They had all kinds of schemes that would keep Penn Square going under new ownership so we would not have to liquidate all those loans. Continental Illinois and the others were trying to give us all their lousy loans. From the FDIC viewpoint, that was a bad deal.

The argument continued through the last days of June and into the July 4 weekend, as Penn Square Bank ran out of money. In the discussions, the money-center banks were supported by Federal Reserve officials, including Volcker, general counsel Michael Bradfield, and John E. Ryan, the Fed's director of supervision and regulation, all of whom feared "severe consequences" for the larger banks if the one in Oklahoma was liquidated.

"The FDIC could have done what they normally do in a bank failure —take out the bad loans and make that up with FDIC money," Bradfield argued. "Or you could put capital into it and take over management control. If you had taken out the bad loans, you could have found a buyer."[4]

Isaac had two objections—the cost and the principle. Reimbursing the insured depositors up to $100,000 would cost the insurance fund a maximum of $240 million, but if the FDIC assumed responsibility for the entire Penn Square operation, the potential loss would be much greater. Penn Square, like any other aggressive bank, had accumulated a huge pool of "off balance sheet" obligations—letters of credit and the loan participations, totaling $3 billion. These commitments didn't appear on the bank's balance sheet of assets and liabilities, but the bank was legally liable for them nonetheless. If the FDIC assumed control, then it would be sued by the holders of these credit instruments and Isaac figured the losses in legal claims could total $500 to $700 million. Among the claimants who would be suing the FDIC would be Continental Illinois and the other banks, trying to get their money back.

Isaac was an apostle of free-market principles and he wanted to teach the bankers a lesson in accountability—a lesson that would also be absorbed by the institutional investors, pension funds, money-market mutual funds, state and local governments, and others, whose money managers parked billions of dollars in banks through large-denomination CDs or commercial paper issued by bank holding companies. In the spirit of financial deregulation, the FDIC chairman thought the losses would be good discipline for banks and bank investors, a strong reminder that they have responsibility for judging risks on their own, instead of simply relying on the government.

"If we bail out this thing," Isaac told the other regulatory officials, "and assume the expense for Continental Illinois, Chase, Seafirst and the others, what kind of signals are we sending to the financial system? That you can engage in the most shoddy banking practices and, in the end, the government will bail you out."

The others thought Isaac was naïve and a little bullheaded. "One person came to the table with such a fixed idea, that it was a good idea to bring discipline to the market," said Bradfield. "But the question is how you get the right discipline on the market without destroying it— the baby with the bath water."

Isaac's principle of free-market risk sounded unassailable in the abstract, but Volcker and his regulatory assistants were worried by a greater, more immediate risk. If the government refused to step in and assume the burden of loss in Penn Square, there could be a general panic among the large investors—the financial institutions that lent billions of dollars every day to large banks like Continental. When they heard the bad news about Continental's losses, prudent money managers would simply stop buying CDs from Continental or the other larger banks that were burned in the questionable loan partnerships. The sudden sense of insecurity might even extend to banks that weren't involved with Penn Square but were exposed on other shaky fronts—such as Citibank, Manufacturers Hanover and the other money-center banks that had lent so heavily to Latin America. When a market panic started, it was impossible to predict which way the crowd would turn or how far it would stampede.

With the speed of a Telex message, money managers across the nation would begin shifting their funds to safer depositories and decline to buy new CDs from any banks that seemed risky. But a bank like Continental could not function if it could not borrow a huge volume of money every day. That was the principle of "managed liabilities" banking that enabled banks to grow aggressively—book the loans first, then borrow the money to fund them. If Continental was unable to sustain its huge daily borrowing, as much as $8 billion a day, its own operation would become imperiled. It was in this manner, literally overnight, that a liquidity crisis starting in an obscure bank in Oklahoma City could spread instantly to Chicago and Seattle and Detroit, perhaps even to New York.

"For the Fed," Isaac said, "the only issue was what effect it would have on the money-center banks. The Federal Reserve position was that a deposit payoff would be catastrophic and we simply had to find a way to work this out. By 'we,' they meant the FDIC."

The Federal Reserve had another reason for avoiding any disturbance in the banking system. A liquidity crisis could force the Fed to alter its monetary policy, pumping up the money supply in order to avert a disaster. "They don't like to see ripples anywhere in the system," Isaac said, "because the ripples cause them to react on monetary policy and they don't like to do that."

To Bradfield, Isaac was making empty debater's points. With Jack Ryan and the Comptroller's supervisor of regulation, Paul Homan, he persisted in trying to change Isaac's mind. If the worst did happen, of course, questions would be raised about both the Federal Reserve officials and the Comptroller, who were jointly responsible for the soundness of banking. How could they have let this pyramid of reckless banking happen in the first place?

At one point in the debates [Isaac said], Paul Homan was pounding the table and saying, "Goddammit, I don't care what it costs. If it costs $1 billion, you've got to bail it out. If you don't, Continental Illinois is going to fail and who knows where it stops." I said, "Paul, if Continental Illinois fails, we will deal with Continental Illinois. We'll recapitalize Continental Illinois and stop it there. We can't stop it here."

The issue was resolved, in a sense, by the "upstream" banks themselves—Continental, Chase, Seafirst and Michigan National—all of whom refused to risk any of their own money to save the situation. They could have taken the responsibility for injecting new capital. When that proposal didn't work out, the federal regulators suggested an alternative: if Continental, Chase and the others would waive their potential claims against Penn Square, that would make it much easier —and cheaper—for the FDIC to assume responsibility and keep Penn Square open. The bankers talked back and forth but, in the end, declined to assume any risk themselves. Chase Manhattan had just been burned by its losses on Drysdale Securities. If Continental and the others were to assume a share of Penn Square's troubles, they would have to forgo the right to sue their own insurance companies, alleging negligence on the part of their own management officers who had bought the participations in Penn Square loans. In other words, the bankers wanted the federal government to take the losses while the banks remained free to cover their own mistakes.

"We wanted the banks to take part in the bailout," Bradfield said, "and when they wouldn't, that's when it collapsed. They all refused to put any money in or forgo their own claims. They didn't want to make any contribution and that killed it."

On the Monday holiday, July 5, all the chief regulators gathered in Volcker's office at the Federal Reserve building, joined by Treasury Secretary Donald Regan, to settle the question. Technically, the Treasury Secretary had no authority to decide the issue for the regulators, but everyone understood that if calamity occurred, it would be the elected government, the President and his officers, not little-known bank regulators, that would have to deal with the damage to the national economy. The Treasury Secretary's opinion was important.

Regan, according to Isaac, asked all the principals: "Does anybody think, if you do a deposit payoff, that there will be chaos, that the financial markets simply can't stand it?"

In Isaac's account, Volcker responded: "I think there's a substantial chance of that."

Volcker's concern was seconded by Todd Conover, the Comptroller. The Fed chairman was also supported by the new vice chairman of the Federal Reserve Board, Preston Martin. Martin, a California financier and businessman, was Ronald Reagan's first appointment to

the Board of Governors, replacing Frederick Schultz. Martin had
served as chairman of the Federal Home Loan Bank Board, which
regulated and lent to savings and loans much as the Fed supervised
commercial banks, so he had a regulator's sensitivities to the potential
risks.

William Isaac, however, repeated his case for disciplining the financial markets: "If we bail out this one, bad as it is, if we take Continental Illinois and the rest of them off the hook and they don't have to pay
a thing, then the markets will know that, no matter what risks they
take, the government will bail them out. Eventually, it's going to lead
down the road to nationalization of the banking system."

What Isaac was suggesting seemed improbable, given the political
power of banking, but his logic was this: if the American taxpayers
someday came to realize that they were actually underwriting all the
risks for private banks, sooner or later the public would demand that
the government take control of bank lending.

The Treasury Secretary sided with the FDIC chairman.

A few hours later, in early evening, the announcement was made.
Penn Square Bank would not open Tuesday morning. The Comptroller
declared the bank insolvent and the Federal Deposit Insurance Corporation seized its assets and placed it in receivership. The insured
depositors would be swiftly reimbursed in the full amount of their
accounts. The other creditors and claimants would have to stand in
line and wait for a share of the bankrupt bank's diminished assets.

In the short run, Isaac was correct. The financial system reacted
defensively when it heard the news, but it did not unravel in fear and
chaos. For the longer term, however, Volcker and the other regulators
were right. There were "severe consequences." Nine months later,
Seattle First was at the edge of failure itself and, to save the situation,
was sold to the Bank of America. Nearly two years later, Continental
Illinois would fall. When nobody else would step in to buy it, the
federal government did.

But the reckless little bank in Oklahoma City produced a far greater
ripple than any of these. When Penn Square failed, it was another,
more dangerous fissure in the American financial system. It sounded
like the rending of fabric, and members of the Federal Open Market
Committee swiftly changed their minds about the correct course for
monetary policy. Instead of following the chairman, the majority now
pleaded, even demanded, that Paul Volcker at last relent.

"Penn Square was very sobering," Governor Emmett Rice said. "It
made believers out of a lot of people. The system was very fragile and
Penn Square confirmed our thinking. A number of us were asking

ourselves if we could take responsibility for what was going to happen if we didn't change policy."

The Federal Open Market Committee convened for a two-day meeting on Wednesday, June 30, right in the middle of the uncertainty over Penn Square. While Volcker and the Fed's regulatory officers argued with the FDIC over how to handle the Oklahoma failure, the FOMC deliberated in the boardroom on the larger questions of economic regulation—M-1, interest rates and the outlook for the real economy. The mood of the meeting was tense, obviously influenced by the cloud of potential crisis hanging over the banking system.

Nancy Teeters felt an uncomfortable sense of vindication. Events were fulfilling the stark warnings she had delivered earlier, but she was still not sure if the others shared her alarm. "The financial fabric did begin to tear, things did begin to rip," she said. "The S & L's were already under water. We were already getting small bank failures. The oil loans were collapsing. A lot of the financial structure was beginning to get very, very shaky."

The random manner in which isolated crises popped up in odd places and threatened wider consequences—first Mexico, then Drysdale, now Penn Square—reminded Teeters of what she had read about the waves of bank failures after 1929. In that disaster, the Federal Reserve had held the money supply too tight for too long, when it should have been pumping liquidity into the financial system.

"After the Penn Square failure, I began to get the feeling we might be headed toward something we hadn't seen since the 1930s," she said. "Here is a bank located in a shopping center in Oklahoma that nobody's ever heard of before, that has participated in billions of dollars of loans and farmed them out to some of the biggest banks in the country. All of a sudden, it fails and no one is sure what happens next."

The chairman himself was worried. Penn Square was a psychological shock to the financial system, involving some of the largest banks. When Volcker considered the debt obligations that were exposed, the strains that were already evident, it lent a sense of urgency to his thinking.

Even Penn Square, however, was not the darkest cloud. Volcker knew that another financial crisis, larger and much more grave, was going to surface soon—the effective default of Mexico. Mexico was "going to blow," as Volcker put it, and it was only a matter of time. On June 30, the Federal Reserve made another overnight loan to the Banco de Mexico so Mexico's central bank could show a positive end-of-the-month balance, but the nation's reserve accounts were dwindling rapidly.

Financial insiders were alert to this impending crisis, though not the general public. In June, Bank of America organized a new $2.5 billion loan for Mexico but had great difficulty persuading other banks to participate in the loan syndication. European banks were refusing to roll over their Mexican loans. Private capital was fleeing the country faster than Mexican banks could borrow from abroad to replenish reserves. Jesus Silva Herzog, the finance minister, was back in Washington, discreetly making the rounds at the Fed and Treasury, informing officials that Mexico would soon be broke.

If Mexico fell, that would be only the beginning. Virtually all of the major debtor nations of Latin America were facing expiration dates on their major loan packages in the coming months. If one Third World nation could no longer pay, especially one that had once been regarded so favorably, then the bankers of Europe and America would be most reluctant to renew loans to the others. All the debtor nations had been undermined by the global recession, nearly all were falling behind. If Mexico failed, lending would stop and the debt crisis would cascade through the Third World, from Mexico to Brazil, Argentina, Peru, Chile, Venezuela and others.[5]

Confronted with these threats, Volcker and his colleagues also had to face up to another disappointing reality. The recovery of the American economy, heralded for so many months by so many forecasters, including the Federal Reserve's, now looked more remote than ever. The incoming economic data on everything from consumer spending to industrial production were all down, not up. The American economy —crucial to world recovery—was sinking still lower. Perhaps the Federal Reserve policy makers should not have been surprised by this, given that the Fed itself had tightened money again back in February, and that through the spring, the Fed had kept short-term interest rates at a punishing level, ignoring the pleas for relief. Nevertheless, they were surprised.

Governor Lyle Gramley recalled:

Early in the year, I was making speeches predicting an upturn in the economy in the second quarter, and when that didn't happen, I said by midyear. By June and July, with each passing statistic, it became increasingly evident that the turnaround wasn't going to be there and something had to be done. If the economy did not turn up soon, a renewed wave of pessimism could spread through the business community and lead to a new curtailment of plans for investment. It became abundantly obvious to me and others that no upturn was developing. Our expectations were thoroughly disappointed. The gloom and doom was beginning to spread.

All three of these realities—the shakiness of the domestic banking system, the looming crisis in Third World debt, the downward slide of the American economy—interacted with one another and all argued for the same thing: the Fed must ease. No matter what M-1 or other monetary aggregates dictated, the world could not take any more of this. If the Federal Reserve did not reverse course quickly, pump up the money supply and bring down interest rates, something far worse than inflation might result.

It was a rare moment of conjunction for the Federal Reserve, when all its diverse responsibilities seemed to fuse in a single powerful moment of crisis. As a governing institution, the Federal Reserve functioned in three distinct though overlapping realms. It manipulated the money supply and the course of the domestic economy. It regulated banks and watched over the financial system at large. It served as unofficial supervisor and lender of last resort for the vast network of global finance, the fate of nations. At this moment, all three of these roles converged on a single, anxious question: could the Federal Reserve get the American economy started again?

If economic activity continued to decline, then the failure of banks, thrifts and other financial institutions would naturally grow worse. Where would the next Penn Square pop up and how far would it spread? And if the U.S. economy did not begin to expand, then the debt problems of the less-developed countries would multiply. America was the major market that bought exports from those debtor nations, but when America was in contraction, its purchases from abroad contracted too. If Americans did not start buying exports again from Mexico or Brazil or the others, there was no way those countries would ever find the income to keep up with their mounting debt payments. Ultimately, their crisis would come home to become America's. As the Fed well understood, the situation literally threatened to collapse the U.S. banking system at its top-heavy apex—the money-center banks of Wall Street that were so overexposed.

No other concern touched more deeply in the institutional mind and memory of the Federal Reserve. This was its original charter, the mantle of responsibility it had inherited in 1913 from J. P. Morgan. The Fed was to protect the safety and soundness of the banking system and, in a crisis, that was the obligation it placed above all others.

"This international debt appeared to be a very, very serious threat to our financial markets," Gramley said. "The overriding concern had to be to provide enough stimulus through monetary policy to turn the U.S. economy and the world economy around and get business activity moving up again. There was no way we could hope to resolve the problem of LDC debt unless we permitted those countries to sell exports again."

As the discussion unfolded in the Federal Open Market Committee, it was obvious that a new consensus had developed. Now was the time to loosen up, the majority argued, and ignore contrary signals from M-1. Six weeks earlier, though many had harbored misgivings, they had gone along with the chairman and kept the money supply tight. Now, they were arguing insistently for easing. They pleaded with Volcker—even demanded—that the Fed must turn its policy around in order to bring down interest rates and stimulate an economic recovery.

"The majority argued strongly and very hotly for ease and Volcker went along with them," Anthony Solomon said. "Maybe Volcker, in a mild way, initiated it." In any case, the too-long reign of M-1 had come to its end.

Frank Morris of the Boston Fed said:

We came to a very critical point. All of our forecasts, the Federal Reserve's and everyone else's, had forecast a third-quarter upturn. But the numbers kept coming in indicating that the economy was still going down, despite the tax cuts that were going into effect. The whole world economy was contracting.

The only thing that was going up was M-1. If we had followed M-1, it would have been a terrible mistake. We would have had to push interest rates up still further. This would have been disastrous for the world. The impact would have been felt everywhere.

Paul Volcker did not disagree. But, in his elliptical manner, the chairman wanted to move to an easier money policy without actually admitting it. Volcker was reluctant to show his hand clearly, even to other members of the Federal Open Market Committee, because he was still hypersensitive about his critics. If the chairman frankly declared himself, both the monetarist Reserve Bank presidents on the FOMC and the skeptical conservatives in the financial markets might accuse him of turning fainthearted. So Volcker preferred to let others make the case in the most strenuous terms and he left an impression with some of his colleagues that they were pulling him along.

"It was getting to the point where we had to ease, regardless," Volcker admitted. "I became particularly antsy about the economy. Clearly, those earlier expectations that the economy would recover were wrong. I'd gotten fairly pessimistic. The strains in the financial system and the LDC debt, all those things together were pushing us. So I jumped when the opening came."

Volcker still felt inhibited by the mystique he himself had helped to create—the fetish of the money numbers. M-1 growth had been running well above its target for six months, yet the economy kept sinking lower and lower—a real-world contradiction that ought to have convinced most anyone that something was wrong with the theory of M-1.

Nevertheless, the monetarists continued to express alarm. In early June, the growth in M-1 had started to accelerate again briefly and the usual voices again warned the financial world that the Federal Reserve was losing control and abandoning principle.

Milton Friedman complained that money growth was "already dangerously high" and must be curbed. Beryl Sprinkel of Treasury insisted that higher inflation would result if the Fed raised its money targets. "Raising the rate of monetary growth still higher," Friedman explained, "might bring down interest rates for a few weeks or even months, but would then surely push them higher again."[6]

The financial markets still seemed mesmerized by this monetarist logic: if the Fed increased the money supply, it would actually raise interest rates. After all, Paul Volcker had been telling Congress the same thing for many months. Volcker could not bring himself to acknowledge bluntly that it wasn't so. Moreover, when M-1 had started to accelerate in June, market interest rates had been pushed higher, anticipating that the Federal Reserve would be compelled to tighten again.

But this time, Volcker knew he couldn't tighten. It was time, finally, to abandon the monetarist formulations that he had used to justify his stringent money control since October 1979. Although he still refused to declare himself, he seized on a brief M-1 decline in late June to declare the monetarist target achieved. It was another precious rationalization, designed to mask the real fears.

At the conclusion of debate, the policy directive adopted by the FOMC was couched in the usual euphemistic language and only insiders would have grasped that the Fed was executing a dramatic reversal. The short-run money targets were raised, instead of lowered. The committee decreed blandly that "somewhat more rapid money growth would be acceptable."

"Well," Anthony Solomon announced dramatically after the roll call, "this is a historic step." Volcker discouraged such talk. "I think you're overstating it, Tony," the chairman chided. Volcker, Solomon said later, "tried to soft-pedal it because he didn't want the monetarists going around shooting at him."

Solomon was right, however. It was a historic moment.

For thirty-three months, the Federal Reserve had imposed the most severe discipline on the U.S. economy—and the world's—ever attempted in the history of the American central bank. The Fed's money policy had forced interest rates up to the highest levels of the twentieth century, levels that would have been called usurious in other times, that would have been impossible to sustain before the deregulation of financial markets. In effect, credit was rationed for two and a half years and the scarce supply of credit was allocated by price—the high price of money effectively eliminated borrowers who were too small or underfinanced to afford the loans.

Despite the initial false start in 1980, the discipline worked. The Gross National Product contracted in real terms by more than $82 billion from its peak and, since 1979, the country had accumulated as much as $600 billion in lost economic output. The excess supply of goods, the declining incomes, the surplus labor—all had worked to force down wages and prices. Price inflation fell dramatically: from above 13 percent to less than 4 percent.

Throughout Volcker's anti-inflation campaign, the nation was instructed by the Fed to watch M-1 and the monetary aggregates as the correct gauge of its monetary policy. But the money numbers zigzagged up and down in a bewildering manner that confused even the economists. The public and the politicians would have had a far more accurate sense of what was happening if they had ignored M-1 and simply followed interest rates and their relative levels. Except for two brief periods in the summer months of 1980 and the last quarter of 1981, the Federal Reserve had succeeded in holding most short-term interest rates above long-term rates for an extraordinary length of time —two and one half years. This abnormality explained things far more reliably than what was happening to M-1 growth or the other aggregates. The inverted condition of interest rates meant scarce credit— the contractionary squeeze that drove away buyers and forced weaker enterprises to retrench or even fail. It was the high price of money, engineered by the government itself, that made economic recovery virtually impossible. As of July 1, 1982, this was still the unnatural condition that the Federal Reserve was imposing on the nation's economy—short-term commercial rates remained higher than long rates.

On July 1, the Federal Reserve turned. Bank reserves would be supplied more generously, the money supply would expand more rapidly and credit conditions would be relaxed. As a result, short-term interest rates promptly started falling. Within three weeks, the Fed Funds rate and other short-term rates would subside at long last to their normal level—below long-term interest rates. This was the historic shift. Now, one could reasonably predict, the economy recovery would at last have a chance to begin.

When the financial markets opened again on Tuesday, July 6, the trauma of Penn Square quickly translated into defensive transactions.

In the stock market, investors dumped shares of Continental Illinois and Chase Manhattan, driving their stock prices lower. In the money market, anxious portfolio managers began moving billions of dollars to safer places.

The movement of funds on a vast scale briefly resembled a game of "hot money," scurrying to find a safe hiding place in the event of a storm. Essentially, that meant moving money out of the largest banks with the greatest risk exposure, particularly those involved in the Penn Square debacle, and parking it instead in smaller and more stable regional banks or even in the safest place of all, short-term Treasury bills. The interest-rate return would be fractionally smaller, but that was preferable to losing everything if one of the major banks failed. The message from Penn Square encouraged the flight of capital: the federal government seemed to be saying it would no longer cover the losses of large-scale depositors, that they must gauge banking risks for themselves.

Continental, among others, faced an immediate crisis of funding. As Continental's certificates of deposit came due, money managers simply declined to renew them and took their funds elsewhere. Or they insisted on purchasing CDs with shorter maturities—three months instead of one year. And they demanded higher interest rates from Continental and others. Money was rushing out of the bank and new money was reluctant to come in.

"We had some rather tense moments," said Michael Bradfield, the Fed's general counsel. "The spread between CDs and governments went through the roof."

While a banking crisis of this sort was virtually invisible to the general public, financial experts could watch it developing in several key numbers. When a bank was having trouble maintaining its deposits, it raised the interest rate offered on its CDs to attract more money. Thus, if an individual bank consistently paid a CD rate far above the market average, this probably meant it had problems. In addition, investors watched the interest-rate spread between bank CDs and competing alternatives such as Treasury bills. When the spread widened between three-month bank CDs and three-month Treasury bills, it was a sure sign that there were a lot of nervous bankers. In the weeks after the Penn Square trauma, compounded by the anxieties over the banks' foreign-debt exposure, this basic spread jumped from 1 percent to 3 percent.

The Federal Advisory Council reported to the Fed:

There is no question but that banks directly involved in the Penn Square affair experienced a sharp deterioration of position in bidding for short-term funds. . . . The larger banks affected were generally able to refund some of their maturities in the Euromarket where quality spreads were narrower. These same banks have found access to the overnight Fed Funds market somewhat more limited as some lenders have either canceled or "rested" lines or authorizations to place money with them. An interesting side effect . . . has been that many good-sized regional banks are being offered greater amounts of CD money than they are used to employing in their funding positions.

The nervous money had to find a safe home somewhere, even in banks that had more money than they needed. When anxieties subsided, the money managers could shift their funds back, but until the storm had cleared, they would take no chances. For banks like Continental Illinois and Seattle First, the funding squeeze reduced profits and simply added to their more fundamental problems.

"Continental's funding began eroding and it continued," said William Isaac. "It turned more and more to Europe, more short-term borrowing, paying premium rates." In other words, Continental's functional base—the managed liabilities it raised daily to fund its bank lending—was becoming narrower and narrower.

For the Fed, the best antidote for rising anxieties in the banking system was easy money.

Open-market operations were conducted against a troubled financial background [the Open Market Desk in New York reported]. . . . Financial markets had to cope with several well-publicized bankruptcies and growing concerns regarding the banking sector's loan exposure to hard-pressed domestic and international borrowers. Large loan losses suffered by several major banks highlighted the potential for difficulties in this area and some major banks encountered investor reluctance to purchase their CDs.

When M-1 failed to expand promptly after the July meeting, Volcker twice directed the Open Market Desk to give it a generous push—simply by adjusting upward the formula for supplying bank reserves. "Two upward adjustments were made when money proved to be unexpectedly weak," the desk reported. "Such judgmental shifts were also made to avoid situations where a mechanical adherence to the path procedures could produce unwanted results."[7] The Fed, in other words, was not going to let its money-supply rules stand in the way of pumping more liquidity into the system.

The money market took on a new glow. In the first week of July, the Federal Funds rate declined modestly. By mid-month it was down to 13.18 percent—160 basis points below its peak—and still falling. All the short-term interest rates in financial markets followed in step—

Treasury bills, commercial paper, bank CDs. On July 19, the Federal Reserve Board cut the Discount rate from 12 to 11.5 percent, the first reduction in seven months and a clear signal to money traders that the Fed intended to let the Federal Funds rate fall still lower. The Discount rate was the "floor price," and when the Fed knocked it down, the markets knew that other rates would follow.

And they did. By the week of July 23, the Fed Funds rate for overnight lending among banks was trading just above 12 percent and falling. A week later, it was at 11 percent and the Federal Reserve Board approved another .5 percent reduction in the Discount rate to 11 percent. The prime rate set by commercial banks, stuck at 16.5 percent since February, fell 200 basis points within a month's time, greatly easing the strains on business borrowers. The prime continued to decline with money-market rates.

A process of ratchetting downward was under way, a step at a time, without any public declarations or explanations. From July to December, the Federal Reserve Board would execute seven reductions in the Discount rate and, in the process, the Fed pulled down short-term interest rates by more than 40 percent. As long as the money markets seemed agreeable, the Federal Reserve would continue easing and even claim that it was following, not leading, this sudden decline in the price of money.

For the Fed, the crucial test was how long-term interest rates would react. If the bondholders were alarmed by the easier money, as Volcker had so long feared, then they would bid up long rates, demanding an "inflation premium" in their returns. If that happened, the prospects for recovery would be dashed. That was the theory, in any case, that had guided the Fed's refusal to ease many months sooner.

But the bondholders applauded the Fed's move. Long-term rates began to decline approximately in tandem with the declining short-term rates and would continue falling for the next four months. The twenty-year Treasury bond rate fell from 14.28 percent in late June to 10.56 in December. Corporate bond rates fell from 15.96 to 12.98 percent. Within three weeks of the July FOMC meeting, the Fed had pulled short-term rates down sharply enough so that all short rates were now below long rates, the natural condition for credit markets.

"The equity markets got a smell of lower interest rates and they took off," said Governor Lyle Gramley.

In early August, as the Fed's turn continued to unfold, an explosive rally started in the stock markets and spilled over into the bond trading. When interest rates declined, equity shares became a more attractive investment, and lower rates also suggested the possibility for economic recovery that would improve corporate profits. On August 17, the stock market recorded the largest one-day jump in its history —up 38.8 points on the Dow. Over the next six months, the index of industrial stocks would increase in value by roughly 50 percent.

The immediate trigger for the rally was an announcement from one of Wall Street's gloomiest voices, Henry Kaufman of Salomon Brothers, the influential "Dr. Doom" who had correctly predicted rising interest rates for so many years. Kaufman reversed himself that day, predicting instead that both long and short rates would continue to decline for the rest of the year. Nothing so cheered the stock markets as a sunny forecast from a dour bond-market economist. If Kaufman saw the turn, then it must be real.

"Rates are coming down like a ton of bricks and many money-market type investments aren't as attractive any more," Charles Comer of Bache Halsey Stuart Shields explained. "There is a lot of cash in the hands of investors." The bond market rallied too, though less dramatically than stocks, as bond trading volume jumped by more than 50 percent. After years of doldrum and depression, it now looked as if financial investments were ready to stage a comeback.[8]

In the aura of good feeling generated by the Fed's discreet change of policy, an important contradiction was generally overlooked. This was not supposed to happen. For months and months, both Paul Volcker and various voices of the financial markets had preached an entirely different scenario: easing money would not lower interest rates, but instead would force them higher. The financial markets would check any easing move by the Fed and, therefore, as Volcker explained repeatedly to congressional critics, the Fed was helpless. It dared not let up lest it lose "credibility" among the bondholders, the long-term investors.

In the actual unfolding of events, the opposite occurred. As soon as financial markets picked up the first hint that the Fed was easing, interest rates were merrily bid downward, both short-term and long-term rates. Instead of being frightened, Wall Street celebrated. Theoretically, this development might be attributed to a sudden and unpredicted change in market sentiment, a new confidence about inflation that developed mysteriously after July 1. This seemed most improbable. A more plausible explanation was that Volcker and the Federal Reserve and the financial-market analysis they relied upon were simply wrong.

If so, the Fed had held money tight and kept interest rates high for many months based on a false premise. It was taking its signals from Wall Street and the signals were mistaken. At least one governor, Emmett Rice, candidly acknowledged as much.

"I think we misinterpreted what the markets wanted," Rice said. "I thought they wanted us to stay tight. After the ease, I was concerned about how the financial markets would react. When they reacted positively, I was surprised."

The "crowds" of Wall Street were, after all, composed of fallible human beings too. The participants in financial markets possibly misled themselves as well as the Federal Reserve. The masculine ideal of toughness, of stern resolve, was as appealing to financial professionals as it was to the technocrats at the central bank.

Market participants talk tough as individuals and they're hard-liners [Emmett Rice said], but they wanted to see interest rates come down and they welcomed it. When they saw rates come down, they were very quick to jump on the bandwagon and benefit from it. If you talk to individuals in the market—dealers, bond salesmen, investment bankers, commercial bankers—they will say: "Stay tight." Yet they welcomed the lower interest rates. It was the same with the Federal Advisory Council, advising us to stay tight. Then we ease and the markets rally and the same advisory council says to us: "You did the right thing."

The misperception had rather large consequences for the rest of the nation. For months, the Federal Reserve had held tight, insisting that this was what the financial markets demanded. The politicians from Congress and the White House, pleading for lower interest rates, were dismissed as mere politicians. Governor Nancy Teeters was ignored too. The economy was driven deeper and deeper into contraction. In effect, the national government's management of the economy was being guided by the self-interested commentaries from a few hundred thousand financial experts in Wall Street. The Fed was steering—or was being steered—by the opinions of bondholders and their representatives and what they alone thought would be good for the nation. Only, in this case, the investors and investment experts from Wall Street were mistaken. Because they were wrong, the Federal Reserve was wrong too.

On August 3, Senator Robert Byrd, the Democratic floor leader, finally introduced the measure that he and other Fed critics had been brandishing for months, the Balanced Monetary Policy Act of 1982. The Federal Reserve would be commanded, by act of Congress, to reduce interest rates to normal levels.

It is time for Congress to wrest control of monetary policy from the hands of a tiny band of monetary ideologues in the White House, the

Administration and the Federal Reserve [Senator Byrd declared]. It is time for basic economic policy once more to be set by those elected officials who must bear the final responsibility. It is time to restore common sense, balance and stability to monetary policy."[9]

The congressional politicians were, in a sense, rolling out their big gun a bit late in the day—after the battle had already been decided. They had no way of knowing this, of course, and the Federal Reserve chairman did nothing to enlighten them. The July FOMC directive was still secret—and vaguely worded, in any case. Since Volcker was denying to his own colleagues that the Fed had executed a fundamental turn in its policy, he could hardly acknowledge it to senators and representatives.

Volcker's strongest hint of the Fed's new direction was contained in his midyear testimony before the House Banking Committee. "The evidence now seems to me strong that the inflationary tide has turned in a fundamental way," Volcker said. Compared to the gloomy caution in his prior assessments of inflation, this sounded like a declaration of victory.

In the meantime, Volcker assured the congressional critics, the Fed recognized the abnormalities in M-1 and the liquidity strains in the financial system and, therefore, would tolerate temporary "bulges" in the money supply. But, otherwise, the chairman repeated his standard vows of vigilance and his usual scolding of Congress for the huge fiscal deficits.

And Volcker simply evaded the question of whether the Fed itself had eased. "Different people have different things in mind when they talk about easing and tightening," he said. "I wouldn't try to straighten that out."[10]

Senator Byrd and the 31 other cosponsors could see that short-term rates were declining, but they were not sure if this was anything more than a temporary blip. Volcker, after all, attributed the falling rates to the "markets," not to any policy change by the Federal Reserve. In the confusion, the angry senators and representatives introduced their bill to strip the Fed of its independence and Volcker continued his lobbying against it.

"Volcker was all over the Hill, trying to talk everyone out of this," a Senate staff aide said. "Volcker just kept saying he hoped Byrd would reconsider. Byrd kept probing him, saying, 'Isn't there anything you can do?' It was a very clever political strategy of the Fed—to absolve themselves of any responsibility."

The Fed-stripping legislation was now an empty threat, however. House Democrats might conceivably have passed the bill, but it was

never evident that Senate Democrats could muster a majority in the
upper chamber to enact such a fundamental reform. It would require
Congress to take responsibility for monetary policy—for the level of
interest rates and for inflation—responsibility that many in Congress
preferred to keep at a mysterious distance in the central bank. More
to the point, the falling interest rates and the stock-market rally—with
the hint of an economic recovery ahead—simply collapsed the congressional zeal for Fed bashing. The momentum for fundamental reform quickly dissipated.

As rates continued to decline in August, Volcker called Senator
Byrd and asked him what he was going to do, now that the pressures
of high rates were subsiding. The senator, according to an aide, assured the Fed chairman: "As long as interest rates are coming down,
we're not going to push it."

Volcker had kept the political critics at bay. Later in the year, as
Congress prepared to adjourn, the Senate did adopt an innocuous
resolution imploring the Federal Reserve to continue driving interest
rates down in order to foster economic growth but "with due regard
for controlling inflation." It was the equivalent of instructing the Fed
to be all good things at once.

Senator Byrd, Representative Henry Reuss and some of the other
reformers persisted in believing that their various hortatory resolutions and their threatened legislation had actually accomplished something. At least they claimed that their actions had induced the Federal
Reserve to change its policy. "Together, we sent a shot across the
Fed's bow this summer and the results speak for themselves," Byrd
boasted to his Senate colleagues.[11]

This was little more than posturing, the kind of adolescent bravado
that might have fooled the public but not the serious players of government. By the time Senator Byrd and his allies had fired their supposed
"shot" at the Fed, Paul Volcker, for reasons of his own, had already
turned the ship around.

The Federal Reserve, it seemed, was right not to take Congress too
seriously. Volcker correctly assumed that, for all their belligerent talk,
the congressional reformers did not really wish to change anything
fundamental. They only wished for the punishment to stop. And, when
it did, they promptly abandoned their threats and tough talk and
retreated from the confrontation. Their performance resembled a
charade, an outburst of angry children resisting a stern parent's
discipline, and that is how the Federal Reserve treated them, like
children.

On the Republican side, politicians also felt a sense of accomplishment, now that Volcker was easing. While they never claimed any

explicit deal with the Federal Reserve chairman, things seemed to be working out as if there had been one. By mid-August, Congress finally enacted a package of almost $100 billion in tax increases, paring down the huge deficits somewhat. And the Fed began easing—pulling down interest rates.

The Senate majority leader, Howard Baker, who had been privately bashing Volcker for more than nine months, reported his satisfaction to White House officials. "Howard Baker saw these interest rates come tumbling down and he declared that Paul Volcker is a fine fellow who keeps his word," David Stockman, the budget director, said.

"I tried to get something to happen," Baker said, "but I'm not sure I did. While I was doing all this bashing and banging, I also enlisted as Volcker's ally." [12]

James Baker, the White House chief of staff, held a less complicated view of the political exchange. With considerable risk and political energy, the White House had helped engineer a major tax increase in an election year in order to reduce the budget deficit. Now that Volcker had gotten what he wanted, the Federal Reserve should engineer a major relaxation of interest rates.

"Jim Baker carried the water," said Lawrence Kudlow. "When the budget reduction was completed, Baker said to Volcker: 'We've done our part—now you do yours.' " There was no suggestion of an explicit deal, but there was an assumption at the White House that one good turn would lead to another. In fact, there was no real connection between the two events. Volcker did not wait for the tax legislation to pass before taking action. The Fed had decided to ease interest rates a full month before final passage of the tax bill was a certainty.

The monetarist economists at the White House and Treasury were, meanwhile, alarmed by what was happening. Thanks to the Fed's decisions in July, M-1 began expanding by more than 10 percent in August. The money supply was ballooning again and they renewed their urgent warnings of future inflation. "Everyone ignored them," Stockman said.

This time the Administration's monetarists were told, in the clearest terms, to keep their complaints to themselves. The White House political advisers were looking at double-digit unemployment and a major debacle for Republican candidates in the November elections. They did not want anyone from the Reagan Administration suggesting that the Federal Reserve ought to tighten money again.

On the contrary, White House officials explicitly assured Volcker that he would encounter no criticism from the Reagan team if the Fed allowed the money numbers to soar above the targets. For James Baker and others, there was a belated regret that they had not taken this step much earlier in the year, when they were allowing monetarists like Beryl Sprinkel to declare the correct position on monetary policy and to encourage Volcker's stringency.

We had thought the recession would be over in the second quarter [William Niskanen of the CEA explained]. By June, it was clear the recession was longer and deeper than we had expected. Starting in mid-July, as industrial production started coming in way low, everybody started running a bit scared. We were going to be in for another three to six months of recession.

There was a very clear signal to the Fed that the Administration wanted much higher money growth, that money growth had to be increased. By then, it was too late to save the election, but the hands-off policy would have been different if we had known the depth and the length of the recession.

As interest rates declined, James Baker personally urged Volcker to do more of the same. A genuine recovery might not develop in time for the election, but falling interest rates—and a surging stock market —provided good news in themselves. Among his colleagues, Baker frequently expressed his frustration with the Fed—that the independent Federal Reserve had been allowed to drive the economy as deeply into contraction as it had, that Volcker had not reacted sooner to the misery and dislocation and financial stress. "From that point on," Stockman said, "Jim Baker was very skeptical about Volcker."

The Federal Reserve chairman's independence, however, was derived in part from the confused purposes in Ronald Reagan's White House. A strong President who knew what he wanted and was willing to demand it forcefully might have been able to move the Fed sooner. But Reagan and his advisers wanted both things at once—tighter money and faster economic growth, rigid control of M-1 and lower interest rates—goals that were fundamentally irreconcilable. Since the President was never willing to resolve his own contradictions, Paul Volcker resolved them for him.

All of the various political pressures directed at the Fed, the threats from Congress and the pleas from the White House, certainly produced caution and a tactical defensiveness at the Federal Reserve. But there was no plausible evidence to indicate that Volcker and his colleagues on the Federal Open Market Committee had turned their monetary policy because they were afraid of what Senator Byrd might do to them, or Senator Baker or Ronald Reagan, for that matter.

What produced the Fed's turn was the policy makers' private fears of financial disorder—the shock waves from Penn Square, the threatening collapse of foreign debtors, the deepening strains on the banking system as the economy failed to recover. In the politics of money, elected politicians could be discounted or outmaneuvered. The distress from ordinary citizens in the real economy could be dismissed as necessary unpleasantness. What the Federal Reserve could not evade, ultimately, was the danger facing the banking system itself.

David Stockman, who was closely allied with Volcker in the internal policy arguments, explained succinctly what finally persuaded the Federal Reserve chairman to relent:

> Volcker is a financial-institutions conservative and that's how he thinks. The thing that impacts on him the most is disorder in the financial community. That's what gets to him. Volcker may keep his powder dry when he sees unemployment numbers that stay too high too long. But, if there's fragility in the financial system, then he moves.

On Friday, the thirteenth of August, Jesus Silva Herzog called once again at the Federal Reserve and the Treasury Department, this time to declare that the game was over. Two weeks before, the Fed had lent another $700 million to Mexico and now that money was virtually gone too. The nation's liquid reserves had dwindled to less than $200 million, but capital was fleeing the country at the rate of at least $100 million a day. On Monday, when the world opened for business, Mexico would be broke.

The United States government could not allow that to happen. If Mexico defaulted on its $80 billion debt, the largest banks of America and Europe would be swamped in the resulting panic. Other debtor nations, faced with the same financial crisis, would no doubt follow Mexico's failure. Investors worldwide would rush to find safe ground, dumping bank stocks and pulling deposits out of any banks that had heavy exposure in Third World loans. The bubble of optimism that had led Citibank and the others to lend so heavily to Mexico, Brazil, Argentina and the rest was about to burst.

The immediate solution, plainly stated, was for the United States to pump a lot of new money into Mexico—over the weekend—before the nation collapsed in insolvency. In the coming months, Mexico faced due dates on $10 billion in loan payments it could not meet, so this time the emergency credit would have to be much larger than the bridging loans the Fed had been providing Mexico since the spring. Once the immediate crisis was averted, then all the threatened parties —commercial banks, central bankers and sovereign nations—would have to work out new terms for dealing with Mexico's long-term solvency.

In crisis, the United States government could move swiftly and on a massive scale. Between Paul Volcker at the Fed and Donald Regan at

Treasury, an unprecedented bailout was arranged in three days of private meetings—$3.5 billion in new loans for Mexico. The Department of Energy agreed to buy $1 billion of oil from Mexico and to pay in advance immediately, instead of paying on delivery. The Department of Agriculture provided another $1 billion, a line of credit for the future purchase of U.S. grain and other food products. Volcker, meanwhile, organized a $1.85 billion loan pool among the central banks of the industrial world, half of the money to be provided by the Fed. All together, this new money would keep Mexico going until a more permanent solution could be worked out. By Sunday evening, the deals were all negotiated and Silva flew home to Mexico City to announce that national bankruptcy had been averted. Mexico, in effect, was now in receivership to the international financiers.

On the following Friday, the Mexican finance minister faced his private creditors. More than a hundred representatives of commercial banks gathered in the auditorium at the New York Fed to hear the details. Anthony Solomon, the New York Fed president, summarized the emergency measures that the government had undertaken on the previous weekend. Then Silva described the larger problems. Mexico needed a ninety-day moratorium from the banks on all the debt payments coming due. It would begin working out the terms for a larger loan from the International Monetary Fund. But it would also require rescheduling of its outstanding debt—and additional loans—from the commercial banks.

The bankers asked a lot of skeptical questions, but they were not in a position to refuse. The decisions made in Washington were essentially a declaration that the U.S. government would take responsibility for sorting out the debt crisis. With that imprimatur, the bankers agreed to begin negotiations on refinancing.

Many smaller regional banks, which had made only limited loans to Mexico and other Latin-American nations, wanted out. Making new loans to Mexico now sounded like "throwing good money after bad." The wise course for a prudent banker would be to take his losses now and get out before things got worse. Some of the bankers gathered at the New York Fed, though they did not say so, intended to do just that. Mexico wasn't their problem—it was Citibank's and Bank of America's and the other majors'.

But the survival of the largest banks in America literally depended on keeping Mexico afloat. And that would require new lending from the private banks, in addition to the publicly financed assistance that would come from governments and the international agencies like the IMF. A creditors' advisory committee was appointed with representatives from Citibank, Chase, Chemical, Morgan Guaranty, Bank of

America, Bankers Trust, Manufacturers Hanover and seven foreign banks. In coming months, these bankers would negotiate the new loan terms with Mexico—and they would make sure that none of their reluctant colleagues from smaller banks backed away from the deal. For purposes of persuasion, the money-center bankers would enlist the authoritative surveillance of the Federal Reserve.

In a formal sense, this was the starting point for what became known as the international debt crisis—actually, a continuing series of crisis points, as one country after another approached the brink of insolvency, then appealed for relief to the Fed, the international lending agencies and the private banks. Within the next year, fourteen other nations would undergo the same trauma that Mexico experienced in August 1982—accepting new conditions of domestic austerity in exchange for new credit from the IMF and the international banks. Each time a nation approached default, the international banking system was threatened anew, and each time, Paul Volcker and his aides from New York and Washington would play the crisis managers.

In a more fundamental sense, the debt crisis had its origins in the collision of purposes within the Federal Reserve itself. In the late seventies and early eighties, the Fed and other regulators had failed to impose prudent limits on the money-center banks and their zealous lending to the Third World. They had issued mild warnings occasionally, but they had not tried to stop the risky lending. Then, starting in 1979, Volcker launched his aggressive campaign to break inflation, rationing money tightly and imposing a stern discipline on the world economy. The global liquidation collided with the mountain of LDC debt.

In theory at least, the debt crisis might have been avoided if the Federal Reserve had not chosen such an abrupt approach to decelerating price inflation. Prudent bankers, certainly, ought to have seen the collision coming and prepared for it. Instead, men like Walter Wriston of Citibank had it both ways: they berated the Fed for its lax control of money and inflation, urging Volcker to be still tougher, while simultaneously they ignored the Fed's mild warnings about the excessive buildup of Third World debt. It was puzzling that such intelligent and worldly-wise financiers did not see the contradiction that was engulfing their banks, but they evidently did not.

Still, even if the bankers had recognized the danger, Volcker's strategy did not give them much time to adjust. The chairman and most members of the Federal Reserve Board had little patience with those who argued for "gradualism" in fighting inflation. The only way to do the job, they decided, was to be swift and sure, to take the pain and get it over with. Only, in this case, the pain did not go away as neatly as they had expected—it would linger on for years and years, especially for the humblest citizens of the less-developed nations.

Bringing a halt to runaway inflation in such an abrupt and extreme manner forced the foreign debtors to the wall—for approximately the same reasons it bankrupted tens of thousands of businesses in the United States. They were heavily dependent on credit, yet the Fed had drastically raised the cost of their borrowing while it simultaneously depressed their sales and incomes. If the world economy had not been pushed down so far, if interest rates had not been forced so high, these debtor nations might have survived the contraction. As it was, they had no time to adjust and really no alternative but to keep borrowing more, just as weakened American corporations had to increase their borrowing to survive the recession. Volcker's great triumph—his single-minded and successful campaign against price inflation—was purchased at a heavy price. It burst the bubble of global debt and rattled the foundations of the international banking system.

The Mexican rescue, however, looked like a triumph of crisis management—in the short term. Within seventy-two hours, Volcker and the other government officials had engineered a massive financial bailout, and when the world's markets opened on Monday morning, there was no crisis, no reason to panic. Very few figures in American politics questioned the intervention. Many drew a deep breath and applauded. The alternative possibilities—what might have happened to the global financial system—were too ominous to contemplate.

For the long term, however, the debt crisis represented a political and economic disaster of historic dimensions—for the struggling nations, for the major international banks, and for the government regulators who were supposed to insure the "safety and soundness" of the financial system. The damage was incalculable because it was diffused deeply and in so many directions.

For poorer countries, the debtors, it produced an era of domestic misery, a steady and unrelenting grinding down of economic aspirations. As bankrupt nations, they must forgo the normal expectations of rising prosperity in order to pay their bankers and, indeed, they would have to keep borrowing more simply to keep up with the interest payments. For the average citizens in a dozen countries, economic life began to resemble a hopeless treadmill. They would see their real standard of living steadily decline as they worked to pay off their nation's old debts. Only the debts did not get smaller.

For the proud banks of Wall Street, the crisis produced an embarrassing dependency on Washington. For all their vigorous rhetoric about the glories of the free market and financial deregulation, the money-center banks would not get out of this mess unless the government stepped in and rescued them. As the IMF lent huge sums to the debtor nations to keep them going, the taxpayers of the United States and other industrial nations were effectively assuming the obligations in behalf of the banks. The more that the public treasuries lent to Mexico and the others, the safer would be the managers and shareholders of Citibank, Morgan Guaranty, Chase and Chemical and the others.

This naked dependency on government did not exactly make the bankers more humble. On the contrary, Wriston and other Wall Street bank executives continued regularly to denounce the meddling of Washington in their business affairs and to demand more freedom from federal regulation, even as they counted on the government to protect them from loss. The bankers were right to be so self-confident, in a sense. This was the way the system was intended to work. The Federal Reserve's fundamental obligation was to protect the banking system, even from its own folly, and it did.

The Federal Reserve performed that role effectively. Whatever private reservations he harbored about shortsighted bankers, Paul Volcker would now serve as their principal advocate and protector, defending their claims in the tendentious negotiations with other sovereign nations, bargaining, pressuring, keeping the complex deals of global finance intact. The necessities of managing the debt crisis— saving the money-center banks—became a powerful preoccupation for the central bank, an obligation that influenced its decisions on both monetary policy and bank regulation.

For Americans at large, there were also costs. The debt crisis produced distorted economic policies from government, particularly at the Fed, and blighted the prospects for trade, growth and general prosperity. If Latin America was compelled to accept austerity, if the debtor nations were forced to restrict their imports and save their money to pay off the banks, then those nations could not buy tractors and grain and appliances and all the other goods they purchased from America in prosperous times. Austerity in Brazil and Argentina meant higher unemployment in Michigan and Ohio. Falling living standards in Mexico and Peru meant depressed farm incomes in Iowa and Kansas.

In August 1982, the debt crisis was only beginning. As Volcker and other financial officials struggled to manage the various moments of crisis in the months and years ahead, the costs would continue. There was a financial price to pay but a much larger price in terms of human suffering. Instead of dissipating gradually, both of these costs would grow larger.[13]

. . .

Continental Illinois had lent $200 million to International Harvester, the farm-implements manufacturer that was on the brink of bankruptcy. It had lent $100 million to Alfa of Mexico and more than $60 million to Braniff airlines, AM International and Wickes, three of the largest corporate bankruptcies of 1982. In addition to the incautious oil loans it had made through Penn Square, Continental had also gambled a huge stake on GHR Companies, a Louisiana oil-and-gas company that was also about to fail as oil prices continued to decline. The federal regulators did not at first discover the full extent of the bad loans, but they could quickly see that Continental Illinois was in even worse shape than the financial markets realized.

William Isaac, chairman of the FDIC, complained:

Continental Illinois continued to make serious mistakes after Penn Square. What should have been done right away was the board of directors should have fired the management, brought in strong management from outside, taken a huge loan write-off and eliminated its dividend to stockholders. They might have failed anyway, but if they had taken these actions promptly, there was a substantial chance they could survive. It could have restored confidence by showing the markets that they were confronting their problems and dealing with them.

None of these remedial steps were taken by Continental Illinois— largely because the Federal Reserve lacked the nerve to invoke its full authority as a bank regulator. After Penn Square collapsed, Paul Volcker also felt that the Chicago bank must shape up, but, unlike Isaac, Volcker was directly responsible, with the Comptroller, for supervising Continental. While the Fed had failed to restrain Continental in its heady days of go-go expansion, it would now attempt to correct things. The Fed's efforts remained totally confidential, largely unknown even to financial insiders. The net outcome, however, was that nothing happened. The episode merely demonstrated again, more vividly, how the Federal Reserve, despite its legendary powers, could be cowed by a major commercial bank.

Shortly after the Penn Square crisis broke, the Federal Reserve chairman began urging the directors of Continental Illinois to clean house and straighten out their troubled portfolio. Volcker met several times with Continental's top executives and members of its board of directors. He reviewed the situation with a special committee appointed by the bank's directors to conduct an internal investigation. Volcker proposed remedial steps to restore soundness. By telephone and in person, he urged the directors to act.

The Federal Reserve chairman's recommendations were rebuffed. The directors of Continental Illinois replied that they would not fire the managers, would not suspend the dividend to shareholders and would not admit the depth of the problems in their loan portfolio.

"Volcker urged them to find out whether they had a temporary funding problem or whether they had a more permanent asset-quality problem," said Michael Bradfield, the Federal Reserve Board's general counsel. "That would determine what kind of action they had to take. In the end, they never answered those questions."

In the second week of August, Volcker put his warning more bluntly to Continental's directors at a meeting at the Fed in Washington. A staff memorandum of the meeting reported:

Chairman Volcker said it was important to deal with this credibility problem as soon as possible. . . . The quality of assets issue following Penn Square raised important questions about the management. . . . It is extremely difficult for officers of the corporation to conduct an independent review of their own activities because of the natural tendency to defend their own past actions. . . . The market won't give much time for this investigation to be completed. . . . The chairman has no fixed plan, but the corporation should consider changes in management and lending policy. . . . Two choices: admit the bank has taken a hard knock but could weather the storm . . . or reduce the third-quarter earnings and clean up the problems.[14]

Continental did not clean up its problems. The bank continued to pay quarterly dividends to its shareholders as though nothing was wrong. Roger Anderson, the aggressive chairman whose high-growth strategy had led the bank into trouble, remained in control as Continental's CEO. A few weeks later, Anderson announced boldly that the bank had dealt with its difficulties and could now go forward confidently, business as usual. The Federal Reserve and the Comptroller knew better, but did nothing to intervene.

"Yeah, maybe we should have nailed them," Bradfield conceded. "It fussed along for a while. Anderson made a statement that everything was fine and they were going to continue on struggling. But it was already too late. They had a $4 to $5 billion hole already."

The Federal Reserve, by reputation, had awesome powers with which to discipline errant banks, but its leverage did not seem so impressive up against the officers and directors of the nation's seventh-largest bank. The Fed declined to use any of its regulatory tools to compel Continental Illinois to shape up. It did not, for instance, threaten to issue a cease-and-desist order to stop dividends or change management. It did not even hint that Continental might be denied Discount privileges. In the crunch, the Fed behaved rather impotently.

What are you going to say [Bradfield pleaded]? Goddamn it, as long as Roger Anderson is chairman of your bank, we're not going to lend any money at the Discount window? You can say it and it's pretty intimidating, but the directors can call your bluff. Legally, you can deny Discount loans if you think there's a risk you won't get your money back. But, as a practical matter, you can't. The consequences of refusing to supply liquidity support to a bank are too severe.

To apply its available powers, the Fed would have had to assume more responsibility for the outcome. If the Fed had imposed direct controls on Continental's affairs, forced the bank to suspend dividends and change its management, the Federal Reserve would have itself been implicated in the fallout. If financial markets became alarmed and the bank failed anyway, Continental stockholders would likely blame Washington. For both the Fed and the Comptroller, it was easier to stick to private pleading and hope for the best.

"When Volcker and Conover presented their recommendations to the Continental Illinois directors," William Isaac related, "the directors said to them: 'Well, this will be the end of this bank and you will be to blame.' It takes real gumption for a regulator to sit there and say, 'I'll take the responsibility, despite your reservations.' We're talking about one of the biggest banks in the world. No one knows what will happen."

Perhaps, as the Federal Reserve's general counsel argued, it was already too late to save Continental Illinois, but that was not a satisfying explanation. If it was too late, then there was a larger question. Why had the Fed allowed the situation to develop in the first place?

"The real failure of supervision," Bradfield agreed, "is that nobody did anything about Continental Illinois in the late seventies and early eighties—when they were following the policy that they would become the fastest-growing lender in the nation, when they were winning management awards and Roger Anderson was named 'banker of the year.' "

Given the political climate, given its own institutional inhibitions, the Federal Reserve did not attempt to slow down banks like Continental Illinois on the upside—when they were expanding their lending agressively. That was when the crisis was seeded and when bank regulators failed to prevent it.

That's the dilemma of regulation [Bradfield explained]. It's so very hard to deal with things when they seem to be working. Who was going to tell the banks not to lend to energy when energy was the hottest part of the economy and running up great profits? Or shipping? Or real estate? In the seventies, the ethos of deregulation and laissez-faire was rising—get the government off the backs of private enterprise. Examiners are affected by that too. On the downside, the examiners are embarrassed and so they want to put everybody to the wall. You have to tell the examiners that some patience is necessary to protect the banking community. . . . How can you be reasonably tough when things are good? It's easy to be tough when things are bad.

Charles Partee, who chaired the Board of Governors' committee on bank supervision, conceded the same failure of federal bank regulation. "It's hard," Partee explained. "In the context of the times, everyone thinks they are doing the right thing. To impose prudential restraints is meddlesome and it restricts profits. If the banking system is expanding rapidly, if they can show they're making good money by the new business, for us to try to be too tough with them, to hold them back, is just not going to be acceptable."

The case of Continental Illinois also demonstrated a profound vulnerability in the American banking system. The federal bank regulators either lacked the will or, as they insisted, the political weight to impose genuine restraint on the largest and most aggressive banks when those banks embarked on their expansionary lending binges. Yet, given the banking strategy called "managed liabilities," there was little else to restrain these bankers, if the regulators didn't. An old-fashioned bank, practicing old-fashioned prudence, would expand its lending only in step with its deposit base. The more deposit customers it could attract, the more loans the bank could make. The modern banks that practiced managed liabilities had no such inhibitions. They simply made new loans, then borrowed the money to fund them. As long as they could borrow freely, there was no internal brake on how fast they could expand.

The result was that huge banking enterprises—virtually all of the most important banks—were balanced precariously on very small foundations. They operated on a small core of permanent depositors and a huge pool of borrowed money. The vulnerability arose—sometimes quite suddenly—when the vast network of money managers, who lent the funds on which these banks operated, decided, for whatever reason, that a bank was itself a risky borrower.

With Continental Illinois, when you get right down to it, here was a $40 billion bank with only $4 billion in deposits [Governor Partee said]. The core of the bank was very, very small. They're selling CDs, getting money from the Eurodollar market, selling commercial paper from the bank holding company. It was an extreme case—but it wasn't all that unusual. Citibank has a small core too. Lots of big banks do.

Without any real restraints on these practices, the modern banking system was thus exposed to a permanent danger of "panics" at the top—virtually the opposite of the old-fashioned "runs" that used to topple smaller banks. Fifty years earlier, when small-town bankers like Marriner Eccles struggled to keep their banks open, the threat was the fear that might spread among ordinary depositors who would rush in to withdraw their accounts. The introduction of federal deposit insurance in 1933 virtually eliminated that danger.

By the 1980s, however, a new danger had succeeded it. A "bank run" of major proportions could swiftly develop if whim or rumors or well-founded fears suddenly swept through the global network of sophisticated investors—money managers, large financial institutions, other bankers. When these people became worried about their money, they did not form lines in the bank lobby; they simply sent Telex messages withdrawing billions of dollars from the CDs issued by the suspect bank. This form of panic did not threaten smaller banks, most of which still depended on a base of permanent depositors to fund their operations. The new variety of "bank runs" struck at the very top of the system—the largest and most important banks. The potential consequences of letting one of them fail seemed too dangerous to entertain.

The Fed was caught, therefore, in its own political dilemma. It could see the risks of reckless credit expansion and was responsible for restraining the banks. Yet, much like elected politicians, the Fed found it difficult to say no. In the era of financial deregulation, the central bank lacked the political self-confidence to really restrain the largest banks. As an institution, the Fed was an assembly of unelected technocrats with no political base of their own. They were ostensibly free of politics, but actually dependent for political protection on the very enterprises the Federal Reserve was supposed to control, the constituency of commercial banks dominated by the largest money-center banks. It took "real gumption" to go against them, as Isaac said.

Whenever the Fed had clearly failed to fulfill its regulatory obligations, its officers often invoked the same excuse—at least privately. They too were vulnerable, they explained, to the informal pressures of politics. Members of Congress would complain. CEOs and stockholders would object. Volcker had offered that excuse, so did Bradfield and Partee. If this was the reality, then behind its aloof image the Federal Reserve was not that different from other "captive" regulatory agencies. The Fed also responded to the mood swings of politics and business, the illusions of conventional opinion and the safe haven of bureaucratic timidity. In the hard cases, when it counted most, the Federal Reserve proved to be a lot less powerful—and a lot more political—than it pretended to be.

For two and a half years, oblivious to critics, Paul Volcker had imposed his will on American economic life. He had stared down U.S. senators and presidential advisers. Yet he could not stare down the directors of an important Chicago bank. When they said no and rejected his advice, the Federal Reserve chairman withdrew and allowed them to have their way.

There was a final, galling insult added to the Fed's failure to prevail over Continental's management. In 1983, with the annual rotation of membership, Roger Anderson, chairman of Continental Illinois, would join the Federal Advisory Council, the select group of twelve commercial bankers who met privately each quarter with the Federal Reserve Board. Volcker had tried to get him fired and failed. Now, as the Continental bank continued to unravel, Roger Anderson would serve as one of Volcker's official advisers.

At a distance, Paul Volcker's execution of monetary policy looked like a virtuoso performance. Despite the confusion and error, Volcker was determined to risk on the side of greater discipline, and because he stuck to that objective, the Federal Reserve succeeded in collapsing price inflation. The reversal of prices was faster and more substantial than even the optimists in the Reagan Administration had expected. And it took nerve. The chairman steered the economy right to the brink—and then pulled back, just in time. His maneuvers were so adroit that many did not recognize what he had engineered until months afterward. By then, the economy would begin to recover its vitality and Paul Volcker would no longer be the subject of attack. In time, the Federal Reserve chairman would be celebrated as the brave and brilliant manager of money.

But, with the brilliance, there was also a quality of blindness, a singlemindedness that stubbornly blocked out the competing realities. Some of the politicians who dealt with him thought so. Senator Howard Baker and Senator Robert Byrd and James Baker at the White House—all got the impression from their private conversations with the Fed chairman that Volcker genuinely didn't grasp the depth of the economic destruction that was unfolding. All they could offer to persuade him were the subjective evaluations of politicians, the random soundings they heard from distressed citizens, including businessmen and bankers, about how bad things were. Volcker was not convinced.

In the technocratic ethic of the Federal Reserve, insulated from mere politics, political complaints were not regarded as reliable evidence. Indeed, it was considered improper for the central bank to respond to the pleadings from politicians, who were presumed to be self-interested and shortsighted. Volcker relied instead on the scientific data of economics, the weekly and monthly numbers on money, prices and other measures that supposedly captured reality in a more objective form. And Volcker relied on the messages from the financial markets—the collective decisions rendered in the daily auctions of the marketplace as well as the informed analysis of the market participants. These analysts were said to be rational and disinterested in a way that democratic politics was not.

In both instances, the Fed was taking its signals from guideposts that proved to be grossly misleading. The monetary theory—the very meaning of the money measures—collapsed and finally had to be abandoned. The financial markets said they wanted one thing and, in the event, it was obvious what they really wanted was the opposite. In any case, when Volcker did finally yield and reverse policy, his decision was not derived from grand economic principle or finely calibrated measures of market sentiment. When the Fed finally turned, the change in monetary policy was forced upon it by events—the harsh necessity of avoiding a breakdown in the financial system.

On the evidence, the politicians were not wrong about what they saw happening to the American economy or what they tried to tell Volcker. The recession, as it turned out, *was* far worse than the Federal Reserve had realized. The politicians' pleas and threats were, of course, partly motivated by crass self-interest—the desire to appease angry voters, the fear of losing elections. But this was the motivation that was supposed to guide government in a representative democracy, the linkage that kept government responsive to the electorate.

For the central bank, the claims that arose randomly from popular discontent were not considered a legitimate guide to policy. That was part of the blindness, but the explanation went deeper. By its very nature, the central bank assumed that destruction was part of its purpose and, once begun, it was natural to let it continue. The process of liquidation, after all, would have no meaning if retrenchment and failure did not occur; this was the "pain" that was supposed to be therapeutic. Given that mind-set, it was easy enough for policy makers to rationalize that if a little harsh medicine would ultimately be good for everyone, then a bit more punishment ought to be even better. Thus, it was in the nature of the Federal Reserve to always go too far.

And it did so again and again in its history—telling itself each time that this was the responsible thing to do. Let "nature" take its course until all excess is purged; do not be dissuaded by the weak-willed politicians. In 1929, the Fed had clung to this self-justification disastrously. In 1982, it relented just short of the brink.

In the politics of money, there were no disinterested players, however. The participants in financial markets, the bondholders and the financial institutions that represented them, instructed the Fed relentlessly and effectively in their own behalf—demanding that the central bank squeeze the real economy still tighter in order to further enhance the value of their financial assets. The commercial bankers who advised the Fed did not, understandably, advocate any policies they thought were in the broad national interest but would be injurious for banks. The officials of the Federal Reserve attended to their own self-interest too. For many months, the Fed was reluctant to lower interest rates, despite the evidence of economic destruction, because it was afraid of losing its own institutional "credibility."

The "money question" was always political, notwithstanding the accepted myth of the Federal Reserve's political independence. In the generic meaning of politics, it could not be otherwise. Whatever was decided by the Federal Reserve, some political interests would be enhanced and others would be injured. The notion that monetary policy could be disinterested—somehow separated from politics in a way that other government policies were not—was the central fallacy inherent in the central bank's protected status. The notion that some political interests—namely, the financial markets, banks and investors—were legitimate voices in deciding the correct course for money policy—and others were not—was the central distortion of political power surrounding the Federal Reserve.

Offensive as this was to democratic principle, the practical result was in some ways worse—it produced distorted judgments by the Fed policy makers. If Volcker and his colleagues had listened more earnestly to the clamoring politicians, the Federal Reserve's errors of excess in the liquidation might have been smaller. The economy and the financial system would not have gotten so close to the edge.

The clearest evidence that Volcker had himself misunderstood the impact of his monetary policy—that he had driven the contraction deeper than even he intended—was contained in the Federal Reserve's own record. By its own testimony, the Federal Open Market Committee had gone too far. Each February, the FOMC was required by law to provide its operating targets and economic projections for the year. Early in 1982, the FOMC members announced the estimates of real economic growth they expected for the year and their projections ranged from a meager growth rate of only .5 percent to a more robust recovery of 3 percent. All the FOMC members, however, predicted positive real growth for 1982. Instead, the economy continued its shrinkage. Real growth was negative for 1982—minus 2.5 percent.

The Fed policy makers misjudged the extent of human dislocation and suffering their money policy would cause. The national unemployment rate reached 10.8 percent in the final quarter of 1982—whereas the Federal Open Market Committee had expected unemployment to peak between 8.25 and 9.5 percent. Several million additional people lost work and incomes as a result. The FOMC had estimated that nominal GNP would grow by 8 to 10.5 percent in 1982. In reality, it expanded by barely more than 3 percent. In sum, the Federal Reserve's stringent monetary policy depressed the economy in 1982 much more than even the Fed planned—about five percentage points below its own forecast for nominal GNP—the equivalent of about $150 billion in unrealized economic activity. It was like an angry father spanking a child and not knowing when to stop.

In general, Federal Reserve officials defended their toughness, but some of them conceded, at least privately, that the monetary discipline had gone too far. William Poole, an academic economist who joined President Reagan's Council of Economic Advisers in 1982 and had served many years as a monetary consultant to the Fed, described what he heard from former colleagues at the central bank: "In private conversations, the Fed people told me: 'If we had known the severity and depth, we probably would have done it more gradually.' "

"We have a crude steering mechanism," the vice president at one Federal Reserve Bank explained. "In retrospect, I wouldn't have steered so close to the edge."

The standard argument used to justify the anomaly of Federal Reserve independence was that neither Congress nor the President could be trusted with money. In the nature of electoral politics, they would always be irresponsible—incapable of restraining themselves or denying the appetites of their constituencies. The federal budget was the vivid proof. Fiscal policy was perennially out of balance and impervious to reform, expanding immoderately in good times and bad. Politicians were not expected to behave otherwise. That was why the central bank must be shielded from the hot breath of voters so it could do the responsible thing, the hard and nasty chore that politicians would not do.

But there was this countervailing reality, one that was usually left out of the argument: the Federal Reserve could be irresponsible too. Just as Congress and the President went to extremes in their budget policies, the central bank was capable of going to extremes in its pursuit of monetary discipline. The Fed demonstrated this impulse most dramatically in the course of the liquidation in 1981–1982, but it was not new behavior, unique to Paul Volcker's regime. When it suppressed the economy, the Federal Reserve usually went too far. Given its own political objectives, the central bank was, like Congress, reluctant to restrain itself—to pursue a moderate, balanced approach to stabilizing money. Gradualism seemed awkward and unconvincing. A moderate policy risked criticism from the Fed's own political constituencies, the bondholders and financial markets. The only way to get the job done was to do it with swift and extreme force.

The single-minded behavior of the Federal Reserve was not so different, in its own way, from the excessive behavior demonstrated by Congress and Presidents. Given the opportunity, both sides exercised their particular powers over the economy in the extreme because, for both, it was politically rewarding to do so. Elected politicians got to do the "fun part" of politics—cutting taxes and increasing spending and creating new government ventures. The Federal Reserve won applause from its audience, the bondholders and associated institutions, when it imposed excessive punishment on the economy. Neither side of the governing equation—not the Fed, not the Congress and Chief Executive—was required to face the consequences of its own excess. Neither side had either the capacity or the incentive to seek balance. Neither was required to think comprehensively about managing the economy.

The governing arrangement, bizarre as it seemed, actually encouraged extreme behavior—and produced wrenching swings back and forth for the American economy. Congress knew that it could pump up the economy recklessly but would not have to answer for the destabilizing effects. The Federal Reserve would eventually come to the rescue and do the dirty work. On the other side, the Fed knew that when it did gain the opening to impose its discipline, it had an incentive to push the stringency as hard and as far as possible, expecting that, sooner or later, the democratic interests being damaged would rally in opposition and force it to retreat.

Congress could not control the brake—money and interest rates—but the Federal Reserve could not control the accelerator—the fiscal stimulus provided by federal spending and tax law. The elected government (and private players in the real economy) pushed toward giddy expansion. The central bank (supported by finance) stepped in and stopped it cold with a devastating contraction. Each power was able only to do its own thing, unchecked by the other, oblivious to the contradictions.

The contradictions grew larger and larger. Over the past two decades, it was evident that the swings back and forth induced by the government's own economic management were becoming more violent. Each cycle produced greater extremes, regardless of which party was in power or which economic doctrine happened to be regnant. The trend moved steadily to new highs and lows—greater fiscal stimulus on one side, harsher monetary discipline on the other. Each time the combat intensified, the damage was magnified for the real interests and real people caught in the middle.

It was not one side or the other that was responsible for this instability—but the unnatural relationship itself. Financial conservatives would blame the profligate spending habits of Congress, liberal voices would blame the willful cruelty of the Fed's high interest rates, but neither complaint addressed the full reality of the governing situation. The real malformation was the pretense that these two powerful levers of government could be rationally managed independently of each other, as though their effects did not constantly interact. The illogical arrangement guaranteed illogical behavior.

The emotional reality of this governing arrangement resembled the warped relationships present in a neurotic family. A psychologist might see the similarity even if an economist or political scientist did not. Like a family trapped in neurotic relationships, the various power elements of the government persisted in repeating obsessive patterns of behavior, playing out the same conflicts over and over again, engaging the same anger and disorder. Their behavior could be mutually destructive and often self-defeating, but they could not help themselves. Each family member clung to his assigned role, unable to alter his responses. Like a troubled family, the power centers of government could not recognize the pathological qualities in their relationships or imagine a way to extricate themselves.

The father figure in this chaotic family was, of course, the Federal Reserve. Personified by its chairman, the Fed presided uneasily over an unruly dinner table of errant children. The chairman's very manner implied paternal authority, yet the noisy children at the table willfully ignored him. The father would instruct and scold, implore and threaten. And still the children blithely misbehaved. Congress and the Executive (and the private economy they represented) played the irrepressible adolescents who went as far as they could, tempting the heavy hand.

Finally, they would push too far. When everything seemed out of control and patience was exhausted, the father punished—and punished with brutal force. The children had known it was coming, yet they could not help themselves. They always misbehaved and they always hoped that somehow they would avoid being punished. "The chairman is the daddy," a staff official of the FOMC had said in a

different context. The metaphor of father and children was embedded
in the mystique of the central bank.

In the recurring drama of excess and punishment, the children
might whine and object, even lash out angrily at the father's authority.
But they did not really challenge the punishment. They had expected
it. The children's role was to misbehave and the father's role was to
inflict pain and restore order.

As a clinician might observe, the pattern of behavior seemed
neurotic because nobody seemed to learn anything from these experiences. Instead, the government repeated the same extremes of
disorder and punishment, and, on both sides, the responses became
more exaggerated. The politicians' impulse for unbridled economic
stimulus escalated and was met by a still heavier hand from the father,
a monetary contraction that was deeper and more destructive than the
previous one. Though the father's punishment became progressively
more severe, it did nothing to improve the behavior of the children.
None of the government's economic managers—either at the Federal
Reserve or in the elected government—seemed to know how to get off
this treadmill.

The other neurotic element was more perverse: the father did not
impose his discipline equally on everyone in the family. The punishment instead was aimed selectively at certain weaker members of the
society. In troubled families, the phenomenon was known as scapegoating. One child in the family would be implicitly singled out by
the others, both parents and siblings, as the one who would absorb the
physical and psychological abuse, in behalf of the entire family. The
scapegoated child usually accepted his fate, persuaded that his suffering was somehow necessary for the family's happiness.

The economic liquidation induced by the Federal Reserve followed
the same warped pattern. Given the methods of monetary discipline
employed by the central bank, the economic losses naturally fell heav-
iest on the weakest and most vulnerable. The economic scapegoating
—the disproportionate suffering by labor and smaller enterprises and,
indeed, by the poorer nations of the world—was useful to the others.
It allowed the father—the Federal Reserve—to exercise his authority
without having to challenge genuinely powerful interests that might
successfully resist. The sacrificial ritual proved gratifying for the family as a whole, so long as one was not designated as the scapegoat.

Errant children, angry father—the metaphor itself suggested the
obvious way out of the government's malformed relationships, though
it was not a resolution that any important political interests, including
elected politicians, were likely to embrace. The children must grow
up. Normal adolescents were eventually allowed—or compelled—to

attain maturity, to accept responsibility for the consequences of their actions. The institutional behavior of representative democracy was, in effect, frozen in immaturity. As long as the stern father was present to indulge their excess, to clean up their mistakes and restore order, the elected government would continue to act like children.

The status quo would most likely endure. The cycles of extremes would probably continue and even become more extreme because the arrangement served the interests of the governing institutions. Each side of the government derived a certain freedom of action from the fractured nature of the government's economic management, an ability to pursue its own goals and evade the obligation for balance and coordination. As long as elected politicians could escape the political responsibility for cleaning up their own mess—for imposing unpopular restraints—then of course they would. As long as the central bank could exercise its power unilaterally, ignoring the collateral injustices, then the Fed had no incentive to moderate its behavior either. In a sense, neither side wished to grow up. Like a troubled family, neither could see the pathology of their behavior.

A reformed system that compelled the coordination of fiscal and monetary policies—and created direct political accountability for the results—was hardly a radical idea, except perhaps among the governing elites of America in the twentieth century. After all, most other industrial nations had such an arrangement—a governing structure in which the central bank was subservient to the elected government and the elected government ultimately had to answer for both interest rates and spending, for both growth and restraint. Political accountability and coordination could be swiftly established by simply designating the Federal Reserve as an agency of the Treasury Department, directly responsive to the wishes of the President (the idea that Paul Volcker once embraced in his college thesis). The process of economic decision making could be made more visible and more open to other voices—the moral claims of the innocent victims.[15]

The combat and instability would continue because its real source was the political contract struck between democracy and capital back in 1913, the implicit decision that democratic politics could not be trusted to act responsibly in the national interest. Therefore, the authority and the responsibilities of elected politicians were permanently curtailed. Put another way, the elected government was allowed to be permanently irresponsible—free to indulge its own follies and protected from the accountability by the higher authority, the nonelected central bank. The creation of the Federal Reserve represented a great retreat from democratic possibilities. The maturing of self-government was forever stunted.

—PART FOUR—

THE RESTORATION OF CAPITAL

─── 15 ───

A GAME OF CHICKEN

Jude Wanniski, the roving advocate for supply-side economics, was among the early winners in the great financial rally touched off by the Federal Reserve. Back in the spring, Wanniski had bought $100,000 in Treasury bonds, putting up $10,000 in cash and borrowing the rest. "I made the bet that Volcker had seen the light and the darkest days were over," Wanniski said. He was a bit premature, but not wrong. After the Federal Reserve turned abruptly to easy money in July and the financial markets rallied explosively in August, Wanniski won his bet. Rising bond prices would give him a $30,000 profit on his $10,000 investment.

"I told my wife we can go ahead and build a new addition on the house," he said. "And we will call it the Volcker Wing. I even put up a sign—the Volcker Wing."[1]

Wanniski's good fortune was a minor example of what was happening across the financial economy. Falling interest rates drove up prices in the stock market at a giddy pace—more than 250 points on the Dow Jones index in six weeks—accurately signaling an imminent recovery for the real economy. Falling interest rates also reinvigorated the bond market. The trading prices on outstanding bonds went up dramatically because they were now more valuable to hold. A twenty-year Treasury bond that collected 14 percent interest was automatically worth much more in the bond market now that newly issued bonds of the same maturity would be earning much lower rates. The optimism generated by new financial wealth was contagious.

"The rally was great for money managers," said Craig Lewis of Investment Counselors of Maryland, Inc., a fund managing $500 million in investors' assets. "We did pretty well. We made 23.1 percent in the equity area and 31 percent in bonds."

The Spangler Group, a small Boston firm managing $60 million, enjoyed a return of 43.7 percent in 1982 from the Fed rally. "Everyone was buying CDs; it was the easiest thing to do," said Mark Emerson. "You try to lock in rates. You try to lock in bonds. Get the money and run."

Other money managers made quick profits by buying the depressed stocks of corporations battered by the recession, confident that recovery was imminent and stocks could not go any lower. "Dire things happening in the economy present unusual opportunities," Dean LeBaron of Batterymarch Financial Management explained.[2]

By early fall, the judgment of Wall Street was that the Federal Reserve had permanently reversed course, even though Paul Volcker had still not admitted it. After two and a half years of constriction, the Fed was now "reflating" the money supply—pumping liquidity into the starved financial system in order to restart the economy and avert additional failures. Financial traders worried abstractly about the long-term implications for money's value, but they were euphoric about the immediate prospects—the recovery of profits.

"Fear vs. Greed—An Old Story Repeats Itself," the Merrill Lynch investment-strategy advisory reported. "The stock market is torn between the fear of reflation . . . and greed for the associated earnings recovery," Merrill Lynch said. ". . . Our scenario calls for the 'greed' to win out on a trend basis."[3]

The markets were right. The Federal Reserve, despite disclaimers and technical evasions, was embarked on the most aggressive, sustained expansion of money in its history, with the possible exception of World War II. Over the next nine months, M-1 would grow by an unprecedented $50 billion. From July to the following March, the pace of money expansion was equivalent to annual growth of 15 percent—more than double the Fed's official targets.

Back in 1928, when Benjamin Strong dominated America's central bank, Strong had explained that the Federal Reserve, if necessary, could always reverse a financial catastrophe simply by "flooding the street with money." Paul Volcker's sudden generosity in the fall of 1982 was the substantial equivalent. While Volcker did not quite "flood the street," his response was inspired by a similar sense of urgency.

By the first of October, the Federal Reserve chairman was finally compelled to concede what he had denied for so many months. The

Federal Reserve must at last abandon the monetarist operating system he had introduced three years earlier—or risk provoking a disaster. The Fed had effectively ignored its M-1 rule in order to ease back in July, but now it would have to go public and admit that it was disregarding the money numbers. Volcker saw no other choice.

Despite the financial rally, the incoming statistics on real economic activity continued to look dismal. While nervous bankers negotiated with Mexico over its debt crisis, other countries were lining up with identical claims of distress. The new monthly unemployment statistics, due out in a few days, would report that U.S. unemployment was still rising—above 10 percent for the first time since before World War II.

Albert Wojnilower, chief economist at First Boston, issued a stark warning: "It is no longer altogether certain that a moderate business upturn can provide enough lift to forestall a cascading of bankruptcies." The danger, he said, is that the Federal Reserve, after three months of easing interest rates, would now tighten again in order to contain the surging growth of M-1. "If we revert to the kind of monetary policy that prevailed prior to midyear," Wojnilower said, "there will be a depression sooner rather than later."[4]

Paul Volcker saw the portents too and delivered essentially the same message to his colleagues on the Federal Open Market Committee. When they met on October 5, the FOMC members immediately recognized the chairman's sense of alarm, because, instead of waiting until last to give his own views, Volcker spoke first. He opened the discussion with a long and gloomy recital of the economic outlook. He reviewed the international debt crisis, country by country, and described his own worries about the fragility of the U.S. financial system.

The surging money numbers dictated that the Fed tighten again— but the Fed didn't dare. The banking system, Volcker warned, would be seriously endangered if the economy did not recover soon. The only sensible course was to disregard the monetary aggregates and continue to push interest rates lower.

This was one crucial instance when Volcker and the Federal Reserve policy makers ignored the formal advice from the commercial bankers. The Federal Advisory Council, three weeks before, had recommended the opposite course. "We also continue to believe very strongly that if the money supply does in fact surge, the Federal Reserve must move promptly to resist," the FAC reported. "Failure to resist in these circumstances would risk losing all the gains in credibility that have been won so painfully over the past few years."[5]

Volcker still worried about the Fed's credibility though. If monetarism was discarded, would the financial markets accuse him of retreat on inflation? His solution was to obscure the meaning of the policy shift as much as possible. In public, the move would be justified by technical complications—an expected distortion in M-1 from the new Super-NOW accounts. The de-emphasis of M-1 would be described as only temporary.

The monetarists on the FOMC knew better. If M-1 was abandoned as the policy rule now, the Fed would be free of the self-imposed restraints it had obeyed since October 6, 1979. "I argued vociferously against downgrading M-1," Lawrence Roos of the St. Louis Fed complained. "We thought it was a cop-out simply because they had lost control of M-1. When you don't get something to work, you dump it in the wastebasket."

In the committee rotation, Roos did not have a vote at the October meeting, but three other Reserve Bank presidents, all monetarists, dissented—Black of Richmond, Horn of Cleveland and Ford of Atlanta. They lost, 9 to 3. The FOMC majority was, if anything, even more nervous than the chairman.

There was concern about the possibility of a general domino fall in Latin America and the consequences that would have on the international financial system [Governor Partee explained]. The economy wasn't too well. There wasn't much sign of resurgence. There didn't seem to be the relationship between money growth and the economic numbers you would have expected. If you are not a dyed-in-the-wool monetarist, it's pretty hard to proceed on an act of faith when these things are happening. You could lose quite a bit—pushing the economy down even further—by being a purist.

Normally, given the Fed's own rules of secrecy, the Federal Open Market Committee's decision would not have become public knowledge for six weeks. This time, somehow, the news flooded Wall Street overnight and the story was promptly leaked to *The Wall Street Journal*. Financial markets loved it.

The Dow Jones was up 37 points the next day. Both short- and long-term interest rates fell. Bond prices jumped $25 for each $1,000 in face value, an extraordinary one-day increase. Major banks cut their prime rate to the lowest level in two years.[6]

Three days later, just to make sure no one missed the message, the Board of Governors reduced the Discount rate again. That meant the Fed intended short-term interest rates to fall further. In four days of furious trading, the stock market surged 115 points, reaching a new peak of 1021 on the Dow index. The financial rally would continue. Thanks to the powerful stimulus of sharply lower interest rates, the economic contraction was about to end.

President Reagan, whose own political stock had been badly tarnished by the long recession, promptly claimed vindication for his economic program. "It's what we've always said," the President declared. "The people are becoming more confident about the economy."[7]

The Federal Reserve chairman was considerably more coy. In a weekend speech before a group of major corporate executives, Volcker insisted that the policy change was merely a "little detour." When press reporters badgered him afterward, the Fed chairman complained that they were making too much of the news, trying to reduce a complex technical matter to a simple, dramatic headline. Finally, Volcker offered to write the headline for them:

FEDERAL RESERVE POLICY REMAINS CONSISTENT;
REWARD IS DECLINING INTEREST RATES

"How do you like that headline?" Volcker asked. The Federal Reserve chairman was as evasive in announcing good news as he had been about the bad.[8]

The Federal Reserve was once again "zooming the money supply," but this time Ronald Reagan did not complain. For many years, as a conservative political leader, Reagan had criticized the political cycles of monetary policy—"pulling the string" and causing recessions, then at election time "flooding the economy with money" and reviving price inflation. The President's monetarist principles were evidently put aside now that the same thing was happening during his own tenure.

The trouble is [David Stockman explained] the President's thinking stops in the past. He can trace the money-supply growth all the way back to the sixties, but his money-growth numbers stop in 1980. He still doesn't realize we did the same thing to the money supply that others did. It's the same with deficits. He doesn't acknowledge our deficits. He can't understand why people keep talking about his position on the deficits. He's been against deficits for forty years. Why should anyone question that?

Reagan's political advisers were not so opaque. Running up to the 1982 congressional elections, James Baker and his deputy, Richard Darman, leaned on Volcker repeatedly to keep cutting the Discount rate—which they hoped would also cut Republican losses in the November elections. When Volcker refused to make a final Discount reduction two weeks before election day, Baker was furious. The stock market fell sharply and overnight polling showed an abrupt drop in

Republican prospects. Republicans lost twenty-six seats in the House and some fingered the Fed chairman. "That's when the White House said, 'We've got to get rid of Volcker,' " Wanniski related. " 'This guy isn't going to play ball in '84 when the President is running.' " [9]

The President developed his own eclectic explanation for what had happened to the economy. The recession could have been avoided entirely, Reagan confided to his associates, if he had never consented to postponing the effective date of the supply-side tax cuts back in 1981. "Reagan still believes this recession wouldn't have happened if the tax cuts were not delayed and the economy wasn't pushed down on its knees," Stockman said. "His view is that we wouldn't have had to go through this at all—or have all these high deficits."

In other words, the President continued to believe in the original logic of his economic recovery program, namely, that the government could somehow tighten money to break inflation while it simultaneously stimulated economic growth with tax cuts. Five quarters of deep recession had persuaded most everyone else, including the President's own advisers, to abandon this fantastic logic.

On the other hand, Reagan also blamed the Federal Reserve for overdoing it. "If that string hadn't been pulled for so long and so hard, we might not have had the depth of recession that we've had," he told one audience. His statement was indisputable, but it conveniently overlooked the fact that the President himself—at two crucial junctures in the spring of 1981 and the winter of 1982—had personally pressured the Fed to tighten its control of money. When the Federal Reserve obliged, it inevitably made the recession worse. [10]

Monetarists in the Reagan Administration voiced the same revisionist criticism of Volcker's management. Treasury Under Secretary Beryl Sprinkel, echoed by Secretary Regan and others, complained after the fact that the Administration had wanted a "gradual" reduction of money growth spread over several years, but instead the Fed had done it swiftly and drastically, causing more economic damage than was necessary. Sprinkel's complaint seemed especially gratuitous. After all, he and the other monetarists had persistently heckled the central bank to be as tough as possible in slowing down money growth. "Gradual reduction," Sprinkel had said himself back in 1981, would be considered the minimum goal. [11]

The monetarists, both inside and outside the Reagan Administration, faced a more fundamental contradiction in their position: their grand theory of the economy was no longer working. [12] Their advice was no longer heeded by the political counselors who ultimately made the policy decisions in the Reagan White House. Political advisers like James Baker had learned from hard experience not to trust the monetarist forecasts or to follow policy recommendations that simply invited higher interest rates and more pain.

In his private memos following the 1982 election, Beryl Sprinkel persisted in sounding the same alarm.

A slowdown of money growth is crucial to a sustained, noninflationary expansion [Sprinkel warned the White House]. Without it, rising interest rates are the inevitable result, once inflationary expectations are aggravated; the positive gains on inflation will be lost and the price we paid for those gains, by enduring a long and severe recession, will be squandered. . . . The economic and political implications are sobering.

This time, however, the Federal Reserve chairman was not summoned to the Oval Office to be scolded by the President. On the contrary, the Fed actually accelerated money growth so that, in one four-week period, M-1 expanded at a startling annual rate of 27 percent. The President's men did not object. The Federal Reserve was abandoning its monetarist principles, but so was the Reagan White House.

The White House senior officials were wise to ignore the monetarists, because none of their dire warnings came true. The most visible public embarrassment was reserved for the father of modern monetarism—Milton Friedman. The acerbic little professor would announce two stark predictions for the economy in subsequent months and both would be spectacularly wrong. First, Friedman declared, a new run-up of price inflation, perhaps approaching double digits, was now inevitable in the next year or so, given the explosive money growth the Federal Reserve was allowing. (Instead, inflation would decline even further.) Next, when Friedman analyzed a slowdown that developed in M-1 growth late in 1983, he boldly predicted that a recession would unfold in the election year of 1984. (That didn't happen either.)

"Now I was wrong, absolutely wrong," Friedman said of his predicted recession. "And I have no good explanation as to why I was wrong."[13]

William Poole offered an explanation for the gross miscalculations by himself and Milton Friedman and the other monetarists. "I think it's fair to say," Poole suggested, "that those of us who have developed strong theories tried to fit the world into the theory rather than the other way around."

If the Federal Reserve was no longer adhering to the money numbers, it would now watch everything—the old eclectic approach that monetarists and markets had scorned. The new approach gave the chairman maximum discretion to be flexible. When asked, Volcker would explain that the Federal Reserve was taking many things into account and there was no single guide to monetary policy. The Fed was withdrawing once again into the mystique of central banking.

For practical purposes, however, the Fed's intentions were now much easier to read. Interest rates were, unambiguously, the thing to watch. More specifically, the financial markets swiftly recognized that the Discount rate—the traditional tool of monetary policy long dismissed as merely symbolic—was now the key indicator of the Fed's decisions. With rates falling, the Discount rate was the effective "floor price" for short-term borrowing, and, save for brief exceptions, the Fed would not allow the Federal Funds rate to trade below its Discount rate (otherwise banks would have no reason to borrow at the Discount window and the Fed would lose its leverage over credit conditions). So Fed watchers watched the Discount decisions with a new intensity.

"The approach used in late 1982 tended to focus market attention on the Discount rate," the Open Market Desk in New York acknowledged. "Sentiment waxed bullish or bearish on prospects for such cuts, usually with each cut generating expectations of further cuts."

Fed officials vigorously denied it, but many money traders assumed the central bank had simply returned to its old pre-1979 operating style—pegging interest rates, adding or withdrawing bank reserves in order to keep the Federal Funds rate at a specified level. William Poole, the monetary expert at the CEA, observed the new pattern. "Starting in about July 1982 the Federal Funds rate became smooth once again, both day to day and especially month to month," Poole noted in a White House memorandum.[14]

After the election, the Federal Reserve Board resumed its downward pressure on interest rates, cutting the Discount rate another half percent on November 19. Other interest rates, short-term and long-term, followed in descent.

On December 13, the board voted another reduction, cutting the Discount to 8.5 percent. It was the seventh reduction in five months —but it was also the last one. This time, the bond market objected. Long-term bond rates, instead of declining further in step with the Fed's easing of short-term rates, turned around and increased slightly. The bond market seemed to be telling the Fed: That's enough. Don't push interest rates any lower.

"If the markets think a Discount cut is inflationary," Henry Wallich explained, "then they will keep interest rates up. As we approached the last Discount cut, the markets were telling us that they didn't like too much ease."

"No question, we got ahead of the markets," said Preston Martin, the new vice chairman of the board.

The Federal Reserve Board got the message. It was a striking and significant example of how influential bond investors could be in determining the government's monetary policy. Interest rates were still abnormally high, but the Discount rate would be lowered no further. Despite continuing pleas from politicians, despite continuing strains on the real economy, the Federal Reserve Board would keep the Discount rate frozen for the next fifteen months.

By January, a dozen or more debtor nations were lining up at the same window, seeking the sort of relief that a business corporation sought when it filed for a Chapter 11 bankruptcy. In this instance, the bankruptcy referee was the International Monetary Fund, assisted directly by the authority of the Federal Reserve, and, one by one, the IMF negotiated "work out" plans for the failed debtors. The rescheduling schemes would prevent default and allow the countries to keep going, but, like any bankrupted borrower, the sovereign nations were compelled to accept the bankers' terms.

Mexico borrowed $3.7 billion from the IMF and another $5 billion from its creditors, the major multinational banks, and rolled over the principal due on its old debt. In exchange, the Mexican government accepted the IMF's terms for austerity: it must reduce its imports drastically as well as domestic government spending in order to build up the reserves to keep up the interest payments on its growing indebtedness.

Brazil borrowed $4.6 billion from the IMF and needed another $3 billion from the banks and accepted similar conditions. Argentina received $1.6 billion from the IMF and a like amount from the private banks. Venezuela, Chile, Peru and a long list of others submitted to similar arrangements. Each accepted international supervision of its domestic economy in order to avoid the trauma of failure and loss of access to international finance.

The process of debt rescheduling for the less-developed nations was not essentially different from the refinancing plans that commercial banks had worked out for such major corporate debtors as International Harvester when it approached failure the year before. Only the stakes were many times larger, especially for the banks. Just as Harvester was too big to fail, too deeply in debt, so were the leading borrowers of Latin America. If any of them was allowed to default, the instant write-off of billions in loan losses would bring down many of the largest banks in the country. In the same sense, however, the rescheduling of old debts did not solve the fundamental problems facing Latin-American debtors any more than it had solved International Harvester's. The debtors were simply given more time to work their way out—permitted to borrow more now at prevailing interest rates in the hope that future economic growth would eventually ameliorate their debt burdens.

Month by month, Paul Volcker was at the center of the crisis management, lending his imprimatur to the IMF terms, pressuring both the debtor nations and the private banks to complete the deals. He dispatched aides to foreign capitals to bargain privately over snarled agreements. He met with bank executives to keep the process on track. Week by week, virtually every country became in turn a momentary subject of crisis. But neither the Fed nor the IMF, the debtor nations nor the money-center banks, could allow the process to break down. If one "work out" failed, then all might swiftly become unraveled and the fragile economic recovery would be interrupted by a global financial crisis.

While Volcker and his counterpart at the IMF, Jacques de Larosiere, succeeded in preventing any ruptures, the sense of progress was in large part illusory. In general, the debt-ridden nations were borrowing billions simply to keep up with the interest payments coming due on their old loans. The due dates on the principal were pushed further and further into the future.

The implicit danger in this process was stated candidly by the Fed's resident authority on international finance, Governor Henry Wallich. Wallich warned: "Situations where a country might begin to rely on rescheduling for the indefinite future should be guarded against. Rescheduling then could become a Ponzi game in which the banks would be lending the borrower the interest so as not to have to treat the ever-mounting loan as nonperforming." [15] Wallich had delivered his warning to bankers back in 1981 before the debt crisis became a visible reality. He did not repeat the point once the reschedulings became commonplace, though, as a practical matter, many of the arrangements did resemble the circular illusions of a "Ponzi game."

The alternative was unthinkable, at least to Paul Volcker and the Federal Reserve. They could not let the debtors default and banks fail. On the other hand, they could not bring themselves to propose more fundamental solutions. In theory at least, the creditor nations of the world, including especially the United States, could have confronted the international debt crisis more forthrightly by acknowledging that the Third World nations were hopelessly overburdened and that general debt relief must be arranged. This would have required immediate losses all around—by the borrowing nations and by the commercial banks that did the original lending. The industrial nations, likewise, would then have to advance major funding to the IMF or the

World Bank so that one of the international lending agencies could underwrite a long-term restructuring of the bad debt—writing off the worthless loans at a loss and spreading out the rest of the debt burden over forty or fifty years.

Former Governor Philip Coldwell, now retired from the Fed and serving as a financial consultant to the Argentine government, was among those convinced that Volcker and the others were simply postponing the inevitable—an international bailout of vast proportions. "Brazil, Argentina and Mexico have just put off the day of the next crisis," Coldwell said. "They're not going to pay off this debt. There is no way the export-income surplus in those countries can increase enough to pay off that debt. Where do they get the money to pay—unless you cut the interest rates by 50 percent?"

A general write-off and long-term restructuring would impose immediate costs on everyone, but they also offered a major advantage for everyone—improved economic prospects for the debtor nations and their trading partners, particularly the United States. As long as the IMF imposed its austerity plans, the LDC debtors must curtail their imports, which, in effect, meant closing major markets for American agriculture and manufacturing.

Like it or not, Americans were interdependent with the world far more than they wished to acknowledge. Major sectors of the American economy could not return to their own full prosperity as long as Latin America was held to an austere financial regimen. In the Midwest, as they figured out the connection, farmers from Iowa complained that they were losing overseas sales for their grain so that banks in New York could collect their interest payments.

Volcker sternly discouraged any talk of debt forgiveness, however, or even concessions on interest rates. "We can't force terms on the banks without creating another crisis of confidence," he argued. The banking system was still recovering from the traumatic fissures of 1982, and the Federal Reserve chairman felt obligated, above all else, to protect the system.

In a sense, the Fed was trying to clean up its own mess. The global recession induced by the Federal Reserve had collapsed Latin economies in the first place, rendered their swollen debt burdens unsustainable and put the major banks at risk. It was perhaps the gravest price that the world—and the United States—would pay for Volcker's zealous assault on inflation. If the Fed chairman had managed the transition more gradually, if he had not steered so close to the edge, the damage to Third World debtors would have been much less severe. Both sovereign nations and their bankers would have had more time to adjust. By driving them to the wall, Volcker was indeed partly responsible for the global dilemma of bankrupt nations. He was obliged to attend.

The same bruised condition applied generally throughout the domestic economy. Debtors, whether they were farmers or home buyers or major corporations, were wounded so deeply by the long recession, it would take years for many of them to recover and many would not make it. The domestic loan failures did not, however, threaten the banking system with the same concentrated force as the foreign debt, and the Federal Reserve did not feel constrained to manage the "work out" for them.

Most Americans had forgotten, if they ever knew, that the United States faced a debt crisis of its own many times during the nineteenth century. Ambitious developers, including state and local governments, would borrow excessively from the banks of Europe to finance railroads or other expansion projects. When ventures failed, the loans were defaulted, sometimes on a massive scale. Vast fortunes in borrowed capital from Britain and the Continent were lost on the American frontier, written off as uncollectible. The recurring scandals and disgrace of default did not inhibit long-term growth for the young Republic or ruin its international credit rating. But, whenever default or forgiveness was suggested for the Third World debts, the idea seemed to outrage Americans, now that they were the creditors.

A larger solution was, in any case, politically impossible. Congress was now angry at the major banks for their gross overcommitments to foreign lending. Despite the deregulation rhetoric of recent years, senators and representatives were pushing the Fed to impose tougher controls on banks. In that hostile environment, neither Volcker nor anyone else could plausibly propose a vast bailout that would require commitments of tens of billions of dollars.

Indeed, as the IMF's lending increased, the Reagan Administration was compelled to ask Congress to authorize an additional U.S. contribution of $8.4 billion to the international fund and the measure was bitterly opposed by both liberals and conservatives. They argued, alternately, that the financial package was a blatant bailout for either the money-center banks or for profligate foreign governments or both. Only intense lobbying by the Administration and the Federal Reserve chairman finally persuaded Congress to approve.

In substance, the critics were correct. The new money from the IMF would be transferred by Telex to Buenos Aires, Rio de Janeiro or Mexico City. But then the money would be swiftly sent back to the creditor banks in New York and elsewhere. The apparent soundness of both debtors and creditors was maintained, but in the process the debtors were drawn still deeper in debt.

A genuine solution, Philip Coldwell predicted, would not be acceptable, either to bankers or politicians, until the consequences of the LDC debt reached a sufficiently frightening level of crisis—when the "Ponzi game" broke down and everyone was forced to acknowledge it. Like all illusions, this one might continue for quite a long time, perhaps many years, but it could also collapse abruptly at any time, shattered by random events.

"The way out of this thing is a shift in the way we treat the LDC debt," Coldwell argued. "The banks would have to take a big hit on their balance sheets, but then it's over. If you give them a definitive hit, then they could say it's behind us. If you get down to a crisis stage, the banks would accept that. They would have no choice."

In the meantime, however, Volcker and his international aides worked assiduously to protect the earnings of the banks, particularly the money-center banks, which were most exposed. In the negotiations over new loans, Volcker usually supported the bankers in their persistent refusal to make any concessions on interest rates. The Fed also took care to instruct its bank examiners to treat the huge portfolios of questionable LDC loans with special solicitude. If the rules were applied too strictly, major banks might be confronted with huge loan write-offs that would wipe out their capital.

The central bank, as regulator and protector, had worked itself into a compromising position. On the one hand, the Fed was trying to gradually extricate the largest banks from their overexposure and preaching sterner discipline for the future. On the other hand, the Fed was bending the banking standards and pressuring hundreds of other wary bankers to make new loans they regarded as dubious.

The survival of the most important money-center banks depended on keeping the rescheduling deals afloat, but dozens of smaller regional banks, with less exposure, wanted out. They were prepared to write off their losses and stop lending to Mexico and the others. Why throw good money after bad? When these bankers balked at committing more money to the new loan packages, they were pressured by the major banks. If that didn't work, they received a friendly call from the president of the local Federal Reserve Bank, urging them to reconsider.

In most cases, the persuasion succeeded, but it also implied an unstated guarantee by the government. The Federal Reserve was coaxing bankers into making new loans that the bankers considered imprudent. Did that commit the Fed to make sure that none of these banks suffered for doing what Volcker had urged upon them? Karin Lissakers, an international finance expert at the Carnegie Endowment, described the risk: "The problem is that by the time the crisis ends, the regulatory authorities may be so deeply compromised by the concessions that they have made to the banks that there is no return." [16]

Volcker, nevertheless, would make slow, steady progress on what he regarded as the primary objective—getting the major money-center banks out of their precarious position. Citibank, Manufacturers Hanover, Morgan and the rest continued rolling over old loans, but their LDC exposure gradually declined as a proportion of their overall portfolios. The major new lending to the troubled nations was now coming from the public agencies—the IMF and the World Bank—and that allowed the commercial banks to moderate their own new commitments. As public sources assumed more of the risk, the largest private banks were able to slowly edge back from the brink.

For the debtors, however, the strategy required a long, bleak future. The IMF's austere conditions not only depressed standards of living for Latin populations, but the nations were compelled to devote most of their export earnings to their debts, so that little or nothing could be invested in economic development for the future. Just as Iowa farmers could no longer sell their grain to Latin America, working citizens of Mexico and Argentina and other countries could no longer look forward to steady improvement in their economic well-being.

"For the first time in the life-span of a majority of the population," Jesus Silva Herzog, the Mexican finance minister, lamented, "we are going to have a deterioration in the standard of living for most of the people of the country." [17]

Governor Charles Partee expressed the same regret. "Now, you can't convince anybody to make a loan to the LDCs," Partee said, "and it's extremely difficult for these countries. There's almost nothing they can do to open access to new credit. So they are being ground down every day by the payments they have to make and they have no chance of getting the new loans that would help their growth."

In Rio de Janeiro, middle-class citizens looted supermarkets, carting off free groceries in a brief and futile rebellion. Brazilians had suffered a .12 percent decline in real per capita disposable income since the beginning of the global recession. In Buenos Aires, amid wildcat strikes and other political unrest, the president of Argentina's central bank was briefly arrested when he returned home from the annual IMF meeting in Washington. He was accused of betraying "national sovereignty" by yielding to the international bankers. [18]

Representative Jim Leach, an Iowa Republican, spoke for the American farmers who were losing export sales:

If there is any scandal at the Fed, it's that they let down on their regulatory function by letting the banks make all these loans in the first place. It's one of the great banking scandals of the century. Yet the Fed now has a monetary policy that holds the people who made the mistakes harmless. It protects the banks in New York at the expense of the Midwest. Someone is paying for the foreign-lending debacle, but it isn't the banks.[19]

These were empty expressions of protest, however. Neither the human distress of deepening poverty in the less-developed countries nor the complaints from American politicians would deflect Volcker and the other managers of international finance from their strategy: to help the banks get well. For the foreseeable future, a dozen nations or more would be held hostage to the past, paying singularly for the mistakes that they and their bankers had made together.

The renewed American prosperity unfolding in 1983 was an utterly different world from the economy that had existed four years earlier. The Federal Reserve had turned the tables on virtually every transaction in American enterprise. The government, in effect, had created new terms for every contract—imposing new conditions for labor's wage settlements and for farm loans, for a family's credit cards and home mortgage, for investments in oil and real estate and shipping, for bonds and stocks, bank CDs and money-market mutual funds. The Fed would continue to steer the economy month to month, but now everything was flowing in the direction it wanted.

The fundamental reversal was in the advantage between lenders and borrowers of every kind. The debtors, from families buying a home to businesses borrowing for new machinery, had benefited powerfully from rising prices—paying back their loans in cheapened dollars. Now it was the creditors' turn. Old debts, contracted when inflation was running high and expected to continue, would now be paid back in "hard" dollars—money that not only retained its value but actually increased in purchasing power as prices continued to fall.

The new terms were visible everywhere, though hardly noticed in general. James McGrady, an Exxon station owner from Baltimore, was paying off a 20 percent loan, contracted when inflation was still in double digits. But now inflation was below 4 percent and the difference would have to come out of the real returns from his business.[20] The implicit subsidy that inflation had provided business borrowers was now reversed.

Young couples who were new homeowners felt the same squeeze in their monthly mortgage payments. When they bought their house, a mortgage at 12 percent or even higher sounded scary, but it was actually a good investment if price inflation was running at 10 percent or above and the couple's wage income was steadily rising too. Inflation would inexorably shrink the burden of their monthly mortgage payments, both in real terms and as a share of their incomes. Meanwhile, the market value of their home would steadily appreciate, accumulating equity for them. But, now that inflation had fallen below 4 percent, their 12 percent mortgage was suddenly a terrible deal. They were paying a real interest rate of 8 percent or higher—unheard of in previous generations.

For decades, the process of homeownership combined with inflation had effectively redistributed wealth from creditors to debtors, across a broad spectrum of citizens. As a practical matter, this was the only way that millions of middle-class families ever managed to accumulate any real wealth over the course of their working lives. When inflation ended, the wealth redistribution was stopped. Now, instead of shrinking, the real cost of the couple's home steadily increased—and, across the nation, housing values stopped rising.

In gross social terms, the "money question" now benefited the "savers"—the 45 percent of American families that were net creditors in financial wealth—at the expense of everyone else. In general, this meant older citizens gained at the expense of the young. Established wealth and enterprise were favored over the smaller and untested ventures. The reversal particularly benefited the minority who owned the bulk of accumulated capital, the 10 percent of Americans who owned 86 percent of the net financial wealth.

For investors deciding where to put their capital, the tables were also turned in a fundamental way: financial assets now flourished and real assets lost their value. Because the dollar was now stabilized and hardening in value, any investment in financial paper, denominated in dollars, was now becoming much more secure and profitable. For the same reasons, investments in tangible assets like land, farm commodities, suburban houses, factories and machines, or oil were now the losers. A harder dollar would buy larger and larger quantities of real things. This basic equation would drive investment choices through the decade: put your money in bonds or other financial instruments, not in new factories, if you want to reap the largest returns.

A study by Salomon Brothers, entitled "What a Difference a Decade Makes," charted the reversed fortunes between real assets and financial assets. In the 1980s, bonds became the most profitable place to store wealth, averaging a return of 20.9 percent. Stocks were the second best, averaging 16.5 percent. Both had suffered negative returns during the inflationary 1970s.

Meanwhile, the tangible things of the economy, from housing to commodities to real manufactured goods, became the losing investments. Their prices were flat or falling because of oversupply; their value was no longer enhanced by general inflation. After discounting inflation, investors in farmland suffered a negative real return of 6.2 percent in the 1980s. Oil investments lost an average of 15.4 percent —virtually wiping out all that oil had gained in the preceding decade.

This new dimension, though largely unrecognized, was launching a perverse new dynamic in the American economy—a kind of rolling liquidation that continued long after the general recession had ended. It was aimed selectively at real goods—suppressing prices and wages. Farmers, oil producers, organized labor—these and other sectors confronted continuing surpluses of whatever they had to sell. The oversupply would continue to depress their products long after the economic expansion was under way and booming—and force continuing failure for the producers of real assets.

The negative returns for real goods severely complicated the debt problems for their producers. As the price of their commodities fell, the value of the collateral on which they had borrowed—whether it was farmland or oil reserves—was automatically downgraded too. Yet they must keep borrowing to stay in business and keep repaying their loans in "harder" dollars. Their real debt burden was increasing while their capacity to borrow was shrinking.

That reversed circumstance was the core equation for what became popularly known as the "farm crisis"—an inexorable squeeze between prices and credit that would drive tens of thousands of American farmers to the wall. These failing farmers were widely described as "inefficient," but nothing had changed about their efficiency except the price they received for their output and the price they paid for their loans.

When producers were caught in such a squeeze, the natural response was to dump more real assets on the marketplace—land or wheat or oil or even idle machines and factories—in an effort to keep up with the shortfall on debts. The desperate selling of more goods, of course, only added to the glut and depressed prices further.

Once this rolling liquidation was under way on a broad front and feeding on itself, the various markets for real assets would keep it going, more or less on their own. As long as unemployment remained high, labor unions would be compelled to accept massive cutbacks in their wage agreements. As long as world agricultural markets were glutted, farmers produced more and sold it for less. Homeowners, having enjoyed robust appreciation in their homes' market value for many years, now noticed that neighborhood real-estate prices were no longer rising, but, in most cities, declining.

The era of inflation was over. To insure that it did not return, the Federal Reserve had only to manage the economy in such a way that the surpluses in goods and labor and productive capacity continued. So long as the surpluses glutted markets, the rolling liquidation of real assets would continue and their prices would be held in check.

Most Americans seemed grateful for the new conditions. Certainly, they did not identify themselves as losers because they were home-owners or workers or borrowers. The reversed fortunes between the economy of finance and the economy of real goods was hardly notice-able to average citizens. What they saw was that the frenzy of price inflation was gone. People were going back to work. A sense of good feeling was spreading through the marketplace.

"The long nightmare of runaway inflation," the President declared, "is now behind us."

Ronald Reagan's ebullient optimism seemed to be confirmed daily in the economic news. The recovery began slowly, amid many fore-casts that it would be weak and unsustainable, but by March the new economic activity was gathering real momentum. The President was triumphant.

"Recession is giving way to a rainbow of recovery, reflecting a re-naissance in enterprise," he announced to a San Francisco business audience. "America is on the mend. . . . Katy, bar the door. We're on our way back."

Ronald Reagan was on the way back too. For more than a year, the President's approval rating in public-opinion polls had fallen steadily as the rate of unemployment increased. By January of 1983, one month after the peak unemployment of 10.8 percent, Reagan's popular sup-port hit a new low point in the Gallup poll—35 percent. In trial heats with potential Democratic challengers for 1984, Reagan lost to both Walter Mondale, the former Vice President, and Senator John Glenn of Ohio. The political talk of Washington was about the likelihood of yet another one-term President.

The economic news turned politics around. In February, when un-employment began to subside, the President's popularity rating sud-denly shot up 5 percent. His standing would continue to improve steadily thereafter. Reagan's political fortunes recovered in an almost perfect inverse ratio to the falling unemployment rate and his re-election prospects brightened accordingly. A second term for Ronald Reagan would depend almost entirely on whether the robust economic recovery continued.

"Something exciting is happening," the President told an audience of Oregon lumber executives. "You can feel it in Klamath Falls and, I think, in towns all across America. . . . I just left a lumber mill that has reopened and I can tell you the whir of the machinery there was music to my ears." [21]

.   .   .

The popularity of the Federal Reserve chairman was not measured by the Gallup poll, but it was clear that Paul Volcker's stature was also vastly enhanced by the economic news, especially among elite opinion makers. After all, Volcker had done what he had promised. Inflation was now subdued. *The New York Times* likened him to a matador, skillfully evading political attackers. His crisis management of the LDC debt problems was compared to St. George battling the dragon.[22]

A Gallup survey of major corporate executives found that they ranked Volcker much more highly than they did the President—51 percent expressed great confidence in the Fed chairman, compared to only 27 percent for Ronald Reagan. Volcker was unloved among small-business men, however. Only 20 percent of them trusted him to do the right thing.[23]

The Wall Street Journal expressed a widely held assessment of the Fed chairman—if it were not for Volcker's leadership, things might have turned out much worse. "Among all top U.S. officials and policy-making agencies, Mr. Volcker and the Federal Reserve Board have shouldered the greatest burden in dealing with international financial turmoil," the *Journal* said. "They have undertaken this role largely by default, given the inexperience of Administration officials. . . . "[24]

One important group did not share this enthusiasm for Paul Volcker —the President's own senior advisers. Treasury Secretary Donald Regan's antagonism was well known. Regan had frequently criticized Volcker's management in public and ordered up an intimidating Treasury study on the Fed's independence. He assured associates that Volcker would not be reappointed when his term as chairman expired in August. What was less well known outside the White House was that presidential counselor Edwin Meese and James Baker, the chief of staff, felt much the same way. Baker resented Volcker's stubbornness in drawing out the recession so severely. He was rankled when Volcker refused to oblige with another Discount cut just before the 1982 election. But, fundamentally, Baker shared Regan's questions about the Federal Reserve's independent political status.

There's an awful lot of power there held by unelected people [an Administration official explained]. That's an awful lot of power with darn little accountability. I'm not sure it's good for a President to be held responsible for monetary policy when he has no control over it. There's a powerful counterargument which is that you don't want politicians messing around with monetary policy for their own benefit, but maybe there's a middle ground somewhere. If the President controlled monetary policy, at least you would have someone accountable for it. After all, the President does have to answer to the public.

Jude Wanniski, who talked regularly with Administration insiders, dined one evening with Volcker and informed the Fed chairman of his bleak prospects. "I told him he had very low chances of being reappointed," Wanniski said, "because he had incurred the wrath of Baker and the White House politicos and they were nervous about '84 and the President's re-election. They had the idea Volcker would not be a team player. They wanted their own man at the Fed—someone who would be inhibited from tightening at the wrong moment." [25]

In Congress, however, Volcker enjoyed a new sense of admiration, even deference. Some critics persisted, but generally members of Congress were respectful, including Republican leaders like Senator Howard Baker who had been so critical during the recession. Paul Volcker had done a nasty, difficult job. He was managing the fragile global financial situation. Meanwhile, the Administration seemed in disarray on its own fiscal problems. The earlier agitation for reforming the Fed simply evaporated.

Volcker was confident enough of his own status to loosen up a bit in public, even joking about his reputation as the hardhearted central banker. "Central bankers are brought up pulling the legs off ants," he quipped at one Washington party.

The President and the Federal Reserve chairman shared in the warming glow of public opinion. Ronald Reagan took personal credit for halting inflation and, though the task was actually done by the Federal Reserve, his claim had some merit. The President, on the whole, had supported Volcker's stringent money policy through most of the recession, even if he disowned any blame for the resulting pain.

Volcker, for his part, thought that the Fed's job was probably made easier by Ronald Reagan's unshakable optimism. Through the dark months, the President had kept telling the people to keep the faith, that there were better times ahead. Sure enough, he was right. The priest and the prince, presiding jointly as public figures, had accomplished their sacred task, the restoration of money. Their miraculous powers were celebrated by a grateful populace.

Yet Ronald Reagan and Paul Volcker were also in a fundamental collision of purposes. Now that the recovery was under way, the President and the Federal Reserve chairman wanted different things from the American economy. Their separate economic policies would pull in contradictory directions. This deeper struggle was hardly visible to the general public and never fully acknowledged by the principals, but it would be the core drama of governance for ensuing years—an epic contest of wills between those who determined fiscal policy and those who controlled monetary policy.

"A game of chicken," as Neil Wallace, an economist at the Minneapolis Fed, aptly called it, played between the two sides of the government. Who would blink first? Who would back off? The President and Congress, who had enacted the highly stimulative $200 billion deficits? Or Paul Volcker, who had vowed to prevent the economy from accelerating into another inflationary run-up? Volcker pleaded with the White House and Congress to retreat, to make major reductions in their deficits. The Reagan Administration complained, meanwhile, that monetary policy must not get in the way of the robust economy. The two formulations were in fundamental conflict, as economist Thomas J. Sargent of the University of Minnesota explained:

> The Federal Reserve [has] resolved to stick to a policy that is feasible only if the budget is approximately balanced, while Congress and the Executive Branch together have determined prospects for taxes and spending that are feasible only if the central bank eventually becomes passive and accommodative. With such mutually infeasible prospects, all that is certain is that one side or the other must eventually give in. Outside parties are thrust into the uncertain position of betting on which side in the game of chicken will eventually capitulate and on how and when.[26]

For innocent bystanders, this contest was much more serious than a political spectacle of divided government. Many citizens and businesses would be punished directly because of the fiscal-monetary collision while others would profit from it—for the visible edge of the conflict was interest rates. The Federal Reserve, blaming market pressures created by the federal deficits, would keep interest rates at extraordinary levels, adding to the burdens of the debtors, foreclosing claims of future economic growth. Whenever there were complaints, the Fed pointed at Congress and the President. Interest rates, it insisted, could not be lowered until the deficits were reduced. The central bank would not moderate its economic policy until the President and Congress yielded first on theirs.

Despite what Fed officials suggested and many politicians assumed to be true, the persistence of high interest rates did not flow ineluctably from the size of the federal deficits. The price of money was naturally influenced by the demand for credit and, obviously, burgeoning federal deficits increased that demand. But, ultimately, the Fed could bring down the price, if it wished, by increasing the supply. In order to safeguard its control over prices, it chose not to do so. Whether its reasons were sound or flawed, wise or wrongheaded, should have been the question for debate because the high interest rates were not, as so many assumed, dictated by impersonal market forces.

The clearest proof of this was visible in what actually happened to interest rates during Paul Volcker's regime—the price of money moved up or down quite independently of what was happening to the federal deficits. Interest rates rose drastically when the deficits were still modest. Later on, interest rates would fall dramatically, even though the deficits were still expanding, reaching record dimensions. If interest rates were simply driven by the market pressures of deficit spending, this could not have occurred. Logically, it had to be something else—or someone else. The "someone else" was Paul Volcker and the policy makers of the Fed.

The contradictory ingredients had been present in the government's macroeconomic policies since 1981, but the situation was now wholly different. The economy was growing again, driven by the tax cuts and huge federal deficits. If the Federal Reserve simply accommodated this powerful fiscal stimulus, it feared it would be acquiescing to a resurgence of the old malady, price inflation. Yet, if the Fed restrained too zealously, it would ruin the good times.

The news media focused intensely, almost exclusively, on only one side of this conflict—the continuing political back and forth over spending and taxes and budget deficits. The press covered the congressional budget debates and the President's reactions in exhaustive daily detail, but in fact the endless arguments between Congress and the White House did not substantially alter the government's fiscal policy. Congress would enact a series of secondary tax increases and additional spending cuts during 1983 and 1984, but the general thrust of fiscal policy remained the same—headed toward annual deficits of $200 billion or more.

The press did not pay much attention to the real game—the Federal Reserve's continuing dominance over management of the American economy. By now, probably, many citizens grasped that Volcker and the Fed had had something to do with the recent recession (*People* magazine had said so). But very few appreciated that the Fed remained in control, now that recession was past and the nation was in recovery. This new chapter was a more subtle exercise of the Fed's power, but also more provocative. Usually, the central bank retreated to a passive role when economic expansions got under way, accommodating the revival of prosperity. This time, the Fed would hang on to its hegemony. It would continue to set the terms for the rest of the government—serving on, unseen, as "economic czar" for the nation.

With the managers of fiscal policy in a stalemate of their own making, the managers of monetary policy held the government's only active lever over the economy. Operating with far less public scrutiny, the Fed would manipulate the rise and fall of the economy on its own. The fate of the Reagan recovery would depend not on the President's decisions or the noisy budget debates but on how Paul Volcker and his colleagues decided to counter the stimulative impact of fiscal policy.

Judging from the past, the Federal Reserve could be expected to lose this contest. That, at least, had usually been the outcome in previous decades. Whenever the federal government grossly accelerated its deficit spending, whether in peacetime or in war, a dramatic run-up of price inflation eventually followed. Economists argued over why this was so, but the linkage was well established in experience. Apparently, the financial markets expected the Fed to lose the struggle. Their skepticism was expressed in the continuing high level of interest rates—investors demanding a higher return now because they expected their dollar assets to be watered down by inflation later. The Fed tacitly legitimized the markets' fears in December when it stopped lowering the Discount rate, accepting the investors' judgment that interest rates must remain at a precautionary level.

While theoretically they were separate functions, monetary policy directly felt the pressures from fiscal policy, in part, because the central bank had a historic obligation to assist the executive branch when it borrowed money. When the Treasury sold bonds, borrowing billions to finance the federal deficits, the government's new debt issue could never be allowed to fail. The financial markets must be able to absorb the new debt paper. Otherwise, the United States government would be profoundly embarrassed before the world and its unassailable creditworthiness suddenly in question. The Fed's monetary officials were responsible for insuring "orderly markets" for government securities, and they regularly coordinated with Treasury debt managers when huge new offerings were made, so the bonds would be sold expeditiously and interest rates would not go berserk.

One way the Fed could insure successful financings by Treasury was simply to guarantee that there was plenty of money available in private hands. If the Fed pumped sufficient liquidity into the banking system, lenders would be able to buy up all the new U.S. debt paper and still be able to serve the competing claims of other borrowers—private business and consumers who also needed credit. As larger and larger federal deficits forced Treasury to borrow more and more, the pressure on the Fed to accommodate naturally grew stronger. If the Fed refused to provide sufficiently, the government's borrowing would squeeze the supply of available credit in the private economy, interest rates would be driven up sharply, some private borrowers would be priced out of the game and economic activity would suffer.

This relationship between money creation and government debt was the reason why, during World War II, the Federal Reserve had reluctantly accepted a totally passive role in supporting the government's enormous borrowings. The central bank had provided whatever money supply was needed to insure that the Treasury could sell its huge offerings of war debt, and interest rates were never allowed to rise above 2 percent. The famous Treasury-Fed Accord of 1951 freed the central bank from its subordinate status, but the Fed still had a fundamental obligation to make sure the federal government could market its debt.

In the extreme, if the Fed was inclined to be too accommodative in this process, the result was what Ronald Reagan and other critics liked to call "printing press money." To economists, the effect was called "monetizing" the debt—a circular game in which the central bank bailed out the Treasury by inflating the currency. The circle went like this: The executive branch borrowed money from the private sector by selling new Treasury notes and bonds. The Fed then diluted the value of this debt by buying up old Treasury notes and bonds from the private sector and paying for them with newly created money. The Federal Reserve, in effect, wound up holding more and more of the government's debt paper in its own cloistered portfolio—and the private economy wound up with a bloated money supply.

Except in wartime, no American government would overtly pursue such a policy and certainly no one at the central bank ever willingly accepted it. Yet, over time, deficit-driven inflations had occurred in approximately that way. This was not because the Fed consciously decided to "monetize" the debt but because the process was much more gradual and ambiguous than the critics of "printing press money" presumed. How much accommodation was too much? There was no easy measure indicating when the effects of "monetizing" began.

The Federal Reserve was expected to support the orderly sale of new Treasury debt issues. It was also not supposed to thwart economic growth. Both obligations encouraged an inclination toward maintaining relaxed credit conditions and stable interest rates. Yielding a step at a time, misjudging the economy or retreating before political pressure, the central bank's inflationary errors of the past had usually been a gradual accumulation of small, unacknowledged surrenders.

This time, however, the Federal Reserve was determined to stand its ground. Paul Volcker had said as much, albeit less bluntly, in his frequent appearances on Capitol Hill, when he repeatedly warned Congress to take corrective action on the deficits. The Fed, he said, was resolved not to yield to the accumulating pressures of the growing debt—Congress and the President should not count on inflation to bail them out of their fiscal deficits. The Federal Reserve did not intend to "chicken out."

Instead, Volcker and the Federal Reserve chose an unprecedented alternative strategy—keeping interest rates at a very high level in the midst of economic recovery. In order to hold its ground, the Fed would "lean against the wind" as it had never done before. Nominal rates had declined, but were still far above normal, as the recovery began. Meanwhile, the real cost of money—because of reduced inflation— was going up at a time when it should have been going down.

The Fed's strategy would satisfy its obligation to assist the executive branch in marketing its burgeoning debt paper. If interest rates were high enough, the Treasury would have no difficulty selling its new bonds. The higher returns available in U.S. financial markets would attract capital from around the world for all sorts of financial invest- ments. The federal government's expanding debt, required by the Reagan Administration's huge deficits, would, in effect, be borrowed from foreigners. The Fed would fulfill its obligation, but real interest rates, instead of subsiding to normal levels, would remain stuck at modern peaks.

As Vice Chairman Preston Martin explained:

> We have to have rates high enough to bring in the capital. All of us have to consider the government financing very seriously. You can overempha- size the importance of the rates in bringing in capital because it's also attracted by the opportunities and the U.S. as a safe haven. But keeping the rates high enough to attract foreign investors is the argument that's made and it's an awareness we all had.

Governor Partee agreed: "We let conditions exist that made the U.S. interest rates look favorable compared to foreign investments. We stayed above the foreign interest rates so the foreign investors would be attracted to the U.S."

When Preston Martin was anxious to get lower interest rates, he first had to satisfy himself that the Treasury would still be able to market its debt. "I made frequent contact with participants in the financial markets on this question," the vice chairman said. "How are the Japanese reacting to these new thirty-year securities? Not the French or the British. What mattered was the Japanese. Are the Jap- anese buying? Fine, if they are, we don't have to raise rates."

. . .

Real interest rates, guided by the Federal Reserve's money-supply policy, became the steering mechanism for its control over the nation's economic expansion. Given the bizarre conflict between monetary and fiscal policy, the extraordinary real rates would attract ample capital to finance the debt. At the same time, the high real rates would enable the Fed to hold back the real economy—forcing it to accept a slower pace of expansion.

None of this was announced as government policy, much less explained fully to average citizens, and the ensuing years were marked by a deep confusion over how the Fed was actually managing money. The public (and many political leaders) kept celebrating the lower nominal interest rates, grateful to the Fed because nominal rates were declining steadily from their recessionary peaks in 1981 and 1982. Yet the actual consequences for the economy were the opposite. Real interest rates, the true measure of money's cost, were not falling at all. Real rates would be kept at historic highs—and even pushed higher.

The arithmetic was not complicated. Price inflation, after all, had fallen drastically since 1981, by about two-thirds. Nominal interest rates had also declined since mid-1982—but only by about one-third. The difference meant that the real return for lenders was increasing dramatically. In other times, the nominal interest rates would have been allowed to fall much lower, but not in 1983. As the Fed regulated the overall supply of credit, it kept the nominal interest rates from subsiding in proportion to the decline in prices. This was the second core reason why finance was now flourishing. Dollars were "hardening" and worth more—but finance was also collecting more dollars on every transaction.

The bondholders, the owners of capital, now actually enjoyed the best real return on their wealth in at least fifty years and probably since the beginning of the twentieth century. Real interest rates went higher in 1983 than the extraordinary levels they had reached in 1981–1982 when the Fed was actively trying to depress the economy. Traditional expectations about the reasonable return on capital were shattered.

The real rate of interest on twenty-year Treasury bonds, for instance, had averaged only .6 percent back in the inflationary months of 1979. It rose sharply to an average of 5.4 percent during the five quarters of the recession. Early in 1983, the real rate on this long-term U.S. debt rose to 6.6 percent and, later in the year, it would go still higher—to 8.4 percent. By comparison, the traditional rule of thumb in financial markets assumed that government long bonds historically yielded a real return of no more than 2 percent, usually less.[27]

The higher real returns, of course, affected every form of financial instrument, not just government securities. For long-term, high-grade corporate bonds, for instance, the real interest rate averaged 8.2 percent in 1983–1984. According to Henry Kaufman of Salomon Brothers, these corporate bonds had averaged a real return of about 1 percent for all of the previous postwar years. Short-term credit was, likewise, more expensive in real terms. The banks' prime lending rate, traditionally pegged at 3 or 4 percent above the rate of inflation, was now kept at a much more profitable spread—more than 7 percent above inflation.[28]

On one level, Volcker's strategy worked. Plenty of lenders, worldwide, were eager to put their money in the United States and collect the record yields. The Treasury issued larger and larger volumes of new debt paper and found plenty of willing lenders. But pegging the real cost of credit at such extraordinary levels also posed a fundamental risk. Could the economy stand it? Could the fledgling recovery take hold and flourish when businesses and consumers were compelled to borrow at such unfavorable terms?

Even some officials inside the Federal Reserve had their doubts.

On March 7, 1983, the Federal Reserve Board was again asked to cut the Discount rate, but this time the request did not come from politicians at the White House. It came from within the Federal Reserve System itself. Like an anxious chorus, the boards of directors at five Federal Reserve Banks—Minneapolis, Chicago, Kansas City, San Francisco and Boston—petitioned the Board of Governors to authorize another reduction in the Discount rate. The governors declined to do so. The Discount rate remained stuck at 8.5 percent. Short-term interest rates were not allowed to decline further.

Two weeks later, the Boston Fed was back again with the same request. The Board of Governors turned it down. In early April, Boston tried again and was again rejected. Three more times, the directors at the Boston Fed petitioned the board in Washington to reduce interest rates further and, each time, they were turned down.

When Boston finally gave up, the Chicago Fed picked up the cause and continued the plea for lower rates. Seven times the Chicago bank asked Washington to lower the Discount rate and seven times Chicago was turned down. The San Francisco Fed and the Philadelphia Fed chimed in too. Even the New York Fed, always closer to the home office than the other regional banks, petitioned for lower rates and was rebuffed. In all, during 1983, different Federal Reserve Banks forwarded twenty-one requests to Washington asking for an additional reduction of the basic borrowing rate. The Board of Governors rejected all of them. The Discount rate remained right where it had been since December 1982.

The frustrated directors of the regional banks eventually yielded to the seven governors in Washington because they had no choice. Among other things, the episode demonstrated the real power relationships within the Federal Reserve System. The twelve Reserve Banks could propose, but the Board of Governors could ignore. The running argument between the central office and the regions, virtually unreported in the press at the time, was especially notable because, for once at least, the conservative officials from the Federal Reserve Banks were advocating a more liberal monetary policy than the Board of Governors was willing to adopt.

Region by region, the Reserve Bank directors were worried that the high level of interest rates was going to smother the economic recovery. Rates ought to be lower at this stage—anyone could look at the rising real cost of credit and see that. Holding the line was Paul Volcker. He knew rates were abnormally high. That was what he intended.

"The economy was still at a very depressed level, even though the recovery had begun," Frank Morris, president of the Boston Fed, explained. "We needed a climate conducive to a high level of capital formation, and to do that, we needed to get the cost of capital down. We were afraid the effect of the very high cost of capital would be to wash out the gains of the Keynesian stimulus from the tax cuts."

New England was primarily a high-tech producer of capital goods—computers, electronics, process-control instruments, machine tools. Morris and the businessmen on his board of directors feared these sectors would be stymied by the high rates, unable to raise capital for their own expansion or to find buyers who could afford to invest in new equipment at these rates.

"When the evidence started coming in in the spring that, in fact, the economy was pulling out of the recession at a very fast clip, we ended our recommendations for rate decreases," Morris said. "When we stopped, the Midwest banks picked it up because their part of the economy still looked pretty grim. Our computer industry looked good, but in their heavy industry nothing was going on."

The Federal Reserve Board, by rejecting all the pleas for lower interest rates, was effectively defining its new strategy—a defensive posture designed to counter the economic stimulus generated by the fiscal deficits from Congress and the President. High real rates would attract investors for the Treasury's debt financing, but a second purpose would simultaneously be served—high interest rates would hold back the real economy.

That was the logic the Federal Reserve intended to pursue for this recovery: it intended to restrain growth and keep the American economy from reaching its full capacity and full employment. Given the economic stimulus already in place from the tax cuts and the Fed's own easier money policy, Volcker and other governors assumed the recovery would be vigorous. But this expansion, unlike earlier cycles in the past, must be braked somewhere short of its full potential.

Preventing full employment was the most direct way to prevent a return of inflation. Typically, it was when the economy approached its productive capacity, when goods and labor became scarce, that the natural competition bid up prices and wages. Employers understood the dynamics of a tight labor market; so did labor unions. The surest way to avoid that point—the risk of inflation driven by an "over-heated" economy—was simply to keep the economy from ever reaching full speed.

Like Volcker's earlier initiative against inflation, when the Fed forced the economy into recession, the implications were never explained to the general public, particularly the Fed's desire to prevent full employment. Stephen H. Axilrod, the staff director of the Fed's monetary policy, explained the choice in straightforward terms:

If you have a lot of demand, you've got to keep interest rates high to keep the demand from overheating the economy. When you're trying to wring out inflation, you have to keep the economy below its potential. The nasty way of putting that is you have to keep unemployment high. If you start from a low enough level, you can still have an economy growing rapidly at high rates of real interest. But you won't have an economy of full employment. You can only risk getting interest rates down to historically acceptable levels when you are convinced the risk of inflation is gone. That's a judgmental point.[29]

For obvious reasons, the Federal Reserve would never state this trade-off explicitly, for it meant that the federal government was actively pursuing an economic policy designed to keep people out of work and to thwart that hallowed goal of American politics—full employment. It also contradicted what the President was telling the public about boundless prosperity.

Occasionally, the minutes of the Federal Open Market Committee meetings hinted obliquely at these intentions. Various anonymous members of the FOMC worried about the possible resumption of "excessive wage settlements." Others expressed satisfaction that "workers' wage demands have been reduced significantly by back-to-back recessions in the past few years and concomitant high unemployment." Rising wages were usually the largest cost component driving price inflation. If wages could be held down by surplus labor, then inflation could be held at bay indefinitely.

But when would the Fed relent and give free rein to the economy? At what point would the central bank decide that the risk of inflation was gone and interest rates could be allowed to fall to normal levels? In large measure, the Federal Reserve would leave that judgment to the financial markets. In his management of economic growth, Volcker accepted the financial markets' expectations of future inflation as the guiding bench mark. If long-term interest rates stayed high in capital markets, that meant investors were still fearful that inflation was going to return. The Fed could have challenged the investors by easing credit conditions and pulling down short-term rates, but it did not. Volcker was convinced the central bank would lose its own restored stature if it went against the markets and permitted too much economic growth.

From time to time, Volcker did attempt to "jawbone" Wall Street sentiments by expressing his own optimism. "If the inflation outlook is as good as I think it is, long-term interest rates are far too high," a "senior Federal Reserve Board official" told *The Wall Street Journal* in April. The "senior official" was identified in the press a day later as Volcker. His veiled efforts did not succeed. Long-term rates remained stubbornly high and the Fed acceded to the anxieties of the bondholders.[30]

In the interest of preserving stable money, the Federal Reserve intended to stand astride the American economy and discreetly frustrate the normal popular ambitions for prosperity—Ronald Reagan's goal and the public's too. Volcker was reasonably explicit about his intentions for the economy. Usually, after a deep recession, the economy bounced back with a booming expansion—like a coiled spring that has been pushed down. This time, Volcker said, his hope was to limit real GNP growth to 3.5 to 4.5 percent in 1983—far short of the 7 to 8 percent growth that would normally be expected in the first year of a recovery. This was not, of course, what the White House political managers had in mind.

A slower expansion, Volcker reasoned, would permit a more durable one—slower but longer-lasting. And Volcker decided to stake out his line of defense early rather than later, before things could get out of hand.

By May, the recovery was barely six months old, and unemployment, though declining steadily, was still above 10 percent. The Federal Reserve chairman decided, nonetheless, that it was not too soon to slow things down.

"It was time to get a little order in the barroom," Volcker said, "or at least to avoid any sense of disorder."

Like a good central banker, Volcker was looking ahead and trying to anticipate. What he saw was a very healthy boom emerging that might swiftly threaten the Fed's control. "You had this great big tax cut accelerating the economy," he said. "You had reviving industry and the money supply had been running pretty darned high. I had no doubt we ought to be tightening up."

Volcker and other Fed veterans from the 1970s were haunted by a perplexing question: When exactly did the Federal Reserve make its big mistakes in the past? At what point in the previous business cycles had the central bank been too accommodative and permitted price inflation to take off? The short answer was that no one knew for certain, but Volcker and others had a strong hunch. They believed that the Fed had lost control early in the previous cycles, when money was easy and everyone was pulling for a strong recovery.

"I think we tended to make mistakes in the past—not at the end of an expansion or the end of boom, not so much in a recession—but by too much stimulus during the early part of an expansion period when things tend to get out of control before you realize it," Volcker said. "I hope we don't make that mistake again."

Lyle Gramley and Charles Partee agreed. As senior staff officials, both men had been seared by the embarrassing episodes of the past—the late 1960s, 1972–1973 and 1977–1978—when the Fed had waited too long to restrain and price inflation had escalated. In each instance, the Federal Reserve was accused of ineptitude or political collusion. Each time, the policy makers were compelled to "slam on the brakes" and force a painful recession in order to stop the inflation.

"During the earlier phase of economic recoveries," Lyle Gramley advised a business audience, "growth in supplies of money and credit has often begun to accelerate because the Federal Reserve did not let credit markets tighten sufficiently while unemployment and excess capacity were still relatively high. That is the mistake we must be particularly careful to avoid. . . ."[31]

"There's a very natural tendency," Partee said, "to want to see good times better than what they are. Some sectors will be lagging behind the overall recovery and utilization will still be below capacity. Business profits may still be low and unemployment may still be higher than it was. So there is a tendency to keep interest rates from pinching as much as they might—then waking up and discovering that you've had too much money growth and you're back in inflation."

When the Federal Open Market Committee met on May 24, Lyle

Gramley stated the case for tightening now. Fiscal policy was very stimulative. The Fed had allowed enormous growth in the money supply already, and as the economic activity picked up, money velocity seemed to be resuming a more normal pattern—people were spending money faster and, thus, multiplying the real economic effect of the swollen money supply.

"We need to throttle back the aggregates," Gramley declared. "The economy doesn't need more stimulus. If we're not willing to throttle back now, when will we be?" The chairman made similar arguments. It was time to apply a little braking action.

But many others on the FOMC couldn't see it. The recovery was "still only a baby," Frank Morris of Boston said, and some regions of the country were still in virtual recession. Even Henry Wallich, usually the hawk, doubted the timing. Anthony Solomon of the New York Fed, usually Volcker's ally on monetary issues, led the charge against the chairman.

"I thought we ought to wait," Solomon said, "because of the LDC debt problems and the overvalued exchange rate. The damage the dollar was doing to the country was already obvious. I didn't feel the strengthening of the economy was so much that it required a tightening."

If the Fed raised interest rates now, even modestly, that would put new pressure on the struggling Latin-American nations that were trying to keep up with their debt payments to the banks. Solomon also worried about adding damage to the trade-sensitive sectors of the American economy by pushing the dollar higher in international exchange. As the higher U.S. interest rates attracted global capital to dollar-denominated financial assets, the increased global demand for dollars raised its exchange value against other currencies. And, as the dollar continued its rise in value, the price disadvantage deepened for American industries, from machine tools to agriculture, against foreign competitors. If the Fed pushed domestic interest rates a notch higher now, the damage to manufacturing and farming would be compounded.

"My inclinations were to vote with the Solomon contingent because I was concerned about LDC debt," Vice Chairman Preston Martin said. "This was one of the few occasions when I didn't vote my inclinations. My sympathy was with the Solomon faction, but I didn't want to see the chairman defeated. I didn't think we could afford that right at that point, with the LDC debt still so fragile. As the voting came around to me, I felt the chairman might well lose. I sort of bit my lip and voted with him."

Volcker was proposing only a modest tightening, but as the roll call unfolded, the chairman discovered he had misjudged the opposition in the committee. The FOMC was split right down the middle and Volcker did not have a majority. "An impasse," he called it.

"Even Volcker, who's very shrewd, sometimes miscalculates what's going on in the committee," Solomon said. "If he had realized that I really meant that this is how I was going to vote and that others would follow me, I don't think he would have pushed it to the same degree."

There was a moment of tension and embarrassment all around the boardroom table. It was obvious the vote was going to be 6 to 6 and the chairman's resolution was going to lose. Then Henry Wallich, though he agreed with Solomon, switched sides and voted with Volcker. That made the final vote 7 to 5.

Afterward, other members needled Wallich about his sudden change of thinking, but he defended his vote. "I think it would have been bad for the chairman and bad for the institution," Wallich explained. "It would have been just bad, period."

The FOMC's tightening in May, modest as it was, produced visible results in the money market. The Federal Funds rate crept upward by 100 basis points over the next eight weeks. Mortgage rates rose about 125 basis points and, in a matter of weeks, the housing industry felt the difference. Sales of new homes and housing construction stopped expanding. With a gentle nudge on interest rates, the Fed was trying to take the edge off the boom.

"The response in real activity was remarkably swift," Frank Morris told a conference of economists. "The new structure of the mortgage market gives the Federal Reserve a powerful tool for moderating the pace of the economic advance. We are likely to see more such 'mid-course corrections' in the future."[32]

In any case, Morris, Solomon and the other dissenters were quickly compelled to concede that Volcker had been right. As more data came in, it was clear the recovery was not moderate, as Volcker had hoped. It was roaring. The real economic growth in the spring quarter exceeded 9 percent. A classic post-recession boom was developing—despite the high level of interest rates or Volcker's modest effort to apply restraint.

Money policy worked with time lags that were hard to predict. For many months before, the Fed had been generously supplying new liquidity to the financial system, pumping in money at unprecedented rates in order to get the economy restarted. Now all that money was at work in the real economy and ample enough to permit a rapid expansion. Neither business borrowers nor families seemed deterred in the least by the high real cost of credit. The Fed's initial attempt to brake gently was barely noticed in the general flourishing of good times.

16

WINNERS AND LOSERS

The headline in the Washington *Times* on April 18 stirred considerable interest because the conservative newspaper was well connected at the Reagan White House. The President, the newspaper declared, has decided not to reappoint Paul Volcker as Federal Reserve chairman. White House aides promptly denied it, but the story was accurate. Treasury Secretary Donald Regan had persuaded the President to decide, first of all, that Volcker would not be given another four-year term as Fed chairman. Later, they could settle on the successor.[1]

"The President did decide not to reappoint Volcker," an Administration official explained, "but it didn't mean anything." As often happened in Washington, the newspaper leak was only the beginning of the argument, not the end. For the next two months, as the White House advisers cast about for a likely alternative, the powerful economic interests and other politicians all expressed their preferences. In the end, they chose Volcker.

Jim Baker was very reluctant to reappoint Volcker [David Stockman said]. Baker felt Volcker had prolonged the recession much longer than necessary. Volcker didn't communicate with him very well. Baker would say: "How can you keep this misery going for five quarters?" Don Regan was adamant about Volcker. He said in private meetings many times: "There's no way we're going to put that guy back in there. He won't take orders."

The problem, however, was agreeing on the successor. Edwin Meese favored Preston Martin, the Fed vice chairman and a like-minded California businessman. Donald Regan liked Walter Wriston of Citibank and also Paul W. McCracken, CEA chairman under Nixon. Alan Greenspan, an outside economics adviser to President Reagan and also a former CEA chairman, was recommended as a candidate whom Wall Street would accept. Beryl Sprinkel was mentioned as a possibility and even Milton Friedman.

The Federal Reserve chairman remained publicly aloof, but privately he expressed his desire for another term. "Volcker knew who his friends were and we talked about it," Stockman said. "He said to me. 'Now is not the time for discontinuity. I am now in the middle of the debt problems and these delicate negotiations. I've got all these deals going and they are based on trust and informal understandings.' " Stockman and Martin Feldstein, the new CEA chairman, lobbied strenuously in Volcker's behalf.

"I pecked at Baker like a hen," Stockman said. "I told him the Fed was doing a pretty credible job and Volcker's the only thing Ronald Reagan has going for him. He's got credibility. The markets trust him. We need to keep him."

Baker and the President's other advisers heard the same message from many quarters. Senator Jake Garn, chairman of Senate Banking, urged the White House to reappoint Volcker. "I wonder, if he is not reappointed, what kind of signals do you send to the marketplace?" Garn said.[2] Howard Baker, the Senate Republican leader, delivered his own endorsement. So did Senator Robert Dole, the Finance chairman.

The U.S. Chamber of Commerce was for reappointment as were the National Association of Manufacturers, the Business Council and *The Wall Street Journal*. The major interests overshadowed the dissenters. The National Association of Home Builders, remembering the devastation of Volcker's recession, urged the President to appoint a more moderate leader for the central bank—Preston Martin, a former developer himself, who would be more sympathetic to the pressures on housing and small business. The home builders organized a coalition of twenty-four small-business organizations in support of Martin's candidacy.

The heavy thunder, however, came from Wall Street—scores of daily calls and letters from bankers and brokers to their contacts in the Reagan Administration, all urging Volcker. The more the financial markets read in the newspapers that the White House men wanted to pick someone else, the more intense the lobbying became. James Baker received a personal plea from an old friend in Houston, Ben

Love of the Texas Commerce Bank, and lots of calls from Wall Street leaders. "Wall Street was bugging us all the time," an aide to Baker said. "They really waged a campaign, just tons of them calling."

Lest there was still any doubt about what Wall Street wanted, a survey of 702 financial-market executives was released by the A. G. Becker Paribas brokerage—77 percent of them wanted Volcker. If he was not to be reappointed, Alan Greenspan was their distant second choice, but only 37 percent expressed special confidence in him. Milton Friedman was third with 11 percent. Preston Martin was sixth with only 7 percent.[3]

The White House advisers resented all the heat from Wall Street and insisted that it counted for little. This President was a "Main Street" Republican, they claimed, who paid little heed to the powerful voices of finance. Nevertheless, the small-business men from "Main Street" who wanted someone else did not get their way. The bankers and brokers from Wall Street did.

"No one had a strong alternative," said David Stockman, who had helped encourage the Wall Street lobbying. "There was a rising crescendo that failure to appoint Volcker would upset the markets. In the end, that was decisive."

"Volcker won by default," an Administration official complained. "It was almost unanimous that it should be somebody other than Volcker, someone we can work with better and with the preferred ideology. But all the parties against Volcker were totally split. You couldn't get three votes for any one person."

The discussions boiled down to a choice between Volcker and Greenspan—then Greenspan withdrew and endorsed Volcker. The President's counselors were confronted with a choice that, for many months, they had promised themselves they would not make.

At that point, the Federal Reserve chairman himself forced the issue. On June 6, Volcker abruptly phoned the White House and arranged for a private meeting with the President. None of the White House senior advisers was included. Volcker and Reagan were alone together in the Oval Office.

"This has dragged on too long and you ought to settle it one way or the other," Volcker told the President. The rumors and speculations were adding to financial uncertainties. The President should make his choice and announce it.

The Fed chairman raised another tantalizing point: if reappointed, he would not necessarily serve out the full four years. Volcker reminded the President that he supported the idea of making the Federal Reserve chairman's tenure roughly coterminous with the President's term, so that a new President could appoint his own Fed chairman within one year after taking office. Legislation to make this change was pending in Congress and Volcker had already endorsed it. A reasonable inference, the kind that politicians might draw from such conversations, was that Volcker was hinting at a compromise—if Reagan reappointed him now, Volcker could step down in midterm and the President, assuming he was re-elected, would be able to choose his own man in 1985 or early 1986.

When Volcker got back to the Fed, Edwin Meese and James Baker came running over to his office. "What did you tell the President?" they asked. Volcker told them the same things he had told their boss. Later, when the substance of these conversations dribbled out into political gossip, it was said that Volcker had promised the White House that he would resign by 1986 and they could appoint their own Fed chairman. This was not the case, but every time this rumor surfaced, financial markets expressed their jitters and the principals denied there was ever such an agreement.

The White House political managers, yielding reluctantly to the inevitability of Volcker's reappointment, nevertheless attempted to establish some ground rules with him for the future course of monetary policy, particularly leading up to the crucial re-election season in 1984. "You don't want a political whore as Fed chairman," one of them explained, "but you don't want someone who is philosophically opposed to your economic policy or partisan in the other direction. We assured ourselves that we could count on him being neutral as a policy maker."

The conversations were never so explicit that they took the form of negotiations. Volcker, for his part, vigorously denied that he had ever discussed the conduct of monetary policy in connection with his reappointment, either with the President or with any of the senior White House advisers. Still, the President's men thought they had an understanding with the Federal Reserve chairman.

I certainly recall a meeting [an Administration official said] where the President would say to Volcker, "I'd like to know that we can count on you." Or rather he'd say, "I'd like to know that your goals and mine are the same—sustained economic growth without inflation." And Volcker agreed with that. We translated that into this understanding: the Fed would provide sufficient growth in the money supply to insure sustained economic growth, without inflation.

Besides the President, the discussion with Volcker included Baker, Donald Regan, Edwin Meese and Michael Deaver, the official said. "There was no suggestion that I'm not going to reappoint you if you don't agree to this, but we may well have discussed that the brakes were shoved on too hard in the recession," the official recalled. "And we made the point that there were no signs of inflation returning now."

The supposed "understanding" meant a lot more to the White House than it did to Paul Volcker. The President's advisers thought they had extracted operating terms from Volcker, an agreement they could hold him to later, if the Fed shifted course and threatened the recovery in the 1984 campaign season. But what exactly did "sufficient" mean? Or "sustained economic growth"?

"It's a perfectly good cliché," a senior White House official complained, "but it's meaningless. It's not a coherent basis for asking the Fed to pursue a specific policy. Volcker can deliver on that commitment with 3 percent money growth and others can say it should be 6 percent. All the parties thought it had meaning, but Volcker could make it mean anything he wanted."

The White House, nevertheless, expected the terms to be honored. As David Stockman said, "Jim Baker thought he had a commitment that nobody was going to screw up the economy in the election year."

On June 18, the President chose his weekly Saturday-morning radio broadcast to announce the news: he was reappointing Paul Volcker to a new four-year term. Volcker, the President declared, is "as dedicated as I am to continuing the fight against inflation." Afterward, Treasury Secretary Regan added an important corollary: "Like the President, Volcker wants the recovery to be sustained and is committed to lower interest rates."[4]

The Treasury Secretary, addressing the National Press Club, was perhaps entitled to a moment of I-told-you-so. For more than two years, the former chief executive of Merrill Lynch had been heckled by the press for his optimism, belittled for his stubborn faith in the principles of supply-side economics. Now it was his turn to cite the economic statistics. The bullish American recovery was redeeming the faith.

> As custodians of the American Dream [Donald Regan boasted], we have nursed it through difficult days. We have brought it into the sunlight. And we will not surrender it to those who would go back to the old, failed dogmas of yesterday. We will now move from recovery to renewal. And we will disperse the dream until it is shared equally by millions who until now have known it only as an abstraction.

Industrial production had soared by 19 percent in the last three months. New orders for durable goods were up 36 percent. Employment in manufacturing jumped by 100,000 for two months running.

Retail sales increased at a 27 percent rate over the last quarter. Autos were up 38 percent from the low point the year before, iron and steel up 44 percent, housing up nearly 50 percent. Consumer confidence, measured by regular polling at the University of Michigan, was soaring to its highest level in ten years.

Donald Regan declared victory and mocked those liberal skeptics who had opposed the President's original doctrine, the program of massive tax cuts for business and individuals. The critics, Regan said, resembled comic-strip characters from *Pogo*, reduced to warning: "We are confronted with insurmountable opportunities."

The recession did last longer than anyone expected [Regan continued]. But all the while, overlooked or simply denied by those who peddle pessimism for their livelihood, the market forces embodied in the Reagan program were gathering momentum. As inflation fell and worker productivity increased, private companies found themselves with more and more internally generated funds. . . .

But our economic program is really aimed at Main Street. . . . What we are seeing is the creation of new opportunities from the grassroots up. We are building a bridge between today's recovery and tomorrow's lasting prosperity. And we are proving that quick fixes, while politically appealing, can never take the place of fundamental market forces and human motivations.[5]

The liberal critics were certainly wrong about one thing—the recovery was not weak, as they had predicted, but as robust and rapid as any of the previous postwar cycles. As the American economy regained its strength, it was clear that the abnormally high level of interest rates was not going to stunt a normal post-recession boom. Economists could worry about the implications, but the high price of money did not seem to inhibit consumers and businesses from rushing to join the action.

Alfred Zeller, who ran a fur shop in St. Johnsbury, Vermont, noticed that, on the contrary, his business improved when interest rates went up. "A lot of my customers are middle-aged, semiretired and retired," Zeller said. "Some are widows whose husbands have left them quite comfortable. All they've got is liquid assets." With higher returns on their money funds, they bought more expensive furs.[6]

William Hamilton, a political consultant for Senator John Glenn, who was seeking the Democratic presidential nomination, found that high interest rates simply did not "personally eat away" at voters. The issue, he concluded, could not be easily packaged by Democrats for the 1984 campaigns.

President Reagan reminded voters repeatedly—and correctly—that nominal interest rates had been cut in half since he took office, from the inflationary frenzy of January 1981 when the prime rate hit 20.5 percent to the current level of 11 percent. What the President did not discuss, of course, was that real interest rates—the exchange of real wealth after discounting for inflation—were actually much higher now and still rising. Though far more significant, real interest rates were another element of money the public didn't understand.[7]

Paul Volcker also blithely dismissed the impact of high interest rates on the different classes of citizens. The subject was too complicated, he claimed, to sort out winners and losers. "Lots of relatively poor people love high interest rates—it depends on how they borrow and save," Volcker insisted. "A lot of older people love high interest. I even get mail, not very much but some, when interest rates go down."

The Federal Reserve Board's own research on financial wealth had, of course, described the implications in starker terms. The Fed studies demonstrated that 55 percent of American families were net debtors in terms of financial assets and that a mere 10 percent of American families owned 86 percent of all the net financial wealth. Paul Volcker said he was unfamiliar with this research.

Keynesian economists, in any case, could claim vindication on a more fundamental point about the economy and they did. This was not a "supply side" recovery, they pointed out; it was Keynesian "demand side." In broad outline, they were correct. Notwithstanding the gloating rhetoric from the President and Donald Regan and other Republicans, the expansion that developed in 1983 did not fulfill any of the supply-side premises articulated back in 1981. On the contrary, the recovery followed the standard Keynesian format for demand stimulus—it was led by consumers spending money on goods in the marketplace, not by savers investing in new capital formation.

The Reagan tax cuts stimulated consumer demand by putting more cash in private hands, and this increased stimulus, combined with the Fed's easing of interest rates, drove the expansion. After several quarters, consumer spending moderated and, as usually occurred, a boom in capital-goods spending developed, producers investing in new productive facilities and equipment.

This was the standard pattern for economic recovery; the sequence and dimensions did not deviate appreciably from past cycles. The effects of the Reagan fiscal policy were not different from what liberal Democrats had done to manipulate economic growth in previous seasons—raising aggregate demand by running federal deficits—only with $200 billion deficits Ronald Reagan's Keynesian push was much bolder than anything Democrats had dared attempt since World War II.

"The paradox," said Charles Schultze, Jimmy Carter's CEA chairman, "is it's the opposite of supply-side economics." The central premise of the new conservative doctrine had been that the across-the-board tax cuts would allow citizens to increase their personal savings—and these savings would flow into capital investment in new factories and equipment, expanding the productive capacity of the nation. Thus, broader prosperity would be created by enhancing the "supply side" of the economy. Nearly the opposite occurred: the savings rate declined, instead of increasing, during the Reagan recovery and fell to record lows the longer the expansion continued.[8]

Rather than savings, it was more accurate to say Reagan's economic revival was powered by debt—living on borrowed money. It was borrowed and spent by the federal government, by businesses and by consumers. As the recovery proceeded, an increasing portion of the accumulating debt was borrowed from abroad—capital supplied by foreign investors. For the first time since 1914, the United States would become a debtor nation again, borrowing more than it lent in international finance.

Ronald Reagan's version of Keynes really was different, however, from what Democrats had done before him, despite the broad similarities. The President's economic policy, combined with the Fed's, effectively inverted the old liberal priorities—as if the principle of income distribution articulated by Marriner Eccles and the other New Dealers had been stood on its head. Instead of pushing money downward, in order to stimulate the consumption of goods by the broadest base of families, the federal government was now discreetly pushing money upward—concentrating income disproportionately in the upper economic brackets.

The reversed redistribution of incomes was masked at first by the general prosperity, but the effects were already visible in 1983. According to the U.S. Census, only families on the top 20 percent of the economic ladder enjoyed real increases in their after-tax household incomes from 1980 to 1983. The others, the bottom 80 percent, actually lost. The highest fifth, families earning $38,000 or more, gained an average of $1,480 per household in real income, and the top 5 percent, earning more than $60,000, gained an average of $3,320. Families in the middle lost about $560 and the working poor lost about $250.

The progressive ladder that had guided liberal redistribution politics for two generations was turned upside down. The wealthiest got most and the least got less. The income share that went to the most pros-

perous families, the top fifth on the ladder, became even more disproportionate, increasing from 40.2 to 42 percent of all U.S. income.[9]

The reversed redistribution flowed from several channels of government action, involving both fiscal policy and the Federal Reserve. The
Reagan Administration's budget cuts had modestly scaled back benefits for lower-income families, while the boom in defense spending
naturally tended to favor high-salaried technical professions. The
across-the-board reduction in tax rates delivered the largest benefits
to taxpayers in the upper brackets. The business tax cuts rewarded
the owners of capital and for corporations offset much of the impact
of high interest rates. The process of liquidation had depressed economic activity generally, but the largest personal losses were absorbed
by labor and small business. All these influences flowed in the same
direction.

Finally, the continuing high level of real interest rates guaranteed a
sustained, regressive redistribution of income upward. The rewards
and penalties were steadily compounded between creditors and
debtors, like compound interest itself. A larger share of incomes automatically flowed to the people who owned most of the net financial
wealth, the well-to-do and the wealthy. The borrowers would owe
more and more. The *rentier* had not only eluded the "euthanasia" that
John Maynard Keynes had prophesied for him in *The General Theory*
of fifty years before. The owner of capital was now receiving far
greater rent for the use of his money than Keynes had ever seen.

In effect, the reward structure of American capitalism was gradually being altered—less for labor, more for capital; a smaller share for
work, a larger one for money. This shift was visible in the shrinking
portion of total U.S. personal income that was derived from wages and
salaries. For many decades, from the 1930s onward, wages and salaries had accounted for about two-thirds of all personal income in the
United States. In the 1970s, the wage share declined proportionately
as government entitlement programs became a larger portion of incomes, mainly Social Security.

In the era of Volcker and Reagan, the wage share shrank much
further—to its lowest level in fifty years—as a larger and larger portion of total U.S. income was claimed by the incomes produced by
money, dividends and interest payments. By 1983, wages and salaries
accounted for only 60.7 percent of total personal income. The following year, the wage share would shrink further—to 59.5 percent—the
lowest level since 1929.

This was the restoration of capital—capital restored to a primacy it
had not enjoyed since before the Great Crash. From 1979 to 1983, the
personal incomes derived from interest grew by more than 70 percent,

an increase of $158 billion, while wage incomes grew by only 33 percent in the same period. When income from stock dividends was included, the returns on capital would claim 20 percent of the whole in 1984, compared to 11 percent in 1979. Money's share of the rewards generated by the American system and apportioned among its citizens had been virtually doubled—primarily by government action—in only five years' time.

But did any of this matter? In the general euphoria, the effects of shifting income shares hardly seemed of consequence to the robust performance of the American economy. America was back and expanding vigorously again. The economy was demonstrating that neither high interest rates nor huge deficits would hold it back. After all, wealthy people spent their money too. The increased discretionary income available to the upper brackets from higher interest rates clearly invigorated the consumer demand.

The well-to-do, one could even say, led the nation to recovery. They bought expensive cars and luxury vacations, jewelry and watches and artwork, boats and bikes and pleasure aircraft, second homes at the beach or in the mountains. Home builders who had nearly gone broke a few years before building moderately priced subdivisions discovered a rich new market in resort condominiums. This upward tilt in the composition of consumer spending was fostering what some business economists called "a two-tier economy," a subtle breakup in the mass-consumption patterns that had driven the American economy since World War II. *Fortune* magazine summarized the implications for its business readers:

> The mass market is splitting apart. Most businessmen don't realize it yet, but the middle class—the principal market for much of what they make—is gradually being pulled apart. Economic forces are propelling one family after another toward the high or low end of the income spectrum. For many marketers, particularly those positioned to sell to the well-to-do, this presages good times. For others used to selling millions of units of their products to middle-income folks, the prospects are altogether darker.[10]

Liberal sensibilities were offended, but the liberal impulse for progressive redistribution of income had been discredited and very few were willing to speak for it now. The question of income shares was regarded as a political issue, a faintly old-fashioned argument about social equity, but not a question of great relevance to economic performance.

Even many liberal Keynesian economists accepted that assumption.

So long as aggregate demand was sufficient to drive an expansionary cycle, they allowed, it did not really matter who got the money or what they bought. In gross economic terms, consumer demand generated by wealthy widows buying new furs with their increased interest income was indistinguishable from the consumer demand of a worker spending his pay raise on a new car. All of it would stimulate production and jobs. This was logical only if one assumed no significant difference between furs and cars.

The Democrats of the 1980s occasionally expressed the wish for a fairer distribution of the rewards, but they fashioned it into a political issue labeled "fairness," not an argument about achieving better economic performance. Most Democrats no longer understood what Marriner Eccles had figured out back in the 1930s—that the progressive distribution of incomes was a necessary prerequisite for healthy economic growth. In a sense, Andrew Mellon, the great Republican theorist from the "roaring twenties," had at last won the argument.

Strangely enough, there was still one group nagged by private doubts about the long-term economic consequences of high interest rates—some of the senior policy makers of the Federal Reserve. Their fitful worrying seemed slightly out of character, since Federal Reserve governors tried to avoid questions of class conflict like the distribution of incomes. Furthermore, they themselves were implicated in the regressive redistribution through their own interest-rate policy, though they insisted this was the unavoidable consequence of the huge federal deficits enacted by Congress and the President. In any case, some at the Fed saw worrisome portents in the lopsided recovery. As Lyle Gramley explained:

> With a sufficiently restrictive monetary policy, you might be able to maintain low inflation for a long period of time. In theory, as an economist, I can imagine that going on for quite a while. Maybe in some theoretical world, you can do that. But—politically—it's going to be dynamite. The effects on the credit-sensitive sectors of the economy are going to be much too severe.

Charles Partee worried about the effects on incomes. "There's been quite a lot of redistribution of income toward the higher-income groups," he said. The high-income creditor classes increase their incomes steadily at the expense of all the borrowers—who must borrow more in order to keep up their spending.

Gramley pointed out a basic disparity in the economic format that the nation was now pursuing: real interest rates were running higher than the real growth rate for the U.S. economy. In fundamental terms, that could not go on forever. A debtor who repeatedly borrows more than the surplus his labor or business enterprise produces will fall further and further behind in his obligations until, sooner or later, the inexorable pressures of compound interest defeat him. This was ancient law in economics, at least as old as Adam Smith, and it had not been repealed. In broad terms, it applied to an entire nation as aptly as it did to individuals.

"If real interest rates exceed growth in the economy—if internal debt is growing faster than GNP—then our problems get worse and worse," Gramley observed. Henry Wallich made the same point about debt: "Only if growth in indebtedness is matched by growth of income-producing assets can the lender be sure that productive use is being made of his funds and that the debt service can be sustained in the years to come." [11]

Wallich's warning was actually directed at commercial banks when they were lending vast sums to less-developed countries, but the logic applied just as well to American families that borrowed more than their future incomes could pay back or businesses that did the same or, for that matter, the American economy as a whole.

The pathological effects—the steady erosion that occurs when real interest rates are higher than the real growth of output—were perhaps easier to visualize in a small enterprise, a farm or any other business venture whose operation depended on credit. The farmer might borrow operating capital at 6 percent real interest, expecting the enterprise to cover the cost and leave a profit. At the end of the season, however, the real earnings surplus that the farmer has produced with the capital amounts to only 4 percent. He must somehow make up the difference—the missing 2 percent—either from his own personal profits or by cutting production costs further or by borrowing still more money to cover the shortfall.

A small-town banker, John A. O'Leary, Jr., president of the Peoples State Bank in Luray, Kansas, put the dilemma in concrete terms:

> The older farmers who bought their land years ago and have it paid off are doing okay. But the young farmer's in bad shape. We break him as soon as we lend him some money. Say he needs $100,000. Our best rate now is 13.5 percent. The first $12,000 he earns he needs to feed his family. It costs at least $9,000 to operate three hundred acres. Another one-third of his income goes to the landlord. If he gets six thousand bushels of wheat out of that land, at $3.50 a bushel, he brings in only $21,000. The equation just won't work. With 6 percent interest rates, he could make it. [12]

The essential point was that the creditor was guaranteed a 13.5 percent return for the use of his capital—but the capital did not produce a 13.5 percent return. The farmer must swallow the loss. The next season, he would try again, and unless his own output expanded miraculously or the price of wheat went up sharply, he would fall further behind, his burden compounded. The *rentier* would still collect his interest. Eventually, he would own the farm.

The federal government itself was caught in a similar dilemma, though no one expected the government to fail. Given its $200 billion annual deficits and the high interest rates it was paying on Treasury bonds, the government's debt burden was expanding much faster than the real economy—the tax base it depended on for revenue. The government's income-producing asset, the private economy which it taxed, was not keeping up with the government's borrowing.

Federal outlays for interest payments rose from $52 billion in 1980 to more than $142 billion by 1986—from 10 percent of all federal revenue to 19 percent. This was an important part of the reversed redistribution of income, since the increasing interest payments went from all American taxpayers to the select minority who were bondholders. The *rentier*'s claim on the taxpayer, one could say, had nearly doubled.

Theoretically, of course, Washington could keep up with the debt simply by devoting more and more of the taxpayers' money to paying the bondholders—and spending less and less on the regular functions of government. Or Washington could raise taxes to close the gap. Neither seemed like a practical option to Congress and the President. Instead, like a debt-burdened young farmer trying to keep going, they decided to do both—to keep spending and to keep borrowing more.

The same debilitating effects worked less obviously on the economy as a whole, when real interest rates exceeded real growth. Many families and businesses, of course, beat the average—their incomes grew faster than their debt burdens and they were able to come out ahead, despite the high cost of credit. Others bumped along and stayed even. Others fell steadily behind. On average, however, the U.S. economy was behind—its output growing more slowly than its debts were growing.

The pressures of this debt squeeze on private borrowers were offset or at least ameliorated in a substantial way by the U.S. tax code. By allowing tax deductions for interest payments, the government effectively reduced the real cost of debt and discreetly subsidized borrowers by forgiving a share of their federal taxes. That softened the effects of the high rates and allowed many businesses and individuals to stay ahead, despite slow growth.

Yet the tax subsidy for borrowers also added a perverse twist: the largest tax savings went to the most prosperous borrowers who paid income taxes at the highest rates. For someone in the 50 percent tax bracket, an interest rate of 13 percent was actually only 6.5 percent after taxes. But, for those in lower tax brackets with less income, the subsidy was much smaller or nonexistent. The interest deduction, originated as a progressive measure to assist debtors and foster easy credit, had a different meaning in an era of permanently high interest rates. In the struggle to cope, the strongest were helped most by the government and many of the weakest were helped not at all.

People did keep borrowing, nonetheless. Credit expanded rapidly as the recovery blossomed, much faster than the Federal Reserve had intended. For a struggling businessman or farmer, the choice sometimes seemed like no choice at all—to stop borrowing was to stop doing business. For families, the spreading optimism and employment, the surging increase in real personal incomes, seemed to promise that they would be able to keep up with their new borrowing. Things were looking up and long-deferred desires were now fulfilled —new cars, new houses, all the good things that the "American dream" promised.

Charles Partee worried about the long-term consequences. The divergence between debtors and creditors bothered him as well as the gross redistribution of incomes that was occurring. The situation reminded the governor of an old, long-forgotten economic theory he had learned in college about the pathology of compound interest.

"I had a little book in college," Partee mused. "I can't remember the name of it, but this book argued that the power of compound interest is such a strong and fundamental force in redistributing incomes, you have to break the impact of compound interest rates every so often and write off the debts—if you don't want to crush people."

Typically, that write-off occurred in recession or, more spectacularly, in an economic collapse. Debtors failed massively and debts were liquidated, so everyone could start over again. The debts could be extinguished, more subtly, through price inflation—ameliorating the burden of the borrowers by depreciating the value of the dollars they must pay back. Partee was not predicting any of these outcomes, but he was bothered by the portents.

> There's been quite a lot of redistribution of income toward the higher-income groups [the governor observed], and that saps the aggregate demand for the economy. It requires consumers to accumulate more and more debt in order to keep spending. You get a good consumption boom —but you have to borrow to get it. The high-income people invest their increased incomes in financial assets—and that money gets borrowed by everyone else.

Charles Partee was describing essentially the same principles articulated by Marriner Eccles fifty years earlier—the economic importance of equitable income distribution. It was the insight that most
liberal Democrats in Congress had forgotten and most Keynesian
economists no longer took seriously. Some governors at the Fed saw
the pathology developing, but they did not feel it was their place to do
anything about it.

"I have no doubt in my mind that the economy would be healthier
with lower interest rates," Gramley said. "It would allocate more savings to real investments, allow the thrifts to improve, help out agriculture, make enormous contributions to the international debt problems.
But the way to get lower interest rates is to do something about the
budget deficits."

Robbin Craven, a twenty-eight-year-old unemployed steelworker in
Homestead, Pennsylvania, tried a series of part-time low-wage jobs—
driving a van for United Cerebral Palsy, security guard at a state
hospital, glass-cleaner demonstrator in the local Sears store. Filling
out yet another job application, Craven joked about his downward
mobility: "What did we used to make in the mill? I can't remember
exactly. I'll just put down: Big Bucks."

Carl Redwood, Jr., another young steelworker, had followed the
same trail of disappointing jobs after he was laid off—security guard,
"meter maid" issuing parking tickets, counselor at a day camp. The
vast mills along the Monongahela River outside Pittsburgh had once
employed twenty-eight thousand basic steelworkers at premium industrial wages; now there were only six thousand jobs left. Redwood
described the big picture:

> No matter how you cut it, with all the people looking for jobs, there's
> not enough jobs, in terms of good steady jobs. We all have to compete
> with each other, unemployed people against each other for a shrinking
> pie. What's happened in this economy is that higher wages have been
> busted down, everyone pushed down to a lower wage, even a minimum
> wage. Yeah, there are people back to work, but what kind of money are
> they making?

As the economic recovery flourished elsewhere and the mills did not
open, anger turned to despair in the Mon Valley and stories of suicide
became a staple of local conversations. Everyone seemed to know
someone who had tried it or succeeded. The county coroner reported
that suicides were up 11 percent "due to economic conditions."

"At first, I was really mad at the corporation executives," said Arnie

Leibowitz, an ex-worker in the Homestead mill. "At one time, I was thinking I was going to blow them away. I could have done it. After a while, I started blaming myself. The day I was committed, I went out on the bridge to jump. I figured this is it: why go on?" Friends "talked him down" and Leibowitz went to a state mental hospital for treatment.

Others like Robbin Craven held on to their good humor. Craven worked at odd jobs and his wife worked as a nurse's aide and they paid their bills, though he said his children did not understand why they could not have new clothes or bikes like other kids.

"At first, I was bitter," he said. "Now I put it all behind me. It's just past, gone. You could stand on the corner and blame them—yell obscenities down over the hill—but it isn't going to do any good. They could care less."[13]

The steel valley's continuing distress was an extreme example, but the pressures of surplus labor described by Carl Redwood pushed wages downward across most sectors of heavy industry in 1983 and afterward—long after the national economy had supposedly regained its health. The United Steelworkers accepted wage cuts and freezes in order to keep selected plants open, but more mills closed anyway. Auto workers gave up substantial wage-and-benefit improvements in new contracts at Ford and General Motors in order to protect job security. Coal miners settled for a $1.40-per-hour raise, compared to $3.60 in their previous contract. Airline machinists and other airline unions accepted wage freezes, deferred raises and what union solidarity had traditionally always opposed—a two-tier pay scale for their members. The younger, newer workers would be paid less than older members for the same work. Oil workers, confronted with the closing of eighty-three refineries, settled for a 20-cent raise at Gulf.

Once the recovery was under way, the American economy created new jobs at an extraordinary pace—nearly five million new jobs added in only twelve months' time, from mid-1983 to the following summer. The unemployment rate moved steadily downward, from nearly 11 percent to an eventual level just above 7 percent. The rising employment generated one of the fastest accelerations in real per capita income ever recorded—up 5.8 percent in the election year of 1984.

But organized labor never really recovered from the recession. The real wages of union workers did not improve once inflation was abated, as Paul Volcker had promised during the painful recession when so many were laid off. Under the pressure of continuing surplus labor and excess capacity in the economy, their real wages declined. In 1983, the first-year raises in the major new labor contracts averaged only 2.5 percent compared to more than 9 percent in 1980 and 1981.

The following year, the percentage was even lower. This was well below the rate of price inflation. They were losing ground.

The bankers on the Federal Advisory Council reported that they were optimistic that inflation would remain subdued—mainly because labor was now subdued. "The fundamental factor explaining continued low inflation is the outlook for unit labor costs," the bankers told the Fed.

Surplus labor and surplus productive capacity were the principal forces behind labor's submission, but labor's weakness was probably also exacerbated by the new tax breaks enacted for business by the Reagan Administration in 1981. The new tax advantages were tilted in favor of capital-intensive buildings and machinery rather than labor-intensive investments. When the boom in capital goods unfolded in late 1983, the spending was devoted largely to purchases of computers and other high-tech equipment that displaced workers—investments that enhanced efficiency but not employment.[14]

The Republican tax changes were good for certain kinds of construction workers, however. Traditionally, when liberal Democratic regimes undertook "pump priming," they launched public-works projects, dams and highways and public buildings, as the way to generate jobs. The Republican program, instead, fostered a nationwide boom in commercial office construction through the generous new depreciation rules provided to business real estate. This created abundant jobs for commercial construction workers, but it also left most major cities with a glut of vacant office space—gleaming new office towers whose owners had trouble filling them with tenants. "They are the Republican equivalent of public works," David Hale of Kemper Financial Services observed.[15]

Organized labor was, if not broken by the process of disinflation and recovery, dramatically weakened. About 1.1 million union workers were compelled to accept pay cuts or freezes in 1983, more than a third of the workers covered by that year's new contracts. The "give backs" to management continued at almost the same pace in subsequent years. As unions hunkered down to deal with the new reality, strikes and work stoppages subsided to the lowest level since World War II.

"It takes a damn fool to strike in a slack labor market, with high unemployment, against a company that might have full inventories," John Zalusky, collective-bargaining specialist at the AFL-CIO, explained.[16]

The rapid expansion of employment was concentrated in nonunionized service sectors—from the highest-paying jobs in finance and technical professions to low-wage work in data processing and franchised food outlets. In heavy industry, where unions dominated, em-

ployment never returned to its pre-recession strength. An estimated
5.1 million workers had been permanently displaced by plant closings
between 1979 and 1984, about half in manufacturing, and the Bureau
of Labor Statistics estimated that only about 60 percent of them found
new jobs.

Union membership declined from 20 million to 17.4 million workers.
Organized labor, which at its peak in the 1950s had represented 35
percent of the American work force, now spoke for only 18 percent.
The political clout of labor, including its influence in the Democratic
Party, declined accordingly.

The Federal Reserve chairman acknowledged that many premier
industrial workers were now worse off, but he did not regard this as
an injustice. Breaking down wages to a lower level was a return to
equilibrium—the classic conservative view of how things were supposed to work.

At the Federal Reserve, officials actually debated among themselves whether 7 percent unemployment—once considered intolerable
—could now be reasonably accepted as the optimum, the "natural
rate of unemployment." In other words, if the Fed allowed unemployment to decline much below that level, would it risk setting off another
round of wage-price inflation? The question was never formally resolved, but the Fed did not try to push unemployment any lower.

The tacit acceptance of 7 percent unemployment as the norm represented another fundamental shift in the American political agenda.
Twenty years before, government economists had considered 4 percent unemployment the national goal, the practical equivalent of full
employment, and it was actually achieved in the 1960s. In the 1970s,
6 percent was reluctantly accepted as the best that might be achieved
without provoking inflation. In the 1980s, the government's economic
policy makers retreated further. There was not much protest from the
public and even the Democratic Party dropped its old rhetoric of full
employment.

There's been very, very little political reaction [Anthony Solomon of the
New York Fed observed]. Unemployment is very demoralizing, particularly for young people who can't find work, but I'd say that 7 percent is
probably what you have to tolerate to avoid a pickup of inflation. If you
had reasonably full flexibility of wages and prices, you could get it down
to 4 percent, but I don't know what you can do to get more flexibility in
wages. You'd have to smash the trade-union movement and there'd still
be some downward price stickiness.

In other words, if labor accepted still more wage concessions, its
members could go back to work. One by one, the major trade unions
grudgingly pursued that bitter formula. Yet the jobs did not return.

Labor would have to yield more. "This is hardball," a Pittsburgh banker explained. "The steelworkers have given up a lot, but they haven't given up enough."

Governor Partee, whose youthful liberal perspective had turned more conservative, was still troubled by the lack of public protest. "Certainly, there are pockets of severe criticism in the steel towns and the Middle West, but there's no voice for the unemployed," Governor Partee lamented. "Maybe it's the majority who feel sort of happy with their lot in life and are unwilling to give up anything for the minority. I don't know. It's a worldwide phenomenon. In Britain, it's 13 percent unemployment. In Germany, it's 9 percent."

While Partee supported the Fed's strategy of restraining the economy from reaching full employment, he did not agree with colleagues who thought 7 percent unemployment was the best that could be achieved. "There's a trap here," Partee said. "What you do is just accept any unemployment number that you get and say that that's what's necessary to avoid any upward pressure on wages and prices."

Nevertheless, as a practical matter, that was what the Federal Reserve did. When the unemployment rate remained stuck just above 7 percent, the Fed accepted that outcome. This meant that about 8.4 million people were officially unemployed and another 1.3 million were described as "discouraged" workers who had stopped registering at the unemployment office. Another 5.7 million people—displaced young workers like Carl Redwood and Robbin Craven—were compelled to work part time or at temporary jobs with wages far below their normal incomes. In all, the "voiceless" minority probably totaled more than 15 million citizens.[17]

Paul Volcker's views on the matter did not change. The heart of his concern was stable money. Driving down price inflation came before other considerations. "I don't know what the right or natural rate of unemployment is," Volcker said, "but I give you one conviction. Over time, you can move unemployment lower if we purge inflation and inflationary expectations than if we don't."

Inflation was running below 4 percent, yet mortgage interest rates remained above 12 percent or higher and, still, young families flocked to buy their first homes. The housing industry was averaging close to 2 million starts, not its best year by far, but still vigorous. Governor Lyle Gramley concluded that people had simply adapted to the new environment of high interest rates.

I bought my first house at 4.75 percent in 1957 [Gramley said]. The most I ever paid on a mortgage was 6 percent. For me, the idea of buying a house with a mortgage of more than 10 percent was unthinkable, unthinkable. My daughter bought a home in July 1983 and her mortgage was 12.5 percent. Because she had seen mortgage rates 6 percent higher, it didn't bother her at all. She thought she was getting a good deal.

Is my daughter any worse off? I don't think so. She bought a smaller house. She pays more of her income for housing. I wouldn't have done it, but people adjust. She will get along with less of other things in her budget. She drives a smaller car. Now, the consequences for others, who can't afford housing at all, that's another matter.

The high price of home mortgages did, in fact, price many people out of the housing market. The National Association of Realtors estimated that 900,000 families were unable to own a home because, no matter how far they stretched, their incomes could not support the monthly payments at such high rates. More and more young people became renters or moved in with their parents.

Those who did buy faced new terms. The new environment for housing was defined by this comparison: in 1970, when the inflation rate was somewhat higher, home mortgages were available at rates between 7 and 8 percent. Now, under similar conditions, mortgage rates were running anywhere from 4 to 7 percent above that level—a huge windfall for the lenders, a huge price increase for the young home buyers.

In the meantime, America's new houses had also gotten smaller, as builders scaled down the square footage in order to make new models affordable. "This is the first generation that in all probability will never live in a home as large or nice as their parents' home," real-estate consultant Lewis Goodkin told *The Wall Street Journal*.[18]

People adapted, but they also became more vulnerable. After years of resistance, most new home buyers now accepted adjustable-rate mortgages that would fluctuate with market rates. This made the initial monthly payments lower, but it also shifted the risk from the lender to the borrower. The creditors for long-term mortgages were now much better protected against the threat of inflation. If prices rose in the future and market interest rates went up, if the Fed tightened credit again, the monthly house payments would go up too and the costs would be absorbed by the homeowners, not the lenders.

The typical young home buyers in the 1980s faced, in addition to the high rates, an entirely different prospect from that of their parents: instead of assuming that their homes would steadily appreciate in value and their real housing costs would steadily shrink, many would encounter the opposite—their home's value was stagnant or declining and their monthly mortgage payments were rising. In the process of breaking inflation, another fundamental element of American economic life had been effectively eliminated—the discreet process by which homeownership had redistributed wealth from creditors to debtors and accumulated real assets for middle-class families.

Many could not keep up with the new terms. Either their family incomes did not rise sufficiently or they were interrupted by temporary unemployment or the high mortgage payments were simply more than they could afford. Mortgage foreclosures, instead of declining after the recession, the normal pattern, increased steadily through the economic recovery and reached record levels.

Elizabeth Laird and her husband, Ray, lost their new home in suburban Houston as oil prices continued to decline and he was laid off by the electronics firm that served offshore oil rigs. In the spring of 1983, they had bought a $63,000 three-bedroom house with fireplace and two-car garage. The mortgage rate was 15.5 percent and the monthly payments were $1,004, but she took a second job to increase their income. "Houston was in the headlines," she said. "Everyone came to Houston and found a job. We thought we were on our way up."

Her husband found another job, then was laid off again. A year later, they were four months behind on the mortgage and they couldn't find a buyer for their home. The Houston real-estate market had collapsed and prices were falling. Mrs. Laird saw neighbors selling $70,000 homes for less than $60,000. Their subdivision was dotted with "foreclosure" stickers. The Lairds filed for bankruptcy and became renters again.

"I don't want to be miserable and I don't want to make my family miserable," she said. "I want to say, 'God, I know you're building character in me.' But, sometimes, I want to ask, 'How much character do I need?' "[19]

The Veterans Administration wound up holding twenty-nine thousand foreclosed homes in 1984, 10 percent more than the year before. The mortgage-insurance industry paid out $425 million on foreclosures in 1985, three times the 1983 losses. The Mortgage Bankers Association of America (where Lyle Gramley would go to work as chief economist after his retirement from the Board of Governors) announced that by mid-1985 mortgage delinquencies reached 6.2 percent of all outstanding mortgages, the highest level in the twenty-two years the association had monitored mortgage payments.[20]

Mike Stout, a young steelworker from Homestead, Pennsylvania, was one of those who fell behind. He was still employed, but his union had accepted a major wage "give back" to management.

When I bought the house at 16 percent, I figured that would add up to $148,000 in interest over thirty years on a $37,000 house. But I figured I would at least get the tax deduction, and if interest rates came down, I could refinance it. Even if my wife lost her job, as long as I was working, I'd be able to keep my head above water. Then the "concessions contract" came along. That took $400 a month off my paycheck and I went from bobbing along with my head just above water to sinking.

A year later, the bank foreclosed and Stout moved to an apartment.

I told the bank they were crazy to foreclose because they'd never be able to sell the house and I was right [he said]. I'll bet there are a hundred and sixty houses for sale in town and nobody's buying. The house is still sitting there, boarded up. In fact, a bunch of kids broke into it and tore it up. It's a real mess.[21]

The fundamental reversal for housing and homeownership, however, was the turning of tables that flowed from the Federal Reserve's successful campaign against price inflation. Through the 1960s and 1970s, owning a home had been a good investment for rich and poor alike, guaranteed to improve their financial status over time. This was so because, despite rising interest rates and rising prices, the value of housing rose faster. Accumulating equity in the family home was a central assumption of what people loosely called the "American dream" and inflation assisted it.

Starting in 1980, the benefits were reversed, not just for new first-time buyers but for every homeowner, young and old. The value of housing began to decline in real terms—that is, housing prices increased less than the general inflation rate. In 1982, inflation was 3.9 percent and house prices increased only 1.2 percent. By 1984, inflation was 3.7 percent but home prices increased an average of only 3.4 percent. By 1985, the median price of houses would be lower, in real terms, than it had been in 1978. The homeowners' equity was no longer accumulating, but, in many towns and cities, shrinking. The wealth-accumulating benefits of "owning your own home" were gone.[22]

The Reagan White House could not have been surprised by this since the CEA chairman, Murray Weidenbaum, had predicted as much in a memorandum to the Cabinet during the recession. "One of the major long-term effects of a lower rate of inflation will be a major redistribution of wealth," Weidenbaum explained. Many "losers," he said, would be people who had bet on continuing price inflation— speculators in art and antiques, farmland and commodities—and they deserved no sympathy. But Weidenbaum's list of "losers" also included the American homeowner.

Most importantly, all homeowners have been "real-estate speculators" and many will experience a loss of wealth [the economist explained].

Those who recently purchased a home at high fixed mortgage rates will experience an unusual loss. Although lower inflation will almost surely increase total real wealth (by increasing productivity), it is important to remember that there is a large vocal constituency (all of the "smart money people" of the 1970s) for higher inflation.[23]

In real estate, the "smart money people" were gone and no one talked much anymore about inflation. Instead, a new word began to appear in the conversations of buyers and sellers, an economic term that a generation of Americans had never heard—"deflation."

In midsummer of 1983, the price of wheat was $3.85 a bushel, a few pennies less than the summer before. Naturally, the grain farmers of the Middle West were losing ground. Faced with the higher cost of credit, their own prices were flat or falling. Since the Consumer Price Index continued to rise moderately, the farmers' real incomes were shrinking.

Crude oil prices were down too—$28.33 a barrel at U.S. refineries, $3 less than in 1982 and still softening. Producers worldwide were offering discounts, trying to keep their shares of customers in a market that had too much supply.[24]

The American auto industry's weekly production was up more than 40 percent from the summer of 1982, but GM, Ford and Chrysler were not raising car prices on the rising demand, as they had done so often in the 1970s. Indeed, the Big Three were now competing for auto buyers by offering price bargains—interest-rate discounts on new auto loans.

Grain, oil, autos—these three staples of the American economy reflected the new reality of disinflation and the obvious benefits for American consumers. Gasoline prices moved steadily lower at the filling station. Food prices no longer escalated with maddening regularity at the supermarket. Auto dealers advertised "specials" that really were special.

Yet bizarre things happened to these prices when products crossed international boundaries. The bushel of wheat that sold for $3.85 in Kansas City now effectively cost $5 or $6 when sold in Europe. In Brazil, a barrel of imported crude oil cost Brazilians the equivalent of $50 or $60 in their own currency. The price of French steel sold in the United States had fallen $125 a ton in less than a year. A Toyota, once delivered in San Francisco for $10,000, could now be marketed in America at a real cost to the Japanese of only $7,500.[25]

The hardy American dollar, created by Paul Volcker's successful campaign against inflation, was the explanation for every one of these anomalies. The dollar continued to rise in value against the world's other major currencies—appreciating by more than 50 percent since 1979—and that altered the terms of trade for every international transaction. French steel, Japanese cars, German machine tools, Korean clothes—all sold cheaper in the U.S. market. American-made tractors and computers, American-grown food and fiber, now cost much more when sold to foreign nations.

The effects were devastating for some—another element in the rolling liquidation that persisted long after the national recession hardened. American grain farmers lost more than a third of their share of the global market from 1981 to 1983 as the export price of their wheat and corn practically doubled (and the debt-burdened Latin-American countries cut back their food imports in order to pay their bank loans). Meanwhile, foreign producers of autos, steel, machine tools, computer chips and a long list of other manufactured products grabbed a larger and larger share of the American domestic market—riding the artificial price advantage provided them by the dollar's rising exchange rate. U.S. imports of manufactured goods rose by 66 percent over four years' time and U.S. exports declined by 16 percent.

With that kind of competition, Detroit could not very well raise its sticker prices—or the wages of auto workers either. "Even after we're all done fixing quality and productivity, and fuel efficiency and performance," Lee Iacocca of Chrysler complained, "the Japanese still have a $2,000 per car advantage in U.S. showrooms. . . . With the yen undervalued against the dollar, by at least 20 percent and probably more, their cars and other products are much cheaper than they would be if the yen reflected its true purchasing power in the open market."

In 1979, the yen had traded at less than 200 yen to the dollar. By 1983, the ratio was 235 yen to the dollar. The German Deutsche mark was worth 54 cents in foreign exchange in 1979. By 1983 it was only 36 cents. The French franc had been close to four to the dollar. By 1983 it was eight to the dollar. In four years' time, the tough monetary policy of the Federal Reserve had totally reversed the dynamics of international exchange. The dollar was so strong that it hurt.

"This idea of jobs chasing the weakest currency and the lowest wages is absolutely crazy," Iacocca declared. That was approximately what was happening: hundreds of thousands, perhaps millions, of U.S. jobs were extinguished, one way or the other, by the strong dollar. The President celebrated the stronger dollar as a sign of America's restored vigor, but in international trade, the advantage flowed to the weakening currencies of Europe and Asia. By 1983, the estimated loss exceeded 1.5 million American jobs, most of them high-wage, unionized jobs in manufacturing.[26]

American exporters like Caterpillar Tractor closed down factories at home as they lost sales overseas. Import-sensitive sectors like steel and copper closed mills and mines as cheaper steel from France and cheaper copper from Chile came in and took away domestic contracts. Finally, the major multinational companies, including Iacocca's Chrysler and the other auto makers, simply exported the jobs. They phased out American plants and moved the production and employment to foreign countries so they too could take advantage of the artificial edge in pricing provided by the lopsided currencies.

One American's loss, however, was another's gain. While certain industries and certain workers suffered, every consumer benefited from the dollar-driven price competition. The import-export pressures were a major force in sustaining the low inflation rate that the Fed had established with the recession. It helped explain why the trade unions were still reeling, still giving up concessions even though the economy was expanding smartly again. Labor's real wages were declining, but, thanks to the dollar exchange, the effective wage differential between U.S. and foreign workers was widening. It also explained why U.S. manufacturers did not dare raise their prices. Only businesses that did not have to compete with foreigners at home or abroad could safely do so.

The new situation, at first, confounded the economic assumptions of both liberal Keynesians and supply-side conservatives. Aggregate demand was increasing rapidly in the U.S. economy, the classic Keynesian formula for expanding output and employment. Yet the formula didn't work because America's producers were losing market shares in their own marketplace. The demand was being satisfied, more and more, by output elsewhere. In a fashion, the supply side was being developed, just as the conservative theory had promised, but the new productive capacity was being built up in Taiwan and West Germany and Japan, not the U.S.A.[27]

"We are decimating our export industries," Anthony Solomon, president of the New York Fed, lamented. "Volcker and I are extremely concerned about the long-term effects of the strong dollar. But we can't do anything about it."

While the hardening dollar helped hold down domestic prices and wages, Solomon could see the longer-term damage to America's manufacturing base. Once an auto company has moved its transmission factory from New Jersey to Brazil, it would not soon move it back again. Once a machine-tool plant in Cincinnati has been closed and dismantled, it would be very expensive to reopen it. In the mercantilist contests among nations, once market shares were lost in international trade, it took a long time to win them back.

"If fiscal policy were not so lax," Solomon complained, "we would have more options to take the dollar into account. As it is, we can't do anything about the dollar, even though it concerns us. I'm being very blunt. Usually, we say that we take a number of things into consideration, including the dollar, but the truth is—our hands are tied."

The Federal Reserve—knowing the damage it was causing—nevertheless allowed the dollar to escalate steadily in value because to do otherwise might have meant the Fed would lose the "game of chicken" with fiscal policy. To curb the dollar's appreciation, the Fed could simply moderate its hard-money policy—back off the high interest rates so that foreign currencies would come into balanced value with America's. That adjustment of monetary policy would have saved U.S. jobs, American market shares, the productive base in industry and agriculture. But the Fed had convinced itself that backing off would mean it was also yielding to the federal budget deficits. In time, this would prove to be a very debatable choice, for it allowed the dollar's devastation to spread and deepen.

But there was never any real debate on the issue. Inside the Fed, Volcker and Solomon, from time to time, brought up the dollar at FOMC meetings and lamented the destruction. But neither of them proposed to do anything about it. The Federal Open Market Committee was locked into Volcker's strategy of resistance. Rightly or wrongly, its members told themselves that the strong dollar was a regrettable but unavoidable side effect of the collision between monetary policy and fiscal policy. The side effect, however, was becoming a central force in American economic life—one of the most devastating new conditions imposed by the 1980s.

The central force driving the dollar upward was the Federal Reserve's determination to keep U.S. interest rates abnormally high—higher than competing interest rates in foreign financial markets. The Federal Reserve held its Discount rate at 8.5 percent while West Germany's Discount was declining to only 4 percent and Japan's to 5 percent. Other interest rates offered for both short-term and long-term investments followed the same pattern. U.S. financial assets paid more and capital inevitably sought out the highest return, wherever it was to be found.

As long as the Fed maintained such a wide differential, the financial wealth of the world would naturally migrate toward the United States, where investments in dollar-denominated assets provided the most attractive interest rates. To moderate this flow, the Fed would have to bring down interest rates and pump up the world's supply of dollars—the very thing it was unwilling to do.

The Federal Reserve can't solve all the world's problems [Lyle Gramley insisted]. The manufacturing sector has become much less competitive. What is needed is a depreciation in the value of the dollar. The way to accomplish that is to reduce the federal budget deficit. I don't think monetary policy can do anything constructively about that. If we tried to bring the dollar down with a highly expansive monetary policy, that would mean destructive consequences.

The heavyweights of American industry were mobilized for political action. Organized labor was already out front on the trade issue, led by the United Auto Workers, aggressively lobbying Congress for legislation to protect the embattled American worker from unfair foreign competition. But corporate executives preferred a more discreet approach. They called on their friends in the Reagan Administration.

"Everyone of us on the business side has seen our companies affected by the distorted currency relationship," Lee L. Morgan, CEO of Caterpillar Tractor, wrote to Treasury Secretary Donald Regan and other Cabinet officers. "And each of us is committed to working with you and your government colleagues to develop a solid understanding of the problem and a good dialogue which can ultimately, I hope, lead to a solution."

When Morgan called at the White House, he was accompanied by some notable corporate names—Borg-Warner, Burroughs, Ford, Cincinnati Milacron, TRW, all members of the Business Roundtable's export committee. What they wanted, Morgan explained, was for the President to impose an emergency surtax on Japanese imports. That would help offset the 35 to 40 percent price disadvantage American companies now suffered because of the lopsided dollar-yen relationship. Their first meeting with Administration officials was held in October 1982, followed by others. The secretaries of State, Treasury and Commerce and other policy makers listened with apparent sympathy, but the businessmen got nowhere.

The Reagan Administration's true feelings were summarized in a Treasury-CEA analysis of the Business Roundtable's complaints against Japan. The paper dismissed the argument that the yen was more undervalued than other foreign currencies. It recommended against any interventions in exchange markets to bring down the dollar. It flatly opposed the idea of an import tax on Japanese products.

The policy recommendations of the paper come out in the right place, OMB economist Lawrence Kudlow reported to his boss. "The protectionist suggestions by various business groups (Ford, Caterpillar Tractor, NAM, Japan-U.S. Business Conference) have been rejected."[28]

The corporations next took their grievances to Congress and, allied with labor unions, they lobbied for new trade legislation to curb imports, particularly from the Japanese. A few industrialists like Iacocca and Robert O. Anderson of the Atlantic Richfield oil company also blamed the Federal Reserve for the dollar's damage. But, given the political sequestration of monetary policy, the central bank was virtually free of blame. The favorite political target, instead, became the Japanese, accused of exploiting American markets while unfairly closing their own to U.S. products.

The exploitation was a two-way street, however. Even Lee Iacocca, though vociferous in his "Japan bashing," acknowledged that an odd and unhealthy symbiosis existed between the two nations. The hardworking Japanese spent less of their incomes on themselves and saved much more than Americans—a surplus of capital that they then lent back to the United States. In the marketing of U.S. government debt, Japan had eclipsed Saudi Arabia as America's most important creditor. As Iacocca pointed out:

> We've been exploiting Japanese initiative and hard work and cheaper wages for a long time. . . . Think about it: The Japanese have been working six days a week, so we can spend *our* Saturdays riding our Honda motorcycles or our Yamaha snowmobiles through the fields. . . . And we have to factor this in: A big part of the Japanese money made in America stays in America—about 77 percent of it in T-bills and other paper that helps finance our crazy budget deficits. . . . So now we're hooked on Japanese *money* as well as TV sets.

In the public debate, the Administration characterized the issue as a choice between "free trade" and "protectionism." It invoked its conservative laissez-faire principles and insisted that governments should not interfere in the free markets that determined the dollar's international value. The Administration, however, was not just blindly following ideology, as some critics assumed. Internally, the Reagan advisers appreciated the political dividends that might be derived from a strong-dollar policy. The strategy involved an implicit decision that some elements of the American economy—industrial labor and manufacturing, agriculture and other commodities—would have to lose so that other economic interests would win.

Martin Feldstein, a Harvard economist who was chairman of the President's Council of Economic Advisers from 1982 to the spring of 1984, described the trade-offs most candidly in a memorandum for the Cabinet:

> Would it be desirable to have a lower exchange value of the dollar? A weaker dollar would raise exports and reduce the substitution of imports for domestically produced goods. As such, it would be welcomed by those U.S. industries that are now being hurt by the strength of the dollar.

But a weaker dollar and smaller trade deficit would also mean less capital inflow from the rest of the world and therefore a lower level of domestic investment in plant and equipment and in housing. The rise in the dollar is a safety valve that reduces pressure on domestic interest rates; the increase in the trade deficit allows the extra demand generated by the budget deficit to spill overseas instead of crowding out domestic investment.

The question of whether it would be desirable to have a lower-valued dollar is equivalent to asking whether it is better to allow the temporary increase in the budget deficit to reduce domestic investment and interest-sensitive consumer spending or to reduce the production of goods for export and of goods that compete with imports from abroad. The answer to this question is clear in principle: it is better to reduce exports and increase imports.

No one in American political life would have ever acknowledged such a choice in public. It sounded unpatriotic. Besides, the Reagan Administration, having enunciated how supply-side doctrine would restore America's economic hegemony, could not very well admit that the actual consequences of government policy were to depress U.S. manufacturing and agriculture while encouraging consumers to buy foreign-made products. The Administration's de facto policy would be good for many sectors—for home-computer sales and housing, for the construction of high-rise office buildings and retailing, for all the thriving service-sector businesses that did not have to compete for sales with foreign rivals. It would be disastrous for farm exports, for heavy industry, for any enterprise whose market was not protected by national boundaries.

The fall in exports and the rise in imports that result from the stronger dollar are clearly causing unemployment and threatening individual firms with possible bankruptcy [the CEA chairman acknowledged]. Perhaps, these adverse effects are more severe than those that would result from an equal decrease in the demand for plant and equipment, housing and other interest-sensitive goods. . . . But at present the burden of proof lies with those who would claim that the industries involved in international trade are more vulnerable. . . .

Feldstein was sanguine about the potential damage, partly because he was confident that the Administration would deliver on its announced intention to reduce the budget deficits. When that occurred, he explained, real interest rates would decline and the pressures driving the dollar upward would dissipate. His confidence was ill-founded. When Martin Feldstein left government and returned to his post at

Harvard, the federal deficit was heading to a new peacetime record, $213 billion.

But the CEA chairman offered another, more basic argument in defense of the strong dollar. It preserved low inflation. The import competition suppressed domestic prices and wages, and, Feldstein warned, if the Federal Reserve were to ease its control of money and bring down the dollar, its victory over inflation would be compromised. Licking inflation was one of the President's proudest accomplishments, a benefit that seemed tangible to every American consumer, and no one in the White House wished to sacrifice it.

"The basic fact is that the value of the dollar can be changed only by modifying the goals for our domestic economy," Feldstein advised. "A lower value of the dollar requires an expansion of the money supply that increases the rate of inflation."[29]

For the short run, it was an astute political strategy for the Reagan Administration to embrace. Despite the long-term economic damage that would be inflicted on America's industrial base, the immediate benefits promised to please a large swath of the American electorate —an outcome sure to enhance Ronald Reagan's re-election campaign in 1984. The President, whether he appreciated it or not, was pursuing a program designed to foster immediate gratification for a maximum number of electoral interests—a high-consumption, low-savings policy that would please both individual voters and economic interests. In another time, were Democrats in power, doing the same thing, Republicans would likely have denounced it as a cynical strategy of "buy now, pay later." Ultimately, the nation would pay an enormous price for the self-indulgence arranged by the government.

But the political strategy, deliberate or otherwise, responded to new realities in the American economy. Manufacturing might still be thought of as the core of America's economic strength, but it was not the dominant force it had once been, any more than farming. Manufacturing employment represented less than a quarter of the whole. Most Americans did not make things for a living. Most Americans sold intangible services, from school-teaching to computer programming, from trashmen to shopkeepers to lawyers and doctors. In relative terms, they would be winners.

The captains of heavy industry, the traditional locus of power within the Republican Party since the days of Lincoln, counted for less too. When the big corporate names from manufacturing lobbied the Republican White House, their failure to get results demonstrated how much their own political influence had declined. Manufacturers of steel, autos, textiles, machine tools and other basic goods were now outclassed in both economic girth and potential electoral strength. As an auto-company lobbyist explained:

> We still think of manufacturing as the "big mule" in politics, but it's not true. The financial sector, the retailing sector, the service sector, are all so much bigger. The strong dollar was good for them and it was good for consumers. It kept prices down and guaranteed cheap goods, while the tax cuts and deficits meant there was plenty of money to spend. It was anti-manufacturing, anti-labor—but it was pro-consumption, pro-services.

What was bad for Chrysler and independent oil drillers and Midwestern farmers was good for Sears, Roebuck and Toyota dealers, Citibank and McDonald's and many others. An approximate sense of who the winners were was conveyed by a sample list of the domestic service sectors that benefited from cheaper prices on manufactured products and commodities, yet were themselves largely exempt from wage-price competition with foreign rivals. These included health services, banking and finance, insurance, real estate, retailing, hotels and restaurants, travel and transport, legal and technical professions, education, the media and communications.

Like housing construction, these service sectors mainly competed in domestic markets, where they did not have to confront foreign competitors and the price disadvantage generated by the lopsided dollar. As a result, these enterprises could continue to increase profits by raising their own prices (and their employees' wages too) and most of them did. While wheat and oil and auto prices sagged, the price index for services continued to advance smartly—up by more than 5 percent in 1983. General inflation and its benefits were gone, but not for everyone.

In terms of its own constituencies, the Republican Party had much to gain from the strong-dollar strategy and little at risk. The "white collar" professional-managerial ranks, the core of Republican voters, would enjoy a continuing rise in their incomes under this scheme, from Main Street retailers to Wall Street stockbrokers. "Blue collar" union members would suffer, but they were overwhelmingly Democratic voters anyway. Farmers, the staunchest of Republicans, could be counted on to vote Republican, regardless.

One other important industrial sector was a major winner under the Reagan-Volcker "strong dollar" recovery strategy—the defense industry. The production of armaments was an important special case, a manufacturing sector that did not suffer from the strong dollar because it was shielded from international competition. The U.S. government simply did not buy very many of its weapons from foreigners. The defense companies and their allied support industries, thus, enjoyed two special advantages: the massive budget increases for defense spending expanded their market enormously and, meanwhile, arms manufacturers benefited from cheaper labor, as wages for skilled industrial workers were depressed generally by the slack employment.

Lee Iacocca of Chrysler, futilely campaigning for assistance to other manufacturing industries, tried to argue that "national defense" involved more than simply buying a strong military.

> The fact is, without a strong industrial base, we can kiss our national security goodbye [Iacocca warned]. We can also kiss goodbye to the majority of this country's high value-added jobs. It was the middle class that made this country great in the first place. Take away America's $8-to-$12-an-hour industrial jobs and you undercut the country. If we don't watch out, I'm afraid we're going to find ourselves armed to the teeth—and with nothing left to defend but drive-in banks, video arcades and McDonald's hamburger stands.

Iacocca's evocative warnings did not persuade. Most Americans seemed to be doing fine or at least doing a lot better. They were enjoying the restored prosperity and buying things again at stable prices, not much concerned about where the things were made. Certainly, the high officials of the Reagan Administration did not intend to tamper with the recovery, now that it was rolling forward so energetically. Their largest worry, it seemed, was whether the Federal Reserve might decide—independently, for its own reasons—to spoil things.

By late November 1983, kibitzing voices were heard again. The President's spokesman, Larry Speakes, pointedly observed to the White House press that the Federal Reserve ought not to let the money supply grow too slowly. The Treasury Secretary worried aloud that the Fed might be getting ready to tighten credit again, given the robust expansion of recent quarters.

"I know they have to be restrictive," Donald Regan said. "My concern is that they not overdo it."

Milton Friedman went further. The Fed had already overdone it, he said. The growth in M-1 had been nearly flat from July to October and, therefore, Friedman predicted, there would be an election-year recession. White House political advisers were not sure they should rely on the monetarist's analysis, but Friedman's bold forecast certainly made them more nervous.

In Congress, Representative Jack Kemp and forty-nine other members sent a letter of protest to the President, charging that Paul Volcker was indeed "playing chicken" with the Reagan recovery and, by implication, with the President's re-election.

"Monetary policy is deliberately being kept unnecessarily tight and the economic expansion held hostage to a tax increase," Kemp and the other Republicans complained. "Mr. Volcker would offer a quid pro quo of monetary ease and lower interest rates in return for a fiscal policy of higher taxes which is more to his liking."[30]

Volcker denied this, of course, but the Federal Reserve chairman had been lobbying on Capitol Hill, urging the legislators to take significant action on the deficits. He warned them that if the deficits were not promptly reduced, interest rates might go even higher. On October 26, Volcker met privately with members of the Senate Finance Committee and urged them to consider various approaches to a major tax increase. Political columnists Rowland Evans and Robert Novak reported: "Finance members left the meeting with this message: if they wanted Volcker's Fed to ease money, they had better get cracking with tax increases."[31]

Shortly afterward, the Finance chairman, Senator Robert Dole of Kansas, did introduce such a measure, a package of revenue increases that would raise $55 billion. President Reagan scotched the idea by repeating what he had said many times before—he would veto any tax-increase legislation that landed on his desk. The "game of chicken" continued between fiscal policy and monetary policy and, so far, neither side had blinked.

The Reagan Administration misunderstood the Fed's predicament, however. The critics looked at M-1 and complained that monetary policy was too tight. At the Federal Reserve, the policy makers looked at the real economy and worried that they had been too loose. By its own standard, the Fed was not being stingy, but too generous.

At the outset, Volcker had vowed to restrain the recovery, to keep it from reaching a runaway boom. But he was behind. At the beginning of 1983, the Federal Open Market Committee had agreed that real economic growth should be held to a modest 3.5 to 4.5 percent, from the last quarter of 1982 to the last quarter of 1983. Instead, the real growth for the year was coming in at 6.3 percent—a much more robust expansion than Volcker had intended.

Despite the Administration's frequent carping, the Federal Reserve appeared to be providing exactly what the White House had asked for —an accommodative money policy. Cynical Democrats around Washington began to wonder if there had, in fact, been a "deal" between the two. Paul Volcker is reappointed. The economy booms. And Ronald Reagan's popularity is restored, just in time for 1984.

The political context was more subtle than these conspiracy theories suggested. The Federal Reserve chairman was, no doubt, inhibited by the surrounding political expectations. He had taken the country (and the Reagan Administration) through a long and punishing recession. Now that the nation was enjoying its recovery, Volcker intended to restrain—but there were limits on how far he dared go.

"There was no way Volcker could have managed a tighter monetary policy and gotten away with it," budget director David Stockman observed. "The Administration would have been all over him. They did a lot of Fed bashing as it was."

Whatever influence the White House "Fed bashing" may have had on Volcker, he clearly had underestimated the strength of the recovery —and the economy's ability to charge forward, despite the high real interest rates. Volcker's monetary policy, in fact, seemed to pose an anomaly: if one looked at the M-1 or interest rates, the money policy looked very tight, extraordinarily tight. But if one looked at the real growth of the economy, the monetary policy looked easy.

The explanation was clear to Fed officials—money's meaning was changing again (and once again leading Milton Friedman into error). After nearly two years of abnormal decline, money's velocity was beginning to accelerate again—returning to its normal trend line. That meant the swollen money supply that the Fed had already pumped into the economy earlier would now translate into greater economic activity—as M-1 turned over faster in different transactions. Maybe, the Fed thought, it was time to take corrective action.

When the Federal Open Market Committee met December 19, some members worried that the economy in 1984 was going to outrun their expectations again, given its momentum and the stimulative fiscal policy. "In particular, it was suggested that the currently high level of confidence among businessmen and large cash flows to business firms favored relatively rapid expansion in business fixed investment," the FOMC minutes reported.

Others were less sanguine, however. They worried that an increase in interest rates now could quickly depress interest-sensitive sectors like housing and send the dollar still higher in foreign-exchange markets, further damaging manufacturing.

One member, Preston Martin, sounded a stronger warning. The economy looked robust at the moment, Martin acknowledged, but business activity and consumer spending would soon be moderating. The FOMC should be thinking about relaxing interest rates, not raising them.

"To me," Martin said, "the pressures of inflation weren't there. The cost push from wages and salaries was very difficult to find anywhere. It seemed to me the probability was now on the other side—that the economy would be slowing down and it might need a little help on interest rates."

Martin's senior colleagues at the Fed discounted the vice chairman. They knew Preston Martin was close to the Californians in the Reagan White House and a favorite of the supply siders. They assumed Martin's economic analysis was heavily influenced by the Administration's natural desire to insure a roaring economy for the President's re-election campaign. The other committee members listened politely as Martin reviewed the weakness in the savings and loan industry and described the potential risks, but they were not impressed.

Because the committee members were themselves divided on the economic outlook, they chose a cautious middle course. The December directive called for "maintaining at least the existing degree of restraint." But it allowed for "the possibility of a slight increase in such restraint, depending on developments. . . ."

Even this modest step bothered Preston Martin, who cast his first dissent as a Federal Reserve governor. Any tightening of money, any increase in interest rates, Martin warned, "would present a threat to the sustainability of the economic expansion. Needed business investment would be more expensive, international debt servicing more burdensome, and interest-sensitive housing more vulnerable." [32]

The majority was worried about the opposite. The Reagan recovery was barely one year old and booming beyond expectations. The Federal Reserve governors figured they were approaching the hard part—the moment when they would have to decide how much prosperity is too much.

──── 17 ────

"MORNING AGAIN IN AMERICA"

When Paul Volcker appeared before the Senate Banking Committee in early February 1984, Senator William Proxmire reminded him, in a friendly way, of the Fed's political history.

"Chairman Volcker," the senator said, "some have argued that the Federal Reserve has historically tried to help the incumbent in the White House during a presidential election year by easing monetary policy. There's one conspicuous exception to that. In October 1979, the new chairman of the Federal Reserve Board instituted a policy of slowing down the rate of increase in the supply of money and I don't think anybody could argue that Paul Volcker was a big help to Jimmy Carter in 1980. . . .

"Do you have an understanding with the Administration," Proxmire asked, "explicit or tacit, that you will follow an accommodative policy in 1984?"

"No, sir," the chairman answered.

"Will you agree to report to this committee and to the House Banking Committee any instances of the Administration bringing pressure on the Federal Reserve to relax its policies?"

Volcker balked. He was in regular communication with Administration officials and properly so, the Fed chairman explained, but he did not interpret those conversations as political pressure.

"Well, Chairman Volcker, you obviously weren't born yesterday," the senator said. "I think you know political pressure when you see it."

"That's right," Volcker said. "That's why I make a distinction. . . . "

Proxmire, the ranking Democrat, was simply inviting the Federal Reserve chairman to come to the Democratic Party for assistance if the Republicans in the White House began to play rough. Most of all, Democrats wanted Volcker to do no more for Ronald Reagan's political fortunes than he had done for Jimmy Carter's.

"Now I know you don't think in political terms and you shouldn't," Proxmire told Volcker at another hearing. "But the fact is that this is an election year and I hope you will treat President Ronald Reagan with the same meticulous disregard for political consequences [with which] you treated President Carter. When Vince Lombardi was coach of the Green Bay Packers, a reporter asked one of the players whether Lombardi showed any unfairness in the treatment of players. The player told the reporter, 'Listen, Coach Lombardi treats us all the same—like dogs.' "[1]

Proxmire's allusion to football was revealing in itself. The Federal Reserve chairman was cast as the coach. Elected politicians were merely players on the team. In fact, the situation sometimes resembled that relationship. The Federal Reserve chairman could not impose his will, but Paul Volcker regularly instructed Congress and the President on how he thought they should alter their economic policies. When politicians tried to do the same to the Federal Reserve, they were scolded in the press for trespassing on the Fed's authority. Players were not supposed to criticize the coach, particularly this coach.

"The political stock of the Federal Reserve right now is very high," Frank Morris of the Boston Fed observed. "The country is breathing a great sigh of relief that we've got inflation behind us and the economy is going again. I don't think this is the proper political season to be knocking the Federal Reserve."

Most Democrats appeared to agree. Except for a few dedicated critics, Democrats were notably quiet about the Federal Reserve's extraordinary strategy for restraining the recovery and preventing full employment. Perhaps, in their innermost thoughts, some wished the Fed to succeed. A sterner monetary policy, after all, would hurt the Republicans in '84, just as it hurt the Democrats back in '80.

Many Republicans, on the other hand, thought that Volcker was already centrally engaged in the politics of 1984—playing his own rough game to achieve his own purpose. By keeping interest rates high, they suspected, the Fed intended to force the President and Congress to come to terms on major deficit reductions. That would require both spending cuts and tax increases in an election year, neither of which would be helpful to the incumbent President. Senator John Heinz of Pennsylvania confronted Volcker with the suspicions.

"You've been in Washington long enough to know that when it comes to getting Congress to bite the tough bullet—in this case, spending—and when it comes to getting the President to bite a tough issue for him—taxes—there's going to have to be a critical reason for the two aforementioned players to do it," Heinz told Volcker. "And you're the only person by following a restrictive, noninflationary monetary policy who can create that crisis."

"It is not our job to artificially provoke a crisis," Volcker protested. "We are not going to go out there and conduct a tight-money policy for the sake of trying to bring leverage on the Congress or on the Administration."[2]

Volcker's repeated complaints about deficits succeeded, however, in diverting the normal political debate, shifting the locus of blame away from monetary policy and toward fiscal policy. "You are playing a kind of game of Russian roulette," Volcker warned the senators, vaguely allowing that the game might end in another recession. When the stock market heard his words, it dropped 24 points.

"A masterful job of redefinition has been performed by the Fed," E. F. Hutton told its clients. "It has essentially removed monetary policy from congressional debate. . . . Quite remarkably, high interest rates—which are correctly seen as a threat to this expansion's long-term viability—have come to be associated with deficits, not with a tightfisted Fed."[3]

A guerrilla band of supply-side Republicans tried to reverse the focus by mounting a frontal attack on the Fed. Congressman Jack Kemp and like-minded conservative reformers accused Volcker of preparing to clamp down again on credit, just as the recovery appeared to be moderating, and thus risking yet another recession induced by monetary policy.[4]

Volcker mostly ignored Kemp's frequent complaints, but privately the chairman worried about the potential for larger political problems. The Fed was always more vulnerable when the political attacks came from the right. The conservative party was the natural reservoir of support for the central bank and "sound money." Many traditional Republican conservatives kept their distance from the aggressive young supply siders like Kemp, but if the New York congressman gathered enough Republican supporters for reforming the Fed, they could make common cause with liberal Democrats and perhaps actually do something.

Volcker suspected, moreover, that Jack Kemp was playing point man for the political managers in the White House. The congressman could say things about the Fed that the White House did not wish to say directly itself. The chairman worried aloud to associates that the Fed was being set up—in case anything went wrong with the economy and the President's campaign.

The White House did, indeed, share Kemp's nervousness about the recovery and the Federal Reserve, but it was not sure what to do about it. In early January, a few weeks before the congressman's attack, Treasury Secretary Donald Regan wrote an unusual memorandum for the President, summarizing anxieties expressed by the Cabinet Council on Economic Affairs: "All members of the Cabinet Council agree that a sustained period of near zero growth in the money supply poses the strong threat of a recession sometime in 1984 and is clearly undesirable. However, the ambiguity of Federal Reserve policy intentions and the accuracy of the policy indicators create some uncertainty regarding the actual course of monetary policy." Regan promised to keep the President posted, as the situation became clearer.[5]

Representative Kemp, meanwhile, continued what the Democrats had abandoned—a legislative campaign to reform the Fed and reduce its political independence. "We need not sit by helplessly, awaiting a third economic recession engineered by the Fed in four years," Kemp complained. "Congress is constitutionally authorized to coin money and regulate its value. The American people can act through Congress to bring monetary policy into line with the Administration's growth-oriented fiscal policies by passing reform legislation."[6]

Dozens of Republicans, mostly younger members who admired Kemp's style and ideas, signed up as cosponsors for his measure to change the Federal Reserve. Among other things, the Kemp bill would make the Secretary of the Treasury a member of the Federal Open Market Committee—restoring the original arrangement of 1913 that gave the Chief Executive direct access to the central bank's deliberations and some influence over its decisions. The Republican reform legislation, though it never advanced, would be brandished from time to time like a threatening sword throughout the campaign season.

The Democratic Party, meanwhile, came to the Federal Reserve's defense. When White House officials planted nasty gibes at Volcker in the press, leading members of the opposition party answered them. Senator Lloyd Bentsen of Texas, the chairman of the Senate Democratic Campaign Committee for the 1984 elections, warned: "I cannot help but reflect on the possibility that the Administration is trying to set up the Fed chairman as a scapegoat in case the economic recovery goes sour between now and the first Tuesday in November." The Fed was doing a good job, the senator declared, and ought to be left alone.

Any problems that developed in the economy would be blamed on the President and the huge federal deficits that flowed from Reagan tax cuts in 1981 (tax cuts that, incidentally, Bentsen and most Democratic senators had voted for).[7]

For the 1984 campaign, the historic positions of the two dominant political parties were reversed. The Democratic Party felt trapped by its own past, still tarnished by the inflationary anxieties experienced under Jimmy Carter, still tagged as the reckless "big spenders." Democratic leaders decided they must convince the public of their newly developed sense of responsibility and so they campaigned for fiscal discipline. Invoking the party's old liberal agenda—full employment, low interest rates, rapid economic growth, aggressive federal management of prosperity—might simply remind voters of the party's old self.[8]

The President's party, meanwhile, had effectively abandoned the old Republican orthodoxy that the Democrats were now attempting to mimic. Republicans, it was true, remained steadfast in their rhetorical loyalty to the idea of a balanced federal budget and fiscal order. In actual performance, however, the conservative party had embraced the opposite—an economy driven by increased federal spending and increased debt, the most stimulative fiscal policy ever attempted in peacetime. The old Republican complaint—that deficit spending ultimately led to ruinous inflation—was conveniently discarded in the presence of Republican deficits.

The role reversal in the two political parties' traditional philosophies was deeper than election-year posturing. Aside from the obvious hypocrisies, it at least suggested that both parties were breaking free of their traditional moorings and, for better or worse, casting about for new sets of beliefs. In terms of managing the economy, what did the Republican Party now stand for? Or the Democrats? It was no longer so easy to summarize either one.

At the very least, new boundaries were being defined for the central debate of American politics: the government's management of the economy through taxes and spending and federal deficits. If a conservative regime could accept $200 billion deficits with equanimity, what would be the new standard for imprudent management in the future —deficits of $300 or $400 billion? Certainly, neither party was soon going to seriously pursue the old Republican objective of balanced budgets. The twisted political alignments of 1984 rested on this paradox: the old "liberal" approach to political management of the economy, denounced as reckless and inflationary, supposedly discredited by two decades of failed promises, seemed to be working wonderfully well for the Republican Party.

Republicans, in fact, now held the symbolic high ground that the Democratic Party had once owned in national politics—the party of growth and prosperity. Through the campaign, the President would be the confident apostle of optimism and limitless opportunity, while the Democratic opposition assumed the role of public scold. The Democratic Party invoked "fairness" as its theme, but it muted the old liberal standards. This shift in emphasis was not entirely new. The Democrats had been shifting rightward in their economic perspective for some years, exemplified by the financial deregulation legislation of 1980. By 1984, instead of attacking the high interest rates, Democrats came to the defense of the Federal Reserve. Partisan stalemate was once again turned to the Fed's advantage.

That fall voters asked a reasonable question—what was so bad about the huge deficits if the economy was flourishing?—and the Democrats never provided a convincing answer. To do so, they would have had to explain the Federal Reserve's "game of chicken" and the consequences of high interest rates. Instead, their presidential nominee, the former Vice President, Walter Mondale, would bravely propose a painful remedy—a major tax increase and substantial budget reductions to restore fiscal order to Washington. For his part, President Reagan bravely proposed an endless vista of "good times" all across America.

Preston Martin, the vice chairman of the Federal Reserve Board and the only Reagan appointee, did not act like a central banker. He was a gregarious western businessman, hearty and direct in manner, a man who sprinkled his conversation with expressions like "hell's bells" and "my goodness." Central bankers, Martin once joked, "are expected to look and act as if they are moving from one funeral to the next."[9] Preston Martin acted as though he was on his way to a family wedding.

Given his personal style, it was easy for Preston Martin's colleagues at the Fed to underestimate him, though the vice chairman had ample practical experience in finance. He had been a housing developer and financier himself. He had chaired the Federal Home Loan Bank Board, which regulated the savings and loan industry. In Los Angeles, Martin had developed his own successful mortgage insurance company, which he had sold to Sears, Roebuck. As chairman of Sears's Seraco Enterprises, Martin was instrumental in making Sears a major player in financial services, through purchase of the Dean Witter Reynolds brokerage.

Still, as he was acutely aware, he did not speak the language of the System. "I became quite a bore," Martin acknowledged. "I reminded them of the thrifts, of small business, of housing. I could see the ears turn off around the table when I made my little speech. But I made it anyway."

It wasn't merely style. Martin saw things differently, and in the opening months of 1984, his perspective was strikingly at odds with the economic analysis of Volcker and other senior governors. They saw the economy roaring forward too fast. Martin saw it slowing down. They thought the Fed should assert some pressure with higher interest rates, lest things get out of control. Martin thought the economic recovery would soon need help and the Fed ought to be thinking about lowering interest rates, not raising them.

A staff officer of the Federal Open Market Committee observed:

Martin doesn't have much influence. He always has to say something. His remarks will always be reflecting what is generally understood to be the Administration's position. Or he will give an update on the thrifts and the housing industry, but it's not particularly sophisticated. His mind operates on the level of platitudes, and he seems not to understand that a good analysis and argument can change minds.

"He speaks his piece," said Charles Partee. "He doesn't seem to me to be trying to bring a group of people with him. He just doesn't structure his argument in a way that you could capture votes by what he's saying. He's usually isolated."

The informal knowledge that Preston Martin wished to succeed Paul Volcker as Federal Reserve chairman did not enhance his influence around the boardroom table. When the vice chairman argued for an easier monetary policy, others inferred that he was simply ingratiating himself with the Reagan White House at Volcker's expense. "It's hard to figure what he's doing and why," an aide to Volcker said. "I can see some consistency in his arguing for an easier policy, but it's not in his own interest to take issue with this particular chairman. Why do you want to pick a fight with Godzilla?"

Alone and discounted by his colleagues, Preston Martin persisted nonetheless in making the case for relaxing monetary policy. The economy, it was true, had accelerated in the first quarter of 1984, surprising everyone with the rapid expansion. Real GNP appeared to be growing at 6 to 7 percent, perhaps even faster. But Martin's business soundings convinced him that sales and production would actually be tapering off in the weeks ahead. Another increase in interest rates at this point could be harmful.

The moment of truth arrived at the March 26 meeting of the Federal Open Market Committee. On its face, it sounded like another dreary argument among economists over competing economic forecasts, but the stakes this time were much more fateful. In direct terms, the Federal Reserve governors were arguing over how much of the booming prosperity they were going to permit Americans to enjoy. The President's generous campaign promises notwithstanding, the central bank would decide the question for itself. Was it time, in William McChesney Martin's celebrated phrase, to take away the punch bowl, now that the party was going good? It was. In a deeper sense, the Fed's governors were implicitly deciding a question of political power too. Did the Federal Reserve claim the authority to cut against all the obvious public aspirations for the unfolding prosperity? It did. And would it have the nerve? It would.

Preston Martin tried to make the case for keeping the robust expansion as vigorous as possible. His own reading of business conditions told him that the boom was about to subside anyway on its own. And there was virtually no sign anywhere that price inflation was about to resume. Why should the Fed step in and spoil things?

I relied on the business data from the Federal Reserve Bank directors a bit more than some of my colleagues [Martin explained]. These directors are people from business who are not looking back; they're looking forward. Their bonuses depend on whether those retail sales goals are realized. The forward indicators looked like this huge surge was calming down and it was going to be a more normal recovery. Inventories had come into line with sales. Wages were not threatening—this was the year of the labor give backs. The boom was coming down. Things really were under control. So I concluded that inflation's not around the corner and we could afford not to tighten.

Within the Board of Governors, Martin's plea was almost bound to fail. Arguing the opposite case in the strongest terms was the second most influential member of the board, Lyle Gramley. "The economy is just growing too fast," Gramley grumbled to associates, "and we let it happen." The present growth rate would lead to trouble down the road. The Fed must ignore the risks of political attack and assert its restraint now. Gramley's argument was aimed not at Preston Martin but at Paul Volcker.

"Lyle Gramley is kind of the conscience of the Fed right now," David Jones, the Fed watcher at Aubrey G. Lanston, explained. "Volcker is behind on where he should be in tightening. Gramley feels the same way. He's very objective and he's usually right." [10]

Gramley himself explained why he took a stern position: "If people say I'm a hawk, there is one reason for it—it's an acute awareness that all of these gains can be lost. All of these costs could be for naught, if we don't keep control of inflation." Gramley was a "System man" and he remembered the 1970s when the Federal Reserve endured its most scornful criticism.

For Gramley and like-minded governors, the choice could no longer be avoided. The FOMC had declined to alter credit conditions at its January meeting, and all the economic news since then told them they had grossly underestimated the force of the expansion. In fact, the economic news was spectacular.

Housing starts jumped in February to an annual rate of 2.2 million units, the strongest construction boom since 1978. Early in the month, auto sales were up 33 percent over the year before. The Commerce Department's survey of businesses reported spending on new plants and equipment would increase in 1984 by a bullish 9.4 percent—then the estimate was revised upward to 13.6 percent. Unemployment was declining steadily, from 10 percent the summer before to 7.8 percent in March.

Paul Volcker worried publicly about the "very strong" economy and whether "bottlenecks" might develop in production and labor that could drive prices upward. "I don't think it is in our interest to see it expand at a maximum rate for two or three quarters," Volcker said, "if it is going to last only two or three quarters." [11]

The bond market was also distressed by the startlingly good news from the buoyant economy. Beginning in early February, long-term interest rates had begun to creep upward and the Fed had allowed market pressures to edge short-term rates higher too. Perhaps, the policy makers thought, this was the beginning of the long-predicted "crowding out"—a collision in credit markets between the federal government's borrowing and the demand for loans from business and consumers.

Stable prices had been secured for more than a year and a half, yet the bond investors were still skeptical. Would the Fed accommodate or would it stand fast? The long-term investors still claimed to be worried that resurgent price inflation was imminent. By late March, the rate on twenty-year Treasury bonds had risen 80 basis points, to above 12 percent.

Wall Street cynics thought this was the point where the Fed might cave in—retreat before the normal political pressures of an election year and yield to faster economic growth. But others took Volcker at his word. David Jones predicted: "The Fed will be tougher than anyone thinks." E. F. Hutton assured its clients: "The Fed will play brakeman for this expansion." [12]

The Federal Reserve chairman had already received opposite instructions from the President. On February 15, Volcker was summoned to the Oval Office for another session intended to put him on notice. Like his earlier meetings with Ronald Reagan, this one was mostly generalities about money and economic growth and inflation. At one point, Volcker delivered one of his rambling meditations on the economy that was so contorted that afterward the President asked Donald Regan and James Baker what the man had said. Neither of them could say.

The White House really delivered its intended message, afterward, in public, by pointedly alerting the press. The President, reporters were told, had asked Volcker to insure that monetary policy would not interrupt healthy economic growth in 1984. "All I am asking . . . in monetary policy is that we have an increase that is commensurate with that growth that can continue the recovery without returning us to inflation," the President told reporters.

Anonymous White House aides put it somewhat more sharply: the Fed must not tighten. Volcker was told, in effect, "We don't care if you err on the top side of the targets, but we do care if you err on the low side," one senior official explained to *The Wall Street Journal*. Columnists Evans and Novak described the White House warning in the most melodramatic terms: "Reagan won't send the Marines down Constitution Avenue to the Federal Reserve, but he seems determined to prevent the central bank from triggering another recession to calm inflationary nightmares of the creditor class."

A week later at a press conference, the President stated his objective more coherently: "I think the Federal Reserve is now on a path of a money-supply increase that is consistent with a sound recovery without inflation. To go one way in excess, they could cause more inflation and I don't think they are planning that. They could go the other way, tighten the strings too much and interfere with the recovery, and I don't think they're going to do that."

Even these mild efforts to influence the Fed were scolded by the press. "The White House is stalking the Federal Board again," a Washington *Post* editorial complained, "in the kind of maneuver that usually turns out to be clever but not wise."[13]

Thus, when the FOMC met in late March, it was another of those excruciating moments when the Federal Reserve had to choose between its audiences. Which power center would the Fed respond to— the White House or the bond market? One side or the other was sure to be disappointed by the FOMC's decision and possibly quite angry. Volcker's old friend and mentor Robert V. Roosa of the investment-banking house of Brown Brothers Harriman described the dilemma: "They are really in a trap with anything they try to do in this situation."[14]

Inside the FOMC, Volcker was also in the middle. Lyle Gramley was arguing for sterner action than Volcker had in mind, given all the competing considerations in the "real world." On the other side, Preston Martin, the only businessman on the board, was warning that tightening credit now could choke off the recovery prematurely. Martin's warning sounded like a preview of what the governors expected to hear from Republicans if Martin was right.

As usual, the debate was conducted not in the broad terms of national goals or social equity but in the esoteric language of monetary analysis. The governors' arguments focused on the obscure measurement known as "capacity utilization," a statistic meant to convey how much of America's productive capacity was now active and how much remained idle. Gramley, joined by Wallich and Partee, argued that capacity utilization, though still quite low, was rising at a threateningly rapid rate. Unemployment was still high, they acknowledged, and prices were flat, but if the Fed did not move swiftly to restrain now, it might soon be too late. The economy would quickly reach its full capacity and another round of inflation could be touched off by the bidding for scarce labor, scarce goods.

"Capacity utilization is a useless standard," Preston Martin countered. The measure, as everyone knew, was based on notoriously unreliable data. More important, as Martin argued, the capacity level of domestic manufacturing was irrelevant in the global economy because U.S. companies and labor had to compete worldwide on prices. It made no sense, he pleaded, to imagine that American corporations and labor unions might somehow bid up wages and prices at the very time they were being hammered down by foreign competitors. Thanks to the rising dollar, American prices were being held down by the cheap imports—and the world had unused productive capacity that was vastly in excess. Martin's analysis did not persuade.[15]

"The two groups had very different views of what was forthcoming in the economy," Martin said. "It was pretty fundamental." If the Fed tightened, Martin warned, the young economic recovery would be suppressed prematurely, robbed of its forward thrust. The "System men" were worried about the opposite—that there was too much momentum.

"I could understand the strong feelings of Wallich and Gramley," Martin said. "They had been in that building in the 1970s and they had seen inflation eat up values and they didn't want to see that happen again." Indeed, the memory of the seventies was invoked by Gramley and others in their arguments. The Fed must stand up now or risk the same ridicule later. To Preston Martin, they sounded like generals refighting the last war instead of the present one. "I haven't seen signs of an overheated economy," Martin declared. "I have seen overheated economists." [16]

The chairman agreed with Gramley and Wallich and the others. The Fed must brake. But Volcker did not wish to brake quite as hard as they proposed. Volcker chose the demands of the bond market over the political community's, but, typically, he attempted to fashion a compromise between the two extremes. His tightening would likely upset the White House Republicans, but it would not upset them nearly as much as what Gramley and Wallich wanted. The move proposed by the chairman was intended to be more in the nature of what Frank Morris had called a "mid-course correction." The FOMC directive would order a measured tightening of credit—pushing short-term interest rates up gradually, no more than 100 to 150 basis points.

Since November 1982, the Fed had been keeping the Federal Funds rate remarkably stable. The prescribed target range was between 6 and 10 percent, and the interest rate for overnight reserve borrowing among banks had been averaging a little above 9.5 percent. Now Volcker proposed that the target range for the Fed Funds rate be raised to 11.5 percent, enough leeway to permit an increase of no more than 150 basis points in short-term interest rates if credit pressures required it. In addition, the FOMC had restored M-1 as an operating target, now that money velocity had returned to a normal trend line, and the chairman's directive proposed "greater restraint" if M-1 grew faster than 6.5 percent.

That was not enough for Lyle Gramley. He thought the Fed should restrain more now or else face a worse choice later on, closer to the election. Henry Wallich agreed and they both dissented. It was Gramley's first dissent in his four years on the Board of Governors. "I don't dissent," he said, "unless it's really a fundamental disagreement, a feeling that the course of policy is really a mistake."

Preston Martin dissented too, but for opposite reasons.

Every time I dissented, people would say I was doing it because I was a Reagan appointee and was worried about the election [he said]. I was very careful not to have contact, either by telephone or in person, with my California friends, with the White House or Treasury during that period because I knew people would think it was political. But that's what they said, understandably. I would probably have said the same thing. It goes with the territory.

The effects of the Fed's tightening were visible almost immediately in the financial markets. The Federal Funds rate moved up about 50 basis points a week after the meeting. The key interest rate also bounced up and down more erratically, a signal to Fed watchers that the Open Market Desk had now returned to targeting the supply of money reflected by M-1 and the other aggregates. That meant interest rates would be allowed to fluctuate more freely, pushed up or down by the demand pressures in the money market.

The consequences were not moderate, however. The move was more like applying a choke-hold to interest-sensitive economic sectors, just as they were charging forward. The mortgage interest rate moved up sharply from around 13 percent a month later. By June, it was at 15 percent and the housing boom retreated swiftly from its February peak. Rates on auto loans went up, too, and auto sales declined accordingly. The economic expansion was confronted now with tighter credit, a rising price for borrowed money. Even though the unemployment rate was still close to 8 percent, the Federal Reserve was applying the brakes.

The bond market was pleased. "The deceleration of the economy is welcome news to the bond market, which has been battered for several weeks," Shearson American Express informed its investor clients. " . . . Despite all the talk of a tighter policy at the Federal Reserve, the monetary authorities have been slow to take decisive action. . . ." [17]

But the Federal Reserve's decision to play brakeman proved to be much more than a "mid-course correction." It effectively marked the end of Ronald Reagan's boom. It drew a line across the future's potential and defined the limits for the unfolding prosperity. The vigorous recovery that had begun eighteen months before would lose its strength rapidly—just as Preston Martin had warned—and that strength would never be regained.

Such a momentous decision by the government—a decision to halt the surging economy—might have been expected to provoke great controversy, especially since the decision was made by an obscure group of unelected technocrats in defiance of the President's wishes and in the midst of an election campaign. Yet there was no public outcry. The "brakeman" was allowed to throw the switch in virtual privacy. Of all the institutions of Washington, none was more deferential toward the Federal Reserve than the press. The news media did not report the significance of what the Fed was doing to the economy, not then and not even later when the effects of the Fed's tightening were fully visible.

Within two months, unemployment would reach its low point— stuck at 7.1 percent—and then begin to creep back upward. Manufacturing's capacity utilization, which had so worried the senior governors, peaked shortly thereafter—far below its potential—and began declining. The dollar's international value was driven still higher by the increase in U.S. interest rates, and the competitive damage was deepened for all the trade-sensitive sectors of the American economy, from farming to autos to machine tools. Within a matter of months, the Federal Reserve would find itself struggling with the opposite problem—trying to re-stimulate the economy to avert a recession.

Preston Martin, the businessman disparaged for his platitudes and sloppy thinking, had been right about the future. The economy decelerated more abruptly than any of the others expected. The Fed's decision to raise interest rates was, as Martin had warned, braking an engine that was already slowing down.

The technocrats who ran the central bank were not only fallible— "not infrequently wrong," as Lyle Gramley once admitted—but they also seemed incapable of listening seriously to competing perspectives. Inside the Fed, Martin's opinions were dismissed as politically inspired—unscientific—much as Nancy Teeters' dissents had been discounted during the long recession because she was regarded as a "knee-jerk liberal." Yet Martin's analysis of what lay ahead for the American economy proved to be more accurate than the expert forecasts from Paul Volcker, Lyle Gramley, Henry Wallich and the Fed's other respected voices.

"I was the only one dissenting on that side," Martin reflected, "and I was right. My God, we just couldn't afford to have an eighteen-month expansion, but it was already slowing down."

If anything, Preston Martin became even less popular among his colleagues at the Federal Reserve Board. They did not concede that he had been correct in March. Soon Martin was making even more dire forecasts about where the economy was headed.

> That's when I began to talk about a "growth recession" [Martin said]. My colleagues didn't like that phrase. It doesn't have a lot of study behind it; it's kind of a journalistic phrase. But that is what we were headed for —a growth recession. Unemployment began creeping up again and we didn't have much real growth. We don't go into a recession, but we also have growth of 2 percent or less.

As the recovery deteriorated, Preston Martin continued to dissent against Paul Volcker's management of money, usually alone. Each time, he was characterized in the press (and in the hallway gossip at the Fed) as politically ambitious, a tool of the White House. But if one searched through the policy record of the Federal Reserve during the Reagan recovery, Preston Martin's dissents were like a crude but reliable leading indicator for turns in the economy. His worries usually came true. Certainly, he was consistently closer to the mark than the other assembled experts at the Federal Reserve Board.

The vice chairman seemed good-humored about his lonely position and the occasional slurs. If he resented the fact that Fed colleagues ignored his opinions, he kept the resentment to himself. He did not try to adapt to their methods of analysis or accept their perspective. Meeting after meeting, the vice chairman continued to deliver the same rambling speeches, knowing that others would pay little attention.

The central bank had its own unwritten protocol and Preston Martin, with a bitter edge in his voice, observed it. "You don't go back to your colleagues and say: 'I told you so. I told you so in March,' " Martin explained. "Oh, no, you never, never do that."

Governor Charles Partee sounded defensive, but did not apologize for the Federal Reserve's decision. "You can look back in retrospect and say now, of course, knowing the economy grew much more slowly from that point on, you can say, 'Sure, we could have let it grow a little longer,' " Partee conceded. "But, as a principle of monetary management, I think it was correct to slow things down."

Paul Volcker was unwilling to concede even that much.

In their own narrow terms, perhaps Volcker and Partee were right. It wasn't a mistake if one accepted the paternal values that guided the Federal Reserve. This was its role in life, to decide what was good for others, even when it knew that the others might disagree. To the Fed, therefore, it did not seem wrong to break the booming economy, just as Americans were enjoying the new glow of prosperity. It was the Federal Reserve's responsibility to maintain order and so it did.

The governors, it was true, had been mistaken in the economic analysis that led them to the fateful decision, but it was not simply their mistakes. Every agent of government will make mistakes at one time or another, just as every human errs. The heart of the matter was the autocratic mind-set of the institution itself, the peculiar perspective that nearly always led the Federal Reserve in the same direction, toward the same sort of choice.

The policy makers were voting, after all, to avoid the one kind of economic risk that mattered most to their institution—the risk to money—and to authorize other kinds of economic loss—lost jobs and incomes, lost production and opportunity, lost equity in society. Even though their fears of inflation proved utterly unfounded, even though the real economy suffered grievously as a result, this was the posture of caution that the Federal Reserve would always find most comfortable. It was the choice its own constituencies in finance and banking would always applaud. In their own minds, central bankers could never be wrong in principle so long as they came down on the side of money.

If any single moment could convey the larger political meaning of the Federal Reserve, perhaps this was such a moment. Baldly stated, the Fed's decision meant that the demands of capital triumphed and democracy lost. Behind the economics, money management was usually a choice over whom to please and whom to disappoint, a political question of who would be made to take the loss, wealth holders or wage earners. In this pivotal instance, as it had done so often in its history, the central bank was deciding to defend wealth and let workers take the loss. The financial side of capitalism would be protected from risk, even excessively enhanced. Enterprise in the productive economy would be restrained, even injured. Opportunities would be canceled, ambitions checked, so that the owners of money would feel more secure about their wealth. The Federal Reserve's ideological values always were inclined toward that choice.

The orderly world described in economics textbooks was, thus, inverted. Economics taught that finance existed to facilitate business and commerce, that the real economy was the core of capitalism and that finance merely served it like a veil. When money's value was given paramount priority, the order was turned upside down. The diverse energies of the real economy, the vast aspirations of Americans generally, would now be suppressed in order to protect the interests of money.

The civic mythology of representative democracy was also exquisitely mocked by these events. In the middle of a presidential election season, the President was impotent. It was not his decision and he could not stop the Federal Reserve from making it. The elected representatives in Congress were not even consulted. Neither branch could object in candid terms without accentuating its own weakness. The American public could hardly protest either, for the public did not know that the unelected government in Washington had decided to end the boom.

Jim Baker was furious and said so in the bluntest terms. The President's chief of staff was attending a private dinner party, surrounded by friends and White House associates. His dinner partners, including Walter Wriston of Citibank, were aghast as Baker vented his anger at Paul Volcker.

"We made a deal," Baker said, according to one who was at his table. "The deal was that if we got the budget under control, the Fed would ease up. That's our part of the bargain. We did our part and now the Fed is double-crossing us. The Fed is tightening."

The White House had not actually gotten the budget under control, but Baker had worked hard at it and made some progress. After much negotiating and arranging, Baker had persuaded the reluctant President to endorse a $150 billion three-year deficit reduction package, including what Ronald Reagan most resisted, tax increases totaling $48 billion. "A down payment" on the deficits, the President called it. The Administration's deficit proposal was a long way from congressional approval (and most of it would be abandoned in the pressures of election-year politics), but Baker still felt "double-crossed" by Paul Volcker.

James Baker had assumed control over most of the major issues in the Reagan White House, including surveillance of the Fed's monetary policy. Theoretical arguments among the Administration's competing economists continued to swirl around him, but Baker decided what the White House would say or do. Without title, he was also functioning as campaign manager for the President's re-election and the Federal Reserve was one of his principal anxieties.

"Baker had the general worries of a full-time political manager," David Stockman said. "He thought he had a commitment that nobody was going to screw up the economy in the election year and now everybody was telling him that the numbers were bad. He didn't want anything that would screw up the economic environment, that's all."

On April 6, the Federal Reserve Board raised its Discount rate to 9 percent, the first change since December 1982. The Discount increase followed in step with the tightening that the Federal Open Market Committee had already authorized. The White House had a sense of what the Fed was doing, but it could not easily react to vague suspicions. On Tuesday, May 8, a tangible event presented itself. Commercial banks raised the prime rate for the second time in six weeks. The White House jumped on the Fed.

"We are disappointed that the prime interest rate has increased to 12.5 percent," Larry Speakes, the White House press spokesman, declared. "Although the economy has been growing at a healthy pace and inflation remains at a low level, it appears the money supply is not accommodating real economic growth."

Baker and Richard Darman, his deputy, sharpened the criticism of the Fed, speaking as the anonymous "senior officials" who were quoted in various press accounts. Other Administration officials were instructed to join the chorus.

For Treasury Secretary Donald Regan, this required a sudden turnabout. On Sunday, he had appeared on a television talk show and declared that the Fed was doing a good job. On Wednesday, Regan attacked the Fed. "You bet your life this has us worried," the Treasury Secretary told reporters. Commerce Secretary Malcolm Baldrige added his voice. "I hope the Fed is looking far enough ahead," Baldrige said.

By Friday, Donald Regan was warning that the Fed might produce another recession if it did not swiftly change its monetary policy. "This is not a campaign against the Fed," Regan said. "It's a campaign against high interest rates."

The Administration's frantic flurry of "Fed bashing" was orchestrated by Baker and Darman, who figured that a public campaign to intimidate Volcker might as well be tried, since private persuasion had clearly failed. At the very least, the White House officials hoped the public criticism would establish a "political predicate" for finger pointing later if the economy did fall apart before the election. "There's a pure political purpose, in terms of laying off blame," an Administration official explained.[18]

Aside from the political objective, Baker and Darman also thought they were right about the economics. For months, they had been listening more attentively to the supply-side advocates, Jack Kemp and Jude Wanniski, argue that Volcker's tight-money strategy could stall out the recovery right in the middle of the campaign. Now events seemed to be confirming the warnings. Within the Reagan Administration, the influence of the competing ideological camps had shifted again. Monetarist advisers, who had been so influential back in 1981 urging a stern monetary policy, were now eclipsed. The supply siders, whose earlier complaints about the Fed had been ignored, were ascendant. At least Baker and Darman took their warnings seriously.

"I said, let's forget about those monetary aggregates, let's keep sufficient growth to keep this wonderful recovery going," an Administration official explained. "There isn't any sign that inflation is coming back and there's a serious risk that the Fed is too tight. What I meant was that there was room for additional growth and no sign of inflation. I think I was right about that. Volcker wasn't letting the recovery go far enough."

The economic argument made by the White House political advisers was perfectly plausible, a legitimate criticism of the Fed's policy that turned out to be correct. "If you looked at all the economic factors," Richard Darman said, "any reasonable person could conclude that there was no inflationary risk in loosening and substantial danger on the other side. We had the merits on our side. It was politically desirable, but it was also reasonable economics."

Yet Volcker brushed the White House comments aside as political complaints. The Fed was used to attack in election seasons. Politicians were expected to defer to the higher judgment of economics. That standard was enforced by the news media, which, once again, criticized the White House for meddling in the Fed's decisions.

The bankers on the Federal Advisory Council, when they met with the Fed in early May, congratulated the governors on their recent tightening. The bankers took note of "the highly charged political atmosphere" and warned that this turbulence "increases the contribution that monetary policy must make to maintaining confidence. . . . "[19]

Volcker, in any case, had his own allies in the White House, and they swiftly mobilized to defend the Federal Reserve. Like other episodes in the Reagan Presidency, when the senior advisers battled for the President's mind, they often did their fighting in public. Martin Feldstein, the CEA chairman, dissented in public. The Fed's tightening was "not inappropriate," he said, contradicting the White House "senior officials."

"I think it would be a terrible mistake to try to push interest rates down by expansionary monetary policy," Feldstein told reporters. He said he was "frankly surprised" to hear the Treasury Secretary advocate the opposite.

The budget director, David Stockman, likewise began lobbying against the anti-Fed broadsides emanating from his White House colleagues. "We called the wrath of God down on Baker after he put that out," Stockman said. "We got lots of Wall Street types to call him to say, 'My God, the markets will go crazy.' So many bricks came down on his head, Baker must have wondered, 'What the hell did I get into?' "

The biggest brick from Wall Street hit on Monday, May 14, when the financial markets opened. The bond market choked on a new issue of thirty-year Treasury bonds and dealers found it difficult to find customers for the $4.75 billion in new government debt. Stock prices declined but bond prices were hit hardest, off by nearly one and a third points. The markets may have simply been reacting to the rising interest rates, but Wall Street analysts blamed the collapse in bonds on the "Fed bashing" in Washington.

The contending factions at the White House quickly negotiated a truce. They agreed that the President must hold an impromptu press conference to calm the financial markets and still the controversy. Federal Reserve officials "are doing the best they can," Reagan declared to reporters, nullifying all previous comments to the contrary. The Administration's public campaign to pressure the Fed ended as abruptly as it had begun.

At the Fed, some governors were more amused than intimidated. "This Administration has been weird," Nancy Teeters said. "On Sunday, the Treasury Secretary is on TV saying we are doing a good job. Then interest rates bump up on Monday and on Wednesday he's attacking us. Then the President has a press conference and says we're doing fine. Within ten days, we went from being white hats to black hats and back again."

Inside the White House, the leading "Fed bashers" proclaimed the exercise a success. "Darman said we've accomplished our purpose," Stockman said. "We've given a warning to the Fed. It's a shot across the bow and now the Fed knows what we expect between now and November."

Both Baker and Darman told associates that their public complaints probably prevented the Fed from adopting an even tougher policy. Volcker was in the middle among his own colleagues at the Fed and the frontal attacks from the White House would make it easier for the Fed chairman to resist the stronger action urged by Gramley and other governors. "They might have been even tighter if we hadn't done that," an Administration official said.

The Federal Reserve, it was true, did hold off from a further decision to tighten money and credit. But the policy makers at the central bank were inhibited by a much larger event than the White House sniping. The Fed was confronted, simultaneously, with another major shock to the American financial system—the collapse of the Continental Illinois National Bank.

The "run" began in Tokyo on Wednesday, May 9, the same day Donald Regan was attacking the Federal Reserve back in Washington. The Commodity News Service had carried a brief wire story reporting "rumors" that a Japanese bank might acquire Continental Illinois in Chicago. When the item was picked up by a Japanese news service, the translator turned "rumors" into "disclosure" and Far Eastern investors holding Continental's certificates of deposit panicked at the implications. That day, as much as $1 billion in Asian money fled from the Continental Illinois bank.

The "run" spread around the globe, with the speed of electronic communications. When financial markets opened in Europe on Thursday, withdrawals from Continental reached the same awesome scale, driven by the same fears. Something was obviously wrong with the Chicago bank. Prudent investors would simply get out of its paper, at least until they could learn more.

In Washington, the Comptroller of the Currency, Todd Conover, issued a vaguely reassuring statement: "The Comptroller's Office is not aware of any significant changes in the bank's operations, as reflected in its published financial statements, that would serve as a basis for these rumors."

Financial markets, foreign and domestic, were not taken in by his artful phrasing. Major depositors worldwide, from brokerages to money-market funds to other commercial banks, continued to pull their money out of Continental CDs and the "run" worsened. Before the close of business on Friday, Continental had to borrow $3.6 billion at the Discount window of the Chicago Federal Reserve Bank in order to make up for its lost deposits. And, in Washington, the heads of the three bank regulatory agencies—the Comptroller, the Federal Deposit Insurance Corporation and the Federal Reserve—gathered in Paul Volcker's office to deal with the crisis.

As swiftly as that, the nation's seventh-largest commercial bank was brought to ruin. But, as Volcker and the other regulators well understood, Continental's collapse had not begun with an erroneous news report forty-eight hours earlier. The real origins went back to the bank's aggressive lending strategy during the late 1970s and early 1980s when the bank was hailed for its brilliant management. The federal regulators had not intervened then to restrain Continental's high-growth strategy, nor had they taken firm action after July 1982, when the failure of the Penn Square Bank in Oklahoma City revealed how reckless Continental's loan officers had been. The Chicago bank was burdened with the $1 billion in bad loans it had purchased from Penn Square and at least another billion from other ventures. But nothing of consequence had been done by Washington regulators to force the bank to clean up its weaknesses. At the time, Roger Anderson, Continental's ambitious chairman, boasted to bank employees: "We have no intention of pulling in our horns."

Indeed, through 1982 and 1983, Continental continued to distribute its regular $2-per-share dividends to stockholders as though nothing had happened. Late in 1983, a new examination by the Comptroller revealed that the bank's condition had deteriorated steadily since the summer of 1982 and was now in even worse shape. Its earnings were declining and the management was maintaining appearances by selling off subsidiaries in order to keep up the dividend payments.

William Isaac, chairman of the FDIC, said he asked the other federal regulators why nothing had been done to discipline the bank. "Why aren't we cutting the dividend? We should have done it back in '82," Isaac said. "The response from the Fed and the Comptroller was: 'You're right, we probably should have done it in '82. But now, if we do it, the markets will panic.' I didn't disagree with that."[20]

Investors were already catching on anyway, at least in American financial markets. Continental continued to offer a much higher rate on its CDs than other money-center banks, a sure sign it was having trouble raising the $8 billion it needed to borrow every day to fund its operations. Even more telling, Continental sold off its profitable credit-card operation to another major bank early in 1984 in a desperate effort to raise funds. "They were dismembering the carcass," Isaac said.

Roger Anderson abruptly retired in February. The bank's stock, which had traded as high as $40 three years before, was declining sharply, down to $12 by early May. Continental Illinois was, in fact, making discreet inquiries among other multinational banks about a merger or take-over, though not apparently in Japan. As American money became more wary, the bank had to rely more and more heavily on investors in Europe and Asia to lend it the billions needed for daily operating funds. When the foreign money suddenly caught on to the dangers, the game was over. The global "run" began.[21]

Back in the summer of 1982, Paul Volcker had privately urged the Chicago bank directors to take drastic remedial action, but he had not ordered them to do so. After the collapse, though he did not reveal what he had attempted, Volcker obliquely conceded some regret that he had not been more forceful. The chairman told a Senate hearing: ". . . one could argue—and the argument becomes even better with hindsight—that it would have been better to look at the dividends right then. I think, with hindsight, that's an unassailable argument."[22]

At the Fed, bank regulators felt, with some merit, that a large share of the blame belonged to William Isaac and the FDIC. By insisting that the Penn Square Bank be liquidated in 1982, with huge losses for "upstream" banks like Continental, Isaac set in motion the unraveling of confidence. When Isaac insisted that only insured depositors up to $100,000 would be reimbursed in the Penn Square failure, that sent a scary message to all large-scale depositors. Isaac had wanted to teach "free market" discipline to the financial markets; instead, he simply frightened them. The complaint against Isaac, however, was also a way to evade the Fed's own culpability—its failure to act when disciplinary action might have made the difference.

In any case, the basic failures of regulation were already history. Now Volcker and the other government agencies faced an immediate crisis of unprecedented dimensions—how to stop what was the largest bank "run" in history, how to rescue Continental Illinois if the "run" couldn't be stopped. They agreed that the FDIC should prepare to make a huge infusion of capital, as much as $2 billion. If the bank's condition did not stabilize, they would try to arrange a take-over by another major bank.

None of the regulators, including Isaac, entertained, even briefly, the option they had followed in Penn Square—paying off only the insured depositors, letting Continental fail and close it doors. If this bank failed, the Comptroller projected, that might lead to another hundred bank failures, mostly small banks that had parked their own money at Continental Illinois. About twenty-three hundred banks were among Continental's large depositors and these assets would be frozen, at least temporarily, if the bank was liquidated. The potential losses to smaller banks were not the real danger, however.

How many of them would fail [Isaac asked aloud]? I don't know. Could we handle it? Yes. But more important was the situation in the largest banks. First Chicago was going to announce big quarterly losses of its own. First Chicago would not have withstood that announcement if we hadn't saved Continental. There would have been a run on Manny Hanny [Manufacturers Hanover]. There were all sorts of rumors about Manny Hanny rippling through the market. Bank of America, Interfirst of Dallas had problems too. Financial Corporation of America [the nation's largest savings and loan] could not have lasted a minute if we had done a deposit payoff at Continental. In my judgment, we would have had worldwide chaos.

This time, whatever the cost, the federal government had to reassure the money managers. If Continental failed, as Governor Charles Partee explained, the corporate treasurers, money managers and local governments that got "burned" there would have a powerful incentive to protect themselves at other banks.

Bank of America was exposed on real estate and other loans, Manny Hanny had a very large exposure on LDC debt [Partee said]. If you were a money manager and there was even the slightest question that you might not be able to get your money out of one of these banks, there was no percentage in maintaining your deposit there. If you had $1 million in Bank of America and you had seen its reports coming out quarter after quarter with these loan losses and then you couldn't get the money, there's no question you'd be fired. You might earn a few extra basis points on interest by keeping your funds there, but if you are wrong, you get fired. It's a very uneven choice.

Over the weekend, Continental's management tried to work out its own rescue by lining up support from the nation's other largest banks. A hastily assembled consortium of sixteen banks, led by Morgan Guaranty, agreed to put up a $4.5 billion loan, a private "safety net" for their troubled competitor. The announcement failed to persuade. When the money markets opened on Monday, May 14, Continental's hemorrhaging resumed.

"The banks tried to get together without government and it didn't work," a Treasury official said. "Then they fell on their knees with hands outspread and said, 'Save us!' "

While Continental borrowed more from the Fed and from its "safety net" of private banks, Volcker, Isaac and Conover worked out the terms for the federal rescue. The three flew to New York on Wednesday to meet with the leading bankers to enlist their support and assistance. The FDIC would guarantee an infusion of at least $1.5 billion and the banks were asked to put up $500 million as an expression of confidence. Present were executives from seven banks—Morgan, Chase, Citibank, Chemical, Manufacturers Hanover, Bankers Trust and Bank of America—who were to sell the package to twenty-five or thirty other major banks. In order not to alarm, the bankers assembled at Morgan Guaranty's uptown branch, rather than at the New York Fed in Wall Street.

The meeting was faintly reminiscent of Wall Street's glorious past, the era when J. P. Morgan and partners could meet among themselves and assemble a package of emergency loans to save the banking system. Several bank executives made patriotic speeches during the meeting, alluding to the Morgan tradition and the spirit of noblesse oblige inherited by Wall Street's most important banks.

The reality was utterly different, however. It was the federal government that would save the banks from possible calamity, including the seven banks assembled at the table. All of them, in varying degrees, were vulnerable to the same sort of panic that had brought down Continental. They all depended heavily on the daily money-market borrowing required by "managed liabilities" banking. They were all overexposed on foreign lending. Even so, Citibank, with characteristic independence, balked at the terms. It demanded ironclad language in the Fed-FDIC agreement to protect itself from loss. The lawyers argued through the night and finally Citibank relented.

On Thursday morning, eight days after the "run" began, the federal regulators announced the largest bailout in the history of banking. The FDIC would pump $4.5 billion in immediate new capital into the bank, assuming liability for the bulk of Continental's bad loans while it searched for a new owner to take over the institution. The Federal Reserve promised that, in the meantime, it would lend whatever was necessary in short-term funds to keep Continental afloat. In the course of fulfilling that promise, the Fed made emergency loans to Continental Illinois that rose to a breathtaking $8 billion.[23]

As Volcker explained to troubled senators:

The operation is the most basic function of the Federal Reserve. It was why it was founded, to serve as a lender of last resort in times of liquidity pressures of this sort, so they don't spread through the rest of the system to innocent parties. . . . That's what a central bank is all about, to provide liquidity in those circumstances. We are just carrying out the most classic function of a central bank.[24]

But the essential and most controversial element of the rescue package was the guarantee to protect everyone, large and small, from any losses. The large depositors could relax. Their money at Continental was safe, effectively insured by the joint announcement from the Federal Reserve and the FDIC. Any liabilities would be assumed by the federal government, that is, by the general public.[25]

A few angry voices were raised. Representative Fernand St. Germain of Rhode Island, who had succeeded Representative Reuss as chairman of House Banking, scornfully called it "a bailout for the powerful." The size of the government's rescue of Continental, St. Germain observed, "dwarfs the combined guarantees and outlays of the federal government in the Lockheed, Chrysler and New York City bailouts." Yet it was arranged, he said, by unelected bureaucrats, with no public debate.

The day after the federal regulators were providing billions to save Continental Illinois, they closed down the Bledsoe County Bank of Pikeville, Tennessee, and the Planters Trust & Savings Bank of Opelousas, Louisiana. Small independent banks complained about the "double standard" implicit in the Continental deal. During the first half of 1984, forty-three banks failed, most of them small agricultural banks forced to close because so many farmers and small businesses were defaulting on their loans.[26] In nearly all cases, the FDIC paid off only the insured depositors and arranged a take-over by a neighboring bank. Large depositors at Continental were treated more generously than large depositors at small banks. Still, Continental's managers were fired in disgrace and its stockholders did lose most of the value of their equity. Very few small bankers would wish to endure the same fate.

The Continental bailout, nevertheless, posed an awkward precedent that federal regulators could not explain away. If there was any doubt before, Continental starkly established that the largest banks would never be allowed to fail, whatever the cost to the government. Badgered on the question in House hearings, the Comptroller conceded that, yes, the eleven largest multinational banks would not be allowed to fail. As a practical reality, the number of protected banks was undoubtedly much larger than that. Probably the largest fifty or even one hundred banks would always be safe because the ripples from their failures would be regarded as too unsettling to tolerate.

The distinction had important consequences for the money market and where investors would place large deposits. Over time, smaller banks would suffer competitively and the largest banks would benefit. Why should a money manager put a $1 million deposit in a smaller bank, where he might lose it above the $100,000 federal insurance guarantee, when he knew all his money would be safe in one of the largest banks, no matter how reckless the managers might be? The federal guarantees of bank safety had inadvertently created unequal discipline between large and small, another incentive for the consolidation of the banking system. As the smaller banks and savings and loans were allowed to fail, their space was taken by the big ones. Citibank, Chase, Chemical and others acquired dozens of failed institutions around the country, establishing far-flung corporate beachheads while they awaited the day when Congress would allow them to become nationwide banks.

The most striking political fact of the Continental rescue, however, was the absence of controversy. Aside from small bankers, there was almost no reaction from the general public and very little criticism from politicians. The dimensions of the crisis were so awesome and complex that perhaps ordinary people felt they could not question the decisions. Another possibility was that most Americans regarded the government intervention as unexceptional. When the largest, most influential enterprises were imperiled, the government would come to their rescue. That was how people expected the American system to work.

Continental stabilized for a time, thanks to the federal promises of support, but skeptical money managers continued to be wary and the bank's funding eroded further. Continental Illinois was shrinking. By midsummer, it was the thirteenth largest bank, not seventh. Meanwhile, the federal regulators could find no willing buyers. Chemical, Citibank and First Chicago all took a look at Continental's books and shared their pessimistic assessments with the government agencies: the bank had $4 billion in bad loans, not $2.7 billion, as the federal regulators had believed. No one offered a good explanation as to why the private bankers found problems that the government regulators did not see. In any case, no one wanted to buy the carcass.

Therefore, in late July, the Continental Illinois bank was nationalized. That term was not used, of course, but that was the meaning of the announcement in Washington. The federal government bought the bank. Unable to find a private buyer, the U.S. government itself became the owner and, until further notice, sole proprietor of the nation's thirteenth largest bank.

The idea of nationalized industries was, of course, offensive to the free-market ethic that still dominated American politics, yet this was done without controversy—and under Ronald Reagan, the most conservative President to govern in many decades. Conservative commentators were silent as the government executed its massive intrusion in the free marketplace. Possibly conservatives were reassured by the understanding that Washington did not intend to operate Continental Illinois as a public bank, its lending policies guided by larger public purposes. Continental would continue to be run like an ordinary commercial bank, strictly devoted to profit making.

The nationalization of Continental was, in fact, a quintessential act of modern liberalism—the state intervening in behalf of private interests and a broad public purpose. In this supposedly conservative era, federal authorities were setting aside the harsh verdict of market competition (and grossly expanding their own involvement in the private economy) in order to protect private citizens from loss—and thereby save the system. Washington was going into big-time banking.

The rescue of Continental also amounted to a vast bailout for the creditor classes. Perhaps that was why the conservative commentators did not complain. The government would save investors from their losses on a scale many times greater than anything it had ever done for endangered debtors, such as the Chrysler Corporation or Lockheed. In the past, conservative scholars and pundits had objected loudly at any federal intervention in the private economy, particularly emergency assistance for failing companies. Now, they hardly seemed to notice. Perhaps they would have been more vocal if the deed had been done by someone other than the conservative champion, Ronald Reagan.

Under the circumstances, the government did not have good alternatives. The FDIC acquired 160 million shares of Continental's stock, fired the management and installed new executives. The purchase price amounted to $5.5 billion (not counting the continuing aid from the Federal Reserve). The assumption was that the government would own Continental until it was back on its feet and operating profitably again, then it would sell the bank back to private investors. By early 1986, the FDIC reported a loss to date of $1.24 billion on the bad loans it has assumed from Continental, but it would be many years before anyone knew the full cost to the public. It might also be many years before the federal government could get out of the banking business.

The banking crisis did not end with the rescue of Continental Illinois, however. Fear and nervousness continued to stalk some of the largest banks in the country. The financial markets buzzed with rumors of another impending crisis, perhaps on the same scale. Before the summer was over, the tremors in American banking would have a direct, distorting impact on the Federal Reserve's monetary policy—and, therefore, damaging consequences for the American economy.

. . .

The value of American farmland had fallen $149 billion in three years, by as much as 50 percent in some areas, and the collateral would keep shrinking as long as agricultural prices remained flat or falling. Thousands more debtors across the South and the Midwest would be driven to the wall, in energy and other commodities as well as farming. The rolling liquidation of real assets was continuing. Ultimately, it brought down banks that had financed production of those real assets.[27]

While the demise of small country banks traumatized local communities and offered a staple feature story for the network television news, the real crisis in banking was at the opposite end of the system —among the largest institutions. While the electorate was distracted by campaign speeches on a host of other themes, federal bank regulators sweated through an anxious summer, tamping out the recurring gossip about who would fail next.

The largest "farm bank" in the nation, after all, was Bank of America in San Francisco, also the nation's largest commercial bank. B of A loans financed the vast enterprises of California agribusiness. But the bank had also financed a largely vacant luxury condo tower in Dallas, now foreclosed. It put up the money for the idle offshore drilling rigs owned by Global Marine in Houston, now in trouble too. It provided billions more for other ventures that were now defaulting. Real estate, oil, agriculture, shipping—Bank of America would be forced to swallow $4.1 billion in failed loans during the first half of the 1980s and yet still would have $7 billion on its books in exposure to other troubled debtors, Mexico, Venezuela and Brazil.

There is weakness in the financial structure [Governor Partee said], but the banks are not weak because they have been foolhardy. Banks have been doing what they've always done, making loans to business and farmers. They are the ones who are weak. There are quite a few companies in financial difficulty, lots of real-estate projects, lots of farmers, including multimillion-dollar agribusiness farms. It's the customers, not the banks.

William Isaac, the FDIC chairman, agreed:

It was very shaky after Continental Illinois. If Continental had not been handled, we would have been in the soup. Crocker of San Francisco was weak, but it had been weak for a long time. First Chicago, Bank of America, Manny Hanny, Interfirst of Dallas, First National of Houston, Financial Corporation of America, Michigan National, Equibank of Pittsburgh. Those are ones that would have been in the soup.

The most striking evidence of the distress was quite visible, though barely noted. Some of the largest and proudest financial institutions were selling off their glamorous headquarters buildings in order to raise capital to offset loan losses. Bank of America, First Chicago, Crocker, Security Pacific, Bank of Boston all sold their modern office towers, then rented them back from the new owners—an appropriate symbol of the forced retreat that was under way.[28]

The general public may have been oblivious to the peril, but financial markets were not. One week after the Continental Illinois rescue in May, the rumors of funding difficulties turned on Manufacturers Hanover Trust in New York, the nation's fourth largest bank. Investors dumped Manny Hanny stock, and its value fell 11 percent in one day, despite the bank's denials. Other major bank shares were driven down too, including even the most prestigious and best-managed ones like Morgan and Citibank. Edward A. Taber, president of the T. Rowe Price money-market fund, explained: "The market is saying, 'Who's next?' "[29]

The New York Fed's Open Market Desk reported the strains more soberly: "The funding problems of Continental cast a long shadow over the financial markets during the late spring and summer." Investors, the New York desk observed, generally executed a "flight to quality," moving money away from any banks perceived as troubled.[30]

Through the summer, the larger banks had to bid up the interest rates offered on their own CDs in order to maintain their own funding. The interest-rate spread between three-month bank CDs and Treasury bills ballooned, from 35 to 160 basis points. Paying more for their own daily borrowing squeezed the banks' profits further, adding to the damage already caused by loan losses.

With an element of poetic justice, commercial banks were now suffering a severe aftershock from the very policies they had urged the Federal Reserve to pursue—the stringent tightening of money and rapid deceleration of price inflation that had destroyed or undermined so many other enterprises. Commercial banks had enjoyed record profits back in 1980 and 1981 when the Fed pushed interest rates to unprecedented peaks, but the severity of the Fed's action had now caught up with them too. The Fed had not given debtors time to adjust to the new reality of disinflation, and because the tables were turned so abruptly on businesses, on farmers, on Latin-American nations, the banks were now stuck with huge portfolios of troubled loans.

Few people made the connection, but, in a sense, this was part of the price still being paid for Volcker's swift and sure assault on inflation. The long and severe contraction of 1982 became the fragility and failure in the banking system in 1984. A more patient approach would have taken longer, but it also would have done less damage to the structure, with fewer victims still struggling to stay afloat years afterward. The stricken debtors, from independent oil drillers to sovereign nations, were now threatening to drag the lenders down with them.

Commercial banks charged off $12.5 billion in loan losses in 1984, more than double the loan-loss provisions of 1981. Their profit rate fell to the lowest level in twenty years. The return on equity for the largest banks had declined from 13.95 percent in 1980 to 9.78 percent. Prodded by federal regulators, they were compelled to raise new capital to protect against more loan failures in the future.

"Usually at this stage in an economic recovery," the Federal Reserve reported, "the quality of loan portfolios would be expected to improve, but loan losses at bank holding companies in 1984 continued to mount." Anthony Solomon of the New York Fed observed: "New York's major money-center banks are running a ratio of 3 to 4 percent of nonperforming loans to total assets. Normally at this stage of a recovery, given that we've had two years of prosperity, it might be as low as 1 to 1.5 percent. That is distressing and shows the fragility."[31]

The public's moral sensibilities about banking's problems were terribly confused. Citizens who felt a tug of sympathy for a small-town banker forced to close his doors might secretly relish the distress of behemoth money-center banks. Yet, in either case, the banker was caught by the same forces, the same mistakes. There was no substantial distinction between large and small except, if anything, the largest banks were usually more generous and imaginative in financing the untested future.

In fact, the bankers in trouble had made essentially the same mistakes that the borrowers had made—they had lent money for new ventures based on assumptions about the future that did not materialize. Bankers had likewise ridden the inflationary curve upward—and were now in trouble because the Federal Reserve turned the tables in its anti-inflation campaign. Despite their preferred position of financial expertise, the bankers, large and small, proved to be no more prescient than farmers, real-estate developers, oil producers or South American governments had been. And, the bankers were no less culpable.

The federal government seemed especially confused by this point. From time to time, various members of the Reagan Administration attributed the debt problems to excessive ambitions generated by the inflation of the past—farmers who had bought too much land and equipment, oil producers who had borrowed recklessly. The CEA chairman, Murray Weidenbaum, had called them all "speculators," gambling that prices would continue to rise forever. Yet, for every farmer or freebooting oilman who had overreached and was subsequently crushed by debt, there was a willing banker who also had been too optimistic, who had made the same bet. It was simply not rational to condemn one side of the debt transaction as reckless and sympathize with the other side as an unfortunate victim. Yet that was essentially the government's posture—it rushed to assist the lenders who had been burned and, simultaneously, left the borrowers to their fate.

This moral confusion between debtors and lenders was especially evident at the Federal Reserve. The Fed worried intensely about helping the banks to overcome their mistakes, yet it dismissed the plight of the failed borrowers as regrettable but unavoidable, even necessary to the process of disinflation. Paul Volcker, for instance, expressed limited sympathy for the bankrupt farmers. Farmers were hurt, yes, but they had put themselves in an unsustainable position. The farmers built up a lot more productive capability than the world is going to buy.

The central bank, in fact, successfully evaded any real public responsibility for what was happening to American farmers and other debtors, much as it had turned aside the complaints from Midwestern farmers destroyed in the Fed's deflation back in the 1920s. The exhaustive press and television coverage on the plight of the failing farmers almost never mentioned any connection with monetary policy or the Federal Reserve. Martha Seger, a finance professor from Central Michigan University, was appointed by President Reagan to succeed Nancy Teeters in mid-1984 as the only woman on the Board of Governors. Governor Seger, as a new member, was struck by how easily the Fed distanced itself from the farm distress. In a conversation reported by Jude Wanniski, Seger remarked: "I'm amazed at how many people there are around here [at the Fed] who insist that we have nothing to do with the farm problem. Nobody here but us chickens!"[32]

For the lenders, however, the financial intermediaries who were also in trouble, the Federal Reserve demonstrated great solicitude. Indeed, Volcker and the other governors went to extraordinary lengths to make sure that the rules of bank regulation were not enforced too zealously in 1983 and 1984. The Federal Reserve (and the Treasury as well) instructed federal bank examiners to apply the accounting standards for bank solvency with due compassion for the special circumstances that troubled bankers found themselves in.

There is no doubt if the examiners were left to themselves, they would have applied their rules in the traditional fashion, put their usual standards on nonperforming loans and so forth, that would have caused enormous problems [a senior officer at the New York Fed explained]. Who knows what would have happened? But the Board of Governors and the Treasury concerned themselves with the details of the accounting rules more closely than ever before. In other times, the board wouldn't have concerned itself with these purely technical questions, but this time they supervised everything very closely, more closely than I've ever seen before. They were making sure the examiners didn't overdo their job.

Special advice went out to examiners on the handling of agribusiness loan losses and on the rules for declaring the international loans past due. When Argentina fell behind on its interest payments, a special grace was granted. If the loans had been declared past due, some of the largest New York banks would have had to write off huge losses immediately. In general, the examiners were told to be tolerant.

Governor Partee, chairman of the Fed's subcommittee on bank supervision, insisted:

We didn't tell the examiners to do anything that would be improper, but we were concerned that they didn't become too righteous in a way that would make the problems worse. . . .

There's the question of when you decide that a bank has made a bad loan. It may be to International Harvester or it may be to Mexico. The loan is in the bank's portfolio; there's no chance that it will be paid back. What do you do with it? There are always people who say you ought to step up and take your medicine. Others of us say, "No, it's better if we try to work it out."

The Fed's solicitous response to the banks' difficulties was, of course, consistent with Volcker's preoccupation with the refinancing of LDC debt. Through 1983 and 1984, Volcker presided like a matchmaker over the new debt packages between the banks and the nations that needed the money, Brazil, Argentina, Mexico and the others, nudging each side toward settlement. If one deal had failed, if one country had defaulted, the whole universe of debt-burdened countries might have given up any attempt to service its loans. At one point, bankers on the Federal Advisory Council complained directly to the governors that Fed bank examiners were being overly zealous toward the banks' shaky LDC loans. "Concern was expressed," the bankers' council reported, "about comments by bank examiners who did not appear to be conversant with the view of the Federal Reserve Board. . . ."

Volcker himself confessed: "We're all being induced to close our eyes to loose banking practices."[33]

But the political climate had changed, and now Congress wanted the Fed and the Treasury to get tough with the banks and impose new regulatory controls. Volcker himself was willing. He had always been skeptical about the deregulation of finance. Still, in the fragile circumstances, the Fed would proceed cautiously.

Gradually, a step at a time, both the Fed and the Comptroller did begin to tighten procedures. They pressed the undercapitalized banks to improve their capital base and meet the higher capital requirements. The largest banks, which had been exempted from the new capital ratios imposed in 1981, were now enjoined to raise more capital and meet the 6 percent minimum. This would, in effect, improve their insurance against future failure if one of the major LDC debtors defaulted.

The Comptroller's office also began applying the sting of public discipline, the legal weapon that regulators had hesitated to invoke against Continental Illinois before its collapse. In an extraordinary move in the autumn, First Chicago and Bank of America were both publicly chastised and compelled to accept a regulatory order that directed them to tighten their lending policies, build up their capital reserves and make provisions to protect themselves against the kind of short-term liquidity crisis that had brought down Continental.

Bankers grumbled at the new heavy-handedness from federal regulators, but the financial markets were hardly panicked by the news. Investors were already quite familiar with the big problems facing these banks, and, if anything, investors may have been reassured to see the federal regulators at last forcing troubled banks to take remedial action.

But the summer's silent crisis in banking was about to have a far more profound impact on the American economy. The jittery behavior of the major banks was disrupting the Federal Reserve's own calculations about the money supply, and the confusion led the central bank into another serious error. The braking effects of the Fed's March tightening would be inadvertently compounded—and the American economy driven to the edge of recession.

Who's next? The managers of the nation's leading banks were surrounded by dark rumors and nervous investors, poised to withdraw billions at the least hint of difficulty. A second tremor jarred their nerves when Financial Corporation of America, the largest savings and loan in the nation, was caught in a funding crisis too. The Los Angeles thrift swiftly lost $8 billion in deposits and federal regulators had to prop it up with huge emergency loans.[34]

Under these circumstances, any bank that was seen borrowing heavily and often from the Fed might become the next candidate for

failure in the market gossip. Overnight, it might be swept away by
panicky investors, just as Continental had been. A Pittsburgh bank
economist put it plainly: "We didn't want to borrow at the Discount
window because of Continental Illinois. If people saw us borrowing a
lot, they would think we were in the same place."

Across the country, nervous bank managers adopted the same strategy—they discreetly hoarded larger pools of excess reserves, just in
case, and they grossly curtailed their routine borrowings from the Fed.
For weeks, the level of Discount borrowing by commercial banks remained mysteriously low—half or less of what the Federal Reserve
anticipated.

The normal hydraulics of money management were thrown off by
this and the effect was perversely damaging. "The banks were not
borrowing as we expected them to do," Volcker explained. "Therefore, the market was tighter than we anticipated." Charles Partee put
it more bluntly. "When the banks stopped borrowing," Partee said,
"we ended up being tighter than we intended."

None of this was instantly clear, however, to the governors or the
Fed's operators. Normally, Federal Reserve technicians relied on the
daily level of Discount borrowing as a major indicator of credit conditions. Discount lending normally went up when money was tight; it
subsided when the money supply was ample and easy. By mid-June,
the normal signals became utterly confused. The Discount borrowing
by banks was subsiding, a signal of excess supply. But the market
interest rates were rising, a sign that conditions were tightening.
Which was it—easy or tight? Should the Fed be withdrawing reserves
or adding more? It couldn't tell for sure.

The confusion misled the Fed's own management because normally
the Open Market Desk assumed that a portion of the new reserves it
provided to the banking system would flow through the Discount window, the rest through open-market transactions. The two valves were
routinely coordinated with each other. But, if one valve got stuck, the
other valve would have to be opened wider—or else the economy
would be starved for money.

That is what happened by midsummer. The Federal Reserve was
slow to recognize that it was the nervous bank managers, not changing
economic conditions, that explained the anomaly. Rather than provide
more money through open-market transactions to make up for the
shortfall at the Discount window, the Federal Reserve allowed the
money supply to get tighter and tighter.

The Federal Funds rate, which the Fed itself had pushed up in
March, rose again in June and July by another 100 to 150 basis points.
Other short-term interest rates moved up accordingly. The ultimate

effect on the real economy—though unintended—was to step still harder on the brake.

When the Federal Open Market Committee met in July, the majority rejected the technicians' interpretation of what was happening and, instead, concluded that the rising interest rates reflected real economic momentum. The economy, they agreed, was slowing down from the booming pace of last winter, but it was still moving along at a "relatively sizable rate of expansion."

Once again, Preston Martin was a minority of one, arguing that the fragile conditions in finance were too grave to let interest rates rise further. Once again, he cited the precarious state of his old industry, the savings and loans. "We just threw them to the wolves," Martin complained. "I argued the situation is too vulnerable. We have to be accommodative because of the vulnerability of key sectors of the economy and of financial markets to the high interest rates."

And, once again, Martin did not persuade. The outcome was further deterioration for the economy. It did not continue to expand smartly, as the FOMC predicted; it slowed down abruptly, almost to a halt. The Fed's management error was reflected in what happened to the money supply. In June, M-1 had grown by nearly 11 percent. In July, M-1 contracted—shrinking by 1 percent.

For the Reagan boom, the inadvertent midsummer tightening was like a final thump—knocking the last wind out of it. Real interest rates were the clearest measure of what the Fed had done to squelch the roaring recovery. In the spring and summer of 1984, the real interest rate on long-term government bonds rose to an extraordinary 9.6 percent—the highest cost of money, in real terms, since Paul Volcker had become chairman in 1979. Real rates were nearly double the punishing conditions the Fed had imposed back in 1982 when it was managing the economic contraction. They were roughly four times higher than the normal cost of money during an expansionary cycle. Worse still, rising real interest rates, inevitably, drove the dollar still higher in foreign exchange, compounding the damage to American producers.

By the fall quarter, the economy was limp, growing at a lackluster rate of 2.1 percent and still weakening. In August, the unemployment rate crept back up to 7.5 percent. Ronald Reagan's boom was over.

"We were a little bit slow to ease," Paul Volcker conceded. "I thought at the time we were a bit late."

Volcker concluded that the Fed must reverse course—and quickly —but the Federal Reserve chairman could not convince his colleagues. When they met on August 21, for once, he did not get his way within the Federal Open Market Committee. Throughout his tenure, there were only a few occasions when Volcker's perspective on monetary policy did not prevail inside the policy-making committee, at least in a compromised form. The August meeting of the FOMC was one of those occasions, perhaps the starkest one.

Volcker was fairly certain about the outlook, but most of the committee members were insisting that the Fed couldn't ease. "The economy's going to come roaring back," they told him.

Arrayed against the chairman in the debate were the senior System men—Gramley, Wallich, Partee—making much the same argument they had made through the year. The Fed had always lost control at this point in earlier cycles. If it did not hold firm now, price inflation would escalate six or nine months hence and the central bank would, once again, have to play a painful game of catch-up. The Fed's primary objective was to maintain stable prices, and it should concentrate on that single goal, not on the competing objective of stimulating the economy.

"Gramley won the argument," an FOMC officer said. "Gramley always expressed concern that if they didn't stay tight now, the next time would be too late with the way the trends are breaking."

Volcker invoked the technical reasons to explain why money was too tight, tighter than they intended. Nervous bankers were staying away from the Discount window and throwing off the normal calculations. The majority did not buy it.

"The committee was reluctant to accept the notion that something exceptional was going on," Governor Partee said. "We were concerned about being too easy."

The sharp division within the Federal Open Market Committee was not revealed by the final vote or by the FOMC's minutes. The chairman himself did not normally dissent, even when he did not get his way. That would suggest internal turmoil at the central bank, not to mention personal embarrassment for its leader. Volcker yielded to the others, and as the FOMC minutes opaquely reported, "All but one member indicated their acceptance of a directive specifying no change at this time in the degree of pressure on reserve positions." The dissenter was Henry Wallich, who as usual wanted the Fed to tighten still more.

Paul Volcker lost. Yet he still got his way. The Federal Reserve chairman went ahead on his own and eased anyway, despite the Federal Open Market Committee's instructions to hold firm. Volcker had only one vote within the FOMC, but he ran the Federal Reserve. In particular, he supervised the daily operations of the Open Market Desk in New York. After the August meeting, Volcker made his own liberal interpretation of the FOMC's directive and told the Open Market Desk to ease.

"I knew what instructions he was giving the New York desk," Anthony Solomon, president of the New York Fed, said, "and I thought he was not faithfully observing the instructions of the FOMC. He got the desk to take major action that went way beyond the framework of the directive. He was taking too much leeway personally."

Volcker shrugged off the "bitching" from other committee members. He had a secondary motive for ignoring the FOMC decision and moving quickly—the approaching fall election. The closer it came to election day, the harder it would be for the Federal Reserve to execute a major policy turn without being accused of politics by one side or the other.

"Volcker thought it was necessary to ease for economic reasons," an FOMC official explained, "but if he waited until after the election, that might be too late. In effect, the window was closing. From Labor Day till election day, the window is closed. He wanted to ease and that was about the last point he could do it without making it look too political."

Some of the FOMC members were not amused. When they saw interest rates declining, they called Tony Solomon at the New York Fed for an explanation. "They called me, they called the desk, asking, 'What's going on?' " Solomon said. "The desk was easing way beyond the directive. The desk was easing because Volcker was telling it to. I told him: 'The substance of what you did is all right, but you should have called a conference call with the committee before you did it. The morale of the FOMC gets shaky.' "

Despite the grumbling from his colleagues, Volcker was right about the economy. It needed help from the Fed—lots of help. The chairman's unilateral decision to relax money policy pulled short-term interest rates down as the Federal Funds rate gradually declined by about 100 basis points. That was not enough, however. The Federal Reserve would have to ease much more than that to keep the recovery alive.

Rather abruptly, the Federal Reserve was compelled to shift its attention from the brake to the accelerator. For many months, the central bank had been worried about slowing down an economic recovery it considered too bullish. Now the Fed was preoccupied with restarting an economy that suddenly seemed dangerously weak.

The enduring image evoked by Ronald Reagan's campaign for reelection was of America in soft focus. His most compelling television commercial conveyed a romanticized vision of everyday life, scenes of ordinary people up and doing, heading for work, raising the flag. "It's morning again in America," the moderator announced in a wise, gentle voice. The camera toured a comfortable community, glimpsing prosperity and good feeling everywhere it turned, a family wedding, a new home with a white picket fence. "Just about everyone in town is thinking the same thing—now that our country is turning around, why would we ever turn back again?"

Before campaign rallies, the President announced the dawning of a new era. "America is back," he said in Ohio, "a giant re-emergent on the scene. Our country is powerful in its renewed spirits, powerful in its economy, powerful in the world economy, and powerful in its ability to defend itself and secure the peace."[35]

For a California audience, the President offered a new slogan for his second term: "You ain't seen nothing yet."

Everywhere he traveled, the crowds waved flags and broke into a spontaneous chant, "U.S.A.—U.S.A.—U.S.A." The nation triumphant. The President invoked the spirit of the Olympic torch that had been carried hand to hand across the country to the Olympic games in Los Angeles, where American athletes won many gold medals amid the patriotic pageantry. "U.S.A.—U.S.A.—U.S.A.," the crowds chanted in joyous self-congratulation.

Thus, with words and pictures, the President fused nationalism and capitalism, the two anchoring ideas of American culture and politics —patriotism and prosperity joined in a single celebration. Ronald Reagan, given his performing skills and sunny personality, evoked the familiar symbols with a melodramatic enthusiasm unmatched in modern politics. The fusion was not, however, new to American politics. The energy of nationhood had always been employed to support the prerogatives of capitalist enterprise.

Sixty years earlier, Thorstein Veblen had written: ". . . the illusions of nationalism allowed the underlying population to believe that the common good was bound up with the business advantage of these captains of solvency into whose service the national establishment was gradually drawn. . . ." And Veblen wrote: "Uncritical devotion to the national pretensions being a meritorious habit, it is also a useful article of camouflage, a shelter for gainful enterprises and transactions which might otherwise be open to doubt, a means of avoiding unfavorable notice and of procuring a profitable line of goodwill."[36]

The patriotic celebration in the fall of 1984, wonderfully effective as a device to re-elect Ronald Reagan, also served as an "article of camouflage." The flag was like a veil that concealed large ironies, great illusions. At the very moment when the Reagan campaign was proclaiming "morning again in America," a dusky pallor was settling over business activity. It was not dawn, but closer to twilight for Ronald Reagan's booming economy.

When the President promised, "You ain't seen nothing yet," the slogan had a droll double meaning. The public, it was true, did not see. Voters believed, reasonably enough from what they had experienced, that the country was headed onward and upward. They did not realize that the roaring phase of expansion had already ended, that the economy was settling into a bumpy routine of fitful starts and stagnation, an era of below-average growth and above-average unemployment.

The news media amplified the illusions. While the business section dutifully reported the slowdown in economic activity, the political coverage on the front page blared a louder message, supporting the President's claims. Americans did not know—and the news media did not tell them—that the rising tide of prosperity was more in the nature of a false, brief surge.[37]

The spirit of nationalism, the warming glow of patriotic fervor that swept the country, was especially ironic. The resurgent American economy was, indeed, leading the global economy back from the worldwide recession. But the U.S. government's economic policies were anything but nationalistic. Domestic industries—manufacturing, agriculture, oil and other minerals—were being decimated by the combined effects of Washington's fiscal and monetary policy. Ronald Reagan's symbol of American revival, the strong dollar, was in reality assisting America's foreign competitors, ceding a larger and larger share of world trade to other nations.

The President's campaign themes could not have been effective, however, if they had not seemed consistent with the authentic human experience of American voters. What most ordinary citizens knew from their own lives appeared to match what the President told them was true. The anxiety of price inflation was gone. Most people were back at work. Most important of all, in immediate political terms, real disposable income per capita was rising throughout the campaign year at an extraordinary pace—up 5 percent. In 1980, when Jimmy Carter was up for re-election, price inflation was above 13 percent and real disposable income was shrinking slightly, thanks to the brief recession. When President Reagan asked, "Are you better off than you were four years ago?," the answer seemed self-evident for the majority of Americans.

The improved economic conditions were summarized in the "misery index," a playful invention of economist Arthur Okun, which politicians of both parties had borrowed for presidential campaigns. The misery index simply added the unemployment rate with the inflation rate as a rough measure of economic discomfort. In 1980, it was more than 19 percent. By 1984, the misery index was down to 11 percent.

Still, a telling dimension of economic distress was missing from that comparison—the historically high level of real interest rates. Democrats, if they had wished to focus on the issue, might have invoked the "hardship index," devised by David P. Eastburn, former president of the Philadelphia Fed. To incorporate the cost of credit as an important element of economic pain, the hardship index simply added the real interest rate on home mortgages to the inflation and unemployment rates. That combination provided a better snapshot of the economic reality facing average citizens. On Eastburn's hardship index, 1980 and 1984 looked identical. In both years, the index was stuck at the uncomfortably high level of 21.[38]

The regressive wealth distribution that flowed from the high interest rates did not easily translate into a political issue. The population, it was true, was starkly divided into net financial debtors and creditors —the 55 percent who were borrowers and the 45 percent who were creditors. The benefits of the high cost of money were flowing to the minority and especially to the wealthy 10 percent who owned most of the net financial wealth. Since this was never talked about in politics, not many voters understood it.

Yet, even if there had been general awareness, it was not certain what the political impact would be. Given the decayed condition of electoral democracy, barely more than half of adult Americans voted in presidential elections. The electorate that actually voted was top-heavy with better-educated, more prosperous Americans—the same people who, on the whole, benefited from the government's high interest rates. Conceivably, a majority of the voting Americans actually liked the high rates. The debtors, though a majority of citizens, counted for less at election time. This helped explain why politicians, particularly Democrats who presumed to speak for the less fortunate, almost never addressed the class implications of debt and interest rates. In speaking for the debtors, many of whom never voted, a candidate risked offending the creditors, who did.

Most citizens, in any case, and most politicians did not assess the condition of economic well-being in these terms. They looked at the present and the recent past, not at implications for the distant future. In 1984, the immediate evidence of rising incomes was a far more convincing reality than the long-term consequences of borrowing money at punishing interest rates. Walter Mondale's campaign for the Presidency could not successfully refute what most citizens believed to be true. America was back, just as the President said.

. . .

"For the Reagan Administration," budget director David Stockman mused, "it was pure luck that the recovery peaked in perfect timing for the election. Then it slowed down and it's been running below trend ever since."

Anthony Solomon expressed the same reaction: "These guys have been incredibly lucky because the Federal Reserve squeezed out the inflationary pressures and the timing happened to be perfect—coming into an election year with a strongly recovering economy and low inflation."

As the economy slowed down sharply in the early fall, the Reagan White House became nervous again about the Federal Reserve, but the political managers agreed that it would be pointless and perhaps counterproductive to revive "Fed bashing" in the midst of a campaign that was going their way. Whatever the Fed did in August or September was not going to substantially alter the economy before November.

"The White House was upset," Stockman said, "but the second-quarter numbers for economic growth had been awfully good. The White House had enough sense to know that nothing the Fed could do now would affect the election."

The Republican Party, gathered in convention in Dallas to nominate Ronald Reagan, did take a swipe at the central bank, however. Despite White House misgivings, the Republican platform included a section inspired by Representative Jack Kemp, which called for reform of the Federal Reserve and a return to the gold standard.

> The Federal Reserve Board's destabilizing actions must . . . stop [the platform declared]. We need coordination between fiscal and monetary policy, timely information about Fed decisions and an end to the uncertainties people face in obtaining money and credit. The Gold Standard may be a useful mechanism for realizing the Federal Reserve's determination to adopt monetary policies needed to sustain price stability.[39]

Like other large controversies surrounding money, the press ignored this one. In 1984, a major political party, the party that held the White House, had proposed a return to the gold standard. Yet the news media paid little attention. Most reporters regarded Kemp's gold crusade as an oddity, arcane and boring. Money seemed too complicated to understand or to explain.

If the Reagan White House was politically lucky about the economy, so in its own way was the Federal Reserve. Because the Fed had switched directions, because prices were clearly under control and the economy was weak, the fall campaign did not produce the same tension that the Fed had weathered in 1980. While Jimmy Carter was making a desperate effort to hold on to the White House, the Fed twice raised the Discount rate and pushed short-term interest rates higher. In the fall of 1984, the Fed was easing interest rates.

On October 2, the Federal Open Market Committee agreed with what Volcker had argued in August. It must relax money and credit, allowing interest to decline further. The move was too tentative for three committee members. Preston Martin dissented, joined by Emmett Rice and Martha Seger, who was the second Reagan appointee. All wanted stronger action to stimulate the economy.

Frederick Schultz, the former vice chairman, visited his old friends at the Fed on the morning of October 19 and ran into Lyle Gramley and Chuck Partee. "Both of them said the same thing to me—'Boy, are we lucky,' " Schultz reported. "Because the Fed didn't have to raise interest rates in the heat of the campaign."

On the morning of October 25, the money-market analyst at Merrill Lynch delivered his daily report on interest rates, which was broadcast to brokers at all the firm's far-flung offices. Short-term interest rates, he predicted, would continue to fall rapidly. "They should call it the Federal Open Market Committee to Re-elect Reagan," he joked.

The President, at that point, did not need any help from the Fed. Reagan carried forty-nine states, the greatest victory in terms of electoral votes since Franklin Roosevelt's landslide in 1936. "You ain't seen nothing yet," the President promised again.

By election day, the Federal Funds rate was trading around 9.7 percent—down by two full percentage points since August. The Federal Reserve Board discreetly waited until two weeks after the election to reduce the Discount rate. Then it reduced the Discount rate again on December 21.

Despite dissents from Lyle Gramley, the Federal Open Market Committee scurried to revive the weakened economy. The FOMC agreed to ease interest rates further at both its November and December meetings. By the end of the year, the Federal Funds rate was below 8 percent for the first time in nearly six years.

The Fed was a bit late. By the final three months of 1984, the booming recovery had been nearly extinguished. Real economic growth for the last quarter fell to an anemic .6 percent—virtually stagnant and dangerously close to contraction. The full scope of what the Federal Reserve had accomplished with its determination to restrain the recovery was now visible in the quarterly growth numbers for the year. First quarter: 11.4 percent real growth. Second quarter: 5.1 percent. Third quarter: 2.1 percent. Fourth quarter: .6 percent.

The recovery had been driven into the ground. Conceivably, as some might claim, the Federal Reserve was not to blame. An economic recovery always slowed down after an initial boom of eighteen to twenty-four months and, therefore, the abrupt subsidence in 1984 might be attributed to "natural forces" of the business cycle. No one, of course, could prove definitively that this was wrong. No one would ever know what might have happened to the U.S. economy if the Fed had not braked it—anymore than one could establish precisely how much economic growth was lost to the nation, jobs and output and income that were permanently forfeited, because the Fed did decide to brake the boom.

But defensive disclaimers after the fact begged the crucial question of intent: Did the Federal Reserve really expect to see the economy subside to nearly zero growth? Is that what the FOMC members had in mind for when they made their policy decisions? Obviously not, judging from the record of their deliberations and their own comments. On the contrary, through most of 1984, the Fed policy makers regularly predicted the opposite danger—an economy running out of control and threatening to create upward pressures on prices again.

If the Federal Reserve believed the recovery would be fading naturally, then why did it raise interest rates and twice apply the brakes? The answer, of course, was that the majority did not believe this. Whatever "natural forces" were moderating the pace of recovery, the Fed did not trust nature to do the job. So it added pressure of its own. The dominant opinion among the FOMC members repeatedly warned about what would happen if the Fed did not act. The majority brushed aside Preston Martin's pleas and even overrode Paul Volcker's in order to stand its ground and prove that, this time, the Federal Reserve would not yield.

In addition to the potential growth lost in 1984, the Fed's strategy may have left larger consequences for the economy. Once the boom was broken, the economy never regained a normal vigor. After the second quarter of 1984, the path of expansion remained below the historic trend line for economic growth, even below the growth rate during the decade of the 1970s, which was universally considered disappointing. The economy did not go into recession; it sputtered and started and disappointed normal expectations.

"It was really scary," Preston Martin said. "We got a stop-go expansion that we are still living with. You have a quarter of 1 percent growth, then a quarter of 3.5 percent, then 2.5 percent, then another quarter of 1 percent. All through that bouncing around, your unemployment stays too high and interest rates stay too high and your real growth is too low."

Yet, in its own terms, the Federal Reserve was triumphant. The central bank had won the "game of chicken." Or, at least, it had not lost. Paul Volcker was utterly unsuccessful in his efforts to persuade Congress to back off and reduce the federal deficits. Despite minor corrective actions, the budget deficits remained huge and would actually reach a new peak in the 1985 fiscal year and a higher one in 1986. Nevertheless, under extreme circumstances, the Fed had not given in. It successfully resisted all the pressures for an easier money policy, including threats and complaints from the White House. Whatever else it got wrong, the Federal Reserve did not repeat its mistakes from the last war.

Prices were steady; money was stable. The central bank and its chairman, after all, had one standard for judging their performance and by that standard they had succeeded. Inflation remained subdued, despite the huge deficits. An economy driven by an enormously stimulative fiscal policy had been kept in check by a steadfast monetary policy. The economy was held back, well short of its potential, but also safe from inflation.

The money question was, as always, a question of values. It depended entirely on what mattered most to the society. If stable money was the nation's first and most important goal, if avoiding the risk of price inflation came before everything else, then Paul Volcker and the Federal Reserve had accomplished the society's highest purpose. But, if only money mattered, then all else must count for less. Jobs, production, home ownership, industrial development, an equitable distribution of incomes and wealth—all of society's competing economic objectives would suffer the consequences of placing money first, as indeed they did. When all these collateral costs were added up, the Federal Reserve's single-minded triumph proved to be quite expensive.

"I'm a lifelong Republican," said Robert O. Anderson, chairman of the Atlantic Richfield oil company, "but I fault the Republicans. Here's a group of free-market, free-enterprise conservatives and they've done more to dismantle American industry than any other group in history. And yet they go around saying everything is great. It's like the Wizard of Oz."

Anderson was also a former board chairman at the Dallas Federal Reserve Bank and he also faulted the Federal Reserve. "I'm a friend of the Fed's," he said, "but I really have been alarmed by what it has done. I told them two years ago that if we didn't alter our course, we were going to kill our industrial sector and that's what happened. In my opinion, the Fed compensated so thoroughly for the tax cuts that nobody even noticed the impact."

To no avail, Anderson personally complained to former colleagues in the System. "When I complain, they simply are silent," he said. "The Fed doesn't respond. It just goes its own way. And the White House has been content just to shut up and let the Fed take the heat."

Anderson was among the industrialists who, for several years, vainly tried to persuade both the Reagan Administration and the Federal Reserve that they must stop the dollar from rising higher and higher in international exchange. For Anderson, the soaring value of the dollar was no mystery. It was mainly driven upward by the high interest rates. "I do not think the high interest rates are any coincidence," Anderson added. "I think they are part of the overall anti-inflation mode."

In the fall of 1984, three weeks before the election, the oilmen and business executives of the Houston Club in Houston, Texas, were startled to hear Anderson deliver an impassioned denunciation of what the Reagan-Volcker government was doing to the American economy.

Everytime I travel abroad, people want to know about this enormous recovery the United States is going through—and I have a little trouble telling them about it [the oil executive said]. Because, to me, it is a white-collar recovery. This recovery has left blue-collar America behind. You don't see the roughnecks out there, you don't see the carpenters, you don't see the steelworkers, you don't see the lumberjacks, you don't see the farmers. The broad spectrum we used to call "Working America" is not in this recovery.

We have been advised by the computer located in the basement of the Federal Reserve building in Washington, D.C., that we are now exceeding the legal speed limit for economic recovery. And that we must somehow slow this vehicle down. But the Blue-Collar America, Working America, Industrial America is not on this boat. We have, in my opinion, a probable growth rate in services, imports, high tech in the 10 percent range. If your desired level is 4.5 percent, you don't have to be very smart to figure out that the other half has to travel at minus 2 percent. And that's just where Industrial America is traveling—minus 2.[40]

Anderson's lament—repeated less vividly by many others in industry and agriculture—was largely ignored during 1984, when the worst of the damage was done. When the Federal Reserve stiffened interest rates to brake the recovery, the dollar escalated in value by another 12 percent against foreign currencies. The index of the dollar's average exchange value with the other major industrial currencies was below 100 at the end of 1980. By the end of 1983, it had risen to 133. By the end of 1984, it was at 149. Neither the Fed nor the Treasury tried to stop it.

Over four years, the cumulative appreciation of the dollar was more than 50 percent—a rough measure of the price disadvantage that the U.S. government had imposed on all the trade-sensitive sectors in the American economy. It was no mystery why American companies were closing domestic factories and moving production abroad or why farmers in Kansas could no longer sell their surplus wheat overseas.

Caterpillar Tractor moved its forklift production from Mentor, Ohio, to Leicester, England. Ford closed a plant in Romeo, Michigan, and shifted the jobs to Belgium and Britain. Du Pont cut more jobs in the United States and built new chemical works in West Germany, France and the Netherlands. Goodyear Tire & Rubber gave up trying to sell huge earthmover tires from Ohio and began making them in Japan.[41]

The flight of U.S. production had ironic consequences for supply-side economics. New plants and factories were indeed being built in America, but they were offset by those that were closed. Economist Gerald Epstein described the actual bottom line: "As a percentage of GNP, net investment was lower in 1984 than in 1979—lower, indeed, than it has been in any recent business-cycle peak . . . industries that are being adversely affected by the high dollar, such as paper, steel and nonelectrical machinery, are cutting back on investment in new plants and equipment."[42]

For agriculture, export markets continued to shrink. Within two years, the trend produced a startling symbol of reversal in America's role as producer of food and fiber. By 1986, it was clear the United States, the most abundant farm country in the world, would become a net importer of agricultural products.

Some cynical farmers and farm-state politicians concluded that the Fed was doing this to them on purpose—in order to bail out the money-center banks burdened by bad foreign loans. The strong dollar helped Latin nations to suppress imports of American food products and, meanwhile, to expand their own exports to the United States—giving them the trade surpluses needed to keep up with their loan payments. Farmers in the Midwest lost in the transaction, while bankers in New York benefited.

Whether or not the farmers were correct in their suspicions about the Fed's motivations, they were certainly right about the results. The farmers might have been shocked to learn that the bankers themselves cited the trade-off in their private advice to the Federal Reserve Board —only the bankers saw it as one of the benefits of the strong dollar. The dollar-induced trade imbalances were hurting agriculture and other sectors, the Federal Advisory Council noted, but they also "provide the LDCs with some much-needed foreign exchange to service debt."

With eloquent anger, Lee Iacocca of Chrysler summarized the overall losses from the strong dollar. Addressing a Washington audience, Iacocca warned:

> People in this town better start realizing that buried somewhere in those numbers, between the highs and lows of these [dollar] swings, are things like 140,000 bankruptcies, three million jobs going overseas and 100,000 fewer farmers, most of whom lost their land. These aren't just bell curves from a textbook. These are real people—human beings trying to eat and buy shoes for their kids and pay off the mortgage.[43]

The soaring dollar's destruction to the domestic economy was a tender subject for Federal Reserve officials. They were notably defensive. Judging from the policy record, the Fed's officials had never fully anticipated how much the dollar would rise as they tightened credit to restrain the recovery. They regretted the consequences. And they offered excuses absolving themselves.

"Our export industries are being wiped out," Anthony Solomon lamented. "Some of them will never come back from this." Solomon emphasized that he and Volcker had always been concerned about the dollar, but he insisted they were unable to act. The Fed could not intervene in foreign-exchange markets to tamp down the rising dollar because the Reagan Administration was ideologically opposed to currency interventions. Even occasional foreign-exchange interventions would not have broken the trend, however, as long as U.S. interest rates were so high.

Paul Volcker, likewise, regretted the consequences but pleaded innocent. "The dollar was a big mistake of the fiscal-monetary policy mix," the chairman acknowledged. "It wasn't our fault but we couldn't do anything about it either. I kept worrying about the dollar coming down with a thud, but by late summer of 1984 it became apparent that this was taking starch out of manufacturing."

Volcker, like Solomon, claimed the Fed was helpless. The central bank could have relaxed domestic interest rates, of course, and that would have brought down the value of the dollar on foreign-exchange markets. But lowering interest rates would have meant surrendering on its main objective—restraining the economy and dampening prices. Volcker said defensively:

> I have more sympathy for taking the dollar into account than anyone else on the committee. But what do you do about it? Should we have been considerably easier, looking at the dollar? In my own terms, I thought that until you had a more settled psychology on inflation and more confidence in the economy, it was going to be hard to ease—particularly when the real source of the difficulty is coming from somewhere else.

"Somewhere else," in the Fed's perspective, was fiscal policy. The central bank justified its own performance—passively tolerating the dollar's gross swing in value—by insisting it could do nothing else in the face of the federal deficits. Paul Volcker, it seemed, was as adept as Ronald Reagan at deflecting blame. Just as the President liked to blame every ill consequence on Jimmy Carter and the sins of the past, Volcker blamed fiscal policy and the budget deficits. When faced with public criticism, the central bank often emphasized its impotence.

Look, all we can do is deal with the macro situation [Governor Partee pleaded]. With the situation we had, manufacturing is hit and foreign imports are high, not because of anything we did, but because of the dollar. What else could we do? The dollar is high because of the deficits, because interest rates are higher in the U.S., because of faith in Reagan and the American economy. What were we supposed to do? Are we supposed to just let money grow and grow to keep interest rates falling? That would guarantee inflation.

The Federal Reserve's self-defense was, to put it charitably, strained. It suggested that the Fed had no discretion in the matter, that there was no other course for monetary policy except the one the Fed had chosen. But that left aside the controversial choices—and mistakes—that the Federal Reserve had made for itself, the extraordinary strategy of high interest rates it followed during recovery and, in particular, the decision to brake the boom in 1984.

Neither of those choices was inevitable, and the excessive nature of what the Fed did was suggested by three different measures. First, real interest rates actually rose to their highest levels as the economy was losing steam—clear evidence that the central bank was overdoing its restraint. Second, economic growth did not simply moderate in 1984, it nearly came to a halt. Third, the general price average did not remain at the moderate level established by the great contraction of 1981–1982, but began falling further—tightening the squeeze on debtors and producers. If it had chosen, the Federal Reserve could have stopped well short of these extremes without yielding to runaway inflation. If the Fed had chosen to be more moderate on interest rates, the devastation from the rising dollar would have been less drastic too.

The Federal Reserve did, however, succeed in evading the blame. Given the divided structure of responsibility in the federal government, everyone could evade blame. Congress and the President left the management of money to the central bank. The central bank pointed the finger back at Congress and the President. The Reagan Administration ignored the rising dollar, even cheered it. The Federal Reserve knew better, but decided it was helpless.

The ambiguity posed the sort of fine-grain question that policy analysts in Washington enjoyed studying. What was the economic cause of the dollar's drastic appreciation? What or who was to blame for the unfortunate devastation—monetary policy or fiscal policy, the Federal Reserve or the executive branch and Congress? Their conclusions were invariably carefully hedged assessments of cause and effect. For the millions of citizens and business enterprises that suffered the consequences, a simpler answer was sufficient: the U.S. government was to blame, all of it.

For most American families, there were two major purchases in life —the car and the house—and no other transactions were as important to their sense of well-being. Yet, something strange was happening in the Reagan recovery: Americans were not buying as many houses and cars as they used to buy. Amid the general euphoria over the revived prosperity, this was like a well-kept secret. The newsmagazines and other media focused, instead, on chronicling the emergence of the Yuppies, a new class of young urban professionals with high incomes and luxurious tastes. As a representative group, the Yuppies could not have been more distant from what was really happening to the patterns of American consumption.

The mass market was shrinking. Automobile sales were booming, of course, in 1984—up 50 percent from Detroit's low point in the recession. Yet the auto industry, including the rising sales volume captured by foreign imports, never recovered the same market that it had enjoyed in the 1970s. As a percentage of the driving-age population, the sale of autos and trucks was actually 16 percent below 1978 and 22 percent below 1973, Morgan Guaranty reported. Compared to the historic consumption patterns, Detroit and Japan and Europe were competing for shares in a smaller market.[44]

The 1980s should have meant, if anything, record car sales. For one thing, the working-age population now included that swollen generation of young people from the "baby boom," new consumers with their own incomes, forming their own households. Furthermore, gasoline prices were declining steadily in the eighties, instead of the steep price increases of the seventies that had raised the cost of owning a car and discouraged buyers. The potential was there, but unfulfilled.

The retreat from home buying was more striking and also more fundamental to the American standard of living. The housing industry surged and ebbed month to month during the recovery, usually following changes in interest rates, but home builders never came close to reaching the potential market of new home buyers in the 1980s. The lost customers in housing naturally extended to durable goods like refrigerators and washing machines that new homeowners would purchase.

Housing starts reached a robust total of 1.7 million units in 1984, nearly double the lowest point of the recession. Yet, during the 1970s, when the pool of potential buyers was much smaller, the housing industry had surpassed 2 million starts a year four times and set a record of 2.4 million new homes in 1972. The decade of the eighties should have broken that record, since the "baby boom" was adding an extra 12 million young families to the pool of potential first-time home buyers. Where did all these buyers go?

"During the 1980s, we have the largest number of new people added to the age group that typically buys homes," said Michael Sumichrast, chief economist for the home builders' association. "The problem is a lot of these young people cannot afford to buy houses. They have no choice but to rent or to double up."[45]

These were the people priced out of the housing market by the high mortgage interest rates or by personal incomes that were too depressed to support a mortgage or by both. Millions of younger families found they could not afford what their parents or even their older brothers and sisters had been able to enjoy prior to the 1980s. If homeownership was the essential element of the "American dream," the dream was becoming more selective.

For the first time in forty years, the percentage of American families that owned their own homes actually decreased during the Reagan Presidency. Though no one talked about it much in the political campaigns, this was a most significant turning point for the pattern of American life. Rising levels of homeownership had been a given since 1940. Stimulated by federal subsidies of various sorts, including the government-imposed ceilings on interest rates, the rate of homeownership among Americans had increased steadily from 44 percent in 1940 to 66 percent by 1980. Starting in 1981, homeownership began to decline for the first time since World War II. By 1984, it was down to 64.5 percent. By 1986, it would fall to 63.9 percent.

"Although the annual declines have been small, they cumulatively offset all of the gains in homeownership achieved during the boom years of the mid-to-late 1970s," the MIT-Harvard Joint Center for Housing Studies reported. In other words, if homeownership was a shared measure of national progress, then the nation had regressed to the pre-1973 level during the era of Reagan and Volcker.[46]

Virtually all of the lost ground was suffered by young people, families under thirty-five years old. Except perhaps for Yuppies, the young families that could buy got smaller homes for their money and were compelled to pay much larger shares of their incomes to keep them.

At age thirty, the average household must now devote 44 percent of its monthly earnings to owning a new home—double what young homeowners had had to pay ten years before.[47]

Given this elemental setback in their living standards, it was particularly ironic that younger people voted so enthusiastically for the President, but then the Democratic Party was also largely silent on the subject. As a practical matter, both political parties had retreated from the goal of universal homeownership, first the Democrats, when they abolished interest-rate controls in 1980, then the Republicans, by adopting an economic strategy that assigned a lower priority to providing homes for people. The decline of homeownership, if the government did nothing to reverse it, represented a major redefinition of the American idea of prosperity.

Throughout the recovery, however, the trend of lost potential was masked by the general abundance of consumption. After all, consumer demand, as defined by economists, was quite strong. Personal income rose vigorously on average. The Reagan recovery was driven largely by personal spending (though, to be sure, a larger share of what Americans bought was imported from abroad). How could both be true—a pro-consumption recovery that was simultaneously losing millions of the potential customers for cars, houses and other goods?

Higher interest rates were part of the answer. The other explanation was the maldistribution of incomes. In the aggregate and on average, the money income available to consumers for buying things looked more than ample. When one looked closer, it was clear that a huge share of the increased money income was going to upper-income families (including the celebrated Yuppies). A decreasing share of national incomes was going to all the families on the bottom half of the economic ladder, people who would also buy cars and houses and other nice things, if they could afford them.

According to the Bureau of the Census, the median real income of the bottom 40 percent had fallen from 1980 to 1984, about $477 per family, a loss of more than 3 percent. The top 10 percent, meanwhile, enjoyed an increase of $5,085 in their median income, an increase of more than 7 percent. The pivotal political decisions of the 1980s, from the Reagan economic program to Volcker's monetary policy, all contributed to the regressive shift in incomes. What was lost by those who depended on wage incomes was gained by those with interest incomes.[48]

Not surprisingly, people whose real incomes were shrinking did not make very good consumers. The economy was carried forward by those who had plenty of money to spend, the upper half. The others, especially young people, simply had to settle for a scaled-down version of the old dream. In general, they were the Americans who were buying fewer cars and houses than they used to buy.

People with inadequate real incomes had one other option—they could borrow the money. By going deeper into debt, they could keep spending and hope that their prospects improved. Millions of families understandably chose that option. Personal debt accumulated rapidly. The increased savings that supply-side economics was supposed to deliver not only did not occur but the savings rate fell to new lows. Families were inclined to borrow rather than forgo purchases, because it was difficult to accept the new reality of their reduced status— especially difficult when the clamor from politics and the news media insisted that Americans were embarked on a new era of prosperity.

The mass market was splitting apart, as *Fortune* magazine had said, but it was also getting smaller. The emerging pattern had profound implications for the future performance of the American economy, not to mention family living standards, yet it did not become an absorbing question for economists. When economists calculated "consumer demand," it was not the sum of what people needed in their lives, the standard that Thorstein Veblen had proposed for an efficient economy. Consumer demand simply consisted of the total money available to the people who could afford to buy things.

For modern economists, the question of which people had the money or what they would spend it on seemed irrelevant. The fact that some families were buying second homes for vacations or third cars while others could not afford their first home or car was considered a social question, not a problem for the economy. Since most modern politicians relied on the economists' definitions, they perhaps did not perceive what had changed.

In the long term, however, if the trends were not reversed, the shrinking mass market would become a political question. Was this what average Americans expected from their economy? Or what political leaders had promised them? To use Lyle Gramley's word, the political implications were dynamite, waiting to explode.

The ultimate irony in Paul Volcker's triumph over inflation was that, in the larger sense, the Federal Reserve actually failed to accomplish its historic purpose. The overriding responsibility of the central bank was to control the overall expansion of credit in the economy, to insure that the society's ambitions did not get ahead of reality and thereby overburden the future with debt. This time, for reasons partly beyond its control, the Federal Reserve was unable to fulfill its most basic function.

Americans, on the contrary, were borrowing during this economic recovery at an unprecedented and dangerous pace, both individuals and institutions, both private business and government. Despite its willingness to impose high interest rates, despite its actions to restrain economic growth, the Fed found itself largely impotent in curbing what Paul Volcker called "a national binge of borrowing."

No one was more troubled by the explosion of debt than the Fed governors themselves. They knew it was like a gun pointed at the future—threatening corporate balance sheets and household solvency alike, inviting widespread failures down the road or, alternately, producing irresistible pressure to bail out debtors by returning to inflation.

Interest rates are the device by which you ration the demand for credit so it won't be excessive [Governor Partee said]. Yet, if you look at the demand for credit now, it's extraordinarily large—it's huge. Government debt is going up, household debt, corporate debt. How can you look at that and conclude that interest rates are too high? I'd say interest rates aren't high enough. Yet I have to admit the economy isn't doing very well. It's a conundrum—extraordinary.

The Federal Reserve chairman worried over the dilemma too. His strategy of restraining the economy on its upswing had required a price for credit that was outrageously high by past standards, real interest rates unmatched in the central bank's own history. Yet borrowers of every kind were not deterred. For 1984, the Federal Open Market Committee set a goal of 8 to 11 percent growth in total domestic debt, but the economy grossly surpassed the Fed's target. The nation's outstanding debt grew by 14.1 percent—the fastest year of new borrowing on record—creating at least $300 billion more in new obligations than the Fed had thought prudent.[49]

This tremendous debt creation worries me [Volcker said]. Why are people making all these bad loans? People can say interest rates are too high and I might agree with that, certainly by historic standards and by the conditions in the economy. But if interest rates are too high, why is debt expanding so fast? Why is debt growing at a record rate relative to GNP? Apparently somebody out there doesn't think interest rates are too high.

Despite the inherited folklore, accumulating new debt was not in itself unhealthy. On the contrary, it was a sign of vigor. After all, the modern American economy would not function without the constant lending and borrowing. In general, if families weren't borrowing, it meant they weren't buying. If corporations did not go into debt, then they also did not build new factories and expand production and em-

ployment for the future. Government debt was creative too, if it stimulated a moribund private economy, if it purchased real economic
resources that would make the society more productive in the future
—roads and canals, schools and universities, basic research labs and
even new factories. By that standard, World War II had been the most
constructive borrowing binge in history.

At every level, from households to government, new debt had to be
judged by two basic questions of quality, the same questions any
careful family would ask itself before taking on a new loan. What was
the borrowed money going to buy—something worthwhile or something frivolous that was not worth the price of going into debt? Sec-
ondly, what was the likelihood that the family would be able to pay off
the loan? These were the same essential tests applied by corporate
managers planning a bond issue or, in theory at least, by government
economists planning a deficit budget.

In the mushrooming debt of the 1980s, it was those two questions
that aroused alarm. A sizable portion of America's new debt was not
buying anything very productive for the future. Much of it was financing immediate consumption, which was invigorating only if consumers
could keep up with the payments. And much of the borrowing was
used for profitable but empty financial speculation. In 1984, for instance, American business accumulated a staggering $140 billion in
new debt that was devoted solely to finance corporate mergers and
take-overs. It did not build any new factories.

As the debt mounted, the second question became more alarming.
The nation as a whole was taking on debt faster than it was enhancing
its ability to repay. Any borrower could do this for a time, counting on
his investment to pay off eventually or assuming his income would
catch up with his debt obligations. But when the American economy
flattened out and lost its robust expansion, the prospects that the
nation could collectively catch up with its mounting loans seemed
more and more questionable.

The dimensions were awesome. The United States's total outstanding debt—government and private—was $7.1 trillion at the end of
1984, nearly doubled since 1977. The alarming point was that domestic
debt had increased by more than 25 percent in 1983 and 1984 alone.
Obviously, debt was growing much faster than the economy as a whole
had grown—and the economy was the source of incomes, profits and
tax revenues that ultimately must pay off these loans.[50]

Over the postwar decades, the nation's total debt, public and private, had expanded in a remarkably steady relationship to the expanding economy—debt normally ran about 40 percent larger than the
Gross National Product. Now, the outstanding debt had become more

than 60 percent larger than GNP. In that situation, the first question became especially relevant—what did this borrowed money buy for the future? In general, not much. The new debt, for the most part, was not enhancing the nation's productive potential—its ability to catch up with the loan payments.

The Fed's inability to restrain the "borrowing binge" was the central contradiction of Paul Volcker's tenure as chairman. If one looked at interest rates, Volcker's monetary policy seemed punishingly stringent. Yet, if one looked at the explosion of credit, Volcker seemed wildly generous. There were two basic explanations. Volcker's own strategy and the central bank's own policies themselves helped to stimulate the rapid debt accumulation. But the other reason for the Fed's loss of control was a political decision. Congress had effectively stripped the Federal Reserve of its ability to constrain debt expansion when it enacted the financial deregulation legislation back in 1980.

Volcker himself had understood the hidden consequences of financial deregulation, though probably few members of Congress who had voted to abolish all remaining interest-rate controls in 1980 appreciated that it would also undermine the Federal Reserve's monetary control. Because of that legislation, the economic recovery that unfolded in 1983 and 1984 was unlike any other in modern experience— the first business cycle since the 1920s that proceeded without any arbitrary federal limits on interest rates. The market was free at last and the market of the 1980s produced the same thing it had produced in the "roaring twenties"—a burgeoning accumulation of dubious loans.

Since New Deal days, the government's various interest-rate ceilings—in addition to subsidizing borrowers—had acted like crude cutoff valves in the plumbing of finance. Once market interest rates reached the legal limits and could go no higher, money flowed away from the financial intermediaries as depositors pulled out, looking for better returns elsewhere. Banks and savings and loans that were losing deposits had no choice but to stop lending. The expansion of new debt naturally moderated (though not without great anguish and uproar from the disappointed borrowers and financial institutions caught in the "credit crunch"). If the Fed wished to slow down borrowing, it simply pushed interest rates closer to the cutoff point—and the supply of new credit was automatically curtailed.

Once the government controls were dismantled, however, the lenders were free to charge whatever the traffic would bear. And the Fed was left with only one lever of restraint—raising interest rates. To curb lending, it had to push rates up literally to a point where the traffic could no longer bear it—depressing the demand for loans by setting an exorbitant price, driving off some loan customers, usually the smallest and weakest.

As Philip Braverman, economist at Briggs Schaedle, explained:

> The emphasis is on making credit too expensive to want, not on reducing access to it. The hope is that the marketplace will allocate credit rationally. The hope is that borrowers won't continue to borrow and lenders will restrain lending. We make the market the only arbiter of credit allocation and whether credit is excessive. But it's perverse—making credit too freely available is ultimately inflationary.[51]

The Fed's single lever—raising interest to exorbitant levels—worked brutishly but effectively during Volcker's first years in office when the Fed's objective was to induce a recession and break inflation. The Fed had to push the prime rate as high as 21 percent to get the desired results and many victims suffered added damage, but the contraction did accomplish its purpose.

Once the economic recovery began, however, the central bank was in a new dilemma. It kept interest rates very high, but it dared not push them still higher and risk killing off the new recovery. As the Fed discovered, even its very high level of interest rates still wasn't high enough to persuade lenders and borrowers to slow down the creation of new debt. The free market distributing new credit was as undisciplined as was the federal government spending more than it took in.

> The only restraining influence you have left [a senior Fed official complained] is interest rates, restraint which works ultimately by bankrupting the customer. It obviously hurts people more. In the typical economist's vision, this is a wonderful world. Interest rates go up half a point and so many points are added to the cost of the loan and therefore lending slows. This is more theoretical than real.
>
> Now, a lot depends on the mood people are in. When we had interest-rate controls, the banks were stuck for funds and they couldn't lend. It didn't depend on the mood the banker was in. Now, without any ceilings, if the lender and the banker are both feeling optimistic, they can go on forever. Or they think they can.

The infectious optimism of Ronald Reagan was shared generally, leading both sides of the credit transaction to overestimate the future. Just as the President was undeterred by the soaring cost of federal debt, so were families and businesses (and their bankers) undeterred by the real debt burdens they took on. Across a broad front of economic activity, both debtors and creditors made high-risk gambles on the future, betting that the loans could somehow be paid off, despite the high interest costs and declining economic growth. Albert Wojnilower, the chief economist at First Boston, had predicted as much in 1980 when the financial deregulation legislation was enacted. By 1984, his warnings were confirmed.

"No doubt," Wojnilower observed, "there exist interest-rate levels high enough to curb private credit demand, but the experience of the 1980s to date, featuring good times and bad, and intervals of double-digit as well as zero inflation, suggests they lie well beyond the range of recent observations." [52]

Beyond that basic explanation, however, the Federal Reserve itself was also implicated in the explosion of debt, in ways that were never acknowledged. The central bank had set out to establish stable money and it succeeded, but its relentless campaign against price inflation also created basic pressures to borrow more—new incentives to get into debt.

By turning the tables on money values, for instance, the Fed essentially shifted the arena of inflationary speculation from tangible assets to financial assets. During the 1970s, as Fed governors often lamented, people borrowed money in order to speculate on real assets—buying houses and farmland, artworks and gold and other commodities, confident that inflation would appreciate their values. In the 1980s, the inflated values and speculative borrowing turned to paper—a bewildering proliferation of new financial instruments that could now deliver quick profits, thanks to the Fed's hard-money policy.

In both instances, people were essentially gambling on the money question, betting on inflation or its opposite. There was nothing about the financial speculation of the 1980s that suggested it was less intense or wasteful than the commodity speculation of the 1970s. When speculators profited on inflation in the seventies by buying houses, farmland, oil leases, the process at least stimulated the production of real goods—more houses, more farm commodities, more oil. Aside from personal profits, the only thing produced by the dizzy run-up of financial prices in the eighties was more paper. When price inflation moved to Wall Street, the Federal Reserve did not challenge it.

The Federal Reserve's stabilization of money was also an underlying cause driving the frenzy of corporate take-over battles in the 1980s—including the "junk bonds" and leveraged buy outs and deepening corporate debt that the central bankers deplored. T. Boone Pickens goes after Unocal. Carl Icahn raids Uniroyal. Capital Cities swallows ABC and General Electric grabs RCA. Ivan Boesky becomes a household name. Instead of the noble function of capital formation, investment bankers were preoccupied by this lucrative game of sharks. The stories of high-stakes combat over corporate ownership were no longer exciting once they became commonplace.

While corporate raiders talked righteously about defending stockholders against slothful corporate managers, the fundamental force that motivated most of these "deals" was a direct result of the changed economic world the Fed had created—real assets languished and financial assets soared. The aim of the corporate manipulations was to extract capital invested in a company's less profitable real assets, its factories and buildings, so the wealth could be redeployed in the financial assets that offered much higher returns. This was accomplished partly by cannibalizing a company, selling off various parts and taking the cash, and by putting the company deeper into debt—borrowing now against its future earnings. Though the techniques differed, the process of recapitalization under way in the eighties was in essence no different from the financial manipulations by J. P. Morgan and his contemporaries early in the century or the speculative stock-market games that financiers played in the 1920s.

Nearly every player profited immediately, from the stockholders who got a higher price for their shares to the investment bankers who collected handsome fees for brokering the deals. The potential losers were mostly in the future—when the weakened corporation, saddled with more debt than it could sustain, failed. The game for today, however, was getting the money out of a company's assets—converting equity ownership into debt. With and without take-overs, U.S. corporations retired $72 billion in corporate stock shares in 1984, replacing it with an equivalent amount of new corporate debt. The future was mortgaged, but nothing had happened to make the future more productive.

"For a corporation, there is one fundamental difference between equity and debt," Governor Partee explained. "You are not required to pay a dividend to stockholders if your profits are down. But if you don't service your debt, you go bankrupt. So corporations are much more exposed than they used to be."

The Federal Reserve deplored the practice and even introduced regulations to curb the use of the "junk bonds" used to finance many of the corporate buy outs. Nonetheless, so long as monetary policy maintained such high real returns for financial investments and simultaneously depressed the return from real assets, smart investors would naturally seek ways to get their capital out of one and into the other.

The financial market's "casino instincts," as Albert Wojnilower called the high-risk games, were also encouraged by the Federal Reserve's protective response to the banking crisis. The blanket guarantee to creditors extended by the government to keep Continental

Illinois afloat sent a message to investors—your money is safe in any bank or brokerage large enough that the Fed cannot let it fail. The risk would be borne by others, including U.S. taxpayers.

Henry Kaufman of Salomon Brothers concluded:

> This growth in credit is nourished by . . . the willingness of our government to spread an official safety net over a variety of participants which tends to reduce the risk of borrowing. No large business corporation is allowed to fail. No large financial institution is allowed to fail. No institution that has depositors is allowed to fail in its obligation to depositors, large or small. Federal credit agencies that get into trouble are not allowed to fail. So there is the kind of official safety net that's spreading and that is perceived by the marketplace.[53]

Finally, the debt explosion was driven substantially by Paul Volcker's own strategy for monetary policy. The high real interest rates, though intended to restrain, actually forced many to borrow more and more, just to keep up with their old debts. This was as true for debt-burdened farmers and oil drillers as it was for Third World countries of Latin America. For that matter, it was also true for the U.S. government. As a practical matter, many borrowers had no choice but to borrow more, even if they knew the added debt was imprudent and the interest costs were exorbitant. Not to borrow meant going under.

Edward Sonnino, a Wall Street portfolio manager, argued:

> These abnormally high interest rates by themselves—whether caused by the budget deficits or by the Fed—have paradoxically been an important, if not the main, cause of skyrocketing debt. Normally, of course, high interest rates deter borrowing. But excessively high interest rates can have the perverse effect of increasing borrowing, which is precisely what has happened over the past few years.[54]

The most visible example of how this worked was the LDC debt (though, of course, it was not a part of the U.S. domestic debt burden). When South American and Caribbean nations reached the peak of their crisis in 1982, they had sunk $330 billion into debt. Everyone agreed they had borrowed too much. Two years later, according to World Bank statistics, these countries were $374 billion in debt— further in the hole.

Their new loans, obligated at the high real interest rates, were devoted mostly to paying the interest due on their old loans. The more they borrowed at the high rates, the more they would need to borrow in the future to pay interest due. Though several countries showed improvement, most were compounding their real debt burdens—the crucial measure of whether they could sustain the lending. In 1981, the foreign debt owed by these countries was 38 percent of their total GNP; by 1984, it was 61 percent. Likewise, their debts were growing faster than their export income was expanding. Paul Volcker's management of the international debt crisis was gradually reducing the exposure of the major U.S. banks but, meanwhile, most of the debtors were in worse shape.

How long could they go on? As long as bankers and international lending agencies would lend them new money so they could keep paying the interest on the old debt. It did resemble a "Ponzi game," as Henry Wallich had suggested.

The effects were less dramatic, but the same erosion was working away on many American borrowers, families and businesses compelled to borrow more to stave off foreclosure or failure. On average, household balance sheets did not look endangered—rising incomes were more or less keeping pace with debt. But that overlooked the maldistribution of incomes and the fact that a large share of America's families were borrowing more because their real incomes were declining. In effect, they borrowed the money from the upper half—the families whose income shares were larger, thanks to high interest rates and other government policies.

"There's been quite a lot of redistribution of income toward the higher-income groups," Governor Partee explained. "It requires consumers to accumulate more and more debt. The high-income people invest their increased income in financial assets—money which gets borrowed by everyone else."

The borrowers were burdened with an additional risk because adjustable-rate loans were now in general use, both for home mortgages and for major business loans. The agreement often gave the borrowers the enticement of a low rate at the start, but one that could escalate sharply in the future. The lending institutions had protected themselves from risk of rising rates and were therefore more willing to lend. The only way the lenders would lose was if their loan customers failed and defaulted.

Even the federal government's huge deficits and rapidly accumulating debt were driven, in part, by the Federal Reserve's monetary policy. Volcker and the Fed, of course, stood foursquare against the deficits and did not think of themselves as partly responsible. But the strategy of high interest rates adopted by the central bank damaged the government's balance sheet too. It slowed down economic growth and therefore reduced tax revenues. Meanwhile, the high rates on Treasury bonds raised the cost of government borrowing enormously —adding as much as $30 or $40 billion to the federal deficits. Like many other debtors, the government had no choice but to pay the higher price and keep on borrowing.

The Federal Reserve, from its own perspective, did not have much choice either. The Fed applied the only lever it had available and in the short term it worked: prices held steady or declined. In the long term, however, the Fed's monetary policy appeared to be perversely self-defeating. Without other controls on the supply of credit, the high interest rates propelled the economy deeper and deeper into debt and created a new instability, the opposite of what Volcker had set out to accomplish. Bloated credit was the usual preamble to inflation. At some future point, the central bank would face a hard choice: should it let all debtors fail or should it bail them out by allowing price inflation to resume?

The Federal Reserve, given the absence of other controls, was in a political bind. If it relaxed the price of money, it would be criticized by the bondholders for yielding, for losing control. Yet if it continued to push so hard, it risked popular fury—eventual bankruptcy for lots of loan customers and devastating loan losses for lots of banks. By the end of 1984, more than seven hundred banks were listed as "problem banks," a list that would eventually grow to twelve hundred. The United States was about to become a net debtor to the rest of the world. A new debt crisis was developing, only this one was centered in the United States, not the Third World. No one in power was doing much to stop it.

Among the most important players in Washington, including the Federal Reserve, there was almost no public discussion of these underlying causes or how to extricate the political economy from the debilitating consequences. The solution was obvious: the federal government would have to reimpose other kinds of controls on banking and credit markets, legal limits that could contain the supply of credit, particularly the most dubious lending, so the Fed would not have to rely solely on the extreme punishment of high interest rates. The new controls could take many forms, from interest-rate ceilings to income-tax penalties to direct regulation by the central bank of how banks and other lending institutions allocated their lending. Controls would mean more equity—but also more stability. If Congress wanted lower interest rates from the Fed, the surest way to get them would be to create different mechanisms to control the expansion of credit.

In the Reagan era's ethos of free markets and less government, there was no prospect that politicians of either party would pursue this solution. Indeed, the political influence of commercial bankers was pushing in the other direction—toward greater freedom from legal restraints. The largest banks sought the power to operate nationwide, a consolidation of financial power that would inevitably centralize the political influence of banking in a handful of very large institutions. They also lobbied for the right to enter into other business sectors—where they would enjoy enormous advantages over competitors since they would still be protected from failure by the federal goverment, thanks to their special status as commercial banks.

Lobbyists from money-center banks (and Reagan administration officials) were outraged when Paul Volcker urged caution on further deregulation. He dragged his feet and lobbied Congress to proceed slowly. But, powerful as he was, the chairman of the central bank was not about to challenge the orthodoxy of his own constituency and become the foremost advocate for the reregulation of finance.

The only voices persistently and persuasively raised in behalf of restoring credit controls were, ironically, from major investment-banking firms of Wall Street—the conservative citadels of capitalism. Financial experts like Henry Kaufman, Albert Wojnilower, Philip Braverman and others warned repeatedly of the risks of the debt explosion and proposed various ideas for imposing new legal limits on lending.[55]

None of their proposals received any serious examination in Washington. Strange as it seemed, leading gurus of Wall Street were urging the federal government to impose new discipline on finance and the leaders of government in Washington would not listen to them. It was another measure of how much the mainstream political opinion had shifted. In the political capital, the new mythology held that the federal government had at last gotten out of the business of regulating finance. And the free market was producing all the benefits predicted for it.

The Wall Street economists knew it wasn't so. The free market was always itself a fiction. The reality, of course, was that the Federal Reserve still regulated credit. It regulated the price. Yet it was unable to control the growth of debt. The 1980s established that trying to control credit by interest rates alone was fundamentally ineffective, in addition to being so inequitable. It was certain to punish the borrowers, especially the weakest ones, while it rewarded the lenders excessively. Yet it also did not prevent folly.

It was possible, of course, that political leaders might in time recognize the injustice and the economic dangers inherent in the Federal Reserve's dilemma and begin to take remedial action. But that was not likely. To reverse fields so abruptly, to abandon the logic of deregulation that both Democrats and Republicans had embraced in the previous decade, would require a dramatic shift in the conventional wisdom shared among the political elites—the elected officials, the economic experts whom they consulted, the news media that communicated acceptable political thinking. All these groups, in general, were committed to the new status quo.

In American history, fundamental shifts in the economic orthodoxy usually did not occur until after there was a large and painful calamity, a visible crisis like the financial collapse of 1929 or the Great Depression that followed. The awful consequences from such an experience discredited the prevailing wisdom and suddenly opened the way for new thinking. It was only after a disaster, unfortunately, that most politicians and most economists were able to entertain ideas they had previously dismissed as unthinkable.

18

THE TRIUMPH
OF MONEY

Catastrophe was general in Iowa. Thousands of farmers faced liquidation on old debts or their banks refused to grant new credit for the approaching growing season. The value of Iowa farmland was decreased by half and small towns withered as the local commerce disappeared. Iowa lost fifty thousand of its citizens. The price of corn, which had been above $3.50 only a few years earlier, fell steadily, headed toward a ruinous low—corn at $1 a bushel.

The Middle West and other regions were trapped in an economic phenomenon beyond the living experience of most Americans—deflation. Since World War II, Americans had become accustomed to one constant, rising prices. In the forty-year upward slope of modern inflation, the only thing that varied was how fast prices were increasing. In 1985, agriculture and other basic producers of the American economy were engulfed by a crisis of the opposite nature—the persistent, crippling effects of falling prices.

On a farm near Unionville, Iowa, a group of distressed farmers gathered in the living room of Clifford and Evelyne Burger to exchange tips on fending off the bank foreclosures, to console one another and to search for answers. The Burgers had been missing debt payments sporadically since 1983; the local bank had just turned down their loan application for spring planting, the money to buy seed and fill their fuel tank for the '85 crop. The Burgers and their friends thought they had found the explanation. Their failure, they decided, was caused by a remote conspiracy of bankers, operating through the Federal Reserve.

"First, the Powers pump up inflation, then they start the propaganda that we have to reduce inflation," Jim Phillips, a grain farmer from Centerville, explained. "They established this policy for the personal gain of the Federal Reserve and the bankers that control it. They saw the coffee shortage, the oil shortage, the sugar shortage. The Powers found out that it works. Why not a money shortage?"

Mrs. Burger distributed an illustrated pamphlet entitled "Billions for Bankers, Debt for the People," a polemical tract on the money question that was circulating widely in Iowa and the other afflicted farm states. The Federal Reserve, the pamphlet explained, was "a system of Banker-owned Mammon that has usurped the mantle of government, disguised itself as our legitimate government, and set about to pauperize and control our people."

The farmers talked quite familiarly about this conspiracy against them, reciting old names and obscure events from the Federal Reserve's early history. A web of international bankers had designed the central bank back in 1913 in order to dominate the world; their unseen control extended to grain companies, major conglomerates, the financial markets and the news media. These manipulations, the farmers earnestly explained, were guided by the "Power 300" and the "Inner Circle" and, ultimately, by the "Zionist Jewish conspiracy."

"Even in the Bible," Cliff Burger interjected, "you're not supposed to have usury. It's usury that's killing us."

"The Federal Reserve dictates to Reagan," said John Sellers, Jr., another young farmer awaiting his foreclosure notice. "Everyone says there is a shortage of money, but it isn't so. If they wanted more money, they pretty well could print it up. The Federal Reserve is the biggest hoax ever played. Ninety-nine percent of the people think it's a branch of the government."

Like others, John Sellers was trying to combat the personal depression that accompanied economic failure. "It's a very gray world and you feel like you're ninety years old," he said. "You're in quicksand and there's no way out. People take to bed and sleep and sleep and sleep." Many blame themselves. "When the hammer finally falls," Sellers said, "you look back at the decisions you made and the decisions you could have made and you go through a terrible period of depression, of guilt."[1]

In Iowa as well as other distressed areas, farmers found some solace in the realization that others were failing too, even some of the best farmers among them who had managed most efficiently. Therefore, it could not be their fault alone. There must be some larger explanation. Some farmers focused their anger on the giant grain-trading companies and accused them of price manipulation. Others blamed the strong dollar and Latin-American debt. Or the crisis was attributed to particular mistakes by Jimmy Carter or Ronald Reagan, Democrats or Republicans.

Others, an intense minority with extreme views, resurrected the old conspiracy theories that had surrounded the Fed's mysterious powers since its origin. The farmers studied the baffling facts of money creation and the anomalous status of the Federal Reserve at the center of elected government and they decided, not illogically, that only a powerful conspiracy could have created such a bizarre arrangement. It was Morgan and Rockefeller and the Jews who had plotted to ruin Iowa. It was the "Powers" that, by controlling money creation, had subverted democracy and usurped the authority of God. The belief in distant conspiracy reflected a shocked disappointment with life, political anger mixed with a deep spiritual distress. In desperate times, confused and powerless people were prepared to believe that their lives were held in thrall by a malevolent hierarchy. The farmers in Iowa were like the Catholic monks of medieval Europe who condemned moneylenders, like the stunned peasants in Colombia who were ensnared by modern capitalism. The farmers in Iowa looked at what money was doing to their lives and they saw the hand of the devil.

There was one other explanation most victims in Iowa and elsewhere did not wish to face—that the American political system itself had decided their fate. The deflation destroying American farmers and other producers was not imposed by remote conspirators, but by their own government in Washington, with the approval or acquiescence of their own elected representatives. The general calamity of falling prices was not a mistake or a random accident of nature or an evil plot. It was the necessary consequence of the economic logic pursued by those who held legitimate political power in the American system, most particularly the Federal Reserve but with the tacit consent of others.

This larger reality was too demoralizing for most victims to accept, even those who understood money and the Federal Reserve's role in the deflation. It was far easier to believe that their distress resulted from mistakes or misguided policy and would soon be relieved if only enough Americans understood what was happening. Faced with failure, they preferred to conclude that an evil cabal had engineered their ruined lives, using the dreadful powers of the Federal Reserve to undermine justice and self-government.

The political logic that propelled their crisis was not secret. Given the choices made in Washington, deflationary destruction was virtually inevitable. The Federal Reserve was determined to drive the rate of inflation lower and lower, regardless of other consequences, and no one of any influence challenged the Fed's objective. Indeed, it was fully endorsed by both political parties. As a practical matter, in order to stabilize money's value at zero inflation or as close as possible, some elements in the economy must be forced into negative levels—held in a state of perpetual losses—in order to offset the rising prices that other economic sectors continued to enjoy. Maintaining the fight against inflation required continuing the liquidation.

The government, especially the Federal Reserve, could not very well acknowledge this unpleasant trade-off, but it was frankly understood in financial markets. With matter-of-fact directness, E. F. Hutton explained the logic to its investment customers:

> To our mind, pockets of deflation and an ad hoc program of bankruptcy containment are as much a part of secular disinflation as are low inflation and declining interest rates. If disinflation in this cycle is to work, there must be losers—those who made or financed wrong bets. These negatives, however, are secondary.[2]

"There must be losers." The losers, as the Hutton newsletter noted, extended far beyond agriculture. They included the workers, managers and owners in many other sectors—real estate, basic commodities, energy. Labor and basic manufacturing could also be regarded as having made "wrong bets." The negative effects of the deflation, however, were not "secondary" pockets, as the brokerage claimed. Taken together, the deflationary losses cut a wide and depressing swath across the American economy, from timber in the Pacific Northwest to the "oil patch" of Texas, Oklahoma and Louisiana, from copper mines and cotton farms in the Southwest to grain states on the northern prairie and famous old industrial cities in the Middle West.

Georgia-Pacific closed nine lumber mills, nearly a quarter of its production. Employment in the copper industry had declined by 63 percent since 1980. Firestone Tire & Rubber, in the same period, shrank from 107,000 to 55,000 employees as it closed plants and reduced management. Tire-industry prices had fallen 7 percent while costs rose by 4 percent. Lead, zinc, silver, orange juice and a long list of other products suffered the same fate as oil, wheat, corn and soybeans.

Deflation, once started, fed on itself and would likely persist as long as the authorities did not alter the terms of money and prices. While commodity prices were always subject to wide swings up and down, reacting to seasonal shifts in supply and demand, the persistence of depressed prices exacerbated the condition. The decreased earnings led producers of all types, from copper miners in Chile to grain farmers in the Middle West, to increase their production, and this response merely exaggerated the market surpluses, driving prices even lower.

Deflation gathered momentum gradually through 1984, and by 1985, it had become a fundamental disorder in the economy. Food commodity prices peaked in the first quarter of 1984 and fell by nearly 12 percent over the next year and a half. The income losses for farmers (but not their shrinking collateral) were offset partially by the government price-support payments (and the cost of federal subsidies for agriculture soared to more than $30 billion). Industrial raw materials, unprotected by government programs, suffered a price decline of 16 percent over the same months. Overall, raw-material prices fell by 40 percent from their peaks in 1980. With so many accumulated losers, the American economy could not be healthy.[3]

The price deflation that unfolded in the middle of the 1980s closely resembled the deflation of the 1920s in its selective damage. The same victims were entrapped by surplus and falling prices in both decades, and their economic predicament likewise was largely ignored—occasionally even applauded—by the rest of the nation. Older Americans remembered the Depression and the general price collapse that followed 1929, when virtually everyone's prices and wages fell dramatically, but this episode was not like that. Instead, the overall price level, reflected in the Consumer Price Index, remained remarkably stable, rising at about 3 percent or less a year, and the economy in general continued to expand modestly, concealing the simultaneous depression under way in its structure.

The regime imposed a basic inequity that was obvious if one looked behind the average price level. While prices fell for commodities and other goods, inflation continued unabated in service industries, sometimes by as much as 6 or 7 percent. The government made no effort to curb the price inflation in the service sectors (or their wage increases), since it was offset by the negative prices in goods-producing sectors. The government, in fact, had created a split-level economy, fiercely divided between winners and losers. If the "hard money" and selective deflation were to continue for many years, the accumulated destruction might eventually begin to resemble the Great Deflation of the 1880s and 1890s, the era that spawned the agrarian revolt known as Populism.

In both the 1920s and the 1980s, the Federal Reserve was the central engine of control, the economic regulator that imposed these terms. The fundamentals of money had not changed in four generations, despite the many innovations elaborated by modern finance and government economic managers. In broad outline, Paul Volcker's management of money and the economy followed the pattern set by Benjamin Strong, the New York Fed president who had dominated America's new central bank during its early decades and whose performance had also been celebrated as a triumph of central banking.

Across six decades, Paul Volcker and Benjamin Strong were like-minded men of finance, who shared the same conservative values. Both were strong-willed crisis managers, esteemed for their awesome grasp of the interlocking complexities of money and banking. Their imperious intellects were also intimidating. Both men assumed the central bank's first obligation was to protect the banking system from crisis and chaos and they worked strenuously to do so. More important, Volcker and Strong were both absorbed—if not obsessed—by a single-minded conception of economic order. For both of them, economic order was defined, above all else, by the stable value of money.

To achieve that ideal, a currency that held constant value, the Federal Reserve proceeded in both decades to first induce a brutal liquidation, the suppression of economic activity designed to break an inflationary surge. Just as the twenties opened with the severe recession engineered by the Federal Reserve in 1920–1921, Volcker's management produced the devastating contraction of 1981–1982. The lever for halting inflation in both cases was a traumatic and unprecedented increase in the price of money—forcing business activity to subside and surpluses to accumulate. The accompanying destruction, it was argued, was the necessary prelude to long-lasting prosperity, an era of order and stability in which all could benefit.

After each contraction, however, in order to preserve the stable price level, the central bank did not give free rein to the economy in recovery. The Federal Reserve, instead, managed money and interest rates in such a way that the surpluses remained—surplus labor, surplus grain, surplus oil, surplus goods—and these surpluses continued to suppress prices and wages. For relatively long periods, therefore, Volcker and Strong each succeeded in maintaining an economy free of inflation. Both men were widely admired for this achievement.

The maintenance of low inflation, however, required a condition of continuing failure for many. The average price level was prevented from rising because certain prices continued to fall. Through the twenties, farmers never really recovered from Benjamin Strong's devastating recession of 1920–1921, and farmers did not recover from Paul Volcker's in the 1980s. Nor did organized labor, nor mines and mills, nor the oil industry and certain other producers.

Stable money was, ultimately, an illusion. It was nothing more than a statistical artifice that concealed harsh realities. In both eras, the Federal Reserve was celebrated for accomplishing what it took to be its highest purpose, the virtual elimination of dollar inflation. Neutral money was the golden mean, what nearly everyone thought they wanted. Yet the ideal was merely an economic abstraction and it was not neutral. It was simply an averaging of gains and losses that produced the comforting illusion of balance.

The condition of stable money conveyed a satisfying sense of social order. Yet the reality was continuing disorder. In the real economy, stable money led to a fiercely inequitable division of advantage: some economic interests continued unrestrained in their ability to raise prices and wages, while others were consigned to permanent decrease and were bound to fail if the condition persisted. The illusion was, naturally, most persuasive to those who were not destroyed by it.

The paradox of money—an economic order that required continuing destruction—was obvious in outline, yet it was largely ignored in both the 1920s and the 1980s. Stable money was a central value in the social mythology created by economics, a core belief of democratic capitalism. In their own lives, people were relieved to see that the anxieties of rising prices were now mostly extinguished. They were disposed to believe that a stable dollar gave no artificial advantage to anyone. An aura of progress and contentment suffused the nation in both eras.

The conservative political context—exemplified by Ronald Reagan and his personal idol from boyhood, Calvin Coolidge—lent encouragement to the Federal Reserve's singular objective of "hard money." With no substantial opposition from politics, the central bank was free to pursue its own idea of economic order and to discount the contradictory evidence of human loss and failure. Competing ideas of economic well-being—abundant growth, full employment, a favorable environment for all sectors—were assumed to be less important. As a political value, money was triumphant. As a social reality, money was more convincing than the tangible suffering of assorted victims.

Indeed, the restoration of stable money produced a smug sense of moral satisfaction, in which the "roaring twenties" served as a crude precedent for the "go-go eighties." Those who succeeded indulged in elaborate fantasies of ostentatious consumption. Those who failed, amid the general prosperity, were blamed for their own mistakes. Farmers and oil producers, it was said, had borrowed excessively in the past, pursuing unrealistic expectations about the future. Their punishment, though regrettable, was justified by their own imprudence. The rationale ignored what had actually transpired: the government itself had drastically and abruptly altered the terms for the future. Its actions put all debtors at a sudden disadvantage, the wise and the unwise alike, with no real opportunity to adjust to the changed circumstances. For the weakest, the only available adjustment was to stop doing business.

The default of producers, it was said further, would enhance the efficiency of the nation, as the weak and marginal were weeded out. Deflationary pressures did indeed force producers to cut their costs and eliminate waste, but the central consequence was merely a consolidation of ownership. Farmland in Iowa did not disappear when its value collapsed and the farmer defaulted on his loans. Nor did oil rigs and reserves in Oklahoma or Texas. They were acquired at depressed prices by other owners who could operate profitably in the new environment of deflation because they had invested so much less. Ownership of family farms passed on to large-scale corporate enterprises. Oil reserves held by failing independent producers became the property of their creditors. The ultimate effect of the liquidation in the 1980s, just as in earlier episodes of deflation, was to further concentrate the ownership of wealth.

With neither political party prepared to represent them on the money question, farmers and the other victims of deflation protested impotently. Their complaints were often misdirected at subsidiary issues, and even when they did challenge monetary policy itself, their arguments were deflected by the Federal Reserve's imposing mystique. Dissent was intimidated by Paul Volcker's awesome reputation.

Just as in the 1920s, the primacy of Volcker and the Fed was essentially an act of political deference. Benjamin Strong's stewardship had been hailed as the first significant triumph of technocratic government, in which disinterested managerial experts took control of policy from the raw and unruly forces of politics. Government would become professionalized, rational and efficient like business, insulated from the random folly of popular opinion. Paul Volcker, the austere technician, oblivious to his own personal gain, enjoyed the same deference. He was admired for his wisdom and competence and, like Ben Strong, for his willingness to defy and dominate elected politicians.

Benjamin Strong's era was described, in Milton Friedman's monetary history, as the "high tide" of the Federal Reserve System. For a number of years, the central bank succeeded in stabilizing money. Volcker's era, for the same reasons, was a second time of triumph for the Fed. Before his death, Strong was widely congratulated for astutely steering the American economy into a "new era"—free of the old excesses, no longer threatened by periodic panics and crashes. So, in his own time, was Paul Volcker. The good feeling generated by stable money in the twenties collapsed abruptly in the autumn of 1929. Paul Volcker's regime, praised for the same accomplishments, was accumulating the same vulnerabilities, the same victims.

Back in the 1920s, Benjamin Strong was once accosted by angry farm leaders, demanding an explanation for the ruinous decline in their prices. He dismissed them coldly. "You inquire as to the man who gave the order for deflation," Strong said. "I know of no order being given."[4]

In February 1985, Paul Volcker had a similar moment of confrontation. A delegation of state legislators from thirteen distressed farm states—Iowa, Nebraska, the Dakotas and others—traveled to Washington to plead for relief. In the magnificent boardroom of the Federal Reserve, the chairman listened to the farm representatives argue for easier money, for lower interest rates and an end to the price deflation. His response chilled them.

"Look," Volcker said, "your constituents are unhappy, mine aren't."[5]

The essence of monetary policy, despite the complexities, was always a choice of values. The men and women who sat around the boardroom table were necessarily preoccupied with technical issues, but the implicit question at the core of their decisions could never be reduced to scientific solution, with a right answer or a wrong one. Which economic goals mattered most? What came first? Paul Volcker's sure-handed management of money had effectively decided the priorities for the nation. Others at the table, a stubborn minority, disagreed with him.

Preston Martin, the vice chairman, declared:

The question is: what are your goals? I think unemployment should be lower than 7 percent. I think 2 percent growth is unsatisfactory. We are accepting a lower-than-trend growth rate and a higher-than-trend unemployment rate. For what reason? What is the public good from that choice? "Well," the others say, "it's fear of inflation—you don't want to bring back inflation." But, look, the inflation of today is a great improvement over the past. Given the improvement in prices we have now, these other goals should be brought to the fore.

Martin's complaint was a fair summary of the continuing argument that took place within the Federal Reserve. Money was still the first priority to Volcker and the majority, who insisted that the one great goal was to protect the gains already made in reducing price inflation. Preston Martin argued that his colleagues, by exaggerating the risk of renewed inflation, were forcing slower than necessary growth for the economy, higher unemployment, spreading financial strains and instability. "What is the public good from that choice?" Martin kept asking.

The Federal Reserve's control produced disappointing results in the real economy. Various forecasters kept predicting a revived boom, but it never materialized. The expansion remained fitful and fainthearted, performing far below the economy's potential and below the historic averages for recovery cycles. From the middle of 1984 onward, after the election-year boom had been broken, the economy settled into a jigsaw pattern of uneven advances—weakening one quarter, then resurgent the next, then weakening again. The Federal Reserve eased or restrained in carefully measured steps, averting a recession but also failing to break out of the lackluster pattern.

"A growth recession must be considered a real threat," Martin complained publicly. The unemployment rate inched up and down slightly, but basically it remained stuck at slightly above 7 percent—the highest unemployment of any postwar recovery—with no prospect of improvement. Capacity utilization in manufacturing remained stuck at 80 percent or below.

Even the Fed's own conservative expectations for the economy were disappointed. Over the subsequent twenty-four months, the economy grew in real terms by less than 2.5 percent. That was only a little better than half of the economic growth the Reagan Administration had expected. It was also far below the growth of 3.5 to 4 percent that the Federal Open Market Committee itself had anticipated.

The general disappointment was crisply summarized by *Fortune* magazine in its report on the 1985 performance of the *Fortune* 500 corporations.

Overall sales moved up only 2.8 percent, less than the inflation rate. Profits sank 19.1 percent, the worst performance since the recession year of 1982. Slack demand, a strong dollar, and fierce international competition all hurt. Metals, transportation equipment, textiles and mining fared poorly. Even computers and office equipment fell 6.2 percent. Only 242 companies among the 500 showed profit increases and 70 lost money—a record. . . .

Unable to wring satisfactory returns from their traditional businesses last year, many of the 500 companies put efforts into rearranging their existing resources and buying new ones. They restructured through mergers and acquisitions, stock repurchases and leveraged buy outs. . . . The combined dollar value (of the corporate restructurings) came to $191.4 billion. That's 54 percent more than in 1984 and equivalent to the combined assets of GM, Exxon, Mobil and ITT. Restructuring is popular because many companies see few incentives to invest in plant and equipment.[6]

In the FOMC debates, Preston Martin had only one consistent ally, Governor Martha Seger, Ronald Reagan's second appointee to the Federal Reserve Board. Through 1985, Martin dissented twice and Seger cast four dissenting votes and, together, they argued repeatedly for an easier money policy "to promote faster economic growth." Lower interest rates would have improved prospects for the *Fortune*

500 and smaller businesses too—stimulating demand by effectively cutting prices, reducing the damage from import competition by bringing down the overvalued dollar.

Inside the Fed, Martha Seger felt even more isolated than Preston Martin. She was a finance professor from Central Michigan State University and a former Michigan state banking commissioner. Seger's credentials were belittled by Democratic senators who had voted against her confirmation. Volcker himself was upset by her appointment because the White House had not consulted him in advance, as was customary. Once on the board, Seger felt ignored. The Fed, she said, was dominated by its male professional staff, which followed the chairman's instructions and denigrated other governors.

"I'm not a part of any discussion before these matters occur," Seger complained. "You are handed an agenda a couple of days in advance. Memos are delivered to our desks. . . . You go in and—bang—you have to vote." The result, she said, was that individual governors were cut out of the policy-making process. "We have very little input into what I call the formulation stage, which I'm not accustomed to," Seger said. "In corporate America, there is input all along the lines. In an auto company, the president of the company isn't exposed to the new models the day he goes down to the auto show."[7]

Seger and Martin, though both were conservative Republicans, were assuming the same lonely role on the Board of Governors that Nancy Teeters, the liberal Democrat, had filled during her tenure. They pulled against the orthodoxy by arguing that the tangible reality of economic loss deserved at least as much consideration as the abstract claims of monetary theory. It was a question of priorities.

"Not having Nancy Teeters around," Martin admitted, "I became the expert on unemployment. I feel there is a real social cost to unemployment that we cannot ignore."

In political terms, it was especially ironic that Ronald Reagan's appointees to the Fed sounded much like liberal Democrats in the internal policy debate over money. Reagan, after all, was the most conservative of Presidents and himself a monetarist. Yet his nominees to the Board of Governors all proved to be to the left of Paul Volcker on the money question's spectrum—more eager to lower interest rates and to foster faster economic growth and lower unemployment. It was never clear whether the President himself understood this role reversal. Nor, for that matter, did the Democratic Party. Democrats, the traditional advocates of easy money, generally sided with Paul Volcker and criticized the Republican appointees whenever they challenged the chairman.

The new alignment inside the Board of Governors was intentional, however. The Treasury and White House officials who had selected Reagan's Fed nominees wanted new governors who would budge Volcker from his hard policy stance and thus stimulate a more robust economy. At the same time, they realized at last that it was counterproductive to attack Volcker directly or, above all, to create an impression that the Reagan Administration was inviting a return to inflation. Instead, they hoped that subtler pressures would turn the Fed. Politicians, regardless of party label or ideological disposition, responded to real disappointments and grievances. In the politics of money, reality was more persuasive than ideology or abstract theory.

Volcker stood his ground. When the economy weakened in the spring quarter of 1985 and many forecasters worried aloud about a possible recession, Volcker relented—but only slightly. The Board of Governors agreed on May 17 to reduce the Discount rate by .5 percent. Economic growth picked up somewhat subsequently as interest rates declined and recession was averted. Except for that limited concession, however, Volcker was unyielding. Despite the gathering deflation and the disappointing business activity, he kept interest rates at the same high level and declined to do more to help the struggling economy.

Volcker's unbending posture was reflected most clearly in the Board of Governors' repeated refusal to grant any additional reductions in the Discount rate, the floor price for credit markets. Throughout 1985, despite the slow growth and accumulating damage from the price deflation, the Federal Reserve Board rejected twelve requests from various Federal Reserve Banks for further reductions in the Discount rate. As a result, short-term interest declined only slightly through the year and the economy continued its stuttering performance. Real interest rates were somewhat lower than the peak levels they had reached in 1984—yet they were still above 7 percent, still higher than the punishing rates the Fed had imposed during the 1981–1982 contraction.

Nine of the petitions for lower rates came from the Dallas Fed, a district where both oil and agriculture, as well as real estate, were caught in the spiral of falling prices. As more producers defaulted, their loan losses were undermining the commercial banks, and some of the major Texas banks were endangered. Both bankers and oilmen feared that a sharp collapse in oil prices would unfold if the Fed provided no relief. The Dallas Federal Reserve Bank, among the most conservative in the System, was pleading week after week for easier money. Its warnings were not heeded.

Paul Volcker's rationale for standing firm was unchanged. Congress must go first, he argued. The Federal Reserve could not push interest rates lower until the federal deficits were reduced substantially. But now Volcker offered a second rationale for holding his ground—his fear that the dollar's value might weaken too much or even collapse on foreign-exchange markets. After appreciating enormously over five years, the dollar had finally peaked in February 1985 and its value began subsiding gradually (responding belatedly to the interest-rate reductions executed by the Fed in late 1984). Now, Volcker claimed, the risk was on the other side: a sudden free fall in the dollar might ignite a burst of price inflation.

The chairman's anxiety about the dollar seemed especially timorous, even precious, considering what was actually occurring in the real economy. The flood of dollar-driven imports was still rising and continuing to decimate U.S. production and jobs. The dollar, in fact, declined steadily and quite dramatically for the next year and a half—with no effect whatsoever on prices and very little relief for America's trade-sensitive sectors. Volcker's stature was such, nonetheless, that few challenged his logic. Whatever happened in the economy, the Federal Reserve chairman always seemed to find another reason not to back off.

In a practical sense, Volcker was guided by an anxiety rarely mentioned: the Federal Reserve refused to lower interest rates because it was afraid to challenge the bondholders. If the Fed pushed down short-term interest rates, the long-term investors in the bond market might disapprove. Their continuing worries about inflation were reflected in the extraordinarily high long-term rates demanded in the bond market. If the Fed eased money, it was supposed that the bond investors would feel threatened by inflation and would react by pushing long-term rates even higher.

Paul Volcker and the Fed, in effect, deferred to the bond market's judgment. They might have challenged it, if they had chosen, simply by driving down interest rates, stimulating faster economic growth, ending the deflation and demonstrating that the investors' anxieties were mistaken (with the risk, of course, that prices would become more buoyant). The bond market could resist for a time by pushing up long rates, but not forever, if the Fed eased sufficiently.

If the Fed had eased, that would have tested the inflationary fears of the investors against reality: was it really impossible, as the bond market seemed to believe, that the nation could achieve no better than 2 percent growth or 7 percent unemployment if it wanted to avoid another spiral of runaway inflation? Must America forever function at less than 80 percent of its capacity? Or were the bondholders, like Federal Reserve officials, fighting the last war—demanding unnecessary insurance against inflation (and excessive returns on their capital) because they had been burned in previous decades?

The answers would never be known because the Federal Reserve chose not to ask the questions. The psychology of the investors was regarded as a fragile thing that the Fed must handle delicately. Easing money must wait upon an improvement in the market psychology. Interest rates could not move lower until bondholders felt more secure about their money.

This crucial linkage between monetary policy and market psychology was obliquely acknowledged in comments by the chairman and others. Volcker was asked, for instance, why he did not challenge the bond market's obsession with inflation more forcefully. After all, inflation had been subdued now for nearly four years and the price average was edging downward. The national economy was operating far below its potential, with slack markets for labor and goods, so an inflation driven by the old wage-price spiral was virtually impossible. How long did it take for the bondholders to be convinced? Why didn't the Fed puncture Wall Street's mind-set by pushing interest rates lower and demonstrating that the fears of inflation were unfounded?

Volcker brushed aside the question with a laugh, as though he had heard the same plea many times. "Some people think we should do more of that," he acknowledged. "But you've got to balance that against the question: will a test that fails damage the process in the other direction? It might build up doubts about your long-term commitment. Are you holding firm against inflation or are you not?"

The sensibilities of the bond market, thus, were ultimately guiding the U.S. government's economic policy. The general desire for a healthier economy was stymied by the particular fears of a particular interest group. The Federal Reserve chairman, having restored the central bank's credibility among financial investors, was unwilling to risk it now by trying to lead them to a lower plateau for the cost of money. Instead, he would follow their lead. When the psychology of investors improved and long rates declined in the marketplace, then the Fed would move too. But it would not go first. And, as long as real interest rates remained so high, the American economy could do no better than fitful stops and starts.

The bond market and its investors enjoyed an enviable position of influence: they profited directly from their own supposed anxieties about the future. In the mythology of economics, markets were treated as disinterested arbiters of reality, individual buyers and sellers who collectively made rational judgments based on the best available information. That is how the Federal Reserve looked upon the bond market. Yet, in the actual scheme of things, the bondholders were not disinterested. They were profit-seeking individuals and institutions that were rewarded handsomely for imposing their priorities on others. Indeed, they had little incentive to relent.

Easier money and a free-running economy threatened the wealth of bondholders and the Fed's tight money enhanced it. In the present time, the investors enjoyed the higher earnings provided by the high interest rates. For the future, the high interest rates effectively blocked the economy from regaining the vigorous growth that might eventually lead to a new condition of rising prices. In short, the bondholders and other financial investors won both ways. They collected the bonus income of high real rates. Meanwhile, the value of their money was not only protected from the dilution of inflation, but their financial wealth was actually magnified in value as monetary policy drove the prices of real assets lower.

Given the exceptional rewards, it was perfectly natural that the bondholders were reluctant to give them up. Endorsing a more moderate monetary policy would have put their own profits at risk. In their own defense, long-term investors would argue that they must protect themselves against potential inflation somewhere off in the future, even if prices were falling at present. No one could say, of course, what might happen to money's value 10 or 20 years hence, but this amounted to protection against a distant tomorrow that was provided to no one else in the economy. Short-term investors could not even make that argument. Their extraordinary returns on six-month or one-year notes were collected right now—paid in "hard dollars" that were utterly unthreatened by price inflation.

Even for the long-term investors, the question was how much insurance they required. By 1985, bond investors had accumulated a huge store of profit against the possibility that inflation might some day return. According to the Shearson Lehman Government/Corporate Bond Index, which added interest income and price appreciation, bond returns had averaged 18.5 percent in the four years since 1981 —the most profitable era for bondholders in the twentieth century. Naturally, they did not wish to see the good times end.[8]

The preferred status of the bondholders and their influence over the Fed's monetary policy were another way of describing the political triumph of money. The bondholder was preoccupied with one thing— preserving the value of wealth accumulated in the past. That was more important to them than fostering the economic possibilities of the future. The political system, by embracing stable money as its preeminent goal, by allowing the Federal Reserve to set the government's economic policy on its own, was unwittingly deferring to the bond market too—and acquiescing to the same reactionary values. In the name of stability, the past was defended, the future was denied.

Like the bondholders, Paul Volcker had a personal incentive to hold his ground—not for financial profit, but in terms of the personal esteem that mattered to public servants. The chairman had established his place in history by his success in breaking inflation and restoring monetary stability. Why should he now put all that at risk? In the absence of any effective counterpressures from the political community, Volcker was naturally inclined to defend his accomplishment. If things were somehow to get out of control again, his name would be forever tarnished by the revived inflation, like other Fed chairmen before him, and his moment of great triumph forgotten. The surest way for the Federal Reserve to prevent that from happening was simply to hold money tight, to keep interest rates high, to yield ground only gradually and reluctantly.

At the Federal Open Market Committee meeting in July 1985, the Fed found itself in a particular bind. Volcker was still instructing financial markets to follow M-1 as the guide to monetary policy, and now M-1 was expanding at a runaway rate of more than 16 percent—more than double the Fed's target. Yet, at the same time, the economy was growing quite weak, having expanded by only .6 percent in the previous quarter. If the Fed stuck by its principles and slowed money growth, a recession seemed likely. Yet if it allowed the money supply to expand out of control, what would happen to its hard-won credibility?

Recession was the risk the Fed dared not take, not so much because of the political attacks that would doubtless follow, but because of a far more threatening prospect. The financial system, given the burgeoning debts and the deteriorating balance sheets of debtors, was becoming dangerously vulnerable. Texas and Oklahoma oil banks were in trouble. Major corporations were overburdened with debt-servicing costs. Hundreds of savings and loans were exposed on shaky real-estate loans. Even the Bank of America, once the largest in the country and now reduced to second place, struggled with huge loan losses in agriculture, oil, shipping, real estate. Latin-American nations depended precariously on selling exports to the U.S. economy in order to keep up with their loan payments to American banks. An economic contraction at this time would threaten all these and perhaps touch off a general sweep of losers—both failed debtors and their creditor banks.

That would be the disaster scenario on the downside [Governor Charles Partee admitted]. Look at all these things—thrifts, farmers, real estate, the corporate debt, the foreign debt. A recession would touch off so many financial problems, spreading through the corporate, agricultural and financial institutions, it would be very difficult to control. It's a hazard. I certainly don't like the looks of what's developing. It's kind of a slow fuse.

The Fed chose, instead, to again disregard M-1 and let the money supply grow. Formally, the FOMC claimed it was merely "rebasing" its money targets, in effect, starting over for the year. But the practical consequence was to accept the runaway money growth because the alternative was too risky. By year's end, M-1 had grown from $563 to $627 billion, up 11 percent. Yet the economy did not revive in a roaring boom, as monetarist economists confidently predicted from the M-1 numbers. The economy remained weak and uneven—despite money.

Sooner or later, overconfident orthodoxy collided with contradictory reality and this was the ultimate embarrassment for monetarism. In the era of disinflation, people simply handled their money differently and so its economic meaning changed unpredictably. The velocity of money was declining sharply again and the usual economic impact attributed to M-1 growth was utterly refuted by the sluggish economy. Even Beryl Sprinkel, the most confident monetarist in the Reagan Administration, conceded that theory was confounded. "Nobody knows where we are going," Sprinkel said.[9]

The inanity of believing that a single number, constructed by economists, could answer the most basic questions of economic policy was demonstrated by the following M-1 statistics. For the five years from 1974 to 1979, M-1 grew by an average of 7 percent. It was a period of excessive money growth and roaring inflation. From 1979 to 1984, M-1 grew by 7.4 percent. Yet that was a period of tight money and shrinking inflation. How could this be so? The short explanation for the anomaly was that M-1 was itself an inconstant value, not the rock of certainty that monetarists claimed.

Milton Friedman, the intellectual father of modern monetarism, was more grudging in admitting defeat. "I don't feel there has been any repudiation of the theory," Friedman insisted. "After all, it's a science in which theories must be tested. So, if we've been wrong about some things, they have to be corrected."[10] After years of self-confident predictions and caustic criticism for his opponents, this was as close as Milton Friedman could bring himself to acknowledging that, in the real world, his theory did not work.

I feel sorry for him [said Charles Partee]. He's an old man now. He spent his life on this theory. Now it's destroyed. The decision to let money go and try to have enough stimulus to keep the economy going pretty much finishes the monetary aggregates. This is the second time we've had to do that and it proved right both times. The aggregates can never again be a

discipline on monetary policy. The next time the aggregates tell you to
tighten when the economy looks weak, you can say: "Look, it would be
suicide to follow them."

The collapse of monetarism as a practical theory involved more than
the embarrassment of selected economists. Volcker and the Federal
Reserve had embraced the money aggregates too and allowed M-1 to
guide their policy decisions. The bankers and financial professionals
of Wall Street had bought into the same belief, an alluring faith that
offered a simple answer to bewildering complexities. Regulating a
single economic variable, the money supply, could somehow produce
order in all the others. The idea was really just a metaphor—a way of
saying that the central bank was willing to concentrate on the abstraction of money alone and to ignore the gross consequences for the real
elements of economic life. It served the Fed's purposes, but monetarism was a costly illusion for the American economy. Belatedly, reluctantly, Volcker abandoned it, this time for good.

Discarding M-1, nevertheless, gave Volcker yet another reason to
be cautious about interest rates. By letting the money supply expand
enormously, the Fed was leaving itself "absolutely wide open to the
next mistake," as Partee put it. The expanded liquidity was pumping
into the system without much effect on the real economy. But if anything happened to change money velocity and alter the transaction
patterns of the public, that liquidity could, theoretically, become sud
den fuel for an inflationary surge.

In that exposed situation, Volcker felt a strong reluctance to take
further risks. He let money go—but he did not lower interest rates
and help the real economy. The chairman now had to explain to financial markets that his abandonment of M-1 was in no way a retreat from
stable money values. This was nothing more than a technical adjustment, he explained. The Fed's commitment remained firm. To prove
it, the Fed kept interest rates from declining.

"We've had a big increase in M-1 during the period and a decline in
the dollar which make me nervous," the chairman said. "I wouldn't
want to test the market too much in the face of that."

Volcker's basic dilemma was only worsened. The instabilities were
accumulating in both finance and the real economy. He couldn't risk
a recession for fear of collapsing debtors and their banks. Yet he
would not give the economy free rein for fear of losing his hold on
stable money.

David Stockman, who left the Reagan Administration in the late
summer, described Volcker's anguish:

I talked to him before I left and he was really agonizing, really between
a rock and a hard place. All these debts, all these huge deficits, so late in

the recovery. What was he going to do? He had no answer, except to keep adjusting a step at a time. The system is headed for dislocations. There's no way around it. But system managers like Volcker will find a way to keep things going. They make loans to people who can't pay them back. They patch things up as best they can.

The Reagan Administration belatedly discovered how to get a handle on Paul Volcker and the Fed—or at least more influence over their decisions. The one legitimate lever the executive branch could use to pressure the Federal Reserve to change its monetary policy was the issue of the dollar's international value. By law and custom, even the Fed accepted that the President had primary responsibility for managing the dollar and the independent central bank was obliged to heed him. Fed officials had always understood this. It took the Reagan Administration four years to figure it out.

When James Baker left the White House in 1985 to become Secretary of the Treasury, he and Richard Darman, the new Deputy Treasury Secretary, acted on the insight. They abandoned the laissez-faire doctrine that Administration conservatives, including the President, had espoused throughout the first term and began working to bring down the overvalued dollar. Two years before, the CEA chairman, Martin Feldstein, had confidently concluded that the losses to American manufacturing were acceptable. By 1985, it was obvious to both the White House and the Fed that their dollar policy had done intolerable damage. The price disadvantage the dollar caused in international trade was continuing to devastate American manufacturing and agriculture; Baker and Darman were responding at last to the complaints corporate executives and labor leaders had been making for four years.

Treasury's new activism involved a return to government interventions in foreign-exchange markets—driving the dollar's price down by flooding the markets with surplus dollars. Baker and Darman also employed private persuasion to coax Volcker toward lower interest rates.

"We agreed from the start that we would not do any Fed bashing if they don't do any Administration bashing," Baker explained. "It's a two-way street. We ought to be free to criticize monetary policy if the Fed criticizes our fiscal policy. But, before we do that, we ought to try to work it out in private."

Baker and Darman were, thus, more sophisticated than their predecessors at Treasury about manipulating the Federal Reserve chairman. They began a series of patient policy consultations intended to enlist Volcker's cooperation and create a united front. The central banks of the world must move in concert, they agreed, to bring down the dollar's value and back off the high level of interest rates that had prevailed worldwide since Volcker's initiative in late 1979. Attacking Volcker directly, the Treasury officials appreciated, was a wasted gesture that accomplished nothing except to upset the financial markets. Using the issue of the dollar as its wedge, the Administration would leverage him instead.

"Volcker's got the power," one Administration official explained. "We don't try to order him around. We have got to work with him."

The visible result of Baker and Darman's discreet campaign was an accord announced on September 22, 1985, by the five leading industrial nations—the U.S., West Germany, Japan, France and Britain—agreeing to coordinate their central banks' efforts to correct the currency imbalances. Paul Volcker lent his imprimatur. It was an implicit acknowledgment that the Fed had allowed the dollar to rise too far in the first place. At the very least, the dollar accord would inhibit the Fed from any future tightening of monetary policy. Raising interest rates again would drive the dollar in the wrong direction—upward.

The Baker initiative succeeded on one level and yet failed to deliver the therapeutic results that were expected for the American economy. The dollar continued a dramatic decline in value, but the damage to trade-sensitive sectors was not reversed. It grew worse, regardless. From its peak in early 1985, the exchange value of the dollar had fallen by nearly one-third in a year and a half, as measured against ten other leading currencies. That brought the dollar roughly back to the same value it had held in late 1981. Yet the United States's trade deficit grew larger and larger, reaching an awesome level above $150 billion a year for 1986—roughly ten times larger than the occasional trade imbalances that had caused alarm in previous decades.

In the mercantilist contest among the great trading nations, America was still losing. Its farmers lost overseas markets and even some of their domestic customers to overseas producers. The same thing happened to other commodities and to a wide range of manufacturing. In part, the continuing damage reflected the delayed effects of the devalued dollar. Eventually, U.S. export-import industries would see the benefits of the new trading terms as foreign competitors were compelled to raise their prices. In the meantime, the loss of American jobs and production became a major political preoccupation. Democrats assailed the Reagan Administration and proposed protective legislation to slow the flow of imports. There was no partisan advantage for Democrats in attacking the Fed, the ultimate source of the trade crisis, and so they blamed Republicans.

But the deepening trade crisis reflected a grim reality of global commerce: once American farmers and manufacturers lost market shares in world trade, it was very difficult to win them back—in many cases impossible. Volcker and Anthony Solomon of the New York Fed had both worried about the long-term consequence during several years as the dollar rose, though they had not done anything to stop it. The regime of the "hard dollar" imposed by the Fed for nearly five years had given foreign competitors a huge price advantage and inflated profit margins too. Now that the dollar was declining, those foreign producers were willing to accept a smaller profit margin rather than raise prices and give up their newly won customers in the U.S.

For many American companies, ones that had closed factories and cut back their employment or moved production overseas, the dollar's decline was too late. For them, the destruction was permanent. In those terms, the Federal Reserve's willingness to let the dollar appreciate so drastically and for so long would prove to be a historic error of monetary policy—one that would take many years for America to overcome. Federal Reserve officials were right to agonize over what they had wrought.

The international money system—regardless of which nations won and which lost—was a financial system that did continuing violence to the real producers. Since "floating" exchange rates were adopted in 1973, letting the free markets set the price of currencies, the dollar had moved through a series of what Lee Iacocca rightly called "violent swings" in value, destabilizing trade relationships each time. As long as the present free-market system was preserved, the extreme swings would continue.

Money was meant to be the neutral agent of commerce. Now it had become the neurotic master. In the 1970s, the dollar's steady decline had injured Arab oil producers and European manufacturers. In the 1980s, when the tables were reversed, American producers suffered far greater losses from the dollar's extraordinary rise. Now the dollar was falling rapidly again as the major central banks tried to correct the imbalance. Neither governments nor their central bankers were able to sustain equilibrium or even to agree on what a fair balance might be. Instead, trade wars were fought through currencies, the mercantile combat among nations that was as old as capitalism itself.

Reforming international exchange, finding some way to stabilize it, would eliminate the violent swings and reduce the artificial influence of money over commerce. But finding a solution was a daunting challenge on every level, from the technical questions to the political. Some conservatives advocated a return to the gold guarantee behind the dollar, a fixed-value exchange rate much like the Bretton Woods agreement that Keynes had devised at the close of World War II. Others argued for a more flexible solution—a target range of currency relationships and a commitment by all governments to keep their money trading within the range.

Difficult as the technical issues were, the heart of the problem was political. To accept a system of permanent exchange values, some nations would have to surrender their temporary trade advantage. To agree worldwide on stabilizing money values, all nations—particularly the United States—would have to yield a measure of their sovereign discretion. Ultimately, the global trading value of currencies reflected each nation's domestic economic policies—how much governments spent and borrowed, how much money growth they permitted, their domestic rates of inflation and their interest rates. Each nation's control over those political questions would be inhibited, even circumscribed, by any international agreement that imposed genuine stability among the rival currencies.

The contest among national currencies was ultimately an expression of the changing realities of power in international politics. When America's economic hegemony was unquestioned, the U.S. dollar was able to impose order on its rivals, just as the British pound sterling had done in the nineteenth century. But now the U.S. was no longer able to dominate its trading partners in global economics. The competitors were stronger and more independent. America itself was becoming a debtor nation again for the first time in four generations.

How could Washington tell Tokyo what to do now that Japan had become America's most important creditor? The Japanese lent the United States many billions to finance its growing federal debt—the surplus capital Japan accumulated from the trade deficit. Americans did not yet fully appreciate that the old order, the economic supremacy they had enjoyed since World War II, was gone.

But if the dollar could no longer rule, who could? Perhaps no single currency. Japan was emergent as the major new force in the global economy, but Japan was neither large enough yet—nor sufficiently self-confident—to take command and impose stability on others. The world seemed trapped between eras, an interregnum like the decades of turmoil between World War I and World War II, when the United States was emerging as the strongest nation but was reluctant to take the role of world leader. Once again, no single nation could set the terms for the others and lead alone. This uncertain condition might endure for many years to come. In the meantime, the strongest nations, it seemed, would have to learn how to share the burden.

Less obviously, the international reform of money would also alter the power relationships within governments: the Federal Reserve would be forced to surrender some of its independent power to decide domestic monetary issues on its own. If governments agreed among themselves to maintain stable currency values, the Fed and other central banks could no longer set interest rates or restrict money growth simply to satisfy their own single-minded purposes. Volcker's dominance, his long run-up of interest rates and the dollar in the 1980s, would not have been possible. Under such a system, the Fed could not have become the "economic czar," as Frederick Schultz had put it.

The paradox of money was that in order to establish a fixed value for the domestic dollar, the Federal Reserve had to permit the destabilizing appreciation of the international dollar. Monetary reform would compel the Fed to balance its objectives, to manage money so that one value was not distorted at the expense of the other. The central bank would thus have to coordinate its monetary policy more closely with the fiscal policy set by the elected government. The Fed's decisions would have to harmonize with the broader economic goals of political leaders.

Reforming the instabilities of international money, thus, contained an ironic possibility: the Federal Reserve would become less powerful. Among the politicians who resented the Fed's independence, only a few understood the implications. Global monetary reform, difficult as the issue would be, was a political opportunity—perhaps the best one available—for elected politics to get control over the unelected Federal Reserve.

"Sensible businessmen do not produce things they cannot sell and certainly they do not build new factories when they have usable factories standing idle."

The observation by businessman and author George P. Brockway, simple and obvious as it seemed, went to the heart of the matter—the fundamental economic disorder that confronted not just the United States, but the world. The contest of currencies, the political controversies over trade restrictions, were the visible struggles that concealed a much deeper malady, one that was shared by all. The U.S. economy and the world's were awash in surpluses—an overabundance of available labor, of foodstuffs and raw materials, of manufactured goods. Worldwide, the existing capacity to produce goods far exceeded the aggregate demand for them—a glut of supply.

Given that basic dilemma, nations naturally fought over market shares and erected trading barriers to protect their own producers. Unemployment remained high in most industrial nations and prices remained depressed—all because the world could produce more goods than its markets could absorb. The United States was operating far below its capacity, but so were Japan and West Germany and other major producers. As Veblen said, the problem of business was always first a question of limiting supply.[11]

The glut was visible in most basic markets: oil and grains, cotton and sugar, steel and copper and other metals. But the excess productive capacity also afflicted many manufactured goods: automobiles and machine tools, personal computers and industrial chemicals, microchips and tape recorders, and many others. The imbalance of supply was, of course, another way of saying that there was inadequate demand. Around the world, there were simply not enough people who had the money to buy all the goods the world's economies could now produce.

The underlying causes of this disorder were deeper than money— economic changes in the world that had been developing for many years. Two decades of global development, led by multinational corporations and financed by bank lending, had greatly enlarged the world's productive capacity, building new factories where none had existed a generation ago, creating a much larger industrial base for the world.

Global auto production, for instance, was once dominated by the United States and Western Europe, but now dozens of other countries shared in the process, most notably Japan, but also Brazil, Korea, Taiwan, Mexico and others. In agriculture, as Third World countries learned how to increase their own food production, they naturally became competitors with America's output. In oil, the soaring prices of the 1970s encouraged both conservation practices by consumers and the development of new sources by producing nations. The long era of inflation put a premium on developing more supply; now the tables were turned and there was too much oil.

The stringent monetary control of the 1980s, led by the Federal Reserve and followed by other central banks, was not the underlying cause, but monetary policy greatly exacerbated the disorder. The high level of interest rates, initiated by the Fed and mimicked proportionately by other central banks, depressed demand worldwide and encouraged the accumulation of surpluses. It was as if all the important governments of the world had decided, simultaneously, to raise the cost of money and price many of their citizens out of the marketplace. Furthermore, the rescue terms that international finance, the IMF and the Fed, imposed on debtor nations in the Third World were guaranteed to shrivel worldwide demand for goods. The nations were required to curb their imports in order to pay the interest on their bank loans. The result was a smaller market of buyers for the world's supply. Finally, the imposition of high interest rates meant that income shares would flow away from those who would buy things—wage earners, debtors—to those who would simply accumulate more wealth —the creditors.

The paradox of the 1980s was that, in a sense, John Maynard Keynes got the last laugh, after all. The American President who came to power focused the debate on improving the "supply side" of the economy. Keynesian "demand side" economics was eclipsed. The Reagan tax cuts, by directing most of the money to investors, would launch a great burst of capital formation, building new factories, developing more supply capacity. Yet the fundamental disorder of the 1980s was essentially the same one that Keynes and the New Deal liberals had identified—there was already too much supply and not enough demand.

The Reagan tax cuts, combined with the Fed's tight money policy, obscured this reality with the anomalous conditions they created. The tax reductions did not produce an investment boom for the very good reason cited by Brockway—why build new factories when you can't sell the goods produced by the old factories? Instead, the fiscal stimulus from the federal deficits drove a boom in consumption—and a burgeoning of debt, both private and public. But, given the overvalued dollar created by the Fed's tight money, a huge share of the American consumption was captured by the cheaper-priced imports instead of by American-made goods. The U.S. market was buying the surplus production of other economies and allowing American producers to suffer the consequences of the supply glut. Americans, in effect, were carrying the world—and borrowing the money to do so.

The disorder of the eighties—excess supply, inadequate demand and the maldistribution of incomes—was parallel to the underlying conditions that led to the collapse of 1929. There were important differences, including the fact that burgeoning debt in the 1920s did not include huge government deficits and that productivity in the 1980's was much weaker. Marriner Eccles, the freethinking banker from Utah who became Federal Reserve chairman, described the maladjustments of the twenties in words that seemed uncannily apt for the present.

In the 1920s, our economy was generally prosperous, not, however, without ups and downs nor without dark spots in different industries. Agriculture was not prospering. The coal industry was sick. While the national income rose to high levels, it was so distributed that the incomes of the majority of families were entirely inadequate and business activity was sustained only by a rapid and unsound increase in the private debt structure, including ever-increasing installment buying of consumption. . . . Foreign loans that ultimately proved to be in large part uncollectible nevertheless furnished an outlet for billions of American savings. . . .

There was an extraordinary expansion of office buildings, hotels, factories and other construction. The giant automobile industry, with all its collateral developments in accessories, servicing and road building, was growing at an unforeseen rate. . . . Our plant, including factories, hotels and office buildings, was becoming excessive. The volume of debt . . . grew too fast, resulting, among other things, in the accumulation in our banking system of a vast amount of assets [or loans] at values that could be sustained only so long as the upward swing of the cycle continued. When this structure finally collapsed, the banks were loaded with unmarketable assets at excessive valuations, the people were weighted down by an excessive burden of debt, and there followed a disastrous deflation that left the country prostrate. . . .[12]

A similar outcome might yet be avoided in the eighties if governments acted to confront the real economic vulnerabilities, though that seemed unlikely. It would require political leaders not only to abandon the economic orthodoxies that had guided their careers, but also to reconsider the very ideas they had disparaged. The world economy, in short, required a new version of Keynesian economics—but a strategy vastly more complex and far-ranging than the original one.

The same basic questions that New Dealers faced in the 1930s were appropriate—how to stimulate demand, how to limit supply. But now answers would have to be devised in terms of global application. The world was no longer divided, as it had been in Keynes's day, between wealthy industrial nations and colonial territories that provided the raw materials. The U.S. no longer dominated, either with its trade or currency, and the economic vulnerabilities confronting it could not be resolved alone. If Mexico or Argentina did not get well, then neither would Iowa. If Japan and West Germany and others did not pursue similar strategies, then any action taken by the United States would only aggravate its own weaknesses. Neither elected governments nor central banks were accustomed to proceeding with unified strategies —absent war or other catastrophe.

To stimulate demand worldwide, governments would, first, have to force interest rates much lower, closer to something resembling the historic rate of return on lending. Lower rates would stimulate both consumer demand and business investment and also relax the burden on debtors, from Midwestern farmers to Latin-American nations. Demand would be stimulated if central banks stopped restraining their countries' economic growth and committed themselves to fostering faster expansion.

Volcker and the Treasury periodically implored Japan and West Germany to lower their interest rates and to provide more stimulus for their economies, but the allied nations were wary—and relatively content. Japan had low unemployment and a trade surplus. West Germany had a deep historic fear of inflation. Both nations and others had been burned in the past by following the American lead and they were reluctant to commit themselves.

"People think I worry about inflation," Volcker said. "They ought to listen to Japan and Germany. The Germans go on ad nauseam about inflation. That's all you hear. In Japan, they think it's nice to have a trade surplus. Low interest rates are not popular in a country with a 20 percent savings rate. Here you attack central bankers for raising interest rates. In Japan, you attack them for not raising interest rates."

Having led the central banks of the world to a high plateau of punishing interest rates, the Federal Reserve could not now get them to back off. Everyone seemed stuck, unable or unwilling to move away from the high cost of money for their own particular reasons. The allies took cautious steps to lower rates slightly and stimulate, but none was adequate.

Aside from the reluctant allies, the U.S. government could not easily extricate itself from its own contradictions. Given the huge deficits, additional fiscal stimulus was out of the question. Yet the Fed feared that if it stimulated by lowering interest rates, capital might flee from U.S. investments, the dollar's value might fall precipitously and the central bankers would lose control of prices. Unless everyone acted together, each party was afraid to act alone.

Faster economic growth would mean higher employment and rising real wages for labor—new buyers for the world's goods—but this time, wages must be driven up worldwide, not just in the United States. At the same time, governments would have to encourage a broader distribution of incomes, the opposite of their economic policies in the eighties, when both tax policy and monetary policy pushed more and more income to the top. The much-celebrated tax reform legislation enacted in 1986 did nothing to reverse the maldistribution of incomes and even exacerbated the imbalance by collapsing the ladder of progressive income-tax rates.

Finally, demand would be stimulated worldwide by refinancing or writing off bad debts—particularly for the Third World nations. Relieving debtors was a way of creating viable consumers. Various proposals to accomplish relief for Latin debtors were beginning to get more serious attention in Congress, but the political obstacles were formidable, including the objections from debtors at home who would demand similar treatment for themselves. Forgiveness, so valued as a human capacity, was always difficult in politics and nearly impossible in economics.

On the supply side, however, the situation was even more difficult because there was no existing political mechanism for dealing with excess capacity and surpluses on an international scale. The only weapon available to governments was to erect individual trade barriers and shield their own markets from the worldwide gluts. In time, the problem of surplus would be resolved by the raw economic forces—the gradual liquidation of producers, whether farms or factories, American or foreign, until the excess capacity was eliminated and world supply came back into balance with the existing demand. The free-market orthodoxy accepted this destruction as the natural process of adjustment.

The political question was whether governments, acting in concert, could devise a less brutal and wasteful means of mediating the surplus among nations—in effect, sharing the burden in order to reduce the pain and disorder. In the 1930s, the New Deal had created a series of supply-control systems for agriculture, oil, labor and other sectors, which worked effectively in the domestic economy for at least a generation. But there was no equivalent vision of how to cope with excess supply on a worldwide scale in the 1980s. Without that thinking, the only plausible solution for politicians was to close their markets to foreign competitors and let someone else's producers swallow the surplus. As long as the world's supply glut threatened, the emerging trade war would likely intensify. As long as supply remained out of balance with demand, the liquidations must continue.

In the present political context, these were forbidden questions. The politics of the eighties celebrated the virtues of free-market forces; activist intervention by governments was scorned. At the Federal Reserve and the White House, policy makers were ruled by conservative orthodoxies that did not allow for such possibilities. The Fed felt encouraged by falling wages and a subdued economy and took these to be evidence of necessary adjustments. Volcker and his colleagues were tolerant of the continuing liquidations, which they believed to be the inescapable cost of restoring order. At the White House, President Reagan and his conservative advisers thought that they had buried Keynes. They were not about to revive his ideas and elaborate on them. Just as in earlier eras, the reigning orthodoxy drifted confidently toward its moment in history—the moment when it too would be repudiated by reality.

"It's a delicious moment of history," the chief economist at E. F. Hutton declared.[13] His exuberance was shared all along Wall Street as both the stock market and the bond market rallied explosively in February 1986, breaking through to historic highs. Everything seemed to be coming together—falling prices, declining interest rates, financial rallies, brighter economic prospects—as if Paul Volcker had planned it that way. The markets were giddy with profit.

Oil prices, after months of predictions, finally did collapse—falling from $26 a barrel to $12 in a few short weeks at the end of 1985. At about the same time, Congress enacted the Gramm-Rudman-Hollings legislation, promising to reduce the federal deficits to zero within five years. The measure was actually nothing more than a declaration of intent, but it cheered investors obsessed with the fear of eventual inflation.

The moment did seem to be a decisive break in the psychology of the financial markets. The stock market, which had been moving upward steadily since the previous May, suddenly took off in almost daily leaps upward. The Dow Jones index rose above 1760—a gain of 500 points in less than nine months. As the rally continued, less spectacularly, the Dow was pushed eventually above 1900.

The significant rally, however, was in the bond market. Bondholders, presumably heartened by the falling oil prices and the congressional promises of deficit reduction, began to accept lower interest rates on long-term paper and to bid up the trading prices for outstanding issues. Bond yields fell to their lowest level since 1978 and bond prices soared proportionately. The interest rate on twenty-year Treasuries declined by more than 2.5 percent over four months, falling below double digits, down to nearly 8 percent. The inflationary fears of the bond market were clearly subsiding at last—exactly what Volcker had been hoping for.

It's psychology [the chairman observed]. Just in the last three months, there has been quite a rally in the bond market for not any obvious reason. The economy wasn't too strong, it's true, but that didn't explain it. Why did the bond market rally? I would interpret this as one stone crumbling in the edifice of inflationary psychology. It didn't disappear but it began to crumble a bit. The reduced rate of inflation has gone on long enough that they began to be believers.

The euphoria of Wall Street investors infected economic forecasters and the good news was swiftly broadcast: the American economy was on the brink of energetic revival, thanks to the twin bonuses of lower oil prices and lower interest rates. In his State of the Union address, President Reagan hailed the "American miracle." *The New York Times* announced the dawning of a new era: an unlimited vista of inflation-free prosperity ahead, unlike anything living Americans had experienced.

The elation was short-lived. Within a few weeks, it became apparent that the supposed benefits of lower oil prices were more than offset by the immediate economic damage they caused—soaring unemployment in the Southwest, a new wave of defaults and threatened banks, renewed crisis for Mexico and other debtor nations that depended on the energy sector. The economy did not take off in the spring, as so many had predicted. It slowed down again to an anemic growth rate of .6 percent.

In fact, a new crisis of debt default was spreading through the economy. The consolidation of ownership that had been rolling up the defaulted producers of real goods was now claiming more victims in finance too. The troubled Bank of America fought off take-over bids. More than 120 banks failed, a modern record. Congress rushed to bail out the depleted insurance fund for bankrupt S & L's and the insolvent federal farm credit system. In Oklahoma, a major bank was "bailed out" by federal regulators before it failed—infused with new capital to forestall collapse. In Houston, the Texas Commerce Bank, twenty-eighth largest in the nation, succumbed to weakness and was acquired by Chemical Bank of New York, the sixth largest. In the deep tides of capitalism, new wealth was widely dispersed on the upside, distributed to new owners in developing regions. Then on the downside some of it was taken back, reconcentrated among the owners of old wealth.

Among other things, the bond market's spontaneous rally seemed to contradict an argument that Volcker and others had promoted since 1981 and that most politicians had come to believe, namely, that the high level of long-term interest rates prevailing through the eighties was the direct function of the swollen federal deficits. Rates were high, it was said, because the huge government borrowing put too much pressure on credit markets—excessive demand chasing limited supply. If that was so, then why were the long-term rates suddenly falling now? The federal deficit was not getting smaller, it was growing larger. In 1986, it would set another new record, $230 billion. The only thing that had changed was the congressional promise to do something substantial about the deficits—next year or the year after (a promise Congress failed to keep). It was not primarily conditions of supply and demand that had held interest rates high. It was a state of mind in the world of finance—the fears of the bondholders, anxious to protect their profits, and the timidity of the Federal Reserve, unwilling to contradict them.

When the psychology did change at last, the reasons were not especially mysterious. Financial investors had tangible cause to feel better about the future. Their inflationary fears were subsiding because, in fact, the selective deflation was simultaneously growing much worse. The plunge in prices for oil and other commodities drove the Consumer Price Index downward toward zero. For the first time in nearly forty years, the average price level actually turned negative —prices falling at a rate of -2.8 percent over three months.

For the owners of financial wealth, this represented a great windfall, regardless of what it did to the real economy. When prices fell for real goods, anyone holding dollars or dollar-denominated financial assets automatically enjoyed the greater purchasing power. The same money would buy more oil or more farmland. The real value of financial assets was magnified by the falling prices. Investors felt more secure about their wealth because the power of their wealth was growing—almost magically.

The ebullient forecasts for the real economy missed this essential point: the owners of financial wealth did not really give up anything when they consented to the decline in nominal interest rates—and borrowers in the real economy did not gain much either. Nominal interest rates fell swiftly, but so did the inflation rate. The real interest rates, therefore, either remained unchanged or actually increased substantially. The yields on long-term Treasury bonds, for instance, declined roughly in step with the falling price level. But the real return on short-term financial assets actually increased since short-term interest rates declined less than prices did. While the inflation rate was falling by nearly 3 percent, interest on one-year Treasury notes declined by only 1.25 percent. The difference meant lenders were actually collecting even higher real interest rates—and borrowers were paying more.

A booming economy was not a likely prospect if the real cost of money was going up. Consumers, home buyers, even businessmen, did feel momentarily cheered as they watched nominal interest rates decline, but the illusion did not erase the facts of the case. The real burden of borrowing was increased for the struggling economy. The simple equation of real interest rates, so little understood outside finance, was combined with the depressing effects of deflation. Together, they guaranteed that a new era could not unfold, despite Wall Street's optimism.

The shunned minority on the Federal Reserve Board finally became the majority. When Lyle Gramley and Charles Partee retired, the President appointed two more governors who shared the perspective of Martha Seger and Preston Martin, the original Reagan appointees. Manuel Johnson, Assistant Secretary of the Treasury and a former economics professor from George Mason University, was a supply sider, confident that faster growth was possible without reviving inflation. Wayne Angell was a Kansas banker and wheat farmer, who called himself a "hard-money Populist." Like the supply siders, Angell argued that the Fed's decisions should be guided by commodity prices—if oil and grain were caught in deflation, as they were, that meant money was too tight and interest rates must be reduced.

The Federal Reserve chairman, who had failed to have his way on only a few occasions in nearly seven years, was now outnumbered on the Board of Governors. Only Henry Wallich, who was recuperating from chemotherapy treatments, and Emmett Rice, who also intended to retire, remained as Volcker's committed allies. The "one-man show," as Martha Seger called it, was about to be disrupted.

Volcker, nonetheless, was even more intransigent. The falling prices and swiftly declining interest rates in the bond market gave the Fed an ideal opportunity to lower short-term rates proportionately. In these circumstances, no one could accuse the chairman of retreating. He would simply be ratifying what the bond market had already decreed. The conditions were ideal for easing money.

Yet the chairman refused to move. He was as stubborn about lowering interest rates as Ronald Reagan was about raising taxes. Volcker insisted on easing short rates only slightly while the long-term rates fell dramatically and the Consumer Price Index dropped below zero— a general deflation. Over four months, long-term bonds had fallen by more than 250 basis points, yet the Fed allowed the Federal Funds rate to decline by only 50 basis points. Given the zero inflation, the effect was to raise the real cost of money—adding to the drag on the weakening economy.

Volcker's rationale reflected his cautious conservatism, his constant fears of what might happen if he yielded. Interest rates were the Fed's single lever of control, and after holding the lever taut for six and a half years, the chairman seemed loath to relax it. This time, he worried, if U.S. interest rates relaxed too much, the flow of international capital might turn away and seek higher returns elsewhere. The value of the dollar might fall swiftly in that event—followed by a surge of domestic price inflation as the terms of trade were suddenly reversed. Volcker argued that the United States could not lower its interest rates unless Japan and West Germany were willing to lower their rates simultaneously.

"Nobody else was ready to move," Volcker said. "My colleagues from the other central banks weren't ready to move and I had no interest in moving without them. I didn't like the implications for the dollar, the interpretations that might be put on it. I was concerned about a slide in the dollar that had already gone too far. The interpretation might be: where's the dollar going to go?"

But Volcker was caught unaware by the intense concerns of his new colleagues on the board. The world's economy was ebbing, and if the Fed did not act quickly to stimulate, deflation and high interest rates could smother the weak expansion. The argument came to a boil at the Board of Governors meeting on February 24. The four Reagan appointees urged a cut in the Discount rate; Volcker and his two allies were opposed. When the roll was called, the chairman did not back off and neither did the other side. Volcker lost the vote, 4–3, his first recorded defeat as Fed chairman. When the news was announced, it would be obvious he had lost control of the Federal Reserve Board.

"I didn't want an argument with the chairman," Preston Martin insisted, "but I didn't have a choice. I thought I could get him to vote with us. I expected him to come along. I was as surprised as anyone when he wouldn't do that and he wound up in the minority."

"I couldn't change," Volcker said. "I didn't have a choice. It was quite apparent that I was going to be in the minority if the majority held to their position. Sometimes, you don't feel that strongly. Sometimes, you do."

Volcker was furious afterward. He talked about resigning immediately. He was the chairman, the man responsible for policy, and the institution could not function otherwise. If the other governors were going to take things into their own hands, maybe they should find someone else to lead them. From the boardroom, still upset, Volcker went to a scheduled luncheon with Treasury Secretary James Baker and expressed his feelings.

The Treasury Secretary discreetly intervened, counseling compromise. The abrupt resignation of Paul Volcker would be a destabilizing event in itself, one the Reagan Administration did not need. In the afternoon, the governors reconvened and agreed to a truce: the Discount reduction would be postponed for two weeks while Volcker tried to persuade the West German and Japanese central banks to take similar action. Volcker would remain as chairman. All of them would try to avoid another embarrassing confrontation in the future.

The episode made visible, for one brief moment, the internal conflict that had long divided the Fed. Whatever satisfaction some governors felt at finally prevailing over Paul Volcker, they were also chastened by the controversy. Martin, whose term as vice chairman was expiring, was accused of usurping power. He left the board shortly afterward when the White House would not promise to appoint him as chairman in 1987, when Volcker's term ended. Manuel Johnson became the new vice chairman and worked on establishing a more settled atmosphere. Volcker patched up his relationships with the new governors, mindful that, if they wished, they could outvote him.

Volcker was still chairman and yet he was no longer chairman in the sense he had been for almost seven years. Instead of being the dominating authority, he was now compelled to be more collegial. Instead of the "System men" who had surrounded him at the board table, arguing if anything that he must be still tougher, he now faced colleagues who were outsiders—less in awe of the institution's folklore and also decidedly different in their perspective on the political economy. By 1987, Henry Wallich and Emmett Rice retired too, replaced by two more Reagan appointees. Robert Heller was an economist, a senior vice president at the Bank of America who shared Wayne Angell's views about pegging monetary policy to the rise and fall of commodity prices. The other was Edward Kelley, an investment counselor from Houston who was a lifelong personal friend of Treasury Secretary James A. Baker.

Now Volcker was all alone. As everyone understood, he was the last "hawk" left at the table. The others did not embarrass him publically again. There were no visible conflicts. But every other member of the Federal Reserve Board held a more generous opinion on the prospects for faster economic growth than the chairman did. His power to control things was ebbing.

The rebellion did succeed in turning Volcker a bit, and, in the aftermath, it was clear that the new governors had been correct in their economic analysis. Real interest rates were too high and going higher. The sluggish economy needed relief from the Fed. If it didn't come soon, the Federal Reserve might induce another economic contraction—the third one in six years—only this time the recession would be inadvertent.

The episode also illustrated, once again, how the democratic political process was deformed by the existence of this separate power center, immune to direct control. The President's men were confined to oblique nudges in order to get their way. And, when they succeeded marginally, the press then accused them of violating the sanctity of the central bank. Congress, instead of confronting the central issues of money and interest rates, plunged into subsidiary debates about trade rules and protective tariffs. Democrats were trapped by their past and Republicans by their accomplishments. Neither party could speak directly to the new inequities created by stable money. Neither party dared to challenge the taboo that protected the Federal Reserve.

The political deformity was deeper than the governing relationships of Washington. Citizens at large did not understand their own interests in the politics of money or how their elected representatives failed to speak for those interests. The money debate hardly existed in

American politics, and where it did, the terms were usually defined by ignorance and misguided prejudice, by numbing discussions of rival economic theories.

One interest group, almost alone, understood its place in the debate —the bondholders, the commercial bankers, the 400,000 financial professionals of Wall Street and their customers, the investors. They were like an ever-present chorus, scolding the Fed or applauding it, demanding that their interests be served by the government before all others. Like any interest group, their opinions were based on narrow values and were often mistaken, but the consequences of Wall Street's wrong judgments and the Fed's flowed into the lives of virtually everyone. The gross distortion of influence would endure so long as neither political party had the presence or courage to challenge it.

The Federal Reserve Board, without further dissent from the chairman, granted three additional Discount reductions in subsequent months of 1986 and nominal interest rates continued downward. Yet the economy still responded fitfully. Real rates were decreasing too, but still remained far above historical levels. The economic impact was obvious, for instance, in mortgage interest rates, which hovered near 10 percent. The lower rate looked inviting to home buyers, but it really wasn't. Twenty years before, when the inflation rate had also been about 1 percent, mortgage rates were between 4 and 5 percent. The real cost of a home mortgage thus remained exorbitant—and lenders were still collecting a huge extra tariff.

Given the Fed's actions, the Discount rate was down to 5.5 percent —the lowest nominal rate in ten years. But the Discount rate was still too high in real terms. To provide genuine stimulus for the economy, some analysts figured the Discount rate would have to go as low as 3 percent. Money was somewhat easier, but it was still punishingly dear. The unanswered question for the makers of monetary policy would be: did they yield too little, too late?

When Charles Partee retired from the Federal Reserve System, in early 1986, he was frankly disillusioned about the presumed certitudes of economics.

> As someone who's been doing this for thirty-five years, it's a very humbling experience [Partee said]. I can't maintain any theory. All I can say is that I have a pretty good sense of the economy. That's all. Nothing ennobling to teach. Nothing to state as a grand principle. Any economist who's going to be honest ought to say just the same thing. Lyle Gramley ought to say the same thing. To tell you the truth, Paul Volcker ought to say the same thing.

The Federal Reserve chairman did, in fact, express his own sense of quandary. Why was there such tremendous creation of new debt when interest rates were so high? Why didn't the productivity of the economy improve now that inflation was gone? How was the financial system going to work its way out of the mountain of questionable debt obligations? The eighties, he agreed, did have parallels with the twenties.

The giddy behavior in financial markets and inflated stock prices were the most obvious resemblances. The dangerous expansion of domestic debt and the international disequilibrium were similar too. Benjamin Strong spent the decade of the 1920s trying to patch the international gold standard back together (and failed spectacularly with the collapse of 1929). Paul Volcker spent the 1980s coping with the currency instability too and trying to keep the international finance system from breaking down. Volcker did not sit around making the-crash-is-coming comparisons with the past. He worried about the dangers of the present.

Volcker's dilemma resembled Benjamin Strong's in a more precise manner. In the summer of 1927, Strong had executed a huge infusion of new liquidity into the banking system, hoping to help European financial markets and to avert a domestic recession. Strong's action, in hindsight, was blamed for bringing on the collapse. Instead of real growth, the excess liquidity flowed into financial speculation, fueling the hectic price run-up on Wall Street that ended abruptly in the Great Crash.

Something similar occurred, starting in the summer of 1985, when the Fed reluctantly allowed money growth to soar. Since the real economy offered such poor prospects, the excess money supply found its way into financial markets, driving up paper prices and allowing Wall Street's great rally. If Volcker acquiesced to the money growth, it simply stimulated financial excess. But if he refused, he might drive the real economy into recession, collapsing debtors and their banks.

With rapid money growth, the financial markets surged for more than two years while the real economy languished, approximately the same divergence that occurred in the late twenties. Stock prices were uncoupled from real value. The resemblance of events was eerily reflected in the Dow Jones index: its upward course in the eighties, as it moved past 2600, was in nearly perfect step with the chart the Dow followed during the fateful bull market of the late twenties.

Even in the best of times, melodramatic scenarios for economic disaster were commonplace and usually fatuous. None had ever come to pass, at least not since 1929. History did not usually repeat itself so neatly. The economy had, nevertheless, developed many of the same vulnerabilities that had led to 1929—in particular, "bubbles" of bad debt that seemed unsustainable. Vacant office buildings were erected with borrowed money, based on occupancy assumptions that could not be fulfilled. Corporate restructurings were financed with "junk bonds" on dubious projections of future profits. If ill-founded hopes were suddenly shattered, the loans behind them might collapse too. Investors would rush to dump the stock shares they owned and financial values would plunge. The bubbles would burst.

In some respects, the underlying conditions of the 1980s were actually less promising. The decade of the twenties, for instance, was an era of enormous expansion in America's industrial base and the capital investment produced extraordinary gains in productivity. During the eighties, both capital formation and productivity improvement were weak. The economy in the twenties also accumulated unsustainable debts, but the borrowing did not include massive deficit spending by the federal government. The present vulnerabilities, in short, rested on a much weaker base.

Charles Partee did not actually subscribe to the disaster scenarios, but in his quandary, he found himself taking them more seriously. Partee laughed nervously at the oddity of it—a retiring Federal Reserve governor, clearing out his office while he speculated on how the next financial collapse might unfold.

Hell, I've got some guy who comes around every six months and tells me about the long cycle and the crash that's coming [Partee said]. I think, well, he's a real oddball. And then I think, well, everything is running on course, just as he told me. First, he says, real estate would crash. Then that would undercut other values, and debt, which is still very high, becomes more risky. This causes a general flight to liquidity—investors getting out of financial instruments—and that would bring down the stock market. I ask him when. He says it might be 1987, but more likely 1989.

Conventional opinion, at least since the 1930s, was comforted by the assumption that governments would never allow such a catastrophe to occur again. The Federal Reserve and other central banks could reverse the event by "flooding the street with money," as Benjamin Strong had said. But that required a willingness to forsake principle and consciously destabilize money. The Fed's failure to act after 1929 was not essentially technical weakness. It was the inability of the governors to understand what was happening, an unwillingness to intervene against what seemed to them natural developments. Would the modern Fed be more perceptive, more willing to act in time? It required decisiveness, even courage, for a central banker to abandon money in order to save the real economy. Charles Partee, for one, was not altogether confident.

"These situations, as they became critical, would force the decision —whether or not to throw money at them," Partee explained. "Do we bring back inflation to prevent these things from happening? Of course, if there was a general collapse, that would be way beyond the scale that open-market operations could deal with."

Partee reassured himself, however, with the knowledge that the economy and the banking system had weathered repeated crises in the recent past, and the gloomy predictions always had been avoided. The Fed would have to muddle through, as Volcker said, patching up weak spots, bailing out the bankrupt banks too large to fail, hoping that, over time, the economy would grow out of its troubles.

"I'm reminded that things looked pretty bad a year or two ago," Partee said. "The banking system was overextended. People were saying the Texas banks were going to go because of oil. West Coast banks have a lot of real-estate loans. New York banks are in way over their heads. Actually, some considerable period of time has gone by and nothing much has happened."

If the historical parallel with the 1920s held true, however, the collapse might not begin in New York or Texas or California, but in Tokyo. Sixty years ago, when the Great Crash developed, the United States was the ascendant new economic power, trying to prop up the enfeebled older power, Great Britain, which could no longer lead. Something similar was occurring in the late 1980s, only now Japan was the rising power and it was the United States that was losing strength and becoming dependent. Under pressure to help the United States, Japan had lowered rates and pumped up its domestic liquidity. But, just as had happened on Wall Street in 1928 and 1929, Japan's enlarged money supply flowed heavily into financial speculation and drove up prices on the Tokyo stock exchange.

In any case, the gap between economic reality and financial illusion was already sufficiently visible in Wall Street. From 1982 to 1987, the value of Dow-Jones stocks had inflated by more than 230 percent. Yet real economic growth had totaled only 20 percent. Industrial production had increased by only 25 percent. Someone was terribly wrong about economic conditions. In the modern financial world, it hardly mattered who crashed first—New York or Tokyo—because the others were sure to follow.

The potential for a modern collapse involved one other underlying vulnerability—the same one Marriner Eccles had identified more than fifty years ago when he tried to figure out what caused the Great

Depression. The economy was being steadily weakened by what Eccles called the "giant suction pump" of maldistribution—economic policies that pulled more and more income away from those who would spend it, pushing millions of families toward the point where they could not consume.

> As mass production has to be accompanied by mass consumption, mass consumption, in turn, implies a distribution of wealth—not of existing wealth, but of wealth as it is currently produced—to provide men with buying power. . . . Instead of achieving that kind of distribution, a giant suction pump had by 1929–30 drawn into a few hands an increasing portion of currently produced wealth. . . . As in a poker game where the chips are concentrated in fewer and fewer hands, the other fellows could stay in the game only by borrowing. When their credit ran out, the game stopped.[14]

The same process was at work. Consumption remained strong because more and more families relied on debt rather than earnings. Personal savings fell to unprecedented levels, as low as 2 percent of current income, and consumer debt levels rose as high as 18 percent. But these averages were misleading because the rising debt burdens were concentrated, naturally enough, on the bottom half of the economic ladder—the families whose income shares had shrunk in the 1980s. In effect, they were borrowing from the upper half in order to keep buying, the debtors relying on the creditors to stay in the game. It was just as well that they did. With business investment dwindling, consumer spending was the principal economic activity keeping the economic expansion alive.

If consumers were eventually forced to pull back, if enough families reached the point where they could borrow no more chips, then the poker game must stop. Recession would follow and all the debt-weakened families and businesses would be at severe risk. When would this occur? The few economic forecasters who were alarmed could not say precisely when. All they could observe with certainty was that the deterioration was under way, and if nothing intervened to reverse it, the game would eventually end.

The surest way to prevent that outcome would be to turn off the "suction pump"—to push more income downward in the society to the debtor families, those who would promptly spend it. Through the tax code, through lower interest rates or through direct aid, the government could prolong and reinvigorate the prosperity by reversing the maldistribution of incomes that had dominated the 1980s. Neither Congress nor the President nor the Federal Reserve, neither Republican nor Democrat, was inclined to embrace this remedy. The idea of progressive distribution of incomes was as passé in the "go-go eighties" as it had been in the "roaring twenties." Old lessons, learned so painfully in past crises, were now forgotten.

Certain principles of money were not subject to alteration by the modern technocratic managers. They might be ignored or forgotten for a time, but they could not be repealed. One of these principles was the ancient biblical injunction against usury. The particular definitions of usury had changed over the centuries, but the moral meaning had not. Usury was present when lenders insisted on terms that were sure to ruin the borrowers.

Like most moral principles, the sin of usury was grounded in practical necessity. It was more than a social plea for fairness or generosity on the part of the wealthy. No social system could tolerate usury, not as a permanent condition, because it led to an economic life that was self-devouring. The *rentier* collected his due until he owned all the property and the peasants had nothing. But who would buy the *rentier*'s grain if he had all the money? And how would the peasants survive?

Modern capitalism, less obviously, was subject to the same pathology. The miracle of compound interest, celebrated for its power to stimulate new ventures and generate new wealth, contained a malevolent potential. The process could not function indefinitely if the creditors got most all of the rewards—the new wealth that was derived from their lending—and the enterprising borrowers got little or none. Interest rates set the terms on which the rewards of capitalism would be divided and interest was usurious when the borrower's rightful share of profit was confiscated by the lender.

Capitalism could not long function in that condition. The creative powers of capital were reversed and the compounding interest became destructive. Instead of distributing the bounty widely, the rewards were steadily concentrated in fewer and fewer hands. The process might go on for quite a long time, but eventually it had to fail, either from social upheaval or economic exhaustion.

Did the Federal Reserve and cooperating forces impose conditions in the decade of the eighties that were a modern equivalent of usury? The question provided a larger context for judging what had transpired. As the decade opened, the legal limits on interest were repealed and the normal political inhibitions were set aside. Lenders would be allowed to collect unlimited rewards, whatever the market dictated. What followed was an era in which the shares were radically redivided. The government itself fostered the redistribution by holding interest rates at unprecedented levels. Creditors received a bloated share. Borrowers accepted terms that, for many, guaranteed their ruin. Like the sixteenth-century French peasants who turned to the usurer, many borrowers did not have much choice. They were ruined anyway if they refused the terms.

"We should not be surprised," economist Kenneth E. Boulding observed, "if the economy is exhibiting some pathological features. . . . If monetary policy causes interest to erode away profit, it creates a bleak future for capitalism." [15] As recently as 1960, net interest was less than 3 percent of the total national income that went to corporations and individuals. In the 1980s, interest claimed 10 or 11 percent of the national income, a severe change in the division of rewards. A larger share for the *rentier* was perhaps justifiable when inflation was alive, depreciating the value of their money. When inflation stopped, however, the terms became scandalous.

Iowa farmers who complained about usury and the Fed were not wrong about their own predicament. Farmers who borrowed money to plant crops, knowing their returns could not possibly cover the interest due, were indeed victims of usurious terms, even if no one else called them that. Sooner or later, if the farmers continued to borrow, the lenders would own their farms. Home buyers, who entered mortgage transactions they could not possibly sustain, could be described as victims too.

For other kinds of enterprises and the economy in general, the question of usury was more difficult to answer. What was obvious was that, throughout the 1980s, creditors collected the greatest returns of this century, whether their wealth was lent to the government or through corporate bonds or bank loans or short-term financial paper. Most individual borrowers seemed able, at least in the short run, to keep up with the swollen interest burdens and retain a share for themselves, albeit a smaller one than they once received. Many of them, however, were like the farmers—falling steadily behind. So too was the economy as a whole.

If this did constitute usury, the ruinous effects for capitalism would not be fully visible immediately. The pathology would be steady and silent, sapping the vigor of the process until one day, perhaps quite dramatically, the underlying malady made itself known. The persuasive evidence suggesting this condition was the level of real interest rates compared to the real growth of the overall economy. In every quarter since 1980, except three, real interest rates had exceeded the real economic growth. That was another way of saying that the share for the creditor was compounding faster than the economy could produce the new wealth to be divided. "It's political dynamite," Lyle

Gramley had observed. "Sooner or later," Preston Martin agreed, "it will sink the ship."

Capitalism had this flaw: there was no natural stop valve to control its appetites. For individuals as well as for great institutions of finance, the natural ambition of capital was always to seek maximum return from wealth. There was nothing in the capitalist process that told investors when they were demanding too much from it, that their collective desire for net gain was undermining the system itself. In the absence of political or social controls, the decrees of church or government, the lenders naturally claimed as much as the marketplace would allow; they had no way to distinguish between their normal desire for profit and the destructiveness of greed. If government endorsed the free rein of the *rentier*, as it had, if politicians removed legal restraints on interest and the regulators of money supported the demands of bondholders, then nothing stood in the way of capital's sinful impulses.

Paul Volcker towered above the pedestrian ranks of politicians and public servants. His stern brilliance intimidated them and his strong-willed expertise outflanked them. Like all mortals, Volcker was fallible but his errors were barely noticed. The Federal Reserve chairman, the men and women of his institution, had accomplished the great goal they had set for themselves in 1979. Indeed, they had achieved much more than most people, including themselves, had thought possible. In a relatively few years and despite an expansionary fiscal policy, the decision makers of the Federal Reserve had brought the rate of price inflation from 13 percent to the practical equivalent of zero. It was a great victory.

The triumph was hollow, however, for the nation. Its moral promises to the victims were not kept. For the entire society, its predicted benefits were not realized. Paul Volcker and the central bank had taken the country and nations around the world through great suffering—the long contraction and its human tragedies, massive failures, dislocated lives, the pain of the continuing liquidation and the losses of deflation. The moral justification offered throughout was that the pain would be worth it. From bankrupt home builders to displaced factory workers, people were told that their sacrifices were necessary to the general good that would come from them. That conviction sustained Volcker and his colleagues as they had to make the nasty decisions and it reassured public opinion too. On the other side of the temporary suffering, the economy would emerge stronger and more stable, better prepared for a long-running prosperity in which all could share the benefits, if they were willing workers.

This moral promise, in the end, could not be kept. The suffering and dislocation, for one thing, proved to be continuing, not temporary. Furthermore, the sacrifices did not lead to anything resembling what the victims had been told to expect. Once money was stabilized, the economy still faced the same underlying problems it had encountered in the era of inflation—only they were now more severe.

Even in terms of Paul Volcker's own stated goals for the economy, the original hopes were mostly disappointed. Starting in 1979, Volcker had regularly predicted that curbing inflation would revive long-term investment in the American economy. The improved climate for capital formation, he said, would lead to greater growth in productivity, the key to larger income shares for everyone in the future. Abroad, the restored value of the dollar would bring stability to the international financial system. Volcker told wage earners that, without inflation, their nominal pay increases would be smaller, but their real wage gains would prove to be larger. He assured Congress that, while interest rates would be higher at first, in the long run interest rates would be lower. None of those objectives was fulfilled. In nearly every instance, something like the opposite occurred.

Volcker did not disagree entirely with that assessment. His original expectations had been thrown askew, he said, by the unforeseen complication of huge federal deficits. Progress toward his original goals—restored long-term investment, greater productivity, international stability, low real interest rates, rising real wages—was taking longer than he had thought it would. The process involved more risks.

"In the gross terms of the recovery of the economy and on inflation, I suppose it's sort of on track," Volcker said. "But the uncertainties are greater than I would have expected. Maybe it was naïve not to expect that. The economic progress looks on track but the surrounding music is not so good."

In fact, the deeper trend lines for the economy did not look "on track" either—at least not toward the brighter future that Volcker had described. By every meaningful indicator, America's economic performance continued to decline in the decade of the 1980s, notwithstanding the President's claims for it or Volcker's predictions. In truth, the 1980s fell far short of what the economy had accomplished in the inflationary 1970s, an era widely described as disappointing. Expansion of economic output in the eighties was roughly one-third less than real economic growth during the previous decade. Real disposable incomes grew more slowly and so did the creation of new jobs. Productivity gains, already weak and troubling in the seventies, were slightly worse in the eighties. Unemployment was persistently higher than ever before. The proportion of citizens living in poverty increased accordingly.

There was only one exception to this bleak picture: prices. Price inflation was gone. The claim that this change would unleash positive forces in economic performance was simply not confirmed by reality. Volcker continued to believe that, given time and the gradual eradication of the various weaknesses, stable money would deliver what he had promised. In the meantime, certain people would have to settle for less. It would be good for them.

Disinterested observers could look at the facts and reach a gloomier conclusion: whatever was fundamentally wrong with the U.S. economy, it had not been fixed—not by Ronald Reagan's supply-side economics and not by Paul Volcker's "hard money." In many ways, these policies had compounded the underlying ailments. The long-term trend line for the American economy was more ominous now than it had been in the 1970s. From the sixties onward, each succeeding decade produced slower growth, higher levels of permanent unemployment and declining real wages, less progress on capital formation and productivity. For many years, all these portentous developments had been blamed on inflation. Now that inflation was gone, it was obvious that something else was responsible, deeper problems in the aging economic structure that remained unattended.

The public was told—and evidently believed—that Paul Volcker and the Federal Reserve had saved the American economy. In truth, the economy was led into greater weakness and graver peril. In fact, altogether, the government in Washington had done great damage to the citizens at large and to economic enterprise in general. Yet the government evaded the moral question that arose from its actions. If the economy was not healthier, if the supposed benefits of stable money had not been realized, then what would the government say to all those people who had been sacrificed?

Despite popular mythology, the Federal Reserve chairman was no longer as powerful as everyone believed, no longer even fully in charge at the Federal Reserve Board. His weakened status became evident to insiders in the early spring of 1987, when the bondholders experienced another of their momentary anxieties over inflation and began again to bid up interest rates. Oil and agricultural prices were reviving slightly; unemployment was subsiding toward 6 percent as the dollar's devastation began to moderate. Though the price improvements were modest, Wall Street analysts quickly characterized it as the long-feared resurgence of inflation. Once again, their fears were not confirmed in reality, but interest rates increased anyway. Commercial banks pushed up their prime lending rate for the first time in three years. The Fed nudged the Federal Funds rate upward.

Paul Volcker wanted the Federal Reserve to do more. But the Board of Governors refused. At least twice in April and May, the chairman suggested informally to his colleagues that the Fed ought to be raising its Discount rate, as an expression of solidarity with the financial markets. He persuaded only Governor Wayne Angell. The other three governors appointed by Ronald Reagan declared, rather bluntly, that they would vote down the chairman if he tried it.

Despite Wall Street's "bull market," the real economy was struggling. Debt defaults were spreading. Governor Martha Seger visited Oklahoma and Texas and described the miseries she had seen there, the continuing failure induced by falling prices and high interest rates. The country was not threatened by inflation, she insisted. It was still suffering from deflation. And it could not stand higher interest rates.

The chairman did not push the question to a formal vote, since he was certain to lose, and so the private confrontation remained private, unknown to the general public. Inside the government, however, the word was about that Paul Volcker had lost control over the Federal Reserve Board. The austere technocrat who had so thoroughly dominated the politics of the 1980s was, at last, at bay.[16]

A week or two later, Volcker lost another important dimension of his power, but in a more subtle manner. John S. Reed, the new chairman at Citibank, took the sort of bold, unilateral action that his predecessor, Walter Wriston, had often initiated. Citibank announced that it was posting a huge loan-loss reserve, $3 billion set aside from profits, to cover its bad loans to Latin America. Other major banks swiftly followed with similar moves. On one level, it was an important first step toward facing reality—the banks accepting the fact that much of their LDC lending would never be repaid and eventually must be written off.

On another plane, however, Citibank's declaration directly outflanked Paul Volcker and undermined his authority as Fed chairman, the crisis manager who had steered the bankers and debtor nations through five years of international debt crisis. Reed and Volcker had quarreled repeatedly in recent months over the easier new terms negotiated for Mexico and other countries. Meanwhile, Brazil suspended interest payments to the banks. Now Citibank was declaring independence from the paternal guidance of the Fed. Henceforth, if necessary, it would go it alone. Armed with its expanded loan-loss reserves, Citibank could stare down the debtor nations' demands for further concessions and, if they threatened default, perhaps the bank would call their bluff. Citibank, followed by the others, was prepared to play a new kind of "hardball" at the bargaining table and that meant the long-running debt crisis was about to enter a turbulent, new phase. For Paul Volcker, it meant he would no longer be able to dictate the terms.

Given these events and the ominous weaknesses developing in the economy, it seemed like the ideal moment for the chairman to retire. His second four-year term ended in August, and, if he left now, history would remember his triumph. Any subsequent disorders would doubtless be blamed on his successor. Yet, despite personal ambivalence, Volcker was willing to continue as chairman—if the President met certain conditions.

The terms were broadcast informally by the chairman's friends and associates: the President should deliver a fulsome declaration of support for Volcker's stewardship. It would serve as a discreet signal to the other governors to follow his leadership. The implication, as one former White House official put it, was: "Volcker wanted the President to give him back his board."

If so, it was an audacious suggestion and the White House had no interest in making such a commitment. After seven years of enduring Volcker's stubborn single-mindedness, the President and supporting politicians would be delighted to finally get their own man in charge at the Fed—especially as they headed into the presidential election year of 1988 with a weakened economy.

"This idea that the President is supposed to beg an appointee to serve again is just not right," an Administration official complained. "Was there some feeling that the President is entitled to his own man? Sure, there was." The Administration wanted a Fed chairman who would not only collaborate more intimately with the White House but who also was sensitive to the present risks of recession.

The question was how to arrange this transition without being accused by Wall Street of dumping the legendary Paul Volcker. The White House floated reassurances in the press that Volcker would almost certainly be reappointed. Meanwhile, it remained silent on the suggested terms for Volcker's reappointment. The oblique signals from the Fed continued. The President's men pretended not to hear them.

On June 2, President Reagan announced, with appropriate regrets, that Paul Volcker had decided to retire. The decision was attributed to the chairman's personal desire to return to private life. The new chairman would be Alan Greenspan, business consultant and former economics advisor to President Ford, an economist sufficiently conservative to reassure Wall Street. Both the press and the financial markets bought the story.

Alan Greenspan was an orthodox conservative Republican who shared the same perspective as Paul Volcker and was actually more conservative on some questions like bank deregulation. Greenspan had even endorsed, at least in principle, the idea of someday restoring the gold standard. On the crucial question of managing the economy, however, the Reagan White House felt satisfied that the new Federal Reserve chairman would be more accommodating and less stubborn than the old one.

Greenspan had a long association with Republican politics and a reputation as a "pragmatist" who liked to work out a consensus with others. Furthermore, for the past year and a half, he had worried aloud at many public forums about the weakened state of the economy and the need to avert a recession at all costs, while so many debtors were in trouble. Finally, whatever his economic inclinations, Greenspan simply did not have the personal stature of Paul Volcker, either in Washington or Wall Street. Surrounded by independent-minded governors, the new chairman would be unable to dominate the Federal Reserve Board the way Volcker had done through most of his tenure. For that matter, he would be less able to intimidate the politicians.

The Volcker era had ended, but money remained triumphant. The government was not yet prepared to shed the agenda Volcker had imposed on it or to repudiate the narrow definition of economic order that he represented. Afterward, as he confided to friends, Volcker was disappointed that the President did not nominate him for another term. He had wanted to be asked and he wasn't. Perhaps, at last, the politicians in Washington had succeeded in outmaneuvering the central banker from Wall Street.

Money was a veil, just as economists said, but what it concealed was the deeper political conflict among classes of citizens. The money question was the political expression of a struggle over shares. When economic growth languished, when the economy persistently disappointed expectations, different groups and interests naturally fought over the dwindling returns, over who would hold onto their shares and who must accept less. In a practical sense, that was all that had happened in the 1980s—a political struggle over diminishing shares. And the bondholders had won, the creditors with accumulated wealth. Their capital was replenished and amply compensated for their earlier grievances against inflation. They held the high ground now and would not yield until forced to do so.

For most of 200 years, America had successfully evaded the contradiction between democracy and capitalism. The nation was able to honor both, so long as it managed to maintain the constant of healthy economic growth. If the broad landscape of work and incomes was expanding generously, distributing new rewards broadly, questions of who owned wealth and other disparities seemed irrelevant to the general prosperity. Economic growth, as many politicians understood intuitively, was the safety valve that relieved the tension between wealth and wage earners, the inherent conflict in democratic capitalism.

The American contradiction was joined, however, when the economy failed to grow robustly. Gradually, but inevitably, the disappointed expectations would feed the conflict between classes, as larger and larger groups of people were compelled to accept smaller shares of prosperity or were left out altogether. Many citizens of influence, led by the wealth holders, were quite content with an economy that grew but slowly. Their own lives went forward prosperously, oblivious to the social deterioration that was underway around them. In time, however, if stagnation persisted long enough, they too would find themselves engulfed by the consequences—bitter social divisions and a vengeful politics aimed at wealth itself. The unanswered question posed by the 1980s was whether the United States has already entered into such an era.

Eventually, the political hegemony of money must end. As history had demonstrated again and again, the economic system could not forever endure stable money. Sooner or later, the pendulum must move back in the other direction, either gradually or violently, if people wished to restore a vigorously expanding economy. If financial speculation and the developing vulnerabilities did indeed reach a climactic point of collapse, the shift in political values might be quite sudden. The confident money orthodoxy that had dominated the decade would be smashed in a single illuminating moment, its illusion of stability finally exposed by the deeper fundamentals that had always been present.

On Monday, October 19, 1987, such a moment arrived. For a month and a half, the stock market had retreated fitfully from its peak above 2700 on the Dow-Jones average. The descent was harrowing, as the market lost as much as 108 points in a single day. Still, financial analysts and most investors maintained their confidence. The economy was healthy, they told one another, and the losses were merely a necessary correction, a temporary pause, in the long bull market that had begun its ascent back in 1982.

Then, on October 19, the stock market crashed. The "crowds" of Wall Street abruptly lost faith and stampeded. The Dow-Jones average fell 508 points, and something on the order of $500 billion in financial wealth was lost in a single day of trading. The following day, financial markets in Asia and Europe panicked too and experienced similar debacles. For Americans, the event was a trauma beyond the experience of anyone except the elderly who remembered 1929.

Market commentators and high government officials hurriedly assured the public that, despite resemblances, this would not be the beginning of another Great Crash. The government was now more sophisticated, they insisted, and so were the professionals of finance. The President declared that the economy was fundamentally sound. His comments sounded eerily like the things Herbert Hoover had said in the autumn of 1929.

In fact, the market collapse was an ominous warning. Whether the economy stabilized or descended into a deeper disaster would depend heavily on whether the people in power had the courage to abandon the discredited orthodoxy and pursue more realistic values. If extreme circumstances developed in subsequent months, their choice might resemble the one Governor Charles Partee had ruminated on two years before: Would the Federal Reserve have the will to abandon money's value in order to save the real economy? The antidote to a general economic collapse was well understood—lower interest rates and rising prices—if the authorities had the nerve to pursue it. For central bankers, it was the hardest choice imaginable—to deliberately debase money in order to save people.

The reinflation of money values would stimulate economic growth but also restore balance and help to heal the wounded. Inflation encouraged the future and, if kept to reasonable proportions, it stimulated general optimism. Rising prices excited what Keynes called the "animal spirits" of businessmen. It gave them the prospect of expanded profit and the courage to plunge forward with new ventures— the "reckless, booming anarchy" that fostered great achievements. The resumption of inflation would mean rising shares for wage earners and an honest return for commodity producers. Rising prices would restore overburdened debtors to solvency, forgiving them their debts by depreciating money. A return to inflation would begin again to discreetly redistribute wealth in a positive direction.

The idea of deliberately destabilizing money was inadmissible. Reviving inflation was beyond discussion. But, perhaps in time, as more people came to understand it, they would demand as the cure what they had been told was the affliction.

Money was like the sacred totem in a primitive culture, a mysterious object that efficiently expressed the larger social reality. In the American culture formed by democratic capitalism, money *was* the sacred totem. The common faith shared by Americans was secular rationalism and the social order was defined by the scientific abstractions surrounding money. Yet religious mystery was still required—priests and ritual, sacred secrets that sustained belief.

If one understood money's secrets, the true nature of the American social reality was made plain. Money revealed compromised ideals in the civic order. Limitations were imposed on the idea of democracy and sovereign citizens passively accepted them. Money defined the social hierarchy, the rank ordering of citizens, which valued some above others. Money expressed the culture's deepest longings and obsessions, the fretful belief that a dead substance could somehow confer immortal life on those who accumulated it. Money was a living creed in American life, as Veblen said, a more convincing reality than human toil or material needs or the tenuous things of the human spirit.

If the secrets of the temple were revealed, the money mystery would dissolve and people would have to look upon these things directly. Taboos uncoded lost their power to persuade. Americans would see the full terms that bound them together as a society, the deals that were made in their name and the harsh rituals. They would stand before the awesome authority to which free citizens deferred. They would know at last what it was they really believed in.

The mystery was necessary, therefore, to sustain social faith. Knowledge was disturbing. Not knowing the secrets was reassuring. If Americans were afraid to look inside the temple, perhaps it was because they feared to see the truth about themselves.

APPENDIX A

The history of U.S. prices from 1800 to 1986—two perspectives. The first chart traces the rise and fall of the general price level and shows the spikes of inflation that accompanied major wars, the great deflation that followed the Civil War, the price collapse after the stock-market crash of 1929 and the long inflationary era that unfolded after World War II. The second chart offers a more realistic perspective on prices because it traces the year-to-year percentage changes in prices over the same period of history. Data are drawn from Historical Statistics of the United States and, after 1929, from the Consumer Price Index of the Bureau of Labor Statistics.

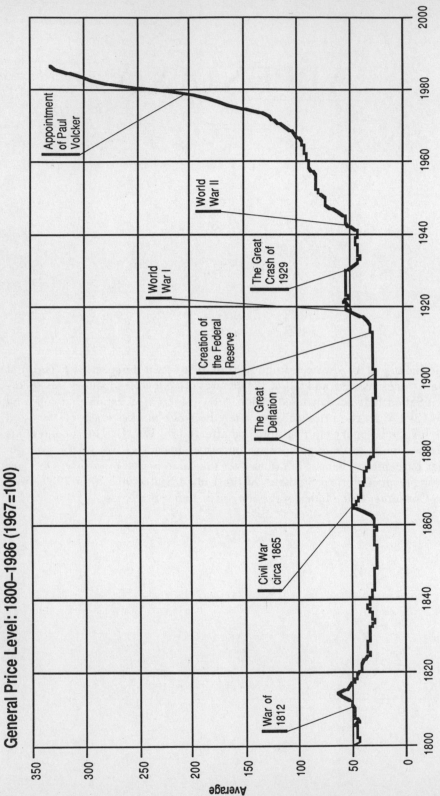

General Price Level: 1800–1986 (1967=100)

General Price Level: Details Showing Dramatic Price Reversals

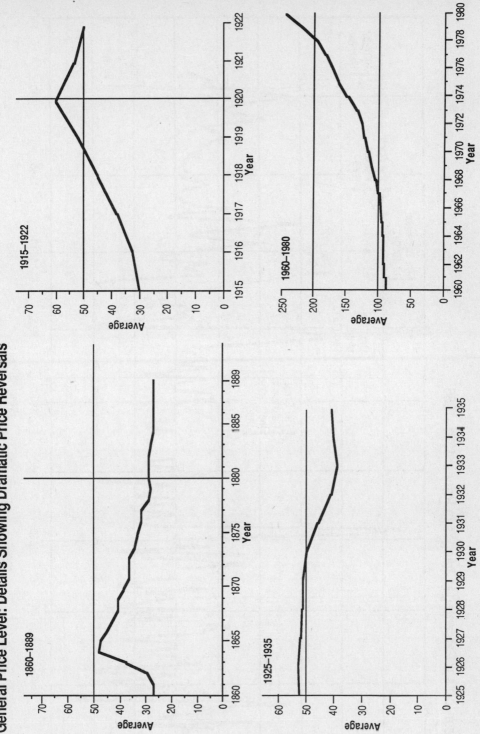

Year-to-Year Percentage Changes in Prices: 1801–1986

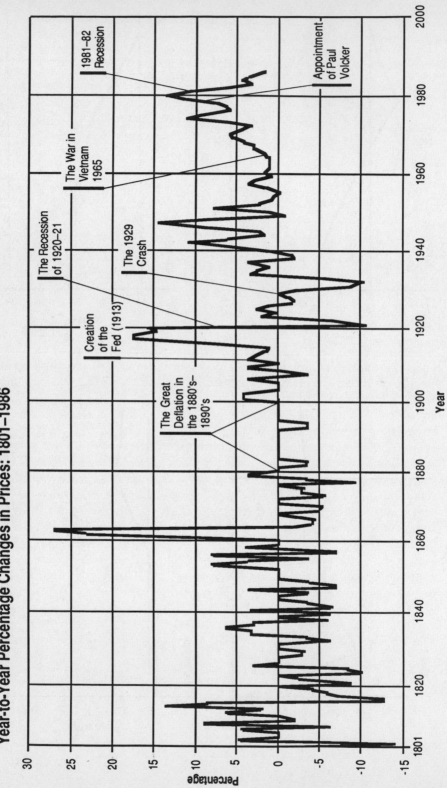

APPENDIX B

Money, Interest Rates and the Economy

The following tables provide an approximate sense of how month-to-month changes in interest rates and money growth interact with the real economy. Monthly changes in growth of the money supply are for the basic aggregate known as M-1. The Federal Funds rate, which applies to overnight lending of excess reserves among commercial banks, is the clearest indicator of Federal Reserve policy because it is the interest rate most reliably controlled by the Fed. The short-term interest rate refers to three-month Treasury bills, a gauge of money-market conditions, and the long-term rate refers to twenty-year Treasury bonds. The inflation rate is the Consumer Price Index for urban population. GNP growth represents the real quarterly growth in the Gross National Product, discounted for inflation. Data are monthly averages from the Annual Statistical Digest of the Federal Reserve Board, the Council of Economic Advisers and the Bureau of Labor Statistics. All interest rates are rounded to the nearest tenth of 1 percent and will not always correspond precisely to the weekly averages used in the text.

1979

	Jan	Feb	Mar	Apr	May	June	July	Aug	Sept	Oct	Nov	Dec
Money Supply	.3	2.3	10.7	18.8	−1.3	15.3	11.2	8.0	7.3	2.2	4.1	6.9
Fed Funds rate	10.1	10.1	10.1	10.1	10.2	10.3	10.5	10.9	11.4	13.8	13.2	13.8
Short-term rate	9.4	9.3	9.5	9.5	9.6	9.1	9.2	9.5	10.3	11.7	11.8	12.0
Long-term rate	9.0	9.0	9.1	9.1	9.2	8.9	8.9	9.0	9.2	10.0	10.4	10.2
Unemployment	5.9	5.9	5.8	5.8	5.6	5.7	5.7	6.0	5.9	6.0	5.9	6.0
Inflation	10.6	14.1	11.6	11.9	14.8	14.0	12.7	12.1	12.5	10.8	11.3	12.6
GNP Growth		3.9			−1.7			4.1			.6	

1980

	Jan	Feb	Mar	Apr	May	June	July	Aug	Sept	Oct	Nov	Dec
Money Supply	6.8	12.8	−.6	−17.2	.9	11.0	13.4	22.8	14.5	13.1	8.1	−10.0
Fed Funds rate	13.8	14.1	17.2	17.6	11.0	9.5	9.0	9.6	10.9	12.8	15.9	18.9
Short-term rate	12.0	12.9	15.2	13.2	8.6	7.1	8.1	9.1	10.3	11.6	13.7	15.5
Long-term rate	10.7	12.2	12.5	11.4	10.4	9.9	10.3	11.1	11.5	11.8	12.4	12.5
Unemployment	6.3	6.2	6.3	6.9	7.5	7.5	7.8	7.7	7.5	7.5	7.5	7.3
Inflation	16.8	15.6	15.6	10.8	10.8	12.0	1.2	9.6	12.0	12.0	13.2	12.0
GNP Growth		3.1			−9.9			2.4			3.8	

1981

	Jan	Feb	Mar	Apr	May	June	July	Aug	Sept	Oct	Nov	Dec
Money Supply	9.8	4.3	14.3	25.2	−11.4	−2.2	2.8	4.8	.3	4.7	9.7	12.4
Fed Funds rate	19.1	15.9	14.7	15.7	18.5	19.1	19.0	17.8	15.9	15.1	13.3	12.4
Short-term rate	15.0	14.8	13.4	13.7	16.3	14.7	15.0	15.5	14.7	13.5	10.9	10.9
Long-term rate	12.3	13.0	12.9	13.5	13.8	13.2	13.9	14.5	15.1	15.1	13.6	13.7
Unemployment	7.5	7.4	7.3	7.2	7.5	7.4	7.2	7.4	7.6	8.0	8.3	8.6
Inflation	9.6	12.0	7.2	4.8	9.6	8.4	13.2	9.6	13.2	4.8	6.0	4.8
GNP Growth		7.9			−1.5			2.2			−5.3	

1982

	Jan	Feb	Mar	Apr	May	June	July	Aug	Sept	Oct	Nov	Dec
Money Supply	19.6	.5	1.6	1.9	8.3	2.7	2.7	10.3	12.8	14.3	13.6	10.6
Fed Funds rate	13.2	14.8	14.7	14.9	14.5	14.2	12.6	10.1	10.3	9.7	9.2	9.0
Short-term rate	12.3	13.5	12.7	12.7	12.1	12.5	11.4	8.7	7.9	7.7	8.1	7.9
Long-term rate	14.6	14.5	13.8	13.6	13.5	14.2	13.8	12.9	12.2	11.0	10.6	10.6
Unemployment	8.6	8.8	9.0	9.3	9.4	9.5	9.8	9.9	10.2	10.5	10.7	10.8
Inflation	3.6	2.4	–3.6	2.4	12.0	12.0	7.2	3.6	2.4	6.0	1.2	–3.6
GNP Growth		–5.9			1.2			–3.2			.6	

1983

	Jan	Feb	Mar	Apr	May	June	July	Aug	Sept	Oct	Nov	Dec
Money Supply	11.5	14.8	13.0	3.6	21.0	10.2	9.4	5.8	3.5	6.2	3.2	5.3
Fed Funds rate	8.7	8.5	8.8	8.8	8.6	9.0	9.4	9.6	9.5	9.5	9.3	9.5
Short-term rate	7.9	8.1	8.4	8.2	8.2	8.8	9.1	9.3	9.0	8.6	8.8	9.0
Long-term rate	10.8	11.0	10.8	10.6	10.7	11.1	11.6	12.0	11.8	11.8	11.9	12.0
Unemployment	10.4	10.4	10.3	10.2	10.1	10.0	9.5	9.5	9.2	8.8	8.4	8.2
Inflation	2.4	0	1.2	8.4	6.0	3.6	4.8	3.6	6.0	3.6	2.4	1.2
GNP Growth		3.5			9.3			6.0			7.3	

1984

	Jan	Feb	Mar	Apr	May	June	July	Aug	Sept	Oct	Nov	Dec
Money Supply	7.6	6.4	7.0	4.3	7.2	10.7	–.9	4.3	5.7	–6.9	11.9	10.2
Fed Funds rate	9.6	9.6	9.9	10.3	10.3	11.1	11.2	11.7	11.3	10.0	9.4	8.4
Short-term rate	8.9	9.1	9.5	9.7	9.8	9.9	10.1	10.5	10.4	9.7	8.6	8.1
Long-term rate	11.8	12.0	12.5	12.7	13.4	13.5	13.4	12.7	12.4	12.0	11.7	11.7
Unemployment	8.0	7.8	7.8	7.8	7.5	7.2	7.5	7.5	7.4	7.3	7.1	7.2
Inflation	7.2	6.0	2.4	6.0	3.6	3.6	3.6	4.8	6.0	3.6	0	1.2
GNP Growth		9.8			5.0			2.3			1.5	

1985

	Jan	Feb	Mar	Apr	May	June	July	Aug	Sept	Oct	Nov	Dec
Money Supply	9.5	13.6	6.1	7.3	14.2	17.3	10.8	17.3	13.3	5.1	11.5	12.6
Fed Funds rate	8.4	8.5	8.6	8.3	8.0	7.5	7.9	7.9	7.9	8.0	8.1	8.3
Short-term rate	7.8	8.3	8.5	8.0	7.5	7.0	7.1	7.1	7.1	7.2	7.2	7.1
Long-term rate	11.6	11.7	12.1	11.7	11.2	10.6	10.7	10.7	10.8	10.7	10.2	9.8
Unemployment	7.4	7.3	7.3	7.3	7.3	7.3	7.3	7.1	7.1	7.1	7.0	6.9
Inflation	2.4	3.6	6.0	4.8	2.4	2.4	2.4	2.4	2.4	3.6	7.2	4.8
GNP Growth		3.1			2.3			4.1			2.1	

1986

	Jan	Feb	Mar	Apr	May	June	July	Aug	Sept	Oct	Nov	Dec
Money Supply	3.6	6.3	15.8	14.4	21.1	14.4	16.4	18.4	10.7	14.4	18.8	30.5
Fed Funds rate	8.1	7.9	7.5	7.0	6.9	6.9	6.6	6.2	5.9	5.9	6.0	6.9
Short-term rate	7.1	7.1	6.6	6.1	6.2	6.2	5.8	5.5	5.2	5.2	5.4	5.5
Long-term rate	9.6	9.1	8.1	7.5	7.8	7.7	7.3	7.3	7.6	7.6	7.4	7.3
Unemployment	6.8	7.2	7.2	7.1	7.2	7.1	7.0	6.8	7.0	6.9	6.9	6.7
Inflation	3.6	−4.8	−4.8	−3.6	2.4	6.0	0	2.4	3.6	2.4	3.6	2.4
GNP Growth		3.8			.6			2.8			1.7	

APPENDIX C

The Federal Open Market Committee releases summary minutes of its meetings six to eight weeks later, on the day after the subsequent meeting. The following is the complete text of the report on the FOMC meeting of May 18, 1981, when the committee decided to tighten—a "substantial deceleration" of money growth—two months before the economy went into recession.

Meeting Held on May 18, 1981

Domestic Policy Directive

The information reviewed at this meeting suggested that growth of real gross national product was slowing in the current quarter from the rapid pace in the first quarter, but activity currently appeared stronger than had been projected at the time of the Committee's meeting on March 31. Real GNP had grown at an annual rate of 6½ percent in the first quarter, according to preliminary estimates of the Commerce Department, and additional data that became available after release of the preliminary estimates suggested that growth had been even more rapid. Average prices, as measured by the fixed-weight price index for gross domestic business product, have continued to rise rapidly in the current quarter, but somewhat less so than earlier in the year.

The dollar value of total retail sales increased slightly further in March but declined appreciably in April, reflecting mainly a sharp drop in sales of new cars in response to the ending of manufacturers' price rebates. Unit sales of new automobiles fell from an annual rate of 10.3 million units in March to 8.1 million units in April. The value of sales excluding automobiles and building materials registered sizable gains in both March and April.

The index of industrial production, which had increased 0.5 percent in March, rose 0.4 percent in April. An increase in auto assemblies, to a rate substantially above the recent pace of sales, was a major factor in the April advance, and output of business equipment and space and defense products exhibited considerable strength. A strike cut production of coal in half and limited the rise in the total industrial production index by about 0.3 percentage point.

Nonfarm payroll employment changed little in March and April after adjustment for strikes, and the unemployment rate was stable at 7.3 percent. In April employment continued to expand in service industries but declined considerably in retail trade establishments and in construction. Small employment gains were recorded in the manufacturing sector, and the average factory workweek edged up 0.1 hour to 40.1 hours.

Private housing starts in March remained at the annual rate of about 1¼ million units recorded in February; during the preceding six months, housing starts had been in a range of 1.4 million to 1.6 million units. Sales of new homes in March continued at the reduced pace of recent months, and sales of existing homes declined further.

Producer prices of finished goods rose at an annual rate of 9½ percent in April, compared with an average rate of 12 percent during the first quarter. The surge of energy prices that had characterized earlier months of the year abated in April, and prices of consumer foods were unchanged. Prices of crude foodstuffs, however, rose sharply. The rise in the consumer price index slowed in March, reflecting a slowing in price increases of energy items and continued moderate increases in food prices and homeownership costs. Prices of other consumer items continued to rise at a relatively rapid pace. Over the first four months of 1981, the rise in the index of average hourly earnings of private nonfarm production workers was slightly less rapid than the pace recorded during 1980.

In foreign exchange markets the trade-weighted value of the dollar against major foreign currencies had risen by about 8½ percent since the final days of March to its highest level in 3½ years. In March the U.S. trade deficit declined sharply, bringing the first-quarter deficit to a level well below the average in 1980. The value and volume of exports rose substantially from the fourth quarter, and the value of imports increased moderately.

At its meeting on March 31, the Committee had decided that open market operations in the period until this meeting should be directed toward behavior of reserve aggregates consistent with growth in M-1B from March to June at an annual rate of 5½ percent or somewhat less, after allowance for the impact of flows into NOW accounts, and growth in M-2 at an annual rate of about 10½ percent. If it appeared during the period before the next regular meeting that fluctuations in the federal funds rate, taken over a period of time, within a range of 13 to 18 percent were likely to be inconsistent with the monetary and related reserve paths, the Manager for Domestic Operations was promptly to notify the Chairman, who would then decide whether the situation called for supplementary instructions from the Committee.

In the latter part of April, incoming data suggested that M-1B, after adjustment for the estimated effects of shifts into NOW accounts, was growing at a rate well above the short-run objectives set forth by the Committee. Consequently, required reserves increased more than the supply of reserves being made available through open market operations. Banks adjusted to the constrained availability of reserves by reducing excess reserves and by increasing borrowings from the Federal Reserve. In the two statement weeks ending May 6, member bank borrowings averaged about $2.4 billion, compared with an average of about $1 billion in the first three statement weeks after the meeting on March 31; and the federal funds rate, which had averaged around 15½ percent in the first three weeks of April, fluctuated within a range of 17 to 20 percent in the last days of April and the first days of May. On May 4 the Board of Governors announced an increase from 13 to 14 percent in Federal Reserve basic discount rates and an increase from 3 to 4 percentage points in the surcharge on frequent borrowings of large institutions.

In a telephone conference on May 6, the Committee agreed that in the brief period before the next regular meeting scheduled for May 18, the reserve path would continue to be set on the basis of the short-run objectives for monetary growth established on March 31. It was recognized that for a time monetary growth might be high in relation to those objectives and that the federal funds rate might continue to exceed the upper end of the range indicated for consultation. In the period remaining until this meeting, bank reserve positions remained under pressure, and federal funds typically traded between 18 and 19 percent.

Growth in M-1B, adjusted for the estimated effects of shifts into NOW accounts, accelerated sharply in April to an annual rate of about 14 percent. But adjusted M-1B had grown from the fourth quarter of 1980 to the first quarter of 1981 at an annual rate of only 1 percent, and its level in April was well within the Committee's longer-run range for that aggregate. M-2 had continued to grow rapidly in April, and its level continued above the upper end of its longer-run range. Growth in the nontransaction component of M-2 slowed markedly, however, as the total of savings and small-denomination time deposits was about unchanged and inflows into money market mutual funds slowed.

Total credit outstanding at U.S. commercial banks registered a slight decline in March and grew at an annual rate of about 4½ percent in April. Holdings of investments changed little over the two months, and growth in loans, particularly business loans, was quite weak. Net issues of commercial paper by nonfinancial corporations declined in April, following expansion at a rapid pace in the first quarter. Issuance of publicly offered bonds remained heavy during April, and the volume of new equity offerings rose considerably.

Short-term market interest rates had risen substantially over the period since the Committee's meeting on March 31: yields on Treasury bills moved up 2¾ to 4 percentage points while yields on private short-term market instruments increased 4½ to 5¼ percentage points. Most long-term interest rates rose to record levels and on balance advanced about 1 percentage point. Over the intermeeting interval, the prime rate charged by commercial banks on short-term business loans was raised in steps from 17½ percent to 19½ percent. In home mortgage markets, average rates on new commitments for fixed-rate loans at savings and loan associations rose above 16 percent, from 15.40 percent at the end of March.

The staff projections presented at this meeting suggested that the surge in growth of real GNP in the first quarter would be followed by much slower growth over the rest of 1981. The rise in the fixed-weight price index for gross domestic business product was projected to moderate as the year progressed but nevertheless to remain rapid.

In the Committee's discussion of the economic situation and outlook, members commented on the considerably greater strength in activity in the first quarter than had been expected, and they continued to stress the difficulties of economic forecasting currently and the importance of adhering to longer-term objectives. While generally anticipating a substantial slowing of growth from the exceptionally rapid pace now indicated for the first quarter, a number of members expressed the view that expansion in activity over the rest of the year was likely to continue to exceed the rates typically being forecast. The observation was made that weakness in demands and activity appeared to be confined to a few sectors, albeit such major ones as housing and automobiles, and that the risks of a significant decline in overall activity appeared to be tempered by the prospect that some accumulated backlogs of demands would be activated whenever interest rates declined. It was also suggested, on the other hand, that high and volatile interest rates could begin to have a cumulative effect in dampening activity, and that little was known about the effects of financial stress that might be developing.

At its meeting on February 2–3, the Committee had adopted the following ranges for growth of the monetary aggregates over the period from the fourth quarter of 1980 to the fourth quarter of 1981: M-1A and M-1B, 3 to 5½ percent and 3½ to 6 percent respectively, after adjustment for the estimated effects of flows into NOW accounts; M-2, 6 to 9 percent; and M-3, 6½ to 9½ percent. It was understood that the distorting effects of shifts into NOW accounts would change during the year and that other short-run factors might cause considerable variation in annual rates of growth from one month to the next and from one quarter to the next.

In the Committee's discussion of policy for the period immediately ahead, it was emphasized that on March 31 the Committee had established an objective for growth of M-1B (adjusted for the estimated effects of shifts into NOW accounts) over the three months from March to June at an annual rate of 5½ percent or somewhat less, and that growth in April had greatly exceeded that pace. According to a staff analysis, some retardation of M-1B growth over the remaining two months of the quarter was to be expected, in light of the greater pressure on bank reserve positions that had developed recently and the apparent slowing of growth in nominal GNP in the current quarter. But growth of M-1B over the two-month period would have to be negligible if the specifications adopted on March 31 were to be realized.

The staff analysis also suggested that growth of M-2 would be less rapid over the second quarter than had been anticipated earlier, reflecting a slowing of growth in savings deposits and small-denomination time deposits as well as continued weakness in money market mutual funds. Thus, growth of the broader monetary aggregates might begin to move down toward their target ranges for growth over the year from the fourth quarter of 1980 to the fourth quarter of 1981.

In considering objectives for monetary growth over the remainder of the quarter, the members in general agreed that a posture of restraint needed to be maintained. They generally agreed with the view that it was particularly important to reduce growth of the monetary aggregates rather quickly, and initial differences in views concerning the precise specifications for monetary growth were relatively narrow. In the discussion, a number of points were emphasized. The indications of continuing strength in economic activity combined with the recent exceptional rise in the income velocity of money posed the risk of pressure for excessive expansion in money and credit as the year developed. Growth of the broader monetary aggregates was already somewhat high relative to the Committee's ranges for the year. The indications of some slowing of the rise in the consumer price index did not appear to reflect as yet any clear relaxation of underlying inflationary pressures, and emphasis was placed on the importance of conveying a clear sense of restraint at a critical time with respect to inflation and inflationary expectations.

With respect to the federal funds rate, it was again stressed that the specification of an intermeeting range for fluctuations over a period of time provided a mechanism for initiating timely consultations between regularly scheduled meetings when it appeared that fluctuations within the specific range were proving to be inconsistent with the objectives for the behavior of the reserve and monetary aggregates. The ranges proposed for the period ahead typically were from 16 or 17 percent to 21 or 22 percent.

At the conclusion of the discussion, the Committee decided to seek behavior of reserve aggregates associated with growth of M-1B from April to June at an annual rate of 3 percent or lower, after allowance for the impact of flows into NOW accounts, and growth in M-2 at an annual rate of about 6 percent. A shortfall in growth of M-1B from the two-month rate of 3 percent would be acceptable, in light of the rapid growth in April and the objective adopted by the Committee on March 31 for growth from March to June at an annual rate of 5½ percent or somewhat less. The members recognized that shifts into NOW accounts would continue to distort measured growth in M-1B to an unpredictable extent and that operational paths would have to be developed in the light of evaluation of those distortions. The Chairman might call for Committee consultation if it appeared to the Manager for Domestic Operations that pursuit of the monetary objectives and related reserve paths during the period before the next meeting was likely to be associated with a federal funds rate persistently outside a range of 16 to 22 percent.

The following domestic policy directive was issued to the Federal Reserve Bank of New York:

The information reviewed at this meeting suggests that real GNP will grow much less rapidly in the current quarter, following the substantial expansion in the first quarter; prices on the average have continued to rise rapidly, although somewhat less so most recently than earlier in the year. The dollar value of total retail sales increased slightly further in March, but it declined appreciably in April when sales of new cars fell in response to the ending of price concessions. Industrial production rose moderately in both months, while nonfarm payroll employment changed little, after adjustment for strikes, and the unemployment rate was stable at 7.3 percent. In March housing starts remained at a reduced pace. Over the first four months of 1981, the rise in the index of average hourly earnings was slightly less rapid than during 1980.

The weighted average value of the dollar against major foreign currencies has risen steadily since the end of March to its highest level in three and a half years. The U.S. trade deficit declined sharply in March, bringing the first-quarter deficit to a level well under the 1980 average.

Growth in M-1B, adjusted for the estimated effects of shifts into NOW accounts, accelerated sharply in April and growth in M-2 remained rapid. Since March, both short-term and long-term market interest rates have risen substantially. On May 4 the Board of Governors announced an increase in Federal Reserve discount rates from 13 to 14 percent and an increase in the surcharge from 3 to 4 percentage points on frequent borrowings of large institutions.

The Federal Open Market Committee seeks to foster monetary and financial conditions that will help to reduce inflation, promote economic growth, and contribute to a sustainable pattern of international transactions. At its meeting in early February, the Committee agreed that these objectives would be furthered by growth of M-1A, M-1B, M-2, and M-3 from the fourth quarter of 1980 to the fourth quarter of 1981 within ranges of 3 to 5½ percent, 3½ to 6 percent, 6 to 9 percent, and 6½ to 9½ percent respectively, abstracting from the impact of introduction of NOW accounts on a nationwide basis. The associated range for bank credit was 6 to 9 percent. These ranges will be reconsidered as conditions warrant.

In the short run the Committee seeks behavior of reserve aggregates consistent with a substantial deceleration of growth in M-1B from April to June to an annual rate of 3 percent or lower, after allowance for the impact of flows into NOW accounts, and with growth in M-2 at an annual rate of about 6 percent. The shortfall in growth of M-1B from the two-month rate specified above would be acceptable, in light of the rapid growth in April and the objective adopted by the Committee on March 31 for growth from March to June at an annual rate of 5½ percent or somewhat less. It is recognized that shifts into NOW accounts will continue to distort measured growth in M-1B to an unpredictable extent, and operational reserve paths will be developed in the light of evaluation of those distortions. The Chairman may call for Committee consultation if it appears to the Manager for Domestic Operations that pursuit of the monetary objectives and related reserve paths during the period before the next meeting is likely to be associated with a federal funds rate persistently outside a range of 16 to 22 percent.

Votes for this action: Messrs. Volcker, Solomon, Boehne, Boykin, Corrigan, Gramley, Partee, Rice, Schultz, Mrs. Teeters, Messrs. Wallich, and Winn. Votes against this action: None. (Mr. Winn voted as an alternate member.)

REFERENCE NOTES

The central source material for this book is drawn from thirty-four interviews with governors of the Federal Reserve Board—Chairman Paul A. Volcker, Vice Chairman Frederick H. Schultz, Henry C. Wallich, Lyle E. Gramley, Nancy H. Teeters, J. Charles Partee, Philip E. Coldwell, Emmett J. Rice, Vice Chairman Preston Martin and Martha R. Seger—and four presidents of Federal Reserve Banks—Anthony M. Solomon of New York, Lawrence K. Roos of St. Louis, Frank E. Morris of Boston and E. Gerald Corrigan of Minneapolis and New York. Other important interviews included, from the Carter Administration, Stuart E. Eizenstat, director of the Domestic Policy Staff; Charles L. Schultze, chairman of the Council of Economic Advisers; and Treasury Secretary G. William Miller; and from the Reagan Administration, David A. Stockman, director of the Office of Management and Budget; Lawrence A. Kudlow, assistant director of the OMB for economic analysis; William A. Niskanen and William Poole of the CEA; Treasury Secretary James A. Baker III; Deputy Treasury Secretary Richard G. Darman; William M. Isaac, Chairman of the Federal Deposit Insurance Corporation; and Treasury assistant secretaries, Paul Craig Roberts and Manuel H. Johnson. Scores of additional interviews were conducted with officials from finance and banking, Congress, the Federal Reserve System and ordinary private citizens from across the United States. Unless otherwise cited in the Notes, statements by individuals are all derived from these personal interviews.

The principal sources for the economic data in the book are the annual reports of the Board of Governors and the *Annual Statistical Digest* published by the Federal Reserve System, as well as the *Economic Report of the President*, prepared each year by the Council of Economic Advisers. Unless otherwise cited in the Notes, the data on monetary policy, financial markets and economic performance are all drawn from these volumes.

CHAPTER 1: The Choice of Wall Street

1. The President's speech, *New York Times*, July 16, 1979. *The New York Times/CBS News* poll was conducted a day after the speech. The political consultant quoted was Peter Hart.

2. The observations of Eugene Sussman and the others, as well as Jay Schmiedeskamp's analysis, are from "The Buying Binge," by William Greider, Washington *Post*, December 17, 1978. The Gallup poll, conducted January 19–22, 1979, found that 27 percent thought a recession was "very likely" in the next twelve months and 35 percent thought it was "fairly likely." The shortened time horizon that inflation caused in public attitudes has been described by Patrick Caddell, public-opinion adviser to President Carter, among others.

3. Market reactions and Cabinet resignations, *New York Times* and *Wall Street Journal*, July 17–20, 1979. The Federal Reserve's senior economists drew the same conclusion about political reactions driving down the dollar. In its confidential economic analysis submitted to the Fed's governors, the staff reported: ". . . the cancellation of a scheduled energy message by the President followed by news reports that the Administration did not plan to decontrol domestic oil prices, triggered further selling pressure on the dollar in early July. Downward pressure on the dollar intensified in mid-July when the announcement of Cabinet resignations heightened uncertainty over U.S. economic policies." "Current Economic and Financial Conditions," Federal Reserve Board Staff, August 8, 1979.

4. The samples of market talk are from *The Wall Street Journal*, May 20, 1983, and May 25, 1984, and the Washington *Post*, May 31, 1984. Perhaps the harshest examples of the "wise guy" tone of Wall Street insiders can be found in *Barron's*, the financial weekly; the most sophisticated and droll, in the books by the pseudonymous "Adam Smith."

5. The statistics on bank deposits are for 1979, from *The American Banker*'s annual listing, "The Hundred Largest Banks in the U.S.," February 29, 1980. The particular deposit totals change from year to year, but only rarely does that alter rankings at the very top. The other four New York banks above $10 billion were Chemical ($29 billion), Bankers Trust ($22 billion), Marine Midland ($12.5 billion) and Irving Trust ($12 billion). The other California banks: Security Pacific National of Los Angeles ($18.5 billion), Wells Fargo ($16 billion) and Crocker National ($12.5 billion) in San Francisco, and United California ($11.7 billion) in Los Angeles. The two Chicago banks were Continental Illinois ($24 billion) and First National ($21 billion). Pittsburgh's was the Mellon Bank ($10 billion). The Texas banks were Republic ($6 billion) and First National ($6 billion) in Dallas, First City National ($5 billion) and Texas Commerce ($4 billion) in Houston.

6. The details on Merrill Lynch and Salomon Brothers are from the firms' annual reports. Statistics on concentration in capital markets in 1979 are from Securities Data Company of New York. The other five brokerages in the top ten were Blyth Eastman Dillon; Lehman Brothers Kuhn Loeb; Kidder, Peabody; Dillon Read; and Prudential-Bache Securities.

7. The world rankings of bank size are from "The 500 Largest Banks in the World," *The American Banker*, February 29, 1980. The annual listings roughly describe how international financial power is changing. By 1983, Japan had eight of the top twenty banks in the world, compared to five in 1979.

8. The nine banks commonly referred to as money-center banks were, in 1979, Chase Manhattan, Bankers Trust, Manufacturers Hanover, Chemical, Citibank,

Morgan Guaranty, First National of Chicago, Bank of America and Security Pacific. Occasionally, the Federal Reserve and others used a broader definition that encompassed sixteen banks, including First National of Boston, Marine Midland, Irving Trust, Mellon, Continental Illinois, Crocker National and Wells Fargo. When Continental Illinois collapsed in 1984, it was replaced on the list by First Interstate of California.

9. The total of 405,830 finance professionals was counted in 1981, compared to 300,680 in 1976. Together, these people handled 72 percent of the dollar volume on the New York Stock Exchange. "Basis for Strategy: A New Census of the Corporate Finance Universe," Dow Jones & Company, 1982.

10. See Marcia Stigum, *The Money Market*, Dow Jones-Irwin, 1983, for the professional's guide to the money market's various financial instruments and how they react to Federal Reserve policy.

11. The approximate sizes of the three main financial markets were derived from the 1979 flow-of-funds accounts compiled by the Federal Reserve. *Annual Statistical Digest*, 1970–1979, Federal Reserve Board.

12. An excellent primer on the Federal Reserve's operations and its relationship to financial markets was published by the Federal Reserve Bank of New York, written by Paul Meek, a senior vice president at the bank, and entitled *U.S. Monetary Policy and Financial Markets*, 1982.

13. See William C. Melton, *Inside the Fed: Making Monetary Policy*, Dow Jones-Irwin, 1985, for the complexities of "Fed watching," as well as a thorough guide to the major technical issues of monetary policy in recent years.

14. Richard Moe provided a sampling of the confidential comments on Paul Volcker and a general description of the sources, but not their names.

15. Paine Webber's marketing strategy, interview, John Lampe, vice president, director of advertising and public relations, November 20, 1984. Bob Simon's comments on Sears, *Advertising Age*, February 13, 1984.

16. "Active Investors: A Survey Concerning Investments and Brokerage Firms," Dow Jones & Company, 1981. "*The Wall Street Journal* Subscriber Study," Dow Jones, 1982.

17. The data on financial assets held by families and the distribution of this wealth are from "Survey of Consumer Finances, 1983," prepared by Robert B. Avery, Gregory E. Elliehausen and Glenn B. Canner of the Federal Reserve Board's Division of Research and Statistics and Thomas A. Gustafson of the Department of Health and Human Services. It was published in two reports, *Federal Reserve Bulletin*, September and December, 1984. The total net financial worth of all households was derived from the Federal Reserve's flow-of-funds accounts for 1979, excluding life-insurance and pension-fund savings since those were not regarded as financial assets in the Federal Reserve study. *Annual Statistical Digest*, 1970–1979, Federal Reserve Board.

18. The approximate proportions of financial assets held directly by households and by various institutions were derived from the 1979 flow-of-funds accounts. The wealth held by tax-exempt foundations and university endowments was derived from "1985 Prospects for Financial Markets," Salomon Brothers, 1984.

19. The stock market and inflation. The index of consumer prices was at 107 in 1969 and reached 212 in 1979. *Economic Report of the President*, 1982.

20. Maxwell Newton discusses the negative real interest rates and the anger of investors in his book *The Fed: Inside the Federal Reserve, the Secret Power Center That Controls the American Economy*, Times Books, 1983.

21. Minarik's conclusions on inflation's impact are from "The Distributional Effects of Inflation and Their Implications," in *Stagflation: The Causes, Effects and Solutions*, Joint Economic Committee, U.S. Congress, 1980. See also Minarik's "The Size Distribution of Income During Inflation," *Review of Income and Wealth*, December 1979. Edward N. Wolff's research is from "The Distributional Effects of the 1969–75 Inflation on Holdings of Household Wealth in the United States," *Review of Income and Wealth*, June 1979. Other studies on inflation in Britain and Canada have found the same distributional effects.

22. Financial numbers and the anonymous Administration official's remark are from *The New York Times* and *The Wall Street Journal*, July 23 and 24, 1979.

23. In his own memoirs, Jimmy Carter makes no mention of the Volcker appointment. See *Keeping Faith: Memoirs of a President*, Bantam, 1982.

24. Lance's warning. Gerald Rafshoon, interview, October 24, 1984. In a separate interview, Bert Lance said he has no recollection of this conversation.

25. The financial markets' reactions to the Volcker appointment are from *The New York Times* and *The Wall Street Journal*, July 26, 1979.

CHAPTER 2: In the Temple

1. "The Federal Reserve Building," Board of Governors, 1937.

2. The District of Columbia's attempt to collect property taxes from the Federal Reserve Board is from an unpublished study on Fed independence done for the Board of Governors, "The Status of the Federal Reserve System in the Federal Government," by Howard H. Hackley, 1972.

3. Wright Patman's critique of the Fed was summarized in *A Primer on Money*, which he wrote as chairman of the Subcommittee on Domestic Finance, published by the House Banking Committee in 1964. His remarks on bankers are from his speech "The ABC's of America's Money System," *Congressional Record*, August 3, 1964.

4. The citizen testimony against Volcker was by Kenneth White, president of the Virginia Taxpayers Association, Senate Banking Committee, July 30, 1979.

5. Wickliffe B. Vennard, Sr., *The Federal Reserve Hoax*, privately published, circa 1962. An excellent sampling of anti-Fed polemics is collected at the Federal Reserve Board library.

6. *Wall Street Journal* editorial, June 4, 1984.

7. The "monks" label was used by Representative Fernand St. Germain (D-R.I.), who became House Banking chairman in 1983.

8. Quoted in Wickliffe B. Vennard, Sr., *The Federal Reserve Hoax* (see above).

9. John Kenneth Galbraith, *Money: Whence It Came, Where It Went*, Houghton Mifflin, 1975.

10. The money aggregates and reserves for August 1979 are from the FRB's *Annual Statistical Digest*, 1970–1979, and are not seasonally adjusted. Federal Reserve analysts make seasonal adjustments in aggregate totals and monetary growth rates as more historical data become available, many months and sometimes years later. In general, I have used the unadjusted statistics whenever possible because they were the data available to Federal Reserve officials at the time they made policy decisions.

11. Eurodollars. Jeffrey Nichols of Argus Research Corporation said the Euromarket "can be considered analytically as a 51st state outside the Federal Reserve System—and not subject to its reserve requirements—but still an integral part of the nation's financial system"; quoted in Michael Moffitt, *The World's*

Money: International Banking from Bretton Woods to the Brink of Insolvency, Simon and Schuster, 1983. The estimate of Eurodollar deposits held by Americans is from *Purposes & Functions*, Federal Reserve Board, 1983. Volcker's pithy remarks on the global dollar are from speeches, October 24, 1978, and October 9, 1979.

12. Bank failures are from the *Annual Report*, Federal Deposit Insurance Corporation, 1979. Business failures are from "Business Failure Record," Dun & Bradstreet Corporation, 1981.

13. The description of internal staff attitudes at the Federal Reserve, the comments on Miller and Burns, and the expectations for Paul Volcker were derived from a series of background interviews with staff members. Merritt Sherman, a retired economist, was particularly helpful in elaborating the history of the institution. Sherman joined the research department of the Federal Reserve Bank of San Francisco in 1926, twelve years after the Fed began operations, and worked in the System for half a century, eventually as secretary to the Board of Governors.

14. Volcker speech at Harvard commencement, June 6, 1985.

15. Statistics on Fed employees, "Budgetary Status of the Federal Reserve System," Congressional Budget Office, 1983.

CHAPTER 3: A Pact with the Devil

1. Volcker on inflation, House Budget Committee, September 5, 1979, and *New York Times*, August 8, 1979.

2. Staff forecast of recession, "Summary and Outlook," Federal Reserve Board Staff, September 12, 1979. The confidential staff reports prepared for meetings of the Federal Open Market Committee are kept confidential for five years, then made available only on request. The contents are quite conventional economic reporting and analysis, divided into three categories: the report known as the "green book" covers international financial conditions including especially dollar exchange rates, the "red book" consists of regional economic conditions reported by the twelve Reserve Banks, and the "blue book" covers proposed options for monetary policy. Given the routine content of these reports, there is no reasonable explanation why they are kept secret so long, other than to protect the Federal Reserve from critical scrutiny and embarrassment. If the outsiders could read these reports six months after they were prepared, the staff's errors and miscalculations would become much more obvious to the public.

3. Lyle E. Gramley, *Wall Street Journal*, August 27, 1979.

4. Market conditions and policy options are from the "blue book," formally entitled "Monetary Aggregates and Money Market Conditions," Federal Reserve Board Staff, September 14, 1979.

5. Minutes, Federal Open Market Committee and Board of Governors, September 18, 1979.

6. *Wall Street Journal*, September 20, 1979.

7. Jack Brod, interview, September 28, 1984.

8. Arthur Bowker, interview, September 24, 1984.

9. Jim Clark, Sandy Shields and Roger Kerndt, interviews, April 4, 1985.

10. National housing prices, Los Angeles *Times*, August 16, 1979.

11. Herbert Young, interview, September 27, 1984.

12. Irvine Ranch, *Business Week*, May 2, 1977.

13. David Parry, interview, October 22, 1984.

14. Bank lending and corporate debt, *Annual Statistical Digest*, 1970–1979, Federal Reserve Board.

15. Samuelson's comment is from "The Radical Economics of Milton Friedman," by John Davenport, *Fortune*, June 1, 1967. *Business Week* called Friedman a "genuine radical" and *The New York Times* described him as an "intellectual radical."

16. Milton Friedman and Anna Jacobson Schwartz, *A Monetary History of the United States, 1867–1960*, Princeton University Press, 1963.

17. Unemployment and inflation in the 1960s, *Economic Report of the President*, 1982.

18. Data on the 1974–1975 recession, *Encyclopedia of Economics*, McGraw-Hill, 1982.

19. A complete set of the semiannual reports of the Shadow Open Market Committee was provided by Professor Karl Brunner of the University of Rochester.

20. The Humphrey-Hawkins legislation of 1978 put into law instructions to the Federal Reserve that had originally been adopted by congressional resolution in 1975.

21. Federal debt as a percentage of GNP, *Statistical Abstract of the United States*, Bureau of the Census, 1983.

22. Volcker on "the long run has caught up with us," speech to the American Bankers Association, October 9, 1979.

23. My brief description of how the management strategies of commercial banks evolved into a more aggressive competition is a capsule summary of a rich and complex story. The development is traced in fascinating detail in two books by Martin Mayer, *The Bankers*, Random House, 1974, and *The Money Bazaars*, E. P. Dutton, 1984. The international implications are lucidly explained by Michael Moffitt, *The World's Money*, Simon and Schuster, 1983.

24. Federal Advisory Council minutes were provided at my request by the Federal Reserve Board, covering the years 1979–1984. To my knowledge, this is only the second time these reports have been made public by the Federal Reserve. In my research, I found only one other instance where the contents of FAC meetings were revealed. John T. Woolley, a political scientist at Washington University, obtained the FAC minutes for 1968–1972, described in *Monetary Politics: The Federal Reserve and the Politics of Monetary Policy*, Cambridge University Press, 1984.

25. Nixon's regrets. Cited in Gregory Fossedal, "The Unaccountable Mystique of Paul Volcker," *American Spectator*, December 1984.

CHAPTER 4: Behavior Modification

1. Albert M. Wojnilower, "The Central Role of Credit Crunches in Recent Financial History," Brookings Economic Papers, 2:1980, Brookings Institution.

2. Market reactions are from *The Wall Street Journal*, October 9 and 10, 1979, and "Report of Open Market Desk Operations, September 18 to November 14, 1979," Federal Reserve Board.

3. Details on how dealers profit from their transactions with the Fed's Open Market Desk are from an interview with Irving Auerbach of Aubrey G. Lanston & Company, December 8, 1983. During the interview, the news arrived that the Fed had executed a $1 billion injection of reserves; Auerbach had predicted $900 million. "I was only $100 million off and in our business that's nothing," he said.

The complaint that the Federal Reserve needlessly "churns" its open-market account has been raised by a number of monetarist economists, most persuasively by William Poole of Brown University.

4. William C. Melton's recollections are from his book *Inside the Fed: Making Monetary Policy*, Dow Jones-Irwin, 1985, which provides, among other things, a splendid description of the uncertainties that Fed watchers face daily in the Fed Funds market.

5. Volcker's comments are from his speech to the American Bankers Association, October 9, 1979, and the *MacNeil/Lehrer Report*, October 10, 1979.

6. Allan Meltzer's reaction is from "Can Volcker Stand Up to Inflation?," by Nicholas von Hoffman, *New York Times Magazine*, December 2, 1979. Other market reactions are from *The Wall Street Journal*, November 15 and December 18, 1979.

7. Interviews and other sources for reactions to October 6 decision are: William Kline, October 2, 1984; James Woulfe, October 3, 1984; Richard LeCates, November 30, 1984; Marvin Berger, May 6, 1985; Jimmy Jackson, October 9, 1984; Vivan Jennings, June 22, 1985; Neal Conover, April 3, 1985; Chemical Bank credit limits, *Wall Street Journal*, December 18, 1979; Portland Teachers Credit Union and Virginia State Employees Credit Union, Joint Economic Committee, November 5, 1979. Illinois usury limit, Chicago Federal Reserve Bank report, November 14, 1979; Suffolk County Federal Savings & Loan, background interview, October 10, 1984; Lina Gray, Department of Labor Federal Credit Union, interview, October 3, 1984; condition of thrifts, John Tuccillo, research director, National Council of Savings Institutions, interview, October 4, 1984; Merrill Lynch Ready Assets, William Hewitt, vice president, interview, October 19, 1984, and Federal Reserve Board flow of funds for 1979–1980; and "Report on Economic Conditions," Federal Open Market Committee, November 14, 1979.

8. The "demand side" influence of monetary policy, *Annual Report, 1981*, Federal Reserve Board.

9. Girard Bank and Bank of America comments, *Wall Street Journal*, October 19, 1979.

10. Bank loan commitments, Albert M. Wojnilower, "The Central Role of Credit Crunches in Recent Financial History," Brookings Institution.

11. The favoritism in bank lending during periods of scarce credit and the new controls that would restore equity were described by Governor Andrew F. Brimmer in "Multi-National Banks and the Management of Monetary Policy in the United States," American Economics Association, December 28, 1972. Similar reforms were proposed unsuccessfully in the early 1980s by Representative Henry Reuss, among others.

12. Morgan Guaranty's estimate of Eurodollar market is from Michael Moffitt, *The World's Money*, Simon and Schuster, 1983.

13. Wallich on Eurodollar leakage, speech, October 11, 1979.

14. *World Financial Markets*, Morgan Guaranty Trust Company, October 1979.

15. *Wall Street Journal* on banks' speculative lending, December 18, 1979.

16. The true dimensions of bank lending to the Hunts' silver speculation were not known until long after the collapse, assembled in investigative hearings by the House Subcommittee on Government Operations and reports submitted to the committee by the Federal Reserve and the Securities and Exchange Commission. "Silver Prices and the Adequacy of Federal Action in the Marketplace, 1979–80," March 31 to May 22, 1980.

17. Federal Advisory Council minutes, November 1, 1979.

18. Volcker's lament was before the Senate Banking Committee, February 19, 1980.

19. Senators Byrd and Proxmire, *Congressional Record*, October 19, 24 and 25, 1979.

20. Congressional complaints about the Fed's money error, House Banking Committee, October 29, 1979.

Throughout the weeks after October 6, Paul Volcker generally avoided making any public predictions of recession. He acknowledged that "a period of adjustment" might be required and agreed with questioners that the economy could contract. Despite this caution, the chairman still found himself in controversy over remarks he made before the Joint Economic Committee on October 17, 1979, where he supposedly predicted a "lower standard of living" for Americans.

What Volcker actually said was a simple statement of self-evident economics, an observation that no economist would dispute:

> I would point out that productivity growth in this country is actually negative in a recent period, and we have had higher oil prices. And, of course, we import 50 percent of our oil, so that the higher revenues going abroad do not go to American citizens. Under those conditions, the standard of living of the average American has to decline. I don't think we can escape that when we're producing less with the same amount of effort, according to the statistics, and we're paying high prices abroad.

Some press accounts suggested that Volcker was proposing a lower standard of living, and many politicians, including the President, were compelled to state publicly that they disagreed with the Federal Reserve chairman. Volcker himself spent much time clarifying his remarks. In fact, Volcker had said precisely the same thing about productivity and living standards two days earlier before the Senate Banking Committee, but none of the reporters at that hearing found his comments newsworthy.

21. Carter press conference on October 9, the San Diego speech on October 11 and the television interview, October 25, are from *Presidential Documents*, 1979.

22. Federal Advisory Council, November 1, 1979.

CHAPTER 5: The Liberal Apology

1. Details on the deregulation legislation in the concluding congressional debates are from the *Congressional Record*, March 26 and 27, 1980, and the conference report dated March 21. House and Senate passed earlier, different bills in 1979 which were combined in conference to form the final measure.

2. Volcker's warnings on the membership problem were taken from an April 2, 1979, speech and testimony before the Senate Banking Committee, February 4, 1980.

3. Kenneth A. Guenther, interviews, September 14, 1983; October 27, 1983; and July 9, 1985.

4. Representative Henry Reuss, interview, August 26, 1983.

5. Daniel Brill, interview, June 29, 1984.

6. The tax implications of the new mandatory reserves were derived from

"Federal Reserve Staff Memorandum on Five-Year Cost Projections for Monetary Improvement Legislation," *Congressional Record*, March 27, 1980.

7. Data on the financial industry's donations to 1980 congressional campaigns were compiled by Common Cause, based on filings at the Federal Election Commission. The banking interests of senators and representatives were revealed in their disclosure statements for 1980, as reported by *Congressional Quarterly*, September 5, 1981.

8. Proxmire remark on the risks of failure, "Big Bank Battle," by Richard A. Rossi, *Dun's Review*, March 1980.

9. Kenneth McLean, interview, July 9, 1985.

10. Reuss remark on the risks of failure, "Big Bank Battle," by Richard A. Rossi (see above).

11. Albert Wojnilower's observation on "freeing" the thrifts is from his "The Central Role of Credit Crunches in Recent Financial History," Brookings Institution.

12. Proxmire's argument is from debate when the Senate first passed the deregulation bill, *Congressional Record*, October 31, 1979. The Senate Banking Committee's report was issued October 15, 1979.

13. Senator Morgan's critique was based on an analysis of winners and losers in deregulation by Henry B. Schecter, economist and urban affairs director of the AFL-CIO, found in the *Congressional Record*, October 31, 1979. Data were from the 1977 Survey of Consumer Credit, Survey Research Center, University of Michigan.

14. Inflation does inflict unconscionable losses on people of modest means, particularly among the retired, who depend on savings to maintain their living standards. A direct solution to this injustice would be provided if the government issued inflation-indexed savings notes or bonds in modest denominations. The "small savers" could be held harmless against inflation. They would receive a much lower interest return but it would be real interest. The government would guarantee to make up any losses due to inflation. Such notes or bonds might be available up to a personal limit of $100,000 or $200,000 so that any citizen could store a generous portion of wealth in absolute safety.

15. The median balance for family checking accounts was $500, thus half of the families had less, as reported in "Survey of Consumers Finance, 1983," *Federal Reserve Bulletin*, December 1984.

16. Wojnilower described how deregulation produced higher interests in a conference speech at the Federal Reserve Bank of St. Louis, October 30, 1981.

17. Edsall's book describes a variety of electoral pressures developing in the 1970s, including the rising volume of campaign contributions from business interests, that drove the Democratic Party toward a more conservative agenda. Thomas B. Edsall, *The New Politics of Inequality*, W. W. Norton, 1984. The declining burden of corporate taxation is from "Inequity & Decline," by Robert S. McIntyre and Dean C. Tipps, Center on Budget and Policy Priorities, 1983.

18. Usury. Jacques Le Goff, "The Usurer and Purgatory," in *The Dawn of Modern Banking*, Yale University Press, 1979.

19. The French usurer of 1540 is from Emmanuel Le Roy Ladurie, *The Peasants of Languedoc*, University of Illinois Press, 1974.

20. John Maynard Keynes's vision, from "Economic Possibilities for Our Grandchildren," *Essays in Persuasion*, Harcourt Brace, 1932, and *The General Theory of Employment, Interest and Money*, Harcourt Brace & World, 1965.

21. Details on Islamic banking were taken from Traute Wohlers-Scharf, *Arab*

and Islamic Banks, Organization for Economic Cooperation and Development, 1983; Roger Cooper, "A Calculator in One Hand and the Koran in the Other," *Euromoney*, November 1981; and Abraham L. Udovitch, "Bankers without Banks: Commerce, Banking and Society in the Islamic World of the Middle Ages," in *The Dawn of Modern Banking*, Yale University Press, 1979.

22. Examples of post-1980 legal usury are from the Washington *Post*, July 31, 1984, and *The Wall Street Journal*, April 8, 1985.

23. Albert Wojnilower's argument on the benefits of interest-rate controls, outlined in his papers previously cited in this chapter, is actually stronger than my description in the text. Wojnilower contends that higher interest rates have little restraining effect and that monetary policy has always relied on supply cutoffs—"credit crunches"—in order to force a slowdown in lending and economic activity. Advocates of deregulation are apt to point out that Wojnilower is not a disinterested witness, since his firm, First Boston, and other investment banking houses benefited competitively from interest-rate regulation. Raising capital for long-term projects, investment bankers naturally attracted investors more easily if the competing opportunities at banks and other institutions were limited on what returns they could offer.

No one in finance is, of course, a neutral observer, but Wojnilower's case speaks for broader public interests. Capital formation, raising funds for new productive capacity, ought to enjoy some preference if long-term economic growth is the goal. Moreover, in Wojnilower's argument, the higher interest rates are themselves a principal source of inflation and instability (a point that faintly echoes the Islamic economists' complaint against the Western banking system).

24. Volcker's comments, House Banking Committee, February 15, 1980.

CHAPTER 6: The Roller Coaster

1. Representative Annunzio's barb, House Banking Committee, July 23, 1980.

2. Details on credit controls, Federal Reserve Board press release, and President Carter's statement, *Presidential Documents*, March 14, 1980.

3. Fred Weimer, interview, December 13, 1984; Duncan Muir, interview, January 2, 1985; Dick Rossi, public relations manager of VISA, December 10, 1984. The added charges for credit imposed by retailers were documented in an evaluation of credit controls by the House Banking Committee, December 4, 1980.

4. Television's impact. The CBS, NBC and ABC evening news coverage for several days following the announcement of credit controls was reviewed from the broadcast archives at Vanderbilt University. Both the tone and content of all three networks were responsible and accurate, devoid of the exaggeration that some viewers attributed to them.

5. Recollections of receiving bricks and two-by-fours in the mail from distraught home builders are frequently offered by top-level Federal Reserve officials. Many still keep the objects on their office desks as souvenirs of battle.

6. Volcker denies paternity for recession, *MacNeil/Lehrer Report*, April 21, 1980.

7. My brief description of the silver debacle depends largely on the compelling narrative by Stephen Fay, *Beyond Greed*, Viking Press, 1982, as well as the subsequent congressional reports cited in Chapter 4.

8. Both Philip Coldwell and a staff member of the Senate Banking Committee described to me how Congress lobbied the Federal Reserve to get assistance for the banks and the Hunts.

9. When the banks arranged the $1.1 billion loan to the Hunts, Volcker insisted on two conditions. First, the Hunts must cease the silver speculation. Second, they must dispose of their vast silver holdings in an orderly manner. The second condition, as it turned out, appeared to be another commandment from the Federal Reserve that the banks would ignore, without consequence.

The Wall Street Journal, October 18, 1984, reported that the Hunts were still holding nearly 60 million ounces of silver. One year later, the *Journal* reported on October 3, 1985, that the Hunts had finally disposed of their hoard, more than five years after the original commitment to do so. The *Journal* said the sell-off was motivated by the Hunts' financial distress, their need to raise large sums of cash to pay off bank loans to their oil enterprises.

10. The 1980 targets for M-1 and other aggregates were announced in *Monetary Policy Report to Congress*, February 19, 1980, in *Annual Report*, Federal Reserve Board, 1980.

For clarity's sake, the statistics used are for the shift-adjusted aggregate, known as M1-B. If the traditional aggregate, now called M1-A, were cited, the money changes up and down would look even more extreme. The distinctions between the two are explained later in the narrative when they become more important in the decision making of 1981.

I am particularly indebted to Philip Braverman, chief economist at Briggs Schaedle in New York, and Daniel Brill, retired research director at the Federal Reserve Board, for explaining the subtle mechanics of how the Fed controls money.

11. John Maynard Keynes, *A Treatise on Money*, Macmillan, 1930.

12. Henry Wallich's analysis is from his speech, "The Limits of Monetary Control," April 3, 1980.

13. Housing starts, *Wall Street Journal*, July 18, 1980.

14. John Paulus, interviews, May 13 and July 3, 1985.

15. Volcker on money supply bouncing back, "A Talk with Paul Volcker," by Andrew Tobias, *New York Times Magazine*, September 19, 1982.

16. Shadow Open Market Committee papers, September 21–22, 1980.

17. Political scientist Edward R. Tufte studied the "electoral-economic cycle" of monetary policy and concluded: "What is probably most important is that the 1972 election was nothing special. Historically, the supply of money increased more rapidly in the two years before presidential elections than in the two years following . . . It appears that anti-inflationary zeal flourishes in the politically slack period after presidential elections, rarely before." The events of 1980 were clearly an exception to Tufte's conclusion. See Edward R. Tufte, *Political Control of the Economy*, Princeton University Press, 1978.

See also David Meiselman, "The Political Monetary Cycle," *Wall Street Journal*, January 10, 1984, for a concise example of the monetarist analysis. Both economics and political science have produced extensive studies attempting to measure the link between the electoral calendar and government economic policies. The problem with most of them is that the results usually imply more than they prove. There is a relationship, no doubt, but it does not have much meaning unless one examines the actual transactions of the policy makers. The statistical evidence is often misleading because it implies that the actual economic results were always what the policy makers intended.

18. Bert Lance, interview, November 19, 1984.

19. Miller's complaint, *Wall Street Journal*, September 12, 1980. Carter's criticism, *Presidential Documents*, October 2, and Carter-Reagan debate, October 28, 1980.

20. Year-after criticisms, *Wall Street Journal*, October 3, 1980.

21. Volcker on 1980s "holding action," speech, November 20, 1980.

CHAPTER 7: The God Almighty Dollar

1. Barton Lidice Benes, interview, November 28, 1984. The Benes exhibit, entitled "Master of Disguise," was at the Federal Reserve Board in November and December, 1984, and later at the Dallas and Cleveland Federal Reserve Banks.

2. Details on the history of money have been drawn from a variety of sources, including John Kenneth Galbraith's *Money: Whence It Came, Where It Went*, Houghton Mifflin, 1975; Wright Patman's *A Primer on Money*, House Banking Committee, 1964; various Federal Reserve System pamphlets; and the works cited subsequently in this chapter.

3. John Maynard Keynes, *A Treatise on Money*, Macmillan, 1930.

4. Sigmund Freud's letters to Wilhelm Fliess in *The Origins of Psychoanalysis*, Basic Books, 1954; "Character and Anal Eroticism," in *Freud Collected Papers*, Volume 2, Leonard and Virginia Woolf and the Institute of Psycho-analysis, 1925; and "Transformation of Instincts," in *Basic Works of Sigmund Freud*, Franklin Library, 1978.

5. Michael T. Taussig's study, *The Devil and Commodity Fetishism in South America*, University of North Carolina Press, 1980, describes the similarities between contemporary peasant myths and the medieval Christian idea of usury as the devil's work. Taussig writes, for instance:

> Whereas the imagery of God or the fertility spirits of nature dominates the ethos of labor in the peasant mode of production, the devil and evil flavor the metaphysics of the capitalist mode of production. . . . Among the displaced Afro-American peasants who are employed as wage workers by the rapidly expanding sugarcane plantations at the southern end of the tropical Cauca Valley in Colombia are some who are supposed to enter into secret contracts with the devil in order to increase their production and hence their wage. . . . Somewhat similarly, displaced Indian peasants who work as wage-earning tin miners in the Bolivian highlands have created work-group rituals to the devil, whom they regard as the true owner of the mine and the mineral. They do this, it is said, to maintain production, to find rich ore-bearing veins and to reduce accidents. Although he is believed to sustain production, the devil is also seen as gluttonous spirit bent on destruction and death.

6. *The Origins of Psychoanalysis* (see above).

7. Georg Simmel, *The Philosophy of Money*, Routledge & Kegan Paul, 1978, and *The Sociology of Georg Simmel*, The Free Press, 1950.

8. Thorstein Veblen, *The Theory of the Leisure Class*, Penguin Books, 1981.

9. Georg Simmel, *The Philosophy of Money* (see above).

10. Norman O. Brown, "Filthy Lucre," in *Life Against Death: The Psychoanalytical Meaning of History*, Wesleyan University Press, 1959.

11. John Maynard Keynes, "Economic Possibilities for Our Grandchildren," in *Essays in Persuasion*, Harcourt Brace, 1932.

CHAPTER 8: Democratic Money

1. Lawrence Goodwyn's powerful account of the Populist experience was an important corrective, rescuing the agrarian reformers from the disparagement by

other modern historians who concentrated on their raw and ugly qualities, the nativist resentments and paranoia, and ignored their intellectual contributions. Goodwyn's full scholarly account was published as *Democratic Promise: The Populist Moment in America*, Oxford University Press, 1976. A condensed version is available as *The Populist Moment: A Short History of the Agrarian Revolt in America*, Oxford University Press, 1978.

2. Details on post–Civil War commodity prices are from Goodwyn (above); Milton Friedman and Anna Jacobson Schwartz, *A Monetary History of the United States, 1867–1960*, Princeton University Press, 1963; and Robert P. Sharkey, *Money, Class and Party: An Economic Study of Civil War and Reconstruction*, Johns Hopkins Press, 1959. Sharkey provides an excellent account of the political struggle surrounding restoration of the gold standard.

3. The discussion of U.S. inflation and deflation under the gold standard is based on the price indexes published in *Historical Statistics of the United States, Colonial Times to 1970*, Census Bureau, 1976.

4. Fernand Braudel, *The Structures of Everyday Life: The Limits of the Possible*, the first of his three-volume history of civilization and capitalism, Harper and Row, 1981.

5. The panic of 1893, Milton Friedman and Anna Jacobson Schwartz, *A Monetary History of the United States, 1867–1960* (see above).

6. The account of Jacksonian values and the destruction of the second Bank of the United States relies on the brilliant essay by Marvin Meyers, *The Jacksonian Persuasion: Politics and Belief*, Stanford University Press, 1957. Bray Hammond's phrase—"reckless, booming anarchy"—appeared in "Jackson, Biddle and the Bank of the United States," *Journal of Economic History*, May 1947.

7. William P. Yohe's analysis, "An Economic Appraisal of the Sub-Treasury Plan," was published as an appendix to Goodwyn's *Democratic Promise and The Populist Moment* (see above). Keynes's salute to the Populists is quoted in Yohe's essay.

8. The most prominent advocate of restoring the gold standard was Alan Greenspan, the financial consultant and former presidential advisor who was nominated in June 1987 as Paul Volcker's successor as Federal Reserve chairman. In a September 1, 1981, essay in *The Wall Street Journal*, "Can the U.S. Return to a Gold Standard?" Greenspan answered in the affirmative but with heavy qualifications. The transition back to gold-based currency would be most difficult but beneficial, Greenspan wrote, because it would compel Congress and the President to limit federal spending. He described himself as "attracted to the prospect of gold convertibility."

"Certainly a gold-based monetary system will not necessarily prevent fiscal imprudence, as twentieth century history clearly demonstrates," Greenspan wrote. "Nonetheless, once achieved, the discipline of the gold standard would surely reinforce anti-inflation policies, and make it far more difficult to resume financial profligacy." Gold, he suggested, might be phased in gradually, by issuing limited amounts of currency backed by a gold guarantee until the full standard was possible.

Greenspan, however, was not counted as a true believer by the *Journal*'s regular contributors, who were zealous advocates of gold. They included Jude Wanniski, president of Polyconomics, a consulting firm, and his associate Alan Reynolds, Rep. Jack Kemp of New York, Lewis E. Lehrman, former president of the Rite Aid Corporation, and the "supply-side" economist Arthur Laffer.

One measure of the intellectual confusion among gold advocates, however, was that they did not agree among themselves on what the correct price of gold ought to be, and their answers ranged widely from $250 to $500 an ounce. As history demonstrated, setting the correct price for gold was always the impossible political question. A price set too low would be disastrously deflationary, ruining producers while it enriched the owners of capital. A price that was too high would be stimulative and inflationary at first, then act as an arbitrary price brake on the economy. For a thorough and persuasive description of all the unresolved problems facing a gold standard, see Anna J. Schwartz, "Alternative Monetary Regime: The Gold Standard," Report of the Commission on the Role of Gold in the Domestic and International Monetary Systems, March 1982.

9. Kelso's analysis of capitalism and ownership can be found in *The Capitalist Manifesto*, with Mortimer J. Adler, Random House, 1958; *Two-Factor Theory: The Economics of Reality*, with Patricia Hetter, Vintage, 1968; and "The Right to Be Productive," with Patricia Hetter, *The Financial Planner*, August–September 1982. Kelso interview, October 9, 1985.

Paul Volcker is among those who have endorsed the idea of employee stock ownership as a way to ameliorate inflationary wage pressures, though Volcker, of course, opposes Kelso's more radical concept for financing broadened ownership through the money-creation system. Volcker told a Texas business audience on November 13, 1983:

I wonder why there has been so much apparent resistance, by labor and management, to planned arrangements for sharing in prosperity and adversity, in the latter instance in ways other than layoffs alone. I am thinking, of course, of profit-sharing plans or other ways of rewarding workers when things are good, without building in a floor on costs that may turn out to be unbearable when things are not. I wonder why more companies have not been successful, or have not made the effort to encourage employee stock ownership.

CHAPTER 9: The Great Compromise

1. *The Wall Street Journal* on J. P. Morgan, quoted in *Literary Digest*, February 17, 1912.

2. Morgan Guaranty's reputation as the "Fed bank" is from background interviews with Fed officials and Volcker's personal friends. "The Morgan bank plays by the rules," an officer of the New York Fed explained. "They really come in and tell us what they're going to do. Citibank would much rather stake out a position, invest in it and challenge us to adjust to it and fight us all the way."

The Federal Reserve, likewise, relied on officers of Morgan Guaranty as a source of financial intelligence. The small circle of people considered social intimates of Paul Volcker included Lewis T. Preston, CEO of the Morgan bank. "We probably get more regular intelligence on what's going on in credit markets from Morgan than from anyone else," the New York Fed officer said.

Morgan Stanley, the investment banking firm that also descended from the house of Morgan, was also close to the Fed, partly because of a number of its senior managers were former executives of the New York Federal Reserve.

3. Roger T. Johnson, *Historical Beginnings . . . The Federal Reserve*, Federal Reserve Bank of Boston, 1977.

4. Gabriel Kolko's analysis of the "conservative triumph" represented in the Federal Reserve Act and other reforms from the Progressive era is supported by his extraordinary historical research—exhaustive evidence unearthed from the private communications of business and banking leaders as well as the legislative draftsmen that confirms the actual political intentions beneath the rhetoric of

reform as well as the economic consequences. Kolko's conclusions challenge both the inherited mythology advanced by most historians and political scientists and the misconceptions that prevailed among reformers at the time, but his analysis makes plausible the subsequent behavior and posture of the Federal Reserve in a way that the competing interpretations do not. If creation of the Fed was intended to break the "money trust," then why did the new institution collaborate so closely with it? Kolko, *The Triumph of Conservatism: A Reinterpretation of American History, 1900–1916*, Macmillan, 1963.

5. The Treasury study on dispersion of banking power is cited by Alexander D. Noyes, "The Money Trust," *Atlantic Monthly*, May 1913.

6. The account of the legislative debates draws upon the *Congressional Record* of 1913 and these accounts: Gabriel Kolko, *The Triumph of Conservatism* (see above); Milton Friedman and Anna Jacobson Schwartz, *A Monetary History of the United States, 1867–1960*, Princeton University Press, 1963; Noyes's "The Money Trust" (see above); Roger T. Johnson, *Historical Beginnings . . . The Federal Reserve* (see above); and Richard H. Timberlake, *The Origins of Central Banking in the United States*, Harvard University Press, 1978.

7. The original system operated differently in that the Federal Reserve Banks provided Discount loans in exchange for any eligible debt paper presented by commerical banks—which meant that the portfolios of the Federal Reserve Banks were composed largely of private loan paper, not Treasury notes and bonds. The modern Fed's holdings, in contrast, are largely government securities. An intriguing and largely unexamined question is the potential economic effect from whether the central bank trades business notes or government debt issues. The orthodox view is that it makes no difference, that the money-creation powers functioned the same, regardless. A senior vice president of the New York Federal Reserve Bank remarked: "As far as the money supply is concerned, we could buy and sell eggs and it would have the same effect." But his example suggests the subtle difference: if the Federal Reserve was "lender of last resort" to the egg market, that would likely encourage egg production and it would certainly help stabilize the market for eggs. Similarly, if the central bank held a substantial portion of its portfolio in private commercial debt paper, the financing for real enterprises in the productive economy, the central bankers would presumably have greater concern for whether their policies were threatening those enterprises with failure. The Fed's portfolio of U.S. debt paper, in other words, permits greater detachment from the real economic consequences.

8. Benjamin Strong's comment is from the biography by Lester V. Chandler, *Benjamin Strong, Central Banker*, The Brookings Institution, 1958.

9. Walter Lippmann, *Public Opinion*, Harcourt, Brace, 1922.

10. Richard Hofstadter, quoted in Roger T. Johnson's history of the Fed (see above), was the leading exponent of the liberal reform perspective, the orthodox interpretation that Gabriel Kolko challenged.

11. Walt Whitman, "Song of Myself," *The Oxford Book of American Verse*, Oxford University Press, 1950. The artist's imaginative interpretation of economics, suggested here but briefly, is another of the great unexplored realms—like the psychology of economics—that scholars have failed to approach, perhaps intimidated by the scientific presumptions of their colleagues, the economists. If artistic expressions speak authentically for the society's inner responses to reality, what people feel and think about their experience, then it seems odd that economic interpretation has mostly ignored the cultural messages from literature, music and film about the nature of American economic life.

12. Details on the Federal Reserve's first two decades are from Milton Fried-

man and Anna Jacobson Schwartz (see above); Lester V. Chandler's biography of Benjamin Strong (see above); and Jane D'Arista, "Federal Reserve Structure and the Development of Monetary Policy: 1915–1935," House Banking Committee, 1971.

13. Andrew Mellon's contribution to tax politics during the 1920s—like the Federal Reserve's role as economic regulator—was seemingly discredited by the Great Crash and, therefore, largely ignored by mainstream discussion of political economy for two generations. Both contributions never lost their relevance, however, and both Mellon's "trickle down" tax policy and the Fed's economic prowess regained political hegemony in the 1980s. An excellent condensed history of the political arguments surrounding the progressive income tax can be found in "From Redistributive to Hegemonic Logic: The Transformation of American Tax Politics, 1894–1963," by Ronald Frederick King, in *Politics & Society*, 1983.

14. 1920s: Robert S. McElvaine, *The Great Depression*, Times Books, 1984.

15. The farmer-Fed dialogue is from "The Federal Reserve Bank and the Farmer and the Stockman," Federal Reserve Bank of Minneapolis, April 1923.

16. Strong's comments on the Federal Reserve caught in the middle are quoted in John Maynard Keynes's *A Treatise on Money*, Macmillan, 1930.

17. Federal Reserve behavior during the great contraction is drawn mainly from Milton Friedman and Anna Jacobson Schwartz and from Jane D'Arista. Strong's prophetic warnings are from Lester V. Chandler's biography. All these works are cited above.

18. Like Kolko's research, Gerald Epstein and Thomas Ferguson's close study of the central bank's archives produced a strikingly different interpretation of the Federal Reserve's performance and actual intentions from 1929 to 1933. In addition to the evidence they unearthed in private letters and discussions, they conducted various economic tests of their thesis and found that the credit data produced by Fed policy supported the conclusion that Fed actions were guided by the earnings condition of commercial banks. Epstein and Ferguson, "Monetary Policy, Loan Liquidation, and Industrial Conflict: The Federal Reserve and the Open Market Operations of 1932," *Journal of Economic History*, December 1984.

CHAPTER 10: Leaning Against the Wind

1. Marriner Eccles's memoir is a neglected gem of American political history, a lucid, idiosyncratic and authoritative account of the New Deal: *Beckoning Frontiers: Public and Personal Recollections*, edited by Sidney Hyman, Alfred A. Knopf, 1951. I have also drawn on Eccles's *Economic Balance and a Balanced Budget*, Da Capo Press, 1973, and L. Dwight Israelson, "Marriner Eccles, Chairman of the Federal Reserve Board," *American Economic Review*, May 1985. The Eccles remarks throughout this chapter, unless otherwise cited, are from these sources.

2. The evolution of Keynesian ideas is from John Kenneth Galbraith's *Money: Whence It Came, Where It Went*, Houghton Mifflin, 1975.

3. A good description of how New Deal reforms influenced commercial and investment banking and their continued relationships can be found in David M. Kotz, *Bank Control of Large Corporations in the United States*, University of California Press, 1978.

4. The reform of the Federal Reserve in 1935 changed the titles of its officers. Originally, the Reserve Bank executives were called governors and only the

chairman of the board held the same title. After 1935, the Reserve Bank officers were called presidents and all board members became governors. To minimize confusion, I have avoided using the title of governor as it was applied in the years from 1913 to 1935.

5. John T. Woolley's research on FOMC voting patterns also found that governors appointed by Democrats tended to be slightly more liberal than governors appointed by Republicans. Woolley, *Monetary Politics*, Cambridge University Press, 1984.

6. The psychological and moral perspectives of Keynes, as well as interesting accounts of his background, are described in various essays in *The End of the Keynesian Era*, edited by Robert Skidelsky, Macmillan, 1977.

7. Eccles's comment on the Fed's obligations to the executive branch is from a speech by his nephew Spencer F. Eccles at the dedication of the Marriner S. Eccles Federal Reserve Board Building, July 28, 1983.

8. Paul Volcker's 1949 senior thesis at Princeton University, "The Problems of Federal Reserve Policy Since World War II."

9. Wright Patman's critique is from his *A Primer on Money*, House Banking Committee, 1964.

10. William McChesney Martin's reminiscence was in *The New York Times*, December 10, 1985.

11. Wright Patman's *A Primer on Money* (see above).

12. John T. Woolley, *Monetary Politics* (see above).

13. Arthur Okun was quoted by Paul Volcker in his New York University lecture "The Rediscovery of the Business Cycle," Free Press, 1978.

14. I am indebted to the British journalist Stephen Fay for sharing his 1979 manuscript on Paul Volcker and allowing me to quote from the material. Volcker's remarks on the 1965 economic policy and his commentary on the shift from fixed to floating exchange rates during the Nixon Administration are drawn from Fay's interviews.

15. Quoted in John Kenneth Galbraith, *Money: Whence It Came, Where It Went* (see above).

16. The gold-dollar imbalance is explained by Robert Triffin, "Correcting the World Monetary Scandal," *Challenge*, January–February 1986. OPEC's role in inflation, *Wall Street Journal*, January 30, 1986.

17. A chapter entitled "Hardball" in William Safire's White House memoir describes the pressure tactics used on Arthur Burns. *Before the Fall*, Doubleday, 1975.

18. Former Governor Andrew F. Brimmer, more than a decade after the 1972 election, delivered a meticulous defense of Arthur Burns's performance that year. Many details are drawn from Brimmer's account, "Politics and Monetary Policy: The Federal Reserve and the Nixon White House," Eastern Economic Association, March 1984. For a broader and less sympathetic interpretation of how politics influences the Fed, see Edward Tufte, *Political Control of the Economy*, Princeton University Press, 1978.

Brimmer and others have particularly attempted to refute a more contentious account of how Burns manipulated policy in 1972 by Sanford Rose, "The Agony of the Federal Reserve," *Fortune*, July 1974. Rose reported, on the basis of confidential sources, that at one point when Burns could not win agreement he returned to the FOMC meeting and announced meaningfully: "I have just talked to the White House." Rose wrote: " . . . the committee got the idea: the White House was determined to try to keep rates from rising." Burns,

Brimmer and other governors have vigorously denied that any such exchange occurred.

19. Burns's exchange with Senator Proxmire, Joint Economic Committee, February 7, 1975.

20. As assortment of internal staff memos to Burns, made available by a former associate, makes it clear that winning reappointment was a major preoccupation in 1977.

21. Volcker's lecture on the "long cycle" was entitled "The Rediscovery of the Business Cycle" (see above).

CHAPTER 11: A Car with Two Drivers

1. President Reagan's statements are from his Inaugural Address, January 20, 1981; address to Congress, February 18, 1981; and an interview with Walter Cronkite, March 3, 1981.

2. Volcker's speeches were before the University of Wisconsin–Milwaukee School of Business Administration, November 20, 1980, and the Tax Foundation dinner in New York City, December 3, 1980.

3. The most complete and informed press coverage of the Federal Reserve could be found, not surprisingly, in *The Wall Street Journal*. Its readers were not only more sophisticated about finance but intensely more interested in monetary policy. For some years, the high quality of the *Journal*'s news coverage was tarnished somewhat by an obvious monetarist bias, relying on the opinions of Milton Friedman and like-minded economists. The *Journal*'s editorial page, meanwhile, advocated the gold standard and criticized the Federal Reserve from that angle. Both perspectives, of course, represented a hard-money bias and were thus compatible with the interests of the *Journal*'s wealthy readership.

In general, press coverage of the central bank failed to scrutinize monetary policy with the same intensity it applied to the rest of government. If, however, Congress or the White House happened to attack the Federal Reserve, the press usually treated their complaints as an embarrassing irregularity, offensive to the way government was supposed to operate. Politicians were inhibited from criticizing monetary policy by the knowledge that they would almost certainly be criticized in the press for intruding on the Federal Reserve's supposed independence.

4. Volcker's remarks are from his speeches cited above. His comments to congressional committees included testimony before the House Banking Committee, February 26, 1981.

5. Bruno Pasquinelli, David Chatham, William Cahill and Lucille Sajec are quoted from their testimony before the House Banking Committee's "Grassroots Hearings on the Economy," September 9 to December 7, 1981.

6. Paul Craig Roberts, interviews, March 22 and June 15, 1984.

7. William Niskanen, interview, April 18, 1985.

8. Beryl Sprinkel's food-and-money comparison was before the House Banking Committee, February 1, 1982.

9. Sprinkel, Jordan and Weidenbaum criticisms of the Fed, *Wall Street Journal*, January 26, April 20 and August 4, 1981. Stockman's was in "Avoiding a GOP Economic Dunkirk," a pre-Inaugural memo he prepared for the President, December 1980.

10. Sprinkel memo, "Memorandum for the Cabinet Council on Economic Affairs, Subject: Domestic Monetary Policy," April 24, 1981.

11. The President's program is detailed in "America's New Beginning: A Program for Economic Recovery," *Presidential Documents*, February 18, 1981.

12. David Stockman, interviews, August 16 and September 22, 1985.

13. Donald Regan speech, Treasury release, March 23, 1981.

14. Stockman's prediction of historic bull market is from the author's *The Education of David Stockman and Other Americans*, E. P. Dutton, 1982.

15. Henry Wallich speech, February 13, 1981.

16. Henry Kaufman's predictions, Washington *Post*, March 6, 1981, and *Wall Street Journal*, May 11, 1981.

17. Donald Regan on bond traders, *Wall Street Journal*, June 1, 1981.

18. The wealth statistics are from the "Survey of Consumer Finances, 1983," *Federal Reserve Bulletin*, September and December 1984. "Financial Characteristics of High-Income Families," based on the same survey, was published separately in the *Federal Reserve Bulletin*, March 1986. The private ownership of government bonds was calculated from the 1981 *Annual Statistical Digest*, Federal Reserve Board.

19. The selected comments from bond-market participants, as well as details on corporate bond issues, were culled from *The Wall Street Journal*'s daily "Credit Markets" column during the month of April 1981.

20. Jack Kemp's complaint, Washington *Post*, May 7, 1981.

21. Sprinkel's analysis is from "Memorandum for the Cabinet Council on Economic Affairs, Subject: Briefing on the State of Financial Markets," undated.

22. Kudlow's analysis is in "Memorandum for the Cabinet Council on Economic Affairs, Subject: Financial Warnings," April 28, 1981.

23. Sprinkel's memo "Briefing on the State of Financial Markets" (see above).

24. Donald Regan's comment on "abolishing the Fed," Paul Craig Roberts, *The Supply-Side Revolution: An Insider's Account of Policymaking in Washington*, Harvard University Press, 1984.

25. The technical reforms that monetarists and the White House urged the Federal Reserve to adopt all dealt with operating refinements in how reserves were controlled in the banking system. The proposals included: contemporaneous reporting of bank reserves instead of the two-week lag that the Federal Reserve permitted, a penalty rate for Discount loans, and targeting operating decisions on a broader measure, the monetary base, instead of the nonborrowed reserves target that the Fed was using. The arguments over techniques involve highly complex questions and are best left to economists who are expert on the functions of money and banking. A full and evenhanded discussion of the operating options, the relative advantages and disadvantages of what the monetarists proposed, can be found in Michael G. Hadjimichalakis, *The Federal Reserve, Money, and Interest Rates: The Volcker Years and Beyond*, Praeger, 1984.

26. Sprinkel comments on the Fed's improvement, *Wall Street Journal*, May 5, 1981, and his Chicago speech, May 29, 1981.

27. Stockman on the Fed's making peace, interview, May 16, 1981.

28. Volcker's speech on gradualism, April 15, 1981.

29. To minimize confusion, the text continues to cite statistics as M-1 rather than M-1B, even though the FOMC was tracking the adjusted aggregate rather than the traditional money measure. The differences in their growth rates varied slightly month to month but followed the same trend line.

30. Peter Fousek, interview, June 26, 1984. Background interviews with numerous staff economists at Reserve Banks and the Federal Reserve Board raised the problem of a "monetarist trap." Many staff members familiar with the FOMC decisions were convinced that the policy makers were more stringent than they

otherwise would have been, both to defend the integrity of their operating method and also to offset the inflationary fears generated in financial markets by the Reagan tax cuts.

31. Michael G. Hadjimichalakis, *The Federal Reserve, Money, and Interest Rates* (see above).

32. One of the Federal Reserve's gravest offenses against democratic self-government is its most obvious trait, the secrecy. The Federal Reserve does not tell citizens the plain truth about what it is doing to the economy and, as a result, many plunge forward innocently into enterprises that the federal government has doomed. What is especially mindless is that frequently private enterprises will be encouraged, even subsidized, by other agencies of the government at the very time the Fed is imposing the adverse conditions.

From time to time, reformers have tried to reconcile this dilemma with marginal proposals—measures requiring the Federal Reserve to be more candid about itself, to report its decisions more promptly and submit its budgets to congressional scrutiny. None of these reforms would likely accomplish much, even if enacted. The Federal Reserve would simply have to devise new ways to avoid frank disclosure of its intentions. It must obscure in order to survive.

Given its anomalous position in the constellation of political power, it is inconceivable that the Federal Reserve could ever speak freely and plainly to the general public. It would be overwhelmed with political complaints, for instance, if it announced in advance that it intended to induce a recession, and probably not even its influential supporters in finance would be able to save it. Citizens would question the decision and the methods of liquidation. Eventually, they would ask why this momentous decision for the entire nation was delegated to an assembly of unelected technocrats, without even the requirement to consult Congress or the President.

The secrecy and evasion are integral to the Federal Reserve's power and it, therefore, fails the minimum prerequisite for representative democracy—that the government must deal honestly with the citizens whom it governs. To resolve the dilemma, the powers of the central bank would have to be relocated elsewhere in the government where decisions could be examined in democratic forums and the decision makers held accountable in democratic elections.

33. Lawrence Kudlow, interviews, October 24, 1983, and July 9, 1985.

34. Roberts's description of the June 5 meeting is from his book *The Supply-Side Revolution* (see above). President Reagan's speech to the nation was on July 27, 1981. The tax bill was signed into law August 13.

35. Manuel H. Johnson, interview, December 3, 1984.

36. Alan Blinder, interview, March 26, 1985.

37. Effective tax rates after 1981 were calculated by the Joint Committee on Taxation, Washington *Post*, November 20, 1984.

38. Volcker's evasive answers, Senate Banking Committee, July 22, 1981.

39. Paul A. Samuelson, "Evaluating Reaganomics," *Challenge*, November–December 1984.

40. Bank prime rate and inflation, David Jones of Aubrey G. Lanston & Company, cited in National Association of Home Builders newsletter, April 1981.

41. Real interest rates on long-term bonds are from Robert A. Johnson, "Anticipated Fiscal Contraction: The Economic Consequences of the Gramm-Rudman-Hollings Bill for the U.S. Economy," Federal Reserve Board, February 1986.

CHAPTER 12: That Old-Time Religion

1. Elizabeth Brock is quoted from her testimony before the House Banking Committee's "Grassroots Hearings on the Economy," September 9 to December 7, 1981 (hereinafter referred to as the "Grassroots Hearings").

2. The details on General Electric's Appliance Park are from Jim Allen, communications director, interview, July 15, 1985.

3. Eldon Kirsch is quoted from his testimony before the Grassroots Hearings.

4. Robert Williams is quoted from his testimony before the Grassroots Hearings.

5. Arthur Estrella and James McCafferty are quoted from their testimony before the Grassroots Hearings.

6. Durward DeChenne, interview, October 8, 1984.

7. Jim Clark, interview, April 4, 1985.

8. Manny Dembs is quoted from his testimony before the Senate Banking Committee, November 20, 1981.

9. Martin Bacal is quoted from his testimony before the Grassroots Hearings.

10. Data on bank profits are from "Profitability of Insured Commercial Banks in 1984," *Federal Reserve Bulletin*, November 1985; "Financial Developments of Bank Holding Companies in 1984," *Federal Reserve Bulletin*, December 1985; and E. Gerald Corrigan, "Are Banks Special?," in *Minneapolis Federal Reserve Bank Annual Report*, 1982. Gerald Epstein's comparisons are from his testimony before the House Banking Committee, July 19, 1983.

11. Federal Advisory Council minutes, September 11, 1981.

12. George Bush's remarks on the French are reported in "Minutes, Cabinet Council on Economic Affairs," July 7, 1981.

13. Dollar appreciation from July 1980 to September 1981 cited by Beryl Sprinkel, "Memorandum for the Cabinet Council on Economic Affairs, Subject: U.S. Exchange Market Intervention Policy," September 16, 1981.

14. Wanniski's letter to Reagan, November 18, 1981, and the President's reply, December 17, 1981.

15. Reagan on the "Carter depression," Lou Cannon, *Reagan*, G. P. Putman, 1982.

16. The President's speech to the nation, September 24, 1981.

17. Reagan's long-standing views on the need for economic pain as the cure for inflation are described by Rowland Evans and Robert Novak, *The Reagan Revolution*, E. P. Dutton, 1981.

18. Public attitudes on recession were reported by Kermit Lansner of the Harris organization, *Making Sense of the News*, Modern Media Institute, 1982.

19. Volcker on the need for tax increases, *Wall Street Journal*, November 12, 1981.

20. Donald Regan on economic recovery, *Wall Street Journal*, November 10, 1981.

21. Sprinkel's analysis is from "Memorandum for Cabinet Council on Economic Affairs, Subject: Financial Market Developments," November 12, 1981.

22. Baker and other Republican leaders' complaints, *New York Times*, September 10, 1981.

23. Howard Baker, interview, January 22, 1986.

24. Volcker speech to National Press Club, September 25, 1981.

25. The unusual stringency of monetary policy in the fall of 1981 is described by former Governor Andrew F. Brimmer in "Monetary Policy and Economic

Activity: Benefits and Costs of Monetarism," *American Economic Review*, May 1983.

26. Details on the capital ratio regulation, *National Journal*, December 17, 1983. The capital data for 1981 are from "Financial Developments of Bank Holding Companies in 1984," *Federal Reserve Bulletin*, December 1985.

27. Walter Wriston's remarks are from "Recycling Revisited," June 4, 1981, and "Going to Hell in a Best-Fit Curve," March 6, 1981; G. A. Costanzo's essay is "The Positive Effect of LDC Lending," May 1981. All published by Citibank. Subsequent remarks by Wriston and Costanzo in this chapter are from the same sources.

28. Henry Wallich's speech on LDC debt, June 2, 1981.

29. Federal Advisory Council minutes, November 6, 1981.

30. William McChesney Martin, quoted in *New York Times*, December 10, 1985.

31. Federal Advisory Council minutes, November 6, 1981.

32. President's press conference, January 19, 1982.

33. Donald Regan quoted in *Wall Street Journal*, January 29, 1982.

34. Sprinkel's warning was in "Memorandum for Cabinet Council on Economic Affairs, Subject: Financial Market Developments," December 18, 1981.

35. Kudlow's warning was in "Memorandum for Cabinet Council on Economic Affairs, Subject: Financial and Economic Update," January 18, 1982.

36. Frank Morris speech, Atlanta, March 17, 1982.

37. President's press conference, February 18, 1982.

38. John Paulus, interview, July 3, 1985.

CHAPTER 13: Slaughter of the Innocents

1. Kudlow's remark was in "Memorandum for Cabinet Council on Economic Affairs, Subject: Financial and Economic Update," January 18, 1982.

2. Thorstein Veblen's commentary in this chapter is from *Absentee Ownership and Business Enterprise in Recent Times: The Case of America*, B. W. Huebsch, 1923.

3. Details on plant closings were compiled by the Bureau of National Affairs, Washington, D.C., 1982.

4. Unemployment by industrial sector was reported by the AFL-CIO research department, 1982.

5. Bankruptcy data were reported in "State of Small Business, 1983," the Small Business Administration, and "1982–83 Business Failure Record," Dun & Bradstreet, 1984.

6. The Urban Institute's calculation of recession losses was described by John L. Palmer and Isabel V. Sawhill, editors, in *The Reagan Record*, Ballinger, 1984.

7. The growth of service jobs was reported by Governor Preston Martin, House Banking Committee, June 1, 1983.

8. John Zanetti, interview, July 3, 1985.

9. Joan Benigno, interview, July 13, 1985.

10. The home builders' "wanted" poster, Len Mills, interview, March 28, 1985.

11. Assailant at the Fed, Washington *Post*, December 8, 1981.

12. John T. Woolley, *Monetary Politics: The Federal Reserve and the Politics of Monetary Policy*, Cambridge University Press, 1984.

13. Most-important citizens were listed in *U.S. News & World Report*, May 10, 1982.

14. *People* magazine's article on Volcker, May 10, 1982.

15. Donald J. Mullineaux, "Monetary Rules and Contracts: Why Theory Loses to Practice," *Business Review*, Federal Reserve Bank of Philadelphia, March/April 1985.

16. *Newsweek*'s extensive profile, February 24, 1986. *People* magazine article (see above).

17. Volcker's speech to the home builders' convention, January 25, 1982.

18. Controlling inflation by other means would require politicians to confront a crucial point. The Federal Reserve gained hegemony and imposed its own solution of liquidation essentially because politicians had failed to address the great governing dilemma that destabilized Keynesian doctrine twenty years before—how to stimulate a robust economy without letting it get out of control. Democratic government knew how to do one but not the other. It was most adept at stimulating the economy but never found the will or the way to manage on the downside, to contain credit and expansion when the economy reached full capacity and inflation approached dangerous levels.

The independent existence of the Federal Reserve probably inhibits such reforms because adopting a different system would require politicians to challenge some of the most powerful interests as well as the free-market mythology. It is far easier to let the central bank deal with the nasty necessities in its own way.

A reformed system, governed by political managers, would begin with the proposition that pushing interest rates as high as 20 percent is unnecessarily destructive as well as grossly inequitable. The traditional argument against the political control of money is that elected politicians will refuse to do the hard part —to impose sufficient pain. Politicians, it is true, naturally hesitate to inflict injury on voters but, rather than a deficiency, this quality would be one of the major benefits of a democratized system. Once in charge, the President and Congress would have to find other ways to control things and they would discover there are many approaches less brutal than the general liquidation.

A democratized system, for instance, could for the first time coordinate all of the government's many levers for influencing private economic behavior—moving them in the same direction to restrain credit and economic expansion. A series of more or less automatic stabilizers might be put in place, to be invoked by the President with congressional approval when inflationary conditions became dangerous. The tax code, for instance, could serve a discreet credit-control system, withdrawing part or all of the federal tax subsidy for interest costs as the economy reached full capacity or runaway inflation. Among other things, this would restrain the largest borrowers first and most effectively—not the weakest. Similar levers could decelerate or shut down the government's own credit-subsidy programs in times of stress or impose temporary tax penalties on wage and price increases. If Congress and the President were in earnest, they could design similar restraints on themselves—a standing provision to curb budget deficits, either through automatic tax increases or spending cuts, that could be employed if inflation got out of hand.

If inflation were controlled in this manner, politicians would discover that monetary policy also had tools for restraint that the Federal Reserve generally did not use. The controls on credit supply that were once so effective with interest-rate ceilings could be restored but made more equitable. That would require rules for lending institutions on how scarce credit was to be allocated so that certain sectors like housing and autos or consumers did not absorb the punishment alone. The rules could be enforced through a system of differential reserve requirements on a bank's loan portfolio, its assets, in addition to the reserve requirements on deposits. The priorities of bank lending could be guided further

through penalty rates at the Discount window—aimed at banks that fueled inflation by making loans for speculation.

The essence of all these ideas is, of course, to restrain more broadly across the
society and thus reduce the special damage that is now directed at a hapless
minority. Until politicians are willing to invent a more sophisticated system to
manage on the downside, the government will no doubt continue to rely on the
crude methods of the Federal Reserve.

19. The discussion of feminine-masculine moral perspectives relies upon Carol
Gilligan, *In a Different Voice: Psychological Theory and Women's Development*,
Harvard University Press, 1982.

20. The examples of congressional "Fed bashing" were drawn from several
exchanges, Senate Budget Committee, March 2, 1982; Joint Economic Committee, June 2, 1982; and Senate floor debate, December 18, 1982.

21. Edward Yardeni testified before the Senate Budget Committee, March 2,
1982. Robert Solow was quoted in *The New York Times*, April 1, 1982.

22. Senate floor debate, *Congressional Record*, December 18, 1982.

23. Dan Brill, interview, June 29, 1984.

24. Howard Baker, interview, January 22, 1986.

25. Liquidity strains were detailed in Lawrence Kudlow, "Financial and Economic Update—a Report on the Current Situation," March 17, 1982.

26. Details on International Harvester are from the company's 1982 annual
report and *The New York Times*, February 19, 1986.

27. Adjustments in monetary policy were described in the annual report of the
Open Market Desk, "Monetary Policy and Open Market Operations in 1982,"
New York Federal Reserve Quarterly Review, Spring 1983.

28. The most intimate account of behind-the-scenes discussions surrounding
Mexico's financial crisis was reported by Joseph Kraft, "The Mexican Rescue,"
Group of Thirty, 1984.

29. Details on the Drysdale failure are from *The Wall Street Journal*, May 20,
1982, and "Monetary Policy and Open Market Operations in 1982" (see above).

30. William M. Isaac, interviews, October 22 and November 14, 1985.

31. Jerry Jordan's comment is from *The Wall Street Journal*, May 28, 1982.

32. Data on profits and bankruptcies were reported in *The Wall Street Journal*,
May 6 and 24, 1982.

33. Lawrence Kudlow's pessimistic analysis was in "Memorandum for the
Cabinet Council on Economic Affairs, Subject: Economic and Financial Update,"
April 16, 1982.

34. Financial-market reactions were reported in *The Wall Street Journal*, May
14, 1982, and the Washington *Post*, May 30, 1982. The survey of money managers
was cited by Donald Regan in a speech, April 26, 1982

35. Nancy Teeters's reaction was reported in the Washington *Post*, May 30,
1982.

CHAPTER 14: The Turn

1. William M. Isaac's remarks throughout this chapter are from interviews,
October 22 and November 14, 1985.

2. Some of the details on Penn Square were drawn from Phillip L. Zweig,
Belly Up: The Collapse of the Penn Square Bank, Crown, 1985.

3. Continental Illinois's rapid growth, *Wall Street Journal*, July 30, 1984. *Dun's
Review* and *Wall Street Journal* accolades mentioned in Chicago *Tribune*, May
27, 1984.

4. Michael Bradfield's remarks throughout this chapter are from a February 6, 1986, interview.

5. The Latin debt problems, *Wall Street Journal*, July 1, 1982.

6. Complaints from Milton Friedman and Beryl Sprinkel are from *The Wall Street Journal*, June 11 and June 28, 1982.

7. Market reactions to Penn Square are from the Federal Advisory Council minutes, September 17, 1982, and "Monetary Policy and Open Market Operations in 1982," *New York Federal Reserve Quarterly Review*, Spring 1983.

8. Stock-market rally and reactions are from the Washington *Post*, August 18, 1982.

9. Senator Byrd's speech on monetary reform was delivered in the Senate on August 3, 1982.

10. Volcker's declaration of progress was made before the House Banking Committee, July 21, 1982, with further comments reported in *The Wall Street Journal*, August 10, 1982.

11. Senator Byrd's claim that political pressure persuaded the Federal Reserve occurred in Senate debate on November 30, 1982.

12. Howard Baker, interview, January 22, 1986.

13. Some details on the debt crisis were drawn from Darrell Delamaide, *Debt Shock: The Full Story of the World Credit Crisis*, Doubleday, 1984.

14. The memorandum on Volcker's meeting with Continental Illinois was read aloud to the author, but not made available, by Michael Bradfield, the general counsel.

15. The idea of making monetary policy directly subservient to the President is hardly a radical notion since central banks in most other industrial nations live comfortably enough with that arrangement. The Bank of England does not raise interest rates (or lower them) without discreetly obtaining permission from the Prime Minister's Secretary of the Exchequer.

A more authentic democratization of the central bank would require a more visible process. The Federal Reserve would be stripped of its independent status and recast as a sub-agency of Treasury with presidential power to remove its chairman like any other appointed officer of government. A more coherent design, though obviously even more disruptive politically, would consolidate all of the government's economic-management powers in one place, a new Cabinet office that combined elements of budget, taxation and monetary policies so that, at last these decisions would be coordinated.

In any of these arrangements, the twelve Federal Reserve Banks would become superfluous institutions. If there is genuine democratic control, there is no reason to let each Reserve Bank president have an independent vote on government economic policy or, for that matter, to let commercial bankers maintain their preferential influence on Federal Reserve policy. The twelve Reserve Banks would be reduced in status to their operating functions, like the regional offices in any federal department.

Once the Chief Executive takes responsibility for managing money, the role of Congress would follow naturally. It would begin to exercise normal congressional oversight, the regular scrutiny of agency operations and budget that it has never applied to the Federal Reserve. Inevitably, Congress would probably claim a more direct role in the making of monetary policy, presumably by enacting periodic instructions for the Executive Branch. Regular resolutions, enacted annually or every six months or even every quarter, could set rough boundaries for monetary policy and provide the public forum for the ongoing economic debate.

One practical advantage is obvious: a visible, accountable management process would exist in which to reconcile the competing forces of fiscal and monetary policy. Certainly, a unified system could not easily repeat the bizarre and devastating collision that occurred in the 1980s, when the federal government attempted simultaneously both to restrain and to stimulate.

A more rational governing system would not, of course, guarantee rational decisions, any more than democracy guarantees equity (or technocratic government guarantees "right" answers). Elected politicians do have certain virtues, however, that technocratic managers usually lack. In politics, they do not pretend to scientific certitude and so they will listen more earnestly to the random evidence of distress from citizens at large. Faced with conflict, politics inclines reflexively toward compromise, an improvised settlement that will lessen the harm to both sides. Furthermore, over time, democracy has the capacity for self-correction. Politicians forced to deal with the consequences of their economic folly might also have to pay the price themselves when they faced disappointed voters.

CHAPTER 15: A Game of Chicken

1. Jude Wanniski, interviews, October 11, 1984, and March 27, 1985.

2. Money managers' comments are from interviews, Craig Lewis, August 14, 1985; Mark Emerson, August 16, 1985; and Dean LeBaron, August 16, 1985.

3. "Fear vs. Greed" is from "Investment Strategy," Merrill Lynch, February 1983.

4. Albert Wojnilower, quoted in Washington *Post*, September 22, 1982.

5. Federal Advisory Council minutes, September 17, 1982.

6. Details on markets' reaction to abandonment of monetarist system are from *The Wall Street Journal*, October 7, 1982, and the Washington *Post* and *The New York Times*, October 8, 1982.

7. President Reagan was quoted in the Washington *Post*, October 8, 1982.

8. Volcker's remarks were at the meeting of the Business Council, October 9, 1982.

9. Jude Wanniski interviews (see above).

10. President Reagan's criticism of the Federal Reserve is quoted in Paul Craig Roberts's *The Supply-Side Revolution*, Harvard University Press, 1984.

11. Beryl Sprinkel's analysis is from "Memorandum for the Cabinet Council on Economic Affairs, Subject: Monetary Policy: The Risks Remain," March 11, 1983.

12. When an economic theory fails, its apostles usually retreat into a series of excuses, explaining that extraordinary conditions that were unforeseeable were responsible, not the theory itself. Monetarists generally took that line of defense, claiming that the temporary distortions would eventually disappear and the money rule would again be viable. Even Paul Volcker was reluctant to dismiss M-1 permanently as a reliable guide to monetary policy.

If M-1 is someday restored, however, it will likely be because the Federal Reserve wants a convenient political cover for severe tightening—not because it believes in the theory's intellectual integrity. The practical disintegration of the monetarist theory was based on three distinct points. First, as Henry Wallich argued in 1979, the dynamic interrelationship between supply, demand and price would always be distorted by holding the supply of money rigid. The other variable—the public's fluctuating demand for money—would then produce sharp and unpredictable swings in the price, and those swings in interest rates would feed back into economic activity, stimulating or dampening in unintended ways—

kicking the economy through the floor and then through the ceiling, as Wallich said.

Second, financial innovation would continuously alter the arbitrary definitions of money that monetarism relied upon for its idea of steady, stable growth. Monetarists claimed that this was a temporary distortion caused by financial deregulation, but the practical history suggested otherwise. Finance was always inventing new ways for people to store their wealth, new hybrid accounts that undermined the old definitions. Money was existential—whatever people thought it was, whatever they were willing to call it. The process of change was not likely to stop in order to accommodate an economic theory.

Finally, starting in late 1981, the basic premise of monetarism—the stable and predictable velocity at which money turned over in circulation—fell apart too. Monetarists conceded as much (long after the fact) but still insisted that velocity would return to normal, that this was an historic aberration. In fact, in turbulent times, velocity usually changed, most dramatically when the central bank was rigidly controlling money, as in the 1920s, and producing sharp interest-rate changes. In other words, monetarism looked like a plausible doctrine—until the Federal Reserve started following it. Then it became unreliable and even destructive.

William McChesney Martin told an interviewer from *The New York Times* in 1985: "They don't really know what the money supply is now, even today. They print some figures—I'm not trying to make fun of it—but a lot of it is just almost superstition." Indeed, the central allure of Friedman's theory was always, in large part, spiritual—a simple act of faith that banished complexities. Believe in one thing and one thing only—the sanctity of money—and all the other bewildering variables would fall into line. In hindsight, it is remarkable that so many influential people fell under the spell.

13. Milton Friedman, interview, July 19, 1984.

14. William Poole is quoted from "Memorandum for the Cabinet Council on Economic Affairs, Subject: Controlling Money Growth," May 16, 1983.

15. Wallich speech before International Conference of Banking Supervisors, September 24, 1981.

16. Karin Lissakers, "Dateline Wall Street: Faustian Finance," *Foreign Policy*, summer, 1983.

17. Jesus Silva Herzog was quoted in *The Wall Street Journal*, August 1, 1983.

18. Argentine episode was reported in the Washington *Post*, October 5, 1983.

19. Jim Leach, interview, November 14, 1985.

20. James McGrady, interview, August 22, 1985.

21. President Reagan's remarks are from the President's Budget Message, January 31, 1983; a speech before the Commonwealth Club, March 4, 1983; and in Klamath Falls, Oregon, March 5, 1983.

22. The "matador" description of Volcker was in a *New York Times* editorial, December 31, 1982, and he was compared to St. George by Darrell Delamaide in *Debt Shock*, Doubleday, 1984.

23. Volcker's standing in public opinion was cited by Kevin Phillips in *The American Political Report*, May 6, 1983.

24. *The Wall Street Journal*'s praise was March 14, 1983.

25. Jude Wanniski interviews (see above).

26. The "game of chicken" metaphor is cited in Thomas J. Sargent, "Confrontations Over Deficits," *New York Times*, August 12, 1983.

27. The question of what caused the high level of real interest rates led to a

continuing debate among economists attempting to define the cause-and-effect linkage between fiscal deficits and tight monetary policy. The Council of Economic Advisers suggested in its 1984 report that a major cause was the business tax cuts enacted by the Reagan Administration, which increased the after-tax return on capital, and, therefore, a higher yield was required for other investments like U.S. bonds to remain competitive. Others attributed the historically high rates to either the huge deficits or the Fed's tight money policy or, more likely, to a combination of the two. See, for instance, Oliver J. Blanchard and Lawrence H. Summers, "Perspectives on High World Real Interest Rates," Brookings Papers on Economic Activity, 2:1984.

Economist William D. Nordhaus of Yale, commenting on the Blanchard-Summers study, argued that the Federal Reserve was itself principally responsible for imposing the extraordinary rates, particularly in the post-recovery years. This is the conclusion which I share, because it seemed to correspond most plausibly with the political events and with subsequent changes in interest rates. Whenever the Fed acted, the level of real rates promptly changed in response, suggesting that the rates were directly the function of monetary policy, not simply "market forces" imposed by the federal deficits.

> Since 1982 . . . a different force has been at work—one that might be called "preemptive monetarism" [Nordhaus explained]. During this period, the Federal Reserve has been forced to keep real interest rates high to pre-empt the actual or prospective effects of the stimulative U.S. fiscal policy. In part, the Federal Reserve seems to have been threatening the Congress with the prospect that real rates would stay high until the deficit was reduced; to some extent, particularly during 1983 and 1984, real interest rates were high because, given the high fiscal deficit, the Federal Reserve's unemployment and inflation targets could be met only with relatively high interest rates.

28. Real rates on corporate bonds are cited in Henry Kaufman, *Interest Rates, the Markets, and the New Financial World*, Times Books, 1986.

29. Stephen H. Axilrod, interview, July 25, 1985.

30. Volcker's "jawboning" of market rates was described in the *National Journal*, June 11, 1983.

31. Volcker and Lyle Gramley actually articulated these new views on the conduct of monetary policy in 1980 when the economy was in recession but quickly recovered. The same principles guided their thinking in 1983. Volcker was quoted in *The Wall Street Journal*, May 12, 1980. Gramley's comment is from a speech, July 17, 1980.

32. Frank Morris's description of the "mid-course correction" was in a speech, November 16, 1983.

CHAPTER 16: Winners and Losers

1. The Washington *Times* story on Volcker's reappointment was April 18, 1983.

2. Senator Garn was quoted in the Washington *Post*, March 10, 1983.

3. The various business endorsements were listed in the *National Journal*, June 11, 1983. The survey of financial executives was reported in *The Wall Street Journal*, June 8, 1983.

4. The President's and Donald Regan's remarks on the reappointment were in the Washington *Post*, June 18, 1983.

5. Donald Regan's speech to the National Press Club was on June 29, 1983.

6. Alfred Zeller's fur sales, *Wall Street Journal*, July 3, 1984.

7. William Hamilton's polling on interest rates, *Wall Street Journal*, January 27, 1984.

8. Charles Schultze on supply-side economics, *Wall Street Journal*, October 10, 1983.

9. The shifting income shares were reported by the Joint Economic Committee, analyzing "After-Tax Money Income Estimates of Households," U.S. Census, July 8, 1985.

10. The changing patterns of mass consumption were reported by Bruce Steinberg, "The Mass Market Is Splitting Apart," *Fortune*, November 28, 1983. A broader description of the economic implications of a shrinking middle class was reported by Robert Kuttner, "The Declining Middle," *The Atlantic*, July 1983.

11. Henry Wallich's warning on debt was from a speech, June 2, 1981.

12. John A. O'Leary, Jr., was quoted in *The New York Times*, October 11, 1983.

13. Robbin Craven, Carl Redwood, Jr., and Arnie Leibowitz were quoted from May 3–4, 1985, interviews in "An American Dream," by the author, *Rolling Stone*, June 20, 1985.

14. Details on labor settlements are from George Ruben, "Modest Labor-Management Bargains Continue in 1984 Despite the Recovery," *Monthly Labor Review*, January 1985, and Robert S. Gay, Anne Peters and Maura Shaughnessy, "Union Settlements and Aggregate Wage Behavior in the 1980s," *Federal Reserve Bulletin*, December 1984.

15. David Hale's comment on Republican "public works" was in *The Wall Street Journal*, January 24, 1985.

16. John Zalusky on strikes, *Washington Post*, March 7, 1985.

17. Data on "Displaced Workers," Bureau of Labor Statistics, November 30, 1984.

18. Lewis Goodkin was quoted in *The Wall Street Journal*, December 7, 1983.

19. Elizabeth Laird, interview, May 28, 1985.

20. Details on mortgage failures are from *The New York Times*, January 25 and February 18, 1985.

21. Mike Stout was quoted from a May 4, 1985, interview in "An American Dream" (see above).

22. Housing deflation data are from "Housing and Housing Finance in an Era of Inflation and Disinflation," Western Economic Association, May 1984, and Jane Bryant Quinn, "The Investment Squeeze on Homes," *Newsweek*, July 8, 1985.

23. Murray Weidenbaum's list of "winners and losers" was in "Memorandum for the Cabinet Council on Economic Affairs, Subject: Adjusting to Lower Inflation," May 14, 1982.

24. Prices of wheat and oil, *New York Times*, August 21, 1983.

25. The examples of exchange-rate effects on prices are from a speech by Robert O. Anderson, chairman of Atlantic Richfield oil company, "How the Dollar Stole Christmas," December 9, 1982.

26. Lee Iacocca's various comments in this chapter on the dollar and Japan are from speeches, June 27, 1983, and June 5, 1986, and testimony before the House Banking Committee, April 28, 1983.

27. Data on trade shifts are from Lee Price, "Trade Problems and Policy from a U.S. Labor Perspective," in *Current U.S. Trade Policy: Analysis, Agenda and Administration*, National Bureau of Economic Research, 1986.

28. The description of business lobbying on the dollar is based on a number of White House documents, including: Lee L. Morgan, letter to Cabinet officers, October 20, 1982; Edwin L. Harper, Memorandum to Cabinet, October 22, 1982; and Lawrence A. Kudlow, "Yen-Dollar Relationships and Japanese Financial Market Restrictions," Memorandum for David A. Stockman, October 26, 1982.

29. Martin Feldstein's defense of the strong dollar was argued in "Memorandum for the Cabinet Council on Economic Affairs, Subject: Is the Dollar Overvalued?," April 8, 1983.

30. Complaints by Larry Speakes, Donald Regan, Milton Friedman and Representative Jack Kemp were described in *The Wall Street Journal*, November 22, December 13 and 14, 1983.

31. Rowland Evans and Robert Novak column, Washington *Post*, November 11, 1983.

32. Preston Martin, interview, June 2, 1986.

CHAPTER 17: "Morning Again in America"

1. Senator Proxmire's remarks on campaign pressures on the Fed were at Senate Banking hearing, February 8 and July 25, 1984.

2. Exchange between Senator John Heinz and Paul Volcker occurred during Senate Banking hearing, February 8, 1984.

3. E. F. Hutton's "Economics: Equity Research," February 13, 1984.

4. Representative Jack Kemp enumerated his complaints in "Six Questions for Chairman Volcker," *Wall Street Journal*, February 7, 1984.

5. Donald Regan's warnings are from "Monetary Policy, Memorandum for the President," January 10, 1984.

6. Representative Kemp's remark is from "Six Questions for Chairman Volcker" (see above).

7. Senator Bentsen's defense of the Federal Reserve was in "The Fed as Scapegoat," Washington *Post*, May 10, 1984.

8. The rightward drift of the Democratic Party's economic policies derived not so much from a supposed increase in conservative sentiment among voters as from the party's increasing dependence on conservative business sectors, including investment bankers, for campaign funds. That thesis was persuasively developed by Thomas Ferguson and Joel Rogers in *Right Turn: The Decline of the Democrats and the Future of American Politics*, Hill and Wang, 1986.

9. Preston Martin's joke was recounted in *The American Banker*, August 5, 1985.

10. David Jones, interview, June 27, 1984.

11. Housing and auto statistics are from *The Wall Street Journal*, February 15 and March 19, 1984. Business spending on new plants and equipment is from the Washington *Post*, March 13, 1984. Volcker was quoted on potential "bottlenecks" in the Washington *Post*, March 1, 1984.

12. David Jones's prediction on the Fed was in the Washington *Post*, January 14, 1984. E. F. Hutton's "brakeman" metaphor was in its "Economics: Equity Research" (see above).

13. Reports of the President's meeting with Volcker and subsequent clarifica-

tions by the White House, as well as press commentaries, appeared in the Washington *Post* on February 16, 22 and 24, 1984, and *The Wall Street Journal*, February 21, 1984.

14. Robert V. Roosa's comment is from *The New York Times*, March 22, 1984.

15. As a practical matter, the Federal Reserve's capacity-utilization index would never reach 100 percent because, as everyone recognized, the index included idle manufacturing facilities that were old and obsolete and would never be active again. In 1979, for instance, when the economy peaked in the last recovery cycle, manufacturing reached 87 percent of its capacity, according to the index. By contrast, the index fell to 72 percent during the recession of 1982.

What alarmed Gramley, Partee and the others in early 1984 was that the utilization index had risen from 79 percent to nearly 82 percent in only three months. If that rapid acceleration were to continue, they feared the economy would soon reach full capacity and inflation would be reignited by scarce supply and scarce labor. In the actual event, the index never went above 82 percent. It subsided eventually to below 80 percent and remained at that subpar level in ensuing years, another measure of how the economy was held far below its potential.

16. Preston Martin's "overheated" remark was quoted in the Washington *Post*, March 14, 1984.

17. The Shearson American Express commentary on the bond market is from its "Economic Research," April 6, 1984.

18. The public comments on "Fed bashing" are from the Washington *Post*, May 9–15, and *The Wall Street Journal*, May 9, 1984.

19. Federal Advisory Council minutes, May 4, 1984.

20. William Isaac's remarks throughout this chapter are from October 22 and November 14, 1985, interviews.

21. Details on the "run" on Continental Illinois are from the Chicago *Tribune*, May 27, 1984.

22. Volcker's acknowledgment of failure to act sooner was made before the Senate Banking Committee, July 25, 1984.

23. Some financial data on the rescue of Continental Illinois are from *The Wall Street Journal*, May 17 and 18 and July 30, 1984.

24. Volcker's explanation was made before the Senate Banking Committee, July 25, 1984.

25. An odd intramural controversy developed over the Fed's enormous emergency loans to Continental Illinois. The Chicago Federal Reserve Bank, which made the loans, had taken $17 billion in assets from Continental as collateral securing its loans, mostly business loan contracts from the bank's portfolio of assets. However, the Chicago Fed had failed to file liens on these assets at the county courthouse, as required by Illinois law, and directors of the Chicago Fed feared that if Continental closed, they would be in a weak legal position to assert their claims. In particular, they feared they might be held personally liable as directors if the Chicago Federal Reserve Bank suffered losses as a result.

Whether or not this was a genuine risk, the Chicago Fed officers periodically warned regulators in Washington that they were going to proceed to file public liens totaling $17 billion in order to protect themselves. If they had, the event might have reignited the fears of money-market investors and restarted the "run" on Continental. To forestall them, the FDIC chairman was compelled to deliver a formal guarantee to the Chicago Federal Reserve Bank, promising to honor all its claims in the event that Continental failed.

26. Bank closings were reported in the Federal Deposit Insurance Corporation 1984 *Annual Report*.

27. Declining farmland values were calculated by the Federal Reserve, reported in the Washington *Post*, December 30, 1984.

28. Details on problems at Bank of America and First Chicago are from *The Wall Street Journal*, December 31, 1984, and the Washington *Post*, February 23, 1986.

29. Edward A. Taber was quoted in *The Wall Street Journal*, May 25, 1984.

30. Details on the Open Market Desk's reactions to the nervousness in banking are drawn from the 1984 *Annual Report* of the New York Federal Reserve Bank.

31. The bank-profit statistics are from previously cited reports in the *Federal Reserve Bulletin*, November and December 1985.

32. Governor Martha Seger's remark on the farm problems was reported by Jude Wanniski in the newsletter from his firm, Polyconomics, March 5, 1985.

33. Karin Lissakers, "Dateline Wall Street: Faustian Finance," *Foreign Policy*, Summer 1983.

34. The crisis at Financial Corporation of America, *New York Times*, August 17, 1984.

35. Richard Brookhiser, *The Outside Story: How Democrats and Republicans Reelected Reagan*, Doubleday, 1986.

36. Thorstein Veblen, *Absentee Ownership and Business Enterprise in Recent Times*, B. W. Huebsch, 1923.

37. The press's failure to focus on the declining economy during the 1984 campaign was especially striking because the initial reports on the decline of real GNP growth were even more drastic than the subsequently revised numbers used in the text. Initially, growth for the third quarter was reported to be 1.6 percent, later revised upward to 2.1 percent. The initial report for the fourth quarter placed growth at 3.9 percent, later revised downward to .6 percent. In either case, political reporters seemed reluctant to question the President's campaign theme of restored prosperity. A subsequent revision several years later moderated the numbers further. First quarter growth was put at 9.8 percent and the fourth quarter was 1.5 percent.

38. David P. Eastburn explained his "hardship index" in a letter to *The Wall Street Journal*, March 22, 1983.

39. The 1984 Republican platform, *Congressional Quarterly*, August 24, 1984.

40. Robert O. Anderson's comments are from an interview, July 17, 1986, and his Houston speech, October 17, 1984.

41. Corporate relocations of production were described in *The Wall Street Journal*, April 9, 1985.

42. Gerald Epstein's commentary was in "The Triple Debt Crisis," *World Policy Journal*, Winter 1986.

43. Lee Iacocca's complaint was in a speech to the American Society of Newspaper Editors, April 10, 1986. His statistics cover 1983–1985. Others have made much higher estimates of the loss of employment caused by the dollar.

44. The lost potential in auto sales was described in *Morgan Economic Quarterly*, June 1985.

45. Michael Sumichrast, interview, September 14, 1983.

46. The decline of homeownership and housing starts is described in "Home Ownership and Housing Affordability in the United States: 1963–1984," Joint Center for Housing Studies, MIT-Harvard, 1985 *Annual Report*.

47. Higher housing costs for young families are described in "The Economic

Future of the Baby Boom," Frank S. Levy and Richard C. Michel, Joint Economic Committee, December 5, 1985.

48. The Census data on incomes were reported by Thomas B. Edsall, "Republican America," *New York Review of Books*, April 24, 1986.

49. The credit expansion for 1984 was reported by the Federal Reserve Board, 1986 *Annual Report*.

50. Statistics on total domestic debt are from James J. O'Leary, former economist at U.S. Trust, reported in the *National Journal*, November 16, 1985.

51. Philip Braverman, interview, June 27, 1984.

52. Albert Wojnilower's commentary is from "Private Credit Demand, Supply and Crunches—How Different Are the 1980s?," delivered before the American Economic Association, December 28, 1984.

53. Henry Kaufman's comment on the "safety net" for finance is from an interview in *Across the Board*, Conference Board, September 1986.

54. Edward Sonnino's analysis is from "Fed Tightness Boosts Borrowing," *Wall Street Journal*, February 21, 1986.

55. As critics from commercial banking would point out, economists from major bond houses were not entirely disinterested in their proposals for new credit controls. If the government imposed supply limits on banking and other forms of short-term credit, more capital would presumably flow to the long-term corporate bonds issued by the investment bankers. The larger social interest would, in fact, be served by that. If long-term capital formation was the highest function of finance and the process that fundamentally determined future prosperity and productivity, then the nation in general would benefit if the government guided wealth in that direction.

In any case, the critique of the bond-market economists who advocated the re-regulation of finance could hardly have been motivated by weak profits. During the 1980's, major brokerages like Salomon Brothers and First Boston enjoyed extraordinary growth and profit.

CHAPTER 18: The Triumph of Money

1. Clifford and Evelyne Burger, Jim Phillips and John Sellers, Jr., interviews, April 4–5, 1985. See also "A Farewell to Farming," by Hank Klibanoff, *Philadelphia Inquirer Magazine*, March 31, 1985.

2. "There must be losers" is from E. F. Hutton's *Investment Strategy*, February 1986. The deflation losers included the Hunt brothers of Texas, who in August 1986 were compelled to file for bankruptcy relief for Placid Oil Company, the center of the family's wealth.

3. Commodity prices are from *The Wall Street Journal*, April 28 and August 19, 1986, and the annual commodity indexes of the *Economist*, Feburary 8, 1986.

4. Lester V. Chandler, *Benjamin Strong, Central Banker*, Brookings Institution, 1958.

5. Joseph Coyne, public affairs director for the Federal Reserve Board, has denied that Volcker made such a comment to the farm-state legislators. Three state legislators attest that they heard Volcker say it, Senators Sandra Scofield and Harry B. Chronister of Nebraska and Representative Norwood Creason of Missouri, letters to *The Wall Street Journal*, October 24 and 27, 1986. Federal Reserve officials often disclaimed responsibility in public for ill consequences they joked about in private. At Paul Volcker's retirement banquet in July 1987, a senior staff official from Oklahoma jokingly awarded the chairman a placque in

recognition that Volcker had reduced his home state to the status of a developing country.

6. *Fortune* 500 summary is from *Fortune*, April 28, 1986.

7. Martha Seger's complaints are in an interview with Nina Easton, *The American Banker*, February 3, 1986.

8. The Shearson Lehman Bond Index was cited in *The Wall Street Journal*, May 10, 1986.

9. Beryl Sprinkel's lament was quoted in *The New York Times*, July 3, 1986. The decline of money velocity in the 1980s was astutely explained by independent economic forecaster A. Gary Shilling in *The Wall Street Journal*, May 20, 1986. Shilling demonstrated that the seesaw pattern of velocity in the 1980s, decreasing and increasing and upsetting monetarist calculations, resembled experience in the 1920s when disinflation also changed the money-holding habits of individuals and businesses. Velocity followed a predictable curve of steady increase only in the decades after World War II, but that fact hardly helped the monetarist theory since that was also the era of inflation. The historical experience charted by Shilling suggested that monetarism's claims about the stable meaning of money were always destabilized in times of disinflation or deflation. The theory, therefore, could not be dependable as the central bank's permanent operating rule unless the central bank also was prepared to allow permanent inflation.

10. Milton Friedman, interview, July 19, 1984.

11. George P. Brockway, economics columnist in *The New Leader*, offered his commentary on the supply disorders in *The New York Times*, November 24, 1985. Edward Dennison, an economist from the Brookings Institution, estimated that the United States had "the largest reserve of unused production capacity since the thirties." While no reliable measure existed for worldwide supply capacity, other leading industrial nations suffered from similar problems in the 1980s. West Germany's capacity utilization declined from 86 to 82.8 percent. Canada's fell from 86 to 76 percent. Japan's utilization rate, calculated on a different base, declined from 91.6 to 85 percent. See the annual report of the Joint Economic Committee, February 1986.

12. Marriner Eccles's analysis is from *Economic Balance and a Balanced Budget*, Da Capo Press, 1973, and *Beckoning Frontiers*, edited by Sidney Hyman, Alfred A. Knopf, 1951.

13. Robert F. Barbera, chief economist of E. F. Hutton, was quoted in *The New York Times*, February 28, 1986.

14. Marriner Eccles, *Beckoning Frontiers* (see above).

15. Kenneth E. Boulding discussed the "pathological features" of interest rates in "Puzzles over Distribution," *Challenge*, November–December 1985.

16. A Federal Reserve Board spokesman denied that the chairman had been rebuffed by the Board of Governors in his attempts to raise the Discount rate, but this account was confirmed by Governor Martha Seger. Except for *Business Week* and columnists Evans and Novak, the press seemed unaware that any conflict had occurred.

ACKNOWLEDGMENTS

My indebtedness to Linda Furry Greider is far greater than the usual thanks an author extends to a spouse for personal support and patience. Through nearly five years, her questions and observations consistently instructed me to see the subject whole—to think in the human dimensions that are much larger than economics. In particular, she encouraged me to examine the psychological subtexts that exist beneath both politics and economics, and to anchor the abstractions of financial economics in the real experiences of real people.

In the reporting for this book, I was fortunate to have as a research assistant a brilliant young reporter, Marilyn Marks, who took a year's leave from her graduate studies to work with me. Her intellectual curiosity and reporter's tenacity were invaluable. She also served as a thoughtful critic of my analysis.

I am of course indebted to Paul Volcker and the other Federal Reserve governors and Reserve Bank presidents who granted me interviews, but I also wish to thank the scores of Federal Reserve System employees, past and present, who helped me to understand the institution. I will mention only a few of them: James H. Oltman, general counsel of the New York Federal Reserve Bank; John Paulus of Morgan Stanley; Daniel Brill, the retired research director; Merritt Sherman, retired secretary to the Board of Governors, and Robert A. Johnson, a staff economist in Washington. Rob Johnson, in particular, was a wonderful teacher and guide through the technical intricacies of monetary economics. I am also grateful to Joseph R. Coyne, public affairs director of the Federal Reserve Board, and Peter H. Bakstansky, who holds the same position at the New York Federal Reserve Bank, for their generous assistance.

The manuscript benefitted from the critical scrutiny of David Smith, A. Thomas Ferguson and Robert A. Johnson, each of whom raised valuable questions about history, politics and economics.

Certain friends were especially important in the advice and encouragement they offered along the way. One was my agent, Lynn Nesbit. Another was Bob Woodward of *The Washington Post*. And I will be forever grateful to Jann Wenner, the editor of *Rolling Stone*, who generously indulged my pursuit of this project.

At Simon & Schuster, I am, most of all, thankful for a brilliant editor, Alice Mayhew, who instantly understood all the reasons why this was an important subject and encouraged me to explore it in the fullest terms. I would also like to thank John Cox, who expertly helped to shape a very long manuscript; Henry Ferris, who supervised production; and Patricia Miller, who provided superb copy editing. In Washington, Katherine Dunbar ably assisted in checking facts.

Finally, on the deepest level, I am indebted to many teachers, formal and informal, who over the years instructed me on how to look at things. I mention especially the late John William Ward, an historian who at Princeton University many years ago taught that history is not a separate subject from politics and economics, religion and literature and social psychology, but that all are pieces from the same fabric. My most important teachers, of course, have been my parents, Harold W. Greider and Gladys McClure Greider, who taught that curiosity, optimism and faith in the democratic ideal are themselves endlessly enriching qualities.

Washington, D.C.
August 15, 1987

INDEX

ABOUT THE AUTHOR

William Greider writes about national affairs for *Rolling Stone*. He was formerly assistant managing editor for *The Washington Post*. Greider is author of *The Education of David Stockman and Other Americans*. He lives in Washington, D.C.

MORE OUTSTANDING TOUCHSTONE BOOKS

THE WORLDLY PHILOSOPHERS
The Lives, Times, and Ideas
of the Great Economic Thinkers
Updated Sixth Edition
by Robert L. Heilbroner
In the most widely read text on the history of economic
thought ever written, the great economic thinkers from
Marx to John Maynard Keynes come to life. We come
to see their ideas not merely as inspired works of the
past but as commentaries that light up our times. "A
living classic."—Leonard Silk. Over 2 million copies
sold worldwide.
0-671-63318-X $9.95

ECONOMICS EXPLAINED
Revised and Updated Edition
by Robert L. Heilbroner & Lester C. Thurow
Two of America's most respected economists illuminate
the vital concerns, trends and challenges of the marketplace. Here is all the economics essential for effective
investing, corporate decision making, or simply
informed citizenship. "Heilbroner and Thurow take the
mystery out."—Library Journal.
0-671-64556-0 $9.95

MAIL COUPON TODAY—NO-RISK 14 DAY FREE TRIAL

Simon & Schuster, Inc.
200 Old Tappan Road
Old Tappan, NJ 07675. Mail Order Dept. SOTT 88
Please send me _____ copies of _____
(If not completely satisfied, you may return for full refund within 14 days.)
☐ Enclose full amount per copy with this coupon: publisher pays
postage and handling: or charge my credit card.
☐ Master Card   ☐ Visa
My credit card number is _____Card expires_____
Signature_____
Name_____
                          (Please Print)
Address_____
City_____ State _____ Zip code_____
or available at your local bookstore   Prices subject to change without notice.